HANDBOOK OF
CHILD AND ADOLESCENT PSYCHOPATHY

Handbook of Child and Adolescent Psychopathy

Edited by

RANDALL T. SALEKIN
DONALD R. LYNAM

THE GUILFORD PRESS
New York London

A Division of Guilford Publications, Inc.
72 Spring Street, New York, NY 10012
www.guilford.com

Printed in the United States of America

This book is printed on acid-free paper.

Last digit is print number: 9 8 7 6 5 4 3 2 1

Library of Congress Cataloging-in-Publication Data

Handbook of child and adolescent psychopathy / edited by Randall T. Salekin, Donald R. Lynam.
p. cm.
Includes bibliographical references and index.
ISBN 978-1-60623-682-6 (hardcover : acid-free paper)
1. Child psychopathology—Handbooks, manuals, etc. I. Salekin, Randall T. II. Lynam, Donald R.
RJ499.3.H263 2010
618.92′89—dc22

2009051596

About the Editors

Randall T. Salekin, PhD, is Professor in the Department of Psychology, Director of the Disruptive Behavior Clinic, and Associate Director of the Center for the Prevention of Youth Behavior Problems at the University of Alabama. He has published in the areas of child and adolescent psychopathy and conduct problems. Dr. Salekin is a recipient of the American Psychology–Law Society's Saleem Shah Award for early career excellence and contributions to the field of psychology and law. He serves on nine editorial boards, is Editor of the *Journal of Psychopathology and Behavioral Assessment*, and is Associate Editor of the *Journal of Abnormal Psychology*.

Donald R. Lynam, PhD, is Professor in the Department of Psychological Sciences at Purdue University. He has published extensively in the areas of adult and juvenile psychopathy, the development of antisocial behavior, and the role of individual differences in deviance. Dr. Lynam is a recipient of the American Psychological Association's Distinguished Scientific Award for Early Career Contribution to Psychology and is a Fellow of the Association for Psychological Science. He formerly served as Associate Editor of the *Journal of Abnormal Psychology* and *Psychological Science*.

Contributors

Henrik Andershed, PhD, School of Law, Psychology, and Social Work, Örebro University, Örebro, Sweden

Rachel Baden, MA, Department of Psychology, University of Alabama, Tuscaloosa, Alabama

R. James R. Blair, PhD, National Institute of Mental Health, Bethesda, Maryland

Angela S. Book, PhD, Department of Psychology, Brock University, St. Catharines, Ontario, Canada

Caroline Boxmeyer, PhD, Center for the Prevention of Youth Behavior Problems, Department of Psychology, University of Alabama, Tuscaloosa, Alabama

David P. Farrington, PhD, Institute of Criminology, Cambridge University, Cambridge, United Kingdom

Adelle E. Forth, PhD, Department of Psychology and Institute of Criminology and Criminal Justice, Carleton University, Ottawa, Ontario, Canada

Paul J. Frick, PhD, Department of Psychology, University of New Orleans, New Orleans, Louisiana

Shabnam Javdani, MA, Department of Psychology, University of Illinois at Urbana–Champaign, Champaign, Illinois

David S. Kosson, PhD, Department of Psychology, Rosalind Franklin University of Medicine and Science, Chicago, Illinois

Julie S. Kotler, PhD, Department of Psychiatry and Behavioral Sciences, University of Washington, Seattle, Washington

Henrik Larsson, PhD, Department of Medical Epidemiology and Biostatistics, Karolinska Institute, Stockholm, Sweden

John E. Lochman, PhD, ABPP, Center for the Prevention of Youth Behavior Problems, Department of Psychology, University of Alabama, Tuscaloosa, Alabama

Donald R. Lynam, PhD, Department of Psychological Sciences, Purdue University, West Lafayette, Indiana

Robert J. McMahon, PhD, Department of Psychology, University of Washington, Seattle, Washington

Christopher J. Patrick, PhD, Department of Psychology, Florida State University, Tallahassee, Florida

Nicole P. Powell, PhD, Center for the Prevention of Youth Behavior Problems, Department of Psychology, University of Alabama, Tuscaloosa, Alabama

Richard Rogers, PhD, Department of Psychology, University of North Texas, Denton, Texas

Naomi Sadeh, MA, Department of Psychology, University of Illinois at Urbana–Champaign, Champaign, Illinois

Randall T. Salekin, PhD, Disruptive Behavior Clinic, Center for the Prevention of Youth Behavior Problems, Department of Psychology, University of Alabama

Kathrin Sevecke, MD, Clinic for Child and Adolescent Psychiatry and Psychotherapy, University of Cologne, Cologne, Germany

Simone Ullrich, PhD, Centre for Psychiatry, Barts and the London School of Medicine and Dentistry, London, United Kingdom

Edelyn Verona, PhD, Department of Psychology, University of Illinois at Urbana–Champaign, Champaign, Illinois

Essi Viding, PhD, Division of Psychology and Language Sciences, University College London, London, United Kingdom

Michael J. Vitacco, PhD, Mendota Mental Health Institute, Madison, Wisconsin

Stuart F. White, MA, Department of Psychology, University of New Orleans, New Orleans, Louisiana

Laura Young, MA, Department of Psychology, University of Alabama, Tuscaloosa, Alabama

Contents

PART V. CONCLUSIONS AND FUTURE DIRECTIONS

1

Child and Adolescent Psychopathy

An Introduction

RANDALL T. SALEKIN
DONALD R. LYNAM

The concept of child psychopathy can be traced to the work of Cleckley (1941), Karpman (1949, 1950), and the McCords (1959/1964). These notable scholars were the first to raise important questions, such as whether psychopathy exists in youth, how early in development it can be identified, whether the disorder is biologically or environmentally determined, and to what extent the disorder is considered treatable (see Salekin & Frick, 2005). However, little progress was made toward better understanding the condition following their initial efforts due to confusion over the defining features of the disorder, a lack of systematic assessment tools, and potential concerns about the pejorative nature of the term.[1] A search of PsycINFO cross-referencing psychopathy with several key terms (i.e., *child*, *children*, *adolescent*, *adolescence*, *juvenile*, *youth*, and *fledgling with psychopathy*) illustrates the slow progress in this area after the work of Cleckley (1941), Karpman (1950), and the McCords (1959/1964). Over a decade after the McCords, between 1978 and 1990, approximately 10 articles per year were published on child and adolescent psychopathy.

Despite meager numbers, some important work occurred during this period, including empirical investigations on psychopathic youth's nonverbal behavior in interpersonal situations (Rimé, Bouvy, Leborgne, & Rouillon, 1978), maternal deprivation and its link to psychopathy in childhood

(Wolkind, 1974), genetic and environmental contributions to psychopathy (Schulsinger, 1972), theoretical work on psychopathy as pathological stimulation seeking (Quay, 1965/1986), and important work on how psychopathic youth respond to aversive cues in school settings (Davies & Maliphant, 1971; Gutiérrez & Eisenman, 1971). While these studies advanced the field, child psychopathy was assessed through widely different and sometimes suspect methodologies (e.g., distinctions between Verbal and Performance IQ scores). In some cases, weak research designs or a lack of sophisticated research technology hampered what studies could offer.

Child and Adolescent Psychopathy Tools Emerge

In the 1990s, the measurement of psychopathy in youth became more systematic. Forth, Hart, and Hare (1990) pioneered research in this area with the first study to evaluate psychopathy in adolescent offenders using an adapted version of the Psychopathy Checklist—Revised (PCL-R; Hare, 1991/2003; Forth, Kosson, & Hare, 2003). Their groundbreaking study showed that psychopathy could be indexed in adolescents. Notably, individuals with high scores on this adapted version of the PCL-R were likely to have more institutional problems and infractions in a young offender rehabilitation institution. Shortly after Forth and colleagues' (1990) study, Frick and Hare (1994/2001) and Lynam (1997) developed psychopathy indices that provided the field with the necessary framework for measuring the concept in children. Their measures have recently been revamped, and alternative versions allow for use with adolescent samples. The Youth Psychopathic Traits Inventory (YPI; Andershed, Kerr, Stattin, & Levander, 2002) was also developed to assess psychopathic traits in nonreferred adolescents. Additional measures developed for the assessment of child and adolescent psychopathy have been added to the family of child and psychopathy indices (Murrie & Cornell, 2000; Rogers, Jackson, Sewell, & Johansen, 2004; Salekin, Ziegler, Larrea, Anthony, & Bennett, 2003). These measures have made it possible for the study of child and adolescent psychopathy to move forward more rapidly and in a more systematic fashion.

We are in the midst of an exciting time in the field of child and adolescent psychopathy as research in this area increases substantially. Across the past decade, there has been a sharp increase in interest in applying the construct of psychopathy to children and adolescents. This is evidenced by the number of articles retrieved from our search of PsycINFO from 1994 to 2009. Using the same qualifiers mentioned earlier, we identified 872 relevant articles through the PsycINFO search engine. Over half of these (i.e., 542) have been identified since the beginning of 2003. Figure 1.1 indicates how interest in the topic has grown very steadily over the past 10 years.

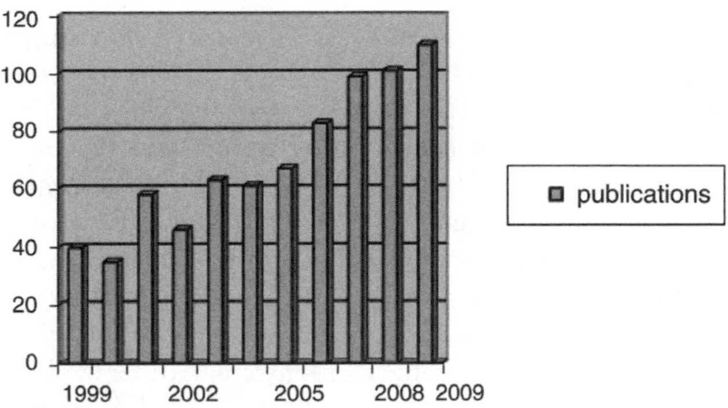

FIGURE 1.1. Publications on child and adolescent psychopathy as a function of publication year.

The interest in child and adolescent psychopathy is also underscored by the special issues dedicated to the topic in *Law and Human Behavior*, *Behavioral Sciences and the Law* (two volumes), *Journal of Abnormal Child Psychology*, *Journal of Clinical Child and Adolescent Psychology*, *Criminal Justice and Behavior*, and most recently *Juvenile Justice and Youth Violence*. In addition to documenting the increasing interest in the topic, Figure 1.1 underscores the rapidly growing empirical base in the literature (e.g., Blair & Coles, 2000; Caldwell, Skeem, Salekin, & Van Rybroek, 2006; Dadds, Fraser, Frost, & Hawes, 2005; Fowles & Kochanska, 2000; Kotler & McMahon, 2005; Loeber, Burke, Pardini, 2009; Lynam, 1996, 1997; Lynam & Gudonis, 2006; Salekin, 2006; Salekin & Debus, 2008; Stickle, Kirkpatrick, & Brush, 2009), with one publication appearing in the inaugural volume of the *Annual Review of Clinical Psychology* (i.e., Lynam & Gudonis, 2005).

In addition, mounting attention to the construct can be seen by the development of indices for child psychopathy in studies that did not originally contain psychopathy scales. One area in which this is particularly notable is longitudinal birth cohorts initiated in the 1970s and 1980s. Within such samples, proxies of psychopathy have been created by drawing on items from existing measures/batteries. This effort reflects the importance of the downward extension of the psychopathy construct and what it might mean in terms of predicting life outcomes. The use of such datasets will likely help the field gain a clearer picture of psychopathy across major developmental periods, especially since such cohorts have now reached adulthood (see Lynam, Caspi, Moffitt, Loeber, & Stouthamer-Loeber, 2007; Obradovic, Pardini, Long, & Loeber, 2007; Pardini & Loeber, 2007). In addition to these factors, the consideration of psychopathy for inclusion in

DSM-V's disruptive behavior section also speaks to its rising importance (Frick & Moffitt, 2010).

The surge in research on child and adolescent psychopathy has extended the study and knowledge of psychopathy immensely. Research has now expanded beyond adolescent boys, with more vigorous research attention being shown to underresearched groups, such as preschool children (Hawes & Dadds, 2005) and girls (Hipwell et al., 2007; Schrum & Salekin, 2006). Progress in genetic research has also revived enthusiasm about the potential for family-history data and biological markers to provide clinically relevant prognostic information (Forsman, Lichtenstein, Andershed, & Larsson, 2008; Viding, Blair, Moffitt, & Plomin, 2005). Groundbreaking research on gene–environment interaction effects in predicting childhood psychopathology outcomes has emerged and helped us understand antisocial behavior more generally (e.g., Caspi et al., 2002) and will, we hope, also begin to shape our understanding of psychopathy.

The Controversy

Extension of the psychopathy concept to youth has not been without controversy, and any such book on child psychopathy would be remiss if this controversy were not mentioned. For instance, Seagrave and Grisso (2002) expressed concerns about whether psychopathy could be applied to youth. These authors were concerned about the concept being overrepresented in youth, such that too many youth would meet the symptomatic definition of psychopathy even though they were not truly psychopathic. Hart, Watt, and Vincent (2002; see also Vincent & Hart, 2002) also expressed unease about the construct validity and temporal stability of child and adolescent psychopathy, using an impressionist painting analogy. Specifically, they stated that the child and adolescent psychopathy construct may look fine from a distance, but "the closer you get, the messier it looks" (p. 241). These important criticisms should be carried forward and kept in mind as research advances in this area. However, as noted earlier, many more advances toward the study of child and adolescent psychopathy have occurred since these early debates.

The ever-increasing research on child psychopathy has helped to fill previously existing research gaps. Research has included attempts to understand the correlates of child and adolescent psychopathy (Blair, Perschardt, Budhani, Mitchell, & Pine, 2006; Dadds et al., 2005), to delineate their trajectories through childhood into adulthood (Burke, Loeber, & Lahey, 2007; Frick, Kimonis, Dandreaux, & Farrell, 2003; Lynam et al., 2007; Salekin, 2008; Salekin & Lochman, 2008), and to differentiate psychopathy from other forms of psychopathology (e.g., conduct disorder) (Kosson, Cyterski, Steuerwald, Neumann, & Walker-Matthews, 2002; Salekin, Leistico, Neumann, DiCicco, & Duros, 2004). These efforts have put us in a better position to answer some of the key questions regarding the potential applicability of psychopathy to child and adolescent populations.

Due to the vast developments in the area of child and adolescent psychopathy, there exists a need for a detailed overview of where the field stands at present, and where it appears to be headed in the future. This handbook on child and adolescent psychopathy was designed to fill this important need. It includes contributions from the world's foremost scientific experts on the topic, and covers chief conceptual and practical issues in the field, providing comprehensive coverage of published empirical work relevant to these key issues. In addition, the handbook offers some guidance as to the practical forensic issues related to risk assessment and the potential changeability of the syndrome.

In editing this handbook, we kept an eye toward providing a comprehensive, integrated overview of existing knowledge in the area. In addition, we wanted to identify priorities for future research in a coordinated way. When examining the etiology of disorders, edited books occasionally run the risk of providing individual views of specific topics that are related to the research priorities of individual contributors, which can lead to narrow opinions about what, in this case, causes psychopathy (Patrick, 2006). To address this issue, we asked authors to be broad in their coverage and where individual chapters focus on somewhat constricted etiological perspectives, we attempted to bring in multiple researchers and perspectives (i.e., additional chapters) to broaden what we know about child and adolescent psychopathy. We did this, in part, knowing that there are still many open questions as to the etiology of child psychopathy, even if significant gains in research have been made in a particular area. We also realize the need for integration across the various perspectives (genetics, temperament, personality, brain functioning, family functioning, parenting practices, etc.) in keeping with the developmental psychopathology macro-paradigm framework (see Kazdin & Kagan, 1994). Much of this research is ongoing in the field, including many strong contributions that attempt to integrate etiological perspectives, all of which will continue to help us better understand psychopathic features in youth.

This handbook on child psychopathy illuminates this exciting and ongoing line of research by addressing what we have learned to date regarding the reliability, construct validity, etiological correlates and mechanisms, and treatment potentiality of child psychopathy. The handbook advances the field of knowledge in many important areas, such as the potential biological paths to psychopathy (Blair, Chapter 7), general personality correlates of child psychopathy (Lynam, Chapter 8), and environmental factors

(Farrington, Ullrich, & Salekin, Chapter 9). In addition, we address how the field might move forward to answer some critical questions that need further exploration, some of which were sparked by the early controversy on this topic and raised primarily by Hart and colleagues (2002), Seagrave and Grisso (2002) and others (e.g., Edens, Skeem, Cruise, & Cauffman, 2001; Farrington, 2005; Rutter, 2005; Salekin, Rosenbaum, Lee, & Lester, 2009). These questions include the following: What is child psychopathy exactly? How does it translate into adult life? Are there successful and less successful transitions from childhood psychopathy to adulthood? This handbook addresses these important questions that continue to require further research with greater precision.

An Overview of This Volume

This handbook is divided into five sections. The first is devoted to chapters that address classification and assessment. In Chapter 2, Christopher J. Patrick provides an overview of the construct of psychopathy and considers a new way to view the construct that includes dimensions of meanness, boldness, and disinhibition. Next, in Chapter 3, John E. Lochman, Nicole P. Powell, Carolyn Boxmeyer, Laura Young, and Rachel Baden provide an overview of the historical conceptions of risk among children by outlining the various ways in which the constructs of disruptive behavior have been divided across the years. In Chapter 4, Julie S. Kotler and Robert J. McMahon review the numerous ways we can now assess psychopathy in youth. They also evaluate the merit of these various assessment tools by highlighting some of the positive and negative aspects of assessment technology for child and adolescent psychopathy, and related issues with respect to classification.

The second section examines the potential etiology of psychopathy in youth. First, Essi Viding and Henrik Larsson (Chapter 5) present an overview of genetic studies related to the development of psychopathy in youth. Their chapter encompasses the latest papers on behavior genetics and psychopathy, and provides a synthesis of the research in this area. As well, these researchers suggest future directions for research in this area. Second, Stuart F. White and Paul J. Frick (Chapter 6) examine the potential causal mechanisms that underlie psychopathy, putting forth callous–unemotional traits as the main component of psychopathy. Then, R. James R. Blair (Chapter 7) examines potential processes underlying child and adolescent psychopathy. Next, Donald R. Lynam (Chapter 8) provides key information on the connections between personality theory and psychopathy. In particular, Lynam links psychopathy to the Big Five factors of personality. Finally, David P. Farrington, Simone Ullrich, and Randall T. Salekin (Chapter 9) examine the relation between psychopathy and the environment, particularly the family environment.

The third section addresses the issues of stability, predictive validity, and comorbidity. Specifically, Henrik Andershed provides, in Chapter 10, a thorough review of research on the stability of psychopathy. In Chapter 11, Adelle E. Forth and Angela S. Book address whether psychopathy predicts the negative outcome of general and violent recidivism. Their chapter overviews previous meta-analytic studies on the topic of psychopathy and recidivism, and also generates new effect size summaries to show the magnitude of effect for predicting recidivism and other negative outcomes. Kathrin Sevecke and David S. Kosson (Chapter 12) address the pertinent topic of comorbidity. There is considerable research to show that psychopathy in youth overlaps with other forms of pathology, and their chapter attempts to help the reader better understand this relation and what it may mean for the concept of child psychopathy.

In the fourth section, several topic areas are covered, including special populations, the treatment of psychopathic youth, and clinical forensic issues. Specifically, Edelyn Verona, Naomi Sadeh, and Shabnam Javdani (Chapter 13) address the important issue of whether gender and culture influence child and adolescent psychopathy. This is a highly significant research area because there may be potential gender and ethnic differences that both affect findings in research studies and have implications for clinical practice. In Chapter 14, Randall T. Salekin addresses the issue of psychopathy and treatment in childhood populations. Particularly, Salekin addresses previous concerns regarding researchers' generally skeptical view regarding the potential for treating psychopathy, then attempts to delineate a road map for change with children and adolescents who may have psychopathic features. Salekin shows that there are important reasons to consider broader inclusion criteria and outcome measures for studies on child and adolescent psychopathy.

Next, Michael J. Vitacco, Randall T. Salekin, and Richard Rogers (Chapter 15) examine the potential utility of psychopathy in child and adolescent forensic cases. Their chapter challenges the notion that psychopathy may offer something beyond a conduct disorder diagnosis in terms of predicting violence. However, the authors recognize and note that psychopathy appears to be equally predictive of negative outcomes, and that the comparability of the two for predicting outcomes remains an open question. Importantly, their chapter points out that there may be many more important reasons to consider the psychopathy construct in forensic settings than recidivism alone. Thus, the chapter recognizes the connection between psychopathy and violence, and highlights its clinical utility as an important construct in understanding youth in forensic settings. In the final section, Randall T. Salekin and Donald R. Lynam (Chapter 16) briefly review the accomplishments thus far of the psychopathy concept and provide guidance regarding directions for research in the field of child and adolescent psychopathy.

To date, there exists no comprehensive handbook on child psychopathy. Because of the surge of research in this area, this volume is unique in its scope, comprehensiveness, and currency of coverage on a topic that is receiving considerable attention for its potential to explain behavior of disruptive youth. Because of its focus on empirical research findings, this handbook will be of particular interest to academics, graduate and undergraduate students in psychology, and researchers in other settings who are interested in youth with disruptive behavior disorders. In addition, it will be of interest to those who do research on juvenile delinquency, violence, crime, and substance abuse. Furthermore, clinical psychiatrists, psychologists, social workers, and other mental health professionals who work with children and adolescents will likely find the volume helpful. It will serve as a highly valuable resource to forensic child and adolescent psychologists and psychiatrists, and juvenile justice scholars due to the breadth of coverage of issues related to clinical assessment, prediction, specialized populations, and intervention. Finally, the book may be of value to those individuals who work in school settings and find persistently troublesome youth difficult to handle. We believe strongly, however, that the term *psychopathy* should not be used in a damaging way, but rather that the concept be used in a constructive manner to understand better the various types of youth as well as to chart ways to help youth lead more prosocial, productive, and meaningful lives.

In closing, we would like to express our gratitude to Kitty Moore and Alice Broussard at The Guilford Press. Their wise counsel throughout was appreciated. We are especially grateful to our colleagues, the esteemed individuals who contributed meaningfully to the book. Our thanks also go out to Caroline Titcomb, Krystal Hedge, Whitney Lester, and Kim Price for their thoughtful comments. We also express our thanks to our families, who supported us through the editing of this handbook. We hope that this handbook helps to further shed light on the concept of child and adolescent psychopathy, as well as to inspire researchers and promote even greater investigation in this key area of research and practice.

Note

1. Concerns about labeling have abated somewhat: Research shows that the term *child psychopathy* does not differ substantially much from conduct disorder in terms of court personnel perception (see Murrie, Boccaccini, McCoy, & Cornell, 2007). Nonetheless, further research is needed on this topic.

References

Andershed, H., Kerr, M., Stattin, H., & Levander, S. (2002). Psychopathic traits in non-referred youths: A new assessment tool. In E. Blaauw & L. Sheridan (Eds.), *Psychopaths: Current international perspectives* (pp. 131–158). Hague, The Netherlands: Elsevier.

Blair, R. J. R., & Coles, M. (2000). Expression recognition and behavioural problems in early adolescence. *Cognitive Development, 15*, 421–434.

Blair, R. J. R., Peschardt, K. S., Budhani, S., Mitchell, D. G. V., & Pine, D. S. (2006). The development of psychopathy. *Journal of Child Psychology and Psychiatry, 47*, 262–275.

Burke, J. D., Loeber, R., & Lahey, B. B. (2007). Adolescent conduct disorder and interpersonal callousness as predictors of psychopathy in young adults. *Journal of Clinical Child and Adolescent Psychology, 36*, 334–346.

Caldwell, M., Skeem, J. L., Salekin, R. T., & Van Rybroek, G. (2006). Treatment response of adolescent offenders with psychopathy features: A 2-year follow-up. *Criminal Justice and Behavior, 33*, 571–596.

Caspi, A., McClay, J., Moffitt, T. E., Mill, J., Martin, J., Craig, I. W., et al. (2002). Role of genotype in the cycle of violence in maltreated children. *Science, 297*, 851–854.

Cleckley, H. (1941). *The mask of sanity*. St. Louis, MO: Mosby.

Dadds, M. R., Fraser, J., Frost, A., & Hawes, D. J. (2005). Disentangling the underlying dimensions of psychopathy and conduct problems in childhood: A community study. *Journal of Consulting and Clinical Psychology, 73*, 400–410.

Davies, J. G. V., & Maliphant, R. (1971). Refractory behavior at school in normal adolescent males in relation to psychopathy and early experience. *Journal of Child Psychology and Psychiatry, 12*, 35–41.

Edens, J. F., Skeem, J. L., Cruise, K. R., & Cauffman, E. (2001). Assessment of "juvenile psychopathy" and its association with violence: A critical review. *Behavioral Sciences and the Law, 19*, 53–80.

Farrington, D. P. (2005). The importance of child and adolescent psychopathy. *Journal of Abnormal Child Psychology, 33*, 489–497.

Forsman, M., Lichtenstein, P., Andershed, H., & Larsson, H. (2008). Genetic effects explain the stability of psychopathic personality from mid- to late adolescence. *Journal of Abnormal Psychology, 117*, 606–617.

Forth, A. E., Hart, S. D., & Hare, R. D. (1990). Assessment of psychopathy in male young offenders. *Psychological Assessment, 2*, 342–344.

Forth, A. E., Kosson, D. S., & Hare, R. D. (2003). *The Psychopathy Checklist: Youth Version*. Toronto: Multi-Health Systems.

Fowles, D. C., & Kochanska, G. (2000). Temperament as a moderator of pathways to conscience in children: The contribution of electrodermal activity. *Psychophysiology, 37*, 788–795.

Frick, P. J., & Hare, R. D. (2001). *Antisocial Process Screening Device (APSD): Technical manual*. Toronto: Multi-Health Systems. (Original work published 1994)

Frick, P. J., Kimonis, E. R., Dandreaux, D. M., & Farell, J. M. (2003). The 4-year stability of psychopathic traits in non-referred youth. *Behavioral Sciences and the Law, 21,* 713–736.

Frick, P. J., & Moffitt, T. E. (2010). *A proposal to the DSM-V Childhood Disorders and ADHD Disruptive Behavior Disorders Work Groups to include a specifier to the diagnosis of conduct disorder based on the presence of callous unemotional traits.* Washington, DC: American Psychiatric Association.

Gutiérrez, M. J., & Eisenman, R. (1971). Verbal conditioning of neurotic and psychopathic delinquients using verbal and non-verbal reinforcers. *Psychological Reports, 29,* 7–10.

Hare, R. D. (2003). *The Hare Psychopathy Checklist—Revised* (2nd ed.). Toronto: Multi-Health Systems. (First edition published 1991)

Hart, S. D., Watt, K., & Vincent, G. M. (2002). Commentary on Seagrave and Grisso: Impressions of the state of the art. *Law an Human Behavior, 26,* 241–245.

Hawes, D. J., & Dadds, M. R. (2005). The treatment of conduct problems in children with callous–unemotional traits. *Journal of Consulting and Clinical Psychology, 73,* 737–741.

Hipwell, A. E., Pardini, D. A., Loeber, R., Sembower, M., Keenan, K., & Stouthamer-Loeber, M. (2007). Callous–unemotional behaviors in young girls: Shared and unique effects relative to conduct problems. *Journal of Clinical Child and Adolescent Psychology, 36,* 293–304.

Karpman, B. (1949). The psychopathic delinquent child. *American Journal of Orthopsychiatry, 20,* 223–265.

Karpman, B. (1950). Psychopathic behavior in infants and children: A critical survey of existing concepts. *American Journal of Orthopsychiatry, 21,* 223–272.

Kazdin, A. E., & Kagan, J. (1994). Models of dysfunction in developmental psychopathology. *Clinical Psychology: Science and Practice, 1,* 35–52.

Kosson, D. S., Cyterski, T. D., Steuerwald, B. L., Neumann, C. S., & Walker-Matthews, S. (2002). The reliability and validity of the Psychopathy Checklist: Youth Version (PCL:YV) in non-incarcerated adolescent males. *Psychological Assessment, 14,* 97–109.

Kotler, J. S., & McMahon, R. J. (2005). Child psychopathy: Theories, measurement, and relations with the development and persistence of conduct problems. *Clinical Child and Family Psychology Review, 8,* 291–325.

Laible, D. J., & Thompson, R. A. (2002). Mother–child conflict in the toddler years: Lessons in emotion, morality, and relationships. *Child Development, 73,* 1187–1203.

Loeber, R., Burke, J., & Pardini, D. A. (2009). Perspectives on oppositional defiant disorder, conduct disorder, and psychopathic features. *Journal of Child Psychology and Psychiatry, 50,* 133–142.

Lynam, D. R. (1996). Early identification of chronic offenders: Who is the fledgling psychopath? *Psychological Bulletin, 120,* 209–234.

Lynam, D. R. (1997). Pursuing the psychopath: Capturing the psychopath in a nomological net. *Journal of Abnormal Psychology, 106,* 425–438.

Lynam, D. R., Caspi, A., Moffitt, T. E., Loeber, R., & Stouthamer-Loeber, M. (2007). Longitudinal evidence that psychopathy scores in early adolescence predict adult psychopathy. *Journal of Abnormal Psychology, 116,* 155–165.

Lynam, D. R., & Gudonis, L. (2006). The development of psychopathy. *Annual Review of Clinical Psychology, 1,* 381–407.

McCord, W., & McCord, J. (1964). *The psychopath: An essay on the criminal mind.* Princeton, NJ: Van Nostrand. (Original work published 1959)

Murrie, D. C., Boccaccini, M. T., McCoy, W., & Cornell, D. G. (2007). Diagnostic labeling in juvenile court: How do psychopathy and conduct disorder findings influence judges? *Journal of Clinical Child and Adolescent Psychology, 36,* 228–241.

Murrie, D. C., & Cornell, D. G. (2000). The Millon Adolescent Clinical Inventory and Psychopathy. *Journal of Personality Assessment, 75,* 110–125.

Obradovic, J., Pardini, D. A., Long, J. D., & Loeber, R. (2007). Measuring interpersonal callousness in boys from childhood to adolescence: An examination of longitudinal invariance and temperoal stability. *Journal of Clinical Child and Adolescent Psychology, 36,* 276–292.

Pardini, D., & Loeber, R. (2007). Interpersonal and affective features of psychopathy in children and adolescents: Advancing a developmental perspective introduction to special section. *Journal of Clinical Child and Adolescent Psychology, 36,* 269–275.

Patrick, C. J. (Ed.). (2006). *Handbook of psychopathy.* New York: Guilford Press.

Quay, H. C. (1965). Psychopathic personality as pathological stimulation seeking. *American Journal of Psychiatry, 122,* 180–183.

Quay, H. C. (1986). Classification. In H. C. Quay & J. S. Werry (Eds.), *Psychopathological disorders of childhood* (3rd ed., pp. 1–42). New York: Wiley.

Rimé, B., Bouvy, H., Leborgne, B., & Rouillon, F. (1978). Psychopathy and nonverbal behavior in an interpersonal situation. *Journal of Abnormal Psychology, 87,* 636–643.

Rogers, R., Jackson, R. L., Sewell, K. W., & Johansen, J. (2004). Predictors of treatment outcome in dually diagnosed antisocial youth. *Behavioral Sciences and the Law, 22,* 215–222.

Rutter, M. (2005). What is the meaning and utility of the psychopathy concept? *Journal of Abnormal Child Psychology, 33,* 499–503.

Salekin, R. T. (2002). Psychopathy and therapeutic pessimism: Clinical lore or clinical reality? *Clinical Psychology Review, 22,* 79–112.

Salekin, R. T. (2006). Psychopathy in children and adolescents. In C. J. Patrick (Ed.), *Handbook of psychopathy* (pp. 389–414). New York: Guilford Press.

Salekin, R. T. (2008). Psychopathy and recidivism from mid-adolescence to young adulthood: Cumulating legal problems and limiting life opportunities. *Journal of Abnormal Psychology, 117,* 386–395.

Salekin, R. T. (2009). Psychopathology and assessment: Contributing knowledge to science and practice. *Journal of Psychopathology and Behavioral Assessment.*

Salekin, R. T., & Debus, S. A. (2008). Assessing child and adolescent psychopathy. In R. Jackson (Ed.), *Learning forensic assessment* (pp. 347–383). New York: Routledge/Taylor & Francis.

Salekin, R. T., & Frick, P. J. (2005). Psychopathy in children and adolescence: The need for a developmental perspective. *Journal of Abnormal Child Psychology, 33,* 403–409.

Salekin, R. T., Leistico, A. R., Neumann, C. S., DiCicco, T. M., & Duros, R. L.

(2004). Psychopathy and comorbidity in a young offender sample: Taking a closer look at psychopathy's potential importance over disruptive behavior disorders. *Journal of Abnormal Psychology, 113*, 416–427.

Salekin, R. T., & Lochman, J. E. (2008). Child and adolescent psychopathy: The search for protective factors. *Criminal Justice and Behavior, 35*, 159–172.

Salekin, R. T., Rosenbaum, J., Lee, Z., & Lester, W. S. (2009). Child and adolescent psychopathy: Like a painting by Monet. *Youth Violence and Juvenile Justice, 7*, 239–255.

Salekin, R. T., Ziegler, T. A., Larrea, M. A., Anthony, V. L., & Bennett, A. (2003). Predicting dangerousness with two Millon Adolescent Clinical Inventory Scales: The importance of egocentric and callous traits. *Journal of Personality Assessment, 80,* 154–163.

Schrum, C. L., & Salekin, R. T. (2006). Psychopathy in adolescent female offenders: An item response theory analysis of the Psychopathy Checklist—Youth Version. *Behavioral Sciences and the Law, 24,* 39–63.

Schulsinger, F. (1972). Psychopathy: Heredity and environment. *International Journal of Mental Health, 1,* 190–206.

Seagrave, D., & Grisso, T. (2002). Adolescent development and the measurement of juvenile psychopathy. *Law and Human Behavior, 26,* 219–239.

Stickle, T. R., Kirkpatrick, N. M., & Brush, L. N. (2009). Callous–unemotional traits and social information processing: Multiple risk factor models for understanding aggressive behavior in antisocial youth. *Law and Human Behavior, 33*, 515–529.

Viding, E., Blair, R. J. R., Moffitt, T. E., & Plomin, R. (2005). Evidence for substantial genetic risk for psychopathy in 7-year olds. *Journal of Child Psychology and Psychiatry, 46,* 592–597.

Vincent, G. M., & Hart, S. D. (2002). Psychopathy in childhood and adolescence: Implications for the assessment and management of multi-problem youths. In R. R. Corrado, R. Roesch, S. D. Hart, & J. K. Gierowski (Eds.), *Multi-problem youth: A foundation for comparative research on needs, interventions, and outcomes* (pp. 150–163). Amsterdam: IOS Press.

Wolkind, S. N. (1974). The components of "affectionless psychopathy" in institutionalized children. *Journal of Child Psychology and Psychiatry, 15*, 215–220.

Part I

Classification and Assessment

2

Conceptualizing the Psychopathic Personality

Disinhibited, Bold, . . . or Just Plain Mean?

CHRISTOPHER J. PATRICK

The field of psychopathy is undergoing important transitions at this point in its history. Vigorous debates are currently underway regarding the conceptual boundaries of the construct and the centrality of criminally deviant behavior in defining and measuring it (e.g., Cooke, Michie, & Hart, 2006; Hare & Neumann, 2006). Renewed attention is being given to alternative methods for assessing psychopathy—including approaches hearkening back to Cleckley's (1941/1976) classic portrayal of the disorder that may have unique value for identifying individuals with psychopathic tendencies outside the walls of correctional settings (e.g., Hall & Benning, 2006; Lilienfeld & Fowler, 2006; Skeem & Cooke, 2009). Interest has grown in the application of advanced quantitative methodologies, including structural equation modeling and item response analysis, to measurement and understanding of psychopathy and related phenomena (cf. Cooke et al., 2006; Krueger, 2006). The study of psychopathy in youth has emerged as a dominant focus within the field and has contributed greatly to our understanding of the origins and development of the syndrome. Neurobiological approaches to the study of psychopathy—from behavioral and molecular genetics to neurochemistry to brain electrophysiology and neuroimaging—have gained momentum and have yielded important clues as to the mechanisms of the disorder.

Growth in knowledge within a discipline invariably serves as inspiration for investigators to reconsider how phenomena under study might best be conceptualized. In this regard, the calls that have arisen for change in how we think about and measure psychopathy can be seen as a natural consequence of the methodological and empirical advances in the field. My aim in this chapter is to discuss varying perspectives advanced over the years regarding the nature and scope of the psychopathy construct and to identify what I believe to be the major themes running through these varying perspectives. These major themes are *disinhibition* (aka externalizing), *boldness* (aka fearless dominance or daringness), and *meanness* (aka callousness or coldheartedness).

I begin with a brief overview of historical conceptualizations of psychopathy predating Cleckley (1941/1976), followed by a discussion of work by Cleckley and his contemporaries. Boldness and disinhibition are highlighted as themes in Cleckley's account of psychopathic hospital patients, in contrast with the emphasis on meanness and disinhibition among writers of Cleckley's time who focused on psychopathy in criminal offender samples. I then review contemporary approaches to the assessment of psychopathy in adult criminal and noncriminal samples, as well as instruments designed to assess psychopathy in delinquents and youth with conduct disorder. Consistent with clinical descriptions of psychopathy in criminal offenders, methods for assessing psychopathy in adult and youthful antisocial samples have emphasized meanness (together with disinhibition) more than boldness. In contrast, boldness appears to be indexed more distinctively by the Psychopathic Personality Inventory (Lilienfeld & Andrews, 1996), a self-report instrument designed to measure traits embodied in Cleckley's conception in nonoffender samples. The last major section of the chapter focuses on defining disinhibition, boldness, and meanness as distinctive phenotypic entities, and considering etiological factors that may give rise to these distinguishable components of the psychopathy construct.

Before Cleckley: Historical Conceptualizations of Psychopathy

Early accounts of the syndrome of psychopathy (e.g., Partridge, 1930; Pinel, 1806/1962; Rush, 1812; Schneider, 1934) assigned prominent emphasis to violent and antisocial behavior, presumably owing to the salience of such behavior in otherwise rational-appearing individuals. Explosive, impulsive, reckless, and irresponsible actions—accompanied often by alcohol or drug problems (e.g., Partridge, 1928a, 1928b; Prichard, 1835) and sometimes by suicidal behavior (e.g., Partridge, 1928b; Pinel, 1806/1962)—emerge repeatedly as themes in these accounts. As I describe further below, these features reflect the disinhibitory (Gorenstein & Newman, 1980) or externalizing (Krueger et al., 2002; Patrick, Hicks, Krueger, & Lang, 2005) component of psychopathy included in modern conceptualizations. For Pinel (1806/1962), explosive violence ("abstract and sanguinary fury") was the most salient clinical feature and, in fact, the second of his three cases would likely have been diagnosed with intermittent explosive disorder according to current clinical criteria rather than psychopathy or antisocial personality disorder. Partridge's (1930) description of the "sociopathic" individual in particular emphasized tendencies toward emotional instability, feelings of inadequacy or inferiority, alienation, and angry aggression. This pattern of emotional volatility and impulsive–reactive violence appears to be more characteristic of highly externalizing individuals (cf. Patrick & Bernat, 2009a) than of individuals who would be considered psychopathic according to contemporary definitions.

A second set of attributes emphasized in these early accounts, which appears somewhat at odds with the features just mentioned, consists of charm, self-assurance, interpersonal dominance, attention seeking, persuasiveness, and affective shallowness. For example, a subgroup of psychopathic individuals that Kraepelin (1904/1915) termed "swindlers" was characterized as glib and charming but lacking in basic morality or loyalty to others; they typically specialized in fraudulence and con artistry, and invariably accumulated large debts that went unpaid. Schneider (1934) identified a similar "self-seeking type" that he described as pleasant and affable, but egocentric, demanding of attention, and superficial in emotional reactions and relations with others. Like Kraepelin's swindlers, self-seeking psychopaths, according to Schneider, were pathologically deceitful and prone to fraudulent behavior. As described in the next section, this set of features was central to Cleckley's (1941/1976) conception of psychopathic personality.

A third prominent emphasis in these historical accounts of psychopathy consists of features relating to brutality, emotional coldness, and callous exploitation of others. For example, one of three psychopathic cases referenced by Pinel (1806/1962), while efficacious and successful in his financial dealings, was described as self-centered and brutally antagonistic in his interactions with others. Rush (1812) emphasized cruelty and viciousness in his account of the psychopath and posited that a deep-rooted "moral depravity" lay at the core of the disorder. An active affectionless type identified by Schneider (1934) was characterized as unscrupulous, cold, and unfeeling. Schneider attributed these tendencies, which he saw as emerging early in life, to a core deficit in emotional sensitivity rather than to a weakness in moral judgment. This emphasis on coldness and cruelty is also evident in the work of later theorists, after Cleckley (1941/1976), who focused on criminal offenders as the basis for their writings on psychopathy (e.g., Craft, 1965, 1966b; Hare, 1970, 1980, 1991, 2003; McCord & McCord, 1964).

Cleckley and His Contemporaries

Modern conceptualizations and measures of psychopathy derive from Hervey Cleckley's monograph, *The Mask of Sanity,* originally published in 1941 (3rd ed., 1955; 5th ed., 1976). Cleckley's account was based on his direct experiences with inpatients at a large psychiatric hospital, which he documented in a series of comprehensive case histories. In an effort to narrow the concept down to a discrete diagnostic entity that could serve as a viable target for study, Cleckley set forth a list of 16 specific criteria for psychopathy. Central to his conception was the idea that psychopathy entails the presence of severe underlying pathology masked by an outward appearance of robust mental health. In contrast with other psychiatric patients who present as confused, agitated, depressed, socially withdrawn, or otherwise disturbed, psychopaths appear on initial contact to be confident, personable, and psychologically well adjusted. It is only through continued observation across a range of settings over time that the psychopath's underlying pathology reveals itself.

Cleckley's (1941/1976) 16 criteria for psychopathy can be grouped into three conceptual categories (Patrick, 2006). The first consists of indicators of positive psychological adjustment: good intelligence and social adeptness, absence of delusions or irrationality, absence of nervousness, and low incidence of suicide. Notably, these characteristics reflect not just the absence of obvious mental disturbance but, in fact, the presence of resiliency and positive adjustment: "The surface of the psychopath ... shows up as equal to or better than normal and gives no hint at all of a disorder within" (Cleckley, 1976, p. 383). At the same time, however, the psychopath, according to Cleckley, exhibits severe behavioral pathology, reflected in a second set of diagnostic indicators: impulsive antisocial acts, irresponsibility (aka "unreliability"), promiscuity, failure to learn from experience, and absence of any clear life plan. With regard to substance use, Cleckley observed that psychopathic patients exhibit enhanced recklessness under the influence of alcohol but not unusual proneness to alcoholism or other addictions. The third cluster of items among Cleckley's criteria consisted of indices of emotional unresponsiveness and impaired social relatedness: lack of remorse or shame, poverty in affective reactions, egocentricity and inability to love, deceitfulness and insincerity, absence of loyalty, and deficient insight.

Notably, Cleckley (1941/1976) did not describe psychopathic patients as antagonistic, violent, or cruel. Indeed, he maintained that the psychopath's deficient emotional sensitivity mitigated against angry, vengeful reactions: "The psychopath is not volcanically explosive, at the mercy of irresistible drives and overwhelming rages of temper. Often he seems scarcely wholehearted, even in wrath or wickedness" (p. 263). In line with this characterization, only a small minority of Cleckley's clinical cases (three of 15) showed consistent signs of belligerence and interpersonal aggressiveness, whereas several (eight of 15) exhibited minimal tendencies of this sort. Furthermore, along with case examples of psychopathic patients whose antisocial acts brought them into repeated contact with the law, Cleckley presented examples of "successful psychopaths" who established careers as physicians, scholars, or businessmen. Cleckley's etiological perspective was that psychopathy reflected a deep-rooted impairment in emotional processing akin to semantic aphasia (in the realm of language processing) or color blindness (in the realm of perceptual processing; cf. Maudsley, 1874). In his view, the occurrence of this core underlying impairment defined the presence of the disorder, rather than any particular overt behavioral expression.

Cleckley's clinical diagnostic account of psychopathy served as direct inspiration for David Lykken's (1957) study of anxiety responses in psychopathic delinquents, generally regarded as the first experimental investigation of this topic. Using Cleckley's criteria as the basis for identifying primary ("true") psychopaths, Lykken reported a number of effects consistent with a deficiency in anxiety or fear, including low scores on a questionnaire measure of risk aversion, diminished electrodermal reactivity to conditioned shock cues, and impaired passive avoidance learning. Cleckley's criteria also served as the basis for subject selection in Robert Hare's program of research on autonomic reactivity in psychopathic offenders during the 1960s and 1970s, which yielded a variety of findings consistent with the idea of a fear deficit (cf. Hare, 1978). Cleckley's conceptualization was also influential in classic neurobiological theories of psychopathy that posited a deficit in the brain's punishment learning system as crucial to the disorder (Fowles, 1980; Gray, 1971).

In contrast, other writers of Cleckley's time who focused on psychopathy in criminal offender samples presented a different picture of the disorder. Drawing on firsthand experiences with criminal and delinquent individuals, as well as written accounts of historic figures, McCord and McCord (1964), in their volume *The Psychopath: An Essay on the Criminal Mind,* emphasized features of affective coldness, social detachment, and dangerousness, along with behavioral disinhibition. These authors described the psychopath as "an asocial, aggressive, highly impulsive person, who feels little or no guilt, and is unable to form lasting bonds of affection with other human beings" (p. 3). For McCord and McCord, the latter two of these characteristics, "guiltlessness" and "lovelessness," comprised the essence of the disorder. Parental rejection/neglect was posited to play a unique etiological role in the emergence of these core characteristics, either as a primary determinant (in cases of severe abuse/neglect) or as an incremental contributor when other distinct pathogenic influences (constitutional proneness toward disinhibition; otherwise adverse environment) were present.

Like Cleckley, McCord and McCord (1964) viewed psychopaths as deficient in emotional reactivity: "In fact, psychopathy is almost the antithesis of neurosis. In terms of emotional sensitivity, the neurotic is 'thin-skinned,' and the psychopath is 'thick-skinned' " (p. 47). However, these authors viewed impairments in anxiety and affective responsiveness in psychopathy as a reflection of profound social disconnectedness ("lovelessness" and "guiltlessness") rather than of a global deficit in affective–motivational capacity. In particular, McCord and McCord maintained that psychopathic individuals, lacking in social conscience and inhibitions against aggression, characteristically responded with rage as opposed to fear in frustrating or threatening situations. Thus, in contrast with Cleckley, who described psychopathic inpatients as neither "deeply vicious" nor "volcanically explosive," McCord and McCord characterized psychopathic criminals as cold, violent, and predatory.

Other writers of Cleckley's era who were concerned with psychopathy in criminal populations also highlighted cruelty and aggressiveness as features of the disorder. Lindner (1944) characterized criminal psychopaths as truculent and antagonistic:

> The psychopathic way of life is characterized by its effects—aggressive behavior, the expression and actional counterpart of a belligerent social attitude, the forceful surmounting of frustration-provoking barriers by acts of voluntary willfulness, as well as by techniques of escape and avoidance the exercise of which removes the psychopath from the frustrating situation. . . . Where any variety of escape is not ready to hand, aggressiveness remains the keynote. . . . (p. 5)

Craft (1966a) identified a "vicious" criminal psychopathic subtype, whom he described as "affectionless, impulsive, and persistently aggressive" (p. 212). Individuals of this sort exhibited early emergence of antisocial behavior and marked resistance to treatment, and, according to Craft, they typically came from highly hostile home environments. Robins (1966, 1978) likewise emphasized early and persistent aggressive antisociality in her empirical accounts of maladjusted youth who developed into adult "sociopaths." Robins's work served as the cornerstone for the modern notion of antisocial personality disorder (APD), included in the third and fourth editions of the *Diagnostic and Statistical Manual of Mental Disorders* (DSM-III, DSM-IV; American Psychiatric Association, 1980, 2000), which emphasizes aggression, destructiveness, and other forms of delinquency in childhood, and behavioral evidence of impulsivity, deception, recklessness, aggressiveness, and criminal deviancy in adulthood.

Summary and Comments

Cleckley (1941/1976) sought to counter historical trends toward overinclusiveness in the use of the term *psychopath* by describing in precise terms a specific diagnostic entity for which he believed the term should be reserved. He portrayed psychopathy as a "masked" pathology: By his account, psychopathic individuals were affable, surgent, and psychologically healthy in their overt social demeanor but impulsive, unreliable, deceptive, and promiscuous in their everyday actions, and superficial in their emotional reactions and relations with people. Cleckley did not view psychopaths as brutally aggressive, predatory, or deliberately cruel. Rather, he characterized the harm they did to others (and the damage they wreaked on themselves) as a by-product of a shallow, venturesome, capricious nature: "In fact, [the psychopath's] most serious damage to others is often largely through their concern for him and their efforts to help him" (p. 262). Other influential writers of Cleckley's time (e.g., Craft, 1965, 1966a, 1966b; Lindner, 1944; McCord & McCord, 1964) likewise sought to clarify and narrow the scope of the diagnosis. However, in contrast with Cleckley, these writers emphasized coldness, viciousness, and exploitativeness in their descriptions.

In terms of referent constructs discussed in the final major section below, Cleckley and his contemporaries similarly highlighted *disinhibition* (proneness to externalizing behavior) in their accounts of psychopathy but differed in the emphasis they assigned to *boldness* versus *meanness* in conceptualizing the disorder. What might account for this crucial difference in emphasis? The most obvious explanation is the difference in subject populations on which these alternative conceptualizations were based. Cleckley's clientele consisted of psychiatric inpatients rather than incarcerated criminal offenders. Many of his psychopathic cases had been committed or referred for psychiatric treatment rather being sent to prison because the antisocial acts they perpetrated were generally of a lesser, nonviolent nature and appeared irrational ("unmotivated") in ways suggestive of an underlying mental disorder. Furthermore, Cleckley's patients came more from high- or middle-class rather than low socioeconomic backgrounds, and in many cases possessed family and other social supports that helped to buffer them against legal consequences. In contrast, other writers of Cleckley's time were concerned with youthful delinquent offenders and adult criminals. These writers sought to delineate a specific subgroup of offenders whose criminal deviancy was distinguished by its amorality, severity, persistence, and recalcitrance to treatment. Individuals of this sort were notable for their aggressiveness, emotional coldness, indifference to the feelings and welfare of others, and cruel victimization. They tended to come from impoverished, abusive backgrounds (e.g., McCord and McCord [1964] identified parental abuse and neglect as distinctively pathogenic for criminal psychopathy) and engaged in serious forms of antisocial behavior that provoked harsh legal penalties.

Modern Conceptualizations of Psychopathy

Psychopathy in Adult Offender Samples

A substantial amount of published empirical research on psychopathy to date has focused on adult criminal (in particular, male) offender samples. Beginning with Lykken's (1957) study of anxiety in psychopathic offenders and continuing through to the early 1980s, Cleckley's criteria were employed as the primary basis for subject selection in experimental studies of psychopathy—including studies by Hare and colleagues on the psychophysiological correlates of the disorder (cf. Hare, 1978). Hare's earlier work employed a global diagnostic approach in which knowledgeable assessors assigned scores from 1 to 7 to indicate the participant's resemblance to Cleckley's prototypic description (1 = clearly nonpsychopathic; 7 = definitely psychopathic). To clarify and systematize the assessment of psychopathy in research, Hare (1980) developed an interview-based inventory, the Psychopathy Checklist—Revised (PCL-R), using the Cleckley prototype ratings as a referent.

The original version of the PCL comprised 22 items distilled from a larger pool of candidate items by selecting those that best discriminated between high and low scorers on the Cleckley global system. Two items ("previous diagnosis as a psychopath," and "antisocial behavior not due to alcohol intoxication") were omitted in the revised PCL (PCL-R; Hare, 1991, 2003), and scoring criteria for the remaining 20 items were modified somewhat. Regarding item content, the affective–interpersonal and behavioral maladjustment features described by Cleckley are well represented in the PCL-R. However, the positive adjustment features identified by Cleckley are not. In particular, the absence of nervousness/neuroticism highlighted by Cleckley is not part of the PCL-R definition. Also omitted are "absence of delusions or irrationality" and "disinclination toward suicide." Although ostensibly similar to Cleckley's "superficial charm and good intelligence" criterion, the "glibness and superficial charm" item of the PCL-R (item 1) is in fact defined in a more deviant manner (i.e., reflecting an excessively talkative, slick, and insincere demeanor).

Patrick (2006) postulated that positive adjustment indicators were omitted from the PCL-R due to the strategy used to develop the original PCL, in which items were chosen to index psychopathy as a unitary construct using Cleckley global ratings as the criterion. Items were selected to be internally consistent with one another, as well as to discriminate between low and high Cleckley groups (Hare, 1980). Accordingly, good discriminating items that correlated with many other candidate items were retained, whereas items that correlated with relatively few other candidate items were eliminated. Given that Cleckley's criteria included more indicators of deviance (12 of 16) than of positive adjustment (4 of 16), and that the development sample for the PCL consisted of prisoners rather than nonincarcerated individuals, it seems likely that the initial candidate pool of items included many more deviance-related indicators, such that positive adjustment indicators dropped out in the selection process. This accounts for why the PCL-R consists of items that are uniformly indicative of deviance—and why overall scores on the PCL-R demonstrate robust positive relations with criterion measures of deviance and maladjustment, including extent and severity of criminal acts, antagonism and aggression, and alcohol and drug problems, but negligible associations with criterion measures of positive adjustment, such as verbal ability, anxiousness, internalizing symptoms, and suicide immunity (Hall, Benning, & Patrick, 2004; Hare, 2003; Lynam & Derefinko, 2006; Smith & Newman, 1990; Verona, Patrick, & Joiner, 2001).

However, despite the fact that the PCL/PCL-R was developed to index psychopathy as a unitary phenomenon, evidence from factor-analytic and correlational–validation studies indicates that it nonetheless taps differentiable component constructs, or factors. The dominant structural model of the PCL-R until recently has been the two-factor model (Hare et al., 1990; Harpur, Hakstian, & Hare, 1988), in which Factor 1 encompasses the interpersonal and affective features of psychopathy, and Factor 2 encompasses the antisocial deviance features. Cooke and Michie (2001) proposed an alternative three-factor model in which Factor 1 is parsed into two components ("arrogant and deceitful interpersonal style," marked by charm, grandiosity, deceitfulness, and manipulation; and "deficient affective experience," comprising absence of remorse, callousness, shallow affect, and failure to accept responsibility) and Factor 2 is pared down to an "impulsive–irresponsible behavioral style" component that comprises five items (boredom proneness, parasitism, impulsivity, irresponsibility, and absence of goals) considered to reflect underlying traits as opposed to behavioral sequelae of those traits. Hare and Neumann (2006) advanced a four-factor model in which Factor 1 is parsed into two "facets" mirroring Cooke and Michie's interpersonal and affective factors, and Factor 2 is divided into a "lifestyle" facet, identical to Cooke and Michie's impulsive–irresponsible factor and an "antisocial" factor encompassing aggressiveness, early behavior problems, juvenile delinquency, revocation of conditional release, and criminal versatility.

Reflecting the unitary conception of psychopathy that guided the PCL-R's development, constituent factors within each of these models show moderate (~.5) correlations with one another. Nonetheless, these separable factors also show diverging relations with various external criterion measures. In the two-factor model, high scores on Factor 1 are associated with higher narcissism and Machiavellianism (Harpur, Hare, & Hakstian, 1989; Hare, 1991; Verona et al., 2001), heightened use of proactive (instrumental/premeditated) aggression (Patrick & Zempolich, 1998; Porter & Woodworth, 2006), and lower empathy (Hare, 2003). In addition, scores on Factor 1 (in particular, variance that is nonredundant with Factor 2) exhibit relations with some measures of adaptive tendencies. For example, Factor 1 shows positive correlations with measures of social dominance (Hare, 1991; Harpur et al., 1989; Verona et al., 2001) and negative correlations with indicators of fearfulness, distress/anxiety, and depression (Harpur et al., 1989; Hicks & Patrick, 2006). Evidence of diminished *physiological* responsiveness to fearful and aversive stimuli has also been reported specifically in relation to Factor 1 (Patrick, 1994, 2007). In contrast, Factor 2 shows selective positive relations with trait measures of aggression, impulsivity, and general sensation seeking (Hare, 1991; Harpur et al, 1989;), as well as child symptoms of DSM APD, and is correlated to a markedly higher degree than Factor 1 with adult APD symptoms and variables reflecting frequency and severity of criminal offending (Hare, 2003; Verona et al., 2001). Factor 2 is also associated more with angry–reactive forms of aggression (Patrick & Zempolich, 1998; Porter & Woodworth, 2006) and measures of alcohol and drug dependence (Hare, 2003; Smith & Newman, 1990) than is Factor 1.

Studies of the external correlates of lower-order components of the PCL-R have also begun to appear in the literature. Skeem, Mulvey, and Grisso (2003) examined the validity of Cooke and Michie's (2001) three factors in relation to violence and other forms of antisocial deviance. They reported that the impulsive–irresponsible ("lifestyle") factor was most related to overall frequency and severity of criminal offending, incidence of property crimes, and substance-related disorders. The affective factor was most related to historical and future violence and crimes against people. The Interpersonal factor was associated to a lesser degree with past and future criminal deviance than either of the other factors.

Hall and colleagues (2004) reported that the interpersonal factor mostly accounted for relations of PCL-R Factor 1 with measures of social efficacy and emotional resilience. The unique variance in the interpersonal factor (i.e., variance distinct from the affective and lifestyle factors) was associated positively with five-factor model (FFM) extraversion, openness, and conscientiousness, and negatively with FFM neuroticism. This factor also showed distinctive positive associations with verbal intelligence and personal and parental socioeconomic status (SES). Scores on the lifestyle factor demonstrated selective relations with indicators of externalizing deviance and maladjustment including personality traits reflecting impulsivity, sensation seeking (disinhibition and boredom facets in particular), anger, alienation, high neuroticism and dysphoria/distress, and low conscientiousness and achievement motivation; fighting in childhood and adulthood; drug and alcohol problems; and low personal SES. As reported by Skeem and colleagues (2003), scores on the affective factor were associated selectively with violent criminal offending (assault, weapons possession, kidnapping, and murder). The most salient personality correlates of the affective factor were aggressiveness, low agreeableness, and low affiliation (low social closeness/communality). Scores on this factor also predicted a reduced incidence of specific fears. The antisocial facet of the PCL-R (cf. Hare & Neumann, 2006), while generally paralleling the lifestyle facet in its relations with criterion measures, showed higher correlations with aggression-related than with impulsivity-related personality traits, and stronger associations with violent criminal charges. All four facets of the PCL-R showed negative zero-order associations with FFM agreeableness (cf. Lynam & Derefinko, 2006), although the associations were more robust for the affective, lifestyle, and antisocial facets than for the interpersonal facet. Parallel findings were reported in a recent study of female offenders (Kennealy, Hicks, & Patrick, 2007).

Psychopathy in Adult Noncriminal Samples

To date, only a small number of studies have been conducted in which adults from the community have been assessed for psychopathy using clinical diagnostic procedures. The first published study of this type (Widom, 1977) recruited individuals through newspaper ads who showed autobiographical evidence of psychopathic characteristics, including impulsivity, aggressiveness, antisocial behavior, and lack of anxiety or guilt. The standardized assessment data for this sample indicated that the target participants were more clearly antisocial–externalizing than clinically psychopathic and would more aptly be characterized as "not currently incarcerated" or "subclinical" than as "noncriminal" or "successful." Other, more recent studies by Raine and colleagues (e.g., Ishikawa, Raine, Lencz, Bihrle, & Lacasse, 2001; Raine et al., 2004) have compared subgroups of individuals with high overall scores on the PCL-R recruited through temporary employment agencies, differentiated by the presence versus absence of prior criminal convictions. Never-convicted psychopathic individuals in these studies did not differ from previously convicted psychopaths in extent of self-reported criminal behavior, presence of psychopathology (i.e., mood/anxiety, substance-related, or psychotic disorders), or self-reported negative affect, with the two psychopathic groups exceeding controls on each of these variables. Based on these findings, never-convicted psychopaths in these PCL-R studies would more accurately be labeled "subclinical" than "noncriminal" or "successful" (cf. Hall & Benning, 2006).

Other published studies have assessed psychopathy in student (e.g., Forth, Brown, Hart, & Hare, 1996; Salekin, Trobst, & Krioukova, 2001), civil psychiatric (e.g., Skeem, Miller, Mulvey, Tiemann, & Monahan, 2005), or at-risk community samples (e.g., Farrington et al., 2006) using an abbreviated Screening Version of the PCL-R (PCL:SV; Hart, Cox, & Hare, 1995) developed for use in forensic and nonforensic samples. However, the range of PCL:SV scores in general community samples tends to be highly restricted, and concerns have been raised regarding the sensitivity of PCL-based ratings for assessing core features of psychopathy in nonincarcerated individuals—particularly in view of the strong emphasis on criminal deviance in the scoring of most PCL items (Skeem & Cooke, 2009; Widiger, 2006). For example, the report of the DSM-IV field trial on APD (Widiger et al., 1996) noted that affective–interpersonal features of psychopathy, as assessed by the PCL:SV, did not contribute incrementally to prediction of psychopathy-related criterion variables over and above APD criteria.

The other major approach used to investigate psychopathy in nonincarcerated adult samples has been self-report assessment. A variety of self-report measures of psychopathy have been developed and utilized over the years (for a review, see Lilienfeld & Fowler, 2006), but these measures for the most part capture mainly the antisocial deviance (Factor 2) component of psychopathy (Hare, 1991, 2003; Harpur et al., 1989; Lilienfeld & Fowler, 2006). A notable exception is the Psychopathic Personality Inventory (PPI; Lilienfeld & Andrews, 1996; Lilienfeld & Widows, 2005), which was developed specifically to assess psychopathy, as described by Cleckley, in nonincarcerated community samples. In contrast with the PCL-R, the development strategy for the PPI did not rely on the assumption of psychopathy as a unitary construct. Instead, an inclusive personality-based approach was taken, with the aim of capturing the full array of trait constructs embodied in Cleckley's description. A comprehensive literature review was undertaken to identify all relevant constructs, and separate unidimensional subscales were developed to assess these varying constructs. Although the PPI was developed with no a priori structural model of psychopathy in mind, exploratory factor analyses of its eight subscales (Benning, Patrick, Hicks, Blonigen, & Krueger, 2003; Benning, Patrick, Salekin, & Leistico, 2005; Ross, Benning, Patrick, Thompson, & Thurston, 2009) have revealed two distinct higher-order factors. Social potency, stress immunity, and fearlessness subscales load preferentially on the first factor (PPI-I) and impulsive nonconformity, blame externalization, Machiavellian egocentricity, and carefree nonplanfulness subscales load on the second factor (PPI-II). Benning, Patrick, Blonigen, Hicks, and Iacono (2005) labeled these two factors fearless dominance and impulsive antisociality. Unlike PCL-R Factors 1 and 2, which are moderately correlated, the two higher-order factors of the PPI are uncorrelated. The eighth subscale of the PPI, coldheartedness (reflecting low sentimentality, low imaginative capacity, and low responsiveness to others' distress), does not load appreciably on either PPI factor; rather, it loads uniquely on a separate factor in an expanded three-factor solution (Benning et al., 2003).

The two higher-order factors of the PPI show meaningful diverging associations with a variety of external criterion variables (Benning et al., 2003; Benning, Patrick, Blonigen, et al., 2005; Benning, Patrick, Salekin, et al., 2005; Blonigen et al., 2005; Douglas et al., 2008; Patrick, Edens, Poythress, & Lilienfeld, 2006; Ross et al., 2009). In general, the correlates of PPI Factors I and II mirror those of the *unique variance* in PCL-R Factor 1 (its interpersonal component, in particular) and of Factor 2, respectively, in relation to a wide range of external criteria described in the preceding section, including narcissism, thrill seeking, empathy, behavioral maladjustment (e.g., impulsivity and aggressiveness, child and adult antisocial behavior, aggression, substance use problems), and core personality dimensions, such as those captured by the FFM.

Psychopathy in Youth with Conduct Disorder

Historically, efforts to investigate psychopathy in childhood and adolescence (e.g., Robins, 1966, 1978) have emphasized the behavioral deviance (externalizing) features of psychopathy more than the core affective–interpersonal features. However, contemporary researchers have systematically endeavored to quantify these core features to delineate a distinct subgroup of youth with conduct disorder who qualify as psychopathic. Much of this work has utilized so-called "downward extensions" (youth-adapted versions; Salekin, 2006) of the PCL-R. Since research on psychopathy in youth comprises the major focus of this volume, I reference this work only briefly to highlight key points of contact with conceptual and empirical work already described.

The earliest of the PCL-R–based approaches to the assessment of psychopathy in youth was the PCL: Youth Version (PCL:YV; Forth, Kosson, & Hare, 1996/2003), a modified, 18-item variant developed for use with adolescent offenders ages 13–18. Research to date indicates that the PCL:YV parallels the PCL-R in terms of factor structure and associations with external criterion measures (Forth et al., 1996/2003). Frick and Hare (2001) devised the 20-item Antisocial Process Screening Device (APSD; formerly the Psychopathy Screening Device; Frick, O'Brien, Wootton, & McBurnett, 1994) to assess psychopathic tendencies in younger children (ages 6–13 years) referred for conduct problems. The APSD is rated by parents or teachers. (A newer self-report version for adolescents ages 13–18 is also available [Loney, Frick, Clements, Ellis, & Kerlin, 2003].) Its items were designed to tap all features of PCL-R psychopathy assessable in children. An initial analysis by Frick and colleagues (1994) revealed two moderately (~.5) correlated but distinctive factors: an impulsivity/conduct problems (I/CP) factor reflecting impulsiveness, behavioral deviance, and inflated self-importance, and a callous–unemotional (CU) factor reflecting tendencies toward interpersonal callousness and emotional insensitivity. Subsequent work (Frick, Boden, & Barry, 2000) suggested that the I/CP factor could be parsed into "impulsive" (bored easily, acts without thinking, fails to plan) and "narcissistic" (high self-importance, brags, uses/cons others) components.

Considerable data have accumulated regarding differences between high I/CP children exhibiting low versus high levels of CU tendencies (for recent reviews, see Frick & Dickens, 2006; Frick & Marsee, 2006; Frick & White, 2008). Compared to nonclinical controls and high CU clinic-referred youth, children high in I/CP but low in CU show IQ (especially Verbal IQ) deficits and difficulty in regulating emotions, as evidenced by higher trait anxiousness and enhanced reactivity to negative emotional stimuli of varying types. In addition, they are prone to reactive (angry–impulsive) aggression but not proactive (instrumental–strategic) aggression. Children high in both CU and I/CP tendencies are lower in trait anxiety and neuroticism, are attracted to activities entailing novelty and risk, show reduced behavioral responsiveness to threatening and affectively distressing stimuli, and have difficulty inhibiting behavior that results in punishment. In addition, high CU children with conduct problems exhibit high levels of both proactive and reactive aggression—and there is evidence that the presence of CU traits prospectively predicts later incidence of aggression and violence over and above I/CP tendencies (Frick, Stickle, Dandreaux, Farrell, & Kimonis, 2005).

A third measure that indexes PCL-R psychopathy in youth is the Child Psychopathy Scale (CPS; Lynam, 1997), which comprises items from existing problem behavior inventories that evidenced empirical relations with items of Hare's PCL-R. A factor analysis of the scale's original 41 items in the CPS development sample (430 boys from the Pittsburgh Youth Study, a longitudinal study of high-risk youth) revealed two distinguishable subsets of items that parallel the PCL-R affective–interpersonal and behavioral deviance factors; these factors were correlated very highly ($r = .95$) rather than moderately. Lynam (1997) reported that high overall scores on the CPS distinguished a subgroup of stable, seriously delinquent boys. More recently, Lynam and colleagues (2005) examined relations between self- and mother-report scores on a revised 55-item version of the CPS and personality dimensions of the FFM (aka the Big Five; John, Caspi, Robins, Moffitt, & Stouthamer-Loeber, 1994). The two factors of the revised CPS were less highly correlated in this study sample, which comprised two cohorts from the Pittsburgh Youth Study. For both self-ratings and mother ratings, overall CPS scores showed marked negative associations with FFM agreeableness (A) and conscientiousness (C), and more modest positive and negative relations, respectively, with neuroticism (N) and openness (O). In one of the two study cohorts, overall CPS ratings by mothers showed a significant *negative* association with extraversion (E). Hierarchical regression analyses revealed that across informants and cohorts, the unique variance in the affective–interpersonal factor was associated negatively with A and (consistently, but to a lesser degree) N. In contrast, the unique variance in the antisocial deviance factor was associated *positively* with N, and negatively with C and (consistently, but to a lesser degree) A.

Summary and Comments

The PCL-R was developed to assess psychopathy as a unitary construct in criminal offender samples. As such, it indexes a distinctly different phenotypic variant of psychopathy than that emphasized by Cleckley (1941/1976) in his descriptions of hospitalized inpatients. High overall scores on the PCL-R are associated with aggressive externalizing tendencies, including low FFM agreeableness (aka high antagonism), low affiliation/communality, low empathy, Machiavellianism, impulsive sensation seeking, and persistent violent offending. This descriptive picture is more in line with the conception of criminal psychopathy advanced by Cleckley's contemporaries than with Cleckley's own portrayal. At the same time, factor-analytic studies indicate that the PCL-R items tap separable interpersonal, affective, and impulsive–irresponsible components that exhibit diverging relations with external criterion measures.[1] The unique variance in the interpersonal component (that associated with the charm and grandiosity items in particular; Patrick et al., 2007) captures some of the adaptive elements of psychopathy emphasized by Cleckley. Furthermore, cluster-analytic studies (Hicks, Markon, Patrick, Krueger, & Newman, 2004; Skeem, Johansson, Andershed, Kerr, & Eno Louden, 2007) have revealed that high PCL-R scorers comprise two distinct subgroups: a (smaller) low-anxious, surgent subgroup akin to the type described by Cleckley (1941/1976), and a (larger) aggressive, unconstrained, socially detached subgroup more akin to that described by McCord and McCord (1964).

The best-known instruments for assessing psychopathy in children and adolescents, devised for use with adjudicated and clinic-referred populations, were constructed to mirror the item coverage of the PCL-R. Accordingly, overall scores on these inventories tap the same aggressive–externalizing variant of psychopathy indexed by overall PCL-R scores. However, like the PCL-R, these instruments contain distinctive subsets of items that show diverging relations with external criteria. The child psychopathy inventory that has been studied most extensively is Frick's APSD. The I/CP factor of the APSD, consistent with findings for Factor 2 of the PCL-R (Patrick et al., 2005), appears to index general disinhibitory (externalizing) tendencies. In contrast, its CU factor is associated with low anxiety and negative emotional reactivity, venturesomeness and thrill seeking, and use of proactive (strategic, goal-oriented) aggression. In addition, children with conduct problems who are high in CU traits are less responsive to treatment and more likely to persist in their deviant behavior—in particular, violence toward others (Frick & Dickens, 2006). Based on these distinctive correlates, Frick and colleagues (2005) have postulated that the presence of CU traits reflects the pathological expression of an underlying fearless temperament.

In contrast with the PCL-R and its youth-adapted variants, the PPI—which was developed to assess trait constructs embodied in Cleckley's conceptualization in a comprehensive manner—indexes psychopathy in terms of two orthogonal, higher-order factors: one reflecting social dominance, stress immunity, and fearlessness, and the other reflecting externalizing deviance. The first PPI factor appears to reflect a purer, more benign expression of underlying temperamental fearlessness (termed *boldness*; see next section) than Factor 1 of the PCL-R, or the CU factor of the APSD—which can be viewed as tapping "meanness" more than boldness. The construct of boldness indexed by PPI-I is likely to be particularly relevant to identification of psychopathic individuals in noncriminal samples—including individuals with psychopathic tendencies who rise to positions of leadership and influence in society (cf. Cleckley, 1941/1976; Lykken, 1995).

Synthesis of Historical and Contemporary Accounts: Disinhibition, Boldness, and Meanness as Distinctive Phenotypic Components of Psychopathy

The foregoing review of historical and contemporary efforts to conceptualize the syndrome of psychopathy reveals three prominent, recurring themes that for ease of reference can be designated disinhibition, boldness, and meanness. Consideration of the broader personality, psychopathology, and neurobiological literatures indicates that these three constructs, although interrelated at some levels empirically and in terms of their mutual connections with the phenomenon of psychopathy, have distinctive phenotypic identities and can be conceptualized, measured, and understood separately. My view is that these three phenotypic constructs represent the key to understanding psychopathy in its varying manifestations: criminal and noncriminal, primary and secondary (cf. Karpman, 1941; Lykken, 1957, 1995; Skeem et al., 2007), stable and aggressive (Hicks et al., 2004), and unsuccessful and successful (Hall & Benning, 2006). Below, I consider each of these key constructs in turn.

Disinhibition

The term *disinhibition* is used here to describe a general phenotypic propensity toward impulse control problems entailing a lack of planfulness and foresight, impaired regulation of affect and urges, insistence on immediate gratification, and deficient behavioral restraint. Related concepts include externalizing (Achenbach & Edelbrock, 1978; Krueger et al., 2002), disinhibitory psychopathology (Gorenstein & Newman, 1980; Sher & Trull, 1994), and low inhibitory control (Kochanska, Murray, & Coy, 1997).[2] In personality terms, disinhibition can be viewed as the nexus of impulsivity and negative affectivity (Krueger, 1999a; Sher & Trull, 1994). Prominent behavioral manifestations of disinhibition include irresponsibility, impatience, impulsive action leading to negative consequences, mistrust and resentfulness, aggressive acting out (in particular, angry–reactive aggression), untrustworthiness, proneness to drug and alcohol problems, and engagement in illicit or other norm-violating activities (Krueger, Markon, Patrick, Benning, & Kramer, 2007).

Disinhibition or externalizing is theorized to reflect impairment in the functioning of anterior brain systems (including the prefrontal cortex and anterior cingulate cortex) that guide and inhibit behavior and regulate emotional responses (Davidson, Putnam, & Larson, 2000; Morgan & Lilienfeld, 2000; Patrick & Bernat, 2009a; Rogers, 2006). Highly externalizing individuals show abnormal brain reactivity, including diminished amplitude of the P300 event-related potential (Patrick, Bernat, et al., 2006) and reduced amplitude of the error-related negativity, a response-locked brain potential that follows the commission of errors in a speeded performance task (Hall, Bernat, & Patrick, 2007); in the case of P300 amplitude reduction, the association with externalizing tendencies has been shown to be mediated by genetic influence (Hicks et al., 2007).

Historic conceptualizations of psychopathy have emphasized this externalizing component to varying degrees, and to an important extent, differences of opinion regarding the appropriate definition and boundaries of the psychopathy construct can be traced to this component. Externalizing encompasses a broad range of pathological behavioral phenomena, including child conduct problems, adult criminal deviance, angry aggression, and addictive behaviors of varying sorts (Krueger et al., 2002, 2007). Some historical writers defined *psychopathy* broadly to include substance-related addictions and other nonnormative behaviors (e.g., sexual deviance of varying kinds that intersect with the externalizing spectrum) (Prichard, 1835); other writers characterized psychopathy in terms that appear more applicable to externalizing individuals (e.g., Arieti, 1963; Partridge, 1928a, 1928b); and still others described subtypes of psychopaths that would more aptly be classified as high externalizers (e.g., Craft, 1966a; Kraepelin, 1904, 1915). Moreover, it can be argued that the traditional notion of the "symptomatic" or secondary psychopath (Karpman, 1941; Lykken, 1957) largely reflects the clinical presentation of the highly externalizing individual.

This is not to say that *externalizing,* defined as the common dispositional factor underlying varying disorders of impulse control, represents an imprecise or amorphous ("wastebasket") entity. To the contrary, behavior genetics research indicates that the general propensity toward problems of this type, reflected by scores on the broad externalizing factor, is heritable to a markedly higher degree (> 80%) than its individual diagnostic indicators, which include conduct disorder and adult antisocial behavior (Krueger et al., 2002). This points to the externalizing construct as a coherent and important target in studies of the neurobiological bases of impulse control problems, including persistent antisocial behavior. The construct of externalizing is also crucial to an understanding of psychopathy. For example, recent research demonstrates that the distinct variance associated with the antisocial deviance component of the PCL-R (Factor 2) largely reflects the externalizing factor (Patrick et al., 2005), and that the impulsive antisociality component of the PPI (PPI-II) exhibits a robust genetic association with scores on the externalizing factor (Blonigen et al., 2005). Based on its known correlates, the I/CP component of Frick and Hare's (2001) APSD also appears to index the externalizing factor.

However, contemporary researchers in the field generally do not view externalizing as equivalent to psychopathy. In particular, as mentioned, externalizing is associated with heightened negative affectivity as opposed to an absence of anxiety or fear. High externalizing is also associated with an increased rather than reduced incidence of internalizing (anxiety, mood) problems in childhood and adulthood (Achenbach & Edelbrock, 1978; Krueger, 1999b), and with a higher rather than lower incidence of suicidal behavior in adult offenders and community participants (Verona & Patrick, 2000; Verona, Sachs-Ericsson, & Joiner, 2004). It is when externalizing tendencies are coupled with dispositional boldness or meanness that a diagnosis of psychopathy is considered applicable.

Boldness

The term *bold* is used here to describe a phenotypic style entailing a capacity to remain calm and focused in situations involving pressure or threat, an ability to recover quickly from stressful events, high self-assurance and social efficacy, and a tolerance for unfamiliarity and danger. Related terms include *fearless dominance* (Benning, Patrick, Blonigen, et al., 2005), *audacity*, *daringness*, *indomitability*, *resiliency* (Block & Block, 1980), and *hardiness* (Kobasa, 1979). In personality terms, boldness can be viewed as the nexus of social dominance, low stress reactivity, and thrill–adventure seeking (Benning et al., 2003; Benning, Patrick, Blonigen, et al., 2005). Prominent behavioral manifestations of boldness include imperturbability, social poise, assertiveness and persuasiveness, bravery, and venturesomeness.

As used here, the term *boldness* is not considered synonymous with the term *fearless*. Rather, fearlessness is conceptualized as an underlying constitutionally based (genotypic) disposition entailing reduced sensitivity of the brain's defensive motivational system to cues signaling threat or punishment (Fowles & Dindo, 2006; Patrick & Bernat, 2006, 2009b). Deviations in responsiveness of the amygdala (e.g., Blair, 2006; Patrick, 1994; Veit et al., 2002) have been posited to play a role in this genotypic disposition. Fearlessness defined in this manner can be considered a key substrate for phenotypic boldness. Consistent with this hypothesis, nonincarcerated individuals who score high on the fearless dominance factor of the PPI (like offenders who score high on Factor 1 of the PCL-R; Patrick, Bradley, & Lang, 1993; Vanman, Mejia, Dawson, Schell, & Raine, 2003) show a marked attenuation of fear-potentiated startle (Benning, Patrick, & Iacono, 2005), and reduced amygdala reactivity when processing affective facial expressions (Gordon, Baird, & End, 2004). In addition, other work has demonstrated that this factor of the PPI represents a low-pole indicator of a broad self-report dimension of fear/fearlessness that fear-potentiated startle indexes physiologically (Vaidyanathan, Patrick, & Bernat, 2009). However, it is likely that other factors such as superior functioning of affective–regulatory circuitry in the brain (cf. Davidson et al., 2000; Ochsner, Bunge, Gross, & Gabrieli, 2002) and parental influences that promote competence and mastery (cf. Masten & Coatsworth, 1998) also contribute to boldness. Furthermore, genotypic fearlessness may be expressed phenotypically in ways other than boldness. For example, as noted below, in the presence of other etiological influences, genotypic fearlessness may also contribute to phenotypic meanness.

Cleckley's (1941/1976) conceptualization of psychopathy emphasized phenotypic boldness, together with disinhibitory (externalizing) tendencies. Cleckley did not view psychopaths as vicious or coldhearted but as personable and ostensibly well-adjusted, albeit markedly unpredictable and untrustworthy in their behavior. Boldness was evident in his case descriptions and diagnostic criteria in terms of poise and high social efficacy, absence of anxiety or neurotic symptoms, diminished emotional responsiveness, imperviousness to punishment (aka "failure to learn by experience"), and low suicidality. Other historical writers concerned with psychopathy in psychiatric patients as opposed to criminal samples (e.g., Kraepelin, 1904,

1914; Schneider, 1934) also identified bold externalizing types. Absence of normal fear reactivity was also emphasized in Hare's classic psychophysiological studies of the 1960s and 1970s (cf. Hare, 1978), and in influential theories of psychopathy advanced subsequently by Fowles (1980) and Lykken (1995).

Lilienfeld's PPI, which was developed to index personality traits embodied in Cleckley's conception of psychopathy in a comprehensive way, includes a broad factor (PPI-I) that directly reflects (within the domain of self-report) the construct of boldness. The subscales that load on this factor are stress immunity, social potency, and (to a lesser degree) fearlessness.[3] Notably, PPI-I is uncorrelated with tendencies toward impulsive antisocial deviance tapped by PPI-II. In this respect, the construct of boldness indexed by PPI-I can be considered a more benign expression of dispositional fearlessness—one that is phenotypically distinct from aggressive externalizing deviance and thus likely to be important for conceptualizing psychopathy in nonviolent, noncriminal samples (cf. Lykken, 1995). The construct of boldness also appears to be tapped somewhat by Factor 1 of the PCL-R (Benning, Patrick, Blonigen, et al., 2005)—in particular, by items comprising the so-called "interpersonal" facet (Hall et al., 2004; Patrick, Hicks, Nichol, & Krueger, 2007). However, the PCL-R interpersonal facet overlaps with the PCL-R's affective, lifestyle, and antisocial facets—indicating that the PCL-R indexes boldness less directly and less distinctively than does the PPI-I. As described below, Factor 1 of the PCL-R as a whole appears to index meanness more than boldness.

Meanness

The term *mean* is used here to describe a constellation of phenotypic attributes, including deficient empathy, disdain for and lack of close attachments with others, rebelliousness, excitement seeking, exploitativeness, and empowerment through cruelty. Terms related to meanness include *callousness* (Frick et al., 1994), *coldheartedness* (Lilienfeld & Widows, 2005), and *antagonism* (Lynam & Derefinko, 2006). With respect to basic dimensions of interpersonal behavior (Leary, 1957; Wiggins, 1982), meanness can be viewed as occupying a position midway between (high) dominance and (low) affiliation (Blackburn, 2006; Harpur, Hare, & Hakstian, 1989). In a joint analysis of basic interpersonal and affective dimensions, Saucier (1992) identified a construct akin to meanness (represented by descriptors such as rough, tough, unemotional, and insensitive) as the nexus of high dominance, low affiliation, and low neuroticism; notably, this configuration of traits mirrors the FFM correlates of PPI coldheartedness, which include low A, low E, and low N (as well as low O; Ross et al., 2009). From this perspective, meanness can be viewed as *agentic disaffiliation*—a motivational style in which pleasure and satisfaction are actively sought without regard for and at the expense of others (cf. Schneider's [1934] "active affectionless" type). In contrast with social withdrawal, which entails passive disengagement from others ("moving away from people"; Horney, 1945), meanness entails active exploitativeness and confrontation ("moving against people"; Horney, 1945). Characteristic behavioral manifestations of meanness include arrogance and verbal derisiveness, defiance of authority, lack of close personal relationships, physical cruelty toward people and animals, predatory (proactive, premeditated) aggression, strategic exploitation of others for gain, and excitement-seeking through destructiveness.

The notion of meanness is central to conceptions of psychopathy in criminal and delinquent samples. McCord and McCord (1964) identified lovelessness and guiltlessness as central to criminal psychopathy. Quay (1964) listed lack of concern for others, an absence of normal affectional bonds, and destructive and assaultive behavior as characteristic features of psychopathy in juvenile offenders. The affective facet of the PCL-R comprises items that reflect McCord and McCord's lovelessness (item 7, "shallow affect," entailing a lack of genuine attachments/love relationships; and item 8, "callous/lack of empathy," which encompasses cruel/sadistic treatment of others, contemptuousness, and destructiveness) and guiltlessness (item 6, "lack of remorse or guilt," and item 16, "failure to accept responsibility"). Notably, the interpersonal items of the PCL-R also include elements of meanness in their definitions: Item 1 ("glibness") includes reference to excessive slickness and is assigned a score of 1 (out of 2) for interviewees who exhibit a "tough guy" demeanor; item 2 ("grandiose sense of self-worth") includes reference to arrogance and superiority over others; the criteria for item 4 ("pathological lying") include routine use of deception in social interactions and enjoyment of deceit; item 5 ("conning/manipulative") refers to predatory exploitation for personal gain, without concern for the welfare of others. The best-known instruments for assessing psychopathy in youth (PCL:YV, CPS, and APSD) were modeled after the PCL-R and likewise emphasize meanness (social and emotional detachment, callousness, and exploitativeness) in their affective–interpersonal items.

A key question is whether meanness can be measured separately from criminal or antisocial behavior. In the case of the PCL-R, a hierarchical (bifactor) analysis revealed that the majority of its items are primarily indicators of a general overarching factor that reflects aggressive externalizing deviance (Patrick et al., 2007). The strongest and purest indicators of this general factor were items reflecting aggressive criminal behavior at varying ages (i.e., items comprising the antisocial facet). However, most of the affective and interpersonal items also showed appreciable loadings on this general factor, and some of these items evidenced stronger relations with the general factor than with secondary affective or interpersonal subfac-

aggressiveness, low communality, and low anxiousness (stress reactivity)—consistent with the distinctive correlates of the PCL-R affective facet and the APSD CU factor noted earlier. Furthermore, higher Coldheartedness was associated with reduced imaginative capacity (low absorption). Related to this, Patrick, Curtin, and Tellegen (2002) reported an opposite pattern of personality correlates (low aggressiveness, high social closeness, high stress reactivity, high absorption) for a well-established measure of emotional empathy (Mehrabian & Epstein, 1972). Elsewhere, Ross and colleagues (2009) reported that higher scores on PPI coldheartedness were associated with lower scores on openness, the FFM trait dimension that is most related to absorption/imaginativeness (Church, 1994). Taken together, these findings suggest that another variable contributing to a callous–antagonistic style may be a lack of imaginative representational capacity (cf. Patrick, Cuthbert, & Lang, 1994).

Conclusions

Historical and contemporary conceptions of psychopathy have emphasized the phenotypic constructs of disinhibition, boldness, and meanness to varying degrees. Since Cleckley, there has been a general consensus that disinhibited (externalizing) behavior is not sufficient for a diagnosis of psychopathy. The psychopathic individual has been viewed as a distinct type of high-externalizing individual—one who is emotionally detached and unperturbed by consequences. Most of the differences of opinion regarding the definition and scope of the construct that have arisen since Cleckley's time can be attributed to a differential emphasis on meanness (predatory exploitativeness, cruelty) versus boldness (venturesomeness, emotional stability). Writers concerned with psychopathy in delinquent youth and in adult antisocial samples (e.g., Frick et al., 1994; Hare, 1980; Lynam, 1997) have placed more emphasis on meanness, whereas writers concerned with psychopathy in inpatient and community samples (e.g., Lilienfeld & Andrews, 1996; Lykken, 1995) have placed more emphasis on boldness. Scores on Hare's PCL-R, designed for use with adult offender samples, index a combination of meanness and externalizing, consistent with historical conceptions of the criminal psychopath (e.g., McCord & McCord, 1964)—with PCL-R Factor 1 weighted more toward meanness and Factor 2 more toward externalizing (Patrick et al., 2005, 2007). The best-known instruments for assessing psychopathy in youth (APSD, CPS, PCL:YV) were modeled after the PCL-R and likewise index meanness more than boldness—as a construct intertwined with externalizing (i.e., the affective–interpersonal factor in each of these instruments is moderately to highly correlated with the behavioral deviance factor).

However, recent research indicates that boldness and meanness can be dissociated psychometrically from disinhibitory (externalizing) tendencies. Lilienfeld's self-report PPI provides for measurement of boldness (aka fearless dominance; Benning, Patrick, Blonigen, et al., 2005) as a distinct phenotypic dimension, independent from externalizing tendencies (aka impulsive antisociality). It will be interesting in future research to examine whether boldness can likewise be dissociated from externalizing in the clinical rating domain, and how boldness assessed in this fashion relates to PCL-R psychopathy. Likewise, Krueger and colleagues (2007) reported evidence of a callous–aggressive subfactor distinguishable from tendencies toward disinhibition/externalizing. Notably, the scale indicators of this callous–aggressive factor closely resembled the item content and known correlates of the CU factor of Frick's APSD. It will be beneficial in future research to examine whether items can be developed to index callous–aggressive tendencies separately from externalizing tendencies, and if so, to evaluate how this construct intersects with affective–interpersonal features of the PCL-R and its youth-oriented counterparts—as well as whether/how it intersects with boldness as indexed by PPI-I. Work of this kind is likely to be of crucial importance in elucidating alternative developmental pathways to psychopathy (cf. Frick & Marsee, 2006).

Research aimed at clarifying and separately operationalizing the constructs of boldness, meanness, and disinhibition also stands to inform our understanding of alternative manifestations of psychopathy—including primary and secondary variants, and successful versus unsuccessful types. Regarding the latter, the concept of psychopathy as aggressive externalizing (meanness + disinhibition), embodied in instruments such as the PCL-R and APSD, is likely to be less pertinent to an understanding of successful psychopathy than the construct of boldness. In particular, individuals high in charm, persuasiveness, imperturbability, and venturesomeness who achieve success in society as political or military leaders (cf. Lykken, 1995) are likely to exemplify boldness more than disinhibition or meanness. The availability of measures such as the PPI that index the boldness component of psychopathy separately from meanness and disinhibition opens the door to investigation of elements of psychopathy that—potentially in combination with moderating factors, such as intellect, creativity, and talent—may be consistent with (or even contribute to) success versus failure in society.

Acknowledgments

Preparation of this chapter was supported by Grant Nos. MH65137, MH072850, and MH089727 from the National Institute of Mental Health.

Notes

1. Items associated with the antisocial component of the PCL-R included in Hare and Neumann's (2006) four-factor model appear to tap the broad aggressive–externalizing dimension underlying the PCL-R as a whole, as opposed to a distinctive subdimension (Patrick et al., 2007).
2. The term *disinhibition* as used here differs from Kagan's (1994) conception of disinhibited temperament in children, which connotes a lack of timidity in novel situations and is associated prospectively with a reduced incidence of anxiety-related problems (Kagan & Snidman, 1999). This conception is more similar to the construct of *boldness* described here.
3. As well as loading to a lesser degree than either stress immunity or social potency on PPI-I, the fearlessness subscale of the PPI also cross-loads reliably on PPI-II. The likely explanation appears to be that PPI fearlessness contains variance related to boredom susceptibility and disinhibition facets of sensation seeking, as well as thrill–adventure seeking and experience seeking facets (cf. Zuckerman, 1979); the thrill–adventure seeking component of PPI fearlessness in particular accounts for its association with PPI-I, whereas the boredom susceptibility and disinhibition components account for its association with PPI-II (cf. Benning, Patrick, Blonigen, et al., 2005).

References

Achenbach, T. M., & Edelbrock, C. S. (1978). The classification of child psychopathology: A review and analysis of empirical efforts. *Psychological Bulletin, 85,* 1275–1301.

American Psychiatric Association. (1980). *Diagnostic and statistical manual of mental disorders* (3rd ed.). Washington, DC: Author.

American Psychiatric Association. (2000). *Diagnostic and statistical manual of mental disorders* (4th ed., text rev.). Washington, DC: Author.

Arieti, S. (1963). Psychopathic personality: Some views on its psychopathology and psychodynamics. *Comprehensive Psychiatry, 4,* 301–312.

Bailey, J. M., LeConteur, A., Gottesman, I. I., Bolton, P., Simonoff, E., Yuzda, E., et al. (1995). Autism as a strongly genetic disorder: Evidence from a British twin study. *Psychological Medicine, 25,* 63–77.

Benning, S. D., Patrick, C. J., Blonigen, D. M., Hicks, B. M., & Iacono, W. G. (2005). Estimating facets of psychopathy from normal personality traits: A step toward community-epidemiological investigations. *Assessment, 12,* 3–18.

Benning, S. D., Patrick, C. J., Hicks, B. M., Blonigen, D. M., & Krueger, R. F. (2003). Factor structure of the Psychopathic Personality Inventory: Validity and implications for clinical assessment. *Psychological Assessment, 15,* 340–350.

Benning, S. D., Patrick, C. J., & Iacono, W. G. (2005). Psychopathy, startle blink modulation, and electrodermal reactivity in twin men. *Psychophysiology, 42,* 753–762.

Benning, S. D., Patrick, C. J., Salekin, R. T., & Leistico, A. R. (2005). Convergent and discriminant validity of psychopathy factors assessed via self-report: A comparison of three instruments. *Assessment, 12,* 270–289.

Blackburn, R. (2006). Other theoretical models of psychopathy. In C. J. Patrick (Ed.), *Handbook of psychopathy* (pp. 35–57). New York: Guilford Press.

Blair, R. J. R. (1995). A cognitive developmental approach to morality: Investigating the psychopath. *Cognition, 57,* 1–29.

Blair, R. J. R. (2006). Subcortical brain systems in psychopathy: The amygdala and associated structures. In C. J. Patrick (Ed.), *Handbook of psychopathy* (pp. 296–312). New York: Guilford Press.

Block, J. H., & Block, J. (1980). The role of ego-control and ego resiliency in the organization of behavior. In W. A. Collins (Ed.), *Development of cognition, affect, and social relations: The Minnesota Symposium on Child Psychology* (Vol. 13, pp. 39–101). Hillsdale, NJ: Erlbaum.

Blonigen, D., Hicks, B., Patrick, C., Krueger, R., Iacono, W., & McGue, M. (2005). Psychopathic personality traits: Heritability and genetic overlap with internalizing and externalizing pathology. *Psychological Medicine, 35,* 637–648.

Caspi, A., McClay, J., Moffitt, T. E., Mill, J., Martin, J, Craig, I. W., et al. (2002). Role of genotype in the cycle of violence in maltreated children. *Science, 297,* 851–854.

Church, A. T. (1994). Relating the Tellegen and five-factor models of personality structure. *Journal of Personality and Social Psychology, 67,* 898–909.

Cleckley, H. (1976). *The mask of sanity* (5th ed.). St. Louis, MO: Mosby. (Original work published 1941; 3rd edition, 1955)

Cooke, D. J., Michie, C., & Hart, S. D. (2006). Facets of psychopathy: Toward clearer measurement. In C. J. Patrick (Ed.), *Handbook of psychopathy* (pp. 91–106). New York: Guilford Press.

Cooke, D. J., & Michie, C. (2001). Refining the construct of psychopathy: Towards a hierarchical model. *Psychological Assessment, 13,* 171–188.

Craft, M. (1965). *Ten studies into psychopathic personality.* Bristol, UK: John Wright.

Craft, M. (1966a). Conclusions. In *Psychopathic disorders and their assessment* (pp. 206–226). New York: Pergamon Press.

Craft, M. (1966b). *Psychopathic disorders and their assessment.* New York: Pergamon Press.

Davidson, R. J., Putnam, K. M., & Larson, C. L. (2000). Dysfunction in the neural circuitry of emotion regulation—a possible prelude to violence. *Science, 289,* 591–594.

Depue, R. A., & Morrone-Strupinsky, J. V. (2005). A neurobehavioral model of affiliative bonding: Implications for conceptualizing a human trait of affiliation. *Behavioral and Brain Sciences, 28,* 313–349.

Douglas, K. S., Lilienfeld, S. O., Skeem, J. L., Poythress, N. G., Edens, J. F., & Patrick, C. J. (2008). Relation of antisocial and psychopathic traits to suicide-related behavior among offenders. *Law and Human Behavior, 32,* 511–525.

Eysenck, H. J. (1977). *Crime and personality* (3rd ed.). London: Routledge & Kegan Paul.

Farrington, D. P., Coid, J. W., Harnett, L, Joliffe, D., Soteriou, N., Turner, R., et al. (2006). *Criminal careers up to age 50 and life success up to age 48: New find-*

ings from the Cambridge Study in Delinquent Development (Research Study 299). London: Home Office.

Forth, A. E., Brown, S. L., Hart, S. D., & Hare, R. D. (1996). The assessment of psychopathy in male and female noncriminals: Reliability and validity. *Personality and Individual Differences, 20,* 531–543.

Forth, A. E., Kosson, D. S., & Hare, R. D. (2003). *The Psychopathy Checklist: Youth Version manual* (2nd ed.). Toronto: Multi-Health Systems. (Original work published 1996)

Fowles, D. C. (1980). The three arousal model: Implications of Gray's two-factor learning theory for heart rate, electrodermal activity, and psychopathy. *Psychophysiology, 17,* 87–104.

Fowles, D. C., & Dindo, L. (2006). A dual-deficit model of psychopathy. In C. J. Patrick (Ed.), *Handbook of psychopathy* (pp. 14–34). New York: Guilford Press.

Frick, P. J., Boden, D. S., & Barry, C. T. (2000). Psychopathic traits and conduct problems in community and clinic-referred samples of children: Further development of the Psychopathy Screening Device. *Psychological Assessment, 12,* 382–393.

Frick, P. J., & Dickens, C. (2006). Current perspectives on conduct disorder. *Current Psychiatry Reports, 8,* 59–72.

Frick, P. J., & Hare, R. D. (2001). *Antisocial Process Screening Device.* Toronto: Multi-Health Systems.

Frick, P. J., & Marsee, M. A. (2006). Psychopathy and developmental pathways to antisocial behavior in youth. In C. J. Patrick (Ed.), *Handbook of psychopathy* (pp. 353–374). New York: Guilford Press.

Frick, P. J., O'Brien, B. S., Wootton, J. M., & McBurnett, K. (1994). Psychopathy and conduct problems in children. *Journal of Abnormal Psychology, 103,* 700–707.

Frick, P. J., Stickle, T. R., Dandreaux, D. M., Farrell, J. M., & Kimonis, E. R. (2005). Callous–unemotional traits in predicting the severity and stability of conduct problems and delinquency. *Journal of Abnormal Child Psychology, 33,* 471–487.

Frick, P. J., & White, S. F. (2008). The importance of callous–unemotional traits for developmental models of aggressive and antisocial behavior. *Journal of Child Psychology and Psychiatry, 49,* 359–375.

Gordon, H. L., Baird, A. A., & End, A. (2004). Functional differences among those high and low on a trait measure of psychopathy. *Biological Psychiatry, 56,* 516–521.

Gorenstein, E. E., & Newman, J. P. (1980). Disinhibitory psychopathology: A new perspective and a model for research. *Psychological Review, 87,* 301–315.

Gray, J. A. (1971). *The psychology of fear and stress.* Cambridge, UK: University of Cambridge Press.

Hall, J. R., & Benning, S. D. (2006). The "successful" psychopath: Adaptive and subclinical manifestations of psychopathy in the general population. In C. J. Patrick (Ed.), *Handbook of psychopathy* (pp. 459–478). New York: Guilford Press.

Hall, J., Benning, S. D., & Patrick, C. J. (2004). Criterion-related validity of the three-factor model of psychopathy: Personality, behavior, and adaptive functioning. *Assessment, 11*, 4–16.

Hall, J. R., Bernat, E. M., & Patrick, C. J. (2007). Externalizing psychopathology and the error-related negativity. *Psychological Science, 18*, 326–333.

Hare, R. D. (1970). *Psychopathy: Theory and research*. New York: Wiley.

Hare, R. D. (1978). Electrodermal and cardiovascular correlates of psychopathy. In R. D. Hare & D. Schalling (Eds.), *Psychopathic behavior: Approaches to research* (pp. 107–143). Chichester, UK: Wiley.

Hare, R. D. (1980). A research scale for the assessment of psychopathy in criminal populations. *Personality and Individual Differences, 1*, 111–119.

Hare, R. D. (1991). *The Hare Psychopathy Checklist—Revised*. Toronto: Multi-Health Systems.

Hare, R. D. (2003). *The Hare Psychopathy Checklist—Revised* (2nd ed.). Toronto: Multi-Health Systems.

Hare, R. D., Harpur, T. J., Hakstian, A. R., Forth, A. E., Hart, S., & Newman, J. P. (1990). The Revised Psychopathy Checklist: Reliability and factor structure. *Psychological Assessment, 2*, 338–341.

Hare, R. D., & Neumann, C. S (2006). The PCL-R assessment of psychopathy: Development, structural properties, and new directions. In C. J. Patrick (Ed.), *Handbook of psychopathy* (pp. 58–88). New York: Guilford Press.

Harpur, T. J., Hakstian, A. R., & Hare, R. D. (1988). Factor structure of the Psychopathy Checklist. *Journal of Consulting and Clinical Psychology, 56*, 741–747.

Harpur, T. J., Hare, R. D., & Hakstian, A. R. (1989). Two-factor conceptualization of psychopathy: Construct validity and assessment implications. *Psychological Assessment, 1*, 6–17.

Hart, S., Cox, D., & Hare, R. D. (1995). *Manual for the Psychopathy Checklist: Screening Version (PCL:SV)*. Toronto: Multi-Health Systems.

Hicks, B. M., Bernat, E. M., Malone, S. M., Iacono, W. G., Patrick, C. J., Krueger, R. F., et al. (2007). Genes mediate the association between P3 amplitude and externalizing disorders. *Psychophysiology, 44*, 98–105.

Hicks, B. M., Markon, K. E., Patrick, C. J., Krueger, R. F., & Newman, J. P. (2004). Identifying psychopathy subtypes on the basis of personality structure. *Psychological Assessment, 16*, 276–288.

Hicks, B. M., & Patrick, C. J. (2006). Psychopathy and negative affectivity: Analyses of suppressor effects reveal distinct relations with trait anxiety, depression, fearfulness, and anger–hostility. *Journal of Abnormal Psychology, 115*, 276–287.

Horney, K. (1945). *Our inner conflicts*. New York: Norton.

Ishikawa, S. S., Raine, A., Lencz, T., Bihrle, S., & Lacasse, L. (2001). Autonomic stress reactivity and executive functions in successful and unsuccessful criminal psychopaths from the community. *Journal of Abnormal Psychology, 110*, 423–432.

John, O. P., Caspi, A., Robins, R. W., Moffitt, T. E., & Stouthamer-Loeber, M. (1994). The "Little Five": Exploring the nomological network of the five-factor model of personality in adolescent boys. *Child Development, 65*, 160–178.

Kagan, J. (1994). *Galen's prophecy: Temperament in human nature*. New York: Basic Books.

Kagan, J., & Snidmon, N. (1999). Early precursors of adult anxiety disorders. *Biological Psychiatry, 46,* 1536–1541.

Karpman, B. (1941). On the need for separating psychopathy into two distinct clinical types: Symptomatic and idiopathic. *Journal of Criminology and Psychopathology, 3,* 112–137.

Kennealy, P. J., Hicks, B. M., & Patrick, C. J. (2007). Validity of factors of the Psychopathy Checklist—Revised in female prisoners: Discriminant relations with antisocial behavior, substance abuse, and personality. *Assessment, 14,* 323–340.

Kobasa, C. S. (1979). Stressful life events, personality, and health: An inquiry into hardiness. *Journal of Personality and Social Psychology, 37,* 1–11.

Kochanska, G. (1997). Multiple pathways to conscience for children with different temperaments: From toddlerhood to age 5. *Developmental Psychology, 33,* 228–240.

Kochanska, G., Murray, K., & Coy, K. C. (1997). Inhibitory control as a contributor to conscience in childhood: From toddler to early school age. *Child Development, 68,* 263–267.

Kraepelin, É. (1904, 1915). *Psychiatrie: Ein lehrbuch* (7th & 8th eds.). Leipzig: Barth.

Krueger, R. F. (1999a). Personality traits in late adolescence predict mental disorders in early adulthood: A prospective–epidemiological study. *Journal of Personality, 67,* 39–65.

Krueger, R. F. (1999b). The structure of common mental disorders. *Archives of General Psychiatry, 56,* 921–926.

Krueger, R. F. (2006). Perspectives on the conceptualization of psychopathy: Toward an integration. In C. J. Patrick (Ed.), *Handbook of psychopathy* (pp. 193–202). New York: Guilford Press.

Krueger, R. F., Hicks, B., Patrick, C. J., Carlson, S., Iacono, W. G., & McGue, M. (2002). Etiologic connections among substance dependence, antisocial behavior, and personality: Modeling the externalizing spectrum. *Journal of Abnormal Psychology, 111,* 411–424.

Krueger, R. F., Markon, K. E., Patrick, C. J., Benning, S. D., & Kramer, M. (2007). Linking antisocial behavior, substance use, and personality: An integrative quantitative model of the adult externalizing spectrum. *Journal of Abnormal Psychology, 116,* 645–666.

Leary, T. (1957). *Interpersonal diagnosis of personality.* New York: Ronald Press.

Lilienfeld, S. O., & Andrews, B. P. (1996). Development and preliminary validation of a self-report measure of psychopathic personality traits in noncriminal populations. *Journal of Personality Assessment, 66,* 488–524.

Lilienfeld, S. O., & Fowler, K. A. (2006). The self-report assessment of psychopathy: Problems, pitfalls, and promises. In C. J. Patrick (Ed.), *Handbook of psychopathy* (pp. 107–132). New York: Guilford Press.

Lilienfeld, S. O., & Widows, M. R. (2005). *Psychopathic Personality Inventory—Revised (PPI-R) professional manual.* Odessa, FL: Psychological Assessment Resources.

Lindner, R. M. (1944). *Rebel without a cause: The story of a criminal psychopath.* New York: Grune & Stratton.

Loney, B. R., Frick, P. J., Clements, C. B., Ellis, M. L., & Kerlin, K. (2003). Callous–unemotional traits, impulsivity, and emotional processing in antisocial adolescents. *Journal of Clinical Child and Adolescent Psychiatry, 32,* 66–80.

Lykken, D. T. (1957). A study of anxiety in the sociopathic personality. *Journal of Abnormal and Clinical Psychology, 55,* 6–10.

Lykken, D. T. (1995). *The antisocial personalities.* Hillsdale, NJ: Erlbaum.

Lynam, D. R. (1996). Early identification of chronic offenders: Who is the fledgling psychopath? *Psychological Bulletin, 120,* 209–234.

Lynam, D. R. (1997). Pursuing the psychopath: Capturing the fledgling psychopath in a nomological net. *Journal of Abnormal Psychology, 106,* 425–438.

Lynam, D. R., Caspi, A., Moffitt, T. E., Raine, A., Loeber, R., & Stouthamer-Loeber, M. (2005). Adolescent psychopathy and the Big Five: Results from two samples. *Journal of Abnormal Child Psychology, 33,* 431–444.

Lynam, D. R., & Derefinko, K. J. (2006). Psychopathy and personality. In C. J. Patrick (Ed.), *Handbook of psychopathy* (pp. 133–155). New York: Guilford Press.

Masten, A., & Coatsworth, J. D. (1998). The development of competence in favorable and unfavorable environments: Lessons from research on successful children. *American Psychologist, 53,* 205–220.

Maudslcy, H. (1874). *Responsibility in mental disease.* London: King.

McCord, W., & McCord, J. (1964). *The psychopath: An essay on the criminal mind.* Princeton, NJ: Van Nostrand.

Mehrabian, A., & Epstein, N. (1972). A measure of emotional empathy. *Journal of Personality, 40,* 525–543.

Morgan, A. B., & Lilienfeld, S. O. (2000). A meta-analytic review of the relation between antisocial behavior and neuropsychological measures of executive function. *Clinical Psychology Review, 20,* 113–136.

Ochsner, K., Bunge, S. A., Gross, J., & Gabrieli, J. D. (2002). Rethinking feelings: An fMRI study of the cognitive regulation of emotion. *Journal of Cognitive Neuroscience, 14,* 1215–1229.

Partridge, G. E. (1928a). Psychopathic personalities among boys in a training school for delinquents. *American Journal of Psychiatry, 8,* 159–186.

Partridge, G. E. (1928b). A study of 50 cases of psychopathic personality. *American Journal of Psychiatry, 7,* 953–973.

Partridge, G. E. (1930). Current conceptions of psychopathic personality. *American Journal of Psychiatry, 10,* 53–99.

Patrick, C. J. (1994). Emotion and psychopathy: Startling new insights. *Psychophysiology, 31,* 319–330.

Patrick, C. J. (2006). Back to the future: Cleckley as a guide to the next generation of psychopathy research. In C. J. Patrick (Ed.), *Handbook of psychopathy* (pp. 605–617). New York: Guilford Press.

Patrick, C. J. (2007). Getting to the heart of psychopathy. In H. Herve & J. C. Yuille (Eds.), *Psychopathy: Theory, research, and social implications* (pp. 207–252). Hillsdale, NJ: Erlbaum.

Patrick, C. J., & Bernat, E. (2009a). From markers to mechanisms: Using psychophysiological measures to elucidate basic processes underlying aggressive externalizing behavior. In S. Hodgins, E. Viding, & A. Plodowski (Eds.), *Persis-*

tent violent offenders: Neurobiology and rehabilitation (pp. 223–250). Oxford, UK: Oxford University Press.

Patrick, C. J., & Bernat, E. (2009b). Neurobiology of psychopathy: A two-process theory. In G. G. Berntson & J. T. Cacioppo (Eds.), *Handbook of neuroscience for the behavioral sciences* (pp. 1110–1131). New York: Wiley.

Patrick, C. J., Bernat, E., Malone, S. M., Iacono, W. G., Krueger, R. F., & McGue, M. K. (2006). P300 amplitude as an indicator of externalizing in adolescent males. *Psychophysiology, 43,* 84–92.

Patrick, C. J., Bradley, M. M., & Lang, P. J. (1993). Emotion in the criminal psychopath: Startle reflex modulation. *Journal of Abnormal Psychology, 102,* 82–92.

Patrick, C. J., Curtin, J. J., & Tellegen, A. (2002). Development and validation of a brief form of the Multidimensional Personality Questionnaire. *Psychological Assessment, 14,* 150–163.

Patrick, C. J., Cuthbert, B. N., & Lang, P. J. (1994) Emotion in the criminal psychopath: Fear image processing. *Journal of Abnormal Psychology, 103,* 523–534.

Patrick, C. J., Edens, J. F., Poythress, N., & Lilienfeld, S. O. (2006). Construct validity of the PPI two-factor model with offenders. *Psychological Assessment, 18,* 204–208.

Patrick, C. J., Hicks, B. M., Krueger, R. F., & Lang, A. R. (2005). Relations between psychopathy facets and externalizing in a criminal offender sample. *Journal of Personality Disorders, 19,* 339–356.

Patrick, C. J., Hicks, B. M., Nichol, P. E., & Krueger, R. F. (2007). A bifactor approach to modeling the structure of the Psychopathy Checklist—Revised. *Journal of Personality Disorders, 21,* 118–141.

Patrick, C. J., & Zempolich, K. A. (1998). Emotion and aggression in the psychopathic personality. *Aggression and Violent Behavior, 3,* 303–338.

Pinel, P. (1962). *A treatise on insanity* (D. Davis, Trans.). New York: Hafner. (Original work published 1806)

Plomin, R., DeFries, J. C., & Loehlin, J. C. (1977). Genotype–environment interaction and correlation in the analysis of human behavior. *Psychological Bulletin, 84,* 309–322.

Porter, S., & Woodworth, M. (2006). Psychopathy and aggression. In C. J. Patrick (Ed.), *Handbook of psychopathy* (pp. 481–494). New York: Guilford Press.

Prichard, J. C. (1835). *A treatise on insanity and other disorders affecting the mind.* London: Sherwood, Gilbert & Piper.

Quay, H. C. (1964). Dimensions of personality in delinquent boys as inferred from the factor analysis of case history data. *Child Development, 35,* 479–484.

Raine, A., Ishikawa, S. S., Arce, E., Lencz, T., Knuth, K. H., Bihrle, S., et al. (2004). Hippocampal structural asymmetry in unsuccessful psychopaths. *Biological Psychiatry, 55,* 185–191.

Robins, L. N. (1966). *Deviant children grown up*. Baltimore: Williams & Wilkins.

Robins, L. N. (1978). Sturdy predictors of adult antisocial behaviour: Replications from longitudinal studies. *Psychological Medicine, 8,* 611–622.

Rogers, R. D. (2006). The functional architecture of the frontal lobes: Implications for research with psychopathic offenders. In C. J. Patrick (Ed.), *Handbook of psychopathy* (pp. 313–333). New York: Guilford Press.

Ross, S. R., Benning, S. D., Patrick, C. J., Thompson, A., & Thurston, A. (2009). Factors of the Psychopathic Personality Inventory: Criterion-related validity and relationship to the BIS/BAS and Five-Factor models of personality. *Assessment, 16,* 71–87.

Rush, B. (1812). *Medical inquiries and observations upon the diseases of the mind.* Philadelphia: Kimber & Richardson.

Salekin, R. T. (2006). Psychopathy in children and adolescents: Key issues in conceptualization and assessment. In C. J. Patrick (Ed.), *Handbook of psychopathy* (pp. 389–414). New York: Guilford Press.

Salekin, R. T., Trobst, K. K., & Krioukova, M. (2001). Construct validity of psychopathy in a community sample: A nomological net approach. *Journal of Personality Disorders, 15,* 425–441.

Saucier, G. (1992). Benchmarks: Integrating affective and interpersonal circles with the Big Five personality factors. *Journal of Personality and Social Psychology, 62,* 1025–1035.

Schneider, K. (1934). *Die psychopathischen personlichkeiten* (3rd ed.). Vienna: Deuticke.

Sher, K. J., & Trull, T. (1994). Personality and disinhibitory psychopathology: Alcoholism and antisocial personality disorder. *Journal of Abnormal Psychology, 103,* 92–102.

Skeem, J. L., & Cooke, D. J. (in press). Is antisocial behavior essential to psychopathy?: Conceptual directions for resolving the debate. *Psychological Assessment.*

Skeem, J. L., Johansson, P., Andershed, H., Kerr, M., & Eno Louden, J. (2007). Two subtypes of psychopathic violent offenders that parallel primary and secondary variants. *Journal of Abnormal Psychology, 116,* 395–409.

Skeem, J. L., Miller, J. D., Mulvey, E. P., Tiemann, J., & Monahan, J. (2005). Using a five-factor lens to explore the relation between personality traits and violence in psychiatric patients. *Journal of Consulting and Clinical Psychology, 73,* 454–465.

Skeem, J. L., Mulvey, E. P., & Grisso, T. (2003). Applicability of traditional and revised models of psychopathy to the Psychopathy Checklist: Screening Version. *Psychological Assessment, 15,* 41–55.

Smith, S. S., & Newman, J. P. (1990). Alcohol and drug abuse-dependence disorders in psychopathic and nonpsychopathic criminal offenders. *Journal of Abnormal Psychology, 99,* 430–439.

Vaidyanathan, U., Patrick, C. J., & Bernat, E. M. (2009). Startle reflex potentiation during aversive picture viewing as an indicator of trait fear. *Psychophysiology, 46,* 75–85.

Vanman, E. J., Mejia, V. Y., Dawson, M. E., Schell, A. M., & Raine, A. (2003). Modification of the startle reflex in a community sample: Do one or two dimensions of psychopathy underlie emotional processing? *Personality and Individual Differences, 35,* 2007–2021.

Veit, R., Flor, H., Erb, M., Lotze, M., Grodd, W., & Birbaumer, N. (2002). Brain circuits involved in emotional learning in antisocial behavior and social phobia in humans. *Neuroscience Letters, 328,* 233–236.

Verona, E., & Patrick, C. J. (2000). Suicide risk in externalizing syndromes: Temperamental and neurobiological underpinnings. In T. E. Joiner (Ed.), *Suicide science: Expanding the boundaries* (pp. 137–173). Boston: Kluwer Academic.

Verona, E., Patrick, C. J., & Joiner, T. E. (2001). Psychopathy, antisocial personality, and suicide risk. *Journal of Abnormal Psychology, 110,* 462–470.

Verona, E., Sachs-Ericsson, N., & Joiner, T. E. (2004). Suicide attempts associated with externalizing psychopathology in an epidemiological sample. *American Journal of Psychiatry, 161,* 444–451.

Weiler, B. L., & Widom, C. S. (1996). Psychopathy and violent behavior in abused and neglected young adults. *Criminal Behavior and Mental Health, 6,* 253–271.

Widiger, T. A. (2006). Psychopathy and DSM-IV psychopathology. In C. J. Patrick (Ed.), *Handbook of psychopathy* (pp. 156–171). New York: Guilford Press.

Widiger, T. A., Cadoret, R., Hare, R., Robins, L., Rutherford, M., Zanarini, M., et al. (1996). DSM-IV antisocial personality disorder field trial. *Journal of Abnormal Psychology, 105,* 3–16.

Widom, C. S. (1977). A methodology for studying noninstitutionalized psychopaths. *Journal of Consulting and Clinical Psychology, 45,* 674–683.

Wiggins, J. S. (1982). Circumplex models of interpersonal behavior in clinical psychology. In P. C. Kendall & J. N. Butcher (Eds.), *Handbook of research methods in clinical psychology* (pp. 183–221). New York: Wiley.

Zuckerman, M. (1979). *Sensation seeking: Beyond the optimal level of arousal.* Hillsdale, NJ: Erlbaum.

3

Historical Conceptions of Risk Subtyping among Children and Adolescents

JOHN E. LOCHMAN
NICOLE P. POWELL
CAROLINE BOXMEYER
LAURA YOUNG
RACHEL BADEN

Psychopathy is just one of a number of constructs that has been used to describe antisocial behavior in children and adolescents. Historically, a range of different approaches has been applied to identify specific patterns of behavior and background characteristics that predict individuals' risk of evidencing psychopathic traits. Some of the earliest applications of multivariate statistical techniques helped to establish aggression and antisocial behavior as key dimensions of childhood psychopathology and also began the tradition of classifying antisocial behavior into different subtypes (Hewitt & Jenkins, 1946; Hinshaw & Lee, 2003). This chapter reviews a number of subtyping approaches that have been applied throughout the past several decades to identify and describe youth who are at risk for psychopathy. Efforts to identify subtypes of antisocial youth based on their social characteristics, developmental trajectories, coexisting psychiatric conditions, nature and severity of antisocial behavior, and personality characteristics are each discussed. These efforts to understand the early risk predictors and varying manifestations of antisocial behavior are critical to the field's ability to provide effective prevention and intervention to individuals whose behavior otherwise exacts a heavy toll on individuals, families, and society.

Subtyping Antisocial Behavior Based on Social Characteristics

Early applications of factor analysis indicated that children with conduct problems varied in their social characteristics (Hewitt & Jenkins, 1946; Hinshaw & Lee, 2003). Social characteristics continue to be a key distinguishing variable among children exhibiting aggressive and antisocial behavior. We describe two different social dimensions that have been used to subtype children with conduct problems to highlight the role of social characteristics in the manifestation of disruptive behavior (see Table 3.1).

Undersocialized versus Socialized Aggressive Conduct Disorder

The third edition of the *Diagnostic and Statistical Manual of Mental Disorders* (DSM-III; American Psychiatric Association, 1980) included the first operational diagnostic criteria for conduct disorder (CD). It also specified subcategories of the diagnosis based on social characteristics. These subcategories were based largely on the work of Hewitt and Jenkins (1946), and differentiated youth with "undersocialized" aggressive CD from those with "socialized" aggressive CD. Both groups were characterized by a repetitive and persistent pattern of aggressive conduct in which the basic rights of others are violated, as manifested by physical violence against persons or property, and/or thefts outside the home involving confrontation with the victim (American Psychiatric Association, 1980). The differentiating feature was that children with the "undersocialized" form of the disorder exhibited a failure to establish a normal degree of affection, empathy, or bond with others, while children with the "socialized" subtype exhibited evidence of social attachments to others.

Subsequent studies have provided both internal and external validation for this empirical distinction (see Quay, Routh, & Shapiro, 1987). The two groups have been shown to vary in the types of delinquent acts committed. Youth with the undersocialized variant commit more overt assaultive and aggressive acts, and typically act alone, while youth with the socialized variant commit covert (e.g., stealing), as well as overt, delinquent acts and often act together with peers (Loeber & Schmalling 1985a, 1985b). Since these subtypes were established, the majority of focus has been on youth with undersocialized forms of antisocial behavior because these youth tend to have a greater number of indicators of psychopathological dysfunction and worse long-term outcomes (Quay et al., 1987). However, despite having better overall prognoses, youth with socialized forms of CD often have higher rates of legal offenses than youth with undersocialized CD (Hanson, Henggeler, Haefele, & Rodick, 1984). Thus, both groups remain important to study and intervention.

Refinements have been made to the diagnostic criteria for CD, and the undersocialized versus socialized distinction is no longer present in the most recent version of DSM (DSM-IV-TR; American Psychiatric Association, 2000). Children who might previously have been diagnosed with undersocialized aggressive CD are similar to those who are currently classified as having an early age of onset of antisocial behavior by DSM-IV-TR. This developmental distinction may reflect differing etiologies for undersocialized and socialized forms of antisocial behavior. While poor parental monitoring has been observed in parents of children with both undersocialized and socialized conduct problems, parents of children with socialized conduct problems were found to be more permissive than parents of those with undersocialized forms of the disorder (Hetherington, Stouwie, & Ridberg, 1971). Thus, the "late starter" distinction in more recent DSM versions may reflect a subgroup of youth who have better social attachments but begin to affiliate with deviant peers as emerging adolescents and, when not well monitored by their parents, develop socialized, covert forms of antisocial behavior. Although the classification taxonomies have changed, the literature suggests that a subgroup of youth exhibit greater interpersonal problems at a younger age, and have more biological and psychosocial risk markers for antisocial behavior, and more stable antisocial traits into adulthood (Loeber, Burke, Lahey, Winters, & Zera, 2000). These youth most likely reflect those previously diagnosed with undersocialized aggressive CD, and are at particularly high risk for showing persistent antisocial traits into adolescence and adulthood.

Aggressive–Rejected versus Aggressive–Nonrejected Youth

Peer status is another social dimension upon which subgroups of aggressive children have been found to differ (Bierman, 2004; Conduct Problems Prevention Research Group, 2004). There is a considerable body of literature demonstrating that aggressive behavior is a strong predictor of peer rejection, particularly among boys (Coie & Dodge, 1998), and that aggression and peer rejection together predict a range of poor adolescent outcomes, including delinquency (Coie, Lochman, Terry, & Hyman, 1992; Lochman & Wayland, 1994). However, this literature also indicates that the relationship between aggression and social status is complex because not all children who exhibit high rates of aggressive behavior are rejected by their peers, and a significant portion of children who are rejected by their peers

TABLE 3.1. Subtypes of Personality Disorders

Subtype	Description	References
Undersocialized versus socialized aggressive CD	Distinguishes groups based on presence or absence of social attachments.	Hewitt & Jenkins (1946)
Aggressive–rejected versus aggressive–nonrejected youth	Distinguishes groups based on level of acceptance or rejection by peers.	Bierman, Smoot, & Aumiller (1993)
ODD versus CD	Distinguishes groups based on DSM-IV-TR diagnostic status.	American Psychological Association (2000)
Early starters versus late starters	Distinguishes groups based on age of onset of antisocial behaviors.	Patterson, DeBaryshe, & Ramsey (1989)
Conduct problems with co-occurring diagnoses	Groups differentiated on the presence or absence of comorbid diagnoses/symptoms including:	
	ADHD	Waschbusch (2002)
	Anxiety	Anderson et al. (1987); Walker et al. (1991)
	Depression	Arredondo & Butler (1994)
Overt versus covert behavior	Distinguishes groups based on presence of overt/confrontative or covert/concealed antisocial behaviors.	Loeber & Schmalling (1985b)
Proactive versus reactive behavior	Distinguishes groups based on presence of proactive/goal directed or reactive aggression.	Dodge & Coie (1987)
Relational versus physical behavior	Characterizes groups based on the manifestation of socially aggressive acts.	Lagerspetz, Bjorkqvist, & Peltonen (1988)
Destructive versus nondestructive behavior	Characterizes groups based on the effects of aggressive acts.	Frick et al. (1993)
Severe versus moderate behavior	Distinguishes groups based on level of severity of aggressive and antisocial behaviors.	Dodge, Price, Bachorowski, & Newman (1990); Slaby & Guerra (1988)
Psychopathic characteristics	Distinguishes groups based on the presence or absence of psychopathic characteristics including:	
	Callous–unemotional traits	Frick et al. (1994); Lynam (1996)
	Impulsivity/conduct problems	Frick et al. (1999)
	Narcissism (grandiose/manipulative)	Raskin & Terry (1988)

do not exhibit high rates of aggression. To understand better the relationship between aggression and peer status, Bierman, Smoot, and Aumiller (1993) compared the characteristics of aggressive boys who were rejected to those who were not. While both groups showed higher rates of physical aggression than nonaggressive–rejected and comparison (neither aggressive nor rejected) peers, the aggressive–rejected boys exhibited more diverse and severe types of conduct problems than the aggressive–nonrejected boys. The more diverse types of disruptive behaviors exhibited by aggressive–rejected boys tended to reflect greater impulsivity and worse behavioral control (e.g., verbal aggression, rule violations, and hyperactivity). In addition, the aggressive–rejected boys exhibited lower adaptive skills on teacher and peer ratings of attentiveness/perceptiveness.

Bierman and colleagues' (1993) findings are consistent with subsequent studies that have found peer rejection in childhood to be strongly associated with attention-deficit/hyperactivity disorder (ADHD), and that children with co-occurring ADHD and aggressive behavior are at greatest risk for peer rejection (Hinshaw & Melnick, 1995). While they often have "controversial" social status, children exhibiting proactive aggression without co-occurring ADHD are less likely to be rejected by their peers (e.g., Milich & Landau, 1988). The relationship between peer rejection and aggressive and antisocial behavior appears to be bidirectional. Not only does aggression predict social rejection in childhood, but peer rejection during childhood has also been causally linked to persistent and escalating levels of antisocial behavior in adolescence (Coie, Terry, Lenox, Lochman, & Hyman, 1995). One potential mechanism underlying this relationship is that children who are rejected by mainstream peers may be increasingly likely to affiliate with deviant peers, from whom they receive reinforcement for aggressive and delinquent acts.

While the current diagnostic taxonomy does not differentiate between aggressive–rejected and aggressive–nonrejected youth, peer rejection is a clear risk marker for early antisocial behavioral patterns and is also a risk factor for the persistence and escalation of these antisocial behaviors. Thus, peer social status should remain a central feature of assessment and intervention for children exhibiting early antisocial behaviors.

Subtyping Antisocial Behavior on the Basis of Developmental Distinctions

In recent decades, many researchers have advanced a developmental framework for organizing and understanding the manifestation and course of antisocial behavior over the lifespan. These researchers have observed that the manifestations of antisocial behavior generally change over time (Loeber & Hay, 1997). For example, a toddler may bite, hit, and throw temper tantrums, while a child in his late school years may shoplift and skip school. Likewise, an adolescent may sell drugs and steal, while an adult may commit fraud and violently aggress against others. Researchers with a developmental perspective have recognized these developmental variations in antisocial behavior and have explored the degree to which early forms of antisocial behavior portend later forms. Consequently, subtyping approaches that have emerged divide the population of antisocial individuals into groups on the basis of developmental variations in antisocial behavior, age of onset for conduct problems, and the course of antisocial behavior over time.

Subtypes of Disruptive Behavior Disorders

Antisocial behavior in children and adolescents can be subtyped on the basis of developmental variations in behavior and the age of onset for conduct problems. This subtyping approach is reflected in DSM-IV-TR (American Psychiatric Association, 2000). DSM-IV-TR presents two diagnoses that are most relevant to the study of antisocial behavior in children and adolescents: oppositional defiant disorder (ODD) and CD.

ODD—initially called "oppositional disorder"—first emerged as a diagnostic category in 1980 with the publication of the DSM-III (McMahon, Wells, & Kotler, 2006). ODD is characterized by a pattern of negativistic, hostile, and defiant behaviors that are evident for at least 6 months (American Psychiatric Association, 2000). These behaviors may include persistent testing of limits, arguing, deliberately annoying others, being touchy or easily annoyed, appearing spiteful or vindictive, and often growing angry or resentful, among others (American Psychiatric Association, 2000). Given that many of these behaviors are quite common in childhood, DSM-IV-TR stipulates that a diagnosis of ODD should be reserved for those individuals whose problem behaviors occur more frequently and result in more serious consequences than those behaviors exhibited by their same-age peers (American Psychiatric Association, 2000). Moreover, DSM-IV-TR requires that these behaviors result in significant academic, social, or occupational impairment. ODD is generally diagnosed before age 8 and no later than early adolescence (American Psychiatric Association, 2000).

While many children exhibit oppositional/disruptive behaviors and ultimately desist in these behaviors over time, a substantial subset of these children gradually progresses to more delinquent acts (Loeber & Farrington, 2000). When these delinquent acts include behaviors that violate societal norms and/or the basic rights of others, CD emerges as a likely diagnostic descriptor. CD first gained recognition as a diagnostic category in 1968, with the publication of DSM-II (McMahon et al., 2006). Since that time, the diagnostic criteria for CD have fluctuated substantially (McMahon et al., 2006). The current diagnostic criteria for CD place symptoms under one of four major headings: aggression to people and animals, destruction of property, deceitfulness or theft, and serious violations of rules (American Psychiatric Association, 2000). At least three (of 15) symptoms must have been present for 12 months, with at least one symptom present in the past 6 months, to warrant a CD diagnosis (American Psychiatric Association, 2000). While symptoms of CD generally emerge in late childhood or early adolescence, they may also appear in early childhood (American Psychiatric Association, 2000). Consequently, DSM-IV-TR presents two subtypes of CD based on age of onset—a childhood-onset type characterized by onset prior to age 10, and an adolescent-onset type characterized by onset after age 10 (American Psychiatric Association, 2000). Many researchers have acknowledged that these age-of-onset distinctions have important implications for the course of antisocial behavior over time.

Early Starters versus Late Starters

As such, another subtyping approach has emerged that groups individuals on the basis of the course of their antisocial behaviors over the lifespan. Researchers who embrace this subtyping approach have identified one group of offenders, termed "early starters" (Patterson, DeBaryshe, & Ramsey, 1989) or *life-course-persistent* offenders (Loeber & Stouthamer-Loeber, 1998; Moffitt, 1993), who commit their first transgression early and persist in offending throughout the lifespan. As McMahon and colleagues (2006) observe, individuals with childhood-onset CD likely fall within this subtype. Patterson and colleagues (1989) maintain that for these "early starters," antisocial behavior is a developmental trait that emerges consistently throughout life but manifests itself differently at each developmental stage. Early manifestations of antisocial behavior often predict later manifestations of antisocial behavior (Patterson et al., 1989). Patterson, Forgatch, Yoerger, and Stoolmiller (1998) clarified these relations further. They demonstrated that high levels of antisocial behavior in childhood significantly related to early arrest (before age 14), and that early arrest significantly related to chronic offenses by age 18. More specifically, Patterson and colleagues found that the majority of chronic offenders (71%) evidenced antisocial behavior in childhood, followed by early arrest, along their path to criminal offending.

While many researchers have noted the stability in antisocial behavior over time, others have acknowledged that a small group does not exhibit early patterns of antisocial behavior, with individuals beginning their criminal careers later in life. Epidemiological data, for example, suggests that the prevalence of antisocial behavior spikes in adolescence (Moffitt, 1993). Moffitt (1993) explores these data further and notes that the prevalence rate of antisocial behavior in boys hovers around 5% at age 11 but jumps to 32% at age 15. These prevalence rates continue to increase until the mid-20s, when most individuals are believed to desist in their antisocial activities (Moffitt, 1993). This subtype of offenders has been termed "late starters" (Patterson et al., 1989), *adolescence-limited offenders* (Moffitt, 1993), or *limited duration* offenders (Loeber & Stouthamer-Loeber, 1998). Individuals with the adolescent-onset type of CD likely fall within this subtype (McMahon et al., 2006).

Many researchers have argued that these two subtypes—the early starters and the late starters—differ in terms of their associated risk factors. Moffitt and Caspi (2001) found that life-course-persistent offenders can be differentiated from adolescence-limited offenders on the basis of risk factors related to parenting, neurocognitive functioning, and child temperament and behavior. Moffitt and Caspi demonstrated that children on the life-course-persistent course experience significantly higher levels of childhood risk in these three domains than their counterparts on the adolescence-limited trajectory. Aguilar, Sroufe, Egeland, and Carlson (2000) also distinguished between early-onset/persistent offenders and adolescence-onset offenders on the basis of childhood risk. However, their results substantially diverge from those highlighted by Moffitt and Caspi. More specifically, Aguilar and colleagues (2000) did not find any significant group differences in early temperament variables. Moreover, they did not find any early group differences in neuropsychological functioning; these differences only emerged in late childhood and early adolescence. Despite the lack of significant, early differences in temperamental and neuropsychological domains, Aguilar and colleagues did identify a number of group differences in psychosocial areas. Specifically, they found that early-onset/persistent offenders were significantly more likely to come from single-parent homes characterized by high levels of stress than were adolescents in the "never antisocial" and time-limited groups. These early-onset/persistent offenders were also significantly more likely to have evidenced avoidant attachment with caregivers at age 12 and 18 months, and to have experienced abusive, neglectful, or otherwise inadequate parenting (Aguilar et al., 2000).

Patterson and colleagues (1989) also emphasized the impact of ineffective parenting practices on children's engagement in the early starter pathway. They discussed the ways in which parents inadvertently reinforce children for bad behaviors and thereby nurture a coercive cycle of parent–child interactions. Patterson and colleagues postulated that this coercive cycle maintains child and adolescent antisocial behavior. Notably, additional parenting factors, such as parental convictions and parental transitions, have been linked to the early-onset course of antisocial behavior in girls (Leve & Chamberlain, 2004). In summary, it appears clear that many factors increase a child's risk for initiating and continuing along the early starter pathway.

While the aforementioned risk factors appear influential in spurring some children on toward the early starter pathway, the concept of "social mimicry"—as presented by Moffitt (1993) in her seminal work—has emerged as the primary explanation for why others pursue antisocial behavior later in life. Moffitt maintains that social mimicry occurs when members of a subgroup of adolescents observe the behavior exhibited by their life-course-persistent antisocial peers and subsequently follow suit. She asserts that these adolescents are motivated by the desire to assert their independence and acquire mature status. These offenders gradually desist in their antisocial behaviors as they gain access to more adult roles and begin to perceive delinquent activities as resulting in punishing rather than rewarding consequences (Moffitt, 1993). As such, the antisocial behavior of these youth is time-limited and is likely more reflective of normative social pressures than of an underlying antisocial trait.

Subtyping Antisocial Behavior on the Basis of Co-Occurring Diagnoses

Decades of research have verified that conduct problems co-occur with other adjustment problems at a much higher rate than would be expected by chance (Angold, Costello, & Erkanli, 1999). Comorbid diagnoses include both externalizing problems, such as ADHD, and internalizing problems, such as anxiety and depression. Several hypotheses have been proposed for the high rate of comorbidity (McMahon & Frick, 2005). In one proposed pathway, additional adjustment problems may stem from conduct problems if, for example, a child's disruptive behaviors lead to peer rejection and result in feelings of depression or anxiety. Alternatively, features of other disorders, such as impulsivity and irritability, may lead to conduct problems. Finally, common risk factors, such as social-cognitive deficits, may be causal sources of conduct problems and other disorders.

Regardless of the mechanisms by which comorbidity occurs, it is clear that comorbid conditions affect the presentation and prognosis for children with conduct problems. Awareness of the impact of comorbid conditions has led some researchers to propose separate diagnostic classifications for conduct problems that co-occur with other diagnoses. However, research to date does not, in general, provide support for distinct categories (e.g., Waschbusch, 2002), and the practice of assigning multiple diagnoses has been upheld. Nonetheless, awareness and understanding of comorbid conditions are important in research and clinical work with children who have conduct problems, and the following section reviews current literature on this topic.

Conduct Problems and Co-Occurring ADHD

ADHD is the diagnosis that most commonly co-occurs with conduct problems; about 50% of children with disruptive behavior exhibit both conduct problems and ADHD (Anderson, Williams, McGee, & Silva, 1987). Comorbidity rates are highest during the preadolescent period, then decline between ages 11 and 15 (Loeber & Keenan, 1994). ADHD appears to precede conduct problems in the majority of cases and is considered to be a causal factor in the development of early-onset conduct problems in boys, though whether this also applies to girls is unclear (Loeber & Keenan, 1994).

Comorbidity rates appear to differ for boys and girls, with several researchers describing stronger correlations between ADHD and conduct problems for girls than for boys (see Loeber & Keenan, 1994). For example, Waschbusch's (2002) meta-analysis of comorbid conduct problems and ADHD revealed comorbidity rates of 36% for boys, as compared to 57% for girls. Furthermore, the meta-analysis suggested that girls with comorbid conduct problems and ADHD were more severely affected than were comorbid boys. Because overall rates of each disorder alone are lower for girls than for boys, the increased likelihood of comorbidity and greater degree of impairment in comorbid girls has been referred to as a *paradoxical gender effect* (Loeber & Keenan, 1994).

Findings from concurrent and prospective research suggest that the presence of ADHD affects the presentation and course of children's conduct problems in important ways. Overall, children with both diagnoses appear to be more severely affected than those with only conduct problems. Compared to children and adolescents who have CD only, youth who have both CD and ADHD display a greater severity and variety of disruptive behaviors, including physical aggression, stealing, and verbal provocation (Beauchaine & Gartner, 2003; Molina, Bukstein, & Lynch, 2002; Thompson, Riggs, Mikulich, & Crowley, 1996; Walker et al., 1991). Youth with comorbid CD and ADHD are also likely to have more severe problems with substance abuse, and to have higher rates of depression and anxiety (Molina et al., 2002; Thompson et al., 1996). In addition, youth with both CD and ADHD may have lower Verbal IQ and more academic problems than youth with CD alone (Forehand, Wierson, Frame, Kempton, & Armistead, 1991; Moffitt, 1990), though these findings have not been consistently replicated (e.g., Thompson et al., 1996).

Several longitudinal studies suggest that youth with comorbid conduct problems and ADHD symptoms have poorer outcomes than those with conduct problems alone (for reviews, see Loeber, Green, Lahey, Frick, & McBurnett, 2000; Lynam, 1996). Results of previous research suggest that when accompanied by ADHD symptoms, conduct problems are more likely to persist and/or escalate into adolescence and adulthood, with comorbid children being at increased risk for later delinquency, criminal activity, and antisocial personality disorder (APD) (Lynam, 1996; Moffitt, 1993). However, a recent study by Washburn and colleagues (2007) did not find the expected association between comorbid CD and ADHD with later APD.

Waschbusch (2002) reviewed four categories of research on comorbid conduct problems and ADHD symptoms, including defining features, associated features, developmental trajectory, and etiology; meta-analyses indicated differences between the comorbid and conduct problems–only groups in each area. Specifically, results indicated that in comparison to children with conduct problems only, the behavior problems of comorbid children are more varied and severe, and that the comorbid condition is associated with lower Verbal IQ, more peer difficulties, and increased social-cognitive deficits. Comorbid children also exhibit behavior problems earlier in life, and these problems tend to be more stable than is the case for children with conduct problems only. Compared to children with conduct problems only, comorbid children are also more likely to have experienced negative parenting and to come from lower socioeconomic status (SES) backgrounds, though the groups do not appear to differ on other etiological factors.

Conduct Problems and Co-Occurring Anxiety

Cross-sectional research indicates that anxiety co-occurs with conduct problems at much higher rates than would be expected by chance alone. A comprehensive literature review by Zoccolillo (1992) suggested a comorbidity rate of 7–30%; however, rates appear to differ based on age and gender. Reviews by Loeber and Keenan (1994) and Russo and Beidel (1994) conclude that among youth with conduct problems, girls are more likely than boys to also have anxiety symptoms, and that these problems most commonly co-occur in middle childhood, then decline during adolescence. In general, conduct problems appear to precede anxiety symptoms, and comorbid children may evidence an earlier onset of conduct problems compared to children with conduct problems only (Loeber & Keenan, 1994).

Multiple research studies have yielded conflicting results on the impact of anxiety symptoms on conduct problems, with some studies documenting a mitigating effect and others, an exacerbating influence. Gray's (1987) neurobiological theory posits that two opposing systems are responsible for aggression (behavioral activation system; BAS) and anxiety (behavioral inhibition system; BIS), and that increased activation of the BIS moderates

BAS activity levels. Several studies have supported this theory, including Walker and colleagues' (1991) comparison of boys with CD and anxiety to boys with CD alone. Walker and colleagues found that boys with both diagnoses were "markedly less deviant" than the single-diagnosis group, in that they had significantly fewer police contacts and school suspensions, and were less likely to be perceived as aggressive by classmates. Woolston and colleagues (1989) reported similar results in their examination of comorbidity among child psychiatric inpatients. Children diagnosed with both CD and an anxiety disorder exhibited lower levels of externalizing behaviors and higher adaptive functioning than those with CD only. Also, O'Brien and Frick (1996) found differences on a measure of reward dominance between children with psychopathic traits only and those who also had anxiety symptoms. Children with psychopathic traits only, but not the comorbid group, exhibited a reward-dominant response style, which is generally maladaptive and associated with antisocial behavior.

Other research has not confirmed a moderating effect of anxiety on conduct problems (e.g., Ollendick, Seligman, & Butcher, 1999; Russo et al., 1993) or suggested that comorbid youth are more severely affected. For example, Anderson and colleagues (1987) found that children with comorbid disruptive behavior disorder and anxiety disorder were rated by parents and teachers as more aggressive and hyperactive than children with only a disruptive behavior disorder. In a longitudinal project, Verhulst and van der Ende (1993) reported that children evidencing high levels of conduct problems, without co-occurring anxiety symptoms, had fewer disruptive behaviors 6 years later than did children who initially had problems in both areas. Loeber, Russo, Stouthamer-Loeber, and Lahey (1994) found that in a sample of 13- to 16-year-old boys, 75% of those with the most severe pattern of externalizing behaviors also had anxiety symptoms, compared to 34.6% of those with moderate and 19.1% of those with more mild conduct problems.

A number of explanations for the conflicting findings on comorbid conduct problems and anxiety have been offered. Some research suggests that age may moderate the effect, with anxiety playing a mitigating role on younger children's conduct problems but exacerbating conduct problems in adolescence (Russo & Beidel, 1994). Differing manifestations of anxiety might also account for the differential findings, with anxiety characterized by inhibition and fear serving as a protective factor, and anxiety characterized by social withdrawal predicting increased impairment (Hinshaw & Lee, 2003). Finally, Ollendick and colleagues (1999) suggested that severity of conduct problems may account for the inconsistent findings, with anxiety being unlikely to mitigate the impact of the most severe conduct problems but potentially acting as a protective factor in subclinically affected youth.

Conduct Problems and Co-Occurring Depression

Depression also frequently co-occurs with conduct problems, with published comorbidity rates ranging from 8.5 to 45.5% among community samples, and even higher rates (up to 76%) among clinic-referred youth (Wolff & Ollendick, 2006). Among children with a diagnosed disruptive behavior disorder, children with CD are significantly more likely also to meet criteria for a mood disorder than children with ODD (Arredondo & Butler, 1994). Gender is also an important factor in comorbidity patterns: Girls are more likely than boys to display the comorbid condition, and prevalence rates increase for girls from childhood to adolescence but decline for boys with age (Loeber & Keenan, 1994). Overall, comorbidity rates are highest during middle adolescence (Beyers & Loeber, 2003), and literature reviews indicate that conduct problems precede depressive symptoms in the majority of cases (Loeber & Keenan, 1994; Wolff & Ollendick, 2006).

Comorbidity research has not yielded a clear picture of how depressive symptoms impact the clinical presentation and course of conduct problems in youth. Some studies have suggested that youth with both types of problems are more severely affected than those with conduct problems only, displaying more impairments at school, at home, and in social relationships (Ezpleta, Domenech, & Angold, 2006), as well as a higher prevalence of CD symptoms (Fleming, Boyle, & Offord, 1993). Children with conduct problems and depressive symptoms may also have an elevated risk for developing CD (Greene et al., 2002), attempting suicide (Fleming et al., 1993; Lewinsohn, Rohde, & Seeley, 1995), and continuing their psychiatric problems into adulthood (Fleming et al., 1993). However, other research has failed to find substantial differences between comorbid and conduct problem–only groups (e.g., Ezpleta, Granero, & Domenech, 2005), or has suggested that comorbid children are less severely affected. For example, Simic and Fombonne (2001) found that, compared to youth with CD only, those with both CD and depressive disorder displayed fewer aggressive and stealing behaviors.

Subtyping Antisocial Behavior on the Basis of Intensity and Qualitative Differences

Although vandalism, running away from home, bullying, and defiance are all forms of antisocial behavior, they clearly represent a diverse list of behaviors. While we can understand them through their grouping in this broader category, it is apparent that antisocial behaviors within this category can vary substantially in regard to method, severity, target, and goal. These subtypes based on more qualitative differences are detailed below.

Overt versus Covert Behavior

Loeber and Schmalling (1985a) examined possible patterns in antisocial behavior. Their meta-analysis of 28 studies of child psychopathology included 11,603 children. Consequently, they identified one dimension, which was termed *overt–covert antisocial behavior*. This was described as a continuum, which at one end was overt, confrontational antisocial behavior and at the other, covert, concealed antisocial behaviors. Loeber and Schmalling defined *overt behaviors* as those involving direct confrontation with or disruption of one's environment (e.g., arguing, temper tantrums, aggression). They defined *covert behaviors* as those occurring without the awareness of adult caretakers (e.g., lying, stealing, fire setting, truancy). Despite these differences, Loeber and Schmalling (1985b) found that noncompliance was central to both forms of antisocial behavior, with similar prevalence at both ends of the continuum. Frick and colleagues (1993) conducted a meta-analysis of 60 studies, which included 28,401 children and adolescents. Like Loeber and Schmalling (1985b), Frick and colleagues found the same covert–overt bipolar dimension among youth with conduct problems.

Since that time, this broad, bipolar, unidimensional description of antisocial behavior has been used to organize and conceptualize many other subtypes of antisocial behavior and aggression. It is also frequently referenced in relation to the developmental trajectories of youth with conduct problems. Loeber and colleagues (1994) proposed that overt and covert conduct problems represent distinct pathways to conduct disorder and delinquency. When defining their theory of delinquency and tracing trajectories of antisocial behavior, Patterson and Yoerger (2002) stated that children with early-onset CD often follow a progression from primarily overt conduct problems through a rapid increase in covert conduct problems. They also reported that while younger delinquent children are more likely to engage in overt behaviors, their older counterparts more readily demonstrate covert behaviors. Archer and Côté (2005) used the overt–covert dimension to elucidate sex differences in antisocial behavior throughout development. They stated that while boys are likely to engage in overt antisocial behavior at a higher rate and at a younger age than girls, this gap narrows during adolescence as girls begin to demonstrate more covert antisocial behavior. Unfortunately, the body of research on the overt–covert dimension of antisocial behavior is weighted toward a greater understanding of overt behaviors, likely due to the readily apparent adverse impact of these behaviors on society. However, because covert antisocial behavior is highly correlated to later overt behavior, there is increasing motivation to expand our understanding of covert behaviors.

Proactive versus Reactive Behavior

Around 1987, Dodge and Coie began examining proactive and reactive aspects of antisocial behavior, two subtypes that differ based on their underlying goals. This subtyping of antisocial behavior has proven to be quite robust across studies (Dodge, Lochman, Harnish, Bates, & Pettit, 1997). *Reactive aggression* is a response to goal blocking and is accompanied by significant autonomic arousal. It is often an impulsive reaction that occurs in response to a preceding condition of perceived or real provocation or frustration, and includes an expression of anger. *Proactive aggression* is thought to be largely an acquired behavior that has been reinforced and is thought to lead to an anticipated reward. For example, proactive aggression may be used to facilitate the attainment of goods from others or dominance over others (e.g., bullying). Thus, it is a more goal-directed and purposeful behavior. The two forms of aggression appear to be differentially related to various types of intervention strategies (Phillips & Lochman, 2003), and are part of different pathways leading to negative adolescent outcomes, such as substance use (Fite, Colder, Lochman, & Wells, 2008).

These two subgroups of aggressors are thought to have different deficits of social information processing. Crick and Dodge (1996) found that whereas proactive aggression is often related to a more positive perception of aggressive acts, it is also related to deficits in response decision processes, including assumptions that aggression is an effective means for obtaining goals. Crick and Dodge also found that proactive aggression is often related to possession of fewer relation-enhancing goals and more self-enhancing goals. However, reactively aggressive youth more often attributed aggressive intent to ambiguous peer behaviors when compared to nonaggressive youth. Reactive aggression is thought to be motivated by perceptions of peers as threatening. Thus, it is apparent that at the heart of proactive and reactive aggression are distinctly different goals. However, Dodge and Coie (1987) found that only a portion of youth displaying conduct problems utilized exclusively proactive or reactive aggression; rather, they often displayed traits of both subtypes. These children typically had more difficulty than their nonaggressive or proactively aggressive peers. However, they seemed to have fewer social information-processing deficits than their reactively aggressive peers.

Relational versus Physical Behavior

Physical aggression has been studied for years, with a greater emphasis in male populations. However, around 1989, researchers began to examine relational aggression as another subtype of common behaviors among children with conduct problems. Whereas *physical aggression* has been defined as a forceful, physical action performed against another person, *relational aggression* is defined as purposeful, manipulative behavior that is directed toward damaging another's self-esteem, social status, or both, and it is also sometimes referred to as *social aggression* or *indirect aggression*. Relational aggression may include things such as rumor spreading, peer group exclusion, or "the silent treatment."

Researchers who have examined the various manifestations of aggression across development have proposed that physical aggression occurs mostly among males and decreases with age (Angold & Costello, 2001; Coie & Dodge, 1998). Studies have also shown that females often aggress against each other in a more covert matter, relying more on relational aggression than their male and nonaggressive counterparts (Angold et al., 1999; Crick & Grotpeter, 1995; Lagerspetz, Bjorkqvist, & Peltonen, 1988). Unlike physical aggression, this problem behavior may actually increase with age (Vaillancourt & Hymel, 2004). Crick and Grotpeter (1995) also found that relationally aggressive children are likely at risk for major adjustment difficulties because they are more often rejected and report greater loneliness, depression, and isolation than their nonrelationally aggressive peers.

Destructive versus Nondestructive Behavior

In 1993, when Frick and colleagues conducted their meta-analysis, which we introduced in relation to the overt–covert dimension of antisocial behavior, they not only found this overt–covert dimension among the 28,401 children and adolescents with conduct problems, but they also described a second, bipolar aspect of antisocial behavior called the destructive–nondestructive dimension. *Destructive behaviors* represented those actions that had direct effects on other people, animals, or property (e.g., cruelty to animals, fire setting, vandalism, bullying). *Nondestructive behaviors* were more self-contained antisocial behaviors (e.g., swearing, breaking rules, running away, truancy).

Frick and colleagues (1993) attempted to integrate the existing overt–covert dimension and their newly defined destructive–nondestructive dimension into two bisecting axes, creating four quadrants containing distinct antisocial behaviors. These included destructive–overt (i.e., aggression), destructive–covert (i.e., property violations), nondestructive–overt (i.e., oppositional), and nondestructive–covert behaviors (i.e., status violations). They proposed that most antisocial and aggressive behaviors can be categorized into one of these quadrants. Frick et al. also reported that these four quadrants corresponded well to the distinctions among norm-violating behaviors made by legal systems and the previous diagnostic conceptualizations of antisocial behavior.

Severe versus Moderate Behavior

A final qualitative dimension of antisocial behavior is severity. Children and adolescents who evidence antisocial or aggressive behaviors are often classified as demonstrating mild, moderate, or severe symptom levels. Mild aggressors often show only low levels of aggressive or antisocial behavior that have less impact on daily functioning when compared to the behavior of their more severe counterparts. Moderate to severe aggressors are often more likely to meet a diagnosis of CD and engage in reactive aggression and violent crimes. There is evidence that level of severity also correlates with these youth's social-cognitive difficulties, with severely aggressive or antisocial behaviors often related to more severe social problem-solving deficiencies (e.g., problem definition, goal orientation, number of solutions, effectiveness of solutions) (Dodge, Price, Bachorowski, & Newman, 1990; Slaby & Guerra, 1988). Short and Simeonson (1986) found that highly aggressive or antisocial traits are often associated with more egocentric perspective-taking styles. Research implies that children and adolescents may follow a variety of paths in reference to severity of symptoms as they develop. Hinshaw and Lee (2003) suggested that some aggressors show consistently mild symptom levels throughout development. However, Moffitt, Caspi, Dickson, Silva, and Stanton (1996) illustrated that there may be variability in symptom levels across development because some youth who show high levels of conduct problems at younger ages may experience a symptom-level decrease, and experience mild to moderate symptom levels into adulthood.

Though many studies examine either community samples of children at risk for aggression or clinical populations of highly aggressive youth, with an emphasis on the former, Lochman and Dodge (1994) compared differences in social-cognitive deficits across level of severity. They found that severely aggressive and antisocial behaviors are related to greater difficulties with cue recall, attributions, social problem solving, and general self-worth. While moderately aggressive boys were found to have some of these same social-cognitive difficulties, their aggression may have been planfully aimed to achieve expected outcomes. Lochman and Dodge also found that when severely and moderately aggressive youth differed in a similar way from their nonaggressive peers, they did so on a continuum, where severely impaired individuals' deficits were more extreme than those of individuals with the moderate classification.

Subtypes Related to Psychopathic Characteristics

It is only in the last decade that research and interest in the concept of psychopathy and its relation to antisocial behavior in adults have begun to move developmentally down to psychopathic characteristics that may be evident in children and adolescents with behavior problems (Salekin, 2006; Salekin, Leistico, Trobst, Schrum, & Lochman, 2005). This work has been fueled by the field's ongoing concern with finding relevant ways to characterize different types of antisocial youth, extending the typologies described in the prior sections of this chapter. The still emerging understanding of psychopathic characteristics in youth was largely initiated by Frick (e.g., Frick, O'Brien, Wootton, & McBurnett, 1994) and Lynam (1996) as they developed downward extensions of the commonly used psychopathy measures for adults (Hare, 1991). Using these measures, investigators have begun examining the role of psychopathic traits in the development and expression of antisocial behavior in children (Lilienfeld, 1998; Lynam, 1998). Many of these studies have focused on the callous (e.g., lack of empathy, manipulativeness) and unemotional (e.g., lack of guilt, emotional constrictedness) traits that represent the cornerstone of the psychopathic personality (Cleckley, 1976; Hare, 1993).

Evidence suggests that callous–unemotional (CU) traits may be evident in a subgroup of antisocial juveniles that exhibits a more severe and chronic pattern of delinquent behavior with a unique etiology (Lochman et al., 2001; Pardini, Lochman, & Frick, 2003; Pardini, 2006). Adjudicated adolescents with high levels of CU traits are more likely to exhibit an early childhood onset of their antisocial behavior (Silverthorn, Frick, & Reynolds, 2001) and to be incarcerated for violent sex offenses (Caputo, Frick, & Brodsky, 1999) than are youth without these traits. Moreover, Christian, Frick, Hill, Tyler, and Frazer (1997) noted that clinic-referred children with conduct problems and CU traits tend to have a greater number and variety of conduct problems, more police contacts, and a stronger family history of APD than children with conduct problems alone. These findings are important given that number and variety of conduct problems (Loeber, 1990), early police contacts (Quay, 1987), family history of APD (Lahey et al., 1995), early onset of conduct problems (Moffitt, 1993) and violent sex offending (Brannon & Troyer, 1995) have all been consistent predictors of poor outcomes in delinquent youth.

In addition, research has shown that youth with CU traits and conduct problems tend to endorse more thrill-seeking activities (Frick et al., 1994), display more passive avoidance errors (Barry et al., 2000), and have a greater sensitivity to reward than to punishment (O'Brien & Frick, 1996) compared to youth with conduct problems alone. In an investigation of sensitivity to consequences in the latter study, children played a computerized game. To earn the maximum number of points, they had to change an initially established, reward-oriented response as the rate of punishment increases during the task. O'Brien and Frick (1996) found that clinic-referred children with high levels of CU traits tended to play more consecutive trials on this task, regardless of whether they had significant conduct problems.

Whereas CU traits have been related to lower levels of behavioral inhibition, the other commonly identified dimension of psychopathy, known as impulsivity/conduct problems (I/CP), has been associated with increased levels of emotional distress (Frick, Lilienfeld, Ellis, Loney, & Silverthorn, 1999). The I/CP factor of psychopathy tends to overlap with DSM symptoms of ADHD, ODD, and CD (Frick, Bodin, & Barry, 2000). This suggests that the I/CP factor identifies a large set of antisocial juveniles, whereas the presence of CU traits specifies a group of children whose antisocial behavior may stem from low levels of fearfulness and a reward-dominant response style.

Recent research has explored how youth's psychopathic traits relate to their broader personality traits, and how they process social information in the moment. Researchers have also increasingly begun to look at the course of development of psychopathic traits over time. The following sections explore these issues in subtypes of youth with psychopathic traits.

CU Traits, Social Cognition, and Anxiety

Because youth with significant CU traits have problems modifying goal-oriented behavior when punished (O'Brien & Frick, 1996), their persistent conduct problems may be due to their difficulties in processing social information and in assessing the likelihood that various outcomes will occur as the result of antisocial behavior. For example, CU traits may be associated with a tendency to overestimate the probability that positive consequences will result from aggression, to underestimate the probability of experiencing negative consequences as the result of violence, and to overvalue aggressive behavior. Pardini and colleagues (2003) investigated this question with a sample of 169 adjudicated youth. Youth with higher levels of CU traits had higher levels of expectations and values associated with the positive consequences of aggression (i.e., tangible rewards, dominance), and lower levels associated with the negative consequences of deviant behavior (i.e., punishment). This pattern of deficient information processing was evident even after controlling for the effects of the I/CP dimension, demographic characteristics, history of abuse, intellectual abilities, and delinquency severity.

Consistent with conceptualizations of emotional characteristics of psychopathic traits, children in this study with high levels of CU traits also had low levels of empathy and fear. In contrast, children who were high on the I/CP dimension but not CU did display emotional distress. Youth with high levels of the I/CP dimension often have dysfunctional family backgrounds, which may cause them to become hypervigilant in very emotional situations (Frick et al., 1999). The CU dimension, on the other hand, has been associated with an emotional processing deficit that may help to buffer the amount of personal distress experienced by youth during threatening events. For empathy development to occur, children must initially experience self-focused emotional distress when they are punished for transgressions or when they see others in pain (Blair, 1999; Kochanska, 1995), but youth with high levels of CU traits have low levels of temperamental fearfulness (Pardini et al., 2003), and thus do not attend to the type punishment that contributes to empathy development.

Psychopathy and Personality

In addition to examining how children with psychopathic features process social and emotional information in the world around them, researchers have begun to examine how psychopathic features might represent aspects of youth's more general personality functioning as it is forming during the adolescent years. Salekin and colleagues (2005) examined personality correlates of 114 adolescent offenders in a detention facility. The presence of high levels of CU traits and I/CP behaviors was associated with adolescents being less conscientious, agreeable, and open. In contrast, these youth with more psychopathic traits scored higher on neuroticism, suggesting that worry and anxiety may accompany psychopathic features in early stages. Thus, it appears that the development of psychopathic features in youth can best be understood as part of their broader personality development.

Grandiose/Manipulative

Recent conceptualizations of psychopathy focus on a third set of characteristics besides CU and I/CP traits as a possible additional key personality component of psychopathy (Cooke & Michie, 2001; Frick et al., 2000; Gustafson & Ritzer, 1995). This third characteristic is an arrogant, grandiose presentation with concern about one's status over others (often referred to as *narcissism*; Barry et al., 2007). Although popular conceptions of grandiosity may equate this construct with extremely high self-esteem, distinctions have been made between the two (Raskin & Terry, 1988). Whereas *grandiosity* is one's emotional investment in establishing superiority over others, self-esteem can be described as a global evaluation of one's goodness, without necessarily being strongly motivated to establish that goodness in the eyes of others.

To explore the relations among the grandiose/manipulative features, which in this study were labeled *narcissism*, self-esteem, and children's aggressive behavior, Barry and colleagues (2007) assessed 160 moderately to highly aggressive preadolescent children with teacher, parent, and child self-report data. Narcissism was found to be unrelated to general self-esteem, providing support that narcissism and self-esteem are different constructs. Consistent with the study's hypotheses, narcissism predicted unique variance in both proactive and reactive aggression, even when researchers controlled for the other dimensions of psychopathy (CU, I/CP), demographic variables associated with narcissism, and the alternative subtype of aggression. As expected, impulsivity was significantly associated with only reactive aggression. CU traits were not related to proactive or reactive aggression once the control variables were entered. Narcissism, but not self-esteem, accounted for unique variance in aggression and conduct problems. These findings suggest the importance of the role of children's narcissism in contributing to their aggressive behaviors, and clarify that narcissism's effects are relatively independent of the other features of psychopathy and of children's general sense of self-esteem.

Changes in Psychopathic Traits over Time

Although there has been an increase in interest in understanding the development of CU traits in youth, longitudinal research in this area is sparse (for an exception, see Frick, Kimonis, Dandreaux, & Farrell, 2003). To address the lack of longitudinal research investigating the possible interactions between child anxiety and parental practices in predicting the development of CU traits in school-age children, Pardini, Lochman, and Powell (2007) examined the development of CU traits across a 1-year period with a sample of 120 moderately to highly aggressive children. Consistent with prior research, CU traits in children displayed a moderate degree of temporal stability and predicted increases in antisocial behavior across time. However, CU traits were changeable across this relatively brief developmental span, and were affected by certain protective factors. Specifically, children who were exposed to lower levels of harsh punishment, and perceived their parent as warm and involved, exhibited decreases in CU traits over time. These parenting practices were also related to reductions in antisocial behavior, suggesting that the co-occurrence of CU traits and antisocial behavior may be partially due to shared environmental influences. In contrast, lower levels of anxiety were uniquely related to increases in CU traits over time, particularly for children who describe their caregivers as exhibiting relatively little warmth and involvement. The results suggest the important protective role of certain parenting practices, especially parent warmth and involvement, in moderating the development of CU traits during these preadolescent years.

In another recent longitudinal study, Barry, Barry, Deming, and Lochman (2008), examined 80 moderately aggressive preadolescents. These adolescents were followed for three annual assessments and, similar to the prior study, had moderately stable psychopathic characteristics over time. This study examined whether children's social relations might affect the development and change of psychopathic traits over time. Although consistent findings were not evident at all time points, partial evidence for moderation was found. The stability of narcissism, or grandiose/manipulative features, was affected by the child's perception of his or her social competence, but, in contrast, the stability of I/CP (i.e., the behavioral dimension of psychopathy) was influenced by the child's social competence, based on teacher ratings, and social preference based on peer ratings. As expected, greater impairments in these social areas were associated with more stable and persistent psychopathic characteristics, including narcissistic, grandiose traits, and I/CP, whereas better social functioning was associated with decreasing levels of psychopathic characteristics across time. These two longitudinal studies both suggest important parent and peer contextual factors that can buffer against, or enhance, the likelihood of psychopathic traits increasing in strength over time.

Conclusion

Over the years there has been a varied and rich history of efforts to identify different ways to create subtypes of youth at different levels of risk for future negative outcomes. These various subtyping methods vary, depending on whether examination is made of youth's social characteristics, their types of psychiatric comorbidities, their behavioral patterns, or, more recently, their personality characteristics associated with psychopathic traits. These efforts to create subtypes have had two principal purposes in the field. First, the various subtype systems permit clinicians and researchers to identify developmental pathways leading to serious antisocial outcomes that develop in different ways for the different subtypes. Second, efforts to identify subtypes of children have considerable implications for how evidence-based interventions developed for youth with conduct problems (e.g., Lochman & Wells, 2003, 2004) may need to be tailored in different ways to target the specific active mechanisms that account for escalating antisocial behavior in the various subtypes.

It is clear that these various efforts to subtype antisocial children likely overlap. For example, there are similarities in the aggressive–rejected versus aggressive–nonrejected subtyping systems and the undersocialized versus socialized categorization of conduct problems. One would expect youth identified as aggressive–rejected to also be classified as undersocialized, whereas aggressive–nonrejected youth would more likely be classified as socialized. Similarly, ADHD symptoms, such as impulsivity, appear to overlap with reactive aggression in youth with conduct problems. Future research can target how many of these subtypes are truly unique, and how others, at least partially, are capturing the same phenomenon.

References

Aguilar, B., Sroufe, L. A., Egeland, B., & Carlson, E. (2000). Distinguishing the early-onset/persistent and adolescence-onset antisocial behavior types: From birth to 16 years. *Development and Psychopathology, 12*, 109–132.

American Psychiatric Association. (1980). *Diagnostic and statistical manual of mental disorders* (3rd ed.). Washington, DC: Author.

American Psychiatric Association. (2000). *Diagnostic and statistical manual of mental disorders* (4th ed., text rev.). Washington, DC: Author.

Anderson, J. C., Williams, S. M., McGee, R., & Silva, P. A. (1987). DSM-III disorders in preadolescent children: Prevalence in a large sample from the general population. *Archives of General Psychiatry, 44*, 69–76.

Angold, A., & Costello, E. (2001). The epidemiology of disorders of conduct: Nosological issues and comorbidity. In J. Hill & B. Maughan (Eds.), *Conduct disorders in childhood and adolescence* (pp. 126–168). New York: Cambridge University Press.

Angold, A., Costello, J. E., & Erkanli, A. (1999). Comorbidity. *Journal of Child Psychology and Psychiatry, 40*, 57–87.

Archer, J., & Côté, S. (2005). Sex differences in aggressive behavior: A developmental and evolutionary perspective. In R. E. Tremblay, W. W. Hartup, & J. Archer (Eds.), *Developmental origins of aggression* (pp. 425–443). New York: Guilford Press.

Arredondo, D. E., & Butler, S. F. (1994). Affective comorbidity in psychiatrically hospitalized adolescents with conduct disorders or oppositional defiant disorder: Should conduct disorder be treated with mood stabilizers? *Journal of Child and Adolescent Psychopharmacology, 4*, 151–158.

Barry, C. T., Frick, P. J., DeShazo, T. M., McCoy, M. G., Ellis, M., & Loney, B. R. (2000). The importance of callous–unemotional traits for extending the concept of psychopathy to children. *Journal of Abnormal Psychology, 109*, 335–340.

Barry, T. D., Barry, C. T., Deming, A. M., & Lochman, J. E. (2008). Stability of psychopathic characteristics in childhood: The influence of social relationships. *Criminal Justice and Behavior, 35*, 243–262.

Barry, T. D., Thompson, A., Barry, C. T., Lochman, J. E., Adler, K., & Hill, K. (2007). The importance of narcissism in predicting proactive and reactive aggression in moderately to highly aggressive children. *Aggressive Behavior, 33*, 185–197.

Beauchaine, T. P., & Gartner, J. (2003). A linear growth curve analysis of inpatient treatment response by conduct-disordered, ADHD, and comorbid preadolescents. *Aggressive Behavior, 29*, 440–456.

Beyers, J., & Loeber, R. (2003). Untangling developmental relations between depressed mood and delinquency in male adolescents. *Journal of Abnormal Child Psychology, 31*, 247–266.

Bierman, K. L. (2004). *Peer rejection: Developmental processes and intervention strategies*. New York: Guilford Press.

Bierman, K. L., Smoot, D. L., & Aumiller, K. (1993). Characteristics of aggressive–rejected, aggressive (nonrejected), and rejected (nonaggressive) boys. *Child Development, 64*, 139–151.

Blair, R. J. R. (1999). Responsiveness to distress cues in the child with psychopathic tendencies. *Personality and Individual Differences, 27,* 135–145.

Brannon, J. M., & Troyer, R. (1995). Adolescent sex offenders: Investigating adult commitment-rates four years later. *International Journal of Offender Therapy and Comparative Criminology, 39,* 317–326.

Caputo, A. A., Frick, P. J., & Brodsky, S. L. (1999). Family violence and juvenile sex offending: Potential mediating role of psychopathic traits and negative attitudes toward women. *Criminal Justice and Behavior, 26,* 338–356.

Christian, R. E., Frick, P. J., Hill, N. L., Tyler, L., & Frazer, D. R. (1997). Psychopathy and conduct problems in children: II. Implications for subtyping children with conduct problems. *Journal of the American Academy of Child and Adolescent Psychiatry, 36,* 233–241.

Cleckley, H. (1976). *The mask of sanity* (5th ed.). St Louis, MO: Mosby.

Coie, J. D., & Dodge, K. A., (1998). Aggression and antisocial behavior. In W. Damon (Series Ed.) & N. Eisenberg (Vol. Ed.), *Handbook of child psychology: Vol. 3. Social, emotional, and personality development* (5th ed., pp. 779–862). New York: Wiley.

Coie, J. D., Lochman, J. E., Terry, R., & Hyman, C. (1992). Predicting early adolescent disorders from childhood aggression and peer rejection. *Journal of Consulting and Clinical Psychology, 60,* 783–792.

Coie, J. D., Terry, R., Lenox, K., Lochman, J. E., & Hyman, C. (1995). Childhood peer rejection and aggression as predictors of stable patterns of adolescent disorder. *Development and Psychopathology, 7,* 697–713.

Conduct Problems Prevention Research Group. (2004). The Fast Track experiment: Translating the developmental model into a prevention design. In J. B. Kupersmidt & K. A. Dodge (Eds.), *Children's peer relations: From development to intervention* (pp. 181–208). Washington, DC: American Psychological Association.

Cooke, D. J., & Michie, C. (2001). Refining the construct of psychopathy: Toward a hierarchical model. *Psychological Assessment, 13,* 171–188.

Crick, N. R., & Dodge, K. A. (1996). Social information-processing mechanisms in reactive and proactive aggression. *Child Development, 67,* 993–1002.

Crick, N. R., & Grotpeter, J. K. (1995). Relational aggression, gender, and social-psychological adjustment. *Child Development, 66*(3), 710–722.

Dodge, K. A., & Coie, J. D. (1987). Social-information-processing factors in reactive and proactive aggression in children's peer groups. *Journal of Personality and Social Psychology, 53*(6), 1146–1158.

Dodge, K. A., Lochman, J. E., Harnish, J. D., Bates, J. E., & Pettit, G. S. (1997). Reactive and proactive aggression in school children and psychiatrically impaired chronically assaultive youth. *Journal of Abnormal Psychology, 106,* 37–51.

Dodge, K. A., Price, J. M., Bachorowski, J., & Newman, J. P. (1990). Hostile attributional biases in severely aggressive adolescents. *Journal of Abnormal Psychology, 99,* 385–392.

Ezpleta, L., Domenech, J. M., & Angold, A. (2006). A comparison of pure and comorbid CD/ODD and depression. *Journal of Child Psychology and Psychiatry, 47,* 704–712.

Ezpleta, L., Granero, R., & Domenech, J. M. (2005). Differential contextual factors of comorbid conduct and depressive disorders in Spanish children. *European Child and Adolescent Psychology, 14,* 282–291.

Fite, P. J., Colder, C. R., Lochman, J. E., & Wells, K. C. (2008). The relation between childhood proactive and reactive aggression and substance use initiation. *Journal of Abnormal Child Psychology, 36,* 261–271.

Fleming, J., Boyle, M., & Offord, D. (1993). The outcome of adolescent depression in the Ontario Child Health Study follow-up. *Journal of the American Academy of Child and Adolescent Psychiatry, 167,* 362–369.

Forehand, R., Wierson, M., Frame, C., Kempton, T., & Armistead, L. (1991). Juvenile delinquency entry and persistence: Do attention problems contribute to conduct problems? *Journal of Behavior Therapy and Experimental Psychiatry, 22,* 261–264.

Frick, P. J., Bodin, D. S., & Barry, C. T. (2000). Psychopathic traits and conduct problems in community and clinic-referred samples of children: Further development of the psychopathy screening device. *Psychological Assessment, 12,* 382–393.

Frick, P. J., Kimonis, E. R., Dandreaux, D. M., & Farrell, J. M. (2003). The 4-year stability of psychopathic traits in non-referred youth. *Behavioral Sciences and the Law, 21,* 713–736.

Frick, P. J., Lahey, B. B., Loeber, R., Tannenbaum, L. E., Van Horn, Y., Christ, M. A. G., et al. (1993). Oppositional defiant disorder and conduct disorder: A meta-analytic review of factor analysis and cross-validation in a clinic sample. *Clinical Psychology Review, 13,* 319–340.

Frick, P. J., Lilienfeld, S. O., Ellis, M., Loney, B., & Silverthorn, P. (1999). The association between anxiety and psychopathy dimensions in children. *Journal of Abnormal Child Psychology, 27,* 383–392.

Frick, P. J., O'Brien, B. S., Wootton, J. M., & McBurnett, K. (1994). Psychopathy and conduct problems in children. *Journal of Abnormal Psychology, 103,* 700–707.

Gray, J. A. (1987). *The psychology of fear and stress* (2nd ed.). Cambridge, UK: Cambridge University Press.

Greene, R. W., Biederman, J., Zerwas, S., Monuteaux, M., Goring, J. C., & Faraone, S. V. (2002). Psychiatric comorbidity, family dysfunction, and social impairment in referred youth with oppositional defiant disorder. *American Journal of Psychiatry, 159,* 1214–1224.

Gustafson, S. B., & Ritzer, D. R. (1995). The dark side of normal: A psychopathy-linked pattern called aberrant self-promotion. *European Journal of Personality, 9,* 147–183.

Hanson, C. L., Henggeler, S. W., Haefele, W. F., & Rodick, J. D. (1984). Demographic, individual, and family relationship correlates of serious and reported crime among adolescents and their siblings. *Journal of Consulting and Clinical Psychology, 52,* 528–538.

Hare, R. D. (1991). *The Hare Psychopathy Checklist—Revised.* Toronto: Multi-Health Systems.

Hare, R. D. (1993). *Without conscience: The disturbing world of the psychopaths among us.* New York: Guilford Press.

Hetherington, E. M., Stouwie, R., & Ridberg, E. H. (1971). Patterns of family interaction and child rearing attitudes to three dimensions of juvenile delinquency. *Journal of Abnormal Child Psychology, 77*, 160–176.

Hewitt, L. E., & Jenkins, R. L. (1946). *Fundamental patterns of maladjustment, the dynamics of their origin*. Springfield: State of Illinois.

Hinshaw, S. P., & Lee, S. S. (2003). Conduct and oppositional defiant disorders. In E. J. Mash & R. A. Barkley (Eds.), *Child psychopathology* (2nd ed., pp. 144–198). New York: Guilford Press.

Hinshaw, S. P., & Melnick, S. M. (1995). Peer relationships in children with attention-deficit hyperactivity disorder with and without comorbid aggression. *Development and Psychopathology, 7*, 627–647.

Kochanska, G. (1995). Children's temperament, mothers' discipline, and security of attachment: Multiple pathways to emerging internalization. *Child Development, 66*, 597–615.

Lagerspetz, K. M., Bjorkqvist, K., & Peltonen, T. (1988). Is indirect aggression typical of females?: Gender differences in aggressiveness in 11- to 12-year-old children. *Aggressive Behavior, 14*, 403–414.

Lahey, B. B., Loeber, R., Hart, E. L., Frick, P. J., Applegate, B., Zhang, Q., et al. (1995). Four-year longitudinal study of conduct disorders: Patterns and predictors of persistence. *Journal of Abnormal Psychology, 104*, 83–93.

Leve, L. D., & Chamberlain, P. (2004). Female juvenile offenders: Defining an early-onset pathway for delinquency. *Journal of Child and Family Studies, 13*, 439–452.

Lewinsohn, P. M., Rohde, P., & Seeley, J. R. (1995). Adolescent psychopathology: III. The clinical consequences of co-morbidity. *Journal of the American Academy of Child and Adolescent Psychiatry, 34*, 510–519.

Lilienfeld, S. O. (1998). Methodological advances and developments in the assessment of psychopathy. *Behaviour Research and Therapy, 36*, 99–125.

Lochman, J. E., Dane, H. E., Magee, T. N., Ellis, M., Pardini, D. A., & Clanton, N. R. (2001). Disruptive behavior disorders: Assessment and intervention. In B. Vance & A, Pumareiga (Eds.), *The clinical assessment of children and youth behavior: Interfacing intervention with assessment* (pp. 231–262). New York: Wiley.

Lochman, J. E., & Dodge, K. A. (1994). Social-cognitive processes of severely violent, moderately aggressive and nonaggressive boys. *Journal of Consulting and Clinical Psychology, 62*(2), 366–374.

Lochman, J. E., & Wayland, K. K. (1994). Aggression, social acceptance, and race as predictors of negative adolescent outcomes. *Journal of the American Academy of Child and Adolescent Psychiatry, 33*, 1026–1035.

Lochman, J. E., & Wells, K. C. (2003). Effectiveness study of Coping Power and classroom intervention with aggressive children: Outcomes at a one-year follow-up. *Behavior Therapy, 34*, 493–515.

Lochman, J. E., & Wells, K. C. (2004). The Coping Power program for preadolescent aggressive boys and their parents: Outcome effects at the one-year follow-up. *Journal of Consulting and Clinical Psychology, 72*, 571–578.

Loeber, R. (1990). Development and risk factors of juvenile antisocial behavior and delinquency. *Clinical Psychology Review, 10*, 1–42.

Loeber, R., Burke, J. D., Lahey, B. A., Winters, A., & Zera, M. (2000). Oppositional defiant disorder and conduct disorder: A review of the past 10 years, part 1. *Journal of the American Academy of Child and Adolescent Psychiatry, 39*, 1468–1484.

Loeber, R., & Farrington, D. P. (2000). Young children who commit crime: Epidemiology, developmental origins, risk factors, early interventions, and policy implications. *Development and Psychopathology, 12*, 737–762.

Loeber, R., Green, S. M., Lahey, B. B., Frick, P. J., & McBurnett, K. (2000). Findings of disruptive behavior disorders from the first decade of the Developmental Trends study. *Clinical Child and Family Psychology Review, 3*, 37–60.

Loeber, R., & Hay, D. (1997). Key issues in the development of aggression and violence from childhood to early adulthood. *Annual Reviews of Psychology, 48*, 371–410.

Loeber, R., & Keenan, K. (1994). Interaction between conduct disorder and its comorbid conditions: Effects of age and gender. *Clinical Psychology Review, 14*, 497–523.

Loeber, R., Russo, M. F., Stouthamer-Loeber, M., & Lahey, B. (1994). Internalizing problems and their relation to the development of disruptive behaviors in adolescence. *Journal of Research on Adolescence, 4*(4), 615–637.

Loeber, R., & Schmalling, K. B. (1985a). Empirical evidence for overt and covert patterns of antisocial conduct problems: A meta-analysis. *Journal of Abnormal Child Psychology, 13*, 337–352.

Loeber, R., & Schmalling, K. B. (1985b). The utility of differentiating between mixed and pure forms of antisocial child behavior. *Journal of Abnormal Child Psychology, 13*, 315–336.

Loeber, R., & Stouthamer-Loeber, M. (1998). Development of juvenile aggression and violence: Some common misconceptions and controversies. *American Psychologist, 53*, 242–259.

Lynam, D. R. (1996). Early identification of chronic offenders: Who is the fledgling psychopath? *Psychological Bulletin, 120*, 209–234.

Lynam, D. R. (1998). Early identification of the fledgling psychopath: Locating the psychopathic child in the current nomenclature. *Journal of Abnormal Psychology, 107*, 556–575.

McMahon, R. J., & Frick, P. J. (2005). Evidence-based assessment of conduct problems in children and adolescents. *Journal of Clinical Child and Adolescent Psychology, 34*, 477– 505.

McMahon, R. J., Wells, K. C., & Kotler, J. S. (2006). Conduct problems. In E. J. Mash & R. A. Barkley (Eds.), *Treatment of childhood disorders* (3rd ed., pp. 137–268). New York: Guilford Press.

Milich, R., & Landau, S. (1988). The role of social status variables in differentiating subgroups of hyperactive children. In L. M. Bloomingdale & J. M. Swanson (Eds.), *Attention deficit disorder* (Vol. 4, pp. 1–16). Oxford, UK: Pergamon Press.

Moffitt, T. E. (1990). Juvenile delinquency and attention deficit disorder: Boys' developmental trajectories from age 13 to age 15. *Child Development, 61*, 893–910.

Moffitt, T. E. (1993). Adolescence-limited and life course persistent antisocial behavior: A developmental typology. *Psychological Review, 100,* 674–701.

Moffitt, T. E., & Caspi, A. (2001). Childhood predictors differentiate life-course persistent and adolescence-limited antisocial pathways among males and females. *Development and Psychopathology, 13,* 355–375.

Moffitt, T. E., Caspi, A., Dickson, N., Silva, P., & Stanton, W. (1996). Childhood-onset versus adolescent-onset antisocial conduct problems in males: Natural history from ages 3 to 18 years. *Development and Psychopathology, 8,* 399–424.

Molina, B. S. G., Bukstein, O. G., & Lynch, K. G. (2002). Attention-deficit/hyperactivity disorder and conduct disorder symptomatology in adolescents with alcohol use disorder. *Psychology of Addictive Behaviors, 16,* 161–164.

O'Brien, B. S., & Frick, P. J. (1996). Reward dominance: Associations with anxiety, conduct problems, and psychopathy in children. *Journal of Abnormal Child Psychology, 24,* 223–240.

Ollendick, T. H., Seligman, L. D., & Butcher, T. (1999). Does anxiety mitigate the behavioral expression of severe conduct disorder in delinquent youth? *Journal of Anxiety Disorders, 13,* 565–574.

Pardini, D. (2006). The callousness pathway to severe violent delinquency. *Aggressive Behavior, 32,* 1–9.

Pardini, D. A., Lochman, J. E., & Frick, P. J. (2003). Callous/unemotional traits and social cognitive processes in adjudicated youth. *Journal of the American Academy of Child and Adolescent Psychiatry, 42,* 364–371.

Pardini, D. A., Lochman, J. E., & Powell, N. (2007). Shared or unique developmental pathways to callous-unemotional traits and antisocial behavior in children? *Journal of Clinical Child and Adolescent Psychology, 36,* 319–333.

Patterson, G. R., DeBaryshe, B. D., & Ramsey, E. (1989). A developmental perspective on antisocial behavior. *American Psychologist, 44,* 329–335.

Patterson, G. R., Forgatch, M. S., Yoerger, K. L., & Stoolmiller, M. (1998). Variables that initiate and maintain an early-onset trajectory for juvenile offending. *Development and Psychopathology, 10,* 531–547.

Patterson, G. R., & Yoerger, K. (2002). A developmental model for early- and late-onset delinquency. In J. B. Reid, G. R. Patterson, & J. Snyder (Eds.), *Antisocial behavior in children and adolescents: A developmental analysis and model for intervention* (pp. 147–172). Washington, DC: American Psychological Association.

Phillips, N. C., & Lochman, J. E. (2003). Experimentally-manipulated change in children's proactive and reactive aggressive behavior. *Aggressive Behavior, 29,* 215–227.

Quay, H. C. (1987). Patterns of delinquent behavior. In H. C. Quay (Ed.), *Handbook of juvenile delinquency* (pp. 118–138). New York: Wiley.

Quay, H. C., Routh, D. K., & Shapiro, S. K. (1987). Psychopathology of childhood: From description to validation. *Annual Reviews in Psychology, 38,* 491–532.

Raskin, R. N., & Terry, H. (1988). A principal-components analysis of the narcissistic personality inventory and further evidence of its construct validity. *Journal of Personality and Social Psychology, 54,* 890–902.

Russo, M. F., & Beidel, D. C. (1994). Comorbidity of childhood anxiety and externalizing disorders: Prevalence, associated characteristics, and validation issues. *Clinical Psychology Review, 14,* 199–221.

Russo, M. F., Stokes, G. S., Lahey, B. B., Christ, M. A. G., McBurnett, K., Loeber, R., et al. (1993). A Sensation Seeking Scale for Children: Further refinement and psychometric development. *Journal of Psychopathology and Behavioral Assessment, 15,* 69–86.

Salekin, R. T. (2006). Psychopathy in children and adolescents: Key issues in conceptualization and assessment. In C. J. Patrick (Ed.), *Handbook of psychopathy* (pp. 389–414). New York: Guilford Press.

Salekin, R. T., Leistico, A. M. R., Trobst, K. K., Schrum, C. L., & Lochman, J. E., (2005). Adolescent psychopathy and personality—the interpersonal circumplex: Expanding evidence of a nomological net. *Journal of Abnormal Child Psychology, 33,* 445–460.

Short, R. J., & Simeonson, R. J. (1986). Social cognition and aggression in delinquent adolescent males. *Adolescence, 21,* 159–176.

Silverthorn, P., Frick, P. J., & Reynolds, R. (2001). Timing of onset and correlates of severe conduct problems in adjudicated girls and boys. *Journal of Psychopathology and Behavioral Assessment, 23,* 171–181.

Simic, M., & Fombonne, E. (2001). Depressive conduct disorder: Symptom patterns and correlates in referred children and adolescents. *Journal of Affective Disorders, 62,* 175–185.

Slaby, R. G., & Guerra, N. G. (1988). Cognitive mediators of aggression in adolescent offenders : 1. Assessment. *Developmental Psychology, 24,* 580–588.

Thompson, L. L., Riggs, P. D., Mikulich, S. K., & Crowley, T. J. (1996). Contribution of ADHD symptoms to substance problems and delinquency in conduct-disordered adolescents. *Journal of Abnormal Child Psychology, 24,* 325–347.

Vaillancourt, T., & Hymel, S. (2004). The social context of children's aggression. In M. M. Moretti, C. L. Odgers, & A. M. Jackson (Eds.), *Girls and aggression: Contributing factors and intervention principles* (pp. 57–73). New York: Kluwer Academic/Plenum Press.

Verhulst, F. C., & van der Ende, J. (1993). "Comorbidity" in an epidemiological sample: A longitudinal perspective. *Journal of Child Psychology and Psychiatry, 34,* 767–783.

Walker, J. L., Lahey, B. B., Russo, M. F., Frick, P. J., Christ, M. A., McBurnett, K., et al. (1991). Anxiety, inhibition, and conduct disorder in children: I. Relations to social impairment. *Journal of the American Academy of Child and Adolescent Psychiatry, 30,* 187–191.

Waschbusch, D. A. (2002). A meta-analytic examination of comorbid hyperactive-impulsive- attention problems and conduct problems. *Psychological Bulletin, 128,* 118–150.

Washburn, J. J., Romero, E. G., Welty, L. J., Abram, K. M., Teplin, L. A., McClelland, G. M., et al. (2007). Development of antisocial personality disorder in detained youth: The predictive value of mental disorders. *Journal of Consulting and Clinical Psychology, 75,* 221–231.

Wolff, J. C., & Ollendick, T. H. (2006). The comorbidity of conduct problems and depression in childhood and adolescence. *Clinical Child and Family Psychology Review, 9*, 201–220.

Woolston, J. L., Rosenthal, S. L., Riddle, M. A., Sparrow, S. S., Cicchetti, D., & Zimmerman, L. (1989). Childhood comorbidity of anxiety/affective disorders and behavior disorders. *Journal of the American Academy of Child and Adolescent Psychiatry, 28*, 707–713.

Zoccolillo, M. (1992). Co-occurrence of conduct disorder and its adult outcomes with depressive and anxiety disorders: A review. *Journal of the American Academy of Child and Adolescent Psychiatry, 31*, 547–556.

4

Assessment of Child and Adolescent Psychopathy

JULIE S. KOTLER
ROBERT J. MCMAHON

In the last several decades, extensive research efforts have identified risk factors and etiological pathways associated with the development and persistence of youth conduct problems, criminality, and violence. In this context, substantial heterogeneity has been uncovered in the developmental trajectories leading to serious conduct problem behavior (e.g., Dodge & Pettit, 2003; Frick & Ellis, 1999). Based on the principle of *equifinality* (i.e., multiple etiological pathways leading to similar outcomes; Sroufe, 1997), it is expected that understanding the diverse developmental pathways leading to antisocial behavior will result in more accurate conceptualizations of this behavior, which will in turn serve as the foundation for successful intervention and prevention efforts.

In this context, there has been increasing interest in exploring "psychopathic traits" in youth because the presence or absence of these traits may help to identify unique etiological processes in the development of antisocial behavior. Many view this avenue of inquiry as particularly promising because the psychopathy construct has been useful in conceptualizing and predicting antisocial behavior in adults (Cleckley, 1976; Frick, 1998; Hare, Hart, & Harpur, 1991). For example, in adult samples, psychopathic traits predict a particularly serious and violent pattern of antisocial behavior that has been shown to be quite resistant to treatment (Hart, Kropp, & Hare, 1988; Serin, 1993). Furthermore, the antisocial behavior associated with adult psychopathy is widely thought to have a relatively different etiology than antisocial behavior in nonpsychopathic adults (Lykken, 1995). However, it is notable that there are also significant concerns about whether the concept of psychopathy should be applied to youth (e.g., Hart, Watt, & Vincent; 2002; Seagrave & Grisso, 2002). Some of the debate surrounding this issue includes (1) conflict about whether delineating psychopathic traits in youth is developmentally appropriate given the malleability of personality during development and the heterogeneity of antisocial youth; (2) questions about the stability of psychopathic traits from youth to adulthood; and (3) concerns about the "psychopathy" label and its use in legal settings (although recently, Murrie, Boccaccini, McCoy, & Cornell [2007] found that behavioral history and personality descriptions influenced judges' decisions, whereas the psychopathy label itself did not).

Current descriptions of the psychopathy construct include interpersonal aspects (e.g., superficial charm, grandiosity, manipulation, and lying); affective aspects (e.g., shallow emotions, absence of guilt, callousness and lack of empathy, lack of responsibility for actions), and a behavioral dimension, including antisocial aspects (e.g., impulsivity, irresponsibility, need for excitement, using others, lack of realistic long-term goals, delinquency) (Cooke & Michie, 2001; Hare, 2003). The most extensively used measure of adult psychopathy is the Psychopathy Checklist (PCL; Hare, 1980; now in a revised form, the Psychopathy Checklist—Revised [PCL-R]; Hare, 1991a, 2003). This "gold standard" assessment tool, intended for use with criminal and incarcerated populations, combines a standardized semistructured interview and a detailed review of correctional institution charts. Additionally, it provides a broad assessment of multiple dimensions of psychopathy, including (1) the affective and interpersonal traits key to classic definitions of psychopathy (e.g., Cleckley, 1976), and (2) lifestyle and antisocial dimensions.

As interest grew in psychopathic traits in children and adolescents, it quickly became clear that the measurement tools used to assess psychopathy in adults, including the PCL-R, were inappropriate for use with children (Edens, Skeem, Cruise, & Cauffman, 2001). For example, a number of the items were inapplicable for children (e.g., "parasitic lifestyle," "many short-term marital relationships"). Additionally, some items (which seemed quite useful as markers of psychopathy in adulthood) measured behaviors that might actually be age-appropriate in children and adolescents. Thus, these items (e.g., "need for stimulation," "impulsivity," "failure to accept responsibility," and "thrill-seeking behaviors") might not accurately distinguish youth with psychopathic traits from their peers. In the context of these issues, research has for two decades focused on accurately assessing the youth psychopathy construct by either (1) adapting adult assessment tools or (2) creating new, developmentally appropriate measures. However, regardless of the strategy utilized in measure development, all commonly used youth psychopathy measures are derived (often both conceptually and in terms of specific items) from the PCL-R (Hare, 1991a, 2003). This chapter is devoted to a discussion of these measures (see Table 4.1 for a summary of measures).

We begin with an in-depth review of two primary categories of measures: (1) the Psychopathy Checklist: Youth Version (PCL:YV; Forth, Kosson, & Hare, 2003), a direct adaptation of the PCL-R for adolescents; and (2) screening measures derived from the PCL-R. For each measure reviewed, we provide (1) brief background information on measure development; (2) a description of the content and structure of the measurement tool; (3) a summary of available psychometric research (i.e., factor structure, reliability data, validity data); and (4) an analysis of the strengths and limitations of the measure. We then compare and contrast the screening measures and the PCL:YV, and provide a summary and analysis of current measurement issues and future research directions. In concluding the chapter, we provide some thoughts on selecting a youth psychopathy assessment tool.

The PCL:YV

Background Information

As noted earlier, the PCL:YV (Forth et al., 2003) is a version of the PCL-R (Hare, 1991b), adapted for use with adolescents. Like the PCL-R, this instrument was designed as a full-scale assessment tool rather than as a screening measure. Thus, it stands apart from the other instruments reviewed in this chapter, and in some cases, serves as a standard of comparison. Early on, studies examining psychopathy in adolescents used the PCL-R and made scoring modifications to adapt individual items for an adolescent population (Forth, Hart, & Hare, 1990). For example, items related to having a "parasitic lifestyle" and "many short-term marriages" were omitted, and the scoring for items related to "juvenile delinquency" and "criminal versatility" was modified because adolescents have had a shorter period of time to develop such behavioral histories. The PCL:YV retains all 20 items from the PCL-R but includes some of these early item-scoring modifications (e.g., changes to item titles and descriptions). Changes to the informational sources and scoring criteria also were intended to tailor the measure for adolescents by focusing more heavily on peer, family, and school adjustment (Neumann, Kosson, Forth, & Hare, 2006).

Measure Description

The PCL:YV is completed by trained raters, includes a thorough record review, and is much more time-intensive and complex than the screening

TABLE 4.1. A Comparison of Child and Adolescent Psychopathy Measures Derived from the PCL-R

Measure	Informant(s)	Age range	No. of items	Scale	Factors	Cutoff points	Reliability/validity data	No. of studies with validity data	Multiple labs conducting research?
PCL:YV[a] (Forth, Kosson, & Hare, 2003)	Skilled rater	13+ years	20 items	0–2	Two factors: interpersonal–affective, socially deviant lifestyle or three to four factors: interpersonal, affective, behavioral (lifestyle/antisocial)	Approx. 30+	Adequate internal consistency. Interrater reliability adequate. Moderate associations with the screening measures. Concurrent/ predictive validity with range of outcomes.	10+	Yes
APSD (Frick & Hare, 2001)	Parent Teacher Youth	4–18 years	20 items	0–2	Two factors: impulsivity–conduct problems, callous–unemotional or three factors: impulsivity, narcissism, callous–unemotional	+1 *SD* in community samples Two factors: a score of 7 or more on I/CP and 4 or more on CU	Adequate internal consistency and reliability for parent–teacher versions. Youth version may not be adequate. Moderate associations with the PCL:YV. Concurrent/ predictive validity with range of outcomes.	10+	Yes
CPS (Lynam, 1997)	Parent	12+ years	12 items: multiple questions for each item	Varies[b]	Total score only; two factors correlated at $r = .95$ were not usable	None reported	Adequate internal consistency. Moderate associations with the PCL:YV. Concurrent/ predictive validity with several outcomes.	3	Yes

TABLE 4.1. *(continued)*

YPI (Andershed, Gustafson, et al., 2002)	Youth	12+ years	50 items: 5 for each of 10 trait scales	1–4	Grandiose/manipulative, callous–unemotional, impulsive/irresponsible	None reported	Adequate internal consistency. Adequate test–retest reliability. Moderate associations with the PCL:YV. Concurrent/predictive validity with several outcomes.	6	Yes
PCS (Murrie & Cornell, 2000)	Youth	12–18 years	20 items from MACI or 16 items revised by Salekin et al. (2003)	True–False	Informal for 16-item version; interpersonal, affective, lifestyle	None reported	Adequate internal consistency (both versions). Moderate associations with the PCL:YV. Concurrent/predictive validity for limited outcomes.	4	Yes

Note. PCL:YV, Psychopathy Checklist: Youth Version; APSD, Antisocial Process Screening Device; CPS, Child Psychopathy Scale; YPI, Youth Psychopathic Traits Inventory; PCS, Psychopathy Content Scale.

[a]Unlike the other measures in the table, the PCL:YV is modeled directly after the PCL-R and is not a screening device. It must be completed by skilled raters and includes a record review.

[b]The items on the CPS are drawn from two well-known measures (i.e., the Child Behavior Checklist [CBCL; Achenbach, 1991] and the California Child *Q*-Set [CCQ; Block & Block, 1980]) that each have their own scales.

measures developed to study youth psychopathy. The 20 items are scored on a 3-point scale (0 = *item definitely does not apply*; 1 = *item may or may not apply* [inconsistencies across file information and interview may be present]; and 2 = *item definitely applies*). The PCL:YV was originally designed and recommended for use with adolescents 13 years of age or older, although some researchers have used it with 12-year-olds (Forth & Burke, 1998; Gretton, Hare, & Catchpole, 2004).

Factor Structure

The PCL:YV items were originally divided into an interpersonal/affective factor and a socially deviant lifestyle factor on an a priori basis, consistent with the originally identified factor structure of the adult PCL-R (Forth et al., 1990). The two factors were used separately or summed for a total score. However, a number of factor-analytic studies have not provided clear support for this two-factor structure in adolescents (e.g., Brandt, Kennedy, Patrick, & Curtin, 1997; Forth et al., 2003; Salekin, Brannen, Zalot, Leistico, & Neumann, 2006). Furthermore, similar to transitions in the adult PCL-R literature (e.g., Cooke & Michie, 2001; Hare & Neumann, 2005), more recent studies on the PCL:YV have found that a three-factor (i.e., 13 items: interpersonal, affective, and behavioral dimensions) or a four-factor (i.e., 18 items: interpersonal, affective, lifestyle, and antisocial dimensions) structure may be more appropriate (e.g., Jones, Cauffman, Miller, & Mulvey, 2006; Kosson, Cyterski, Steuerwald, Neumann, & Walker-Matthews, 2002; Salekin et al., 2006; Sevecke, Pukrop, Kosson, & Krischer, 2007). For example, in a large-scale study involving confirmatory factor analyses across five samples of incarcerated males (*N* = 100+ youth for each sample), Neumann and colleagues (2006) found that the three-factor model had adequate fit. However, their results indicated that the four-factor model was somewhat more robust overall. Additionally, Vitacco, Neumann, Caldwell, Leistico, and Van Rybroek (2006) reported that the four-factor model had some incremental validity over the three-factor model in predicting a correlate of psychopathy, instrumental aggression. Because the identification of a four-factor model is a relatively recent development, and most of the extant research is focused on two- and three-factor models, more data are needed to determine the most stable and interpretable factor structure. While most of the research on the structure of the PCL:YV has utilized populations of adolescent males, Schrum and Salekin (2006) recruited a population of 123 adolescent female offenders. Using an item response theory analysis, they found that the interpersonal and affective components of the PCL:YV (rather than the behavioral components) seemed to best discriminate the underlying psychopathy construct. These findings suggest that while aspects of the measure may be applicable to females, additional studies with female youth are needed before conclusive statements can be made about the structure and validity of psychopathy in this population.

Psychometric Data

Forth and colleagues examined the PCL-R adapted for adolescents and the final version of this adaptation, the PCL:YV, in two early studies of incarcerated and community adolescent males (PCL-R adaptation: Forth et al., 1990; PCL:YV: Forth, 1995). In these samples, interrater reliability and internal consistency for the PCL:YV ratings were adequate (i.e., intraclass correlation coefficient [ICC] = .99, alpha = .90). As expected, the PCL:YV score in young offender populations was much higher than the mean score of community adolescents (*M* = 26.30 and *M* = 3.62, respectively). A significant proportion (34%) of the young offender population scored above 30 (an informal cutoff point on the measure). In both samples, the total psychopathy score was related to antisocial/violent behavior, providing some preliminary construct validity. Forth and Burke (1998) also found significant correlations between the number of overall conduct disorder symptoms and the total PCL:YV score, as well as individual factor scores.

Toupin, Mercier, Dery, Cote, and Hodgins (1996) also reported on the reliability and validity of the PCL-R revision for adolescents in a sample of 52 adolescent boys with conduct disorder. Internal consistency was good (alpha = .89) and the interitem correlations were similar to those found in adult samples studied with the PCL-R. Items were correlated with independent ratings scales, including measures of self-esteem, alcohol and drug use, and delinquency, suggesting some convergent validity. Scores on the adolescent version of the PCL-R were also related to delinquency, aggressive behavior, alcohol use, and aggressive conduct disorder symptoms at a 1-year follow-up, providing evidence of predictive validity.

Other research groups have examined the reliability and validity of the PCL:YV. For example, Kosson and colleagues (2002) utilized a sample of 115 adolescent males on probation. Measures of reliability were adequate and similar to those found in the earlier studies. Additionally, PCL:YV ratings predicted concurrent antisocial behavior, interpersonal behaviors commonly associated with psychopathy, and lack of attachment to parents. Dolan and Rennie (2006) conducted a replication study with 115 incarcerated adolescent males in the United Kingdom, and also found adequate reliability, concurrent associations with indices of antisocial/externalizing behavior, and predictive relations with institutional violence at a 3-month follow-up.

Additional work has focused explicitly on the predictive validity of the PCL:YV. Corrado, Vincent, Hart, and Cohen (2004) administered the PCL:YV to 182 male adolescent offenders to examine relations between

PCL:YV scores and both general and violent recidivism (measured at a 14.5-month average follow-up). They found that both two- and three-factor models fit the data and significantly predicted both general and violent recidivism. However, Corrado and colleagues noted that variance in general recidivism was primarily explained by the behavioral psychopathic factor alone (conduct problems and impulsivity), while a combination of factors best explained variance in violent recidivism. Extending findings on predictive validity of the PCL:YV into adulthood, Gretton and colleagues (2004) retrospectively coded criminal file information on 157 adolescent boys. These authors reported that PCL:YV scores were positively correlated with violence 10 years later, after controlling for conduct disorder, age at first offense, and history of violent/nonviolent offending. Schmidt, McKinnon, Chattha, and Brownlee (2006) examined the PCL:YV in a multiethnic community sample of 130 adjudicated male and female adolescents. At a mean follow-up of 3 years, the PCL:YV predicted general and violent recidivism in male European American and Native Canadian youth. Notably, concurrent associations and predictive validity were significantly weaker for females, providing further evidence that the applicability of the PCL:YV to this population remains a concern. Recently, Salekin (2008), examining a sample of 130 children and adolescents involved in court assessments, showed that after controlling for a host of variables relating to offending, PCL:YV scores predicted general and violent recidivism over a 3- to 4-year period from midadolescence to young adulthood.

Finally, recent meta-analytic work has added to the PCL:YV knowledge base. Leistico, Salekin, DeCoster, and Rogers (2008) showed that adolescent psychopathy is predictive of negative outcomes such as violent and nonviolent recidivism, as well as institutional infractions, and that the effect is no different than that found with adults. Edens and Campbell (2007) suggest that caution may be appropriate when considering the concurrent and predictive validity of the PCL:YV. Examining effect sizes for relations between psychopathy scores and institutional misconduct in 15 studies (N = 1,310), these authors found only modest weighted mean correlations (r = .24 to .28). Additionally, there was significant variability in the strength of positive relations between PCL:YV scores and aggressive/violent institutional behavior (e.g., correlations between aggressive misconduct and PCL:YV scores ranged from $r = .14$ in unpublished studies to $r = .33$ in published reports). Taken together, these findings suggest that relations between psychopathy and institutional conduct problems may be somewhat weaker than often stated. Another meta-analysis, conducted by McCoy and Edens (2006), addressed concerns that black and white youth may differ in levels of measured psychopathic traits. Examining 16 studies ($N = 2,199$), these authors found only a very small mean difference ($d = 0.20$, $p = .03$) in levels of psychopathic traits between black and white adolescents as measured by the PCL family of instruments (this difference is equivalent to black youth scoring an average of 1.5 points higher than white youth on a 40-point scale). Although there was certainly significant variability across the studies examined, these results do not support fears of widespread racial bias in the assessment of psychopathy in adolescents, at least as measured by the PCL:YV. However, given the limited research base with minority youth, McCoy and Edens still strongly caution against making inferences about understudied populations based on PCL:YV scores because findings neither establish that the same underlying construct is being measured across ethnic groups nor demonstrate that predictive validity is equivalent.

Strengths and Limitations

The PCL:YV has received substantial research attention over the last two decades and serves as a standard of comparison for many of the other youth psychopathy measures. Compared with the screening measures presented in this chapter, the in-depth, comprehensive nature of the PCL:YV is both a strength and a challenge. Clearly, having interviews and a record review completed by a highly-trained rater is likely to provide a more complete view of a youth's psychopathic traits and is less subject to issues of reporter bias. These aspects may be especially important if youth psychopathy assessments are used in forensic settings. However, because not all juveniles have an extensive history of documented behavior, little information may be available on which to base ratings. Furthermore, the necessity of a record review limits the measure's use with nonoffender populations (as these youth are not likely to have a documented history of behavior), increasing the difficulty of establishing measure generalizability. There is also debate about the feasibility of the downward extension of this measure (although other screening measures are subject to similar concerns). While the authors of the PCL:YV certainly made efforts to modify PCL-R items to make them more developmentally appropriate, there are concerns that a number of items still seem to be more appropriate for adults (e.g., those related to work and relationship histories; Edens et al., 2001).

Screening Measures Derived from the PCL-R

The Antisocial Process Screening Device

Background Information

To test models of psychopathy directly in diverse populations of children and adolescents, Frick and Hare (2001) developed a juvenile psychopathy screening measure, the Antisocial Process Screening Device (APSD; originally called the Psychopathy Screening Device [PSD]). The APSD was modeled directly after the PCL-R (Hare, 1991a), in that all elements of the PCL-R were also included in the APSD, unless they were absolutely not relevant for children (e.g., multiple marriages). Currently, the APSD is the most extensively utilized and tested youth psychopathy screening measure.

Measure Description

The APSD is a 20-item questionnaire available in parent/caregiver, teacher, and youth self-report formats. Scoring is based on a 3-point scale: 0 (*not at all true*), 1 (*sometimes true*), or 2 (*definitely true*). Parent and teacher ratings can be examined separately or combined by item to obtain a composite score. Although age ranges for the measure have not been absolutely specified, the APSD has been used with youth from 4 to 18 years of age.

Factor Structure

Frick, O'Brien, Wootton, and McBurnett (1994) initially examined the psychometric properties of the parent- and teacher-report forms of the APSD in a sample of 95 clinic-referred children ages 6–13. Consistent with the adult literature at the time, initial findings identified two correlated (r = .50) factors similar to those found on the PCL-R. An impulsivity/conduct problems (I/CP) factor included items such as (1) becomes angry when corrected, (2) thinks he or she is more important than others, (3) acts without thinking, (4) blames others for mistakes, (5) teases other people, (6) engages in risky or dangerous activities, and (7) gets bored easily. The authors suggested that this factor is similar to behavioral descriptions of psychopathy (i.e., the deviant lifestyle factor of the PCL-R and criteria for the antisocial personality disorder diagnostic group in DSM-III). A callous–unemotional (CU) factor included items such as (several reverse scored) (1) feels bad or guilty, (2) emotions seem shallow, (3) acts charming in ways that seem insincere, and (4) is concerned about the feelings of others. Frick and colleagues described this factor as representing the psychological/personality dimension of psychopathy (similar to the PCL-R interpersonal/affective factor). Further psychometric evaluation suggested adequate internal consistency (I/CP factor alpha = .82; CU factor alpha = .73; Frick et al., 1994) and test–retest reliability (reliability coefficients = .87 for the I/CP factor and .73 for the CU factor; McBurnett, Tamm, Noell, Pfiffner, & Frick, 1994).

However, preliminary results on the factor structure of the APSD revealed a discrepancy with traditional views of psychopathy in the adult literature. Specifically, several items that would typically load on the interpersonal/affective factor of the PCL-R (i.e., an exaggerated sense of self-worth, failure to accept responsibility for actions, and a tendency toward boredom) were associated with the I/CP factor rather than being associated with the CU factor (Frick et al., 1994). While no explanation for the loading of these items on the I/CP factor was immediately evident, it has been suggested that these inconsistencies with the adult literature may result from a problem with the construct validity of the measure, or may suggest developmental differences in the psychopathy construct itself (Lilienfeld, 1998).

In a second wave of research, Frick, Bodin, and Barry (2000) examined two larger samples of children using both parent and teacher report on the APSD: (1) a community sample of 1,136 third to seventh graders, and (2) a clinic sample of 160 children between the ages of 6 and 13. Based on factor analyses completed on these samples, Frick and colleagues proposed that a three-factor model may be a more useful way to examine psychopathic features in children (although data also supported a two-factor solution). Specifically, several items that originally loaded on the I/CP factor formed a separate factor that was stable across both parent and teacher ratings. Frick and colleagues described these items as being related to narcissism and egocentrism (e.g., thinks he or she is more important, brags excessively, uses or "cons" others) and labeled this third factor *narcissism* (a CU factor was also present in the three-factor solution, and the other factor in this model, composed mainly of remaining I/CP items, was termed *impulsivity*). It should be noted that the correlation between the narcissism factor and the impulsivity factor was quite high in both samples ($r = .66$ in the community sample; $r = .61$ in the clinic sample). Correlations between the CU factor and these two factors were somewhat lower but still highly significant (CU and narcissism: $r = .55$ in the community sample, $r = .52$ in the clinic sample; CU and impulsivity: $r = .57$ in the community sample, $r = .49$ in the clinic sample).

According to Frick and colleagues (2000), the three-factor solution provided several possible benefits. First, isolating narcissism items might facilitate research clarifying relations between narcissism and impulsivity in youth samples (rather than with CU traits, as would be expected from adult samples). Second, in spite of high factor correlations, findings from this study indicated that the narcissism factor may have some different associations than the impulsivity factor (i.e., narcissism seemed more related to oppositional defiant disorder [ODD], while impulsivity was more related to attention-deficit/hyperactivity disorder [ADHD]). Thus, separating these factors would facilitate further examination of these unique associations. Finally, Frick and colleagues argued that the APSD three-factor model aligned with findings supporting a three-factor structure for the PCL-R (Cooke & Michie, 2001).

In an effort to clarify the factor structure and the psychometric properties of the APSD in an independent sample, Kotler, McMahon, and the Conduct Problems Prevention Research Group (2002, 2003) completed principal components analyses and confirmatory factor analyses using parent-report APSD data from two samples of seventh-grade youth (a normative sample and a high-risk sample) in the Fast Track program (Conduct Problems Prevention Research Group, 1992). Results from the principal components analyses on the normative sample indicated that either a two- or a three-factor structure could be appropriate for the APSD data, consistent with findings from Frick and colleagues (2000). However, results from the confirmatory factor analyses on the high-risk sample showed that a three-factor solution fit the data significantly better than a two-factor solution. Confirmatory factor analyses conducted by gender indicated that the three-factor solution fit adequately for the sample of high-risk boys but only marginally for the sample of high-risk girls.

Psychometric Data

Frick and colleagues (e.g., Christian, Frick, Hill, Tyler, & Frazer, 1997; Frick et al., 1994; O'Brien & Frick, 1996), and several other research groups, have identified numerous relations between parent and teacher forms of the APSD and constructs that are theoretically relevant for psychopathy. For example, higher scores on the APSD, especially the CU factor, designate a subgroup of children with more serious antisocial behavior, earlier contact with the juvenile justice system (Christian et al., 1997), and more severe and predatory types of juvenile offending (Caputo, Frick, & Brodsky, 1999). Furthermore, while the I/CP factor is correlated with other measures of conduct problems (r = .5 to .7; Frick et al., 1994), the CU factor is related to a number of temperamental characteristics that have been connected with the psychopathy construct in the adult literature, including (1) sensation seeking (Frick et al., 1994), (2) a reward-oriented response style (O'Brien & Frick, 1996), and (3) fearlessness (Barry et al., 2000). Blair, in research with clinic-referred children, demonstrated that APSD total scores predict electrodermal responses to distress cues and threatening stimuli (Blair, 1999), as well as differences in moral reasoning (Blair, 1997). Recent studies have also provided some initial data on the parent- and teacher-report forms of the APSD with regard to stability and relations with parenting practices. Using the parent-report APSD, Frick, Kimonis, Dandreaux, and Farrell (2003) found that CU traits were quite stable over a 4-year period (third through seventh grade; r = .93). However, their results also suggested that higher levels of positive parenting (youth report) were related to decreases in CU traits at the 4-year follow-up. Combining parent and teacher reports on the APSD, Pardini, Lochman, and Powell (2007) found only moderate stability (r = .59) in the CU factor over a 1-year period in a sample of 120 aggressive fifth graders. Their results also indicated that higher levels of parental warmth and involvement at baseline were associated with decreases in CU traits. Such change in CU factor scores over a 1-year period is notable in the context of the typical conceptualization of psychopathy as a stable personality characteristic.

More recently, increased use of the Youth Self-Report form of the APSD (APSD-Y) has provided psychometric data on this version of the measure. Murrie and Cornell (2002) examined relations between self- and staff-report on the APSD and found no significant correlation (total APSD score only). Poythress and colleagues (2006) reviewed a number of their datasets containing APSD-Y data to evaluate the measure's internal consistency. Their findings suggested some concerns in this regard, especially with respect to the CU scale (narcissism median alpha = .69; impulsivity median alpha = .53; CU median alpha = .46). However, other authors, examining primarily institutionalized samples of youth, have found more promising results. Vitacco, Rogers, and Neumann (2003) found support for a three-factor model on the APSD-Y using confirmatory factor analysis. Additionally, these authors found that the CU scale and the Narcissism scale differentiated between maximum security and local detention populations. Furthermore, additional concurrent and predictive validity has been demonstrated in terms of severity of offenses, number of arrests, early onset of offending, and severity of institutional antisocial behavior (e.g., Caputo et al., 1999; Kruh, Frick, & Clements, 2005; Salekin, Leistico, Neumann, DiCicco, & Duros, 2004; Silverthorn, Frick, & Reynolds, 2001). Muñoz and Frick (2007) have also completed a study examining the psychometric properties of the APSD-Y. In a sample of 91 nonreferred adolescents, self-report on the APSD was found to be moderately correlated with APSD parent ratings, and scores were moderately stable across 1- and 2-year follow-up assessments. However, these authors also noted concerns about the internal consistency of the subscales, which was generally below accepted levels and lower than the parent-report version of the APSD (i.e., alpha = .50 to .68 for ASPD-Y compared to alpha = .65 to .82 for parent report). As part of a study described previously, Salekin (2008) examined the predictive validity of the APSD-Y and, after controlling for 14 variables related to offending, found that it accounted for 3% of the variance in general recidivism.

Strengths and Limitations

The APSD (parent, teacher, and youth self-report forms) has a number of strengths. It is a short and easily administered measure that can be used to screen for child psychopathy via multiple reporters. The APSD is associated with adult psychopathy measures in terms of both its factor structure and its relations with a variety of personality and behavioral outcome measures. Both the total APSD scale and the individual factors are related to a range of individual characteristics and problem behaviors that are of primary interest in conduct problem research. However, several limitations of the measure must also be considered. One of the most serious limitations of the APSD is the difficulty identifying a clear and stable factor structure with adequate internal consistency for all factors. Frick and colleagues (2000) have also identified a number of other limitations of the APSD. First, the instability of the impulsivity/narcissism factor from one sample to another indicates that these constructs may not be adequately captured by the limited number of APSD items. Second, items on the CU factor seem to have limited variance (especially in community samples), which is likely due to the limited response scale of the APSD (0 to 2–point scale). Third, all of the reverse-scored items load on the CU factor, which raises concerns about whether the response set is influencing the factor structure of the scale (although unique relations between the CU factor and a variety of other outcome measures support the theoretical utility of the CU factor). Other authors have noted a specific concern about the self-report adaptation of the APSD, arguing that, because the APSD was not designed with self-report in mind, the items are straightforward measures of traits that are obviously negative in many cases and may be likely to increase response bias (Andershed, Kerr, Stattin, & Levander, 2002).

The Development of CU-Specific Measures

It is notable that, because of interest in the CU dimension as a possible explanatory factor in the etiology and prediction of serious conduct problems, several authors have attempted to address some of the limitations noted earlier by developing CU-specific measures. Frick (2004) developed the 24-item self-report, Inventory of Callous–Unemotional Traits (ICU). For each of the four items in the original APSD-Y CU factor, five additional items (positively and negatively worded) assessing similar content were written, and the Likert rating scale was expanded to four points. Preliminary studies have demonstrated internal consistency and construct validity (Essau, Sasagawa, & Frick, 2006; Kimonis, Frick, Muñoz, & Aucoin, 2007; Muñoz, Frick, Kimonis, & Aucoin, 2008). Pardini, Obradović, and Loeber (2006) have also developed an eight-item parent- and teacher-report measure of interpersonal callousness (IC) using items from the Child Behavior Checklist (CBCL; Achenbach, 1991a), the Teacher's Report Form (TRF; Achenbach, 1991b), and supplemental items developed by investigators. Using data from the Pittsburgh Youth Study (a longitudinal project tracking the development of delinquency over time in normative and high-risk youth; Loeber, Farrington, Stouthamer-Loeber, & Van Kammen, 1998), results provided initial evidence of internal consistency, construct validity, and stability in IC over 9 years of assessment (Obradović, Pardini, Long, & Loeber, 2007). Finally, Dadds, Fraser, Frost, and Hawes (2005) have also created a new CU scale by combing the items from the parent-report APSD CU factor with negatively correlated items from the Prosocial Behavior scale of the Strengths and Difficulties Questionnaire (SDQ; Goodman, 1997). Similar to the other measures, Dadds, El Masry, Wimalaweera, and Guastella (2008) have demonstrated preliminary internal consistency and construct validity for their CU scale and have also provided initial evidence of scale specificity and sensitivity to change (Hawes & Dadds, 2007). In a subset of the sample, CU scores dropped after a parent-training intervention, an unexpected result given that CU traits are often thought to be stable personality constructs.

The Child Psychopathy Scale

Background Information

Similar to the APSD, the Child Psychopathy Scale (CPS; Lynam, 1997) is theoretically based on the PCL-R (Hare, 1991a). However, the items that make up the scale are drawn from the CBCL (Achenbach, 1991a) and the California Child Q-Set (CCQ; Block & Block, 1980). Items on the CBCL and CCQ were used to create scales similar to items on the PCL-R (e.g., the CBCL item "doesn't seem to feel guilty after misbehaving" and the CCQ item "he often feels guilty" [reverse scored] were combined into a "scale" to correspond to the PCL-R item "lack of remorse or guilt"). This item mapping was completed for 12 of the 20 items on the PCL-R. Two PCL-R items were not included because they measure antisocial behavior, and the authors designed the CPS to serve as a pure measure of personality. Additionally, according to Lynam (1997), the six other items on the PCL-R either did not reflect developmentally appropriate behaviors (e.g., "many short-term marital relationships"), could not be operationalized, or did not correlate with other items; thus, matching scales were not created on the CPS.

Measure Description

As noted earlier, the CPS contains 12 brief scales. Each "scale" is composed of items drawn from the CBCL and/or the CCQ. The number of items representing each scale ranges from two to seven. CBCL items are based on a 3-point response scale, whereas scores on the CCQ range from 1 to 9. Most of the scales showed adequate internal reliability, and the overall measure had high internal consistency (alpha = .91).

Psychometric Data

Lynam (1997) reported that a confirmatory factor analysis of the CPS "scales" was consistent with a two-factor model (i.e., an interpersonal–affective factor and a behaviorally oriented factor similar to the PCL-R two-factor structure), but the extremely high correlation between the factors ($r = .95$) indicated that they were indistinguishable. Thus, only the total CPS score was used for further analyses.

Examining a sample of 403 boys, age 12.5 years (subjects from the Pittsburgh Youth Study; Loeber et al., 1998), Lynam (1997) found that the CPS score correlated with measures of impulsivity (measured by multiple informants). Additionally, the CPS was positively correlated with the frequency of externalizing disorders and negatively correlated with the incidence of internalizing disorders. Finally, CPS scores independently predicted delinquency above and beyond other predictors, which included prior delinquency, socioeconomic status, IQ, and impulsivity. More recently, Lynam, Caspi, Moffitt, Loeber, and Stouthamer-Loeber (2007; Lynam, Derefinko, Caspi, Loeber, & Stouthamer-Loeber, 2007) assessed psychopathy in a subsample of 271 boys from the Pittsburgh Youth Study at the age of 24, using the Psychopathy Checklist: Screening Version (PCL:SV; Hart, Cox, & Hare, 1995). Lynam, Caspi, and colleagues (2007) reported that psychopathy from early adolescence to early adulthood was moderately stable ($r = .31$), irrespective of initial risk status or initial psychopathy level, and after they controlled for 13 other constructs (e.g., demographic information, parenting, delinquency). Additionally, utilizing the same sample from the Pittsburgh Youth Study, Lynam, Derefinko, and colleagues (2007) created an "empirical rating" index of psychopathy using 26 items from the CCQ (administered at age 12.5 years) that were significantly correlated with psychopathy scores in adulthood (measured by the PCL:SV at 24 years of age). The scores on this "empirical rating" index were compared to scores on an "expert rating" index of psychopathy, composed of 21 items from the CCQ identified by experts as defining the prototypical "fledgling psychopath" (at approximately 13 years old). Scores on both the "empirical rating" index and the "expert rating" index were compared to the original CPS scores. Using item content analyses, Lynam, Derfinko, and colleagues demonstrated significant overlap among the three indices. Additionally, when overlapping CCQ items were removed, there was still considerable item convergence. The authors suggested that these results provide support for the content validity of the CPS as a downward translation of the PCL-R (Hare, 1991a).

Strengths and Limitations

The findings just described provide initial support for the reliability, consistency, and validity of the CPS. A notable strength of the CPS is its use of multiple items to assess each psychopathic characteristic, which is likely to improve the measure's construct validity. Additionally, Lynam and colleagues have made unique efforts to examine the content validity of the CPS, and have provided supportive psychometric data in this domain. Furthermore, if resources are limited, this measure provides a method for assessing youth psychopathy using data from commonly used behavioral measures that are not psychopathy specific (i.e., the CBCL and CCQ). However, compared to the PCL:YV and the APSD, the CPS has been used in a very limited number of samples. Research with additional diverse samples is needed to examine further its psychometric properties. A 55-item version of the CPS is undergoing validation testing.

The Youth Psychopathic Traits Inventory

Background Information

The Youth Psychopathic Traits Inventory (YPI; Andershed, Kerr, et al., 2002), a self-report psychopathy instrument theoretically based on the three-factor model of the PCL-R (Hare, 1991a), was specifically designed to address many of the challenges that make the self-report of psychopathy difficult. First, because deceitfulness, lying, and manipulation are core psychopathic characteristics, it is hard to get truthful responses to questions about clearly negative personality characteristics (e.g., shallow affect, lack of guilt; Harpur, Hare, & Hakstian, 1989). Second, at least in adult populations, individuals with psychopathic traits tend to lack insight into their own behavior. Thus, even though, to an objective observer, they may lack empathy, they might not see themselves as callous and might not endorse these traits positively (Andershed, Kerr, et al., 2002). With these concerns in mind, the authors endeavored to develop an instrument that did not tempt people with psychopathic traits to lie; they also made an effort to present many psychopathic traits in a manner that a person with these traits might view as admirable.

Measure Description

The YPI contains 10 scales designed to measure 10 core personality traits (e.g., grandiosity, lying, manipulation, callousness, unemotionality, impulsivity, thrill seeking) associated with psychopathy. Each scale is composed of five items. Respondents are asked to rate the degree to which individual items applies to them on a 4-point Likert scale. This measure is designed for use with youth age 12 and older.

Psychometric Data

Andershed, Kerr, and colleagues (2002) initially examined the measure in a large community sample of eighth-grade students in Sweden ($N = 1,024$).

The 10 scales had acceptable internal consistency (most in the alpha = .7–.8 range). Boys generally had higher scores than girls on several of the scales, including grandiosity, manipulation, lying, callousness, unemotionality, remorselessness, irresponsibility, and impulsivity. Factor analyses suggested three factors that were consistent across gender: a grandiose/manipulative factor, a CU factor, and an impulsive/irresponsible factor. Higher scores on the YPI were related to higher scores on measures of conduct problems. Hyperactivity, impulsivity, and attention problems were also positively correlated with scores on the YPI. Cluster analyses suggested that youth with high scores on all three factors and conduct problems showed more severe problem behaviors than youth with elevations only on the impulsive/irresponsible factor and conduct problems.

Several other research groups have also examined the psychometric properties of the YPI. Skeem and Cauffman (2003) administered the YPI to a group of 160 serious adolescent offenders. They reported that the YPI demonstrated test–retest reliability (ICC = .74 for the total score). In addition, the YPI was positively correlated with both violent/aggressive infractions and property/substance abuse infractions and negatively correlated with an anxiety measure. In a sample of 115 adolescent males with conduct disorder, Dolan and Rennie (2006) reported that the YPI was moderately successful at predicting subsequent institutional infractions (although less accurate than the PCL:YV). Poythress, Dembo, Wareham, and Greenbaum (2006) compared the YPI to the APSD-Y in a sample of 165 adolescents in a juvenile diversion program. For both measures, internal consistency on the affective dimension (i.e., CU traits) was low (APSD-Y alpha = .45; YPI alpha = .57). On the other two subscales (grandiose/manipulative [YPI] or narcissism [APSD-Y] and impulsivity), the YPI demonstrated superior internal consistency (APSD-Y narcissism alpha = .61, YPI grandiose/manipulative alpha = .91; APSD-Y impulsivity alpha = .57, YPI impulsive/irresponsible alpha = .82). Both measures demonstrated construct validity, showing positive relations with age of delinquency onset, delinquent behaviors, gang history, history of abuse, and drug use. Finally, a structural equation model relating the YPI to delinquency and drug use showed adequate fit, whereas a similar model for the APSD-Y did not have acceptable fit.

Strengths and Limitations

The YPI is particularly interesting because it is designed to address a number of inherent problems with the self-assessment of psychopathy. Using multiple items to measure each core personality trait is a strength as well. Overall, the psychometric data for this instrument are somewhat stronger than those reported for the other available self-report measures. However, more research using this measure needs to explore issues of consistency between youth report on the YPI and adult report on other psychopathy measures.

The Psychopathy Content Scale

Background Information

While the Psychopathy Content Scale (PCS; Murrie & Cornell, 2000) is theoretically based on the content of the PCL-R (Hare, 1991a), the scale is constructed from items drawn from the Millon Adolescent Clinical Inventory (MACI; Millon, 1993), a self-report measure designed for use with clinical and correctional adolescent populations. The authors chose MACI items that were conceptually related to the psychopathy construct. These items were reviewed by experienced forensic psychologists to verify that they were conceptually appropriate.

Measure Description

This self-report scale includes 20 true–false items drawn from the MACI. Although many of the items chosen represent affective, interpersonal, or behavioral characteristics consistent with the psychopathy construct, the scale cannot be mapped easily onto a model of psychopathy with an explicit factor structure (e.g., the Cooke & Michie [2001] three-factor structure). No specific age range is stated, but studies utilizing the PCS have included adolescents from 12 to 18 years of age.

Psychometric Data

In the initial examination of this measure, Murrie and Cornell (2000) utilized a sample of 90 adolescents between the ages of 12 and 17, hospitalized in a state psychiatric hospital. The PCL-R was also completed for all subjects. The PCS distinguished youth with high psychopathy scores (PCL-R score > 22) from those with low psychopathy scores (PCL-R score < 10) in 83% of the cases. Sensitivity for the scale was 85% and specificity was 81%. The scale also demonstrated good internal consistency (alpha = .87).

Additional research with this measure has provided some preliminary validity data. Loper, Hoffschmidt, and Ash (2001) examined the PCS in a sample of 82 incarcerated male and female adolescent offenders. Scores on the PCS were positively related to instrumental violence and violent offending, and negatively related to measures of empathy, guilt, and remorse. Furthermore, Salekin, Ziegler, Larrea, Anthony, and Bennett (2003) examined the PCS in a sample of 55 male and female offenders. They found only weak, nonsignificant correlations between the PCS score and youth recidivism at a 2-year follow-up. However, the authors also examined a revised, 16-item version (P-16) of the measure (alpha = .86) designed to align better with the three-factor model of psychopathy identified by Cooke and Michie (2001) and Frick and Hare (2001). The total score on this revised measure was a significant predictor of recidivism, violent recidivism, and number of offenses. Furthermore, results indicated that the affective and interpersonal components of the scale were particularly salient in the relationship with general and violent recidivism (correlations ranging from $r = .35$ to $r = .46$).

Strengths and Limitations

The PCS and the 16-item adaptation constructed by Salekin and colleagues (2003) are quickly and easily administered self-report instruments. Because the items come from the MACI, a measure originally developed for self-report (similar to the YPI), wording of some items may be somewhat less susceptible to bias compared to the APSD-Y. However, only preliminary psychometric data are available at this time for both the PCS and the 16-item adaptation, and additional data are needed to determine how these measures compare to the other self-report instruments.

Comparing the PCL-R–Derived Screening Measures with the PCL:YV

As described throughout this chapter, the primary measurement tools in the field of youth psychopathy are based on the PCL-R. However, there are a number of core differences between the PCL-R–derived screening measures and the PCL:YV. First, PCL:YV ratings come from expert, formally trained raters. As a result, there is much higher interrater agreement compared to parent/caregiver-, teacher- and youth-report measures. Also, the PCL:YV rater is a fairly objective informant, whereas most of the screening measures depend on ratings from persons closely associated with a youth, if not the youth him- or herself. Finally, PCL:YV ratings are based on multiple sources and domains of information, whereas most rating scales assess an individual opinion (although, certainly, the opinions of multiple/varied raters can be collected). Given these core measurement differences, it is not surprising that a number of studies have focused on the comparison of one or more of the youth psychopathy screening measures with the full-scale assessment of youth psychopathy (i.e., the PCL:YV).

Murrie and Cornell (2002) assessed psychopathy with screening measures (i.e., staff- and youth-report versions of the APSD) and the PCL:YV in 117 male juvenile offenders ranging in age from 13 to 18 years. There were moderate correlations between the APSD screening measures and the PCL:YV (r = .30–.49), and scores on the screening measures resulted in moderately accurate identification of youth with high scores on the PCL:YV (67–82%). Unfortunately, information on relations between individual factors is not available because only the total score was examined.

Both Lee, Vincent, Hart, and Corrado (2003) and Vitacco and colleagues (2003) conducted studies comparing youth self-report on the APSD with scores on the PCL:YV in adolescent offender samples. Similar to the previous study, these research groups reported moderate concurrent validity between these two measures (r = .40 and r = .62, respectively; total psychopathy score). Lee and colleagues also examined correlations between the three-factor APSD and a three-factor model of the PCL:YV. Findings revealed only weak associations (r = .20–.37 for the three factors).

A study by Salekin and colleagues (2004) also provides a comparison of screening measures and the PCL:YV. To examine the convergent and discriminant validity of three measures of youth psychopathy, they assessed psychopathic traits in a sample of 130 child and adolescent offenders (mean age = 14.9 years) using several measures, including the PCL:YV and the APSD. Using scores over 30 on the PCL:YV as a criterion for psychopathy, they found that 21.5 % of their juvenile offender sample qualified. They also measured a broad range of DSM-IV (American Psychiatric Association, 2000) Axis I diagnoses. The psychopathy scales actually correlated more highly with a conduct disorder diagnosis (r = .50–.59) than with each other (r = .35–.49). Furthermore, there were correlations between the psychopathy measures and other Axis I diagnoses (e.g., ADHD, depression, adjustment disorder, substance abuse disorder). This was especially true for the APSD. However, it is important to note that, although the psychopathy measures were significantly correlated with other Axis I diagnoses (especially conduct disorder and ODD), these correlations were less than the correlations between (1) the conduct disorder and ODD diagnoses themselves and (2) these two diagnoses and other Axis I disorders. Thus, these results suggest that even with far from perfect discriminant and convergent validity, the psychopathy measures are still likely to offer some utility in classification of antisocial youth beyond that of traditional conduct disorder and ODD diagnoses (Salekin et al., 2004). Finally, data from this study also indicated that the PCL:YV was the only psychopathy measure to predict violent and nonviolent offenses beyond the predictive power of conduct disorder and ODD diagnoses.

A group of studies has compared self-report instruments with the PCL:YV. Skeem and Cauffmann (2003) compared the YPI to the PCL:YV in a sample of 160 serious adolescent offenders. The YPI moderately correlated with a three-factor structure for the PCL:YV (r = .30 for the total score). In a sample of 115 adolescent males with conduct disorder, Dolan and Rennie

(2006) also found moderate correlations between the YPI and PCL:YV in the lifestyle/social deviance domain. However, notably, these authors did not find correlations between the measures in the affective domain. Murrie and Cornell (2000) reported that their PCS was positively correlated with the PCL-R ($r = .60$). In a second study comparing the PCS and the PCL:YV specifically, Murrie and Cornell also reported a moderate positive correlation ($r = .49$) and noted that the PCS correctly classified about three-fourths of the youth scoring above or below a cutoff of 25 on the PCL:YV. Salekin (2008) found that both the APSD-Y and the PCL:YV predicted general recidivism (the PCL:YV was a better predictor of violent recidivism), suggesting that even a brief self-report measure of adolescent psychopathy can provide sensitive and specific information regarding future conduct problem outcomes.

Taken together, these results suggest that the screening measures and the PCL:YV have a moderate correspondence. Given these findings, it is worth noting that personality ratings (and even behavioral ratings) from multiple sources often generate only moderate correlations (Meyer et al., 2001). Furthermore, as discussed previously, the psychopathy construct includes deceitfulness, lying, and manipulation as core characteristics, presenting significant challenges for the self-assessment screening measures (Harpur et al., 1989), especially when compared with the trained-rater/record review format used for the PCL:YV. Thus, on the whole, while the modest associations between the screening measures and the PCL:YV do provide support for the construct validity of adolescent psychopathy, they also suggest that caution is needed when selecting a measure and comparing findings across measures, as these tools are certainly not equivalent.

Summary and Analysis of Child and Adolescent Psychopathy Measures

While some of the measures described in this chapter take items directly from the PCL-R and others use alternate items measuring similar constructs, all purport to measure a psychopathy construct that is consistent with that described by Hare and colleagues (1991). Furthermore, all of the measures have items/scales that address the affective, interpersonal, and behavioral dimensions of the psychopathy construct. Thus, all can be viewed as attempting to capture aspects of the "psychopathic personality" (affective/interpersonal components), as well as the deviant lifestyle and antisocial behaviors typically associated with that personality. Moreover, although many questions remain, the pattern of relations between the youth psychopathy measures and temperamental and behavioral characteristics suggests that the assessment tools discussed in this chapter are capturing a construct that appears similar to conceptualizations of adult psychopathy. Finally, all of the measures described in this chapter have been examined in terms of their psychometric properties, at least preliminarily. Overall, as the extensive measurement research described in this chapter highlights, significant progress has been made in the assessment of psychopathy in children and adolescents in the last two decades.

However, a number of very significant measurement issues remain unresolved. First, although attempts have been made to adapt and develop measures appropriate for youth, the feasibility of extending the adult psychopathy measures to youth is still questionable given the dramatic social and behavioral changes that occur between childhood, adolescence, and adulthood (Hart et al., 2002; Seagrave & Grisso, 2002). This question of downward extension is even more salient because (1) adult conceptualizations of psychopathy are still being debated (e.g., factor structure); (2) there is no clear developmental model of psychopathy informing its measurement (Frick, 1998; Silverman & Ollendick, 1999); and (3) age differences (within youth samples) in psychopathic traits have not been adequately examined.

Second, specific differences between the factor structures of adult and youth psychopathy measures have not been adequately explained (e.g., on the APSD, the narcissism factor is highly correlated with the impulsivity factor, but based on the adult literature, we would expect the narcissism and CU factors to be more highly related). At this time, a number of possible explanations for these differences exist and cannot be differentiated based on current research, including (1) real developmental differences, (2) lack of equivalence between an in-depth diagnostic tool (the PCL-R) and the brief questionnaire format of most of the youth measures, and (3) poor measure development (e.g., inadequate translation of adult items for youth populations; use of items that are not applicable for children and/or adolescents; use of adult items that may be applicable to youth populations but have different meanings in a developmental context, too few items, or an inadequate sampling of behavior).

Third, even ignoring comparisons with the adult research literature and examining youth psychopathy studies only, factor structures are not adequately stable within or across measures. For several measures, multiple possible factor structures have been identified in different samples. In some cases, even within the same sample, both two- and three-factor structures fit the data, and there is neither a compelling theoretical nor data-driven basis for selecting one over the other. Additionally, for some assessment tools, the assumed factor structure has not been empirically validated, and, in all cases, additional replication efforts in community, clinical, and/or offender samples are needed. This constantly changing landscape in terms of factor structure negatively impacts the reliability of the youth psychopathy measures, the ability to compare measures, and the accurate operationalization of the psychopathy construct (e.g., Salekin et al., 2006).

Fourth, as discussed in detail previously, correlations between different raters on the same measure, and between different measures, range from nonsignificant at worst, to low-to-moderate at best. While these issues are certainly not unique to the child psychopathy literature, they remain an obstacle in the effort to identify and clearly operationalize a youth psychopathy construct.

Fifth, it is not clear that the current youth psychopathy assessment tools are adequate for use with samples of girls or ethnic minorities (see Verona, Sadeh, & Javdani, Chapter 13, this volume). Findings suggest that factor structures may not be consistent across gender and ethnicity, and that relations among psychopathy, conduct problems, and other behavioral and temperamental characteristics identified in samples of boys and white youth may not be easily generalized.

Finally, some problematic assessment issues are due to gaps in the current research that need to be addressed. For example, some of the measures reviewed lack adequate reliability and validity data. Moreover, information on stability of the psychopathy construct, related developmental trajectories, and continuity between youth and adult psychopathy is growing but still limited. In many cases, results have been based on a small number of samples obtained by a few research groups, and this limited diversity in datasets has contributed to the inadequate assessment of issues that affect measurement accuracy (e.g., age, gender, and ethnicity differences, as noted earlier). However, as the youth psychopathy knowledge base continues to grow at a rapid pace, we are hopeful that many of these issues will continue to be addressed.

Selecting a Youth Psychopathy Assessment Tool

While there is certainly no absolute heuristic for selecting a child and/or adolescent psychopathy assessment tool, consideration of a number of factors should facilitate choosing among the current options. First, it is essential to consider the research setting and the youth population to be examined. For example, in a correctional setting, with available records and sufficient resources, the full scale PCL:YV might be the obvious measure of choice. However, in community or clinical populations, where records may be unavailable, or in settings where assessment resources are limited, a screening measure is likely to be more appropriate. Second, the age of subjects is also an important consideration. Only the APSD and CPS were developed for use with children; moreover, self-report measures would not be appropriate for younger, preadolescent subjects. Furthermore, when assessing psychopathy in childhood, the availability of both teacher and parent forms of the APSD is an asset (by middle school, teacher report may be less reliable given the limited student contact time for individual teachers). For older adolescent populations, a self-report measure may be ideal, used either alone or combined with another screening measure or the PCL:YV, if appropriate. While the YPI currently seems to have the strongest psychometric data among the available self-report measures, researchers wanting to explore relations between multiple reporters on the same measure may want to consider using various versions of the APSD. Third, it is important to consider available resources. Researchers working in a setting where assessment administration time is very limited (e.g., a psychiatric hospital) may want to consider obtaining their psychopathy data from a broader clinical tool like the MACI (the PCS and P-16 were based on a subset of MACI items), or using the CPS, with its items drawn from other, commonly administered measures (i.e., the CBCL and the CCQ). Finally, all of the assessment tools presented in this chapter have significant strengths and limitations. However, careful measure selection, followed by consideration of the measure-specific psychometric data, can make a substantial difference in our ability to answer specific research questions and continue to move the field of child and adolescent psychopathy forward.

References

Achenbach, T. M. (1991a). *Manual for the Child Behavior Checklist/4–18 and 1991 Profile*. Burlington: University of Vermont, Department of Psychiatry.

Achenbach, T. M. (1991b). *Manual for the Teacher's Report Form and 1991 Profile*. Burlington: University of Vermont, Department of Psychiatry.

American Psychiatric Association. (2000). *Diagnostic and statistical manual of mental disorders* (4th ed., text rev.). Washington, DC: Author.

Andershed, H., Gustafson, S. B., Kerr, M., & Stattin, H. (2002). The usefulness of self-reported psychopathy-like traits in the study of antisocial behavior among non-referred adolescents. *European Journal of Personality, 16*, 383–402.

Andershed, H., Kerr, M., Stattin, H., & Levander, S. (2002). Psychopathic traits in non-referred youths: Initial test of a new assessment tool. In E. Blaauw & L. Sheridan, (Eds.), *Psychopaths: Current international perspectives* (pp. 131–158). Hague, The Netherlands: Elsevier.

Barry, C. T., Frick, P. J., DeShazo, T. M., McCoy, M. G., Ellis, M., & Loney, B. R. (2000). The importance of callous–unemotional traits for extending the concept of psychopathy to children. *Journal of Abnormal Psychology, 109*, 335–340.

Blair, R. J. R. (1997). Moral reasoning and the child with psychopathic tendencies. *Personality and Individual Differences, 22*, 731–739.

Blair, R. J. R. (1999). Responsiveness to distress cues in the child with psychopathic tendencies. *Personality and Individual Differences, 27*, 135–145.

Block, J., & Block, J. H. (1980). *The California Child Q-Set*. Palo Alto, CA: Consulting Psychologists Press.

Brandt, J. R., Kennedy, W. A., Patrick, C. J., & Curtin, J. J. (1997). Assessment of psychopathy in a population of incarcerated adolescent offenders. *Psychological Assessment, 9,* 429–435.

Caputo, A. A., Frick, P. J., & Brodsky, S. L. (1999). Family violence and juvenile sex offending: Potential mediating roles of psychopathic traits and negative attitudes toward women. *Criminal Justice and Behavior, 26,* 338–356.

Christian, R. E., Frick, P. J., Hill, N. L., Tyler, L., & Frazer, D. R. (1997). Psychopathy and conduct problems in children: II. Implications for subtyping children with conduct problems. *Journal of the American Academy of Child and Adolescent Psychiatry, 36,* 233–241.

Cleckley, H. (1976). *The mask of sanity* (5th ed.). St. Louis, MO: Mosby.

Conduct Problems Prevention Research Group. (1992). A developmental and clinical model for the prevention of conduct disorder: The FAST Track program. *Development and Psychopathology, 4,* 509–527.

Cooke, D. J., & Michie, C. (2001). Refining the construct of psychopathy: Towards a hierarchical model. *Psychological Assessment, 13,* 171–188.

Corrado, R. R., Vincent, G. M., Hart, S. D., & Cohen, I. M. (2004). Predictive validity of the Psychopathy Checklist: Youth Version for general and violent recidivism. *Behavioral Sciences and the Law, 22,* 5–22.

Dadds, M. R., El Masry, Y., Wimalaweera, S., & Guastella, A. J. (2008). Reduced eye gaze explains "fear blindness" in childhood psychopathy traits. *Journal of the American Academy of Child and Adolescent Psychiatry, 47,* 455–463.

Dadds, M. R., Fraser, J., Frost, A., & Hawes, D. (2005). Disentangling the underlying dimensions of psychopathy and conduct problems in childhood: A community study. *Journal of Consulting and Clinical Psychology, 73,* 400–410.

Dodge, K. A., & Pettit, G. S. (2003). A biopsychosocial model of the development of chronic conduct problems in adolescence. *Developmental Psychology, 39,* 349–371.

Dolan, M. C., & Rennie, C. E. (2006). Reliability and validity of the Psychopathy Checklist: Youth Version in a UK sample of conduct disordered boys. *Personality and Individual Differences, 40,* 65–75.

Edens, J. F., & Campbell, J. S. (2007). Identifying youths at risk for institutional misconduct: A meta-analytic investigation of the Psychopathy Checklist measures. *Psychological Services, 4,* 13–27.

Edens, J. F., Skeem, J. L., Cruise, K. R., & Cauffman, E. (2001). Assessment of "juvenile psychopathy" and its association with violence: A critical review. *Behavioral Sciences and the Law, 19,* 53–80.

Essau, C. A., Sasagawa, S., & Frick, P. J. (2006). Callous–unemotional traits in a community sample of adolescents. *Assessment, 13,* 454–469.

Forth, A. E. (1995). *Psychopathy and young offenders: Prevalence, family background, and violence* (Program Branch User's Report). Ottawa: Minister of the Solicitor General of Canada.

Forth, A. E., & Burke, H. C. (1998). Psychopathy in adolescence: Assessment, violence, and developmental precursors. In D. J. Cooke, A. E. Forth, & R. D.

Hare (Eds.), *Psychopathy: Theory, research, and implications for society* (pp. 205–229). New York: Kluwer Academic.

Forth, A. E., Hart, S. D., & Hare, R. D. (1990). Assessment of psychopathy in male young offenders. *Psychological Assessment, 2*, 342–344.

Forth, A. E., Kosson, D. S., & Hare, R. D. (2003). *The Psychopathy Checklist: Youth Version*. Toronto: Multi-Health Systems.

Frick, P. J. (1998). *Conduct disorders and severe antisocial behavior*. New York: Plenum Press.

Frick, P. J. (2004). *The Inventory of Callous–Unemotional Traits: Unpublished rating scale*. New Orleans: University of New Orleans.

Frick, P. J., Bodin, S. D., & Barry, C. T. (2000). Psychopathic traits and conduct problems in community and clinic-referred samples of children: Further development of the Psychopathy Screening Device. *Psychological Assessment, 12*, 382–393.

Frick, P. J., & Ellis, M. (1999). Callous–unemotional traits and subtypes of conduct disorder. *Clinical Child and Family Psychology Review, 2*, 149–168.

Frick, P. J., & Hare, R. D. (2001). *The Antisocial Process Screening Device (APSD)*. Toronto: Multi-Health Systems.

Frick, P. J., Kimonis, E. R., Dandreaux, D. M., & Farrell, F. M. (2003). The 4-year stability of psychopathic traits in non-referred youth. *Behavioral Sciences and the Law, 21*, 713–736.

Frick, P. J., O'Brien, B. S., Wootton, J. M., & McBurnett, K. (1994). Psychopathy and conduct problems in children. *Journal of Abnormal Psychology, 103*, 700–707.

Goodman, R. (1997). The Strengths and Difficulties Questionnaire: A research note. *Journal of Child and Adolescent Psychiatry, 38*, 581–586.

Gretton, H. M., Hare, R. D., & Catchpole, R. E. H. (2004). Psychopathy and offending from adolescence to adulthood: A 10–year follow-up. *Journal of Consulting and Clinical Psychology, 72*, 636–645.

Hare, R. D. (1980). *The Hare Psychopathy Checklist*. North Tonawanda, NY: Multi-Health Systems.

Hare, R. D. (1991a). *The Hare Psychopathy Checklist—Revised*. Toronto: Multi-Health Systems.

Hare, R. D. (1991b). *The Hare Psychopathy Checklist—Revised manual*. Toronto: Multi-Health Systems.

Hare, R. D. (2003). *The Hare Psychopathy Checklist—Revised* (2nd ed.). Toronto: Multi-Health Systems.

Hare, R. D., Hart, S. D., & Harpur, T. J. (1991). Psychopathy and the DSM-IV criteria for antisocial personality disorder. *Journal of Abnormal Psychology, 100*, 392–398.

Hare, R. D., & Neumann, C. S. (2005). The structure of psychopathy. *Current Psychiatry Reports, 7*, 1–32.

Harpur, T. J., Hare, R. D., & Hakstian, A. R. (1989). Two-factor conceptualization of psychopathy: Construct validity and assessment implications. *Psychological Assessment, 1*, 6–17.

Hart, S. D., Cox, D. N., & Hare, R. D. (1995). *The Hare Psychopathy Checklist: Screening Version (PCL:SV)*. North Tonawanda, NY: Multi-Health Systems.

Hart, S. D., Kropp, P. R., & Hare, R. D. (1988). Performance of male psychopaths following conditional release from prison. *Journal of Consulting and Clinical Psychology, 56,* 227–232.

Hart, S. D., Watt, K. A., & Vincent, G. M. (2002). Commentary on Seagrave and Grisso: Impressions of the state of the art. *Law and Human Behavior, 26,* 241–245.

Hawes, D. J., & Dadds, M. R. (2007). Stability and malleability of callous–unemotional traits during treatment for childhood conduct problems. *Journal of Clinical Child and Adolescent Psychology, 36,* 347–355.

Jones, S., Cauffman, E., Miller, J. D., & Mulvey, E. (2006). Investigating different factor structures of the Psychopathy Checklist: Youth Version: Confirmatory factor analytic findings. *Psychological Assessment, 18,* 33–48.

Kimonis, E. R., Frick, P. J., Muñoz, L. C., & Aucoin, K. J. (2007). Can a laboratory measure of emotional processing enhance the statistical prediction of aggression and delinquency in detained adolescents with callous–unemotional traits? *Journal of Abnormal Child Psychology, 35,* 773–785.

Kosson, D. S., Cyterski, T. D., Steuerwald, B. L., Neumann, C. S., & Walker-Matthews, S. (2002). The reliability and validity of the Psychopathy Checklist: Youth Version (PCL:YV) in nonincarcerated adolescent males. *Psychological Assessment, 14,* 97–109.

Kotler, J. S., McMahon, R. J., & the Conduct Problems Prevention Research Group. (2002, November). *Relations among callous–unemotional traits, narcissism, and conduct problems: Subsequent behavioral and social adjustment in early adolescence.* Poster presented at the annual meeting of the Association for Advancement of Behavior Therapy, Reno, NV.

Kotler, J. S., McMahon, R. J., & the Conduct Problems Prevention Research Group. (2003, November). *A re-examination of the psychometric properties of the Antisocial Process Screening Device in samples of normative and high-risk youth.* Poster presented at the annual meeting of the Association for Advancement of Behavior Therapy, Boston.

Kruh, I. P., Frick, P. J., & Clements, C. B. (2005). Historical and personality correlates to the violence patterns of juveniles tried as adults. *Criminal Justice and Behavior, 32,* 69–96.

Lee, Z., Vincent, G. M., Hart, S. D., & Corrado, R. R. (2003). The validity of the Antisocial Process Screening Device as a self-report measure of psychopathy in adolescent offenders. *Behavioral Sciences and the Law, 21,* 771–786.

Leistico, A. R., Salekin, R. T., DeCoster, J., & Rogers, R. (2008). A large-scale meta-analysis relating the Hare measures of psychopathy to antisocial conduct. *Law and Human Behavior, 32,* 28–45.

Lilienfeld, S. O. (1998). Methodological advances and developments in the assessment of psychopathy. *Behaviour Research and Therapy, 36,* 99–125.

Loeber, R., Farrington, D. P., Stouthamer-Loeber, M., & Van Kammen, W. B. (1998). *Antisocial behavior and mental health problems: Explanatory factors in childhood and adolescence.* Mahwah, NJ: Erlbaum.

Loper, A., Hoffschmidt, S., & Ash, E. (2001). Personality features and characteristics of violent events committed by juvenile offenders. *Behavioral Sciences and the Law, 19,* 81–96.

Lykken, D. T. (1995). *The antisocial personalities*. Hillsdale, NJ: Erlbaum.

Lynam, D. R. (1997). Pursuing the psychopath: Capturing the fledgling psychopath in a nomological net. *Journal of Abnormal Psychology, 106*, 425–438.

Lynam, D. R., Caspi, A., Moffitt, T. E., Loeber, R., & Stouthamer-Loeber, M. (2007). Longitudinal evidence that psychopathy scores in early adolescence predict adult psychopathy. *Journal of Abnormal Psychology, 116*, 155–165.

Lynam, D. R., Derefinko, K. J., Caspi, A., Loeber, R., & Stouthamer-Loeber, M. (2007). The content validity of juvenile psychopathy: An empirical examination. *Psychological Assessment, 19*, 363–367.

McBurnett, K., Tamm, L., Noell, G., Pfiffner, L. J., & Frick, P. J. (1994). *"Psychopathy" dimensions in normal children*. Paper presented at the annual meeting of the Society for Research in Child and Adolescent Psychopathology, London.

McCoy, W. K., & Edens, J. F. (2006). Do black and white youths differ in levels of psychopathy traits?: A meta-analysis of the Psychopathy Checklist measures. *Journal of Consulting and Clinical Psychology, 74*, 386–392.

Meyer, G. J., Finn, S. E., Eyde, L. D., Kay, G. G., Moreland, K. L., Dies, R. R., et al. (2001). Psychological testing and psychological assessment: A review of evidence and issues. *American Psychologist, 56*, 128–165.

Millon, T. (1993). *Millon Adolescent Clinical Inventory manual*. Minneapolis, MN: National Computer Systems.

Muñoz, L. C., & Frick, P. J. (2007). The reliability, stability, and predictive validity of the self-report version of the Antisocial Process Screening Device. *Scandinavian Journal of Psychology, 48*, 299–312.

Muñoz, L. C., Frick, P. J., Kimonis, E. R., & Aucoin, K. J. (2008). Types of aggression, responsiveness to provocation, and callous–unemotional traits in detained adolescents. *Journal of Abnormal Child Psychology, 36*, 15–28.

Murrie, D. C., Boccaccini, M. T., McCoy, W., & Cornell, D. G. (2007). Diagnostic labeling in juvenile court: How do descriptions of psychopathy and conduct disorder influence judges? *Journal of Clinical Child and Adolescent Psychology, 36*, 228–241.

Murrie, D. C., & Cornell, D. G. (2000). The Millon Adolescent Clinical Inventory and psychopathy. *Journal of Personality Assessment, 75*, 110–125.

Murrie, D. C., & Cornell, D. G. (2002). Psychopathy screening of incarcerated juveniles: A comparison of measures. *Psychological Assessment, 14*, 390–396.

Neumann, C. S., Kosson, D. S., Forth, A. E., & Hare, R. D. (2006). Factor structure of the Hare Psychopathy Checklist: Youth Version (PCL:YV) in incarcerated adolescents. *Psychological Assessment, 18*, 142–154.

Obradović, J., Pardini, D. A., Long, J. A., & Loeber, R. (2007). Measuring interpersonal callousness in boys from childhood to adolescence: An examination of longitudinal invariance and temporal stability. *Journal of Clinical Child and Adolescent Psychology, 36*, 276–292.

O'Brien, B. S., & Frick, P. J. (1996). Reward dominance: Associations with anxiety, conduct problems, and psychopathy in children. *Journal of Abnormal Child Psychology, 24*, 223–240.

Pardini, D., Obradović, J., & Loeber, R. (2006). Interpersonal callousness, hyperactivity/impulsivity, inattention and conduct problems as precursors to delinquency persistence in boys: A comparison of three grade-based cohorts. *Journal of Clinical Child and Adolescent Psychology, 35,* 46–59.

Pardini, D. A., Lochman, J. E., & Powell, N. (2007). The development of callous–unemotional traits and antisocial behavior in children: Are there shared and/or unique predictors? *Journal of Clinical Child and Adolescent Psychology, 36,* 319–333.

Poythress, N. G., Dembo, R., Wareham, J., & Greenbaum, P. (2006). Construct validity of the Youth Psychopathic Features Inventory (YPI) and the Antisocial Process Screening Device (ASPD) with justice involved adolescents. *Criminal Justice and Behavior, 33,* 26–55.

Poythress, N. G., Douglas, K. S., Falkenbach, D., Cruise, K., Murrie, D. C., & Vitacco, M. (2006). Internal consistency reliability of the self-report Antisocial Process Screening Device. *Assessment, 13,* 107–113.

Salekin, R. T. (2008). Psychopathy and recidivism from mid-adolescence to young adulthood: Cumulating legal problems and limiting life opportunities. *Journal of Abnormal Psychology, 117,* 386–395.

Salekin, R. T., Brannen, D. N., Zalot, A. A., Leistico, A., & Neumann, C. S. (2006). Factor structure of psychopathy in youth: Testing the applicability of the new four-factor model. *Criminal Justice and Behavior, 33,* 135–157.

Salekin, R. T., Leistico, A. R., Neumann, C. S., DiCicco, T. M., & Duros, R. L. (2004). Psychopathy and comorbidity in a young offender sample: Taking a closer look at psychopathy's potential importance over disruptive behavior disorders. *Journal of Abnormal Psychology, 113,* 416–427.

Salekin, R. T., Ziegler, T. A., Larrea, M. A., Anthony, V. L., & Bennett, A. D. (2003). Predicting dangerousness with two Millon Adolescent Clinical Inventory psychopathy scales: The importance of egocentric and callous traits. *Journal of Personality Assessment, 80,* 154–163.

Schmidt, F., McKinnon, L., Chattha, H. K., & Brownlee, K. (2006). Concurrent and predictive validity of the Psychopathy Checklist: Youth Version across gender and ethnicity. *Psychological Assessment, 18,* 393–401.

Schrum, C. L., & Salekin, R. T. (2006). Psychopathy in adolescent female offenders: An item response theory analysis of the Psychopathy Checklist: Youth Version. *Behavioral Sciences and the Law, 24,* 39–63.

Seagrave, D., & Grisso, T. (2002). Adolescent development and the measurement of juvenile psychopathy. *Law and Human Behavior, 26,* 219–239.

Serin, R. C. (1993). Diagnosis of psychopathology with and without an interview. *Journal of Clinical Psychology, 49,* 367–372.

Sevecke, K., Pukrop, R., Kosson, D. S., & Krischer, M. K. (2009). Factor structure of the Hare Psychopathy Checklist: Youth Version in German female and male detainees and community adolescents. *Psychological Assessment, 21,* 45–56.

Silverman, W. K., & Ollendick, T. H. (Eds.). (1999). *Developmental issues in the clinical treatment of children.* Boston: Allyn & Bacon.

Silverthorn, P., Frick, P. J., & Reynolds, R. (2001). Timing of onset and correlates of severe conduct problems in adjudicated girls and boys. *Journal of Psychopathology and Behavioral Assessment, 23,* 171–181.

Skeem, J. L., & Cauffman, E. (2003). Views of the downward extension: Comparing the youth version of the Psychopathy Checklist with the Youth Psychopathic Traits Inventory. *Behavioral Sciences and the Law, 21,* 737–770.

Sroufe, L. A. (1997). Psychopathology as an outcome of development. *Development and Psychopathology, 9,* 251–268.

Toupin, J., Mercier, H., Dery, M., Cote, G., & Hodgins, S. (1996). Validity of the PCL-R for adolescents. *Issues in Criminal and Legal Psychology, 24,* 143–145.

Vitacco, M. J., Neumann, C. S., Caldwell, M. F., Leistico, A., & Van Rybroek, G. J. (2006). Testing factor models of the Psychopathy Checklist: Youth Version and their association with instrumental aggression. *Journal of Personality Assessment, 87,* 74–83.

Vitacco, M. J., Rogers, R., & Neumann, C. S. (2003). The Antisocial Process Screening Device: An examination of its construct and criterion-related validity. *Assessment, 10,* 143–150.

Part II

Etiological Theories

5

Genetics of Child and Adolescent Psychopathy

ESSI VIDING
HENRIK LARSSON

Individuals with criminal psychopathy effect extreme harm to those around them. Not only do these individuals represent a significant tax burden, but they also leave a trail of emotional havoc in their wake. Since most individuals with criminal psychopathy have started their antisocial behavior early in life, several researchers have proposed extending the study of core psychopathic personality characteristics into childhood (Frick & Marsee, 2006; Salekin, 2006). Despite some reservations about labeling children with psychopathic traits, research into this area has been seen as an important endeavor from the point of view of prevention and intervention (see Lynam, Caspi, Moffitt, Loeber, & Stouthamer-Loeber, 2007, for a discussion of this issue).

Psychopathy syndrome[1] in both childhood and adulthood involves both affective–interpersonal impairment (e.g., lack of empathy, lack of guilt, shallow emotions, superficial charm) and overt impulsive, irresponsible, and antisocial behavior (Blair, Peschardt, Budhani, Mitchell, & Pine, 2006; Frick & Marsee, 2006). The symptom profile of psychopathy is discussed extensively in other chapters in this book. In short, individuals with psychopathy represent a subset of persons who meet diagnostic criteria for conduct disorder (CD) in childhood or antisocial personality disorder (APD) in adulthood (Blair et al., 2006). However, formal diagnostic criteria for child and adult antisocial behavior syndromes do not distinguish subgroups of antisocial individuals on the basis of their (CU) callous–unemotional profile (American Psychiatric Association, 1994; Hart & Hare, 1997).

Psychopathic personality traits may predispose children to life-course-persistent antisocial behavior of a particularly serious nature (Frick & Hare, 2001; Frick & Marsee, 2006). Given the early emergence of antisocial behavior in individuals with criminal psychopathy and its long-term impact, even as compared with other antisocial individuals, there has been recent interest in genetically informative research into psychopathy. Such research has scope to be informative relative to not only genetic risk but also the nature of the environmental risk associated with psychopathy. The current research base consists of several twin studies, but only four published molecular genetics studies to date have specifically focused on psychopathy (rather than a broader construct of antisocial behavior). Only one study to date has examined potential environmental risk factors for psychopathy in the context of genetically informative studies. Only a subset of the studies has focused on children or adolescents.

Taking genetic information into account adds an important level of analysis when we attempt to understand psychopathic personality traits as a potential risk factor for persistent antisocial behavior. Genetic information can help us to validate whether the large group of children and youth with conduct problems can be meaningfully subtyped into more homogeneous groupings. For example, our lab has studied whether the heritability of antisocial behavior varies as a function of co-occurring CU traits. Twin studies focusing on different components of psychopathic personality have predictably documented significant heritable influences but, more interestingly, a lack of shared environmental influences. This information has practical implications for understanding environmental risk related to development of adult psychopathy (and the prevention thereof) and is discussed later in this chapter. Large-scale twin studies have also enabled study of common versus unique genetic and environmental influences on various aspects of psychopathic personality, study of the etiology of stability and change in psychopathic personality, and study of etiological overlap between psychopathic personality and antisocial/externalizing behaviors in children and youth. The strength of the child and youth studies lies in the fact that they address important etiological questions before the accrual of negative consequences that are relevant for samples of criminal psychopaths (e.g., extensive substance abuse) may have muddied the etiological picture. Genetically informative studies of child and youth psychopathy thus have a great potential to provide relevant information for prevention and treatment. These themes are discussed in the last section of this chapter.

In this chapter, we attempt to review the current knowledge base of the genetics of child/adolescent psychopathy. We primarily concentrate on twin study findings that have dominated the genetic research into psychopathy. To assist the reader, we first provide a brief discussion of the basic premise of the twin method. We have also included a brief overview of quantitative genetics findings of antisocial behavior and adult psychopathy. The existing twin data make five important points with regard to child/adolescent psychopathy, and these are discussed in turn:

1. Psychopathic personality traits show heritable and nonshared environmental influences in childhood/adolescence.
2. The same genetic and environmental influences are important in accounting for individual differences in psychopathic personality traits for both males and females (although the magnitude of their influence may vary between sexes).
3. Genetic factors are important in explaining covariance among different aspects of psychopathic personality.
4. Genetic factors account for stability of psychopathic personality across development.
5. Genetic factors contribute to the relationship between psychopathic personality traits and antisocial behavior.

In addition to the twin data, we also briefly and selectively review molecular genetics, environmental, and gene–environment interplay research on antisocial behavior and psychopathy, and point out what we consider to be relevant new research directions, as well as potential translational implications of "genetics of child/adolescent psychopathy" research.

The Twin Method

The twin method is a natural experiment that relies on the different levels of genetic relatedness between identical and fraternal twin pairs to estimate the contribution of genetic and environmental factors to individual differences, or extreme scores in a phenotype of interest. *Phenotype* includes any behavior or characteristic that is measured separately for each twin, such as twins' scores on an antisocial behavior checklist. Statistical model-fitting techniques and regression analyses methods incorporating genetic relatedness parameters are used to investigate the etiology of the phenotype of choice. These techniques are not covered in detail in this chapter, but for the interested reader there are textbooks available on the topic (Plomin, DeFries, McClearn, & McGuffin, 2008). The basic premise of the twin method is this: If identical twins, who share 100% of their genetic material, appear more similar than do fraternal twins on a trait, who share on average 50% of their genetic material (like any siblings), then we infer that there are genetic influences on a trait. Identical twins' genetic similarity is twice that of fraternal twins. If nothing apart from genes influences behavior, then we would expect identical twins to be twice as similar with respect to the phenotypic measure as fraternal twins. *Shared environmental influences*—environmental influences that make twins similar to each other—are inferred if fraternal twin similarity is more than half of the identical twin similarity (as expected from sharing 50%, as opposed to 100%, of their genes). Finally, if identical twins are not 100% similar on a trait (as would be expected if only genes influenced a trait), nonshared environmental influences are inferred, that is, environmental influences that make twins different from each other. The nonshared environmental estimate also includes measurement error.

Quantitative Genetic Findings of Antisocial Behavior and Adult Psychopathy

Various conceptualizations of antisocial behavior have received more attention in behavioral genetic research than psychopathy. A meta-analysis, including 51 twin and adoption studies, estimated that, on average, 41% of the variance on antisocial behavior is due to genetic factors (additive and nonadditive genetic effects), about 16% is due to shared environmental factors, and about 43% is due to nonshared environmental factors (Rhee & Waldman, 2002). The finding of a heritability estimate of 41% for adolescent and adult antisocial behavior is substantially lower than the estimate of 82% reported in a study on childhood antisocial behavior that is pervasive across settings (Arseneault et al., 2003). Furthermore, stability in antisocial behavior from childhood to adolescence (Eley, Lichtenstein, & Moffitt, 2003) and childhood-onset antisocial behavior have also been found to have a strong genetic component (Taylor, Iacono, & McGue, 2000). It is not known what proportion of the samples in these twin studies have included psychopathic individuals, although it is plausible that they have represented a subset of individuals sampled and have therefore contributed to the estimates of heritable and environmental influences. Based on the phenotypic data on individuals with psychopathy, it is possible to argue that studies of early-onset, pervasive, and stable antisocial behavior may bear particular relevance for psychopathy.

Studies of adult samples examining the heritability of psychopathic traits have indicated moderately strong influences of genetic and nonshared environmental factors (Waldman & Rhee, 2006). For example, Blonigen, Carlson, Krueger, and Patrick (2003) used a self-report measure, the Psychopathic Personality Inventory (PPI; Lilienfeld & Andrews, 1996), in a sample of adult male twins to examine the genetic and environmental influences on psychopathic personality traits. Individual differences in all eight dimensions measured by the PPI (i.e., Machievellian egocentricity, social potency, fearlessness, coldheartedness, impulsive nonconformity, blame externalization, carefree nonplanfulness, stress immunity) were associated with genetic and nonshared environmental effects. Genetic effects explained 29–56% of variation of the respective dimensions of the PPI. Shared environmental effects were not found for any of the PPI facets (Blonigen et al., 2003).

Psychopathic Personality Traits Show Heritable and Nonshared Environmental Influences in Childhood/Adolescence

To date, at least 13 published twin studies have examined the etiology of child/youth psychopathy and its various components. These studies come from the United States, Sweden, and the United Kingdom. The samples in these studies vary in size from moderate (398 twin pairs) to large (3,687 twin pairs), represent different age ranges (7–24 years), and have used a range of instruments to assess different aspects of psychopathic personality. All studies except one (Taylor, Loney, Bobadilla, Iacono, & McGue, 2003), include information from both sexes, with a similar male–female composition (46–48% males). In this section we concentrate on reviewing the univariate data on psychopathic personality (variously measured) from these studies. The univariate findings document the relative importance of heritable and environmental influences on psychopathic personality in children and youth.

Taylor and colleagues used items from a self-report questionnaire, the Minnesota Temperament Inventory (Loney, Taylor, Butler, & Iacono, 2002), to assess the CU (e.g., "I don't experience very deep emotions") and impulsive–antisocial (e.g., "I am unreliable") dimensions of adolescent psychopathy (Taylor et al., 2003). This self-report questionnaire was distributed to a sample of 398 adolescent male twin pairs (16–18 years old) from the Minnesota Twin Family Study. In this study, genetic effects accounted for around 40% of the variation in both the CU and the impulsive–antisocial factor. Nonshared environmental effects explained all of the remaining variance, whereas the influences of shared environment seemed to be of no importance (Taylor et al., 2003).

Blonigen, Hicks, Krueger, Patrick, and Iacono (2005, 2006) used factor scores on the primary scales of the self-report Multidimensional Personality Questionnaire (MPQ) to index the two main dimensions of the PPI (Lilienfeld & Andrews, 1996): the fearless dominance dimension (from here on, the "CU–grandiose/manipulative" dimension, for the sake of consistency across the chapters in this book) and the impulsive–antisocial dimension. In their first report on this sample of adolescents, Blonigen and colleagues reported data from 626 seventeen-year-old male and female twin pairs. Genetic influences accounted for 45% of the variance in the CU–grandiose/manipulative dimension and 49% of the variance in the impulsive–antisocial dimension. The remainder of the variance in each dimension was accounted for by nonshared environmental influences. Very similar findings were reported for the same sample at age 24. Genetic influences accounted for 42% of the variance in the CU–grandiose/manipulative dimension and 49% in the impulsive–antisocial dimension. The remainder of the variance in each dimension was accounted for by nonshared environmental influences.

Viding and colleagues studied the heritability of teacher-rated CU traits in the Twins Early Development Study (TEDS) sample of over 3,500 7-year-old twin pairs (both boys and girls) (Viding, Blair, Moffitt, & Plomin, 2005; Viding, Frick, & Plomin, 2007). The CU scale in the TEDS analyses consisted of seven items: three Antisocial Process Screening Device items (Frick & Hare, 2001), as well as four items from the Strengths and Difficulties Questionnaire (SDQ; Goodman, 1997). Individual differences in CU traits were strongly heritable (67% of the phenotypic variance was due to genetic influences) (Viding et al., 2007). The group difference in CU traits between those scoring in the top 10% of the TEDS sample and the rest of the TEDS children was also strongly heritable (h^{g2} = .67). The group heritability estimates were very similar regardless of whether the CU traits occurred with (h^{g2} = .80) or without (h^{g2} = .68) elevated levels of conduct problems (Larsson, Viding, & Plomin, 2008). None of the shared environmental estimates for CU in these different analyses differed significantly from zero. However, nonshared environmental influences made a significant contribution to CU traits at age 7, both across the continuum and at the extremes.

Larsson, Andershed, and Lichtenstein (2006) used a sample 1,100 16-year-old male and female twin pairs from the Twin study of Child and Adolescent Development (TCHAD; Lichtenstein, Tuvblad, Larsson, & Carlstrom, 2007) to examine the heritability of three psychopathic trait dimensions: CU, grandiosity/manipulation, and impulsivity/irresponsibility. The 50-item, self-report Youth Psychopathic Traits Inventory (YPI) was used to measure these traits (Andershed, Kerr, Stattin, & Levander, 2002). For the grandiose/manipulative dimension, the heritability was estimated at 51%. Nonshared environmental effects explained almost all of the remaining variance, whereas the influence of shared environmental effects seemed to be of minimal importance. Similar patterns, with considerable heritable and little shared environmental influences, were evident for the other two dimensions as well; that is, genetic effects accounted for 43 and 56% of the variation in the CU and impulsivity/irresponsibility dimensions, respectively.

Various aspects of psychopathic personality in children/adolescents show moderate to strong genetic influence and moderate nonshared environmental influence. Shared environmental influences on psychopathic personality traits were not detected in any of the studies, suggesting that the environmental factors making members of the twin pair similar to each other do not account for individual differences in psychopathic personality in children/adolescents. These results are in line with previous adult data on psychopathic personality traits (Blonigen et al., 2003), as well as data on other personality dimensions (Bouchard & Loehlin, 2001), and suggest that there is moderate to strong genetic vulnerability to psychopathic personality. Importantly, these results do not preclude that environmental factors (e.g., parental characteristics) exert an influence on psychopathic personality traits. However, such factors may act in a child-specific manner (represented by nonshared environmental variance) or via the process of gene–environment interplay.

In addition to reporting univariate heritabilities for various aspects of psychopathic personality, most of the studies reviewed here have also addressed multivariate questions of etiology of covariance between different aspects of psychopathic personality, origins of stability of psychopathic personality across development, and the etiological relationship between psychopathic personality traits and antisocial behavior. The subsequent sections review findings from these analyses.

The Same Genetic and Environmental Influences Are Important in Accounting for Individual Differences in Psychopathic Personality Traits for Both Males and Females

Two studies (Larsson et al., 2006; Viding et al., 2007) have incorporated dizygotic, opposite-sex twin pairs in their analyses to explore the potential role of qualitative sex differences (i.e., different genes and environments influencing phenotypic variation for males and females) in the etiology of psychopathy. Neither of these studies found support for qualitative sex differences in the genetic and environmental influences on psychopathic traits. Few studies have also assessed the impact of quantitative sex differences (i.e., the same genetic and environmental influences affecting males and females to a different degree). Most studies found little evidence of quantitative sex differences (e.g., Blonigen et al., 2006; Larsson et al., 2006), but there is also some support for a higher heritability of CU traits for males (Viding et al., 2007). The findings so far indicate that although males and females show mean differences in psychopathic personality trait scores at the phenotypic level, the etiological influences on individual differences in these traits are similar for both genders.

Genetic Factors Are Important in Explaining Covariance among Different Aspects of Psychopathic Personality

Two twin studies to date have employed models to study the origins of covariance among different aspects of psychopathic personality. In the first study to address this issue, Taylor and colleagues (2003) reported that half of the covariation between CU traits and impulsivity–antisocial behavior at 16–18 years of age was due to genetic factors (53%), while nonshared environmental factors explained the remaining part of the covariation (47%). This study also found support for some independence in the etiology underlying the two trait dimensions; that is, approximately half of the total genetic variance in CU was unique to that personality dimension, which clearly suggests that the CU and impulsive–antisocial dimensions can be differentiated etiologically.

Larsson and colleagues (2006) used the YPI in a sample of 16-year-old twin pairs from the aforementioned TCHAD study to examine the etiology underlying the covariation among the three psychopathic trait dimensions (i.e., CU, grandiosity/manipulation, and impulsivity/irresponsibility). The authors used multivariate model fitting techniques to study the shared covariance among the three psychopathic personality dimensions simultaneously. They found that a common pathway model provided the best fit of the data, which indicates that the three dimensions of psychopathic personality are significantly linked to a highly heritable common latent factor. The relatively high heritability (63%) for the latent psychopathic personality factor makes it a novel target for future research.

In summary, studies investigating the etiology of covariance among different aspects of psychopathic personality suggest that common genes are important.[3]

Genetic Factors Account for Stability of Psychopathic Personality across Development

Two twin studies to date have explored the genetic and environmental contributions to the stability of psychopathic personality traits in adolescence. Blonigen and colleagues (2006) used scales derived from the MPQ to examine the genetic and environmental contribution to stability of CU–grandiose/manipulative (what they called fearless dominance) and impulsive–antisocial dimensions from adolescence to early adulthood. The authors applied model-fitting analyses on MPQ information from two time points 7 years apart, when the twins were 17 and 24 years old. Their results indicate that the heritability of the fearless dominance and impulsive–antisocial dimension remained consistent across time. Furthermore, the decomposition of the covariance across time for fearless dominance and impulsive–antisocial dimensions revealed that 58% of the stability in fearless dominance and 62% of the stability in the impulsive–antisocial dimensions were due to genetic influences. This result indicates that the relatively high stability in these traits is substantially influence by genetic factors (see also Andershed, Chapter 10, this volume).

Forsman, Larsson, Andershed, and Lichtenstein (2008) measured CU, grandiose/manipulative, and impulsive/irresponsible dimensions with the YPI, and examined genetic and environmental contribution to the stability of psychopathic personality between ages 16 and 19 in the TCHAD sample. The authors focused on a hierarchical model of psychopathic personality, in which a higher-order general factor substantially explained the variation in the three psychopathic personality dimensions both in mid- and late adolescence. Results showed that the observed test–retest correlation of the higher-order psychopathic personality factor was high ($r = .60$). In addition, as much as 90% of the test–retest correlation was explained by genetic factors. However, they also found evidence for specific genetic stability in the CU and impulsive/irresponsible dimensions. For example, 13% of unique genetic effects in the CU dimension at age 19 were shared with corresponding effects at age 16. Thus, their model provides evidence for etiological generality and specificity for the stability of psychopathic personality between mid- and late adolescence.

In summary, longitudinal twin studies have found that the stability in psychopathic personality traits from adolescence to early adulthood is substantially influenced by genetic factors. Nothing is known about how genetic and environmental factors contribute to psychopathic traits during the transition from childhood to adolescence. It would therefore be interesting to explore how genetic and environmental factors influence different developmental trajectories for antisocial children with and without CU traits. Another important research goal for future longitudinal twin studies of psychopathic personality traits is to test developmental hypothesis about different patterns of gene–environment correlations and gene–environment interaction.

Genetic Factors Contribute to the Relationship between Psychopathic Personality Traits and Antisocial Behavior

Blonigen and colleagues (2005) used a sample of adolescent twin pairs (626 pairs of 17-year-old male and female twins) from the Minnesota Twin Family Study to examine the etiological connection between psychopathic personality traits and broad domains of externalizing behavior (antisocial behavior, substance abuse). They found a moderate positive genetic correlation ($r^g = .49$) between the impulsive–antisocial dimension and externalizing behavior, and modest positive genetic correlation ($r^g = .16$) between CU–grandiose/manipulative dimension and externalizing behavior (stronger for males, $r^g = .35$).

Larsson and colleagues (2007) conducted another twin study using the aforementioned TCHAD sample. Theory-driven multivariate twin models were applied to self-report assessments of psychopathic personality (YPI) and adolescent antisocial behavior. The authors found that a common genetic factor contributed substantially to the three psychopathic personality dimensions (grandiose/manipulative, CU, and impulsive/irresponsible) and antisocial behavior measured at ages 13–14 and 16–17 years. This is in line with the Blonigen and colleagues (2005) study that reported a genetic overlap between self-reported psychopathic personality traits and externalizing psychopathology.

A study by Forsman and colleagues (2007) represents another example of how twin research designs can be used to study the nature of association between psychopathic personality traits and various forms of externalizing psychopathology. This study used a longitudinal design to compare identical and fraternal twins discordant for parent-rated externalizing behavior in childhood (at ages 8–9 and 13–14 years) on self-reported scores on psychopathic personality traits in adolescence (at age 16–17 years). This study found that externalizing behavior in childhood was associated with higher levels of psychopathic personality traits (YPI) in adolescence among boys but not girls. The comparison of identical and fraternal twins suggested that genetic factors were responsible for the association between externalizing behavior and psychopathic personality traits.

Another study by Forsman, Lichtenstein, Andershed, and Larsson (2009) using the TCHAD sample (n = 2,255 twins) showed that psychopathic personality (measured with the YPI) in adolescence predicted antisocial behavior in early adulthood, over and above both concurrent and preexisting levels of antisocial behavior. Their study also showed that the association between adolescent psychopathic personality and adult antisocial behavior was mainly explained by genetic effects—a result that can be interpreted as a genetically influenced personality-driven process, where individuals are predisposed to higher risk of involvement in antisocial behavior because of their antisocially prone personality

Viding and colleagues (2007) examined the extent to which genetic influences contribute to the overlap between CU traits and antisocial behavior at age 7. The analyses in this study were conducted on the same TEDS sample of twins used in Viding and colleagues (2005). Teachers provided ratings of CU traits and antisocial behavior, and analyses were performed across the continuum of scores and at the extreme ends of the distribution. The findings demonstrated, most importantly, that there is a substantial genetic overlap between CU traits and antisocial behavior in both boys and girls. Common genetic influences operate to bring about both of these problems, assessed as dimensions, and even more so at the high extremes.

Finally, twin data have also informed the utility of using psychopathic personality traits to subtype individuals with antisocial behavior. Viding and colleagues (2005) used information from TEDS to investigate whether the etiology of teacher-rated antisocial behavior differs as a function of teacher-rated CU traits. Antisocial behavior was assessed using the SDQ five-item Conduct Problem scale. The authors separated children with elevated levels of antisocial behavior (in the top 10% for the TEDS sample) into two groups based on their CU score (in the top 10% or not). Antisocial behavior in children with CU was under strong genetic influence (h^{g2} = .81) and no influence of shared environment. In contrast, antisocial behavior in children without elevated levels of CU traits showed moderate genetic influence (h^{g2} = .30) and substantial environmental influence (c^{g2} = .34, e^{g2} = .26). Viding, Jones, Frick, Moffitt, and Plomin (2008) have recently replicated the finding of different heritability estimates for the CU and non-CU groups using the 9-year teacher data from TEDS. Their results indicate that the heritability differences hold even after hyperactivity scores of the children are controlled for, suggesting that the result is not driven by any differences in hyperactivity between the two groups. Taken together, these findings clearly suggests that while the CU subtype is genetically vulnerable to antisocial behavior, the non-CU subtype manifests a more strongly environmental etiology of antisocial behavior.

In summary, twin studies that have examined the overlap between psychopathic personality traits and antisocial behavior have all shown that common genetic influences account for much of the covariation between psychopathic personality traits and antisocial behavior. In addition, data on young twins suggest that early-onset antisocial behavior is more heritable for the group of children with concomitant CU traits and antisocial behavior. These findings are consistent with the notion that a common set of genes influences psychopathic personality traits and antisocial behavior (as well as other disorders on the externalizing spectrum) and in line with the hypothesis that a shared set of genes affects various externalizing psychopathology (Krueger et al., 2002). However, there are other feasible, competing explanations of the observed finding. For example, the findings are congruent with genetic influences that act indirectly on antisocial (externalizing) behavior via psychopathic personality traits (Goldsmith & Gottesman, 1996). Multilevel methodological approaches (e.g., measured genes, brain functioning, neuropsychological measures) can be helpful when the shared versus unique etiological processes between psychopathic personality traits and antisocial behavior are explored, especially since twin studies only conceptualize these processes as latent genetic and environmental factors. For example, molecular genetic studies could concentrate on testing the hypothesis that risk genes that eventually emerge for psychopathic personality traits would also increase the risk for antisocial behavior (and, conversely, test for an association of theoretically plausible risk genes for antisocial behavior with psychopathic personality traits).

Molecular Genetic Studies

Most of the molecular genetic research that is relevant for psychopathy has used association analysis to explore the impact of *candidate genes* (i.e., genes whose function suggests that they might be associated with a trait). Association studies usually use a case–control design to compare allelic frequencies in unrelated affected and unaffected individuals in the population. An allele in a gene is said to be associated with a trait if it occurs at a significantly higher frequency in the affected group of individuals compared to the unaffected group.

Despite the substantial literature demonstrating a heritable component of psychopathic traits, we know of only four published studies that have looked at the association between candidate genes and psychopathy measures. Three previous studies have focused on the phenotype of adult psychopathy. These studies are limited as they involved small samples of adults with substance abuse and only focused on a few candidate genes. The first of these studies found no association between psychopathy and either of the Taq1 single nucleotide polymorphisms (SNPs) located in the 3′-untranslated region of the dopamine D2 receptor gene (*DRD2*) (Smith et al., 1993). Two recent studies of a small sample of adult patients with alcoholism and found an association between psychopathy and specific allelic variants of cannabinoid receptor type 1 and fatty acid amide hydrolase (Hoenicka et al., 2006), as well as psychopathy scores and *DRD2 C957T* polymorphism and ankyrin repeat and kinase domain containing 1 (*ANKK1*) gene's (*Taq1A*) polymorphism acting epistatically (Ponce et al., 2008). An additional study on a relatively small sample of adolescents with ADHD recently reported associations between the *val* allele of the cathecol-o-methyl-transferase gene, the low activity allele of monoamine oxidase A gene (MAOA-L), the short allele of the *5HTT* gene (*5HTTs*), and "emotional dysfunction" scores of psychopathy (Fowler et al., 2009). The latter two of these associations were unexpected based on imaging genetic data suggesting that *MAOA-L* and *5HTTs* confer opposite patterns of amygdala reactivity (heightened) to that typically seen in individuals with psychopathy (dampened) (e.g., Meyer-Lindenberg et al., 2006; Munafo, Brown, & Hariri, 2008; see below for further discussion on MAOA and imaging genetics). Research on molecular genetics of psychopathy is still very much in its infancy. Molecular genetic research on antisocial behavior, on the other hand, has received more attention. Below we review research on molecular genetics of antisocial behavior and relate it to potential investigations in the field of psychopathy.

Genes regulating serotonergic neurotransmission, in particular monoamine oxidase A (*MAOA*), have been highlighted in the search for a genetic predisposition to antisocial behavior (Lesch, 2003). The *MAOA* gene contains a well-characterized functional polymorphism consisting of a variable number of tandem repeats in the promoter region, with high- (*MAOA-H*) and low-activity (*MAOA-L*) allelic variants. The *MAOA-H* variant is associated with lower concentration of intracellular serotonin, whereas *MAOA-L* variant is associated with higher concentration of intracellular serotonin. Recent research suggests that genetic vulnerability to antisocial behavior conferred by *MAOA-L* may only become evident in the presence of an environmental trigger, such as maltreatment (e.g., Caspi et al., 2002; Kim-Cohen et al., 2006). Despite the demonstration of genetic influences on individual differences in antisocial behavior, it is important to note that no genes *for* antisocial behavior exist. Instead, genes code for proteins that influence characteristics, such as neurocognitive vulnerabilities, that may in turn increase risk for antisocial behavior. Thus, although genetic risk alone may be of little consequence for behavior in favorable conditions, genetic vulnerability may still manifest at the level of brain/cognition. Imaging genetics studies attest to genotype differences associated with variation in brain structure and function in nonclinical samples (Meyer-Lindenberg & Weinberger, 2006). We can think of this as the neural fingerprint; ready to translate into disordered behavior in the presence of unfortunate environmental triggers.

Meyer-Lindenberg and colleagues (2006) provided the first demonstration of the *MAOA-L* genotype's association with a pattern of neural hypersensitivity to emotional stimuli. Specifically, they reported increased amygdalar activity coupled with lesser activity in the frontal regulatory regions in *MAOA-L* compared with *MAOA-H* carriers. Similar findings have been reported in subsequent studies (reviewed in Buckholtz &Meyer-Lindenberg, 2008). Buckholtz and Meyer-Lindenberg speculate that the brain imaging findings of poor emotion regulation in *MAOA-L* carriers relate to threat reactive and impulsive rather than psychopathic antisocial behavior. They based this speculation on the finding that individuals with psychopathy display underreactivity of the brain's emotional circuit, particularly the amygdala (Birbaumer et al., 2005; Kiehl et al., 2001).

As highlighted earlier, while behavioral genetics data suggest heritability of psychopathy, a molecular level account of the disorder remains in its infancy. Suggestions have been made that psychopathy might be related to anomalies in noradrenergic neurotransmission (Blair, Mitchell, & Blair, 2005). It is also interesting to note that some studies have reported increased vulnerability to antisocial behavior in the presence of the *MAOA-H* allele (e.g., Manuck et al., 1999). This may reflect false positive findings, but it is also possible to speculate that the amygdalar hypo- as opposed to hyperreactivity seen in individuals with psychopathy may be influenced by *MAOA-H*, rather than *MAOA-L* genotype. This suggestion remains highly speculative, and as for any behavior, the genetic influences are not be limited to a single candidate gene. However, it is entirely possible that different alleles of the same gene may predispose to different types of antisocial syndromes.

In addition to *MAOA*, other genes influencing the reactivity of the brain's affect circuitry, such as the serotonin transporter gene (*5-HTT*), could also play a role in psychopathy. Finally, new technologies, such as DNA pooling,[4] are enabling genomewide association studies that search for novel single nucleotide polymorphisms (SNPs) that may be associated with psychopathy syndrome. We have recently conducted such study and preliminary data is suggestive of some SNPs in or near neurodevelopmental genes that may be associated with psychopathy syndrome (Viding et al., in press). Once it is established whether these findings replicate, such SNPs could be assessed in relation to psychopathy/antisocial behavior in several existing studies beyond our own collaborations. They could also be incorporated into imaging genetic investigations of psychopathy.

Genetic Studies Informing on Environmental Risk

Although a growing body of evidence points toward some genetic risk for psychopathy, this risk is likely to act in conjunction with environmental factors. One way to examine the causal role of environmental risk factors in the development of any trait or behavior is to use behavioral genetic research designs. These designs make use of "natural experiments" to disentangle the normally inseparable contribution of genes and environments, as well as to study gene–environment interplay (Moffitt, 2005). These studies encompass both twin and adoption methods, and more recently studies of measured genes and environments (see the section on molecular genetics highlighting gene–environment interaction). Unfortunately, none of the studies to date has focused on psychopathy syndrome.

Given the different levels of genetic and environmental risk tentatively associated with psychopathic and nonpsychopathic antisocial behavior (Viding et al., 2005), it may be interesting to see whether putative environmental risk factors operate differently on the two subtypes. For example, there is some suggestive evidence that antisocial behavior in children with CU traits may be less strongly associated with poor parental practices than in children without these traits (Lynam, Loeber, & Stouthamer-Loeber, 2008; Oxford, Cavell, & Hughes, 2003; Wootton, Frick, Shelton, & Silverthorn, 1997), which suggest a moderating role of CU traits on the relationship between negative parenting and children's antisocial behavior. We are in the process of extending this research line by charting both common and unique environmental risk factors for antisocial behavior in these two etiologically distinct subtypes.

Since nonshared environment appears to be important for the etiology of psychopathic traits, a twin design comparing identical twins discordant for psychopathic traits could be an interesting analytic avenue on which to focus. Caspi and colleagues (2004) used this design to good effect when they demonstrated that discrepancies in maternal negative emotion/hostility toward identical twins was related to discrepancies in future teacher-rated antisocial behavior. This finding held even after researchers controlled for previous levels of antisocial behavior and suggests that when two genetically identical individuals receive discrepant treatment, the individual who is the focus of more negative emotionality is also the individual most at risk for developing antisocial behavior. This type of design strongly demonstrates an environmental effect, since effects of the child genotype can be ruled out by effectively comparing "genetic clones."

We have recently replicated the findings reported by Caspi and colleagues (2004) on antisocial behavior using a sample of children (2,254 twin pairs, between 7 and 12 years old) from the TEDS sample (Viding et al., 2009). We found that the twins who had received more negative parental discipline at age 7 were more likely to have higher levels of conduct problems at age 12 than their co-twins. However, this finding was not replicated for CU. Although there was a phenotypic relationship between negative parental discipline and CU, we did not find a longitudinal environmental effect of differential negative parental discipline on differences in subsequent CU between the twins. This finding may be explained by the fact that the relationship between parental practices and CU in children could reflect passive and/or evocative gene-environment correlation (i.e., genetic endowment within families), which would not be revealed in a design that focuses on nonshared environment (i.e., MZ twin differences design). In sum, we found that during the transition to early adolescence, negative parental discipline was a nonshared environmental risk factor for antisocial behavior, but not for CU.

Existing behavioral genetic research also indicates that children's genetically influenced antisocial behavior evokes negative parenting (e.g., Larsson, Viding, Rijsdijk, & Plomin, 2008). One process that may explain this finding is likely to be an evocative gene–environment correlation, in which genetically influenced child predispositions elicit responses, such as negative parenting, that in turn influence development of antisocial behavior (Moffitt, 2005). Unfortunately, the role of evocative gene–environment correlation in the context of psychopathic personality traits has not been studied in a behavioral genetic framework. Future studies may therefore benefit from including careful assessments of proximal environmental components (e.g., maltreatment, parent–child conflict, parental negativity, and inconsistent–harsh parenting) in the twin study design. Both twin designs and designs of measured genes and environments have been used to demonstrate that gene–environment interaction (G × E) seems to bring about antisocial behavior (e.g., Jaffee et al., 2005; Kim-Cohen et al., 2006; see the previous the discussion of the *MAOA* G × E findings). No studies to date have investigated G × E in relation to psychopathy in either adult or child samples. It is important to note that treatment of antisocial behavior may be thought of as a "reverse" G × E, where an individual's genetic makeup may limit the success of a particular intervention. Given some preliminary data indicating that children with CU traits may respond differently to parenting and interventions than their antisocial peers (e.g., Hawes & Dadds, 2005; Hipwell et al., 2007; Wootton et al., 1997), it would be of interest to understand how the genetic susceptibility to antisocial behavior in this population could be best moderated with suitable environmental buffering.

The Future of Genetic Research: Psychopathy and Translational Considerations

One interesting, new avenue of genetic research in childhood/adolescent psychopathy is imaging genetics. Because there is now a wealth of data on the neurocognitive profile associated with child/adolescent psychopathy (see Blair, Chapter 7, this volume), there is the potential to combine multiple levels of analyses to chart the genes–brain–behavior pathway associated with development of psychopathy.

The research base into genetic influences on child/adolescent psychopathy is still sparse and requires considerable replication and extension before any policy or treatment recommendations can be based on these findings (see Salekin, Chapter 14, this volume). However, current studies that suggest genetic vulnerability to psychopathic personality traits, as well as etiological differences between children with and without CU-type antisocial behavior, tie in with much of the neurocognitive, behavioral, and treatment research base on psychopathy. The existing, nongenetic research base strongly suggests that these children/adolescents form a specific, particularly high-risk group of youngsters (Frick & Marsee, 2006). Currently, treatment programs for antisocial behavior do not routinely assess the effects of psychopathic personality traits on outcome success. Frick (2001) has emphasized that although there are prevention programs that address the needs of primarily impulsive antisocial behavior, less is known about possible prevention and treatment of antisocial behavior in individuals who lack empathy and remorse. Children with psychopathic personality traits manifest strong on self interest and get motivated by rewards, but do not characteristically process others' distress or react to punishment. These are cognitive strengths and limitations that have to be worked with to produce change in behavior (see also Salekin, Chapter 14, this volume).

Behavioral genetic research should caution against entertaining ideas of gene therapy for antisocial behavior. Genes that have common variants in the population are more than likely to have functions, some desirable, others not desirable. Hence, a risk gene may have many functions over and above increasing risk for disorder. When this information is combined with the fact that genes interact in complex systems, as well as with environmental risk factors, it seems pertinent to conclude that removal of the effects of one gene via gene therapy is unlikely to be effective (Nuffield Council on Bioethics, 2002). This does not mean that genotype information will be irrelevant for therapeutic intervention. For example, demonstration of genetically (and, consequently, cognitively) heterogeneous subtypes of early-onset antisocial behavior suggests the possibility of subtype-specific gene variants that index risk for different cognitive deficits. An early knowledge of such risk genes has potential to guide prevention efforts prior to the emergence of clear, overt behavioral markers for the disorder. As cognitive-behavioral approaches are likely to feature strongly in the antisocial behavior intervention, developing better understanding of the genes–brain–cognition–behavior pathways for particular subtypes—especially within a longitudinal, developmental framework—could provide crucial insights for intervention. All such intervention plans must proceed hand in hand with extensive ethical consultation.

Summary

Genetic research into psychopathy is off to a very promising start, with several research groups in different countries publishing in the area. Overall, psychopathic traits appear to be moderately to strongly heritable and show little shared environmental influence. The same genetic and environmental influences appear to be important in accounting for individual differences in psychopathic personality traits for both males and females. Genetic factors are important in explaining covariance among different aspects of psychopathic personality and stability of psychopathic personality across development. Furthermore, common genes contribute to the relationship between psychopathic personality traits and antisocial behavior. Much more work using genetically informative study designs is required. First of all, quantitative genetic research findings need more replications. Second, the molecular genetic research base on psychopathy needs to start in earnest. Third, environmental risk can be studied in a particularly informative way using behavioral genetic designs, but to date this has not been done with psychopathy. New avenues, such as imaging genetic studies should also be encouraged. Genetic research into psychopathy is too much in its infancy to inform current policymaking and treatment planning. However, there is promise for an important contribution, as long as ethical issues are carefully considered along the way.

Acknowledgments

Our work was supported by grants from the U.K. Department of Health (No. MRD 12-37) and Medical Research Council (No. G0401170) to Essi Viding, and by a postdoctoral stipend from the Swedish Council for Working Life and Social Research (Project No. 2005-1356) to Henrik Larsson.

Notes

1. We wish to note that we are aware of the controversies of calling children/adolescents psychopaths. The terms *psychopathy syndrome*, *individuals (children/youth) with psychopathy*, and *children with antisocial behavior and callous–unemotional traits* (AB/CU+) are used interchangeably throughout this chapter. However, we do not have a strong preference for a particular label for this group of youngsters.
2. h_{g2} denotes group heritability estimate, which is the proportion of the group differences between a "case" and the rest of the sample that is due to heritable influences.
3. Note that Blonigen and colleagues (2005) did not report a significant phenotypic correlation between CU–grandiose/manipulative and irresponsible–antisocial dimensions, and, as such, data from this study are not included in the discussion of the etiology of covariance between different dimensions of psychopathic personality. The authors suggest that their data is compatible with the view that largely distinct genetic influences are responsible for variation in the CU–grandiose/manipulative and irresponsible–antisocial dimensions. However, the lack of phenotypic and genetic correlations between the two dimensions (as derived from the MPQ) is not in line with reports using other instruments to index psychopathic personality. This discrepancy clearly warrants further investigation.
4. *DNA pooling* refers to a genetic screening method that combines DNA from many individuals in a single molecular genetic analysis to generate a representation of allele frequencies. A DNA pool can thus be generated for all cases and all controls, and allele frequencies can be compared between these pools.

References

Andershed, H., Kerr, M., Stattin, H., & Levander, S. (2002). Psychopathic traits in non-referred youths: Initial test of a new assessment tool. In E. Blaauw & L. Sheridan (Eds.), *Psychopaths: Current international perspectives* (pp. 131–158). Hague, The Netherlands: Elsevier.

Arseneault, L., Moffitt, T. E., Caspi, A., Taylor, A., Rijsdijk, F. V., Jaffee, S. R., et al. (2003). Strong genetic effects on cross-situational antisocial behavior among 5-year-old children according to mothers, teachers, examiner-observers, and twins' self-reports. *Journal of Child Psychology and Psychiatry and Allied Disciplines, 44*(6), 832–848.

Birbaumer, N., Veit, R., Lotze, M., Erb, M., Hermann, C., Grodd, W., et al. (2005). Deficient fear conditioning in psychopathy: A functional magnetic resonance imaging study. *Archives of General Psychiatry, 62*(7), 799–805.

Blair, R. J. R., Mitchell, D. G. V., & Blair, K. S. (2005). *The psychopath: Emotion and the brain.* Oxford, UK: Blackwell.

Blair, R. J. R., Peschardt, K. S., Budhani, S., Mitchell, D. G. V., & Pine, D. S. (2006). The development of psychopathy. *Journal of Child Psychology and Psychiatry, 47*(3), 262–275.

Blonigen, D. M., Carlson, S. R., Krueger, R. F., & Patrick, C. J. (2003). A twin study of self-reported psychopathic personality traits. *Personality and Individual Differences, 35*, 179–197.

Blonigen, D. M., Hicks, B. M., Krueger, R. F., Patrick, C. J., & Iacono, W. G. (2005). Psychopathic personality traits: Heritability and genetic overlap with internalizing and externalizing psychopathology. *Psychological Medicine, 35*, 637–648.

Blonigen, D. M., Hicks, B. M., Krueger, R. F., Patrick, C. J., & Iacono, W. G. (2006). Continuity and change in psychopathic traits as measured via normal-range personality: A longitudinal-biometric study. *Journal of Abnormal Psychology, 115*, 85–95.

Bouchard, T. J., & Loehlin, J. C. (2001). Genes, evolution, and personality. *Behavior Genetics, 31*, 243–273.

Buckholtz, J. W., & Meyer-Lindenberg, A. (2008). MAOA and the neurogenetic architecture of human aggression. *Trends in Neurosciences, 31*, 120–129.

Caspi, A., McClay, J., Moffitt, T., Mill, J., Martin, J., Craig, I. W., et al. (2002). Role of genotype in the cycle of violence in maltreated children. *Science, 297*, 851–854.

Caspi, A., Moffitt, T. E., Morgan, J., Rutter, M., Taylor, A., Arseneault, L., et al. (2004). Maternal expressed emotion predicts children's antisocial behavior problems: Using monozygotic-twin differences to identify environmental effects on behavioral development. *Developmental Psychology, 40*(2), 149–161.

Eley, T. C., Lichtenstein, P., & Moffitt, T. E. (2003). A longitudinal behavioral genetic analysis of the etiology of aggressive and nonaggressive antisocial behavior. *Development and Psychopathology, 15*, 383–402.

Forsman, M., Larsson, H., Andershed, H., & Lichtenstein, P. (2007). Persistent disruptive childhood behavior and psychopathic personality in adolescence: A twin study. *British Journal of Developmental Psychology, 25*, 383–398.

Forsman, M., Lichtenstein P., Andershed H., & Larsson H. (2008). Genetic effects explain the stability of psychopathic personality from mid- to late adolescence. *Journal of Abnormal Psychology, 117*, 606–617.

Forsman, M., Lichtenstein P., Andershed H., & Larsson H. (2009). A longitudinal twin study of the direction of effects between psychopathic personality and antisocial behaviour. *Journal of Child Psychology and Psychiatry and Allied Disciplines, 51*(1), 39–47.

Fowler, T., Langley, K., Rice, F., van den Bree, M., Ross, K., Wilkinson, L. S., et al. (2009). Psychopathy trait scores in adolescents with childhood ADHD: The contribution of genotypes affecting MAOA, 5HTT and COMT activity. *Psychiatric Genetics, 19*(6), 312–319.

Frick, P. J. (2001). Effective interventions for children and adolescents with conduct disorder. *Canadian Journal of Psychiatry, 46*(7), 597–608.

Frick, P. J., & Hare, R. D. (2001). *Antisocial Process Screening Device*. Toronto: Multi Health Systems.

Frick, P. J., & Marsee, M. A. (2006). Psychopathy and developmental pathways to antisocial behavior in youth. In C. J. Patrick (Ed.), *Handbook of psychopathy* (pp. 353–374). New York: Guilford Press.

Goldsmith, H., & Gottesman, I. I. (1996). Heritable variability and variable heritability in developmental psychopathology. In J. J. Haugaard & M. F. Lenzenweger (Eds.), *Frontiers of developmental psychopathology* (pp. 5–43). New York: Oxford University Press.

Goodman, R. (1997). The Strengths and Difficulties Questionnaire: A research note. *Journal of Child Psychology and Psychiatry and Allied Disciplines, 38*(5), 581–586.

Hawes, D. J., & Dadds, M. R. (2005). The treatment of conduct problems in children with callous–unemotional traits. *Journal of Consulting and Clinical Psychology, 73*(4), 737–741.

Hipwell, A. E., Pardini, D. A., Loeber, R., Sembower, M., Keenan, K., & Stouthamer-Loeber, M. (2007). Callous–unemotional behaviors in young girls: Shared and unique effects relative to conduct problems. *Journal of Clinical Child and Adolescent Psychology*, *36*, 293–304.

Hoenicka, J., Ponce, G., Jiménez-Arriero, M. A., Ampuero, I., Rodríguez-Jiménez, R., Rubio, G., et al. (2006). Association in alcoholic patients between psychopathic traits and the additive effect of allelic forms of the *CNR1* and *FAAH* endocannabinoid genes, and the 3' region of the *DRD2* gene. *Neurotoxicity Research, 11*, 51–60.

Jaffee, S. R., Caspi, A., Moffitt, T. E., Dodge, K. A., Rutter, M., Taylor, A., et al. (2005). Nature x nurture: Genetic vulnerabilities interact with physical maltreatment to promote conduct problems. *Development and Psychopathology, 17*, 67–84.

Kiehl, K. A., Smith, A. M., Hare, R. D., Mendrek, A., Forster, B. B., Brink, J., et al. (2001). Limbic abnormalities in affective processing by criminal psychopaths as revealed by functional magnetic resonance imaging. *Biological Psychiatry, 50*(9), 677–684.

Kim-Cohen, J., Caspi, A., Taylor, A., Williams, B., Newcombe, R., Craig, I. W., et al. (2006). *MAOA*, maltreatment, and gene–environment interaction predicting children's mental health: New evidence and a meta-analysis. *Molecular Psychiatry, 11*(10), 903–913.

Krueger, R. F., Hicks, B. M., Patrick, C. J., Carlson, S. R., Iacono, W. G., & McGue, M. (2002). Etiologic connections among substance dependence, antisocial behavior and personality: Modeling the externalizing spectrum. *Journal of Abnormal Psychology, 111*(3), 411–424.

Larsson, H., Andershed, H., & Lichtenstein, P. (2006). A genetic factor explains most of the variation in the psychopathic personality. *Journal of Abnormal Psychology, 115*, 221–230.

Larsson, H., Tuvblad, C., Rijsdijk, F., Andershed, H., Grann, M., & Lichtenstein, P.

(2007). A common genetic factor explains the association between psychopathic personality and antisocial behavior. *Psychological Medicine, 37*, 15–26.

Larsson, H., Viding, E.,& Plomin, R. (2008). Callous–unemotional traits and antisocial behavior: Genetic, environmental and early childhood influences. *Criminal Justice and Behaviour, 35*(2), 197–211.

Larsson, H., Viding, E., Rijsdijk, F. V., & Plomin, R. (2008). Relationships between parental negativity and childhood antisocial behavior over time: A bidirectional effect model in a longitudinal genetically informative design. *Journal of Abnormal Child Psychology, 36*(5), 633–645.

Lesch, K. P. (2003). The serotonergic dimension of aggression and violence. In M. P. Mattson (Ed.), *Neurobiology of aggression: Understanding and preventing violence* (pp. 33–64). Totowa, NJ: Humana Press.

Lichtenstein, P., Tuvblad, C., Larsson, H., & Carlstrom, E. (2007). The Swedish Twin study of Child and Adolescent Development: The TCHAD study. *Twin Research and Human Genetics, 10*, 67–73.

Lilienfeld, S. O., & Andrews, B. P. (1996). Development and preliminary validation of a self-report measure of psychopathic personality. *Journal of Personality Assessment, 66*, 488–524.

Loney, B. R., Taylor, J., Butler, M., & Iacono, W. G. (2002). *The Minnesota Temperament Inventory: A psychometric study of adolescent self-reported psychopathy*. Unpublished manuscript, University of Minnesota.

Lynam, D. R., Caspi, A., Moffitt, T. E., Loeber, R., & Stouthamer-Loeber, M. (2007). Longitudinal evidence that psychopathy scores in early adolescence predict adult psychopathy. *Journal of Abnormal Psychology, 116*, 155–165.

Lynam, D. R., Loeber, R., & Stouthamer-Loeber, M. (2008). The stability of psychopathy from adolescence into adulthood. *Criminal Justice and Behavior, 35*, 228–243.

Manuck, S. B., Flory, J. D., Ferrell, R. E., Dent, K. M., Mann, J. J., & Muldoon, M. F. (1999). Aggression and anger-related traits associated with a polymorphism of the tryptophan hydroxylase gene. *Biological Psychiatry, 45*(5), 603–614.

Meyer-Lindenberg, A., Buckholtz, J. W., Kolachana, B., Hariri, A. R., Pezawas, L., Blasi, G., et al. (2006). Neural mechanisms of genetic risk for impulsivity and violence in humans. *Proceedings of the National Academy of Sciences USA, 103*(16), 6269–6274.

Meyer-Lindenberg, A., & Weinberger, D. (2006). Intermediate phenotypes and genetic mechanisms of psychiatric disorders. *Nature Reviews Neuroscience, 7*(10), 818–827.

Moffitt, T. E. (2005). The new look of behavioral genetics in developmental psychopathology: Gene–environment interplay in antisocial behaviors. *Psychological Bulletin, 131*, 533–554.

Munafo, M. R., Brown, S. M., & Hariri, A. R. (2008). Serotonin transporter (*5-HTTLPR*) genotype and amygdala activation: A meta-analysis. *Biological Psychiatry*, *63*, 852–857.

Nuffield Council of Bioethics. (2002). *Genetics and human behavior: The ethical context*. London: Author.

Oxford, M., Cavell, T., & Hughes, J. (2003). Callous–unemotional traits moderate the relation between ineffective parenting and child externalizing problems: A partial replication and extension. *Journal of Clinical Child and Adolescent Psychology, 32*, 577–585.

Plomin, R., DeFries, J., McClearn, G., & McGuffin, P. (2008). *Behavioral genetics* (5th ed.). New York: Worth.

Ponce, G., Hoenicka, J., Jiménez-Arriero, M. A., Rodriguez-Jiménez, M. D., Aragüés, M., Martin-Suñé, N., et al. (2008). DRD2 and *ANKK1* genotype in alcohol-dependent patients with psychopathic traits: association and interaction study. *British Journal of Psychiatry, 193*, 121–125.

Rhee, S. H., & Waldman, I. D. (2002). Genetic and environmental influences on antisocial behavior: A meta-analysis of twin and adoption studies. *Psychological Bulletin, 128*(3), 490–529.

Salekin, R. T. (2006). Psychopathy in children and adolescents: Key issues in conceptualization and assessment. In C. J. Patrick (Ed.), *Handbook of psychopathy* (pp. 389–414). New York: Guilford Press.

Smith, S. S., Newman, J. P., Evans, A., Pickens, R., Wydeven, J., Uhl, G. R., et al. (1993). Comorbid psychopathy is not associated with increased D2 dopamine receptor TaqI A or B gene marker frequencies in incarcerated substance abusers. *Biological Psychiatry, 33*, 845–848.

Taylor, J., Iacono, W. G., & McGue, M. (2000). Evidence for a genetic etiology of early-onset delinquency. *Journal of Abnormal Psychology, 109*(4), 634–643.

Taylor, J., Loney, B. R., Bobadilla, L., Iacono, W. G., & McGue, M. (2003). Genetic and environmental influences on psychopathy trait dimensions in a community sample of male twins. *Journal of Abnormal Child Psychology, 31*(6), 633–645.

Viding, E., Blair, R. J. R., Moffitt, T. E., & Plomin, R. (2005). Evidence for substantial genetic risk for psychopathy in 7-year-olds. *Journal of Child Psychology and Psychiatry, 46*, 592–597.

Viding, E., Fontaine, N. M. G., Oliver, B. R., & Plomin, R. (2009). Negative parental discipline, conduct problems and callous-unemotional traits: A monozygotic twin differences study. *British Journal of Psychiatry, 195*, 414–419.

Viding, E., Frick, P. J., & Plomin, R. (2007). Aetiology of the relationship between callous–unemotional traits and conduct problems in childhood. *British Journal of Psychiatry, 49*, S33–S38.

Viding, E., Hanscombe, K., Curtis, C. J. C., Davis, O. S. P., Meaburn, E. L., & Plomin, R. (in press). In search of genes associated with risk for psychopathic tendencies in children: A two-stage genome-wide association study of pooled DNA. *Journal of Child Psychology and Psychiatry*.

Viding, E., Jones, A. P., Frick, P., Moffitt, T. E., & Plomin, R. (2008). Heritability of antisocial behaviour at nine years: Do callous–unemotional traits matter? *Developmental Science, 11*(1), 17–22.

Waldman, I. D., & Rhee, S. H. (2006). Genetic and environmental influences on psychopathy and antisocial behavior. In C. Patrick (Ed.), *Handbook of psychopathy* (pp. 205–228). New York: Guilford Press.

Wootton, J. M., Frick, P. J., Shelton, K. K., & Silverthorn, P. (1997). Ineffective parenting and childhood conduct problems: The moderating role of callous–unemotional traits. *Journal of Consulting and Clinical Psychology, 65*(2), 301–308.

6

Callous–Unemotional Traits and Their Importance to Causal Models of Severe Antisocial Behavior in Youth

STUART F. WHITE
PAUL J. FRICK

Research on antisocial and aggressive youth, including those diagnosed with conduct disorder (American Psychiatric Association, 2000), has consistently indicated great heterogeneity within antisocial youth in terms of their behavioral characteristics, and the developmental course and causes of their behavior problems (Frick, 2006; Lahey, Moffitt, & Caspi, 2003). This finding has led to a number of attempts to divide antisocial youth into more homogeneous groups (Frick & Marsee, 2006). This research is critical for etiological theories of antisocial and aggressive behavior. Specifically, if youth with the same outcome (e.g., conduct disorder, delinquency) have different causal processes leading to their behavioral disturbance, it is critical to be able to divide youth appropriately into distinct groups to study and to better understand the mechanisms operating in the various causal pathways.

One important causal pathway for understanding aggressive and antisocial behavior in youth is distinguished by the presence of callous–unemotional (CU) traits (i.e., lack of guilt, lack of empathy, callous use of others). CU traits are prominent in most conceptualizations of psychopathy in adults (Cleckley, 1976; Hare, 1999), and the construct of psychopathy in adults has designated a particular severe and violent group of antisocial adults (Hemphill, 2007; Porter & Woodworth, 2006). Importantly, most definitions of psychopathy include several other dimensions, including impulsivity/irresponsibility and narcissism/grandiosity (Cooke, Michie, & Hart, 2006). However, while all three dimensions (i.e., impulsivity, narcissism, CU traits) are related to antisocial behavior in both youth and adults, there is some evidence that CU traits are most important for designating a distinct subgroup of antisocial adults (Cooke & Michie, 1997) and youth (Caputo, Frick, & Brodsky, 1999; Christian, Frick, Hill, Tyler, & Frazer, 1997). For example, in samples of youth, impulsivity and narcissism have been found to be higher in children with early-onset severe behavior problems (Christian et al., 1997) and in serious juvenile offenders (Caputo et al., 1999), but it is CU traits that seem to designate a distinct group of youth who show severe antisocial behavior. The focus of this chapter is to review research supporting the importance of this subgroup of antisocial youth that is high on CU traits.

CU Traits and the Severity and Stability of Antisocial and Aggressive Behavior

A comprehensive review of the research on the association between psychopathy and the severity and stability of antisocial behavior is included in other chapters of this volume (Forth & Brook, Chapter 11; Andershed, Chapter 10) and elsewhere (Edens, Campbell, & Weir, 2007; Frick & Dickens, 2006; Salekin, 2008). However, to summarize this literature, Leistico, Salekin, DeCoster, and Rogers (2008) conducted a large-scale meta-analysis on psychopathy with 95 nonoverlapping studies (N_{total} = 15,826; 2,553 adolescents) and found that adolescents scoring high on psychopathy scales were as likely to offend in the future as adults scoring high on psychopathy, with effect sizes of $d = 0.50$ for overall recidivism, and $d = 0.47$ and $d = 0.59$ for violent and nonviolent recidivism, respectively. This meta-analysis also reported that psychopathy was linked to institutional infractions, with an effect size of $d = 0.53$. Frick and Dickens (2006) reported on a qualitative review of 24 published studies using 22 independent samples. Ten of these studies showed a concurrent association between CU traits and measures of aggressive, antisocial, or delinquent behavior, and 14 studies showed a predictive relationship, with follow-up intervals ranging from 6 months to 10 years. These authors further reported on five studies that showed CU traits were associated with poorer treatment outcomes. Importantly, these studies included community ($N = 6$), clinic-referred ($N = 4$), and forensic ($N = 13$) samples, with samples ranging in age from 4 to 20.

Frick and White (2008) expanded on this review by comparing CU traits to other dimensions of psychopathy in terms of their association with conduct problems, aggression, and delinquency. Overall, CU traits were less strongly associated with conduct problem measures compared to narcissism and impulsivity. Furthermore, they generally showed similar associations with aggression and delinquency compared to the other dimensions. However, CU traits seemed to be most useful in designating a distinct group of more severely aggressive and violent antisocial youth (Enebrink, Anderson, & Langstrom, 2005; Frick, Cornell, Barry, Bodin, & Dane, 2003; Kruh, Frick, & Clements, 2005), who initiated their delinquency at an earlier age (Christian et al., 1997; Frick, Stickle, Dandreaux, Farrell, & Kimonis, 2005; Silverthorn, Frick, & Reynolds, 2001), who were at increased risk for future offending (Pardini, Obradović, & Loeber, 2006; Salekin, Ziegler, Larrea, Anthony, & Bennett, 2003), and who showed a more stable pattern of offending (Frick et al., 2005).

One finding that strongly suggests antisocial youth with CU traits may also have an etiology distinct from other antisocial youth comes from a large (*N* = 3,687 twin pairs) twin study by Viding, Blair, Moffitt, and Plomin (2005). These authors selected 7-year-old twins who were elevated on a measure of conduct problems, and further divided them into groups that were high and low on CU traits. Overall, the heritability for the high conduct problem group was substantial (.68), but the estimate was very different for those high on CU traits (.81) and low on CU traits (.30). These findings were replicated in the same sample 2 years later at age 9 (Viding, Jones, Frick, Moffitt, & Plomin, 2008). Importantly, these studies indicated that the differences in heritability could not be attributed to differences in either the severity of conduct problems (Viding et al., 2005) or the level of impulsivity (Viding et al., 2008).

Although the results of this large twin study provide strong support for the contention that distinct causal factors are operating for the two groups of youth with conduct problems, they do not provide clues as to what specific causal processes may be operating for the two groups. In the next section, we review findings showing several distinct emotional, cognitive, and familial characteristics of antisocial youth with CU traits that could inform such etiological models.

Distinct Emotional, Cognitive, and Familial Characteristics of Antisocial Youth with CU Traits

Emotional Reactivity and CU Traits in Youth

A consistent finding in research with adults with psychopathic traits is that they show a number of deficits in how they process emotional stimuli (Levenston, Patrick, Bradley, & Lang, 2000; Patrick, 1994; Patrick, Bradley, & Lang, 1993; Williamson, Harpur, & Hare, 1991). Specifically, using several different types of laboratory paradigms to assess emotional reactivity, these studies all demonstrated that individuals scoring high on psychopathic traits generally showed no differences from other antisocial individuals in how they process positive emotional stimuli, but they showed consistent deficits in how they process negative emotional stimuli. Based on this research, deficits in the processing of negative emotional stimuli have been critical to many etiological theories of psychopathy (Hare, 1998; Lykken, 1995; Patrick, 2007).

Importantly, similar emotional processing deficits have also been found in samples of youth with CU traits, when these traits are either assessed alone or with other dimensions of psychopathy. For example, Blair (1999) reported that boys (ages 8–17) with CU traits were significantly less responsive to distress cues in pictures, but not threatening cues, than other boys with behavioral problems and community controls. Similar findings were reported by Sharp, Van Goozen, and Goodyer (2006), who studied 659 nonreferred children (ages 7–11) and reported that youth scoring high on a measure that included CU traits self-reported less arousal to pictures with unpleasant, but not pleasant, content. Kimonis, Frick, Fazekas, and Loney (2006) reported similar findings that nonreferred boys and girls (ages 6–13) with CU traits showed deficits in their processing of pictures with distress cues but not of pictures with positive emotional content. However, this was true only for youth who also scored high on conduct problems. Also, youth who scored high on conduct problems but low on CU traits showed an enhanced orienting response to distressing pictures. This finding was replicated in a sample of 88 detained adolescent (ages 13–18) boys (Kimonis, Frick, Muñoz, & Aucoin, 2008).

Finally, in one study assessing emotional reactivity, Loney, Frick Clements, Ellis, and Kerlin (2003) examined the relationship between CU traits and cognitive orienting responses to negative, positive, and neutral stimuli in a sample of 60 adolescent boys (ages 12–18) with criminal involvement, referred to a day treatment program. These authors used the emotional lexical decision paradigm that has been used to assess emotional deficits in adults with psychopathy (Kiehl et al., 2004; Williamson et al., 1991). In this task, participants are required to indicate whether or not a string of letters forms a real word. The response speed in recognizing words of emotional and nonemotional content was compared. As in previous studies, there were no associations between level of CU traits and processing of words with positive emotional content. However, CU traits were negatively associated with the speed of processing words of negative emotional content, indicating less facilitation in participants' speed of recognition. Interestingly, this was one of the few studies to test the specificity of the association to the CU dimension of psychopathy. The results suggested that the deficits were not associated with the impulsivity and narcissism dimensions. Furthermore, and consistent with findings in adults (Williamson et al., 1991), there was no association between level of CU traits and youth ratings of the emotional content of the words, suggesting that the emotional deficits were largely confined to the degree of reactivity to the emotional content and were not apparent in participants' recognition of the emotional content of words.

Thus, all these studies converge to suggest that youth with CU traits show deficits in their reactivity to certain types of emotional stimuli. Furthermore, this deficit is not found in relation to positive emotional stimuli, and it seems to be most evident in response to stimuli depicting distress in others. Finally, the results of Loney and colleagues (2003) suggest that these emotional deficits may not be apparent in tasks that assess the child's ability to recognize emotions. However, several studies have documented at least some types of deficits in emotional recognition in youth with CU traits.

Emotional Recognition and CU Traits in Youth

Blair and Coles (2000) studied a community sample of older children (ages 11–14). Participants in this study were shown a series of human faces depicting various emotions (e.g., happiness, anger, fear, sadness, and disgust) and asked to identify the emotion being displayed. CU traits were associated with the number of errors in identifying sad and fearful expressions. These results were replicated in a clinic-referred sample of boys (Stevens, Charman, & Blair, 2001), and using vocal tones as opposed to facial expressions (Blair, Budhani, Colledge, & Scott, 2005). Furthermore, Blair, Colledge, Murray, and Mitchell (2001) found that, on a task that asked participants to identify the emotional expression as quickly as possible as the face gradually came into focus, boys (ages 9 to 17) with CU traits were significantly slower to recognize sad and fearful expressions.

Dadds, El Masry, Wimalaweera, and Guastella (2008) and Dadds and colleagues (2006) also studied emotional recognition in samples of boys (ages 8–15). Similar to other emotional recognition tasks, participants were required to distinguish happiness, sadness, anger, disgust, fear, or neutral facial expressions. As in past studies, youth scoring high on CU traits made more errors in recognizing fearful facial expression but not other emotions. However, the deficit did not appear when participants were instructed to attend to the eyes of the faces, but it became significant again when participants were asked to attend to mouths. The results were extended when Dadds and colleagues (2008) documented that youth with CU traits naturally focus less on the eyes in facial expressions compared to youth scoring low on CU traits, which could account for their deficits in identifying fear in others.

Taken together, these studies suggest that children with CU traits may have difficulties recognizing certain emotions. As was the case with emotional reactivity, the deficit does not appear to be generalized to all emotions but instead seems to be specific to distress or fear in others. Furthermore, the results of Dadds and colleagues (2006) suggest that this may be due to a skills deficit (e.g., lack of attention to eyes) that can be altered under certain instruction sets. However, it is difficult to reconcile these findings of deficits in emotional recognition with the findings of Loney and colleagues (2003) and findings from adults (Williamson et al., 1991) in which youth with CU traits or adults with psychopathic traits showed deficits in emotional reactivity but not emotional recognition. It could be that the deficits in recognition are only apparent on tasks involving human faces, whereas the stimuli used by Loney and colleagues involved emotional words. Alternatively, the studies that assessed recognition deficits generally included younger children, and it may be that over the course of development, youth with CU traits learn to overcome any deficits in emotional recognition. Thus, while it is clear that youth with CU traits experience deficits in the processing of certain emotional stimuli, the type and pervasiveness of these deficits require further testing.

Cognitive Characteristics of CU Traits in Youth

Although many causal models for psychopathy in adults focus on potential emotional deficits, one proposed major alternative model focuses on neurocognitive deficits (Newman & Schmitt, 1998). Early studies suggested that psychopathic prisoners may have deficits in their responsiveness to punishment cues (Schmauk, 1970). However, later studies suggested that this deficit was only found under conditions in which a previously rewarded response was punished (Newman, Patterson, & Kosson, 1987). There is evidence that youth with CU traits also show differences in their responsivity to rewards and punishments compared to other antisocial youth.

For example, several studies have shown that children who score high on CU traits show less responsivity to punishment once a reward-oriented response set is established (Barry et al., 2000; Fisher & Blair 1998). To explore these deficits to punishment contingencies further in youth with CU traits, Blair, Colledge, and Mitchell (2001) utilized a task in which four decks of cards were available for play, with two decks having greater rewards combined with greater punishment (for a net loss), and two having lesser rewards and lesser punishments (for a net gain). The boys with CU traits were significantly less likely than boys without psychopathic traits to avoid the risky packs of cards. In a second task, participants were required to make discriminations between sets of shapes and lines. The task required both intradimensional and extradimensional discrimination shifts, and immediate feedback was given after each trial. Contrary to expectations, the boys with CU traits did no worse than other boys. The authors contended that the immediate and clear feedback in the second task, compared to the subtle feedback of the card-playing task, was responsible for the differences in results.

In an effort to investigate sensitivity to reward and punishment displayed by youth with CU traits in social settings, Pardini, Lochman, and Frick (2003) studied detained adolescents' (ages 11–18) responses to eight vignettes depicting peers involved in aggressive acts in various age-appropriate social contexts. Youth were asked how likely and how important were various possible outcomes to the aggressive interpersonal situations. In this ethnically diverse sample of boys and girls, CU traits were associated with responses indicating a tendency to emphasize the positive and rewarding aspects of aggression, to value the importance of being dominant in aggressive interactions, and to minimize the potential of punishment for being aggressive.

Another type of cognitive deficit that has been investigated in youth with CU traits focuses on moral reasoning. Blair and colleagues (Blair, Monson, & Frederickson, 2001; Fisher & Blair, 1998) found that youth with higher levels of CU traits were less likely to distinguish correctly between actions that are wrong given only a certain context (conventional) and actions that are always wrong (moral). Youth with high levels of CU traits recognized that certain behaviors were against the rules and could result in punishment, but they did not view behaviors as wrong because of the potential harm to others.

One final difference in cognitive functioning between youth with CU traits and other antisocial youth is in the area of intelligence. Specifically, there is some evidence that antisocial youth with CU traits show less impairment in intelligence, particularly in the area of Verbal IQ, than other antisocial youth (Loney, Frick, Ellis, & McCoy, 1998; Salekin, Neumann, Leistico, & Zalot, 2004). Interestingly, Muñoz, Frick, Kimonis, and Aucoin (2008) did not find that detained adolescents (ages 13–18) with CU traits showed higher Verbal IQ scores than those scoring low on these traits. However, they did report that Verbal IQ was negatively associated with violent delinquency in youth scoring low on CU traits but positively associated with violent delinquency in youth scoring high on CU traits.

Taken together, these studies have documented a number of cognitive differences between antisocial youth with and without significant levels of CU traits. Specifically, youth scoring high on CU traits seem less sensitive to cues for punishment when a reward-dominant response set is primed; they have difficulties in making age-appropriate moral distinctions; they tend to emphasize the positive and rewarding aspects of aggressive behavior; and they do not consistently show the same level of verbal deficits as other antisocial youth.

Dysfunctional Parenting and CU Traits in Youth

Failure in parental socialization is a central component of most theories developed to explain the etiology of conduct problems (e.g., Patterson, Reid, & Dishion, 1992), and ineffective parenting strategies have been linked repeatedly to the development of antisocial behavior in a large number of studies (Frick, 1998; Loeber & Stouthamer-Loeber, 1986). However, there is evidence to suggest that the association between conduct problems and dysfunctional parenting practices may be different for youth with and without CU traits. Wootton, Frick, Shelton, and Silverthorn (1997) studied a sample of both nonreferred and clinic-referred youth, ages 6–13. They studied the dimensions of parenting that have most consistently been related to conduct problems and delinquency in past research (Shelton, Frick, & Wootton, 1996): low parental involvement, failure to use positive reinforcement, poor monitoring and supervision, inconsistent discipline, and use of corporal punishment. They reported that a composite of these dysfunctional parenting practices showed an interaction with CU traits in predicting conduct problems in this preadolescent sample. Specifically, these ineffective parenting strategies were strongly related to conduct problems in children without these traits, but unrelated to conduct problems in children high on CU traits.

These findings have been replicated in several different samples. Oxford, Cavell, and Hughes (2003) found a similar interaction between CU traits and ineffective parenting for predicting conduct problems in a sample of 243 second- and third-grade students recruited for a program designed to prevent later substance abuse and delinquency. Hipwell and colleagues (2007) also replicated this interaction in a large (N = 990) sample of young girls (ages 7–8). Specifically, a measure of harsh parenting was highly (r = .47) related to conduct problems in girls scoring low on CU traits but only moderately related (r = .33) in girls with moderate CU traits, and weakly related (r = .19) in girls scoring high on CU traits. Finally, Edens, Skopp, and Cahill (2008) reported that harsh and inconsistent discipline was associated with more conduct problems, but only in adolescents scoring low on CU traits in a sample of 76 juvenile offenders (mean age 15.63). Interestingly, Edens and colleagues specifically tested whether this moderation of the association between parenting and conduct problems was due to the CU dimension, or whether other dimensions of psychopathy also showed this effect, and they found that the moderation effect was found only for the CU dimension.

Thus, there is now relatively consistent evidence to suggest that conduct problems are more strongly related to many types of ineffective parenting practices in the absence of CU traits. It is important to note, however, that these findings should not be interpreted to suggest that other parenting dimensions, or other factors within the family context, may not be related to conduct problems in youth with CU traits. It is possible that the dimensions of parenting studied in this body of research (i.e., methods of parental socialization) are less related to conduct problems in youth with CU traits, but that other aspects of parenting (e.g., the parent–child relationship) could still play an important role in the development and maintenance of conduct problems in these youth (Fowles & Kochanska, 2000; Lynam, Loeber, & Stouthamer-Loeber, 2008; Robison, Frick, & Morris, 2005). Furthermore, these findings do not necessarily suggest that parental socialization practices may not influence the onset or stability of the CU traits themselves. For example, Frick, Kimonis, Dandreaux, and Farrell (2003) found that more effective parental socialization practices were related to a decrease in the level of CU traits in children over a 4-year study period.

Implications for Causal Models of Antisocial Youth with CU Traits

This review suggests that a growing body of research indicates that a number of emotional, cognitive, and family factors differ in antisocial youth with and without CU traits. Although some of the studies used measures that included CU traits with other dimensions of psychopathy (i.e., narcissism and impulsivity), the few studies that directly compared the different dimensions support the contention that the CU dimension is most important for designating a distinct group of antisocial youth. The next important step is to develop causal models that use this research to explain the developmental processes involved in the etiology of these traits, and/or the antisocial and aggressive behavior displayed by youth with them. Several initial attempts to integrate research on the normal development of empathy, guilt, and other aspects of conscience, and research on characteristics of antisocial youth with CU traits show promise for advancing these causal models.

Temperament and Conscience Development

Many of the characteristics of youth with CU traits closely resemble a temperament that has been described as behaviorally uninhibited or fearless (Frick & Morris, 2004; Pardini, 2006). For example, Kagan, Reznik, and Snidman (1988) define *behaviorally inhibited children* as being shy, quiet, timid, and skittish in unfamiliar settings, while *behaviorally uninhibited children* are sociable, talkative, and affectively spontaneous in novel situations and when exposed to new people. Furthermore, uninhibited children tend to seek out novel and dangerous activities, and show less physiological arousal to unfamiliar people and circumstances. Similarly, Rothbart (1981) has identified a similar temperamental dimension referred to as "fearfulness." Originally conceptualized as "approach" by Thomas, Chess, Birch, Hertzig, and Korn (1963), this dimension deals with reactions to novel or intense stimuli, with children falling on a continuum between low reaction to novel stimuli (fearless temperament) and high reaction to novel stimuli (fearful temperament). Many of these characteristics of behaviorally uninhibited and fearless children are quite consistent with some of the emotional and cognitive characteristics identified in youth with CU traits.

Importantly, there is also evidence that children with this uninhibited or fearless temperament score lower on measures of conscience development (Asendorpf & Nunner-Winkler, 1992; Kochanska, DeVet, Goldman, Murray, & Putnam, 1994; Kochanska, Gross, Lin, & Nichols, 2002). This association is found when the temperament is rated by behavioral measures of fearful inhibitions (e.g., avoidance of novel, strange, or threatening stimuli) and by psychophysiological indexes of reactivity to threatening stimuli (Fowles & Kochanska, 2000). Furthermore, this link has also been documented in prospective studies, with a measure of fearlessness in toddlers predicting parent ratings of guilt and shame at ages 6 and 7 (Rothbart, Ahadi, & Hershey, 1994).

Based on these findings, Kochanska (1993) proposed a theory to explain how behaviorally inhibited and behaviorally uninhibited temperaments can influence the development of conscience. She proposed that the anxiety and discomforting arousal that follow wrongdoing and punishment are integral in the development of an internal system that functions to inhibit misbehavior, even in the absence of the punishing agent. Kochanska (1991) labeled the negative arousal prompted by prohibited behaviors as *deviation anxiety.* To avoid experiencing this deviation anxiety, children learn to adopt the behaviors deemed appropriate by major socializing agents, such as parents and teachers. Kochanska (1993) proposed that behaviorally inhibited children are predisposed to experience higher rates of this deviation anxiety, whereas fearless and behaviorally uninhibited children are not. Thus, the low-level arousal may impede conscience development. Dadds and Salmon (2003) proposed a similar model that also focused on the child's responsiveness to parental socialization attempts and, in particular, sensitivity to punishment.

Several findings support this emphasis on differences in the child's responsivity to rewards and punishment for understanding the development of CU traits and explaining severe and stable pattern of antisocial and aggressive behavior. First, Kochanska (1995, 1997; Fowles & Kochanska, 2000) demonstrated that relatively fearless children did not show enhanced conscience development when they were exposed to mild, consistent, and low-power assertive parenting that was most effective for other children (Fowles & Kochanska, 2000; Kochanska, 1995, 1997). Presumably, such parenting measures did not result in the level of deviation arousal that would be necessary to internalize parental norms. Second, in a sample of 169 detained adolescents (ages 11–18), Pardini (2006) reported that scores on a measure of fearlessness were correlated with a measure of CU traits, but this association was mediated by a measure of punishment insensitivity. Furthermore, the associations of both fearless temperament and punishment insensitivity with violent delinquency were mediated by the youth levels of CU traits. Third, Hawes and Dadds (2005) studied the effectiveness of a parenting intervention for boys, ages 4–9, referred to a mental health clinic for conduct problems. They reported that children with CU traits showed a less overall positive response to this treatment than other children with conduct problems. However, this differential effectiveness was not consistently found across all phases of the treatment; that is, children with and without CU traits seemed to respond equally well to the first part of the intervention that focused on teaching methods of using positive reinforcement to parents to encourage prosocial behavior. In contrast, the group with CU traits did not show added improvement with the second part of the intervention that focused on teaching parents more effective punishment strategies.

Blair and colleagues (Blair, 1995; Blair, Colledge, Murray, et al., 2001; Blair, Jones, Clark, & Smith, 1997) have also proposed a theoretical model focusing more specifically on the development of empathetic concern in response to the distress in others. They suggest that humans are biologically prepared to respond to distress cues in others with increased autonomic activity, in what they have labeled the violence inhibition mechanism (VIM). This negative emotional response develops before the infant or toddler is cognitively able to take the perspective of others, such as when a young child becomes upset in response to the cries of another child (Blair, 1995). According to this model, these early negative emotional responses to the distress of others become conditioned to behaviors in the child that lead to distress in others. Through a process of conditioning, the child learns to inhibit such behaviors as a way of avoiding this negative arousal. Children with the behaviorally uninhibited temperament may not experience this negative arousal and, as a result, do not experience this conditioning.

Temperament and Parenting Interactions in the Development of Conscience

All of these models suggest possible developmental mechanisms to explain why children with a behaviorally uninhibited temperament may be at increased risk for problems in conscience development. These theories all could be important for understanding the development of CU traits, conceptualized as a severe deficit in conscience. However, such models are not meant to imply that all children with a fearless and uninhibited temperament will have problems in their conscience development. Instead, understanding both the normative processes involved in conscience development and how they may go awry in some youth can provide the basis for possible protective mechanisms that could enhance development in temperamentally at-risk youth.

For example, Kochanska (1997; Kochanska & Murray, 2000) proposed that the parent–child relationship, especially responsiveness toward each other, may be the more critical socialization component for uninhibited children. This aspect of parenting does not rely on punishment-related arousal for internalization, and instead focuses on the positive qualities of the parent–child relationship (Kochanska & Murray, 2000). In support of this proposal, attachment security was shown to be predictive of conscience development in temperamentally fearless children (Kochanska, 1995, 1997).

Cornell and Frick (2007) specifically tested several interactions between behavioral inhibition and parenting in predicting scores on measures of guilt and empathy in young (ages 3–5 years) children; that is, these authors studied preschool children nominated by their teachers as being highly behaviorally inhibited or highly uninhibited. These temperamental categories showed two interactions with parenting in predicting measures of parent-rated guilt and empathy. First, there was an interaction with parental consistency in discipline, such that children who were behaviorally inhibited showed higher levels of guilt, irrespective of the consistency of parenting. However, uninhibited children showed higher levels of guilt only when parental consistency was high. Second, there was an interaction between authoritarian parenting (i.e., use of strong, rule- and obedience-oriented parenting), such that authoritarian parenting was unrelated to parent ratings of guilt in behaviorally inhibited children but positively related to levels of guilt in uninhibited children. The authors interpreted these findings to suggest that behaviorally inhibited children are predisposed to develop appropriate levels of guilt and often do so, even with less than optimal parenting. However, behaviorally uninhibited children require stronger and more consistent parenting to develop appropriate levels of guilt.

Summary and Conclusions

In summary, there is a rather substantial body of research to suggest that CU traits are important for designating an important subgroup of antisocial, aggressive, conduct disordered, or delinquent youth. The subgroup with high levels of CU traits shows an especially severe, aggressive, and chronic pattern of antisocial behavior. Furthermore, these youth show a number of distinct emotional, cognitive, and familial characteristics compared to other antisocial youth that provide some clues as to the unique causal processes that may underlie their antisocial behavior. Finally, many of these characteristics of antisocial youth with CU traits are very similar to those displayed by adults with psychopathic traits.

However, it is important to note that this link between CU traits in youth and psychopathy in adults needs to be made very cautiously for a number of reasons. First, the term *psychopath* has quite pejorative connotations and could thus be quite stigmatizing to a child or adolescent (Murrie, Boccaccini, McCoy, & Cornell, 2007), and be used to justify legal decisions (e.g., transfer of a juvenile to adult court) that have serious consequences to the youth (Seagrave & Grisso, 2002). Second, one of the reasons for the pejorative connotations is the fact that the construct of psychopathy is often associated with lack of amenability to treatment, despite the fact that there is research to suggest otherwise (Salekin, 2002). Third, only a few published studies have followed youth with CU traits into adulthood to estimate the actual degree of stability of the construct over an extended period of time (Burke, Loeber, & Lahey, 2007; Lynam, Caspi, Moffitt, Loeber, & Stouthamer-Loeber, 2007). The results of these studies suggest that, consistent with other personality traits, there is some level of stability in CU traits from childhood to adulthood. However, the amount variance in adult measures accounted for by child measures is rather small (e.g., < 10%).

Rather than viewing the limited stability as a problem with the construct in youth (e.g., Seagrave & Grisso, 2002), we view this finding as an important reason for studying it in youth. Such instability allows for the testing of factors that can either enhance the stability or contribute to its desistance. For example, Frick, Kimonis, and colleagues (2003) studied the 4-year stability of CU traits in older children transitioning into high school. They documented relatively strong stability over this developmental period and noted that it was especially rare for youth low on CU traits to develop high levels of these traits during this developmental period. However, a significant number of youth showed a substantial decrease in their rate of CU traits (see Lynam et al., 2007, for a similar pattern). Importantly, lower level of conduct problems, higher socioeconomic status, and more effective parenting practices all were predictors of a decrease in CU traits over time.

More studies that investigate factors associated with desistance in these traits over time could be very important for guiding the development of more effective treatments for youth with CU traits. Unfortunately, there have been very few tests of treatments directly targeting youth with CU traits, as reviewed elsewhere in this book (Salekin, Chapter 14). However, understanding which factors might be involved in the development of the antisocial and aggressive behavior displayed by youth with CU traits, and how these factors differ from the causal processes operating for other antisocial youth, could help in the design of more effective interventions. Specifically, such research could be critical for guiding interventions that can be tailored to the unique needs of the different subgroups of antisocial youth (Frick, 2006).

Even more importantly, studying the different developmental trajectories of various subgroups of youth who eventually become highly antisocial and aggressive may be very important for prevention efforts. In this chapter, we have tried to link research on CU traits with research on the normal development of empathy, guilt, and other aspects of conscience. We framed this research as being critical for causal models by providing clues to potential manifestations of these traits earlier in development, and by determining how temperamental and contextual factors are involved in both the normal and abnormal development of conscience. However, such findings could also be critical for designing more effective prevention programs that foster prosocial development in children at risk for problems, before their behavior causes problems for themselves and others in their environment.

Clearly, much more work is needed to understand more fully the causal processes leading to antisocial behavior in different subgroups of youth. However, by defining potentially more etiologically homogenous subgroups of antisocial youth, CU traits could be critical for guiding future studies in this area. We have focused in this chapter on some of the unique emotional, cognitive, and familial characteristics of youth with and without CU traits. However, evidence also indicates that there may be distinct neurological correlates to the two groups, as reviewed in another chapter in this book (Blair, Chapter 7) and in other publications (Blair, Mitchell, & Blair, 2005). For example, there are several lines of both direct and indirect evidence that deficits in amygdala functioning could be implicated in some of the deficits exhibited by youth scoring high on CU traits (see Blair, Mitchell, et al., 2005). First, in terms of indirect evidence, individuals with damage to the amygdala have difficulty identifying emotions in others, particularly fear and distress (Davis & Whalen, 2001). Furthermore, this damage specifically impairs a person's ability to interpret emotions based on looking at the eyes of others (Whalen et al., 2004). Thus, these deficits are very similar to those found in youth with CU traits (e.g., Dadds et al., 2006, 2008). More direct evidence comes from brain imaging studies showing lower levels of activation in the amygdala of youth with CU traits, while exposed to fearful facial expressions (Deeley et al., 2006; Marsh et al., 2008). Also, boys who score high on CU traits show differences in both their resting (Loney, Butler, Lima, Counts, & Eckel, 2006) and stress-induced (O'Leary, Loney, & Eckel, 2007) levels of cortisol, a hormone related to stress and emotional reactivity. Cortisol indexes activity in the hypothalamic–pituitary–adrenal axis, which is also linked to amygdalar functioning.

Thus, the research clearly suggests that the presence of CU traits designates a distinct group of antisocial youth who differ behaviorally, emotionally, cognitively, and neurologically from other antisocial youth. As a result, CU traits should be an important part of causal theories of antisocial and aggressive behavior in youth, and some method of subtyping youth using these traits should be considered in the design of future studies of antisocial and aggressive behavior. Furthermore, this method of subtyping antisocial youth could provide an important link to conceptualizations of adult psychopathy and allow this research on youth to be informed by the decades of research on this construct in adult samples.

References

American Psychiatric Association. (2000). *Diagnostic and statistical manual of mental disorders* (4th ed., text rev.). Washington, DC: Author.

Asendorpf, J. B., & Nunner-Winkler, G. (1992). Children's moral motive strength and temperamental inhibition reduce their immoral behavior in real moral conflicts. *Child Development, 63,* 1223–1235.

Barry, C. T., Frick, P. J., DeShazo, T. M., McCoy, M., Ellis, M., & Loney, B. R. (2000). The importance of callous–unemotional traits for extending the concept of psychopathy to children. *Journal of Abnormal Psychology, 109,* 335–340.

Blair, R. J. R. (1995). A cognitive developmental approach to morality: Investigating the psychopath. *Cognition, 57,* 1–29.

Blair, R. J. R. (1999). Responsiveness to distress cues in the child with psychopathic tendencies. *Personality and Individual Differences, 27,* 135–145.

Blair, R. J. R., Budhani, S., Colledge, E., & Scott, S. (2005). Deafness to fear in boys with psychopathic tendencies. *Journal of Child Psychology and Psychiatry, 46,* 327–336.

Blair, R. J. R., & Coles, M. (2000). Expression recognition and behavioural problems in early adolescence. *Cognitive Development, 15,* 421–434.

Blair, R. J. R., Colledge, E., & Mitchell, D. G. V. (2001). Somatic markers and response reversal: Is there orbitofrontal cortex dysfunction in boys with psychopathic tendencies? *Journal of Abnormal Child Psychology, 29,* 499–511.

Blair, R. J. R., Colledge, E., Murray, L., & Mitchell, D. V. G. (2001). A selective impairment in the processing of sad and fearful expressions in children with psychopathic tendencies. *Journal of Abnormal Child Psychology, 29,* 491–498.

Blair, R. J. R., Jones, L., Clark, F., & Smith, M. (1997). The psychopathic individual: A lack of responsiveness to distress cues? *Psychophysiology, 34*(2), 192–198.

Blair, R. J. R., Mitchell, D., & Blair, K. (2005). *The psychopath: Emotion and the brain.* Malden, MA: Blackwell.

Blair, R. J. R., Monson, J., & Frederickson, N. (2001). Moral reasoning and conduct problems in children with emotional and behavioural difficulties. *Personality and Individual Differences, 31,* 799–811.

Burke, J. D., Loeber, R., & Lahey, B. B. (2007). Adolescent conduct disorder and interpersonal callousness as predictors of psychopathy in young adults. *Journal of Clinical Child and Adolescent Psychology, 36,* 334–346.

Caputo, A. A., Frick, P. J., & Brodsky, S. L. (1999). Family violence and juvenile sex offending: The potential mediating role of psychopathic traits and negative attitudes towards women. *Criminal Justice and Behavior, 26,* 338–356.

Christian, R. E., Frick, P. J., Hill, N. L., Tyler, L., & Frazer, D. (1997). Psychopathy and conduct problems in children: II. Implications for subtyping children with conduct problems. *Journal of the American Academy of Child and Adolescent Psychiatry, 36,* 233–241.

Cleckley, H. (1976). *The mask of sanity.* St. Louis, MO: Mosby.

Cooke, D. J., & Michie, C. (1997). An item response theory analysis of the Hare Psychopathy Checklist. *Psychological Assessment, 9,* 3–14.

Cooke, D. J., Michie, C., & Hart, S. D. (2006). Facets of clinical psychopathy: Toward clearer measurement. In C. J. Patrick (Ed.), *The handbook of psychopathy* (pp. 91–106). New York: Guilford Press.

Cornell, A. H., & Frick, P. J. (2007). The moderating effects of parenting styles in the association between behavioral inhibition and parent-reported guilt and empathy in preschool children. *Journal of Clinical Child and Adolescent Psychology, 36,* 305–318.

Dadds, M. R., El Masry, Y., Wimalaweera, S., & Guastella, A. J. (2008). Reduced eye gaze explains "fear blindness" in childhood psychopathic traits. *Journal of the American Academy of Child and Adolescent Psychiatry, 47*(4), 455–463.

Dadds, M. R., Perry, Y., Hawes, D. J., Merz, S., Riddell, A. C., Haines, D. H., et al. (2006). Attention to the eyes and fear-recognition deficits in child psychopathy. *British Journal of Psychiatry, 189,* 280–281.

Dadds, M. R., & Salmon, K. (2003). Punishment insensitivity and parenting: Temperament and learning as interacting risks for antisocial behavior. *Clinical Child and Family Psychology Review, 6,* 69–86.

Davis, M., & Whalen, P. J. (2001). The amygdala: Vigilance and emotion. *Molecular Psychiatry, 6,* 13–34.

Deeley, Q., Daly, E., Surguladze, S., Tunstall, N., Mezey, G., Beer, D., et al. (2006). Facial emotion processing in criminal psychopathy. *British Journal of Psychiatry, 189,* 533–539.

Edens, J. F., Campbell, J. S., & Weir, J. M. (2007). Youth psychopathy and criminal recidivism: A meta-analysis of the psychopathy checklist measures. *Law and Human Behavior, 31, 53–75.*

Edens, J. F., Skopp, N. A., & Cahill, M. A. (2008). Psychopathic features moderate the relationship between harsh and inconsistent parental discipline and adolescent antisocial behavior. *Journal of Clinical Child and Adolescent Psychology, 37,* 472–476.

Enebrink, P., Anderson, H., & Langstrom, N. (2005). Callous–unemotional traits are associated with clinical severity in referred boys with conduct problems. *Nordic Journal of Psychiatry, 59,* 431–440.

Fisher, L., & Blair, R. J. R. (1998). Cognitive impairment and its relationship to psychopathic tendencies in children with emotional and behavioral difficulties. *Journal of Abnormal Child Psychology, 26,* 511–519.

Fowles, D. C., & Kochanska, G. (2000). Temperament as a moderator of pathways to conscience in children: The contribution of electrodermal activity. *Psychophysiology, 37,* 788–795.

Frick, P. J. (1998). *Conduct disorders and severe antisocial behavior.* New York: Plenum Press.

Frick, P. J. (2006). Developmental pathways to conduct disorder. *Child and Adolescent Psychiatric Clinics of North America, 15,* 311–331.

Frick, P. J., Cornell, A. H., Barry, C. T., Bodin, S. D., & Dane, H. E. (2003). Callous–unemotional traits and conduct problems in the prediction of conduct problem severity, aggression, and self-report of delinquency. *Journal of Abnormal Child Psychology, 31,* 457–470.

Frick, P. J., & Dickens, C. (2006). Current perspectives on conduct disorder. *Current Psychiatry Reports, 8, 59–72.*

Frick, P. J., Kimonis, E. R., Dandreaux, D. M., & Farrell, J. M. (2003). The 4-year stability of psychopathic traits in non-referred youth. *Behavioral Sciences and the Law, 21,* 713–736.

Frick, P. J., & Marsee, M. A. (2006). Psychopathy and developmental pathways to antisocial behavior in youth. In C. J. Patrick (Ed.), *Handbook of psychopathy* (pp. 353–374). New York: Guilford Press.

Frick, P. J., & Morris, A. S. (2004). Temperament and developmental pathways to conduct problems. *Journal of Clinical Child and Adolescent Psychology, 33,* 54–68.

Frick, P. J., Stickle, T. R., Dandreaux, D. M., Farrell, J. M., & Kimonis, E. R. (2005). Callous–unemotional traits in predicting the severity and stability of conduct problems and delinquency. *Journal of Abnormal Child Psychology, 33,* 471–487.

Frick, P. J., & White, S. F. (2008). The importance of callous–unemotional traits for developmental models of aggressive and antisocial behavior. *Journal of Child Psychology and Psychiatry, 49*(4), 359–375.

Hare, R. D. (1998). The Hare PCL-R: Some issues concerning its use and misuse. *Legal and Criminological Psychology, 3,* 99–119.

Hare, R. D. (1999). *Without conscience: The disturbing world of the psychopaths among us.* New York: Guilford Press.

Hawes, D. J., & Dadds, M. R. (2005). The treatment of conduct problems in children with callous–unemotional traits. *Journal of Consulting and Clinical Psychology, 73,* 737–741.

Hemphill, J. F. (2007). The Hare Psychopathy Checklist and recidivism: Methodological issues and critically evaluating empirical evidence. In H. Herve & J. C. Yuille (Eds.), *The psychopath: Theory, research, and practice* (pp. 141–170). Mahwah, NJ: Erlbaum.

Hipwell, A. E., Pardini, D., Loeber, R., Sembower, M., Keenan, K., & Stouthamer-Loeber, M. (2007). Callous–unemotional behaviors in young girls: Shared and unique effects relative to conduct problems. *Journal of Clinical Child and Adolescent Psychology, 36,* 293–304.

Kagan, J., Reznik, J. S., & Snidman, N. (1988). Biological bases of childhood shyness. *Science, 240,* 167–171.

Kiehl, K. A., Smith, A. M., Mendrek, A., Forster, B. B., Hare, R. D., & Liddle, P. F. (2004). Temporal lobe abnormalities in semantic processing by criminal psychopaths as revealed by functional magnetic resonance imaging. *Psychiatry Research: Neuroimaging, 130,* 297–312.

Kimonis, E. R., Frick, P. J., Fazekas, H., & Loney, B. R. (2006). Psychopathy, aggression, and the emotional processing of emotional stimuli in non-referred girls and boys. *Behavioral Sciences and the Law, 24,* 21–37.

Kimonis, E. R., Frick, P. J., Muñoz, L. C., & Aucoin, K. J. (2008). Callous–unemotional traits and the emotional processing of distress cues in detained boys: Testing the moderating role of aggression, exposure to community violence, and histories of abuse. *Development and Psychopathology, 49*(4), 414–421.

Kochanska, G. (1991). Socialization and temperament in the development of guilt and conscience. *Child Development, 62,* 1379–1392.

Kochanska, G. (1993). Toward a synthesis of parental socialization and child temperament in early development of conscience. *Child Development, 64,* 325–347.

Kochanska, G. (1995). Children's temperament, mother's discipline, and security of attachment: Multiple pathways to emerging internalization. *Child Development, 66,* 597–615.

Kochanska, G. (1997). Multiple pathways to conscience for children with different temperaments: From toddlerhood to age 5. *Developmental Psychology, 33,* 228–240.

Kochanska, G., DeVet, K., Goldman, M., Murray, K., & Putnam, S. P. (1994). Maternal reports of conscience development and temperament in young children. *Child Development, 65,* 852–868.

Kochanska, G., Gross, J. N., Lin, M., & Nichols, K. E. (2002). Guilt in young children: Development, determinants, and relations with a broader system of standards. *Child Development, 73,* 461–482.

Kochanska, G., & Murray K. (2000). Mother–child mutually responsive orientation and conscience development: From toddler to early school age. *Child Development, 71,* 417–431.

Kruh, I. P., Frick, P. J., & Clements, C. B. (2005). Historical and personality correlates to the violence patterns of juveniles tried as adults. *Criminal Justice and Behavior, 32,* 69–96.

Lahey, B. B., Moffitt, T. E., & Caspi, A. (2003). *Causes of conduct disorder and juvenile delinquency.* New York: Guilford Press.

Leistico, A. R., Salekin, R. T., DeCoster, J., & Rogers, R. (2008). A large-scale meta-analysis relating the Hare measures of psychopathy to antisocial conduct. *Law and Human Behavior, 32,* 28–45.

Levenston, G. K., Patrick, C. J., Bradley, M. M., & Lang, P. J. (2000). The psychopath as observer: Emotion and attention in picture processing. *Journal of Abnormal Psychology, 109,* 373–385.

Loeber, R., & Stouthamer-Loeber, M. (1986). Family factors as correlates and predictors of juvenile conduct problems and delinquency. In M. Tonry & N. Morris (Eds.), *Crime and justice* (Vol. 7, pp. 29–149). Chicago: University of Chicago Press.

Loney, B. R., Butler, M. A., Lima, E. N., Counts, C. A., & Eckel, L. A. (2006). The relation between salivary cortisol, callous–unemotional traits, and conduct problems in an adolescent non-referred sample. *Journal of Child Psychology and Psychiatry, 47,* 30–36.

Loney, B. R., Frick, P. J., Clements, C. B., Ellis, M. L., & Kerlin, K. (2003). Callous–unemotional traits, impulsivity, and emotional processing in adolescents with antisocial behavior problems. *Journal of Clinical Child and Adolescent Psychology, 32,* 66–80.

Loney, B. R., Frick, P. J., Ellis, M. L., & McCoy, M. G. (1998). Intelligence, callous–unemotional traits, and antisocial behavior. *Journal of Psychopathology and Behavioral Assessment, 20,* 231–247.

Lykken, D. (1995). *The antisocial personalities.* Hillsdale, NJ: Erlbaum.

Lynam, D. R., Caspi, A., Moffitt, T. E., Loeber, R., & Stouthamer-Loeber, M. (2007). Longitudinal evidence that psychopathy scores in early adolescence predict adult psychopathy. *Journal of Abnormal Psychology, 116,* 155–165.

Lynam, D. R., Loeber, R., & Stouthamer-Loeber, M. (2008). The stability of psychopathy from adolescence into adulthood: The search for moderators. *Criminal Justice and Behavior, 35*(2), 228–243.

Marsh, A. A., Finger, E. C., Mitchell, D. G., Reid, M. E., Sims, C., Kosson, D. S., et al. (2008). Reduced amygdala response to fearful expressions in children and adolescents with callous–unemotional traits and disruptive behavior disorders. *American Journal of Psychiatry, 165,* 712–720.

Muñoz, L. C., Frick, P. J., Kimonis, E. R., & Aucoin, K. J. (2008). Verbal ability and delinquency: Testing the moderating role of psychopathic traits. *Journal of Child Psychology and Psychiatry, 49*(4), 414–421.

Murrie, D. C., Boccaccini, M. T., McCoy, W., & Cornell, D. G. (2007). Diagnostic labeling in juvenile court: How do descriptions of psychopathy and conduct disorder influence judges? *Journal of Clinical Child and Adolescent Psychology, 36,* 228–241.

Newman, J. P., Patterson, M. C., & Kosson, D. S. (1987). Response perseveration in psychopaths. *Journal of Abnormal Psychology, 96,* 145–148.

Newman, J. P., & Schmitt, W. A. (1998). Passive avoidance in psychopathic offenders: A replication and extension. *Journal of Abnormal Psychology, 107,* 527–532.

O'Leary, M. M., Loney, B. R., & Eckel, L. A. (2007). Gender differences in the association between psychopathic personality traits and cortisol response to induced stress. *Psychoneuroendocrinology, 32,* 183–191.

Oxford, M., Cavell, T. A., & Hughes, J. N. (2003). Callous/unemotional traits moderate the relation between ineffective parenting and child externalizing problems: A partial replication and extension. *Journal of Clinical Child and Adolescent Psychology, 32,* 577–585.

Pardini, D. A. (2006). The callousness pathway to severe violent delinquency. *Aggressive Behavior, 32,* 1–9.

Pardini, D. A., Lochman, J. E., & Frick, P. J. (2003). Callous/unemotional traits and social-cognitive processes in adjudicated youths. *Journal of the American Academy of Child and Adolescent Psychiatry, 42,* 364–371.

Pardini, D. A., Obradović, J., & Loeber, R. (2006). Interpersonal callousness, hyperactivity/impulsivity, inattention, and conduct problems as precursors to delinquency persistence in boys: A comparison of three grade-based cohorts. *Journal of Clinical Child and Adolescent Psychology, 35,* 46–59.

Patrick, C. J. (1994). Emotion and psychopathy: Startling new insights. *Psychophysiology, 31,* 319–330.

Patrick, C. J. (2007). Getting to the heart of psychopathy. In H. Herve & J. C. Yuille (Eds.), *The psychopath: Theory, research, and practice* (pp. 207–252). Mahwah, NJ: Erlbaum.

Patrick, C. J., Bradley, M. M., & Lang, P. J. (1993). Emotion in the criminal psychopath: Startle reflex modulation. *Journal of Abnormal Psychology, 102,* 82–92.

Patterson, G. R., Reid, J. B., & Dishion, T. J. (1998). *Antisocial boys.* Eugene, OR: Castalia.

Porter, S., & Woodworth, M. (2006). Psychopathy and aggression. In C. J. Patrick (Ed.), *Handbook of psychopathy* (pp. 481–494). New York: Guilford Press.

Robison, S. D., Frick, P. J., & Morris, A. S. (2005). Temperament and parenting: Implications for understanding developmental pathways to conduct disorder. *Minerva Pediatrica, 57,* 373–388.

Rothbart, M. K. (1981). Measurement of temperament in infancy. *Child Development, 52*(2), 569–578.

Rothbart, M. K., Ahadi, S. A., & Hershey, K. (1994). Temperament and social behavior in childhood. *Merrill–Palmer Quarterly, 40,* 21–39.

Salekin, R. T. (2002). Psychopathy and therapeutic pessimism: Clinical lore or clinical reality? *Clinical Psychology Review, 22,* 79–112.

Salekin, R. T. (2008). Psychopathy and recidivism from mid-adolescence to young adulthood: Cumulating legal problems and limiting life opportunities. *Journal of Abnormal Psychology, 117,* 386–395.

Salekin, R. T., Neumann, C. S., Leistico, A. R., & Zalot, A. A. (2004). Psychopathy in youth and intelligence: An investigation of Cleckley's hypothesis. *Journal of Clinical Child and Adolescent Psychology, 33,* 731–742.

Salekin, R. T., Ziegler, T. A., Larrea, M. A., Anthony, V. L., & Bennett, A. D. (2003). Predicting dangerousness with two Millon Adolescent Clinical Inventory psychopathy scales: The importance of egocentric and callous traits. *Journal of Personality Assessment, 80,* 154–163.

Seagrave, D., & Grisso, T. (2002). Adolescent development and the measurement of juvenile psychopathy. *Law and Human Behavior, 26,* 219–239.

Schmauk, F. J. (1970). Punishment, arousal, and avoidance learning in sociopaths. *Journal of Abnormal Psychology, 76,* 325–335.

Sharp, C., Van Goozen, S., & Goodyer, I. (2006). Children's subjective emotional reactivity to affective pictures: Gender differences and their antisocial correlates in an unselected sample of 7- to 11-year olds. *Journal of Child Psychology and Psychiatry, 47,* 143–150.

Shelton, K. K., Frick, P. J., & Wootton, J. (1996). Assessment of parenting practices in families of elementary school-age children. *Journal of Clinical Child Psychology, 25,* 317–329.

Silverthorn, P., Frick, P. J., & Reynolds, R. (2001). Timing of onset and correlates of severe conduct problems in adjudicated girls and boys. *Journal of Psychopathology and Behavioral Assessment, 23,* 171–181.

Stevens, D., Charman, T., & Blair, R. J. R. (2001). Recognition of emotion in facial expressions and vocal tones in children with psychopathic tendencies. *Journal of Genetic Psychology, 162,* 201–211.

Thomas, A., Chess, S., Birch, H. G., Hertzig, M. E., & Korn, S. (1963). *Behavioral individuality in early childhood.* New York: New York University Press.

Viding, E., Blair, R. J. R., Moffitt, T. E., & Plomin, R. (2005). Evidence for substantial genetic risk for psychopathy in 7-year-olds. *Journal of Child Psychology and Psychiatry, 46,* 1–6.

Viding, E., Jones, A. P., Frick, P. J., Moffitt, T. E., & Plomin, R. (2008). Heritability of antisocial behaviour at age 9: Do callous–unemotional traits matter? *Developmental Science, 11,* 17–22.

Whalen, P. J., Kagan, J., Cook, R. G., Davis, F. C., Kim, H., Polis, S., et al. (2004). Human amygdala responsivity to masked fearful eye whites. *Science, 306,* 2061.

Williamson, S., Harpur, T. J., & Hare, R. D. (1991). Abnormal processing of affective words by psychopaths. *Psychophysiology, 28,* 260–273.

Wootton, J. M., Frick, P. J., Shelton, K. K., & Silverthorn, P. (1997). Ineffective parenting and childhood conduct problems: The moderating role of callous–unemotional traits. *Journal of Consulting and Clinical Psychology, 65,* 301–308.

7

A Cognitive Neuroscience Perspective on Child and Adolescent Psychopathy

R. JAMES R. BLAIR

Our goal in this chapter is to consider child and adolescent psychopathy from the perspective of cognitive neuroscience. As such, the chapter begins with a very brief description of the disorder, particularly those aspects of the classification that confer the greatest potential insights with regard to a cognitive neuroscience–based account. Following this, there is some consideration of the similarities and dissimilarities in the expression of psychopathy in adolescents and adults. Then, dominant models of psychopathy are considered and, in particular, a division is made between the influential attention-based account of Newman (Hiatt & Newman, 2006; MacCoon, Wallace, & Newman, 2004) and the range of emotion-based positions (e.g., Blair, Mitchell, & Blair, 2005; Frick & Marsee, 2006; Kiehl, 2006; Lykken, 1995; Patrick, 1994; Salekin, 2006). The similarities and differences between these emotion-based positions are described. The chapter ends with an elaboration of one of the emotion-based positions: the integrated emotion systems model (Blair, 2004, 2006, 2007).

What Is Psychopathy?

The disorder of *psychopathy* involves at least two core components: emotional dysfunction and antisocial behavior (Frick, 1995; Hare, 1991). However, whether at least a third and fourth dimension should be added is frequently debated (Cooke, Michie, & Hart, 2006; Frick, Bodin, & Barry, 2000; Neumann, Kosson, Forth, & Hare, 2006; Salekin, Brannen, Zalot, Leistico, & Neumann, 2006). Thus, in addition to the emotional dysfunction (i.e., callous–unemotional [CU] traits and reduced guilt, empathy, and attachment to significant others) and antisocial behavior, there is reference in both child and adult samples to an arrogant and deceitful interpersonal style involving narcissism, and conning and manipulative behavior. Others also consider impulsivity to be important. Thus, some have divided the concept of psychopathy into interpersonal and affective components, and impulsive and antisocial components (Hare, 2003).

There are many forms of psychiatric condition, in addition to psychopathy, that significantly increase the risk for antisocial behavior, particularly threat/frustration-based reactive aggression (Blair, in press). Thus, antisocial behavior, per se, is not a unique defining feature of the disorder. However, it should be noted that psychopathy is the only *psychiatric condition* that significantly increases the risk for goal-directed *instrumental* aggression (social and individual variables also increase the risk for instrumental aggression; e.g., lower socioeconomic status and lower IQ). The increased risk for instrumental and reactive aggression in individuals with psychopathic traits has been documented in both child and adult populations (Cornell et al., 1996; Frick, Cornell, Barry, Bodin, & Dane, 2003). Another feature specific to individuals with the disorder relative to other psychiatric conditions and, additionally, other antisocial individuals, is the emotional dysfunction, the CU traits (Cooke & Michie, 1997).

The disorder is developmental. Recent work has confirmed the stability of CU traits in particular and the disorder more generally from childhood into adulthood. Thus, CU traits have been shown to be relatively stable from late childhood to early adolescence (Frick, Kimonis, Dandreaux, & Farrell, 2003; Lynam, Caspi, Moffitt, Loeber, & Stouthamer-Loeber, 2007; Muñoz & Frick, 2007; Obradović, Pardini, Long, & Loeber, 2007). Moreover, CU traits indexed in clinic-referred boys ages 7–12 have been shown to predict adult measures of psychopathy at ages 18–19 (Burke, Loeber, & Lahey, 2007). Similarly, Lynam and colleagues (2007) reported early measures of CU-related traits at age 13 predicted adult measures of psychopathy at age 24.

Comparing Adolescents and Adults with Psychopathy

Direct empirical comparisons between adolescent and adult populations with psychopathy have not been made. This likely reflects the practical difficulties of doing so. Different scales are used to identify psychopathy in adolescent and adult populations. Moreover, there is sufficient debate regarding appropriate cutoff scores on the Psychopathy Checklist—Revised (PCL-R) in adult populations to discourage direct comparisons of adults with adolescents (where no agreed-upon cutoffs for classification have been provided for any of the currently available indices).

However, two strands of data suggest that adolescents and adults with psychopathy can be compared with one another. The first strand is the longitudinal data referred to earlier. CU traits indexed in adolescence predict adult psychopathy (Burke et al., 2007; Lynam et al., 2007) and offending through to adulthood (Salekin, 2008). These data suggest that the syndrome identified by the measures designed for adolescents may be the same syndrome identified by the measures designed for adult populations. The second strand is the neurocognitive data. Some of the core impairments identified in adults with psychopathy are also seen in adolescents with psychopathy (Forth, Kosson, & Hare, 2003). According to some researchers, these include impairments in both auditory (Blair et al., 2002; Blair, Budhani, Colledge, & Scott, 2005) and facial expression recognition (Blair, Colledge, Murray, & Mitchell, 2001; Blair et al., 2004), in extinction (Newman, Patterson, & Kosson, 1987; O'Brien & Frick, 1996), and in reversal learning (Budhani & Blair, 2005; Budhani, Richell, & Blair, 2006). With respect to impairments in expression recognition and aversive conditioning, research appears to suggest some similarities between adolescent and adult populations.

It is notable, however, that the impairment in reversal learning is more pronounced in adult relative to adolescent populations. Reversal learning paradigms in which the contingency change is highly salient (the always-rewarded response becomes the always-punished response) do not reveal any impairment in adolescent populations (Blair, Colledge, & Mitchell, 2001). However, they do reveal impairment in adult populations (Mitchell, Colledge, Leonard, & Blair, 2002). In contrast, reversal learning paradigms in which the contingency change is less salient (in probabilistic reversal learning paradigms) reveal impairment in both adolescent and adult populations (Budhani & Blair, 2005; Budhani et al., 2006).

It is unclear why in some research studies there appear to be greater response reversal impairment in adults with psychopathy than in adolescents with psychopathic tendencies. However, there are several possibilities. First, the adolescent samples may just be less serious cases than the adult populations and more sensitive measures may be needed to reveal the reversal learning impairment. Second, and more interestingly, the potential genetic anomalies associated with psychopathy might affect the development of the amygdala and orbitofrontal cortex independently of one another. Genetic contribution might affect the functioning of the amygdala at an early age but progressively affect the functioning of the orbitofrontal cortex with age. Third, the amygdala and orbitofrontal cortex are massively interconnected (Amaral, Price, Pitkanen, & Carmichael, 1992), and a reduction in afferent input from the amygdala could disrupt the development of orbitofrontal cortex to an increasingly greater degree as development progresses. Animal research does suggest that amygdalar dysfunction leads to aberrant development of the amygdala (Machado, Snyder, Cherry, Lavenex, & Amaral, 2008). Fourth, psychopathy is associated with elevated levels of alcohol and polydrug abuse (Hemphill, Hart, & Hare, 1994). Alcohol and drug-dependent individuals show impairment on measures assessing the functioning of orbitofrontal cortex (Bechara et al., 2001; Rogers & Robbins, 2001). Thus, it is also possible that the apparent developmental effect seen here is simply a consequence of the lifestyle chosen by psychopathic individuals. To distinguish between these possibilities, it will be necessary to compare the careful longitudinal studies that have shown the developmental nature of the classification (Burke et al., 2007; Lynam et al., 2007) with studies that examine age-related changes (or their absence) in neurocognitive performance and the causal factors associated with these changes.

Neurocognitive Models of Psychopathy

There are two main classes of neurocognitive models of psychopathy. The first suggests that psychopathy reflects an attentional impairment (Hiatt & Newman, 2006; MacCoon et al., 2004). The second class suggests that psychopathy reflects a specific form of emotional dysfunction (Blair, Mitchell, et al., 2005; Frick & Marsee, 2006; Kiehl, 2006; Lykken, 1995; Patrick, 1994). These distinct models and their supporting evidence are now briefly described.

Psychopathy: An Attentional Impairment?

Newman and colleagues have provided an influential, attention-based model of psychopathy: the response modulation (RM) hypothesis (Lorenz & Newman, 2002; Newman, 1998; Newman, Brinkley, Lorenz, Hiatt, & MacCoon, 2007). This cognitive model suggests that RM involves "a rapid and relatively automatic, i.e., non-effortful or involuntary shift of attention from the effortful organization and implementation of goal-directed behavior to its evaluation" (Newman, Schmitt, & Voss, 1997, p. 564). This "brief and highly automatic shift of attention ... enables individuals to monitor and, if relevant, use information that is peripheral to their dominant response set; i.e., deliberate focus of attention" (Lorenz & Newman, 2002, p. 92). Within this view, the core impairment with respect to psychopathy is thought to relate to reduced RM. According to this view, "the impulsivity, poor passive avoidance, and emotion-processing deficits of individuals with psychopathy may all be understood as a failure to process the meaning of information that is peripheral or incidental to their deliberate focus of attention"

(Lorenz & Newman, 2002, p. 92). It has been suggested that RM impairment in psychopathy might reflect "a deficit in automatically allocating top down attention" (MacCoon et al., 2004, p. 429). Thus, according to Newman's position, individuals with psychopathy are less able to use top-down attentional mechanisms to shift "automatically to nondominant cues that suggest a more adaptive response" (MacCoon et al., 2004, p. 429).

The RM hypothesis faces difficulties (for a critical review, see Blair & Mitchell, 2009). In particular, it is worth briefly noting that it remains unclear how top-down attentional systems determine which nondominant cues suggest a more adaptive response. As yet the computations driving this automatic shifting have yet to be specified. Moreover, in at least one class of paradigms, individuals with psychopathy have been found to be unimpaired in shifting attention to nondominant cues. These are the attentional set-shifting tasks; for example, the Wisconsin Card Sorting Test and the extradimensional set-shifting component of the intradimensional/extradimensional (ID/ED) task. Individuals with psychopathy, adults and adolescents, show no impairment on these tasks (Blair, Colledge, Murray, et al., 2001; LaPierre, Braun, & Hodgins, 1995; Mitchell et al., 2002).

The RM hypothesis has received considerable attention in work with adults with psychopathy (for reviews, see Hiatt & Newman, 2006; MacCoon et al., 2004). However, it has received rather less attention in child and adolescent populations. In particular, there has been no use of measures that emotion-based models cannot account for (e.g., reduced facilitation for high-frequency words in lexical decision tasks or reduced distraction for spatially distinct distracters in certain forms of Stroop tasks) (Hiatt, Schmitt, & Newman, 2004; Lorenz & Newman, 2002).

There has been work examining performance on two tasks developed by Newman and colleagues: the passive avoidance task (Newman & Kosson, 1986) and the card playing extinction task (Newman et al., 1987). In passive avoidance paradigms, participants must learn to approach (respond to) those stimuli that become associated with reward, and to avoid (not respond to) those stimuli that become associated with punishment (Newman & Kosson, 1986). In the card playing extinction task, participants learn to respond to a card that initially is associated with reward but becomes progressively more associated with punishment (Newman et al., 1987). Adults with psychopathy have repeatedly demonstrated impairment on these tasks; specifically, they fail to learn to avoid the stimuli associated with punishment (Newman & Kosson, 1986; Newman et al., 1987; Newman & Schmitt, 1998) as have adolescents with psychopathic tendencies (Fisher & Blair, 1998; O'Brien & Frick, 1996).

There have been suggestions that data from passive avoidance and extinction paradigms can be considered evidence for an attentional viewpoint (Hiatt & Newman, 2006; MacCoon et al., 2004; Newman et al., 2007). It is argued that "psychopaths appear to have difficulty accommodating secondary or contextual cues that indicate the need to suspend responding and self-evaluate behavior when already engaged in a primary, goal-directed task (Hiatt & Newman, 2006, p. 347). However, it should be noted that these tasks, or very close analogues, have received considerable attention from systems neuroscientists (Ambrogi Lorenzini, Baldi, Bucherelli, Sacchetti, & Tassoni, 1999; Gallagher, McMahan, & Schoenbaum, 1999; Gallagher & Schoenbaum, 1999; Schoenbaum, Chiba, & Gallagher, 1999; Schoenbaum, Nugent, Saddoris, & Setlow, 2002; Schoenbaum & Roesch, 2005). This systems neuroscience work has stressed stimulus–reinforcement learning and relearning, and the importance of the amygdala and orbitofrontal cortex, that is, information compatible with an emotion-based account (see below). This work has not stressed attention and regions critical for attention, such as dorsolateral prefrontal and parietal cortex. One potential limitation is that these findings are based on animal research, and the situation is different in humans. However, functional magnetic resonance imaging (fMRI) work examining passive avoidance learning and operant extinction in adult humans has been highly consistent with this animal literature (see below; Finger et al., 2008; Kosson et al., 2006).

Moreover, it is unclear how such data are compatible with classic models of top-down attentional control in which the RM hypothesis must be based. Attention is the result of the competition for neural representation that occurs when multiple stimuli are present (Desimone & Duncan, 1995; Duncan, 1998). Which stimuli win this competition and are "attended to" is a product of both bottom-up sensory-driven mechanisms (e.g., visual salience) and top-down influences generated outside of sensory cortices (e.g., executive attention). In the passive avoidance and card playing extinction tasks briefly described earlier, there are trials in which the participant receives punishment. However, there are no representational competitors to this punishment information that could suppress its processing. Reward information may have been delivered, but this would have occurred on a previous trial at least several seconds earlier.

In conclusion, the RM hypothesis has received relatively little empirical investigation with adolescent populations. Data suggest that adolescents with psychopathy show no impairment in shifting attention to nondominant cues in one class of paradigms: the attentional set-shifting tasks, such as the extradimensional set-shifting component of the ID/ED task (Blair, Colledge, Murray, et al., 2001). Moreover, data that have been held up as evidence for the RM hypothesis (e.g., from the passive avoidance and card playing extinction paradigms) could be conceptualized as more compatible with emotion-based accounts, which are explained in further detail below. In conclusion, the literature on adolescents with psychopathic tendencies cannot currently be considered to provide strong support for the RM hypothesis.

Emotion Dysfunction in Psychopathy

A variety of researchers have suggested that psychopathy reflects a specific form of emotional dysfunction (Blair, Mitchell, et al., 2005; Frick & Marsee, 2006; Kiehl, 2006; Lykken, 1995; Patrick, 1994; Salekin, 2006). In this section of the chapter, I consider this position and attempt to highlight the slight differences in the various positions. First, I consider positions regarding anatomical impairment. Here Patrick (1994), Blair (e.g., 2003b, 2007), and Kiehl (2006) have articulated distinguishable models. Second, I consider positions regarding the nature of the cognitive impairment.

Emotion Dysfunction at the Anatomical Level

Within this literature, at the anatomical level, there is some support for the notion that the amygdala is dysfunctional (Blair, Mitchell, et al., 2005; Dadds et al., 2006; Kiehl, 2006; Patrick, 1994; Viding, 2004). This potential dysfunction was first proposed by Patrick (1994), and the position has been developed and extended by Blair (2003b, 2007; Blair & Frith, 2000). Specifically, whereas Patrick focused on the role of the amygdala in punishment processing, Blair has argued that (1) not all forms of punishment processing are impaired; (2) the amygdala's role in reward processing may also be compromised; (3) the role for the amygdala in specific aspects of social cognition does not appear impaired in psychopathy; and (4) the impairment should be characterized as an impairment in stimulus reinforcement learning. These issues are expanded below.

It is also possible that there are other deficits; however, the extent to which neural systems other than the amygdala are also implicated remains unclear. Blair and colleagues also suggest a dysfunction in the ventromedial prefrontal cortex (vmPFC) in psychopathy (Blair, 2007; Blair, Mitchell, et al., 2005). In contrast, Kiehl (2006) has implicated a considerably greater variety of structures, including anterior and posterior cingulate, superior temporal cortex, and hippocampus, what he has termed the paralimbic system. fMRI studies involving both adults and adolescents with psychopathic tendencies have begun to show some support for the hypothesis of dysfunctional responding in both the amygdala and vmPFC of adults and adolescents with psychopathic tendencies (e.g., Birbaumer et al., 2005; Finger et al., 2008; Gordon, Baird, & End, 2004; Kiehl et al., 2001; Marsh et al., 2008; Rilling et al., 2007). The importance of the vmPFC is underscored in research with nonhuman primates. Interestingly, a recent study examining reversal learning reported that adolescents with psychopathic tendencies failed to show the reduction in vmPFC activity associated with an unexpected punished response (Finger et al., 2008). This is notable because work with nonhuman primates suggests that the amygdala is not thought to be critical for reversal learning, unlike the vmPFC (see Murray & Izquierdo, 2007). In other words, the reversal learning data suggest that psychopathy may reflect impairment in vmPFC functioning that is independent of, and additional to, amygdalar impairment.

The neuroimaging literature on psychopathy has also suggested anomalous activity in other structures, specifically, the dorsal anterior cingulate cortex (Kiehl et al., 2001), inferior frontal cortex (Gordon et al., 2004), parietal cortex (Marsh et al., 2008), posterior cingulate cortex (Marsh et al., 2008), insula (Birbaumer et al., 2005; Marsh et al., 2008), and caudate (Finger et al., 2008). These findings led to Kiehl's (2006) paralimbic hypothesis. However, there has been a lack of consistency in the results, with only one or two studies reporting atypical activity in each of these regions. Although these results possibly reflect real differences, it is also possible that they reflect stochastic influences and/or reduced input from core regions in the particular task studied. In short, currently the data do not appear to support the degree of impairment that the paralimbic hypothesis suggests.

However, one region identified by Kiehl and neglected until recently by Blair may be important—the superior temporal cortex (STC). Atypical activity in this region was seen in the majority of the fMRI studies cited earlier (Birbaumer et al., 2005; Finger et al., 2008; Kiehl et al., 2001; Marsh et al., 2008). These include the two studies of adolescents with psychopathic tendencies (Finger et al., 2008; Marsh et al., 2008). The STC has considerable reciprocal connections with the amygdala (Amaral et al., 1992); thus, the atypical activity in this region in individuals with psychopathic tendencies may be a consequence of the amygdalar dysfunction. Moreover, the suggestion of STC dysfunction in psychopathy, unlike the evidence for amygdalar and vmPFC dysfunction (see below), remains currently unsubstantiated by neuropsychological findings (therefore, we cannot be sure that they do not simply reflect reduced input from dysfunctional core regions). However, it should be noted that Kiehl and colleagues (2004) observed that adults with psychopathy showed reduced recruitment of right STC when responding to abstract relative to concrete words in the context of a lexical decision task. Due to the nature of the stimuli, these data are unlikely to reflect reciprocal interaction with the amygdala and, if replicated, may suggest STC dysfunction that is independent of amygdalar dysfunction.

Emotion Dysfunction at the Cognitive Level

With respect to the nature of the functional impairment, all of the emotion-based positions agree that the processing of punishment information is disrupted (Blair, Mitchell, et al., 2005; Frick & Marsee, 2006; Kiehl, 2006; Lykken, 1995; Patrick, 1994). There are two core differences in the details, however. First, in contrast to the other emotion positions, Blair (2006; Blair,

Mitchell, et al., 2005) has argued that there are multiple, relatively independent systems that respond to punishment/threat. This suggestion follows arguments generated by systems neuroscience work (Amaral, 2003; Baxter & Murray, 2002). Importantly, the suggestion is that not all of threat/punishment systems are impaired in psychopathy (Blair, 2006; Blair, Mitchell, et al., 2005). The argument has been made that stimulus–reinforcement learning (learning to associate a value with an object) can be distinguished from stimulus–response learning (learning to make a response to gain a reward or avoid a punishment) (Baxter & Murray, 2002). Examples of stimulus–reinforcement learning tasks include aversive conditioning and the passive avoidance task described earlier; the individual learns that the object associated with shock or punishment is bad, and the object associated with reward is good. Examples of stimulus–response tasks include conditional learning paradigms and object discrimination. In these tasks, the individual does not learn that an object is rewarding or punishing. The object may elicit either reward or punishment: Whether it does or not is a function of the *response* made to the object. Importantly, while stimulus–reinforcement learning is reliant on the amygdala, stimulus–response learning does not appear to be (Baxter & Murray, 2002).

Newman challenged early fear dysfunction accounts (Lykken, 1995; Patrick, 1994) by use of *punishment-only* versions of the passive avoidance paradigm, in which individuals must learn to respond to some stimuli (if they do not respond, they are punished) and withhold responses from other stimuli (if they do not withhold, they are punished). Newman (1998) showed that adults with psychopathy failed to show impairment on punishment-only versions of the passive avoidance paradigm despite their notable impairment on the standard version. These data were clearly problematic for the fear dysfunction positions because these positions should predict impairment whenever punishment information needs to be processed. However, there is a substantial difference between the classic passive avoidance paradigm and the punishment-only version. In the classic paradigm, the individual learns to respond to the "good" stimuli and withhold responses to the "bad" stimuli. However, in the punishment-only version, there are no good and bad stimuli to guide responding. Whether one receives punishment or nothing is determined by one's response to the stimulus; one must learn either to respond or to withhold a response to avoid punishment. In short, the punishment-only passive avoidance paradigm is a stimulus–response learning task. As such, Blair has argued it is independent of the amygdalar dysfunction seen in psychopathy.

Second, there is some debate within the literature regarding the extent to which reward processing is disrupted. Some authors have argued that the deficit only implicates punishment information (Frick & Marsee, 2006; Lykken, 1995). However, Blair, Mitchell, and colleagues (2005) believe that stimulus–reward association formation and use is also dysfunctional, just to a lesser extent than stimulus–punishment association formation and use. While there are data suggesting that this view does apply to adults with psychopathy (Blair, Mitchell, et al., 2005; Verona, Patrick, Curtin, Bradley, & Lang, 2004), this view has yet to be substantiated empirically in adolescents with psychopathic tendencies.

The Development of Psychopathy: A Cognitive Neuroscience Approach

While there have been suggestions that psychopathy might be a developmental consequence of early physical/sexual abuse or early neglect (Rutter, 2005), the theme of this chapter argues against this etiological explanation. Considerable work has examined the impact of trauma/extreme stress and threat on development of the brain. Some of this work, whether conducted in humans or other mammalian species, has shown support for the notion that neglect and other stressors increase emotional responsiveness to threatening stimuli (Bremner & Vermetten, 2001; Rauch, Shin, & Phelps, 2006; Rilling et al., 2001). For example, individuals with posttraumatic stress disorder (PTSD), an anxiety disorder that can develop following exposure to extreme threat, is associated with increased amygdalar responses to fearful facial expressions (Rauch et al., 2006). However, some research has shown an opposite effect, reduced amygdalar responses to fearful facial expressions, in both adolescents and adults with psychopathic tendencies (Gordon et al., 2004; Marsh et al., 2008). Moreover, some research has shown that psychopathy may be protective for PTSD and other anxiety disorders (Verona, Patrick, & Joiner, 2001).

In contrast to the suggestion of a social basis, the suggestion of a genetic contribution to the disorder has received considerable support in recent years (Blonigen, Hicks, Krueger, Patrick, & Iacono, 2005; Viding, Blair, Moffitt, & Plomin, 2005). In one of the largest studies, involving around 3,500 twin pairs, CU traits were shown to be strongly heritable (67% heritability) at 7 years (Viding et al., 2005). Unfortunately, however, nothing is yet known about psychopathy at the molecular genetic level. Of course, this situation is likely to change rapidly in the next few years.

A Cognitive Neuroscience Model

The suggestion is that the genetic contribution acts to decrease the functional integrity of the amygdala and vmPFC. Recent research suggests that several genes, including, for example, the serotonin transporter (*5-HTTLPR*) gene, may have polymorphisms associated with decreased amygdalar and vmPFC responsiveness to emotional stimuli (e.g., [LL] homozygotes for *5-HTTLPR*) (Hariri et al., 2002, 2005; Pezawas et al., 2005). However, it should be noted that no studies have yet shown an association between LL homozygosity and CU traits.

As noted earlier, the amygdala is critical for stimulus–reinforcement learning (Baxter & Murray, 2002; Everitt, Cardinal, Parkinson, & Robbins, 2003). Stimulus–reinforcement learning is necessary for aversive conditioning, the augmentation of the startle reflex following the presentation of visual threat primes, and passive avoidance learning. Damage to the amygdala disrupts performance in all three of these measures (Davis & Whalen, 2001; LeDoux, 2007; Schoenbaum & Roesch, 2005). Similarly, psychopathy, at least in adulthood, is associated with impaired performance on all three of these measures (Flor, Birbaumer, Hermann, Ziegler, & Patrick, 2002; Levenston, Patrick, Bradley, & Lang, 2000; Newman & Kosson, 1986). These three indices have received less attention in adolescent populations with respect to psychopathy. However, the literature has long shown that reduced aversive conditioning is associated with a poorer prognosis in adolescent aggressive populations (Raine, Venables, & Williams, 1996). Moreover, there are data showing reduced startle reflex in the context of negative images in adolescent populations with severe behavioral problems (Fairchild, Van Goozen, Stollery, & Goodyer, 2008).

The amygdala is also critically involved in responding to expressions of fearfulness and, to a lesser extent, sadness. Damage to the amygdala particularly disrupts the recognition of fearfulness expressions (Adolphs, 2002), and fMRI studies have revealed amygdalar activation to fearful and, to a lesser extent, sad expressions (Blair, Morris, Frith, Perrett, & Dolan, 1999; Murphy, Nimmo-Smith, & Lawrence, 2003). Psychopathy is also associated with impaired recognition of fearful and sad facial expressions in some studies (for a meta-analytic review, see Marsh & Blair, 2008). Importantly, this impairment is also seen in adolescent samples (Blair, Colledge, Murray, et al., 2001). And, adolescents with conduct disorder and callous–unemotional traits (CD+CU) show reduced amygdalar responses to fearful expressions relative to comparison samples (Marsh et al., 2008). Moreover, it is also seen for fearful vocal affect (Blair, Budhani, et al., 2005), and both adult and adolescent samples show reduced autonomic activity to the distress of others (Aniskiewicz, 1979; Blair, 1999; Blair, Jones, Clark, & Smith, 1997). However, it should be noted that not all studies produce the facial fear result (Wilson, Demetrioff, & Porter, 2008).

Nonetheless, there exists some evidence for this contention, and the suggestion is that expressions of fear and sadness serve as social reinforcers that are particularly important for moral socialization (Blair, 2003a). As such, they allow caregivers to teach the societal valence of objects and actions to the developing individual (Blair, 2003a). This suggestion was at the heart of the earlier violence inhibition mechanism (VIM) model; stimuli associated with the sadness/fear of others, in healthy developing children, are to be avoided (Blair, 1995). A considerable body of work attests to the power of facial expressions to transmit valence information in both humans and other primates (Blair, 2003a; Klinnert, Emde, Butterfield, & Campos, 1987; Mineka & Cook, 1993).

The integrated emotion systems (IES) model (Blair, 2006), an expansion of the VIM model, keeps the basic suggestion of a mechanism necessary for making associations between representations of acts that harm others and the aversive reinforcement of the victim's distress. However, it places this suggestion within a cognitive neuroscience framework; that is, it suggests that this form of stimulus–reinforcement learning is simply one of the types of stimulus–reinforcement learning mediated by the amygdala that is dysfunctional in psychopathy. In short, the suggestion remains that individuals with psychopathy are less able to take advantage of "moral social referencing." They are less likely to learn to avoid actions that might harm others. In line with this, several studies have demonstrated that adolescents with psychopathy (high CU traits) are more difficult to socialize through standard parenting techniques than are comparison adolescents (Oxford, Cavell, & Hughes, 2003; Wootton, Frick, Shelton, & Silverthorn, 1997).

One major extension of the IES model over the earlier VIM position is the suggestion of dysfunction in psychopathy in output systems from the architecture that mediates basic stimulus–reinforcement learning. Specifically, the amygdala is thought to output reinforcement expectancy information to vmPFC, which represents this outcome information by allowing its use for successful decision making (Saddoris, Gallagher, & Schoenbaum, 2005; Schoenbaum & Roesch, 2005). It may be that the functioning of vmPFC is also dysfunctional in psychopathy. Behaviorally, this is expressed as impairment on decision-making tasks reliant on stimulus–reinforcement association information. Such tasks include passive avoidance learning and the differential reward–punishment task. Individuals with psychopathy show impairment on both these tasks (Blair, Leonard, Morton, & Blair, 2006; Newman & Kosson, 1986). fMRI work shows the important role of the amygdala and vmPFC in the successful performance of these tasks (Blair, Marsh, et al., 2006; Kosson et al., 2006).

vmPFC dysfunction is also expressed as impairment on reversal learning tasks. Impairment in reversal learning is seen in both adults and adolescents with psychopathic traits (Budhani & Blair, 2005; Budhani et al., 2006). The vmPFC potentially has two important roles during reversal learning. First, it may play a role in signaling prediction errors in response to errors during the reversal phase (trials in which a previously rewarded response is now punished) (Budhani, Marsh, Pine, & Blair, 2007). The vmPFC does show a significant *reduction* in activity during reversal errors (Budhani et al., 2007) as well as in other paradigms involving reinforcement prediction errors (McClure, Berns, & Montague, 2003; O'Doherty, Dayan, Friston, Critchley, & Dolan, 2003; Yacubian et al., 2006). Recent research shows that adolescents with psychopathy do not show this reduction in activity during reversal errors (Finger et al., 2008).

Second, vmPFC may orchestrate reversal learning by representing the reinforcement associated with the two responses. As the old correct response becomes more frequently punished, the expectancy of reward associated with it decreases. At the same time, the expectancy of reward associated with the now-correct response increases. When the expectancy of reward associated with the now-correct response is greater than the expectancy of reward associated with the old correct response, participants should switch their responding (cf. Hampton, Bossaerts, & O'Doherty, 2006). If vmPFC is dysfunctional, then this representation of reward expectancies is impaired; thus, the switch occurs after more trials and is potentially less permanent; the individual may switch back to the old response because the guide of the outcome representation is deficient.

With respect to the second option, it is interesting to note the behavioral performance of adults with psychopathy on reversal learning paradigms (Budhani et al., 2006). Budhani and colleagues (2006) examined the impact of reward and punishment information on participants' responding on the subsequent trial. In particular, they examined whether (1) having been punished for making an incorrect response, participants shifted away from the incorrect response (lose–shift) or inappropriately stayed with it (lose–stay); and (2) having been rewarded for making the correct response, participants stayed with this correct response on the subsequent trial (win–stay) or inappropriately shifted their response (win–shift).

Adults with psychopathy were as likely as comparison individuals to shift away from a punished incorrect response (data that are again problematic for the undifferentiated punishment-based emotion accounts of psychopathy). These data may suggest appropriate recruitment of dorsomedial and inferior frontal cortex to punished reversal errors (i.e., appropriate recruitment of regions necessary for altering subsequent behavior). However, adults with psychopathy were significantly less likely than comparison individuals to stay with the same response having made a rewarded correct response (i.e., they were more likely to revert to the previously rewarded, now no longer correct, response) (Budhani et al., 2006). If, as suggested earlier, vmPFC is necessary for the representation of outcome expectancies used in response selection, and if vmPFC is dysfunctional in psychopathy, then it would be expected that participants' response selection would be impaired. This should be particularly evident in a situation where the outcome expectancy that guided the successful response had been associated with reward.

It is argued that the vmPFC dysfunction, and particularly the consequent impaired decision making and reversal learning, may relate to the increased frustration-based reactive aggression seen in psychopathy (Blair, 2004). Individuals engage in actions in the expectation of achieving their goals, but because of these impairments, their behavioral choices are suboptimal, leading to aggression, and particularly frustration-based reactive aggression. While this theory accounts for aggression, it is also necessary to start work on theories that deal with the covert behaviors of psychopathic individuals (e.g., theft).

Conclusions

Psychopathy is a developmental disorder that is present by late childhood/ early adolescence and continues to be displayed into adulthood. It is marked, in part, by a specific form of emotion dysfunction; clinically, individuals with the disorder, in adolescence and adulthood, present with reduced guilt and empathy. This emotion dysfunction appears to disrupt significantly the ability of the individual to be socialized and significantly increases the risk that the individual will display heightened levels of antisocial behavior.

With the caveat that less work has been conducted with adolescents with psychopathy, it appears that the impairments seen in adolescents and adults with the disorder may be similar. Impairments in both adolescents and adults with psychopathy are seen in expression recognition, in aversive conditioning, on the emotion lexical decision task, and in extinction (but see other research for alternative opinions; Farrington, Ullrich, & Salekin, Chapter 9, this volume). Impairments in both adolescents and adults with psychopathy are also seen in reversal learning. However, for this impairment to be seen in adolescents with psychopathy, it is necessary to reduce the salience of the contingency change (rather than a switch from always being reinforced for making the response to always being punished for it, the contingency change may involve a switch from an 80% probability of reward for making the response to an 80% probability of punishment for making it). As yet, it remains unclear why adolescents with psychopathy show milder impairment in reversal learning relative to adults with the disorder.

There are two dominant classes of theoretical account of psychopathy: the attention-based response set modulation account and the various emotion-based positions. Few data in support of the response set modulation account have been generated from work with adolescents with the disorder. In particular, there has been no use of measures for which emotion-based models cannot account (e.g., reduced facilitation for high-frequency words in lexical decision tasks or reduced distraction for spatially distinct distracters in certain forms of Stroop tasks) (Hiatt et al., 2004; Lorenz & Newman, 2002). However, considerable data have been generated in support of emotion-based accounts.

The emotion-based positions share notable similarities. For example, all those who have made reference to putative anatomical substrates have assumed that amygdalar dysfunction is part of the condition. In addition, all assume that at least some forms of punishment-based processing are disrupted in psychopathy. There are differences in the details, however. Blair (2007) implicates the amygdala and vmPFC in particular, while Kiehl (2006) implicates considerably more structures. The disruption in punishment processing is confined to the use of punishment information in stimulus–reinforcement learning according to Blair, although such differentiations have not been made by other theorists.

Importantly, the emotion-based positions allow an empirically tractable account of why impairment seen in the disorder should lead to development of the disorder. The last section of this chapter offered one such account: the IES position. The basic suggestion is that reduced processing of social reinforcers related to the distress of others (fearful and sad expressions) coupled with a reduced ability to perform stimulus–reinforcement learning severely compromises the ability of the child to profit from moral socialization. These impairments are a consequence of amygdalar dysfunction. Given amygdalar dysfunction, there will be reduced transmission of reinforcement expectancy information to vmPFC, a region that itself appears dysfunctional in psychopathy. This results in disrupted decision making and impaired reversal learning. Such functional impairments are likely to increase frustration and may contribute to the increased frustration-based reactive aggression seen in individuals with this disorder. However, this theory requires formal testing, and other theoretical models, including RM theory, may also be shown to have support, as research evolves on child and adolescent psychopathy.

Acknowledgments

This research was supported by the Intramural Research Program of the National Institute of Mental Health, National Institutes of Health.

References

Adolphs, R. (2002). Neural systems for recognizing emotion. *Current Opinions in Neurobiology, 12*(2), 169–177.

Amaral, D. G. (2003). The amygdala, social behavior, and danger detection. *Annals of the New York Academy of Sciences, 1000*, 337–347.

Amaral, D. G., Price, J. L., Pitkanen, A., & Carmichael, S. T. (1992). Anatomical organization of the primate amygdaloid complex. In J. P. Aggleton (Ed.), *The amygdala: Neurobiological aspects of emotion, memory, and mental dysfunction* (pp. 1–66). New York: Wiley.

Ambrogi Lorenzini, C. G., Baldi, E., Bucherelli, C., Sacchetti, B., & Tassoni, G. (1999). Neural topography and chronology of memory consolidation: A review of functional inactivation findings. *Neurobiology of Learning and Memory, 71*, 1–18.

Aniskiewicz, A. S. (1979). Autonomic components of vicarious conditioning and psychopathy. *Journal of Clinical Psychology, 35*, 60–67.

Baxter, M. G., & Murray, E. A. (2002). The amygdala and reward. *Nature Reviews Neuroscience, 3*(7), 563–573.

Bechara, A., Dolan, S., Denburg, N., Hindes, A., Anderson, S. W., & Nathan, P. E. (2001). Decision-making deficits, linked to a dysfunctional ventromedial prefrontal cortex, revealed in alcohol and stimulant abusers. *Neuropsychologia, 39*(4), 376–389.

Birbaumer, N., Veit, R., Lotze, M., Erb, M., Hermann, C., Grodd, W., et al. (2005). Deficient fear conditioning in psychopathy: A functional magnetic resonance imaging study. *Archives of General Psychiatry, 62*(7), 799–805.

Blair, K. S., Leonard, A., Morton, J., & Blair, R. J. R. (2006). Impaired decision making on the basis of both reward and punishment information in individuals with psychopathy. *Personality and Individual Differences, 41*, 155–165.

Blair, K. S., Marsh, A. A., Morton, J., Vythilingham, M., Jones, M., Mondillo, K., et al. (2006). Choosing the lesser of two evils, the better of two goods: Specifying the roles of ventromedial prefrontal cortex and dorsal anterior cingulate cortex in object choice. *Journal of Neuroscience, 26*(44), 11379–11386.

Blair, R. J. R. (1995). A cognitive developmental approach to morality: Investigating the psychopath. *Cognition, 57*, 1–29.

Blair, R. J. R. (1999). Responsiveness to distress cues in the child with psychopathic tendencies. *Personality and Individual Differences, 27*, 135–145.

Blair, R. J. R. (2003a). Facial expressions, their communicatory functions and neurocognitive substrates. *Philosophical Transactions of the Royal Society of London B: Biological Sciences, 358*(1431), 561–572.

Blair, R. J. R. (2003b). Neurobiological basis of psychopathy. *British Journal of Psychiatry, 182*, 5–7.

Blair, R. J. R. (2004). The roles of orbital frontal cortex in the modulation of antisocial behavior. *Brain and Cognition, 55*(1), 198–208.

Blair, R. J. R. (2006). The emergence of psychopathy: Implications for the neuropsychological approach to developmental disorders. *Cognition, 101*, 414–442.

Blair, R. J. R. (2007). The amygdala and ventromedial prefrontal cortex in morality and psychopathy. *Trends in Cognitive Sciences, 11*(9), 387–392.

Blair, R. J. (in press). Psychopathy, frustration, and reactive aggression: The role of ventromedial prefrontal cortex. *British Journal of Psychology*.

Blair, R. J. R., Budhani, S., Colledge, E., & Scott, S. (2005). Deafness to fear in boys with psychopathic tendencies. *Journal of Child Psychology and Psychiatry, 46*(3), 327–336.

Blair, R. J. R., Colledge, E., & Mitchell, D. G. (2001). Somatic markers and response reversal: Is there orbitofrontal cortex dysfunction in boys with psychopathic tendencies? *Journal of Abnormal Child Psychology, 29*(6), 499–511.

Blair, R. J. R., Colledge, E., Murray, L., & Mitchell, D. G. (2001). A selective impairment in the processing of sad and fearful expressions in children with psychopathic tendencies. *Journal of Abnormal Child Psychology, 29*(6), 491–498.

Blair, R. J. R., & Frith, U. (2000). Neuro-cognitive explanations of the antisocial personality disorders. *Criminal Behaviour and Mental Health, 10*(4), S66–S82.

Blair, R. J. R., Jones, L., Clark, F., & Smith, M. (1997). The psychopathic individual: A lack of responsiveness to distress cues? *Psychophysiology, 34*, 192–198.

Blair, R. J., & Mitchell, D. G. (2009). Psychopathy, attention and emotion. *Psychological Medicine, 39*(4), 543–555.

Blair, R. J. R., Mitchell, D. G. V., & Blair, K. S. (2005). *The psychopath: Emotion and the brain*. Oxford, UK: Blackwell.

Blair, R. J. R., Mitchell, D. G. V., Colledge, E., Leonard, R. A., Shine, J. H., Murray, L. K., et al. (2004). Reduced sensitivity to other's fearful expressions in psychopathic individuals. *Personality and Individual Differences, 37*, 1111–1121.

Blair, R. J. R., Mitchell, D. G., Richell, R. A., Kelly, S., Leonard, A., Newman, C., et al. (2002). Turning a deaf ear to fear: impaired recognition of vocal affect in psychopathic individuals. *Journal of Abnormal Psychology, 111*(4), 682–686.

Blair, R. J. R., Morris, J. S., Frith, C. D., Perrett, D. I., & Dolan, R. (1999). Dissociable neural responses to facial expressions of sadness and anger. *Brain, 122*, 883–893.

Blonigen, D. M., Hicks, B. M., Krueger, R. F., Patrick, C. J., & Iacono, W. G. (2005). Psychopathic personality traits: heritability and genetic overlap with internalizing and externalizing psychopathology. *Psychological Medicine, 35*, 637–648.

Bremner, J. D., & Vermetten, E. (2001). Stress and development: Behavioral and biological consequences. *Development and Psychopathology, 13*, 473–489.

Budhani, S., & Blair, R. J. (2005). Response reversal and children with psychopathic tendencies: Success is a function of salience of contingency change. *Journal of Child Psychology and Psychiatry, 46*(9), 972–981.

Budhani, S., Marsh, A. A., Pine, D. S., & Blair, R. J. (2007). Neural correlates of response reversal: Considering acquisition. *NeuroImage, 34*(4), 1754–1765.

Budhani, S., Richell, R. A., & Blair, R. J. (2006). Impaired reversal but intact acquisition: Probabilistic response reversal deficits in adult individuals with psychopathy. *Journal of Abnormal Psychology, 115*(3), 552–558.

Burke, J. D., Loeber, R., & Lahey, B. B. (2007). Adolescent conduct disorder and interpersonal callousness as predictors of psychopathy in young adults. *Journal of Clinical Child and Adolescent Psychology, 36*, 334–346.

Cooke, D. J., & Michie, C. (1997). An item response theory evaluation of Hare's Psychopathy Checklist. *Psychological Assessment, 9*, 2–13.

Cooke, D. J., Michie, C., & Hart, S. D. (2006). Facets of clinical psychopathy: Toward clearer measurement. In C. J. Patrick (Ed.), *Handbook of psychopathy* (pp. 91–106). New York: Guilford Press.

Cornell, D. G., Warren, J., Hawk, G., Stafford, E., Oram, G., & Pine, D. (1996). Psychopathy in instrumental and reactive violent offenders. *Journal of Consulting and Clinical Psychology, 64*, 783–790.

Dadds, M. R., Perry, Y., Hawes, D. J., Merz, S., Riddell, A. C., Haines, D. J., et al. (2006). Attention to the eyes and fear-recognition deficits in child psychopathy. *British Journal of Psychiatry, 189*, 280–281.

Davis, M., & Whalen, P. J. (2001). The amygdala: Vigilance and emotion. *Molecular Psychiatry, 6*(1), 13–34.

Desimone, R., & Duncan, J. (1995). Neural mechanisms of selective visual attention. *Annual Review of Neuroscience, 18*, 193–222.

Duncan, J. (1998). Converging levels of analysis in the cognitive neuroscience of visual attention. *Philosophical Transactions of the Royal Society of London B: Biological Sciences, 353*, 1307–1317.

Everitt, B. J., Cardinal, R. N., Parkinson, J. A., & Robbins, T. W. (2003). Appetitive behavior: Impact of amygdala-dependent mechanisms of emotional learning. *Annals of the New York Academy of Sciences, 985*, 233–250.

Fairchild, G., Van Goozen, S. H., Stollery, S. J., & Goodyer, I. M. (2008). Fear conditioning and affective modulation of the startle reflect in male adolescents with early-onset or adolescence-onset conduct disorder and healthy control subjects. *Biological Psychiatry, 63*(3), 279–285.

Finger, E. C., Marsh, A. A., Mitchell, D. G. V., Reid, M. E., Sims, C., Budhani, S., et al. (2008). Abnormal ventromedial prefrontal cortex function in children with callous and unemotional traits during reversal learning. *Archives of General Psychiatry, 65*(5), 586–594.

Fisher, L., & Blair, R. J. R. (1998). Cognitive impairment and its relationship to psychopathic tendencies in children with emotional and behavioural difficulties. *Journal of Abnormal Child Psychology, 26*, 511–519.

Flor, H., Birbaumer, N., Hermann, C., Ziegler, S., & Patrick, C. J. (2002). Aversive Pavlovian conditioning in psychopaths: Peripheral and central correlates. *Psychophysiology, 39*, 505–518.

Forth, A. E., Kosson, D. S., & Hare, R. D. (2003). *The Psychopathy Checklist—Youth Version*. Toronto: Multi-Health Systems.

Frick, P. J. (1995). Callous–unemotional traits and conduct problems: A two-factor model of psychopathy in children. *Issues in Criminological and Legal Psychology, 24*, 47–51.

Frick, P. J., Bodin, S. D., & Barry, C. T. (2000). Psychopathic traits and conduct problems in community and clinic-referred samples of children: further development of the psychopathy screening device. *Psychological Assessment, 12*(4), 382–393.

Frick, P. J., Cornell, A. H., Barry, C. T., Bodin, S. D., & Dane, H. E. (2003). Callous–unemotional traits and conduct problems in the prediction of conduct problem severity, aggression, and self-report delinquency. *Journal of Abnormal Child Psychology, 31*, 457–470.

Frick, P. J., Kimonis, E. R., Dandreaux, D. M., & Farrell, J. M. (2003). The 4-year stability of psychopathic traits in non-referred youth. *Behavioral Sciences and the Law, 21*, 713–736.

Frick, P. J., & Marsee, M. A. (2006). Psychopathy and developmental pathways to antisocial behavior in youth. In C. J. Patrick (Ed.), *Handbook of psychopathy* (pp. 353–374). New York: Guilford Press.

Gallagher, M., McMahan, R. W., & Schoenbaum, G. (1999). Orbitofrontal cortex and representation of incentive value in associative learning. *Journal of Neuroscience, 19*, 6610–6614.

Gallagher, M., & Schoenbaum, G. (1999). Functions of the amygdala and related forebrain areas in attention and cognition. *Annals of the New York Academy of Sciences, 877*, 397–411.

Gordon, H. L., Baird, A. A., & End, A. (2004). Functional differences among those high and low on a trait measure of psychopathy. *Biological Psychiatry, 56*(7), 516–521.

Hampton, A. N., Bossaerts, P., & O'Doherty, J. P. (2006). The role of the ventromedial prefrontal cortex in abstract state-based inference during decision making in humans. *Journal of Neuroscience, 26*(32), 8360–8367.

Hare, R. D. (1991). *The Hare Psychopathy Checklist—Revised*. Toronto: Multi-Health Systems.

Hare, R. D. (2003). *Hare Psychopathy Checklist—Revised (PCL-R)* (2nd ed.). Toronto: Multi-Health Systems.

Hariri, A. R., Drabant, E. M., Muñoz, K. E., Kolachana, B. S., Mattay, V. S., Egan, M. F., et al. (2005). A susceptibility gene for affective disorders and the response of the human amygdala. *Archives of General Psychiatry, 62*(2), 146–152.

Hariri, A. R., Mattay, V. S., Tessitore, A., Kolachana, B., Fera, F., Goldman, D., et al. (2002). Serotonin transporter genetic variation and the response of the human amygdala. *Science, 297*, 400–403.

Hemphill, J. F., Hart, S. D., & Hare, R. D. (1994). Psychopathy and substance use. *Journal of Personality Disorders, 8*(3), 169–180.

Hiatt, K. D., & Newman, J. P. (2006). Understanding psychopathy: The cognitive side. In C. J. Patrick (Ed.), *Handbook of psychopathy* (pp. 334–352). New York: Guilford Press.

Hiatt, K. D., Schmitt, W. A., & Newman, J. P. (2004). Stroop tasks reveal abnormal selective attention among psychopathic offenders. *Neuropsychology, 18*, 50–59.

Kiehl, K. A. (2006). A cognitive neuroscience perspective on psychopathy: Evidence for paralimbic system dysfunction. *Psychiatry Research, 142*(2–3), 107–128.

Kiehl, K. A., Smith, A. M., Hare, R. D., Mendrek, A., Forster, B. B., Brink, J., et al. (2001). Limbic abnormalities in affective processing by criminal psychopaths as revealed by functional magnetic resonance imaging. *Biological Psychiatry, 50*, 677–684.

Kiehl, K. A., Smith, A. M., Mendrek, A., Forster, B. B., Hare, R. D., & Liddle, P. F. (2004). Temporal lobe abnormalities in semantic processing by criminal psychopaths as revealed by functional magnetic resonance imaging. *Psychiatry Research, 130*(1), 27–42.

Klinnert, M. D., Emde, R. N., Butterfield, P., & Campos, J. J. (1987). Social referencing: The infant's use of emotional signals from a friendly adult with mother present. *Annual Progress in Child Psychiatry and Child Development, 22*, 427–432.

Kosson, D. S., Budhani, S., Nakic, M., Chen, G., Saad, Z. S., Vythilingam, M., et al. (2006). The role of the amygdala and rostral anterior cingulate in encoding expected outcomes during learning. *NeuroImage, 29*(4), 1161–1172.

LaPierre, D., Braun, C. M. J., & Hodgins, S. (1995). Ventral frontal deficits in psychopathy: Neuropsychological test findings. *Neuropsychologia, 33*, 139–151.

LeDoux, J. (2007). The amygdala. *Current Biology, 17*(20), R868–R874.

Levenston, G. K., Patrick, C. J., Bradley, M. M., & Lang, P. J. (2000). The psychopath as observer: Emotion and attention in picture processing. *Journal of Abnormal Psychology, 109*, 373–386.

Lorenz, A. R., & Newman, J. P. (2002). Deficient response modulation and emotion processing in low-anxious Caucasian psychopathic offenders: Results from a lexical decision task. *Emotion, 2*(2), 91–104.

Lykken, D. T. (1995). *The antisocial personalities*. Hillsdale, NJ: Erlbaum.

Lynam, D. R., Caspi, A., Moffitt, T. E., Loeber, R., & Stouthamer-Loeber, M. (2007). Longitudinal evidence that psychopathy scores in early adolescence predict adult psychopathy. *Journal of Abnormal Psychology, 116*(1), 155–165.

MacCoon, D. G., Wallace, J. F., & Newman, J. P. (2004). Self-regulation: Context-appropriate balanced attention. In R. F. Baumeister & K. D. Vohs (Eds.), *Handbook of self-regulation: Research, theory, and applications* (pp. 422–446). New York: Guilford Press.

Machado, C. J., Snyder, A. Z., Cherry, S. R., Lavenex, P., & Amaral, D. G. (2008). Effects of neonatal amygdala or hippocampus lesions on resting brain metabolism in the macaque monkey: A microPET imaging study. *NeuroImage, 39*(2), 832–846.

Marsh, A. A., & Blair, R. J. (2008). Deficits in facial affect recognition among antisocial populations: A meta-analysis. *Neuroscience and Biobehavioral Reviews, 32*(3), 454–465.

Marsh, A. A., Finger, E. C., Mitchell, D. G. V., Reid, M. E., Sims, C., Kosson, D. S., et al. (2008). Reduced amygdala response to fearful expressions in adolescents with callous–unemotional traits and disruptive behavior disorders. *American Journal of Psychiatry, 165*(6), 712–720.

McClure, S. M., Berns, G. S., & Montague, P. R. (2003). Temporal prediction errors in a passive learning task activate human striatum. *Neuron, 38*(2), 339–346.

Mineka, S., & Cook, M. (1993). Mechanisms involved in the observational conditioning of fear. *Journal of Experimental Psychology: General, 122*, 23–38.

Mitchell, D. G. V., Colledge, E., Leonard, A., & Blair, R. J. R. (2002). Risky decisions and response reversal: Is there evidence of orbitofrontal cortex dysfunction in psychopathic individuals? *Neuropsychologia, 40*, 2013–2022.

Muñoz, L. C., & Frick, P. J. (2007). The reliability, stability, and predictive utility of the self-report version of the Antisocial Process Screening Device. *Scandinavian Journal of Psychology, 48*, 299–312.

Murphy, F. C., Nimmo-Smith, I., & Lawrence, A. D. (2003). Functional neuroanatomy of emotions: A meta-analysis. *Cognitive, Affective, and Behavioral Neuroscience, 3*(3), 207–233.

Murray, E. A., & Izquierdo, A. (2007). Orbitofrontal cortex and amygdala contributions to affect and action in primates. *Annals of the New York Academy of Sciences, 1121*, 273–296.

Neumann, C. S., Kosson, D. S., Forth, A. E., & Hare, R. D. (2006). Factor structure of the Hare Psychopathy Checklist: Youth Version (PCL: YV) in incarcerated adolescents. *Psychological Assessment, 18*, 142–154.

Newman, J. P. (1998). Psychopathic behaviour: An information processing perspective. In D. J. Cooke, A. E. Forth, & R. D. Hare (Eds.), *Psychopathy: Theory, research and implications for society* (pp. 81–105). Dordrecht, The Netherlands: Kluwer Academic.

Newman, J. P., Brinkley, C. A., Lorenz, A. R., Hiatt, K. D., & MacCoon, D. G. (2007). Psychopathy as psychopathology: Beyond the clinical utility of the Psychopathy Checklist—Revised. In H. Herve & J. C. Yuille (Eds.), *The psychopath: Theory, research, and practice* (pp. 173–206). Mahwah, NJ: Erlbaum.

Newman, J. P., & Kosson, D. S. (1986). Passive avoidance learning in psychopathic and nonpsychopathic offenders. *Journal of Abnormal Psychology, 95*, 252–256.

Newman, J. P., Patterson, C. M., & Kosson, D. S. (1987). Response perseveration in psychopaths. *Journal of Abnormal Psychology, 96*, 145–148.

Newman, J. P., & Schmitt, W. A. (1998). Passive avoidance in psychopathic offenders: A replication and extension. *Journal of Abnormal Psychology, 107*, 527–532.

Newman, J. P., Schmitt, W. A., & Voss, W. D. (1997). The impact of motivationally neutral cues on psychopathic individuals: Assessing the generality of the response modulation hypothesis. *Journal of Abnormal Psychology, 106*, 563–575.

O'Brien, B. S., & Frick, P. J. (1996). Reward dominance: Associations with anxiety, conduct problems, and psychopathy in children. *Journal of Abnormal Child Psychology, 24*, 223–240.

O'Doherty, J. P., Dayan, P., Friston, K., Critchley, H., & Dolan, R. J. (2003). Temporal difference models and reward-related learning in the human brain. *Neuron, 38*(2), 329–337.

Obradović, J., Pardini, D., Long, J., & Loeber, R. (2007). Measuring interpersonal callousness in boys from childhood to adolescence: An examination of longitudinal invariance and temporal stability. *Journal of Clinical Child and Adolescent Psychology, 36*, 276–292.

Oxford, M., Cavell, T. A., & Hughes, J. N. (2003). Callous–unemotional traits moderate the relation between ineffective parenting and child externalizing problems: A partial replication and extension. *Journal of Clinical Child and Adolescent Psychology, 32*, 577–585.

Patrick, C. J. (1994). Emotion and psychopathy: Startling new insights. *Psychophysiology, 31*, 319–330.

Pezawas, L., Meyer-Lindenberg, A., Drabant, E. M., Verchinski, B. A., Muñoz, K. E., Kolachana, B. S., et al. (2005). 5–HTTLPR polymorphism impacts human cingulate–amygdala interactions: A genetic susceptibility mechanism for depression. *Nature Neuroscience, 8*(6), 828–834.

Raine, A., Venables, P. H., & Williams, M. (1996). Better autonomic conditioning and faster electrodermal half-recovery time at age 15 years as possible protective factors against crime at age 29 years. *Developmental Psychology, 32*, 624–630.

Rauch, S. L., Shin, L. M., & Phelps, E. A. (2006). Neurocircuitry models of posttraumatic stress disorder and extinction: Human neuroimaging research—past, present, and future. *Biological Psychiatry, 60*, 376–382.

Rilling, J. K., Glenn, A. L., Jairam, M. R., Pagnoni, G., Goldsmith, D. R., Elfenbein, H. A., et al. (2007). Neural correlates of social cooperation and noncooperation as a function of psychopathy. *Biological Psychiatry, 61*, 1260–1271.

Rilling, J. K., Winslow, J. T., O'Brien, D., Gutman, D. A., Hoffman, J. M., & Kilts, C. D. (2001). Neural correlates of maternal separation in rhesus monkeys. *Biological Psychiatry, 49*, 146–157.

Rogers, R. D., & Robbins, T. W. (2001). Investigating the neurocognitive deficits associated with chronic drug misuse. *Current Opinion in Neurobiology, 11*, 250–257.

Rutter, M. (2005). Commentary: What is the meaning and utility of the psychopathy concept? *Journal of Abnormal Child Psychology, 33*, 499–503.

Saddoris, M. P., Gallagher, M., & Schoenbaum, G. (2005). Rapid associative encoding in basolateral amygdala depends on connections with orbitofrontal cortex. *Neuron, 46*, 321–331.

Salekin, R. T. (2006). Psychopathy in children and adolescents: Key issues in conceptualization and assessment. In C. J. Patrick (Ed.), *Handbook of psychopathy* (pp. 389–414). New York: Guilford Press.

Salekin, R. T. (2008). Psychopathy and recidivism from mid-adolescence to young adulthood: Cumulating legal problems and limiting life opportunities. *Journal of Abnormal Psychology, 117*, 386–395.

Salekin, R. T., Brannen, D. N., Zalot, A. A., Leistico, A. R., & Neumann, C. S. (2006). Factor structure of psychopathy in youth: Testing the new four factor model. *Criminal Justice and Behavior, 33*, 135–157.

Schoenbaum, G., Chiba, A. A., & Gallagher, M. (1999). Neural encoding in orbitofrontal cortex and basolateral amygdala during olfactory discrimination learning. *Journal of Neuroscience, 19*, 1876–1884.

Schoenbaum, G., Nugent, S. L., Saddoris, M. P., & Setlow, B. (2002). Orbitofrontal lesions in rats impair reversal but not acquisition of go, no-go odor discriminations. *NeuroReport, 13*, 885–890.

Schoenbaum, G., & Roesch, M. (2005). Orbitofrontal cortex, associative learning, and expectancies. *Neuron, 47*, 633–636.

Verona, E., Patrick, C. J., Curtin, J. J., Bradley, M. M., & Lang, P. J. (2004). Psy-

chopathy and physiological response to emotionally evocative sounds. *Journal of Abnormal Psychology, 113*, 99–108.
Verona, E., Patrick, C. J., & Joiner, T. E. (2001). Psychopathy, antisocial personality, and suicide risk. *Journal of Abnormal Psychology, 110*, 462–470.
Viding, E. (2004). Annotation: Understanding the development of psychopathy. *Journal of Child Psychology and Psychiatry and Allied Disciplines, 45*, 1329–1337.
Viding, E., Blair, R. J. R., Moffitt, T. E., & Plomin, R. (2005). Evidence for substantial genetic risk for psychopathy in 7-year-olds. *Journal of Child Psychology and Psychiatry, 46*, 592–597.
Wilson, K., Demetrioff, S., & Porter, S. (2008). A pawn by any other name?: Social information processing as a function of psychopathic traits. *Journal of Research in Personality, 42*, 1651–1656.
Wootton, J. M., Frick, P. J., Shelton, K. K., & Silverthorn, P. (1997). Ineffective parenting and childhood conduct problems: The moderating role of callous–unemotional traits. *Journal of Consulting and Clinical Psychology, 65*, 292–300.
Yacubian, J., Glascher, J., Schroeder, K., Sommer, T., Braus, D. F., & Buchel, C. (2006). Dissociable systems for gain- and loss-related value predictions and errors of prediction in the human brain. *Journal of Neuroscience, 26*, 9530–9537.

8

Child and Adolescent Psychopathy and Personality

DONALD R. LYNAM

My main premise in this chapter is that juvenile psychopathy is best understood as a constellation of endogenous, enduring predispositions to think, act, and feel in certain characteristic ways. More specifically, I argue that psychopathy in children, adolescents, and adults is a constellation of traits drawn from a model of general personality functioning, namely, the five-factor model of personality (FFM; McCrae & Costa, 2003).

It may surprise some to read "personality" rather than "temperament" as the central explanatory construct for a syndrome in children and adolescents. There are, however, several reasons for relying on personality rather than temperament. First, although some may draw distinctions between the two constructs, there appears to be no firm line of demarcation. The distinction seems to be more accidental, with researchers who study individual differences in children referencing them as temperaments, and those studying such differences in adults referencing them as personality traits. Both McAdams (1996) and McCrae and Costa (2003) view personality traits as biologically based tendencies to think, act, and feel in certain characteristic ways. Second, empirical work supports links between the two types of explanatory constructs; for example, Rothbart, Ahadi, and Evans (2000) report moderate to large correlations between four temperament traits and four of the domains within the FFM. Third, even if one wishes to maintain a distinction between personality and temperament, the FFM functions much like a temperament system presumably should. As embodied in the NEO Personality Inventory—Revised (NEO PI-R; Costa & McCrae, 1992), the dimensions of the FFM show high heritabilities (Yamagata et al., 2006), temporal stability across the lifespan (Roberts & DelVecchio, 2000), and etic and emic cross-cultural support (Ashton & Lee, 2001; Church, 2001; McCrae et al., 2005). Additionally, the FFM can be applied to children and adolescents (e.g., Digman & Shmelyov, 1996) and to nonhuman animal species (e.g., Gosling & John, 1999; King & Figuererdo, 1997).

Although other potential personality models might be employed, I draw primarily on the FFM. As assessed via the NEO PI-R (Costa & McCrae, 1992), the model includes five broad domains, each with six specific facets, providing a reasonably comprehensive lexicon of 30 facets (see Table 8.1). At the domain level, the FFM includes neuroticism (vs. emotional stability), extraversion (vs. introversion), openness (vs. closedness) to experience, agreeableness (vs. antagonism), and conscientiousness (or constraint). Two domains, extraversion (E) and agreeableness (A), assess an individual's orientation toward others. E assesses an individual's proneness to positive emotions and sociability. A is concerned with an individual's interpersonal relationships and strategies; people high in A tend to be trusting, straightforward, and empathetic, whereas those who score low tend to be manipulative, arrogant, and unconcerned about others. The domain of N assesses emotional adjustment and stability. C relates to the "control of impulses," as well as the ability to plan, organize, and complete behavioral tasks. The domain O refers to an individual's interest in culture and the preference for new activities and emotions.

I draw on this model over others for several reasons. First, I find its derivation compelling. The FFM was originally derived within the lexical paradigm suggesting that what is most important or meaningful to people is encoded within the language. As noted by Widiger and Trull (2007), "Language can be understood as a sedimentary deposit of the observations of persons over the thousands of years of the language's development and transformation" (p. 74). Under this approach, the most important aspects of personality are those with greatest representation in the language. Such an approach virtually ensures that important aspects of personality are represented in the model (Ashton & Lee, 2001; John & Srivastava, 1999). Second, there is much research supporting the validity of the FFM. In addition to research demonstrating high heritability, temporal stability, and cross-cultural consistency, the FFM enjoys considerable empirical support in the form of convergent and discriminant validaty across self, peer, and spouse ratings (Costa & McCrae, 1988), and relations to important outcomes (Ozer & Benet-Martínez, 2006), including academic achievement (Digman & Takemoto-Chock, 1981), antisocial behavior (Miller, Lynam, & Leukefeld, 2003), substance use and abuse (Flory, Lynam, Milich, Leukefeld, & Clayton, 2002), and risky sexual behavior (Miller et al., 2004). Perhaps most importantly, most of the work in adults and almost all of the work in children and adolescents has been conducted using the FFM. Thus, the FFM

TABLE 8.1. FFM Facet-Level Profiles of Psychopathy in Adults

	Expert prototype	PCL-R translation	Mean PPI correlations	Mean HSRP correlations
Neuroticism				
Anxiety	1.47	0	–.34	–.27
Angry hostility	3.87	1	.14	.25
Depression	1.40	0	–.04	–.03
Self-consciousness	1.07	–1	–.26	–.20
Impulsiveness	4.53	1	.12	.13
Vulnerability	1.47	0	–.13	–.10
Extraversion				
Warmth	1.73	–1	–.19	–.22
Gregariousness	3.67	0	.05	.00
Assertiveness	4.47	0	.28	.23
Activity	3.67	0	.05	.08
Excitement seeking	4.73	1	.30	.27
Positive emotions	2.53	–1	–.08	–.11
Openness				
Fantasy	3.07	0	.11	.10
Aesthetics	2.33	0	.05	–.04
Feelings	1.80	0	–.14	–.15
Actions	4.27	0	.26	.16
Ideas	3.53	0	.11	.13
Values	2.87	0	.01	.00
Agreeableness				
Trust	1.73	–2	–.22	–.31
Straightforwardness	1.13	–2	–.58	–.63
Altruism	1.33	–2	–.38	–.43
Compliance	1.33	–2	–.42	–.51
Modesty	1.00	–2	–.35	–.39
Tendermindedness	1.27	–2	–.29	–.38
Conscientiousness				
Competence	4.20	0	–.22	–.16
Order	2.60	0	–.30	–.19
Dutifulness	1.20	–2	–.34	–.29
Achievement striving	3.07	–2	–.23	–.14
Self-discipline	1.87	–2	–.28	–.19
Deliberation	1.60	–2	–.51	–.38
Similarity indices				
PCL-R translation	.70			
PPI	.81	.79		
HSRP	.83	.83	.96	

provides a common language that allows comparisons to be made across developmental periods.

Psychopathy as Personality: Research in Adults

The argument that psychopathy is personality can first be made by reference to clinical descriptions of psychopathy. Cleckley's (1941/1976) seminal description of psychopaths is a study in personality. By looking across the lives of individuals, Cleckley deduced their consistent patterns of behavior (i.e., their personalities). Cleckley's list of 16 criteria for psychopathy is replete with personality traits. Nine of his diagnostic criteria are fairly standard personality descriptors: interpersonally charming, (absence of) nervousness, unreliability, insincerity, (lack of) shame, poor judgment, egocentricity, affectively impoverished, and interpersonally unresponsive. Five of the remaining seven characteristics reference "enduring patterns" of behavior and can therefore be considered to assess personality: inadequately motivated antisocial behavior, fantastic and uninviting behavior with drink and sometimes without, suicide rarely carried out, an impersonal sex life, and failure to follow any life plan. The emphasis on personality is also found in Hare's influential operationalization of psychopathy, the 20-item Hare Psychopathy Checklist—Revised (PCL-R; 2003). In the PCL-R, 13 of the 20 items assessed represent standard personality descriptors: glibness, grandiosity, need for stimulation, untruthfulness, manipulativeness, lack of guilt, shallow affect, callousness, poor behavioral control, lack of planning, impulsivity, irresponsibility, and failure to accept responsibility. At least four of the remaining seven items reference enduring behavior patterns: parasitic lifestyle, promiscuous sexual behavior, many short-term marital relations, and criminal versatility.

That psychopathy can be understood as a particular set of personality traits, on the other hand, is made best by reference to empirical work. Multiple studies have examined the relations between the broad domains of the FFM and various measures of psychopathy in adults. The top portion of Table 8.2 presents the results from a meta-analysis of nine studies reporting such relations. As can be seen, the strongest zero-order correlate of psychopathy among adults is A, with a large, average weighted r of –.47; the moderate r of –.30 for C is the next largest correlate. Both relations are relatively robust, in that all nine studies have reported negative relations between these domains and psychopathy. By themselves, these relations suggest that the psychopathic individual is antagonistic (i.e. suspicious, deceptive, exploitive, combative, arrogant, and callous), has trouble controlling his or her impulses, and endorses nontraditional values and standards. The remaining domains show weak but significant relations, on average, to total

TABLE 8.2. Results of Meta-Analysis on the Relations of Structural Models of Personality to Psychopathy

	Unweighted mean effect size	Weighted mean effect size	95% Confidence interval	No. of studies	Total *N*	Range of effect sizes
Adults						
Neuroticism	0.04	0.06***	0.03 to 0.10	8	2,672	–0.34 to 0.36
Extraversion	–0.02	–0.05***	–0.10 to –0.02	9	2,942	–0.25 to 0.34
Openness	–0.01	–0.04*	–0.08 to –0.00	7	2,548	–0.21 to 0.24
Agreeableness	–0.44	–0.47***	–0.54 to –0.47	9	2,942	–0.65 to –0.25
Conscientiousness	–0.29	–0.30***	–0.35 to –0.27	9	2,942	–0.12 to –0.46
Youth						
Neuroticism	0.21	0.15***	0.12 to 0.19	6	3722	–0.08 to 0.49
Extraversion	–0.12	–0.13***	–0.16 to –0.10	6	3,722	–0.26 to –0.02
Openness	–0.19	–0.16***	–0.19 to –0.12	6	3,722	–0.33 to –0.04
Agreeableness	–0.59	–0.55***	–0.57 to –0.52	6	3,722	–0.65 to –0.39
Conscientiousness	–0.47	–0.42***	0.45 to –0.40	6	3,722	–0.62 to –0.21

Note. Studies in the adult meta-analysis include Paulhus and Williams (2002); Lynam, Whiteside, and Jones (1999); Harpur, Hare, and Hakstian (1989); Harpur, Hart, and Hare (2002); Lynam (2002); Skeem, Miller, Mulvey, Tiemann, ansd Monahan (2005); and Hicklin and Widiger (2005).

*$p < .05$; ***$p < .001$.

psychopathy scores; these relations, however, are not consistent across studies, potentially reflecting differences in the content of several psychopathy scales (Hicklin & Widiger, 2005).

Because the FFM domains are broad, comprising multiple facets, the domain-level profile of psychopathy tends to lacks specificity (Clark, 1993). Several personality disorders manifest similar relations to A and C as psychopathy (Saulsman & Page, 2004). A more compelling case for a specific FFM profile of psychopathy comes from work at the facet level. Several studies have shown that fidelity and resolution are much higher at the facet level; as noted by Saulsman and Page (2004), "When each personality dimension is broken down into their respective facets, finer detail regarding within-disorder and across-disorder observations will emerge for the personality disorders" (p. 1077). Resolution is gained at the facet level because a personality disorder might be related to only one or two facets within a domain, or even be related differentially to facets within a domain. Both are true in the case of psychopathy.

My colleagues and I have explored the FFM profile of psychopathy using multiple approaches—expert ratings, empirical relations, and "translations" of extant instruments into the trait language of the FFM. The profiles that emerge across each approach are extremely consistent with one another. One approach is to have psychopathy experts describe the personalities of prototypic psychopaths in the language of the FFM. Such descriptions are useful because the descriptions are not bound by any particular operationalization of psychopathy. Additionally, aggregating the ratings brings out in stark contrast the aspects on which experts agree, and blunt the idiosyncratic elements of each description. Miller, Lynam, Widiger, and Leukefeld (2001) wrote to 21 nationally known psychopathy researchers and asked each to "rate the prototytpical, classic Cleckley psychopath" on each of 30 bipolar scales that correspond to the 30 facets of the FFM. For example, to assess the facet of straightforwardness (a facet of A), experts were asked, "To what extent is the male [or female] psychopath honest, genuine, and sincere versus deceptive and manipulative?" Response choices ranged from 1 (*Extremely low*) to 5 (*Extremely high*). Sixteen experts returned the ratings. The experts' mean rating on each of the facets are given in Table 8.1. There was strong agreement in the descriptions of the prototypic psychopath, an internal consistency finding that is itself encouraging. Taking any facet with a mean score lower than 2 (low) or higher than 4 (high) as characteristic, the profile indicates that the prototypic psychopath is low in all facets of agreeableness (A), three facets of conscientiousness (C; dutifulness, self-discipline, and deliberation), four facets of neuroticism (N; anxiety, depression, self-consciousness, and vulnerability), and warmth (E); in contrast, the prototypic psychopath was rated as high in impulsiveness (N) and excitement seeking (E).

A second approach is to examine the correlations between scores on psychopathy assessments and facet scores on the NEO PI-R. My colleagues and I (Derefinko & Lynam, 2006; Hicklin & Widiger, 2005) have collected data on over 1,000 participants using the NEO PI-R and the Hare Self-Report Psychopathy Scale (HSRP; Williams, Paulhus, & Hare, 2007) or the Psychopathic Personality Inventory (PPI; Lilienfeld & Andrews, 1995). In Table 8.1, I have aggregated these studies to present empirically derived FFM profiles for the HSRP and PPI. According to both profiles, psychopathy is characterized by low levels of A, especially straightforwardness, altruism, compliance, and modesty. Psychopathic individuals are also low in C, especially the facets of self-discipline and deliberation. As with expert ratings, psychopathy shows a complex profile in relation to the facets of N and

E. Within N, psychopathy is negatively associated with anxiety and self-consciousness but positively associated with angry hostility and impulsiveness. Similarly, within E, psychopathy is negatively related to warmth but positively related to assertiveness and excitement seeking.

A final approach to generating a personality profile of psychopathy based on the FFM is to translate the criteria for psychopathy into the language of the FFM. I proposed earlier that all of the core features of psychopathy operationalized in Hare's (2003) PCL-R have an explicit representation within one or more facets of the FFM (Widiger & Lynam, 1998). Table 8.1 provides this translation of the PCL-R items into the facets of the FFM. This profile was generated by assigning a score of 0 to a facet that does not appear in any item translation (e.g., anxiety), a score of +1 (*high*) or –1 (*low*) to a facet that appears in the translation of only one PCL-R item (e.g., angry hostility), and a score of +2 (*high*) or –2 (*low*) to a facet that appears in the translation of more than one item (e.g., any facet of A). From this profile, the psychopath appears to score very low in all facets of A except trust, and in four out of six facets of C (dutifulness, achievement striving, self-discipline, and deliberation). Additionally, the psychopath scores somewhat low in self-consciousness from N, and warmth and positive emotions from E. Finally, the psychopath is rated as scoring somewhat high in angry hostility and impulsiveness from N, and excitement seeking from E.

In the bottom of Table 8.1, I present similarity indices for each profile. Where both profiles are in the same metric (i.e., for the HSRP and PPI correlations), the similarity is an intraclass correlation that takes into account similarity in both shape and magnitude. Otherwise, the similarity coefficient is a simple Pearson correlation coefficient. As can be seen from these indices, there is high agreement among the profiles derived from the different methods. The correlational profiles for the two self-report assessments are virtually identical. The lowest similarity coefficient is between the PCL-R translation and the expert ratings; my colleagues and I have previously speculated that this might be due to the fact that experts were unconstrained by any particular definition or conceptualization of psychopathy.

Not only is the psychopathic personality profile robustly recovered, but the profile also seems capable of standing in for psychopathy. Several studies in adults have found that FFM-assessed psychopathy shows high convergence with explicit measures of psychopathy and expected relations with psychopathy-related criteria. Convergent correlations among FFM psychopathy, PPI, and HSRP indices ranged from .63 to .81 (Derefinko & Lynam, 2006). In studies of both undergraduates and drug-using samples (Derefinko & Lynam, 2007; Miller & Lynam, 2003; Miller et al., 2001), FFM psychopathy has been found to be robustly related to antisocial behavior, number of arrests, multiple forms of aggression (inside and outside of the laboratory), substance use and abuse, risky sexual behavior, and hostile social information processing.

Psychopathy as Personality: Research in Children and Adolescents

At the adult level, the consistency of the FFM psychopathy profile across methods, studies, and instruments, along with the ability of FFM-assessed psychopathy to recreate the nomological network around psychopathy, provides support for understanding psychopathy as a specific constellation of FFM traits. Research on child and adolescent psychopathy only strengthens the argument. Not only is the FFM profile of adult psychopathy remarkably robust across methods, but it is also quite similar to the profile for juvenile psychopathy. Recently, there have been a number of studies examining the relations between the domains and facets of the FFM and juvenile psychopathy. Within this area, various approaches have also been used.

In one of the earliest reports, I provided information on the results of an expert rating project for child psychopathy, similar to the one reported for adults earlier (Lynam, 2002). Specifically, I asked 14 psychopathy experts to rate the prototypic fledgling psychopath as described by Cleckley (1941/1976) using the 100 items of the Common Language Q-Sort (CLQ; Caspi et al., 1992). Specifically, I asked for a "criterion definition of the fledgling psychopath as studied by you and your colleagues and as described by Cleckley. We say 'fledgling' because we would like you to extrapolate downward several years and tell us, using the language of the California Q-Sort, what the adult psychopath looks like as a young adolescent, about 13 years old." Eight of 14 experts returned their Q-sorts of the fledgling psychopath, which were then used to construct a prototype by averaging across raters for each of the 100 items. Agreement among the returned Q-sorts was excellent; the average interrater reliability for each rater ranged from .61 to .87, with a mean of .73, which can be taken as the reliability of the composite profile. Eleven items had average ratings of 2.5 or less on the 1- to 9-point scale ranging from *most uncharacteristic* to *most characteristic*; 10 items had average ratings of 7.5 or more on this scale. Because the CLQ items have been mapped to FFM space (John, Caspi, Robins, Moffitt, & Stouthamer-Loeber, 1994; Robins, John, & Caspi, 1994), it is possible to discuss these 21 items in FFM terms. Of the 21 items, 10 were indicators of single domains—five assessed antagonism, three assessed low C, and two assessed low N. The remaining 11 items were interstitial blends of two or more domains; fully 10 of these represented blends of low A and low C, and one represented a blend of low N and high E.

In an effort to examine the validity of translating the adult conception of psychopathy downward developmentally, the expert profile described earlier was treated as an endogenously derived instrument and was compared to two other CLQ profiles (Lynam, Derefinko, Caspi, Loeber, & Stouthamer-Loeber, 2007). One of the profiles was based on the Childhood Psychopathy Scale (CPS; Lynam, 1997), which was originally developed from archived items to operationalize, in childhood and adolescence, the *personality* traits found in the PCL-R (Hare, 2003). The CLQ was one instrument available in the archive, and 16 of the items used in the CPS were taken from the CLQ. The other profile we created empirically by correlating each CLQ item with psychopathy assessed 11 years later; 26 CLQ items comprised this index. The overlap among CLQ items across profile derivation methods was quite high, with content validity coefficients above .90 and convergent validities above .80. More germane to the present purposes, however, are the mappings of the CLQ items to FFM domains. Of the 36 items that appear on at least one index (out of a possible 63, if there was no overlap), 30 of them are indicators of low A, low C, or blends of low A and low C. The remaining six items are indicators or blends of low N, low O, and/or low E.

A handful of empirical studies reporting correlations between juvenile psychopathy assessments and the FFM are available to examine the relations between the FFM domains and psychopathy among children and adolescents. Five studies providing six effect sizes were identified for this chapter. Salekin, Leistico, Trobst, Schrum, and Lochman (2005) reported on the correlations between FFM domains and total scores on the Antisocial Process Screening Device (APSD), the CPS, and the Hare Psychopathy Checklist: Youth Version (PCL:YV) in a sample of 114 youth. Essau, Sasagawa, and Frick (2006) reported the relations with Frick's Inventory of Callous and Unemotional Traits (ICU; Essau et al., 2006) in a large sample of 1,443 youth. Lynam and colleagues (2005) reported correlations for two samples (*N*'s = 405 and 435) of male adolescents in relation to total scores on the CPS. Finally, unpublished data from two studies were also incorporated. Correlations between the FFM and total scores on the Youth Psychopathic Traits Inventory (YPI; Andershed, Kerr, Stattin, & Levander, 2002) and the PCL:YV (Forth, Kosson, & Hare, 2003) were available for 1,166 youth involved in the Pathways to Desistance study, a multisite, longitudinal study of serious juvenile offenders (Mulvey et al., 2004; Schubert et al., 2004). Data from a sample of 385 late adolescents reporting relations to the YPI, ICU, and CPS were also used (Lynam, Miller, Gaughan, Heyde, & Leukfeld, 2009). Results from a meta-analysis of these studies appear in Table 8.2. These results are quite similar to those obtained among adults. Juvenile psychopathy is strongly negatively related to agreeableness (A) and conscientiousness (C). It is weakly negatively related to extraversion (E) and openness (O), and weakly positively related to neuroticism (N).

TABLE 8.3. FFM Facet-Level Correlation Profiles of Juvenile Psychopathy

	Undergraduate sample		Pathways to Desistance study		
	YPI	CPS	YPI	PCL:YV	Average *r*
Neuroticism					
Anxiety	–.21	–.09	.02	.02	–.07
Angry Hostility	.26	.38	.24	.17	.26
Depression	–.03	.08	.31	.10	.12
Self-consciousness	–.16	–.10	.12	–.04	–.05
Impulsiveness	.12	.23	.13	.08	.14
Vulnerability	.08	.27	.04	.02	.10
Extraversion					
Warmth	–.32	–.37	–.29	–.18	–.29
Gregariousness	–.02	–.03	.04	–.05	–.02
Assertiveness	.02	.09	–.06	.04	.02
Activity	–.01	–.01	.07	.01	.02
Excitement seeking	.06	.00	.32	.12	.13
Positive emotions	–.29	–.30	–.10	–.10	–.20
Openness					
Fantasy	–.05	–.07	.06	.05	.00
Aesthetics	–.09	–.15	–.07	.03	–.07
Feelings	–.28	–.30	.03	.06	–.12
Actions	.10	.06	–.07	.07	.04
Ideas	–.07	–.18	–.12	.00	–.10
Values	–.18	–.14	–.10	–.09	–.13
Agreeableness					
Trust	–.35	–.40	–.10	–.15	–.25
Straightforwardness	–.57	–.53	–.56	–.24	–.48
Altruism	–.50	–.58	–.25	–.12	–.36
Compliance	–.36	–.43	–.36	–.23	–.35
Modesty	–.46	–.40	–.10	–.06	–.26
Tendermindedness	–.33	–.36	–.09	–.05	–.21
Conscientiousness					
Competence	–.24	–.37	–.15	–.08	–.21
Order	–.15	–.26	–.20	–.02	–.16
Dutifulness	–.37	–.50	–.13	–.09	–.27
Achievement striving	–.17	–.30	–.15	–.09	–.18
Self-discipline	–.22	–.34	–.14	–.09	–.20
Deliberation	–.36	–.49	–.34	–.18	–.34
Similarity indices					
CPS Total	.94				
Pathways YPI	.73	.77			
Pathways PCL:SV	.82	.82	.87		

TABLE 8.3. *(continued)*

Adult experts	.73	.57	.40	.53	.60
PPI	.83	.74	.67	.77	.81
HSRP	.89	.78	.72	.81	.87
Translation	.83	.82	.69	.81	.84

Note. YPI, Youth Psychopathic Traits Inventory; CPS, Child Psychopathy Scale; PCL:YV, Psychopathy Checklist: Youth Version; PCL:SV, Psychopathy Checklist: Screening Version; PPI, Psychopathy Personality Inventory; HSRP, Hare Self-Report Psychopathy Scale.

Not only are the relations at the juvenile level similar to those obtained among adults at FFM domain levels, the facet-level results are also quite similar. Table 8.3 provides the correlations between the 30 NEO PI-R facets and four psychopathy total scores from the undergraduate samples and the Pathways to Desistance study. It also provides the average correlation across the four columns and correlations between the columns. The first point to notice is the high degree of similarity in the correlational profiles for the various instruments across the two samples. Correlations with the PCL:YV tend to be a bit lower, presumably reflecting the different sources but, in general, correspondence is high. Profile similarities, indexed by Pearson's *r*, ranged from .73 for the YPI across the two samples to .94 between the measures in the undergraduate sample. Thus, the average correlational profile provided in the last column would appear to offer an adequate summary. According to this average profile, youth psychopathy is characterized by low scores on all facets of A, especially straightforwardness, altruism, and compliance. It is also characterized by low scores on several facets of C, especially, dutifulness and deliberation. Finally, juvenile psychopathy shows a complex pattern of relations to the facets within E and N. Within E, juvenile psychopathy is correlated positively with excitement seeking but negatively with warmth and positive emotions. Within N, it is moderately positively correlated with angry hostility; weakly positively correlated with depression, impulsiveness, and vulnerability; and weakly negatively correlated with anxiety and self-consciousness.

In general, the personality profile of psychopathy is similar across methods of derivation and specific assessments. It also appears similar across developmental period; the personality of the psychopathic adult is the personality of the psychopathic youth. The similarities between the juvenile and adult psychopathy profiles presented in Table 8.1 range from .60 for the expert profile to .87 for the HSRP profile (shown in the bottom of Table 8.3). This should not be surprising given what we know about the stability of personality in general. Block (1993) provided evidence for the impressive 10-year stability of ego control (a specific constellation of FFM traits), reporting a retest correlation of .67 between age 14 and age 23. In their meta-analysis, Roberts and DelVecchio (2000) found a moderate to large stability coefficient for each of the five factors across ages 12 to 17.9. Although the coefficients from the meta-analysis do not suggest that personality is immutable across adolescence, they are not dissimilar from the results found for stabilities in early to mid adulthood.

Corollary: Basic Traits Represent the Basic Elements of Psychopathy

Across youth and adults, approaches and instruments, a consistent profile of psychopathy emerges. The profile consists of a high degree of interpersonal antagonism (i.e., low on all facets of A), a lack of inhibitory control (i.e., N5: impulsiveness; E5: excitement seeking; low C5: self-discipline; and low C6: deliberation), a general absence of negative self-directed affect (i.e., low N1: anxiety and N4: self-consciousness), little warmth and few positive emotions (i.e., low E1 and E6), feelings of anger and hostility (i.e., high A2), and a description as undependable and unethical (i.e., low C4). There is at least one point of divergence between the juvenile and adult profiles. The psychopathic adult profiles include negative relations, with multiple facets within N, notably, anxiety, self-consciousness, and vulnerability; that is, the adult psychopath is relatively immune to worry, shame, and stress. This is less true among psychopathic youth, who are at least mildly stress reactive.

A corollary to my argument that psychopathy is personality is that these FFM traits constitute the long-searched-for basic elements of psychopathy. Much current work in psychopathy in both adults and youth is aimed at uncovering the basic structure of psychopathy itself. These attempts frequently rely on factor analyses of psychopathy scales and have led to much debate in the literature regarding the appropriate factor structure of a single scale; for example, two- (Harpur, Hare, & Hakstian, 1989), three- (Cooke & Michie, 2001; Skeem, Mulvey, & Grisso, 2003), and four-factor models (Hill, Neumann, & Rogers, 2004) of the PCL-R and its derivatives have received empirical support. Within the child and adolescent literature, recovering the right number of factors and being able to map them to extant factors is seen as an almost required validity step for youth psychopathy inventories. Along with Widiger, I have argued (Lynam & Widiger, 2007) that the repeated factor analyses of the PCL-R, its derivatives, or any psychopathy assessment, are unlikely to yield the basic dimensions of psychopathy itself. The crux of our argument is that the "items" in the psychopathy assessments are themselves complex mixtures of different personality traits, or compounds, and that factor analyses of such compounds cannot yield basic elements. The alternative is to begin with a set of basic, elemental traits, such as those found in the FFM.

I have previously discussed some of the issues within the psychopathy field that can be resolved by conceptualizing psychopathy at the more elemental level (see Lynam, 2002; Lynam & Derefinko, 2006; Lynam & Widiger, 2007). These include understanding comorbidity between personality disorders (including psychopathy), understanding sex differences in the personality disorders, making sense of the diversity of putative psychopathic deficits, and organizing the various conceptualizations of successful psychopathy. In the next several pages, I illustrate the utility of the elemental approach in two final examples from the child and adolescent psychopathy field. Then I discuss a few additional benefits of understanding psychopathy as a constellation of these elemental traits.

Suppression

Previous studies, at both the youth and adult levels, have revealed the presence of cooperative suppressor effects for the factors of several psychopathy instruments, particularly in relation to negative affect. The characteristic finding is little or no relation between psychopathy factors and negative affect at the zero-order level, but significant opposite relations once the factors are partialed from one another (e.g., Frick, Lilienfeld, Ellis, Loney, & Silverthorn, 1999; Hicks & Patrick, 2006). I have suggested previously (Lynam, Hoyle, & Newman, 2006) that such relations are likely due to the representations of different facets of neuroticism in the various factors; that is, these compound factors include different, but related, basic elements. For illustrative purposes, I use data from 381 undergraduates who completed the ICU along with the NEO PI-R. Within this sample, there is a small cooperative suppressor relation between the Callousness and Uncaring scales on N; the nature of the suppression is such that neither scale is related to N by itself; betas equal –.05 and .06 for Callous and Uncaring, respectively. However, when both scales are included in a simultaneous regression, their relations to N become larger and marginally significant; betas equal –.10 and .10 for Callous and Uncaring, respectively.

An examination of the zero-order relations between the ICU scales and the facets of N shed light on the nature of this suppressor effect; callousness and uncaring scales bear somewhat differential relations to the facets of N. Callousness, with a small nonsignificant negative correlation to N, is significantly negatively related to N1 and N4 (r's = –.23 and –.11), and significantly positively related to N2 (r = .16), whereas uncaring, with a small nonsignificant positive correlation to N, is significantly positively related to N2 and N6 (r's = .14 and .15) and significantly negatively related to N1

($r = -.14$). It is in these relations that the key to the suppressor effect exists. The result of partialing uncaring from callousness is the removal of variance associated with N2 and N6, the two facets countervailing the general negative relation to N. The result of partialing callousness from uncaring is the removal of variance associated with N1 and N4, the two facets countervailing the general positive relation to N. To demonstrate this is the reason behind the suppressor, I examined whether N2/N6 and N1/N4 can stand in for uncaring and callousness. When N is regressed onto callousness, N2, and N6, the effect for callousness changes from –.05 at the zero-order level to –.16 ($p < .001$). Similarly, when N is regressed onto uncaring, N1, and N4, the effect for uncaring changes from .06 at the zero-order level to .13 ($p < .001$). Such an understanding of these suppressor relations is available only at the level of fidelity provided by the FFM facets.

Factor Structure and Genetics of the YPI

As a second example, I offer a reinterpretation of several findings regarding the YPI (Andershed et al., 2002), which comprises 10 scales, with three higher-order factors that in turn are overlaid by a second-order factor referred to as psychopathy. A behavioral genetic study of this structure (Larsson, Andershed, & Lichtenstein, 2006) found evidence of high heritability for the general psychopathy factor, and specific additional genetic effects for

TABLE 8.4. Correlations between five-factor model (FFM) Domains and the Scales and Factors of the Youth Psychopathic Traits Inventory (YPI)

YPI scales	N	E	O	A	C
Grandiose/Manipulative	.02	–.05	–.11	–.61	–.19
Dishonest charm	.02	.01	–.09	–.54	–.15
Grandiose	–.07	–.05	–.13	–.46	–.02
Lying	.13	–.07	–.08	–.46	–.28
Manipulative	.00	–.04	–.08	–.56	–.18
Callous/Unemotional	–.14	–.30	–.29	–.56	–.17
Remorseless	.01	–.19	–.16	–.47	–.21
Unemotional	–.20	–.25	–.21	–.43	–.14
Callous	–.17	–.33	–.37	–.51	–.08
Impulsive/Irresponsible	.15	.08	.00	–.39	–.51
Thrill seeking	.02	.28	.13	–.29	–.22
Impulsive	.16	.16	.00	–.31	–.44
Irresponsible	.17	–.20	–.10	–.36	–.54

two of the higher-order factors (i.e., callous–unemotional [CU] and impulsive/irresponsible [II]) but no specific genetic effect for the third (i.e., grandiose/manipulative [GM]). An examination of the correlations between the FFM domains and YPI scales and factors offers an alternative account for the factor structure and the genetics findings. As can be seen in Table 8.4, low levels of A saturate the scales of the YPI, especially the GM factor and its subscales, which have few relations with the other domains. The II factor and its subscales are fairly strongly negatively correlated with C. Finally, the CU factor and its scales show negative correlations with N, E, and O, particularly for the unemotional and callous scales. This pattern of correlations suggests an alternative interpretation of the higher-order factor structure of the 10 scales. The highest-order psychopathy factor, what is shared across all scales, captures antagonism (or low A); this is what creates the general positive manifold. The GM factor is a fairly pure indicator of A. The other two factors are distinguished from the first and from each other by their relations to the other domains. The II factor assesses C, in addition to A; the CU factor assesses low E, low N, and low O, in addition to A.

To test this, I used data from 379 undergraduate participants who completed both the YPI and NEO PI-R to fit a model relating the FFM domains to the YPI. Along with Larsson and colleagues (2006), scores for the first-order factors were used as observed indicators of a higher-order psychopathy factor. The structural equation model proceeded in several steps; results are shown in Table 8.5. First, I ran a baseline model without any relations between the YPI and FFM domains. Next, I allowed A to predict the latent

TABLE 8.5. Results from Models Examining the Relations between FFM Domains and YPI Scales and Factors

	General model (domains to factors)					
	df	χ^2	Δ in χ^2	CFI	RMSEA	RMSEA 90% confidence interval
Measurement model	17	480		.55	.27	.25 to .29
Path from A to YPI psychopathy	16	285	195 (1)***	.74	.21	.19 to .23
Path from C to impulsive/irresponsible	15	179	106 (1)***	.84	.17	.15 to .19
Paths from N, E, and O to callous–unemotional	12	77	102 (3)***	.94	.12	.10 to .15
Path from E to impulsive/irresponsible	11	34	43 (1)***	.98	.07	.05 to .10

***$p < .001$.

psychopathy factor; this resulted in a significant improvement in fit. A was strongly negatively related to the latent psychopathy factor and accounted for 47% of the variance in this latent factor. In the following steps, I added a path between C and the II factor, paths between N, E, and O and the CU factor, and a path between E and the II factor, which reflects the positive relations that E bears to two of the scales. At each step, the fit of the model was improved. At the final step, the model fit the data quite well, with a comparative fit index (CFI) of .98 and a root mean square error of approximation (RMSEA) of .07.

Figure 8.1 provides estimates from the final model. The figure underscores the alternative interpretation of the YPI structure and genetics. A is strongly negatively related to the latent psychopathy factor; GM is a pure indicator of the latent factor. The other scales, in addition to reflecting A/latent psychopathy, are blends of the other domains. CU is negatively related to N, E, and O; II is strongly negatively related to C and positively related to E. Under this interpretation, the genetic factor common to all scales and reflected in the latent psychopathy factor is the genetics of A; the specific genetic factors for the two subscales reflect the genetics of the other FFM domains. It is worth noting that model fit is improved by allowing A to predict each of the three scales individually (CI = .99, RMSEA = .06), by modeling the YPI using the 10 subscales and allowing domains to bear relations to specific subscales (e.g., E to Thrill seeking), or by modeling the FFM domains using the facets and allowing specific facet to subscale relations.

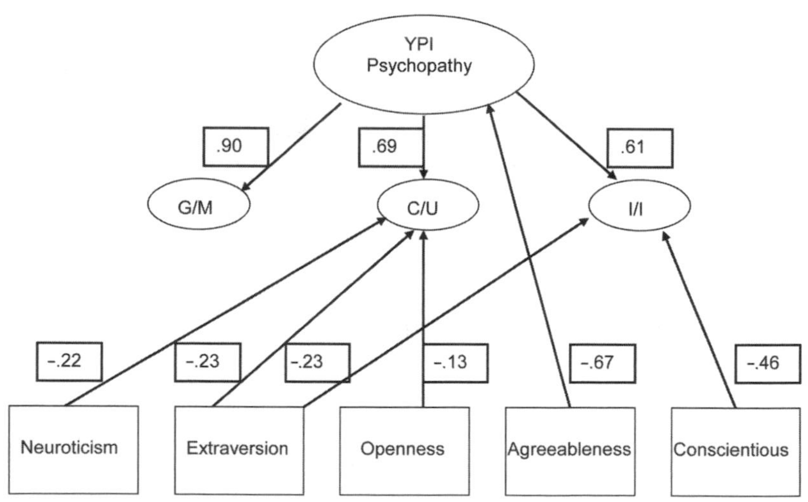

FIGURE 8.1. Final model relating the FFM domains to YPI factors.

Other Potential Benefits

Conceptualizing psychopathy as a constellation of the 18 or so facets described throughout this chapter has implications for assessment and theory building. In terms of assessment, the consensus elemental traits provide an index of the content that psychopathy scales should have and provide a common language for comparison across them. These traits might also serve as the basis for new measurement development. There are several facet-level assessments available at the adult level (e.g., the NEO PI-R, the Five-Factor Model Rating Form [FFM-RF; Mullins-Sweatt, Jamerson, Samuel, Olson, & Widiger, 2006], the Structured Interview for the FFM [Trull & Widiger, 1997], and the International Personality Item Pool [IPIP] approximation to the FFM Facet Scales [Goldberg, 1999]). Fewer assessments are available at the adolescent level, although the NEO PI-R and the NEO PI-3 have been used successfully with children and adolescents (McCrae, Martin, & Costa, 2005), and the FFM-RF can likely be used with this population as well. These extant assessments have been criticized, however, for potentially failing to include the more maladaptive ends of personality functioning (Haigler & Widiger, 2001). Developing new scales, particularly ones designed for use by mothers, teachers, adolescents, and children, would fill an important gap. Doing so with the elemental facets as the basis would circumvent the issues faced by current explicit measures of psychopathy, namely, the problem of compound traits. By conceptualizing psychopathy in terms of these elemental traits, some concerns about labeling children and adolescents as psychopathic may be ameliorated. Instead of talking about psychopathy per se, one can talk about a particular personality profile and describe the elemental traits that are involved.

By thinking at the elemental trait level, researchers and theorists can build psychopathy from the bottom up. One can examine which elements are most central, which are peripheral, and which are unnecessary to the construct of psychopathy. One can ask which elements are important for which particular outcomes (e.g., institutional aggression, recidivism, treatment resistance). One can also study the possibility of combinatorial effects; that is, one can search for synergistic effects in which specific combinations of elements give rise to emergent properties. One can more clearly ask which effects developmentally precede others. Working with the basic elements of the FFM to study psychopathy may also allow for a better connection to basic research in development and personality, where the focus is at more elemental rather than more compound levels often used in clinical psychology. As previously noted, empirical work has tied specific temperament dimensions to specific personality dimensions; to the extent that the developmental processes underlying those temperament dimensions are known, this information can be mapped onto the traits that comprise psychopathy. Some basic research in personality is aimed at elucidating the mechanisms that underlie specific traits. For example, several researchers are studying the basic processes underlying agreeableness (e.g., Graziano & Tobin, 2002). Meier, Robinson, and Wilkowski (2006) found that the behavioral link between an aggressive cue and later aggression was stronger among individuals low in agreeableness. Many researchers are also examining the personality pathways to impulsive behavior (e.g., Whiteside & Lynam, 2001). Bechara (2005) has recently placed the four traits related to impulsive behavior (i.e., N5: impulsiveness, E5: excitement seeking, C5: self-discipline, and C6: deliberation), into a larger neurocognitive framework rooted in neurology. Even more researchers are examining the self-relevant negative affects, including anxiety, depression, and shame/guilt, and how these emotions relate to behavior (e.g., Beer, Heerey, Keltner, Scabini, & Knight, 2003). With the basic traits, it is possible to bridge this research directly into theories on the development and nature of psychopathy.

Conclusion

In this chapter, I have argued that psychopathy is a specific configuration of elemental personality traits drawn from the FFM. I have summarized research at both the adult and child/adolescent levels. This research shows excellent convergence in terms of the defining traits across methods within a developmental period, and across developmental periods. At this point, the psychopathic individual, adult, adolescent, or child, can be described as *interpersonally antagonistic* (i.e., suspicious [A1], manipulative [A2], selfish [A3], oppositional [A4], arrogant [A5], callous [A6], and interpersonally cold [E1]); *pan-impulsive* (i.e., easily tempted [N5], daring [E5], negligent [C5], and rash [C6]); *lacking several self-directed negative emotions* (i.e., unconcerned [N1] and shameless [N4]); *high in anger* (N2); *low in positive emotions* (E6); and *undependable* (C4). This chapter has reviewed the benefits of construing psychopathy in terms of these elemental traits.

References

Andershed, H., Kerr, M., Stattin, H., & Levander, S. (2002). Psychopathic traits in non-referred youths: A new assessment tool. In E. Blaauw & L. Sheridan (Eds.), *Psychopaths: Current international perspectives* (pp. 131–158). Hague, The Netherlands: Elsevier.

Ashton, M. C., & Lee, K. (2001). A theoretical basis for the major dimensions of personality. *European Journal of Personality, 15,* 327–353.

Bechara, A. (2005). Decision making, impulse control and loss of willpower to resist drugs: A neurocognitive perspective. *Nature Neuroscience, 8,* 1458–1463.

Beer, J. S., Heerey, E. A., Keltner, D. Scabini, D., & Knight, R. T. (2003). The regulatory function of self-conscious emotion: Insights from patients with orbitofrontal damage. *Journal of Personality and Social Psychology, 85*, 594–604.

Block, J. (1993). Studying personality the long way. In D. Funder, R. Parke, C. Tomlinson-Keasy, & K. Widaman (Eds.), *Studying lives through time: Personality and development* (pp. 9–41). Washington, DC: American Psychological Association.

Caspi, A., Block, J., Block, J. H., Klopp, B., Lynam, D., Moffitt, T. E., et al. (1992). "Common-language" version of the California Child Q-Set for personality assessment. *Psychological Assessment, 4*, 512–523.

Church, T. A. (2001). Personality measurement in cross-cultural perspective. *Journal of Personality, 69*, 979–1006.

Clark, L. A. (1993). Personality disorder diagnosis: Limitations of the five-factor model. *Psychological Inquiry, 4*, 100–104.

Cleckley, H. (1976). *The mask of sanity* (5th ed.). St. Louis, MO: Mosby. (Original work published 1941)

Cooke, D. J., & Michie, C. (2001). Refining the construct of psychopathy: Towards a hierarchical model. *Psychological Assessment, 13*, 171–188.

Costa, P. T., & McCrae, R. R. (1988). Personality in adulthood: A six-year longitudinal of self-reports and spouse ratings on the NEO Personality Inventory. *Journal of Personality and Social Psychology, 54*, 853–863.

Costa, P. T., & McCrae, R. R. (1992). *Revised NEO Personality Inventory (NEO-PI-R) and NEO Five-Factor Inventory (NEO-FFI) professional manual.* Odessa, FL: Psychological Assessment Resources.

Derefinko, K. J., & Lynam, D. R. (2006). Convergence and divergence among self-report psychopathy measures: A personality-based approach. *Journal of Personality Disorders, 20*, 261–280.

Derefinko, K. J., & Lynam, D. R. (2007). Using the FFM to conceptualize psychopathy: A test using a drug abusing sample. *Journal of Personality Disorders, 21*, 638–656.

Digman, J. M., & Shmelyov, A. G. (1996). The structure of temperament and personality in Russian children. *Journal of Personality and Social Psychology, 71*, 341–351.

Digman, J. M., & Takemoto-Chock, N. K. (1981). Factors in the natural language of personality: Re-analysis, comparison, and interpretation of six major studies. *Multivariate Behavioral Research, 16*, 149–170.

Essau, C. A., Sasagawa, S., & Frick, P. J. (2006). Callous–unemotional traits in a community sample of adolescents. *Assessment, 13*, 454–469.

Flory, K., Lynam, D., Milich, R., Leukefeld, C., & Clayton, R. (2002). The relations among personality, symptoms of alcohol and marijuana abuse, and symptoms of comorbid psychopathology: Results from a community sample. *Experimental and Clinical Psychopharmacology, 10*(4), 425–434.

Forth, A. E., Kosson, D. S., & Hare, R. D. (2003). *Manual for the Hare Psychopathy Checklist: Youth Version* . Toronto: Multi-Health Systems.

Frick, P. J., Lilienfeld, S. O., Ellis, M., Loney, B., & Silverthorn, P. (1999). The association between anxiety and psychopathy dimensions in children. *Journal of Abnormal Child Psychology, 27*, 383–392.

Goldberg, L. R. (1999). A broad-bandwidth, public domain, personality inventory measuring the lower-level facets of several five-factor models. In I. Mervielde, I. Deary, F. De Fruyt, & F. Ostendorf (Eds.), *Personality psychology in Europe* (Vol. 7, pp. 7–28). Tilburg, The Netherlands: Tilburg University Press.

Gosling, S. D., & John, O. P. (1999). Personality dimensions in nonhuman animals: A cross-species review. *Current Directions in Psychological Science, 8, 69–75.*

Graziano, W. G., & Tobin, R. (2002). Agreeableness: Dimension of personality or social desirability artifact? *Journal of Personality, 70,* 695–727.

Haigler, E. D., & Widiger, T. A. (2001). Experimental manipulation of NEO-PI-R items. *Journal of Personality Assessment, 77,* 339–358.

Hare, R. D. (2003). *Manual for the Psychopathy Checklist—Revised* (2nd ed.). Toronto: Multi-Health Systems.

Harpur, T., Hare, R., & Hakstian, A. (1989). Two-factor conceptualization of psychopathy: Construct validity and assessment implications. *Psychological Assessment, 1,* 6–17.

Harpur, T. J., Hart, S. D., & Hare, R. D. (2002). Personality of the psychopath. In P. T. Costa & T. A. Widiger (Eds.), *Personality disorders and the five-factor model of personality* (2nd ed., pp. 299–324). Washington, DC: American Psychological Association.

Hicklin, J., & Widiger, T. A. (2005). Similarities and differences among antisocial and psychopathic self-report inventories form the perspective of general personality functioning. *European Journal of Personality, 19,* 325–342.

Hicks, B. M., & Patrick, C. J. (2006). Psychopathy and negative emotional: Analyses of suppressor effects reveal distinct relations with emotional distress, fearfulness, and anger–hostility. *Journal of Abnormal Psychology, 115,* 276–287.

Hill, C. D., Neumann, C. S., & Rogers, R. (2004). Confirmatory factor analysis of the Psychopathy Checklist: Screening Version in offenders with Axis I disorders. *Psychological Assessment, 16,* 90–95.

John, O. P., Caspi, A., Robins, R. W., Moffitt, T. E., & Stouthamer-Loeber, M. (1994). The "Little Five": Exploring the nomological network of the five-factor model of personality in adolescent boys. *Child Development, 65,* 160–178.

John, O. P., & Srivastava, S. (1999). The Big Five trait taxonomy: History, measurement, and theoretical perspectives. In L. A. Pervin & O. P. John (Eds.), *Handbook of personality: Theory and research* (2nd ed., pp. 102–138). New York: Guilford Press.

King, J. E., & Figueredo, A. J. (1997). The five-factor model plus dominance in chimpanzee personality. *Journal of Research in Personality, 31,* 257–271.

Larsson, H., Andershed, H., & Lichtenstein, P. (2006). A genetic factor explains most of the variation in the psychopathic personality. *Journal of Abnormal Psychology, 115,* 221–230.

Lynam, D. R. (1997). Pursuing the psychopath: Capturing the fledgling psychopath in a nomological net. *Journal of Abnormal Psychology, 106,* 425–438.

Lynam, D. R. (2002). Psychopathy from the perspective of the five factor model. In P. T. Costa & T. A. Widiger (Eds.), *Personality disorders and the five-factor model of personality* (2nd ed., pp. 325–350). Washington, DC: American Psychological Association.

Lynam, D. R., Caspi, A., Moffitt, T. E., Raine, A., Loeber, R., & Stouthamer-Loeber, M. (2005). Adolescent psychopathy and the Big Five: Results from two samples. *Journal of Abnormal Child Psychology, 33*, 431–443.

Lynam, D. R., & Derefinko, K. J. (2006). Psychopathy and personality. In C. J. Patrick (Ed.), *Handbook of psychopathy* (pp. 133–155). New York: Guilford Press.

Lynam, D. R., Derefinko, K. J., Caspi, A., Loeber, R., & Stouthamer-Loeber, M. (2007). The content validity of juvenile psychopathy: An empirical examination. *Psychological Assessment, 19*, 363–367.

Lynam, D. R., Hoyle, R. H., & Newman, J. P. (2006). The perils of partialling: Cautionary tales from aggression and psychopathy. *Assessment, 13*, 328–341.

Lynam, D. R., Miller, J. D., Gaughan, E. T., Heyde, B., & Leukfeld, C. (2009). *The five-factor model and externalizing behavior*. Manuscript submitted for publication.

Lynam, D. R., Whiteside, S., & Jones, S. (1999). Self-reported psychopathy: A validation study. *Journal of Personality Assessment, 73*, 110–132.

Lynam, D. R., & Widiger, T. A. (2007). Using a general model of personality to identify the basic elements of psychopathy. *Journal of Personality Disorders, 21*, 160–178.

McAdams, D. P. (1996). Personality, modernity, and the storied self: A contemporary framework for studying persons. *Psychological Inquiry, 7*, 295–321.

McCrae, R. R., & Costa, P. T. (2003). *Personality in adulthood: A five-factor theory perspective* (2nd ed.). New York: Guilford Press.

McCrae, R. R., Martin, T. A., & Costa, P. T. (2005). Age trends and age norms for the NEO Personality Inventory-3 in adolescents and adults. *Assessment, 12*, 363–373.

McCrae, R. R., Terracciano, A., & 78 Members of the Personality Profiles of Cultures Project. (2005). Universal features of personality traits from the observer's perspective: Data from 50 cultures. *Journal of Personality and Social Psychology, 88*, 547–561.

Meier, B. P., Robinson, M. D., & Wilkowski, B. M. (2006). Turning the other cheek: Agreeableness and the regulation of aggression-related primes. *Psychological Science, 17*, 136–142.

Miller, J. D., & Lynam, D. R. (2003). Psychopathy and the five-factor model of personality: A replication and extension. *Journal of Personality Assessment, 81*(2), 168–178.

Miller, J. D., & Lynam, D. R., & Leukefeld, C. (2003). Examining antisocial behavior through the use of the five factor model facets. *Aggressive Behavior, 29*, 497–514.

Miller, J. D., Lynam, D. R., Widiger, T. A., & Leukefeld, C. (2001). Personality disorders as extreme variants of common personality dimensions: Can the five-factor model adequately represent psychopathy? *Journal of Personality, 69*, 253–276.

Miller, J. D., Lynam, D. R., Zimmerman, R., Logan, T. K., Leukefeld, C., & Clayton, R. (2004). The utility of the five factor model in understanding risky sexual behavior. *Personality and Individual Differences, 36*, 1611–1626.

Mullins-Sweatt, S. N., Jamerson, J. E., Samuel, D. B., Olson, D. R., & Widiger, T. A. (2006). Psychometric properties of an abbreviated instrument of the five-factor model. *Assessment, 13*, 119–137.

Mulvey, E., Steinberg, L., Fagan, J., Cauffman, E., Piquero, A., Chassin, L., et al. (2004). Theory and research on desistance from antisocial activity among adolescent serious offenders. *Journal of Youth Violence and Juvenile Justice, 2*, 213–236.

Ozer, D. J., & Benet-Martínez, V. (2006). Personality and the prediction of consequential outcomes. *Annual Review of Psychology, 57*, 401–421.

Paulhus, D. L., & Williams, K. M. (2002). The dark triad of personality: Narcissism, Machaivellianism, and psychopathy. *Journal of Research in Personality, 36*, 556–563.

Roberts, B. W., & DelVecchio, W. F. (2000). The rank-order consistency of personality traits from childhood to old age: A quantitative review of longitudinal studies. *Psychological Bulletin, 126*, 3–25.

Robins, R. W., John, O. P., & Caspi, A. (1994). Major dimensions of personality in early adolescence: The Big Five and beyond. In C. F. Halverson, G. A. Kohnstamm, & R. P. Martin (Eds.), *The developing structure of temperament and personality from infancy to adulthood* (pp. 267–291). Hillsdale, NJ: Erlbaum.

Rothbart, M. K., Ahadi, S. A., & Evans, D. E. (2000). Temperament and personality: Origins and outcomes. *Journal of Personality and Social Psychology, 78*, 122–135.

Salekin, R. T., Leistico, A. R., Trobst, K. K., Schrum, C. L., & Lochman, J. E. (2005). Adolescent psychopathy and personality theory—the interpersonal circumplex: Expanding evidence of a nomological net. *Journal of Abnormal Child Psychology, 33*, 445–460.

Saulsman, L. M., & Page, A. C. (2004). The five-factor model and personality disorder empirical literature: A meta-analytic review. *Clinical Psychology Review, 23*, 1055–1085.

Schubert, C., Mulvey, E., Steinberg, L., Cauffman, E., Losoya, S., Hecker, T., et al. (2004). Operational lessons from the pathways to desistance project. *Journal of Youth Violence and Juvenile Justice, 2*, 237–255.

Skeem, J. L., Miller, J. D., Mulvey, E., Tiemann, J., & Monahan, J. (2005). Using a five-factor lens to explore the relation between personality traits and violence in psychiatric patients. *Journal of Consulting and Clinical Psychology, 73*, 454–465.

Skeem, J. L., Mulvey, E. P., & Grisso, T. (2003). Applicability of traditional and revised models of psychopathy to the Psychopathy Checklist: Screening Version. *Psychological Assessment, 15*, 41–55.

Trull, T. J., & Widiger, T. A. (1997). *Structured interview for the five factor model of personality*. Odessa, FL: Psychological Assessment Resources.

Whiteside, S. P., & Lynam, D. R. (2001). The five factor model and impulsivity: Using a structural model of personality to understand impulsivity. *Personality and Individual Differences, 30*, 669–689.

Widiger, T. A., & Lynam, D. R. (1998). Psychopathy and the five-factor model of personality. In T. Millon, E. Simonsen, M. Birket-Smith, & R. D. Davis (Eds.),

Psychopathy: Antisocial, criminal, and violent behavior (pp. 171–187). New York: Guilford Press.

Widiger, T. A., & Trull, T. J. (2007). Plate tectonics in the classification of personality disorder: Shifting to a dimensional model. *American Psychologist, 62*, 71–83.

Williams, K., Paulhus, D. L., & Hare, R. D. (2007). Capturing the four-factor structure of psychopathy in college students via self-report. *Journal of Personality Assessment, 88*, 205–219.

Yamagata, S., Suzuki, A., Ando, J., One, Y., Kijima, N., Yoshimura, K., et al. (2006). Is the genetic structure of human personality universal?: A cross-cultural twin study from North America, Europe, and Asia. *Journal of Personality and Social Psychology, 90*, 987–998.

9

Environmental Influences on Child and Adolescent Psychopathy

DAVID P. FARRINGTON
SIMONE ULLRICH
RANDALL T. SALEKIN

Psychopathy

Child and adolescent psychopathy has emerged as an important clinical construct. As operationally defined by the Psychopathy Checklist: Youth Version (PCL:YV) and adult counterpart measures (Forth, Kosson, & Hare, 2003; Hare, 2003; Hart, Cox, & Hare, 1995), psychopathy is a multidimensional construct. It encompasses key descriptive elements, such as low remorse; impulsiveness; and a cold, callous, and calculating personality; as well as behavioral elements, such as impulsive, antisocial, and even criminal conduct (Salekin, 2006). Cooke, Michie, Hart, and Clark (2004) and others (e.g., Blackburn, 1998) have suggested that psychopathy should be operationally defined only by the personality trait elements of the disorder. These authors contend that psychopathy is defined by an arrogant and deceitful interpersonal style (ADI), deficient affective experience (DAE), and impulsive and irresponsible behavior (IIB). Cooke and colleagues also proposed that these personality factors lead to criminal and antisocial behavior (ANT). While Cooke and colleagues and Blackburn (1998) reinvigorated discussions on this issue, many years earlier, Cleckley (1941) also had suggested that a psychopathic personality causes moral transgressions and antisocial behavior.

In the past, ADI and DAE have been subsumed under the interpersonal–affective components of psychopathy (Factor 1, henceforth referred to as F1, also called *psychopathic traits*), and IIB and ANT have been encompassed within irresponsible–antisocial lifestyle components (Factor 2, henceforth referred to as F2, also called *social deviance*). While there has been considerable research on the biological and neurocognitive causes of psychopathy, less attention has been paid to its social origins. Although biology and the environment are, of course, inextricably intertwined, environmental factors may be particularly important for researchers who study child and adolescent psychopathy because it is likely that they interact with biology and impact youth to result in a psychopathic personality.

Our purpose in this chapter is to review the environmental forces that may have some impact on the development of psychopathy. Specifically, we review and present new findings on social predictors of psychopathy and its two broad subfactors (F1 and F2). We limit our discussion to the two traditional factors of psychopathy and do not discuss other attempts to deconstruct psychopathy, for example into disinhibition, boldness, and meanness (Patrick, Fowles, & Krueger, 2009). Also, because of the scope of this chapter, we do not review research on related constructs, such as conduct disorder (CD) or oppositional defiant disorder (ODD). We do, however, focus on six specific predictors of psychopathy, including parental, childrearing, family, socioeconomic, peer, school, and neighborhood factors.

In this chapter, we assume that child/adolescent psychopathy is a meaningful concept (Farrington, 2005a; Salekin & Frick, 2005), while recognizing that this view does not go unchallenged (e.g., Hart, Watt, & Vincent, 2002; Johnstone & Cooke, 2004, 2009; Seagrave & Grisso, 2002; Sharp & Kine, 2008). We also assume that there is stability in the psychopathic personality from childhood to adulthood, as Lynam, Caspi, Moffitt, Loeber, and Stouthamer-Loeber (2007) found, and that findings on psychopathy in adults are therefore pertinent to children and adolescents. Other scholars have also noted that personality traits in general, and psychopathic traits in particular, tend to be relatively stable over time (e.g., Frick, Kimonis, Dandreaux, & Farrell, 2003; Obradović, Pardini, Long, & Loeber, 2007; Roberts & DelVecchio, 2000; Ullrich, Paelecke, Kahle, & Marneros, 2003).

Longitudinal Surveys: Environmental Effects on the Development of Psychopathy

The best method of determining whether a social factor predicts later psychopathy is a prospective longitudinal survey, and the emphasis in this chapter is on findings obtained in such surveys (see Kalb, Farrington, & Loeber, 2001; Loeber & Farrington, 1997). Longitudinal studies avoid retrospective bias (e.g., in which parents' memories about their childrearing practices are biased by the knowledge that their child has become a psychopath) and help in establishing causal order. Also, psychopaths emerge naturally from an initially nonpsychopathic population in community surveys. This eliminates the need to select a control group, which can be problematic. As noted by Farrington (2005b), a number of problems can occur in choosing control groups. For instance, utilizing and subsequently contrasting extreme groups (e.g., psychopaths vs. nonpsychopathic nonoffenders) may result in an overestimate of the magnitude of the relation between predictor variables and psychopathy. Alternatively, comparing (more or less psychopathic) offender groups may result in inadequate variation between subgroups to detect relationships with psychopathy. We devote less attention to findings obtained with offender samples than to results acquired with community and mixed (offender plus nonoffender) samples.

A few other concerns are worth noting here before we start our review. Specifically, retrospective case–control studies of psychopaths (cases) and nonpsychopathic offenders (controls) are dubious because retrospective bias is problematic, causal ordering is not certain, and the study design may not elucidate the development of psychopathy in the general population. When studying the causes of psychopathy, prospective probabilities are more appropriate than retrospective probabilities. As noted by Kraemer and colleagues (1997), only risk factors that can vary over time within individuals can be established as causes of a disorder. With this in mind, we do not review static variables, such as gender and race (for gender and psychopathy, see two special issues of *Behavioral Sciences and the Law*: Vols. 23[6], 2005, and 24[1], 2006; for race and psychopathy, see Sullivan & Kosson, 2006).

As stated elsewhere (Farrington, 2006), there are very few prospective longitudinal surveys that specifically investigate the development of psychopathy. This is, as noted in the opening paragraphs of this chapter, at least partly due to the research focus in psychopathy on individual and biological factors rather than on social or environmental influences (Herpertz & Sass, 2000). Because of the lack of research on environmental factors that might influence the development of child and adolescent psychopathy, much of this chapter reviews knowledge gained in longitudinal surveys of delinquency that can help shed light on the child and adolescent psychopathy construct. Despite being centered on delinquency, these surveys may be at least as relevant as retrospective studies of psychopathy, particularly since we know that psychopathy is highly linked with persistent, serious, and violent offending. As Hart and Hare (1997, p. 22) put it, "Psychopaths are responsible for a disproportionate amount of crime in our society."

For some time now, researchers have known that the overlap between psychopathy and delinquency is caused, at least in part, by the inclusion of antisocial items in measures of psychopathy. This makes it difficult to know for sure which social background features are related to psychopathic personality, and which are related to antisocial behavior. However, the early factor models for psychopathy delineated by Harpur, Hare, and Hakstian (1989), and later factor models developed by Cooke and Michie (2001) and Hare (2003), allow for a more precise examination of these potential relations. Specifically, we assume that the interpersonal–affective (F1) score is a measure of the classic psychopathic personality, whereas the irresponsible–antisocial (F2) score is a measure of irresponsible and antisocial behavior. It seems probable that the predictive validity of child/adolescent psychopathy in relation to subsequent offending is largely driven by the antisocial items (Corrado, Vincent, Hart, & Cohen, 2004; Salekin, 2008), although F1 also appears to have some predictive merit. For example, in their large-scale meta-analysis of studies relating psychopathy to antisocial conduct, Leistico, Salekin, DeCoster, and Rogers (2008) found that the mean weighted *d* value effect size for predicting recidivism was 0.37 for F1 and 0.64 for F2. Thus, Leistico and her colleagues showed that both factors are predictive but, clearly, F2 was more predictive than F1.

Two Key Research Investigations on the Social Origins of Psychopathy: The Cambridge and Pittsburgh Studies

Two major studies can inform what we know about the development of child and adolescent psychopathy. In this chapter, we discuss these two studies in some detail and present new findings from one, the Cambridge Study in Delinquent Development. The Cambridge study is a 40-year prospective longitudinal survey of the development of offending and antisocial behavior. In this survey, 411 London boys have been followed up from ages 8 to 48 with in-person interviews (Farrington, 2003; Farrington et al., 2006). A wide variety of individual, family, and socioeconomic risk factors were indexed at ages 8–10, before the boys had an opportunity to be convicted. Later, at age 48, 365 of the 394 men who were still alive were interviewed (93%). For such a large time span, this retention rate, by any standard, is impressive.

Of the 365 men who completed a social interview, 304 (83%) also completed a medical interview. In this, participants completed two well-known, and well-validated, structured interviews: the Structured Clinical Interview for DSM-IV Personality Disorders (SCID-II; First, Gibbon, Spitzer, Williams, & Benjamin, 1997) and the Psychopathy Checklist: Screening Version (PCL:SV; Hart et al., 1995); see Rogers (2001) for information on validity. Psychopathy assessments in this survey are based on the adult years from ages 18 to 48. In the Cambridge sample, PCL:SV scores on the 12-item scale ranged from 0 to 17 (out of a possible maximum of 24), with a mean of 3.5 and a standard deviation of 3.8 (see also Farrington, 2006, 2007).

Up to the age of 50, 167 men (41%) were convicted out of a possible 404 at risk. Convictions were only tabulated for the more serious "standard list" offenses, excluding driving-related and other minor crimes. Representative offenses included theft, burglary, violence, vandalism, fraud, and drug use. Of the convicted men, 28 were classified as chronic offenders because they had 10 or more convictions. These chronic offenders, who constituted 7% of the sample, accounted for 52% of all convictions. These findings are consistent with other research on persistent offenders (Moffitt, 2003).

Another key longitudinal survey that has examined the development of psychopathy is the Pittsburgh Youth Study. This is a lengthy follow-up survey of three samples of approximately 500 Pittsburgh boys, first studied at ages 7, 10, and 13. The youngest and oldest cohorts were followed up to ages 25 and 30, respectively, by researchers using numerous assessment measures (Loeber, Farrington, Stouthamer-Loeber, & White, 2008). The middle sample was administered the Childhood Psychopathy Scale at age 13 and the PCL:SV at age 24 (Lynam et al., 2007). This study was one of the first to show that there is modest stability in psychopathy from childhood to young adulthood ($r = 0.31$). While these two studies have been important in understanding the development of psychopathy, we should note other, relevant longitudinal data on psychopathy that have helped us better understand the social origins of psychopathy, including research by Weiler and Widom (1996) in Indianapolis; Lang, af Klinteberg, and Alm (2002) in Stockholm; and Fowler and colleagues (2009) in the United Kingdom.

Psychopathy versus Number of Convictions

When PCL:SV scores were compared with number of convictions in the Cambridge study, we noted that there were qualitative differences between men scoring 10 or more on the PCL:SV and the remainder. Specifically, all except one (97%) of the 33 men scoring 10 points or more (11% of the sample) were convicted, compared with 46 out of 73 men scoring 4–9 points (63%) and only 43 out of 197 men scoring 0–3 points (22%). Almost half (45%) of the men scoring 10 or more points were chronic offenders, compared with 2% of the remainder (see Table 9.1). The vast majority of chronic offenders who completed the medical interview (15 out of 20) scored 10 or more on the PCL:SV.

We must acknowledge, however, that even the most psychopathic males in this community sample would not likely be classified as clinical "psychopaths." Hart and colleagues (1995), in the PCL:SV manual, state that a "high" score in a community sample is 16 or more. In the Cambridge sample, only two men achieved this score, suggesting that few of the "most psychopathic" men suffered from a severe personality disorder. However,

TABLE 9.1. Psychopathy Checklist: Screening Version Scores versus Convictions

Scale	Score	*N*	Convicted %	Convicted OR	Chronic %	Chronic OR
Interpersonal–affective	0–3	272	35.7	6.2*	2.9	20.8*
(Factor 1)	4+	31	77.4		38.7	
Irresponsible–antisocial	0–6	271	33.9	18.8*	2.6	25.8*
(Factor 2)	7+	32	90.6		40.6	
Total	0–9	270	33.0	65.1*	1.9	44.2*
	10+	33	97.0		45.5	

Note. OR, odds ratio.

$^{*}p < .05$.

based on the distribution of scores in the sample, and because we know that psychopathy is nontaxonomic (see Murrie et al., 2007), it is accurate to say that 33 males were the "most psychopathic" according to the PCL:SV.

Table 9.1 also displays relations between the two traditional psychopathy factor scores and convictions. In the interest of comparability, the highest 10% on each factor scale was contrasted with the remaining 90%. Both interpersonal–affective (F1) scores and irresponsible–antisocial (F2) scores were significantly related to convictions and to chronic offending, as in the Leistico and colleagues (2008) meta-analysis. In addition, the scores were significantly correlated ($r = .65$). Perhaps not surprisingly, irresponsible antisocial scale scores were more strongly linked to convictions and to chronic offending.

Societal Factors

Although Hare (1970) mainly emphasized the role of biological factors in psychopathy, and recent research has continued this trend, he also indicated that having an antisocial or psychopathic parent, parental substance use, inconsistent parental discipline, and separation from a parent all influenced the development of psychopathy (in interaction with genetic predisposition). Other researchers have also noted the potential importance of parenting, although they may have offered slightly different perspectives than Hare (e.g., Lykken, 1995). Despite the small number of contemporary research studies in this area, several projects on these and other environmental factors can shed further light on the development of psychopathy. We hope that these important studies might also help to open up new avenues for research in this crucial but neglected area of study.

Childrearing Practices

It is evident that harsh or punitive discipline (involving physical punishment) predicts offending, as the review by Haapasalo and Pokela (1999) indicated. In a follow-up study of nearly 700 Nottingham children, the Newsons (1989) found that physical punishment at ages 7 and 11 predicted later convictions (see Table 9.2). These researchers discovered that 40% of the offenders had been hit or beaten at age 11, compared with 14% of nonoffenders. Unpredictable or inconsistent discipline is also linked to delinquency (West & Farrington, 1973, p. 51). This can involve either erratic discipline by one parent, who sometimes inappropriately ignores bad behavior and sometimes punishes it severely, or inconsistency between two parents, in which one parent is tolerant or indulgent and the other is harshly punitive. Other researchers have also shown the link between antisocial behavior and punitive parenting (e.g., Fergusson, Horwood, & Lynskey, 1994; Patterson, Reid, & Dishion, 1992; Silva, 1990).

Just as inappropriate methods of responding to bad behavior predict offending, low positive reinforcement (not praising) of good behavior by a parent is also a predictor (Farrington & Loeber, 1999). In an English twin study, Larsson, Viding, and Plomin (2008) reported that negative parenting (including harsh parental discipline) was associated with the combination of callous–unemotional traits and antisocial behavior. However, inconsistent parenting and poor monitoring were unrelated to callous–unemotional psychopathic traits in another study with Hispanic girls in Texas (Vitacco, Neumann, Ramos, & Roberts, 2003).

Distant, cold, and rejecting parents are inclined to have delinquent children, as noted by McCord (1979) in the Cambridge–Somerville study, in Boston. McCord (1997) also found that parental warmth can buffer against the effects of physical punishment. Whereas 51% of boys with emotionally distant and cold, physically punishing mothers were convicted in her study, only 21% of boys with warm, physically punishing mothers were convicted—similar to the 23% of boys with warm, nonpunitive mothers who were convicted. The father's warmth was also a protective factor against his physical punishment. These findings replicate some of the McCords' earlier findings. Specifically, many years before, McCord and McCord (1964) concluded that parental rejection was the most critical factor in the development of psychopathy, possibly because it facilitated the development of a cold, unemotional, detached, callous personality. Following in the footsteps of the McCords, other researchers (e.g., Frodi, Dernevik, & Sepa, 1999; Saltaris, 2002) have also proposed that the initiation of child and adolescent psychopathy lies in early problems of attachment to the family, and particularly to parental figures.

TABLE 9.2. Major Studies of Childrearing Practices and Psychopathy/ Antisocial Behavior

Researcher	Parenting method	Sample	Outcome
	Punishment		
Newson & Newson (1989)	Physical punishment	700 Nottingham children	More convictions
Patterson, Reid, & Dishion (1992)	Punitiveness	206 Oregon boys	More antisocial behavior
West & Farrington (1973)	Erratic discipline	411 London boys	More convictions
	Reinforcement		
Farrington & Loeber (1999)	Low parental reinforcement	508 Pittsburgh boys	More delinquency
Larsson, Viding, & Plomin (2008)	Negative parenting	4,152 English children	High antisocial behavior and callous–unemotional traits
	Cold/Distant		
McCord (1979)	Parental rejection and coldness	253 Cambridge–Somerville boys	More convictions
McCord (1997)	Warmth as a protective factor	232 Cambridge–Somerville boys	Fewer convictions
	Involvement		
Lewis, Newson, & Newson (1982)	Low parental involvement	700 Nottingham children	More convictions
West & Farrington (1973)	Low parental involvement	411 London boys	More convictions
	Supervision		
Marshall & Cooke (1999)	Poor parental supervision, poor parental discipline and neglect	50 psychopaths, 55 nonpsychopaths	More psychopathic inmates had these conditions during their childhood.
Salekin & Lochman (2008)	Poor parenting practices	Multiple samples	Psychopathic youth had poor parenting in their background.

Note. This table does not include an exhaustive list of studies that have addressed the development of psychopathy or antisocial behavior from social origins, but rather includes several important survey investigations.

Low levels of parental involvement in the child's activities foreshadow later offending, as the Newsons discovered in their Nottingham survey (Lewis, Newson, & Newson, 1982). In the Cambridge study, having a father who never participated in the boy's hobbies or leisure activities increased his risk of conviction twofold (West & Farrington, 1973, p. 57), and this was the most important predictor of persistence in offending after age 21 as opposed to desistance (Farrington & Hawkins, 1991). Similarly, poor communication between the parent and the child predicted offending in the Pittsburgh Youth Study (Farrington & Loeber, 1999), and low family cohesiveness was the most important predictor of violence in the Chicago Youth Development Study (Gorman-Smith, Tolan, Zelli, & Huesmann, 1996).

Marshall and Cooke (1999) contrasted psychopathic and nonpsychopathic inmates in Scotland using the Psychopathy Checklist—Revised (PCL-R). They discovered that significantly more of the psychopathic inmates reported experiencing parental indifference or neglect, poor parental supervision, and poor parental discipline. In the Cambridge Study, poor parental supervision, indexed at age 8, significantly predicted high psychopathy scores; specifically, 24% of boys who were poorly supervised at age 8 (because their parents did not know where they were when they went out) had high psychopathy scores at age 48, compared with 8% of the remainder (odds ratio [OR] = 3.6, 95% confidence interval [CI] = 1.7 to 8.0). This is quite a large effect; see Cohen (1996).

In a series of studies on protective factors against youth psychopathy (see Salekin & Lochman, 2008), poor parenting was linked to psychopathy early in childhood, even if parental factors were not statistically significant as moderators in adolescence. Salekin and Lochman (2008) suggested that parenting may exert its greatest influence during childhood, and difficulties that arise after childhood may be harder to reverse even if parenting practices are improved. This notion, however, requires much more research, since measures of parental practices require more precision to detect what is occurring in families across adolescence.

Table 9.3 shows 25 chief childhood risk factors that were significantly linked to total psychopathy scores in the Cambridge study. Given that relationships with psychopathy have been presented before (see Farrington, 2006, 2007), Table 9.3 shows relationships with the traditional two-factor model, including the interpersonal–affective (F1) and irresponsible–antisocial (F2) scores, dichotomized as in Table 9.1. The risk factors were dichotomized into the worst quarter (approximately) versus the remaining three quarters.

Table 9.4 shows which childhood risk factors were unique predictors of psychopathy and high F1 and F2 scores (based on logistic regression analyses). Only explanatory risk factors were included in these analyses; trou-

TABLE 9.3. Childhood Predictors of PCL:SV Scores

	% Interpersonal–affective (Factor 1)			% Irresponsible–antisocial (Factor 2)		
Risk factor at ages 8–10	No	Yes	OR	No	Yes	OR
Poor supervision	8.3	14.5	1.9	7.4	23.6	3.9*
Harsh discipline	7.7	16.0	2.3*	8.6	16.0	2.0
Father uninvolved	5.0	20.0	4.7*	6.7	16.9	2.7*
Physical neglect	7.7	28.6	4.8*	8.1	31.4	5.2*
Disrupted family	8.8	15.4	1.9	6.7	24.6	4.6*
Parental disagreement	8.8	13.9	1.7	7.3	17.7	2.7*
Large family size	7.4	19.2	3.0*	6.9	21.9	3.8*
Convicted father	6.1	22.2	4.4*	7.0	22.2	3.8*
Convicted mother	8.8	23.3	3.2*	8.4	30.0	4.7*
Delinquent sibling	8.5	25.0	3.6*	8.5	28.1	4.2*
Young mother	9.4	12.9	1.4	8.1	18.6	2.6*
Depressed mother	7.7	14.9	2.1	6.6	19.1	3.3*
Low family income	6.8	22.1	3.9*	7.2	22.1	3.6*
Low social class	8.4	18.5	2.5*	8.4	20.4	2.8*
Poor housing	8.2	13.3	1.7	6.5	16.7	2.9*
Unpopular	6.9	17.6	2.9*	9.4	13.2	1.5
Delinquent school	6.8	17.6	2.9*	8.2	19.6	2.7*
Low Nonverbal IQ	7.9	16.9	2.4*	8.8	15.6	1.9
Low Verbal IQ	7.0	20.8	3.5*	10.0	12.5	1.3
Low school track	6.9	18.2	3.0*	8.3	15.9	2.1
High daring	8.1	15.2	2.0	7.6	17.4	2.6*
Poor concentration	8.2	18.3	2.5*	8.2	20.0	2.8*
High impulsivity	7.5	17.9	2.7*	8.8	15.4	1.9
Dishonest	8.6	15.9	2.0	6.1	22.2	4.4*
Troublesome	8.7	16.1	2.0	8.3	19.4	2.7*

Note. OR, odds ratio.
*$p < .05$.

blesomeness and dishonesty were not included because they are measures of antisocial behavior. However, tautological issues may also arise in using impulsivity or daring as predictors of psychopathy (Farrington, 2005a; Salekin, Brannen, Zalot, Leistico, Neumann, 2006). One-tailed tests were used because all the predictions are directional.

Table 9.3 shows that poor parental supervision was much more strongly related to the irresponsible–antisocial (F2) score than to the interpersonal–affective (F1) score. In contrast, low involvement of the father in the boy's activities was a stronger predictor of the interpersonal–affective score (F1). Harsh or erratic parental discipline predicted both scores roughly equally. None of these three risk factors was shown to be an independent predictor, as can be seen in Table 9.4.

Child Psychopathy May Stem from Child Abuse and Neglect

Research has shown a relationship between physical abuse or neglect in childhood and offending later in life. The best known study of this was conducted by Widom (1989) in Indianapolis. She used court records to identify over 900 children who had been abused or neglected before age 11, then compared them with a matched control group. The court records allowed Widom to "go back in time" to look at abuse, thereby providing for a natural follow-up. Her results showed that abused or neglected children were more likely to be arrested as juveniles and as adults than were the controls. Moreover, they were more frequently arrested for juvenile violence (Maxfield & Widom, 1996). Child sexual abuse, and child physical abuse and neglect, also predicted adult arrests for sexual crimes (Widom & Ames,

TABLE 9.4. Independent Predictors of PCL:SV Scores

Scale	LRCS change	*p*	Partial OR	*p*
Interpersonal–affective (Factor 1)				
Convicted father	13.69	.0001	3.3	.002
Low family income	7.76	.003	2.7	.010
High impulsivity	1.79	.091	1.8	.088
Irresponsible–antisocial (Factor 2)				
Disrupted family	14.01	.0001	3.7	.001
Depressed mother	7.62	.003	2.9	.007
Large family size	6.56	.005	2.3	.031
Poor supervision	2.78	.048	2.2	.045
Total				
Low family income	18.30	.0001	2.8	.014
Convicted father	9.68	.001	3.0	.005
High daring	8.51	.002	3.2	.004
Depressed mother	3.87	.025	2.3	.026
Poor concentration	2.29	.065	1.9	.074
Delinquent sibling	1.80	.090	2.1	.086

Note. LRCS, likelihood ratio chi-squared; OR, odds ratio.

p values one-tailed.

1994). Most importantly, in terms of the development of child and adolescent psychopathy, Luntz and Widom (1994) found that child abuse predicts adult antisocial personality disorder, and Weiler and Widom (1996) showed that child abuse predicts high PCL-R scores in adulthood across both gender and race.

The findings noted by Widom (1996) have been backed by other researchers as well. An extensive review by Malinosky-Rummell and Hansen (1993) showed evidence that being physically abused as a child subsequently predicts violent and nonviolent offending. For example, in the Cambridge–Somerville study in Boston, McCord (1983) found that approximately half of the abused or neglected boys suffered a number of subsequent problems in later life, including being convicted for serious crimes, becoming alcoholic or mentally ill, or even dying before age 35. In Germany, criminal boys who had been abused or neglected were inclined to have high PCL:YV scores (Krischer & Sevecke, 2008). Likewise, in a retrospective study conducted in Canada, Campbell, Porter, and Santor (2004) found that high scoring PCL:SV delinquents were more likely than low scorers to have suffered physical abuse.

In Stockholm, Lang and colleagues (2002) reported that boys who were abused or neglected at ages 11–14 were inclined to have high PCL scores at age 36 and also to become violent at some time during the follow-up. Retrospective studies of offenders by Koivisto and Haapasalo (1996) in Finland and by Patrick, Zempolich, and Levenston (1997) in Florida found positive correlations between early child abuse and high PCL-R scores, but Marshall and Cooke (1999) in Scotland reported no difference in physical abuse histories between psychopathic and nonpsychopathic inmates. In the Cambridge study, physical neglect of the boy at age 8 was a solid predictor of both interpersonal–affective (F1) and irresponsible–antisocial (F2) scores (Table 9.3).

Disrupted Families and Parental Discord

Bowlby (1951), over a half-century ago, argued that it is essential that a child experience a warm, loving, and continuous relationship with a mother figure in the first 5 years of life. He also suggested that children who suffered maternal deprivation because of a broken home might become "affectionless characters," with no close or meaningful emotional relationships. However, most studies of disbanded families have focused on the loss of the father rather than the mother because the loss of a father occurs much more frequently. In general, research has shown that children who are separated from a biological parent are more likely to offend than are children from cohesive families. For example, Kolvin, Miller, Fleeting, and Kolvin (1988), in a birth cohort study of children born in Newcastle-upon-Tyne, found that boys who experienced divorce or separation in their first 5 years of life had a twofold risk of conviction up to age 32 (53% as opposed to 28%).

McCord (1982), in Boston, conducted an important study of the later serious offending (up to age 45) of boys from homes substantively changed by loss of the biological father. She discovered that the prevalence of offending was high for boys from broken homes without affectionate mothers (62%), and for those from unbroken homes characterized by parental conflict (52%), regardless of whether they had affectionate mothers. The prevalence of offending was low for those from cohesive homes without conflict (26%) and—importantly—equally low for boys from broken homes with affectionate mothers (22%). These results indicate that parental conflict may contribute to family breakdown and youth offending. They also suggest that a connected and caring mother might to some degree be able to compensate for the loss of a father.

Wells and Rankin (1991) conducted a meta-analysis of studies on family makeup and delinquency, and showed that broken homes are more strongly related to delinquency when caused by parental separation or divorce rather than by death. In the Cambridge study, being reared in a disrupted family (separation from a parent before the 10th birthday for reasons other than death or hospitalization) predicted high antisocial personality scores at age 32 (Farrington, 2000) and high irresponsible–antisocial scores (F2), but not high interpersonal–affective (F1) scores. Coming from a disrupted family was the strongest predictor of high irresponsible–antisocial (F2) scores in a logistic regression analysis (see Table 9.4). Although the retrospective study in Finland by Koivisto and Haapasalo (1996) showed a correlation between broken homes and high PCL-R scores, Patrick and colleagues (1997), in Florida, reported that psychopathic inmates were less likely than nonpsychopathic inmates to come from single-parent homes.

Numerous studies show that parental discord and interparental violence predict subsequent antisocial behavior (see Buehler et al., 1997; Kolbo, Blakely, & Engleman, 1996). In the Christchurch Health and Development Study in New Zealand, children who witnessed violence between their parents self-reported engaging in more violence and property offenses (Fergusson & Horwood, 1998). The predictability of witnessing father-initiated violence was robust and maintained its significant predictability even after researchers controlled for other risk factors (e.g., parental criminality, parental substance abuse, parental physical punishment, a young mother, and low family income). In addition, parental discord also predicted offending in both the Cambridge and Pittsburgh studies (Farrington & Loeber, 1999). Table 9.3 shows that parental disagreement at age 8 significantly predicted high irresponsible–antisocial (F2) scores but not high interpersonal–affective (F1) scores.

Large Family Size and Psychopathy

A large number of children in the family is a robust predictor of offending (Ellis, 1988; Fischer, 1984). Large family size was similarly predictive in the Cambridge and Pittsburgh studies (Farrington & Loeber, 1999). In the Cambridge study, having four or more siblings by his 10th birthday doubled a boy's risk of being convicted as a juvenile (West & Farrington, 1973, p. 31). Large family size was the most important independent predictor of convictions up to age 32 in a logistic regression analysis; 58% of boys from large families were convicted up to this age (Farrington, 1993). Being part of a big family at the 10th birthday also predicted chronic offending (Farrington & West, 1993), high scores on an antisocial personality scale at age 32 (Farrington, 2000), and high interpersonal–affective (F1) and irresponsible–antisocial (F2) scores (Table 9.3). Coming from a large family was also a significant independent predictor of high irresponsible–antisocial (F2) scores (Table 9.4).

Antisocial Parents Have Antisocial Children

Numerous studies have shown that criminal and antisocial parents tend to have criminal and antisocial children (McCord, 1977; Robins, 1979). The most extensive research on the concentration of offending in families was conducted in the Cambridge study. Having a convicted family member (convicted father, mother, brother, or sister) predicted a boy's own convictions, and all four relatives were independently important as predictors (Farrington, Barnes, & Lambert, 1996). Same-sex relationships were stronger than opposite-sex relationships, and older siblings were stronger predictors than younger siblings. Only 6% of the families accounted for half of all the convictions of all family members.

The Pittsburgh Youth Study showed findings similar to those in the Cambridge study. Arrests of fathers, mothers, brothers, sisters, uncles, aunts, grandfathers, and grandmothers all predicted the boy's own delinquency (Farrington, Jolliffe, Loeber, Stouthamer-Loeber, & Kalb, 2001). In the Pittsburgh study, the most important relative was the father; arrests of the father predicted the boy's delinquency, independent of all other arrested relatives. Again, a small proportion (only 8%) of families accounted for 43% of arrested family members.

To date, no longitudinal study has specifically linked psychopathy of parents to psychopathy of children. Nonetheless, in Copenhagen, Brennan, Mednick, and Mednick (1993) found that parental psychopathology (including psychopathy) predicted violence by sons up to age 22. In addition, Harris, Rice, and Lalumiere (2001) reported that antisociality in parents (identified on the basis of a composite measure incorporating parental criminality and alcoholism, along with child abuse and neglect) was related to higher psychopathy scores in a sample of violent offenders obtained from a maximum security psychiatric hospital in Canada.

In the Cambridge study, having a convicted parent or a delinquent older sibling by the 10th birthday was consistently among the best predictors at ages 8–10 of the boy's later antisocial behavior. Apart from behavioral measures, such as troublesomeness, they were the most robust predictors of juvenile convictions (Farrington, 1992a) and chronic offending (Farrington & West, 1993). Having a convicted parent was the strongest predictor of scoring high on an antisocial personality measure at age 32 (Farrington, 2000). Table 9.3 shows that having a convicted father, a convicted mother, or a delinquent sibling by the 10th birthday significantly predicts high interpersonal–affective (F1) and irresponsible–antisocial (F2) scores. A convicted father was the best independent predictor of high irresponsible/antisocial scores (F2), and a convicted father and a delinquent sibling were independent predictors of total psychopathy scores (Table 9.4).

Other Potentially Important Parental Characteristics

Many other parental characteristics predict antisocial behavior. For example, early childbearing, or teenage pregnancy, are risk factors. Morash and Rucker (1989) analyzed results from four surveys in the United States and England (including the Cambridge study) and found that teenage mothers coincide with low-income families, and are inclined to have welfare support and absent biological fathers. In addition, they are more likely to use poor childrearing practices, and their children are often characterized by poor school performance and conduct problems, including delinquency. However, the presence of the biological father protects against many of these adverse factors (see below). Likewise, a large-scale study in Washington State found that children of teenage or unmarried mothers had a significantly increased risk of offending (Conseur, Rivara, Barnoski, & Emanuel, 1997). Boys born to unmarried mothers age 17 or less were found to have an 11-fold increase in the risk of chronic offending compared with boys born to married mothers age 20 or more.

In both the Cambridge and Pittsburgh studies, the age of the mother at her first birth was only a moderate predictor of the boy's later delinquency (Farrington & Loeber, 1999). In the Cambridge study, 27% of sons of young mothers were convicted as juveniles, compared with 18% of the remainder. More specific analyses in this study indicated that teenage mothers who went on to have large numbers of children were particularly likely to have convicted sons (Nagin, Pogarsky, & Farrington, 1997). Table 9.3 shows that boys born to mothers in their teen years at the time of their first birth were significantly more likely to have high irresponsible–antisocial (F2) scores. Having a young mother also predicted high scores on an antisocial personality scale at age 32 (Farrington, 2000).

Parental stress, anxiety, and/or depression also predicted delinquency in the Pittsburgh Youth Study (Loeber, Farrington, Stouthamer-Loeber, & van Kammen, 1998). In a large-scale study in England, Barker and Maughan (2009) found that anxiety and depression in prenatal women were significant predictors of conduct problems in children. In the Cambridge study, having an anxious or depressed mother predicted a boy's high scores on an antisocial personality scale at age 18 but not at age 32 (Farrington, 2000). Table 9.3 shows that having an anxious or depressed mother predicts high irresponsible–antisocial (F2) scores, and Table 9.4 shows that a depressed mother is an independent predictor of high irresponsible–antisocial (F2) scores and total psychopathy scores. Having a father with depressive symptoms did not predict psychopathy.

Parental substance use also foreshadows antisocial behavior by children according to findings in the Pittsburgh Youth Study (Loeber et al., 1998). Smoking by the mother during pregnancy is a salient risk factor. Smoking was related to psychopathy scores in a sample of children with attention-deficit/hyperactivity disorder (ADHD) (Fowler et al., 2009). A large-scale follow-up of a general population cohort in Finland showed that maternal smoking during pregnancy doubled the risk of violent or persistent offending by male offspring, after researchers controlled for other biopsychosocial risk factors (Rasanen et al., 1999). When maternal smoking was combined with (1) a teenage mother, (2) a single-parent family, and (3) an unwanted pregnancy, the risk of offending increased 10-fold. Clearly, other substance use and abuse problems (e.g., alcohol use, illicit drug use) are likely to be even more detrimental to the healthy development of youth.

Socioeconomic Factors: Poorer Youth Are at Risk

Speaking generally, coming from an affluent family serves as a protective factor against antisocial behavior, and particularly against violence. Research has shown that being reared in a low social class family predicts later violence. For example, in the U.S. National Youth Survey, prevalence rates for self-reported assault and robbery were about twice as high among low-class youth as among middle-class youth (Elliott, Huizinga, & Menard, 1989). In Project Metropolitan in Stockholm (Wikström, 1985) and in the Dunedin Study in New Zealand (Henry, Caspi, Moffitt, & Silva, 1996), low socioeconomic status (SES) of a boy's family—based on the father's occupation—predicted later violent crimes.

Low SES is a less consistent predictor of general offending, but it continues to have some predictive value, especially when examined in the context of other important variables, such as low income; that is, one source of variance is whether it is measured by income and housing or by occupational prestige. In the Cambridge study, low family income and poor housing predicted self-reported and official juvenile and adult offending. However, low parental occupational prestige predicted only self-reported offending (Farrington, 1992a, 1992b). In addition, low family income and low SES (but not poor housing) significantly predicted chronic offending (Farrington & West, 1993) and high scores on an antisocial personality scale at age 32 (Farrington, 2000). Table 9.3 indicates that low family income at age 8 and low social class at ages 8–10 (based on occupational prestige) predicted psychopathy. Specifically, low family income predicted high interpersonal–affective (F1) and irresponsible–antisocial (F2) scores, whereas poor housing at ages 8–10 predicted only high irresponsible–antisocial (F2) scores. Being poor was the most important independent predictor of total psychopathy scores, and it was also an independent predictor of high interpersonal–affective (F1) scores (Table 9.4).

In addition, Lynam, Loeber, and Stouthamer-Loeber (2008) noted that growing up in wealthier families protects youth against the development of psychopathy. Specifically, they stated that "boys who were low in psychopathy at age 13, who grew up poorer, who had antisocial friends, and who experienced more physical punishment became more psychopathic over time" (p. 238). This study is important because it not only addresses the issue of SES but it also encapsulates a number of the previously discussed risk factors in this chapter.

Child and Adolescent Psychopathy and Peer Influence

It is clear that having delinquent friends is an important predictor of offending (Lipsey & Derzon, 1998). Less well known is whether antisocial peers facilitate adolescent antisocial behavior, or whether it is merely the case that "birds of a feather flock together." Delinquents may have delinquent friends because of co-offending, which is particularly common under age 21 (Moffitt, 2003; Reiss & Farrington, 1991). However, Elliott and Menard (1996), in the U.S. National Youth Survey, deduced that delinquent friends influence an adolescent's own delinquency, and that the reverse is also true. Delinquent friends were not measured until age 14 in the Cambridge study, but chronic offenders significantly tended to have them (Farrington & West, 1993).

There is little doubt that highly aggressive children are inclined to be rejected by many of their peers (Coie, Dodge, & Kupersmidt, 1990). Coie and Miller-Johnson (2001) discovered that the boys who were both aggressive and rejected by their classmates became the self-reported and official offenders. In the Oregon Youth Study, peer rejection at ages 9–10 significantly predicted adult antisocial behavior at ages 23–24 (Nelson & Dishion, 2004). In Stockholm, Freidenfelt and af Klinteberg (2003) noted that unpopularity predicted high PCL scores among hyperactive boys but not nonhyperactive boys. In another Swedish study, Muñoz, Kerr, and Besic (2008) discovered that youth who scored high on psychopathic traits reported that their peer relationships were more conflictual than others. They also found that having one friend who was doing well in school served as a protective factor for a psychopathic youth.

In the retrospective study by Campbell and colleagues (2004), having numerous friends was not related to high PCL:SV scores. However, Barry, Barry, Deming, and Lochman (2008) found that social competence serves as a protective factor against future offending. Low popularity at ages 8–10 was only a marginal predictor of adolescent aggression and teenage violence in the Cambridge study (Farrington, 1989). It significantly predicted chronic offending (Farrington & West, 1993) but not high antisocial personality scores at age 32 (Farrington, 2000). Low popularity significantly predicted high interpersonal–affective (F1) scores (Table 9.3).

Neighborhood and School Contextual Factors

The extent to which child and adolescent psychopathy is linked to neighborhood and school factors is not all that well established. However, it is relatively well known that delinquents disproportionately attend schools with high delinquency rates, with high levels of distrust between teachers and students, low commitment to the school by students, and at times unclear and inconsistently enforced rules (Graham, 1988). In the Cambridge study, attending a school with a high delinquency rate at age 11 predicted a boy's own delinquency (Farrington, 1992a), as well as his chronic offending (Farrington & West, 1993) and high scores on an antisocial personality scale at age 32 (Farrington, 2000). Table 9.3 shows that attending a school with a high delinquency rate predicts psychopathy scores and, specifically, high interpersonal–affective (F1) and irresponsible–antisocial (F2) psychopathy scores.

Numerous research studies indicate that boys residing in urban areas are more violent than those living in rural ones. In the U.S. National Youth Survey, the prevalence of self-reported assault and robbery was considerably higher among urban youth (Elliott et al., 1989). Within urban areas, boys residing in high-crime neighborhoods are more violent than those living in low-crime neighborhoods. In the Rochester Youth Development Study, residing in a high crime neighborhood significantly predicted self-reported violence (Thornberry, Huizinga, & Loeber, 1995). Likewise, in the Pittsburgh Youth Study, residing in a bad neighborhood predicted both reported and official violence (Farrington, 1998).

Additional Risk Factors

Table 9.3 also outlines the extent to which other, well-known risk factors, measured at ages 8–10 in the Cambridge study, predicted high interpersonal–affective (F1) and irresponsible–antisocial (F2) psychopathy scores. Low Nonverbal IQ, low Verbal IQ, and assignment to low-achieving classes all predicted high interpersonal–affective (F1) scores but not high irresponsible–antisocial (F2) scores. High sensation-seeking or daring behavior (taking many risks) predicted high irresponsible–antisocial (F2) scores, poor concentration or restlessness predicted both scores (F1 and F2), and high impulsivity on psychomotor tests predicted high interpersonal–affective (F1) scores. High dishonesty (rated by peers) and high troublesomeness (rated by peers and teachers) significantly predicted only high irresponsible–antisocial (F2) scores. High daring was an important independent predictor of high total psychopathy scores (Table 9.4).

Delineating the Developmental Path of Psychopathy

It is a very complex task to determine the precise causal mechanisms that link family factors—such as parental criminality, young mothers, large family size, poor parental supervision, child abuse, or disrupted families—to later psychopathy. This is because these factors tend to be intertwined with each other and are also related to other risk factors, such as low family income, poor housing, impulsiveness, low IQ, and low school attainment. Just as it is difficult to know the main underlying family causal mechanisms, it is equally difficult to know the chief underlying mechanisms in other domains of life. It is, of course, also important to study the interactive effects of different types of risk factors.

With child psychopathy emerging as a relevant construct, and its manifestation occurring early in life, it is important to investigate the ontogeny of the disorder and the sequential effects of risk factors on psychopathy. A number of researchers have suggested that socioeconomic standing affects offending through its effect on family factors (see Dodge, Pettit, & Bates, 1994; Larzelere & Patterson, 1990; Stern & Smith, 1995). For instance, in the Pittsburgh Youth Study, researchers proposed that socioeconomic and neighborhood factors (e.g., poor housing) influence family factors (e.g., poor supervision), which in turn influence child factors (e.g., low guilt), which in turn influence offending (Loeber et al., 1998, p. 10). There may also be sequential effects of some family factors on others (e.g., if young mothers tend to use poor childrearing methods; see Conger, Patterson, & Ge, 1995), or of family factors on other risk factors (e.g., if antisocial parents tend to have low incomes and live in poor neighborhoods).

Based on our results, the most important childhood risk factors for high psychopathic traits or interpersonal–affective scores (F1) are a convicted father, low family income, high impulsivity, an uninvolved father, low popularity, and low intelligence/achievement. It may be that poverty, combined with family criminality and parental rejection, creates a low-achieving, unattached child and, potentially, the psychopathic personality, which in turn leads to rejection by peers. Lynam and colleagues' (2008) results also suggest that low income and other factors promote growth in psychopathy scores over time.

The most important childhood risk factors for high social deviance or irresponsible–antisocial scores (F2) are parental conflict and a disrupted family, a depressed mother, a young mother, large family size, and poor parental supervision. In the logistic regression analysis, there was a near-significant ($p = .056$, two-tailed) interaction between being reared in a large family and having a depressed mother. If neither risk factor was present, 6% of boys had high irresponsible–antisocial scores, similar to the percentage with only large family size (9%) or only a depressed mother (9%). However, if large family size co-occurred with a depressed mother, 43% of boys had high irresponsible–antisocial scores.

Similar to the notions put forward by Blackburn (1998), Cooke and colleagues (2004) and even earlier by Cleckley (1941/1976), it has been suggested that a psychopathic personality causes an irresponsible and antisocial lifestyle, especially with exposure to environmental risk factors such as a young, separated, depressed mother with a large family, who is unable to supervise or monitor her children effectively. Looking at this issue from a protective factor framework (Salekin & Lochman, 2008), competent parenting early on, good peer influence (peers interested in school), and social competence can all protect against the development of psychopathy. In essence, these environmental influences may be key in setting the moral compass of children, and may be especially important for children and adolescents at risk for psychopathy.

Conclusions and Future Directions

Although child/adolescent psychopathy has received a great deal of research attention in the past decade, much more scientific research on the development of psychopathy is needed. More effort should be directed toward integrating the personality constructs underlying psychopathy, especially an arrogant and deceitful interpersonal style and deficient affective experience, with larger systems of personality constructs (Lynam et al., 2005; Salekin, Leistico, Trobst, Schrum, & Lochman, 2005; Widiger, 1998). In addition, research is required on the development of more unbiased, valid, and reliable instruments to measure psychopathy, particularly in children and adolescents, as Johnstone and Cooke (2004, 2009) suggested. And it is desirable to have measures that are not contaminated by antisocial behavior, and that do not rely on open-ended questions.

Alternatively, as in this chapter, researchers could examine the constituent factors of psychopathy (personality vs. behavior). In addition, bottom-up attempts at developing child and adolescent psychopathy measures (Salekin, 2006; Salekin, Rogers, & Machin, 2001) rather than using adult derivative measures could prove fruitful. Also, as we have noted elsewhere, it is important to supplement self-report data with other information (e.g., from case files and/or interviews). Finally, more research is needed on protective factors against psychopathy (Salekin & Lochman, 2008).

The goal should be to chart out and test developmental theories of psychopathy and its core constructs, such as low remorse and egocentricity (see Farrington, 2005a). There is a great need for prospective longitudinal surveys with high-risk community samples to investigate the link between psychopathic parents and psychopathic children. More randomized experiments are needed to evaluate psychosocial interventions (see Farrington, 2005a; Farrington & Welsh, 2005; Salekin, Chapter 14, this volume), with large samples, incorporating long-term downstream outcome indices of psychopathy. In principle, a considerable amount of knowledge can be gleaned from such experiments, which are designed to reveal more about causal effects of social factors (Robins, 1992).

There is little doubt of the importance of the child and adolescent construct of psychopathy, the need to develop better operational definitions of the underlying concepts, and the demand to advance knowledge about the development, explanation, prevention, and treatment of psychopathy. Ambitious, coordinated programs of research on psychopathy, focusing on international multidisciplinary collaboration and aiming to train a new generation of biopsychosocial researchers, are needed. Given the enormous social costs of psychopathy, the benefits of such a large-scale coordinated program of research should easily outweigh its costs. And, of course, a reduction in the number of psychopathic children/adolescents and victims in their wake would greatly increase collective human well-being.

Acknowledgments

Data collection on participants ages 8–10 in the Cambridge Study in Delinquent Development was funded by the Home Office and directed by Professor Donald West. The medical interview at age 48 was funded by the U.K. National Programme on Forensic Mental Health, and the interview was conducted by Dr. Crystal Romilly, under the supervision of Professor Jeremy Coid. The PCL:SV was scored by Drs. Crystal Romilly and Simone Ullrich.

References

Barker, E. D., & Maughan, B. (2009). Differentiating early-onset persistent versus childhood-limited conduct problem youth. *American Journal of Psychiatry, 166,* 900–908.

Barry, T. D., Barry, C. T., Deming, A. M., & Lochman, J. E. (2008). Stability of psychopathic characteristics in childhood: The influence of social relationships. *Criminal Justice and Behavior, 35,* 244–262.

Blackburn, R. (1998). Psychopathy and personality disorder: Implications of interpersonal theory. In D. Cooke, A. Forth, & R. D. Hare (Eds.), *Psychopathy: Theory, research and practice* (pp. 269–301). Dordrecht, The Netherlands: Kluwer.

Bowlby, J. (1951). *Maternal care and mental health.* Geneva: World Health Organization.

Brennan, P. A., Mednick, B. R., & Mednick, S. A. (1993). Parental psychopathology, congenital factors, and violence. In S. Hodgins (Ed.), *Mental disorder and crime* (pp. 244–261). Newbury Park, CA: Sage.

Buehler, C., Anthony, C., Krishnakumar, A., Stone, G., Gerard, J., & Pemberton, S. (1997). Interparental conflict and youth problem behaviors: A meta-analysis. *Journal of Child and Family Studies, 6,* 233–247.

Campbell, M. A., Porter, S., & Santor, D. (2004). Psychopathic traits in adolescent offenders: An evaluation of criminal history, clinical, and psychosocial correlates. *Behavioral Sciences and the Law, 22,* 23–47.

Cleckley, H. (1941). *The mask of sanity.* St. Louis, MO: Mosby.

Cohen, P. (1996). Childhood risks for young adult symptoms of personality disorder. *Multivariate Behavioral Research, 31,* 121–148.

Coie, J. D., Dodge, K. A., & Kupersmidt, J. (1990). Peer group behavior and social status. In S. R. Asher & J. D. Coie (Eds.), *Peer rejection in childhood* (pp. 17–59). Cambridge, UK: Cambridge University Press.

Coie, J. D., & Miller-Johnson, S. (2001). Peer factors and interventions. In R. Loeber & D. P. Farrington (Eds.), *Child delinquents: Development, intervention, and service needs* (pp. 191–209). Thousand Oaks, CA: Sage.

Conger, R. D., Patterson, G. R., & Ge, X. (1995). It takes two to replicate: A mediational model for the impact of parents' stress on adolescent adjustment. *Child Development, 66,* 80–97.

Conseur, A., Rivara, F. P., Barnoski, R., & Emanuel, I. (1997). Maternal and perinatal risk factors for later delinquency. *Pediatrics, 99,* 785–790.

Cooke, D. J., & Michie, C. (2001). Refining the construct of psychopathy: Towards a hierarchical model. *Psychological Assessment, 13,* 171–188.

Cooke, D. J., Michie, C., Hart, S. D., & Clark, D. A. (2004). Reconstructing psychopathy: Clarifying the significance of antisocial and socially deviant behavior in the diagnosis of psychopathic personality disorder. *Journal of Personality Disorders, 18,* 337–357.

Corrado, R. R., Vincent, G. M., Hart, S. D., & Cohen, I. M. (2004). Predictive validity of the Psychopathy Checklist: Youth Version for general and violent recidivism. *Behavioral Sciences and the Law, 22,* 5–22.

Dodge, K. A., Pettit, G. S., & Bates, J. E. (1994). Socialization mediators of the relation between socioeconomic status and child conduct problems. *Child Development, 65*, 649–665.

Elliott, D. S., Huizinga, D., & Menard, S. (1989). *Multiple problem youth.* New York: Springer-Verlag.

Elliott, D. S., & Menard, S. (1996). Delinquent friends and delinquent behavior: Temporal and developmental patterns. In J. D. Hawkins (Ed.), *Delinquency and crime: Current theories* (pp. 28–67). Cambridge, UK: Cambridge University Press.

Ellis, L. (1988). The victimful–victimless crime distinction, and seven universal demographic correlates of victimful criminal behavior. *Personality and Individual Differences, 3*, 525–548.

Farrington, D. P. (1989). Early predictors of adolescent aggression and adult violence. *Violence and Victims, 4*, 79–100.

Farrington, D. P. (1992a). Explaining the beginning, progress, and ending of antisocial behavior from birth to adulthood. In J. McCord (Ed.), *Facts, frameworks and forecasts: Advances in criminological theory* (Vol. 3, pp. 253–286). New Brunswick, NJ: Transaction.

Farrington, D. P. (1992b). Juvenile delinquency. In J. C. Coleman (Ed.), *The school years* (2nd ed., pp. 123–163). London: Routledge.

Farrington, D. P. (1993). Childhood origins of teenage antisocial behaviour and adult social dysfunction. *Journal of the Royal Society of Medicine, 86*, 13–17.

Farrington, D. P. (1998). Predictors, causes, and correlates of youth violence. In M. Tonry & M. H. Moore (Eds.), *Youth violence* (pp. 421–475). Chicago: University of Chicago Press.

Farrington, D. P. (2000). Psychosocial predictors of adult antisocial personality and adult convictions. *Behavioral Sciences and the Law, 18*, 605–622.

Farrington, D. P. (2003). Key results from the first 40 years of the Cambridge Study in Delinquent Development. In T. P. Thornberry & M. D. Krohn (Eds.), *Taking stock of delinquency* (pp. 137–183). New York: Kluwer Academic/Plenum Press.

Farrington, D. P. (2005a). The importance of child and adolescent psychopathy. *Journal of Abnormal Child Psychology, 33*, 489–497.

Farrington, D. P. (Ed.). (2005b). *Integrated developmental and life-course theories of offending (Advances in criminological theory, Vol. 14)*. New Brunswick, NJ: Transaction.

Farrington, D. P. (2006). Family background and psychopathy. In C. J. Patrick (Ed.), *Handbook of psychopathy* (pp. 229–250). New York: Guilford Press.

Farrington, D. P. (2007). Social origins of psychopathy. In A. R. Felthous & H. Sass (Eds.), *International handbook on psychopathic disorders and the law: Vol. 1. Diagnosis and treatment* (pp. 319–334). New York: Wiley.

Farrington, D. P., Barnes, G., & Lambert, S. (1996). The concentration of offending in families. *Legal and Criminological Psychology, 1*, 47–63.

Farrington, D. P., Coid, J. W., Harnett, L., Jolliffe, D., Soteriou, N., Turner, R., et al. (2006). *Criminal careers and life success: New findings from the Cambridge Study in Delinquent Development.* London: Home Office (Findings No. 281).

Farrington, D. P., & Hawkins, J. D. (1991). Predicting participation, early onset, and later persistence in officially recorded offending. *Criminal Behavior and Mental Health*, *1*, 1–33.

Farrington, D. P., Jolliffe, D., Loeber, R., Stouthamer-Loeber, M., & Kalb, L. M. (2001). The concentration of offenders in families, and family criminality in the prediction of boys' delinquency. *Journal of Adolescence*, *24*, 579–596.

Farrington, D. P., & Loeber, R. (1999). Transatlantic replicability of risk factors in the development of delinquency. In P. Cohen, C. Slomkowski, & L. N. Robins (Eds.), *Historical and geographical influences on psychopathology* (pp. 299–329). Mahwah, NJ: Erlbaum.

Farrington, D. P., & Welsh, B. C. (2005). Randomized experiments in criminology: What have we learned in the last two decades? *Journal of Experimental Criminology*, *1*, 9–38.

Farrington, D. P., & West, D. J. (1993). Criminal, penal, and life histories of chronic offenders: Risk and protective factors and early identification. *Criminal Behavior and Mental Health*, *3*, 492–523.

Fergusson, D. M., & Horwood, L. J. (1998). Exposure to interparental violence in childhood and psychosocial adjustment in young adulthood. *Child Abuse and Neglect*, *22*, 339–357.

Fergusson, D. M., Horwood, L. J., & Lynskey, M. (1994). The childhoods of multiple problem adolescents: A 15–year longitudinal study. *Journal of Child Psychology and Psychiatry*, *35*, 1123–1140.

First, M. B., Gibbon, M., Spitzer, R. L., Williams, J. B. W., & Benjamin, L. (1997). *Structured Clinical Interviews for DSM-IV Axis II personality disorders*. Washington, DC: American Psychiatric Press.

Fischer, D. G. (1984). Family size and delinquency. *Perceptual and Motor Skills*, *58*, 527–534.

Forth, A. E., Kosson, D. S., & Hare, R. D. (2003). *The Psychopathy Checklist: Youth Version manual*. Toronto: Multi-Health Systems.

Fowler, T., Langley, K., Rice, F., Whittinger, N., Ross, K., van Goozen, S., et al. (2009). Psychopathy traits in adolescents with childhood attention-deficit hyperactivity disorder. *British Journal of Psychiatry*, *194*, 62–67.

Freidenfelt, J., & af Klinteberg, B. (2003). Are negative social and psychological childhood characteristics of significant importance in the development of psychosocial functioning? *International Journal of Forensic Mental Health*, *2*, 181–193.

Frick, P. J., Kimonis, E. R., Dandreaux, D. M., & Farrell, J. M. (2003). The 4-year stability of psychopathic traits in non-referred youth. *Behavioral Sciences and the Law*, *21*, 713–736.

Frodi, A., Dernevik, M., & Sepa, A. (1999). Psychopathy: Roots in early attachment relationships? *Forensic Update*, *58*, 5–8.

Gorman-Smith, D., Tolan, P. H., Zelli, A., & Huesmann, L. R. (1996). The relation of family functioning to violence among inner-city minority youths. *Journal of Family Psychology*, *10*, 115–129.

Graham, J. (1988). *Schools, disruptive behaviour and delinquency*. London: Her Majesty's Stationery Office.

Haapasalo, J., & Pokela, E. (1999). Child-rearing and child abuse antecedents of criminality. *Aggression and Violent Behavior, 1*, 107–127.

Hare, R. D. (1970). *Psychopathy: Theory and research.* New York: Wiley.

Hare, R. D. (2003). *The Psychopathy Checklist—Revised* (2nd ed.). Toronto: Multi-Health Systems.

Harpur, T., Hare, R. D., & Hakstian, R. (1989). A two-factor conceptualization of psychopathy: Construct validity and implications for assessment. *Psychological Assessment, 1*, 6–17.

Harris, G. T., Rice, M. E., & Lalumiere, M. (2001). Criminal violence: The roles of psychopathy, neurodevelopmental insults, and antisocial parenting. *Criminal Justice and Behavior, 28*, 402–426.

Hart, S. D., Cox, D. N., & Hare, R. D. (1995). *The Hare Psychopathy Checklist: Screening Version.* Toronto: Multi-Health Systems.

Hart, S. D., & Hare, R. D. (1997). Psychopathy: Assessment and association with criminal conduct. In D. M. Stoff, J. Breiling, & J. D. Maser (Eds.), *Handbook of antisocial behavior* (pp. 22–35). New York: Wiley.

Hart, S. D., Watt, K. A., & Vincent, G. A. (2002). Commentary on Seagrave and Grisso: Impressions of the state of the art. *Law and Human Behavior, 26*, 241–245.

Henry, B., Caspi, A., Moffitt, T. E., & Silva, P. A. (1996). Temperamental and familial predictors of violent and nonviolent criminal convictions: Age 3 to age 18. *Developmental Psychology, 32*, 614–623.

Herpertz, S. C., & Sass, H. (2000). Emotional deficiency and psychopathy. *Behavioral Sciences and the Law, 18*, 567–580.

Johnstone, L., & Cooke, D. J. (2004). Psychopathic-like traits in childhood: Conceptual and measurement concerns. *Behavioral Sciences and the Law, 22*, 103–125.

Johnstone, L., & Cooke, D. J. (2009). Conceptualizing psychopathic-like traits in children and adolescents: Promise or peril? *Neuropsychiatrie, 23*(Suppl. 1), S54–S63.

Kalb, L. M., Farrington, D. P., & Loeber, R. (2001). Leading longitudinal studies on delinquency, substance use, sexual behavior, and mental health problems with childhood samples. In R. Loeber & D. P. Farrington (Eds.), *Child delinquents: Development, intervention, and service needs* (pp. 415–423). Thousand Oaks, CA: Sage.

Koivisto, H., & Haapasalo, J. (1996). Childhood maltreatment and adulthood psychopathy in light of file-based assessments among mental state examinees. *Studies on Crime and Crime Prevention, 5*, 91–104.

Kolbo, J. R., Blakely, E. H., & Engleman, D. (1996). Children who witness domestic violence: A review of empirical literature. *Journal of Interpersonal Violence, 11*, 281–293.

Kolvin, I., Miller, F. J. W., Fleeting, M., & Kolvin, P. A. (1988). Social and parenting factors affecting criminal-offence rates: Findings from the Newcastle Thousand Family Study (1947–1980). *British Journal of Psychiatry, 152*, 80–90.

Kraemer, H. C., Kazdin, A. E., Offord, D. R., Kessler, R. C., Jensen, P. S., & Kupfer, D. J. (1997). Coming to terms with the terms of risk. *Archives of General Psychiatry, 54*, 337–343.

Krischer, M. K., & Sevecke, K. (2008). Early traumatization and psychopathy in female and male juvenile offenders. *International Journal of Law and Psychiatry, 31*, 253–262.

Lang, S., af Klinteberg, B., & Alm, P.-O. (2002). Adult psychopathy and violent behavior in males with early neglect and abuse. *Acta Psychiatrica Scandinavica, 106*, 93–100.

Larsson, H., Viding, E., & Plomin, R. (2008). Callous–unemotional traits and antisocial behavior: Genetic, environmental, and early parenting characteristics. *Criminal Justice and Behavior, 35*, 197–211.

Larzelere, R. E., & Patterson, G. R. (1990). Parental management: Mediator of the effect of socioeconomic status on early delinquency. *Criminology, 28*, 301–324.

Leistico, A. M. R., Salekin, R. T., DeCoster, J., & Rogers, R. (2008). A large-scale meta-analysis relating the Hare measures of psychopathy to antisocial conduct. *Law and Human Behavior, 32*, 28–45.

Lewis, C., Newson, E., & Newson, J. (1982). Father participation through childhood and its relationship with career aspirations and delinquency. In N. Beail & J. McGuire (Eds.), *Fathers: Psychological perspectives* (pp. 174–193). London: Junction.

Lipsey, M. W., & Derzon, J. H. (1998). Predictors of violent or serious delinquency in adolescence and early adulthood: A synthesis of longitudinal research. In R. Loeber & D. P. Farrington (Eds.), *Serious and violent juvenile offenders: Risk factors and successful interventions* (pp. 86–105). Thousand Oaks, CA: Sage.

Loeber, R., & Farrington, D. P. (1997). Strategies and yields of longitudinal studies on antisocial behavior. In D. M. Stoff, J. Breiling, & J. D. Maser (Eds.), *Handbook of antisocial behavior* (pp. 125–139). New York: Wiley.

Loeber, R., Farrington, D. P., Stouthamer-Loeber, M., & van Kammen, W. B. (1998). *Antisocial behavior and mental health problems.* Mahwah, NJ: Erlbaum.

Loeber, R., Farrington, D. P., Stouthamer-Loeber, M., & White, H. R. (2008). *Violence and serious theft: Development and prediction from childhood to adulthood.* New York: Routledge.

Luntz, B. K., & Widom, C. S. (1994). Antisocial personality disorder in abused and neglected children. *American Journal of Psychiatry, 151*, 670–674.

Lykken, D. T. (1995). *The antisocial personalities.* Hillsdale, NJ: Erlbaum.

Lynam, D. R., Caspi, A., Moffitt, T. E., Loeber, R., & Stouthamer-Loeber, M. (2007). Longitudinal evidence that psychopathy scores in early adolescence predict adult psychopathy. *Journal of Abnormal Psychology, 116*, 155–165.

Lynam, D. R., Caspi, A., Moffitt, T. E., Raine, A., Loeber, R., & Stouthamer-Loeber, M. (2005). Adolescent psychopathy and the Big Five: Results from two samples. *Journal of Abnormal Child Psychology, 33*, 431–443.

Lynam, D. R., Loeber, R., & Stouthamer-Loeber, M. (2008). The stability of psychopathy from adolescence into adulthood: The search for moderators. *Criminal Justice and Behavior, 35*, 228–243.

McCord, J. (1977). A comparative study of two generations of native Americans. In R. F. Meier (Ed.), *Theory in criminology* (pp. 83–92). Beverly Hills, CA: Sage.

McCord, J. (1979). Some child-rearing antecedents of criminal behavior in adult men. *Journal of Personality and Social Psychology, 37*, 1477–1486.

McCord, J. (1982). A longitudinal view of the relationship between paternal absence and crime. In J. Gunn & D. P. Farrington (Eds.), *Abnormal offenders, delinquency, and the criminal justice system* (pp. 113–128). Chichester, UK: Wiley.

McCord, J. (1983). A forty year perspective on effects of child abuse and neglect. *Child Abuse and Neglect, 7*, 265–270.

McCord, J. (1997). On discipline. *Psychological Inquiry, 8*, 215–217.

McCord, W., & McCord, J. (1964). *The psychopath: An essay on the criminal mind.* Princeton, NJ: Van Nostrand.

Malinosky-Rummell, R., & Hansen, D. J. (1993). Long-term consequences of childhood physical abuse. *Psychological Bulletin, 114*, 68–79.

Marshall, L. A., & Cooke, D. J. (1999). The childhood experiences of psychopaths: A retrospective study of familial and social factors. *Journal of Personality Disorders, 13*, 211–225.

Maxfield, M. G., & Widom, C. S. (1996). The cycle of violence revisited six years later. *Archives of Pediatrics and Adolescent Medicine, 150*, 390–395.

Moffitt, T. E. (2003). Life-course-persistent and adolescence-limited antisocial behavior: A ten-year research review and a research agenda. In B. B. Lahey, T. E. Moffitt, & A. Caspi (Eds.), *Causes of conduct disorder and juvenile delinquency* (pp. 49–75). New York: Guilford Press.

Morash, M., & Rucker, L. (1989). An exploratory study of the connection of mother's age at childbearing to her children's delinquency in four data sets. *Crime and Delinquency, 35*, 45–93.

Muñoz, L. C., Kerr, M., & Besic, N. (2008). The peer relationships of youths with psychopathic personality traits: A matter of perspective. *Criminal Justice and Behavior, 35*, 212–227.

Murrie, D. C., Marcus, D. K., Douglas, K. S., Lee, Z., Salekin, R. T., & Vincent, G. (2007). Youth with psychopathy features are not a discrete class: A taxometric analysis. *Journal of Child Psychology and Psychiatry, 48*, 714–723.

Nagin, D. S., Pogarsky, G., & Farrington, D. P. (1997). Adolescent mothers and the criminal behavior of their children. *Law and Society Review, 31*, 137–162.

Nelson, S. E., & Dishion, T. J. (2004). From boys to men: Predicting adult adaptation from middle childhood sociometric status. *Development and Psychopathology, 16*, 441–459.

Newson, J., & Newson, E. (1989). *The extent of parental physical punishment in the UK*. London: Approach.

Obradović, J., Pardini, D. A., Long, J. D., & Loeber, R. (2007). Measuring interpersonal callousness in boys from childhood to adolescence: An examination of longitudinal invariance and temporal stability. *Journal of Clinical Child and Adolescent Psychology, 36*, 276–292.

Patrick, C. J., Fowles, D. C., & Krueger, R. F. (2009). Triarchic conceptualization of psychopathy: Developmental origins of disinhibition, boldness, and meanness. *Development and Psychopathology, 21*, 913–938.

Patrick, C. J., Zempolich, K. A., & Levenston, G. K. (1997). Emotionality and violent behavior in psychopaths: A biosocial analysis. In A. Raine, P. A. Brennan, D. P. Farrington, & S. A. Mednick (Eds.), *Biosocial bases of violence* (pp. 145–161). New York: Plenum Press.

Patterson, G., R., Reid, J. B., & Dishion, T. J. (1992). *Antisocial boys*. Eugene, OR: Castalia.

Rasanen, P., Hakko, H., Isohanni, M., Hodgins, S., Jarvelin, M., & Tilhonen, J. (1999). Maternal smoking during pregnancy and risk of criminal behavior among adult male offspring in the Northern Finland 1966 birth cohort. *American Journal of Psychiatry, 156*, 857–862.

Reiss, A. J., & Farrington, D. P. (1991). Advancing knowledge about co-offending: Results from a prospective longitudinal survey of London males. *Journal of Criminal Law and Criminology*, *82*, 360–395.

Roberts, B. W., & DelVecchio, W. F. (2000). The rank-order consistency of personality traits from childhood to old age: A quantitative review of longitudinal studies. *Psychological Bulletin, 126*, 3–25.

Robins, L. N. (1979). Sturdy childhood predictors of adult outcomes: Replications from longitudinal studies. In J. E. Barrett, R. M. Rose, & G. L. Klerman (Eds.), *Stress and mental disorder* (pp. 219–235). New York: Raven Press.

Robins, L. N. (1992). The role of prevention experiments in discovering causes of children's antisocial behavior. In J. McCord & R. E. Tremblay (Eds.), *Preventing antisocial behavior: Interventions from birth through adolescence* (pp. 3–18). New York: Guilford Press.

Rogers, R. (2001). *Handbook of diagnostic and structured interviewing*. New York: Guilford Press.

Salekin, R. T. (2006). Psychopathy in children and adolescents: Key issues in conceptualization and assessment. In C. J. Patrick (Eds.), *Handbook of psychopathy* (pp. 389–414). New York: Guilford Press.

Salekin, R. T. (2008). Psychopathy and recidivism from mid-adolescence to young adulthood: Cumulating legal problems and limiting life opportunities. *Journal of Abnormal Psychology, 117*, 386–395.

Salekin, R. T., Brannen, D., Zalot, A., Leistico, A. R., & Neumann, C. S. (2006). Factor structure of psychopathy in youth: Testing the applicability of the new four-factor model. *Criminal Justice and Behavior, 33*, 135–157.

Salekin, R. T., & Frick, P. J. (2005). Psychopathy in children and adolescents: The need for a developmental perspective. *Journal of Abnormal Child Psychology, 33*, 403–409.

Salekin, R. T., Leistico, A.-M. R., Trobst, K. K., Schrum, C. L., & Lochman, J. E. (2005). Adolescent psychopathy and the interpersonal circumplex: Expanding evidence of a nomological net. *Journal of Abnormal Child Psychology*, *33*, 445–460.

Salekin, R. T., & Lochman, J. E. (2008). Child and adolescent psychopathy: The search for protective factors. *Criminal Justice and Behavior, 35*, 159–172.

Salekin, R. T., Rogers, R., & Machin, D. (2001). Psychopathy in youth: Pursuing diagnostic clarity. *Journal of Youth and Adolescence, 30,* 173–195.

Saltaris, C. (2002). Psychopathy in juvenile offenders: Can temperament and attachment be considered as robust developmental precursors? *Clinical Psychology Review*, *22*, 729–752.

Seagrave, D., & Grisso, T. (2002). Adolescent development and the measurement of juvenile psychopathy. *Law and Human Behavior*, *26*, 219–239.

Sharp, C., & Kine, S. (2008). The assessment of juvenile psychopathy: Strengths and weaknesses of currently used questionnaire measures. *Child and Adolescent Mental Health*, *13*, 85–95.

Silva, P. A. (1990). The Dunedin Multidisciplinary Health and Development Study: A 15 year longitudinal study. *Pediatric and Perinatal Epidemiology*, *4*, 96–127.

Stern, S. B., & Smith, C. A. (1995). Family processes and delinquency in an ecological context. *Social Service Review*, *69*, 705–731.

Sullivan, E. A., & Kosson, D. S. (2006). Ethnic and cultural variations in psychopathy. In C. J. Patrick (Ed.), *Handbook of psychopathy* (pp. 437–458). New York: Guilford Press.

Thornberry, T. P., Huizinga, D., & Loeber, R. (1995). The prevention of serious delinquency and violence: Implications from the program of research on the causes and correlates of delinquency. In J. C. Howell, B. Krisberg, J. D. Hawkins, & J. J. Wilson (Eds.), *Sourcebook on serious, violent and chronic juvenile offenders* (pp. 213–237). Thousand Oaks, CA: Sage.

Ullrich, S., Paelecke, M., Kahle, I., & Marneros, A. (2003). Categorical and dimensional assessment of psychopathy in German offenders: Prevalence, gender and age specific effects. *Der Nervenarzt*, *74*, 1002–1008.

Vitacco, M. J., Neumann, C. S., Ramos, V., & Roberts, M. K. (2003). Ineffective parenting: A precursor to psychopathic traits and delinquency in Hispanic females. *Annals of the New York Academy of Sciences*, *1008*, 300–303.

Weiler, B. L., & Widom, C. S. (1996). Psychopathy and violent behavior in abused and neglected young adults. *Criminal Behavior and Mental Health*, *6*, 253–271.

Wells, L. E., & Rankin, J. H. (1991). Families and delinquency: A meta-analysis of the impact of broken homes. *Social Problems*, *38*, 71–93.

West, D. J., & Farrington, D. P. (1973). *Who becomes delinquent?* London: Heinemann.

Widiger, T. (1998). Psychopathy and normal personality. In D. J. Cooke, A. E. Forth, & R. D. Hare (Eds.), *Psychopathy: Theory, research, and implications for society* (pp. 47–68). Dordrecht, The Netherlands: Kluwer.

Widom, C. S. (1989). The cycle of violence. *Science*, *244*, 160–166.

Widom, C. S., & Ames, M. A. (1994). Criminal consequences of childhood sexual victimization. *Child Abuse and Neglect*, *18*, 303–318.

Wikström, P.-O. H. (1985). *Everyday violence in contemporary Sweden*. Stockholm: National Council for Crime Prevention.

Part III

Stability, Predictive Validity, and Comorbidity

10

Stability and Change of Psychopathic Traits

What Do We Know?

HENRIK ANDERSHED

Many studies have devoted themselves to the question of whether the psychopathy construct can be meaningfully applied to youth during the last decade or so. Results have generally been promising and have given rise to a rapidly growing body of research on the topic (for reviews, see Forth & Book, 2007; Lynam & Gudonis, 2005; Salekin, 2006). A central question is to what extent psychopathic traits are stable from youth to adulthood (Salekin, Rosenbaum, & Lee, 2008). This chapter reviews what is known from research concerning stability and change of psychopathic traits, and also suggests ways forward for future research.

There have been several concerns over the correctness in applying this concept to youth (e.g., Edens, Skeem, Cruise, & Cauffman, 2001; Seagrave & Grisso, 2002). One major concern that has been put forth is that several characteristics of adult psychopathy may be normative and temporary characteristics for some youth during adolescence and, because of this, a concept of juvenile psychopathy may not be valid and useful (Edens et al., 2001; Seagrave & Grisso, 2002). This concern emphasizes the need for studies exploring the stability of psychopathic personality during childhood and adolescence, and not least, from youth to adulthood. If the psychopathy construct is to prove useful for youth, one can argue that evidence needs to show that it is relatively stable over time, into adulthood, and that it has some predictive utility. Put another way, to know the implications of the presence of a psychopathic personality in a young person, we need to know to what extent the presence of this personality in young age predict the presence of the same traits years later.

A conceptual differentiation that is important to this review, and probably the psychopathy field more broadly, is the differentiation between the terms *psychopathy* and *psychopathic traits*. Psychopathy is generally seen as a syndrome comprising a constellation of extreme interpersonal, affective, and behavioral/lifestyle traits and behaviors (see Cooke & Michie, 2001; Hare, 2003). Psychopathic traits, on the other hand, can be defined as the individual traits/symptoms and behaviors that make up the syndrome of psychopathy. A rather common phenomenon in the literature is the use of the term *psychopathy* to refer to individual psychopathic traits or to subfactors of psychopathy, such as callous–unemotional (CU) traits. It can be argued that the most important issue to focus on here is to what extent and how psychopathy, rather than psychopathic traits, is stable over time. This is important because it is at least theoretically possible that individual psychopathic traits are more or less stable when they exist apart or as a part of the other traits and dimensions of the psychopathy syndrome. For example, CU traits alone, without a person's interpersonal and behavioral traits, may be more or less stable than when they exist together with interpersonal and behavioral traits. Having said this, most studies to date have focused on psychopathic traits (e.g., CU traits) and studied them as separate dimensions rather than as part of a syndrome of psychopathy.

This narrative review focuses exclusively on prospective longitudinal studies with a minimum follow-up period of 1 year. In terms of the review of so-called "rank-order" stability, the following labels are used throughout this chapter to indicate the degree of stability: *low* = r under .30; *moderate* = r between .30 and .49; *high* = r between .50 and .69; *very high* = r of .70 and higher.

Different Ways to Study and Understand Stability

A basic question when thinking about psychopathy and stability is how stable we should expect it to be, and what implications this has for the usefulness of the psychopathy construct in youth. On the one hand, if there is basically no stability over time, without intervening explanations, there will be no predictive usefulness of the construct. In the other extreme, if there is an extremely high degree of stability, which typically is assumed for personality disorders in general, as well for psychopathy, there would definitely be a predicitve value of the construct. However, the value for interventions would be limited in the sense that one may interpret this knowledge in a way to conclude that interventions would be a waste of time and resources. The more realistic expectation concerning how stable psychopathy and psychopathic traits are over time probably lies somewhere in between these two extreme positions. In some people, it will be quite stable; for others, it will not. A broad question of interest, then, is whether the group of people whose psychopathy stays stable over time is in the majority or the minority. Is it common or uncommon that psychopathy stays stable during childhood and adolescence, and from youth to adulthood?

Before going into the empirical part of the review, the fact that stability and change can be studied in several different ways merits some attention. In the literature, one very common way to study stability has been simply to investigate correlations between personality scores across two points in time (i.e., as in test–retest correlations). This is often referred to as *rank-order stability* and reflects the extent to which the relative ordering of individuals on a given personality trait is maintained over time. Another perspective and measure of stability is *mean-level stability*, which refers to the extent to which the average trait level of a population is maintained over time, indicating whether the sample as a whole is staying on the same levels, or if they are increasing or decreasing on a trait. It is typically assessed by studying the mean levels of the specific traits at two points in time (Roberts, Caspi, & Moffitt, 2001).

Rank-order and mean-level stability are two of the most common indices used to track continuity and change in personality development. However, a focus on these indices limits understanding of personality development to a population-level phenomenon. It overlooks alternative perspectives on personality change at individual levels, which can be referred to as *individual differences* in stability, or *individual-level stability*. This refers to the magnitude of increase or decrease exhibited by each individual over time on any given trait. Furthermore, individual differences in change can be, and often are, unrelated to population indices of change. In fact, a given population may demonstrate robust individual differences in change while showing absolutely no mean-level changes. For example, at the individual level, one may find that a large proportion of the population increases on a trait substantially, whereas an equally large proportion decreases substantially, so that the groups effectively cancel each other out, resulting in no population-level change but substantial changes in specific subgroups of individuals. Hence, there can be meaningful individual-level change even when there is substantial stability at the population level (Roberts et al., 2001).

The three types of stability measures described so far all focus on personality traits singly, one at a time. In contrast, *ipsative stability (or person-centered stability/change)* is about stability in the configuration of variables (e.g., factors of psychopathy) within an individual across time. This type of stability and change is typically assessed with some form of profile similarity analysis; that is, it focuses on multiple dimensions within an individual rather than on a single dimension across persons. It reflects how much a *person's personality configuration* changes rather than how much any given trait changes (Roberts et al., 2001). This type of stability measure is of particular interest because one can argue that it is the most relevant measure when investigating the stability of psychopathy. This can be argued because psychopathy is a collection or constellation of several different traits and behaviors or dimensions/factors, rather than a single trait or behavior. That being said, unfortunately, not a single study so far in the literature has studied the ipsative stability of psychopathy.

Clues from Theory and Research on the Stability of Normal Personality and Personality Disorders

In trying to answer the question of how stable we should expect psychopathy and psychopathic traits to be, we may take clues from theory and research on normal personality and personality disorders in general. The comparison between normal personality and psychopathy is likely to be relevant because there is evidence that psychopathy is a continuous dimensional construct rather than a qualitatively distinct category; that is, people can be seen as more or less psychopathic, and there is no distinct cutoff to differentiate between nonpsychopaths and psychopaths (e.g., Edens, Marcus, Lilienfeld, & Poythress, 2006; Murrie et al., 2007; Walters, Duncan, & Mitchell-Perez, 2007). Accordingly, there is evidence that psychopathy can be understood as an extreme version of a "normal" personality profile (Lynam & Derefinko, 2006; Lynam & Widiger, 2007; Salekin, Leistico, Trobst, Schrum, & Lochman, 2005); therefore, research on stability and change of normal personality would be relevant to review here.

Theoretically, there are arguments both for and against the stability of normal personality. A personality "trait" perspective would argue that personality traits are only to some extent susceptible to environmental influences and would thus be quite stable over time (e.g., McCrae et al., 2000). A contextual or environmental perspective, on the other hand, talks about the importance of life changes, experiences, and role transitions in personality development. From this perspective, personality should be quite fluid, unstable, and thus relatively sensitive and prone to change, perhaps especially during developmental periods characterized by rapid cognitive, physical, and social changes, as in early adolescence, for example (e.g., Lewis, 1999). Research broadly supports both of these perspectives. Meta-analyses that focus on the five-factor model of personality (Fraley & Roberts, 2005; Roberts & DelVecchio, 2000) show that the rank-order stability of personality is generally moderate, even from childhood to early adulthood. Stability tends to increase somewhat with age, from moderate in childhood to high at around age 30, then very high between ages 50 and 70. Stability tends to decrease as the time interval between measurements increases, but it does not vary clearly across the various Big Five traits or by gender. Thus, the rank-order stability of normal personality traits seems to be at least moderate, even during childhood and adolescence (Fraley & Roberts 2005; Roberts & DelVecchio, 2000).

In terms of mean-level stability of normal personality, a large meta-analysis synthesized data from over 90 longitudinal studies spanning the period from age 10 to 101 (Roberts, Walton, & Viechtbauer, 2006). Results showed that individuals tend to increase in social dominance, emotional stability, and conscientiousness in young adulthood (ages 20–40). Individuals tend to increase on measures of social vitality and openness in adolescence, then decrease in these domains in old age. The traits of agreeableness changed only in old age. Of the six personality trait categories studied in the meta-analysis, four demonstrated significant change in middle and old age. Gender was found to have minimal effects on change. Studies looking at large time spans and those based on younger cohorts showed greater change. Importantly, the majority of personality change seems to occur in young adulthood, not in adolescence, as one might hypothesize. Furthermore, for certain trait categories, the review shows that change occurs well past young adulthood, demonstrating the continued plasticity of personality in adulthood (Roberts et al., 2006).

One of the few studies of individual-level stability in normal personality reveal that between 9 and 27% of individuals demonstrate change on measures of the Big Five personality factors over a 4-year period during late adolescence/young adulthood (Robins, Fraley, Roberts, & Trzesniewski, 2001). Another study that looked at stability and change of personality from late adolescence/early adulthood to adulthood (ages 18–26) found that greater than chance levels of change occurred on the individual level, sometimes despite the lack of population mean-level change (Roberts et al., 2001). More commonly, people did not change significantly on any given trait across the 8-year span of the study. Rates of absolute stability ranged from 72 to 90%. A small percentage showed relatively unstable profiles over time. Thus, this study showed that the percentage of the population that remains the same in personality is quite large indeed, and the probability that someone will change a great deal during this specific developmental period seems quite small (Roberts et al., 2001).

Most studies that have looked at ipsative change and stability in personality have used the so-called *Q*-sort methodology, in which continuity and change are indexed by computing correlations across a ranked set of attributes at Time 1 with the corresponding set of ranked attributes at Time 2. The higher the correlation, the more the constellation of traits within the individual is interpreted to be stable (see Ozer, 1993). The average *Q*-correlations between childhood and adolescence, and between early and late adolescence, have proven to be very high (Asendorpf & van Aken, 1991; Block, 1971; Ozer & Gjerde, 1989), and those between late adolescence and adulthood have been shown to be high (Block, 1971). Despite these quite high levels of similarity of personality constellations over time, many individuals have very low and even negative *Q*-correlations that indicate major changes in their personality profiles over time (Asendorpf & van Aken, 1991; Block, 1971; Ozer & Gjerde, 1989). Personality constellation similarity over time can also be indexed across the scales of a common personality questionnaire using profile correlations and so-called D2 (distance function) indices. One study found that the mean Big Five profile correlation during late adolescence/young adulthood was .61 (with a range from –.95 to .97 on the individual level) (Robins et al., 2001). Another study of persons ages 18–26 found that it is very common for a person's personality configuration to stay the same over this 8-year period (Roberts et al., 2001). As much as 93% of the sample had profile correlations ranging from .30 to 1.0, and only 1% of the sample showed a zero or negative profile correlation over time. Thus, in this study, only a very small proportion of young adults experienced large personality changes between ages 18 and 26 (Roberts et al., 2001).

Psychopathy in adulthood is considered as serious a personality disorder as those defined and measured with the *Diagnostic and Statistical Manual of Mental Disorders* (DSM-IV-TR; American Psychiatric Association, 2000). Psychopathy has a partial overlap in traits and behaviors primarily with not only antisocial personality disorder but also narcissistic personality disorder and borderline personality disorder according to the DSM system. Hence, it is likely that the literature on the stability of these personality disorders has value and gives some clues concerning the extent to which we can expect psychopathy and psychopathic traits to be stable. One of the primary assumptions in both descriptive (e.g., DSM-IV-TR) and theoretical (e.g., Millon, Meagher, & Grossman, 2001) models of personality disorders is that these conditions reflect pathology that is quite stable and rigid over time. Empirically the studies show, in some contrast to the theoretical assumptions about very high degree of stability over time, that the rank-order stability of personality disorder symptoms during adulthood is moderate to high at best, and categorical diagnostic stability is low to moderate (e.g., Durbin & Klein, 2006; Lenzenweger, Johnson, & Willett, 2004). Thus, the clues from studies on personality disorders say that psychopathy may not be absolutely stable in adulthood as is often assumed.

I now turn to the review of studies that more directly examined stability of psychopathic traits. I start with a review of studies looking at stability during youth and then move on to studies looking at stability from youth to adulthood. Finally, I turn to studies looking at stability during adulthood.

Stability of Psychopathic Traits

Stability during Childhood and Adolescence

Dadds, Fraser, Frost, and Hawes (2005) studied the 1-year rank-order stability of the three factors of the parent version of the Antisocial Process Screening Device (APSD; Frick & Hare, 2001) in a community sample of 780 boys and girls ages 4–9 years. The rank-order stabilities were high over the 1-year period: CU traits (.55), narcissism (.63), and impulsivity/conduct problems (.64). Gender-separate analyses of stability were not presented (Dadds et al., 2005).

Barry, Barry, Deming, and Lochman (2008) studied the 1-, 2-, and 3-year rank-order stability of the three factors of the APSD (Frick & Hare, 2001) in a small sample (*N* = 76) of children recruited as part of a larger investigation of the effectiveness of a school-based prevention program for moderately aggressive children who ranged in age from 9 to 12 years at the time of the initial assessment. Both boys and girls were included, and the three factors were found not to be significantly related to gender or ethnicity. Within-informant rank-order stability (using parents as informants across time points) over 1 year was high for CU traits (.57–.64), high for narcissism as well (.61–.70), and high to very high for impulsivity/conduct problems (.68–.73). Two-year CU trait stability was high (.60); narcissism was very high (.81); and impulsivity/conduct problems was very high (.74). Cross-informant rank-order stabilities (using parents at one time point and the teacher at the other) were clearly lower for all three factors (Barry et al., 2008).

Frick, Kimonis, Dandreaux, and Farrell (2003) studied the rank-order stability of scores on the three factors of the parent-, teacher-, and self-rated versions of the APSD (Frick & Hare, 2001) across 2, 3, and 4 years in a small (*N* = 98) sample of children in the third, fourth, sixth, and seventh grades at the first assessment. The study included both males and females, but gender-separate analyses were not conducted. The sample was selected from a larger population in order to overrepresent individuals scoring high on the two dimensions of the APSD—CU traits and impulsivity/conduct problems. Parent-reported rank-order stability was very high (> .70) for all three of the APSD factors over 2, 3, and 4 years. Cross-informant stabilities (e.g., using youth reports at Time 1 and parent reports at follow-ups) were lower, most often moderate in magnitude. This study also investigated the individual-level stability of CU traits and found that a majority (about 60%)

of the children who were initially low on CU traits stayed low across all points of assessment. Among the children initially high on CU traits, change was more common. Only around 30% of these children stayed high on CU traits across the 4 years (Frick et al., 2003).

Obradović, Pardini, Long, and Loeber (2007) studied rank-order stability of CU traits in the youngest age cohort of the Pittsburgh Youth Study (Loeber, Farrington, Stouthamer-Loeber, & Van Kammen, 1998). A total of 503 boys were assessed annually from ages 8 to 16. The Parent- and Teacher-Report version of the interpersonal callousness scale (IC; Pardini, Obradović, & Loeber, 2006) was used as the measure of psychopathic traits. Significant rank-order stability was found across all 9 years of assessment, and stability was highest between adjacent assessments and declined steadily as the time between assessments increased. One- and 2-year correlations were moderate to high (.49 and .61) based on teacher reports, and very high (.71–.84) based on parent reports. Three- to 8-year correlations ranged from low to high (.27–.53) based on teacher reports, and from high to very high (.50–.74) based on parent reports. The stability of teacher report of CU traits was weaker than that of parent report, a finding that may partially be explained by the fact that teachers generally changed with every year of assessment, while parents remained the same (Obradović et al., 2007).

Pardini, Lochman, and Powell (2007) investigated the 1-year rank-order stability of CU traits using the APSD (Frick & Hare, 2001) in a sample of 120 youth who ranged in age from 9 to 12 years at the initial assessment. This study included both males and females, but gender-separate analyses were not conducted. The 1-year rank-order stability of CU traits was high (.59) using combined parent and teacher reports of CU traits.

Muñoz and Frick (2007) investigated the 2-year rank-order and mean-level stability of the three factors of the APSD (Frick & Hare, 2001) in a small sample (N = 91) of youth with an average age of about 13 at the initial assessment. The sample was recruited from a large, communitywide screening, where youth with conduct problems and high levels of psychopathic traits were oversampled. This study included both males and females, but presented no gender-separate analyses concerning stability. The 2-year rank-order stability based on self-reports of the APSD total scale was high (.64), CU traits were moderate (.48), Narcissism was moderate (.43), and impulsivity/conduct problems were high (.58). The 2-year rank-order stability based on parent reports of the APSD total scale (.77), CU traits (.71), and narcissism were very high (.74), and impulsivity/conduct problems was high (.65). In terms of mean-level stability, all three factors tended to increase slightly over the 2 years (Muñoz & Frick, 2007).

Muñoz, Kerr, and Bésic (2008) followed a community sample of 12- to 15-year-olds over 4 years (N = 667) and used the Youth Psychopathic Traits

Inventory (YPI; Andershed, Kerr, Stattin, & Levander, 2002), a self-report measure of psychopathic traits. Cross-year correlations (rank-order stabilities) of the total YPI score were reported to be high (.52–.67). Both boys and girls were studied, but gender-separate analyses of stability were not presented (Muñoz et al., 2008).

Pardini and Loeber (2008) studied rank-order, mean-level and individual-level stability in the oldest age cohort of the Pittsburgh Youth Study (Loeber et al., 1998). The sample of 506 boys between ages 14 and 18 was followed annually. The parent-report version of the IC (Pardini et al., 2006) was used to measure psychopathic traits. The rank-order stability of these traits was high during the 1-year span (.61–.69), and moderate during the 4-year span (.49). A latent model describing a relatively flat, stable development of these traits for the sample as a whole during these years fitted the data well. However, in terms of mean-level stability, the traits tended to decrease slightly between ages 14 and 18. Also, as was evident in the individual-level stability analyses, some individuals stayed stable over time, whereas others decreased or increased between ages 14 and 18 (Pardini & Loeber, 2008).

Stability from Youth to Adulthood

Lynam, Caspi, Moffitt, Loeber, and Stouthamer-Loeber (2007) assessed the stability of juvenile psychopathy from age 13, using the mother-reported Childhood Psychopathy Scale (CPS; Lynam, 1997), to age 24, using the interviewer-rated Psychopathy Checklist: Screening Version (PCL:SV; Hart, Cox, & Hare, 1995). Data from over 250 male participants of the middle age-cohort sample of the Pittsburgh Youth Study (Loeber et al., 1998) were used. Despite the long time lag, different sources, and different methods of assessment, the rank-order stability was moderate (.31). Diagnostic stability was somewhat lower. The stability was not influenced by initial risk status and initial levels of psychopathic traits, and it held even after adjustment for several other variables at age 13. Total scores on the CPS at age 13 were more strongly related to PCL:SV Facets 3 (Lifestyle) and 4 (Antisocial) than to Facets 1 (Interpersonal) and 2 (Affective) at age 24 (Lynam et al., 2007).

Blonigen, Hicks, Krueger, Patrick, and Iacono (2006) used the Psychopathic Personality Inventory (PPI; Lilienfeld & Andrews, 1996) to examine the stability of psychopathic traits from ages 17–24 years in sample of 920 twins. Rank-order stabilities of the two PPI factors fearless dominance (FD) and impulsivity/antisociality (IA) were high (.60 and .53, respectively). Mean-level stability was also investigated and showed that the IA factor decreased, whereas the FD factor remained relatively stable (Blonigen et al., 2006).

Forsman, Lichtenstein, Andershed, and Larsson (2008) assessed 1,480 male and female twin pairs with the YPI (Andershed et al., 2002) at age 16–17 years (i.e., midadolescence) and again at age 19–20 (i.e., late adolescence/young adulthood). Rank-order, mean-level, and individual-level stability of the three YPI dimensions were investigated. Results showed rank-order stability to be moderate to high in all three dimensions; that is, grandiose/manipulative (interpersonal), callous–unemotional (affective), and impulsive/irresponsible (Behavioral) (range from .43 to .61, and from .51 to .58 among boys and girls, respectively). The impulsive/irresponsible dimension showed the highest rank-order stability among both males (.61) and females (.58). Rank-order stability was also assessed concerning a latent psychopathy construct consisting of the covariation of the three dimensions of the YPI. The correlation between this latent construct at ages 16–17 and 19–20 was high (.60). In terms of mean-level stability, there were small but statistically significant increases for all three psychopathic personality dimensions among boys. For girls, there was a statistically significant increase in the impulsive/irresponsible dimension only. Individual-level stability was studied for all three YPI dimensions. For both girls and boys, a clear majority stayed at approximately the same level on all three dimensions from age 16–17 to age 19–20. For those who exhibited change, both decreases and increases occurred, but increases were more common. Most change was observed in the impulsive/irresponsible dimension among boys, where an *increase* by far was the most common pattern of change (Forsman et al., 2008).

Loney, Taylor, Butler, and Iacono (2007) investigated 6-year stability during the transition to young adulthood in 475 males using the self-report Minnesota Temperament Inventory comprising two dimensions: antisocial and detachment. Participants were ages 16–18 at the initial assessment. Detachment and antisocial features displayed moderate rank-order stability (.40 and .41, respectively) across the transition from adolescence to adulthood. In terms of mean-level stability, significant decreases over time were observed in both dimensions (Loney et al., 2007).

Stability of Psychopathic Traits during Adulthood

Rutherford, Cacciola, Alterman, McKay, and Cook (1999) investigated the 2-year rank-order and mean-level stability of psychopathy using the Psychopathy Checklist—Revised (PCL-R; Hare, 1991) in 200 male (mean age at first assessment = 40) and 25 female (mean age at first assessment =37) methadone patients. For the total PCL-R, rank-order stabilities were high (.60 and .65) for men and women, respectively. On Factor 1 (interpersonal–affective), stabilities were high (.63) for females and moderate (.43) for males. On Factor 2 (behavioral–lifestyle), stabilities were moderate (.50) for females and high (.60) for males. Among males, the total PCL-R mean-level score increased significantly over the 2 years, but not among females. However, Factor 2 scores increased significantly among both males and females (Rutherford et al., 1999).

Summary, Conclusions, and Ways Forward

The majority of existing studies show that the rank-order stability during childhood and adolescence, and from youth to adulthood, is moderate to high. Most of these studies included only males. The few studies that included females show quite similar findings in terms of rank-order stability compared to what has been found in males. Stability is higher when the same informant is used across assessments. Based on this narrative review, the similarities in the stability of normal personality, personality disorders, and psychopathic traits are quite striking. The common finding in all of these fields is that the traits and behaviors we are assessing show moderate to high stability over a period of several years. The studies investigating mean-level stability generally show significant but not dramatic changes over time. Studies of individual-level stability show that there is substantial stability from youth to adulthood, but that certainly a smaller group of youth change in personality during the transition from youth to adulthood. This seems to be the case among both males and females (e.g., Forsman et al., 2008).

Although now several studies are looking at stability of psychopathic traits and psychopathy over time, more research needs to focus on stability and change, particularly on understanding individual, as well as ipsative, stability and change. Not a single study so far has studied the ipsative stability of psychopathy. Basically all research thus far has studied psychopathic traits as separate symptoms (i.e., the individual traits or factors) despite the fact that most researchers would concur that psychopathy is a syndrome of several traits/symptoms (i.e., the constellation of interpersonal, affective, and behavioral deficits). Studying ipsative stability and change can thus be argued to be the most relevant thing to do when the interest is in psychopathy rather than individual psychopathic traits. A focus on ipsative and individual-level stability gives a focus on individuals rather than on variables (which is rather the case in rank-order and mean-level stability). In this perspective as well, ipsative and individual-level stability should be a priority because research focused on individuals rather than variables can be argued to be more informative for clinical practice (Andershed & Andershed, 2008).

An important critical point against the use of the psychopathy construct with youth (Edens et al., 2001; Seagrave & Grisso, 2002) is that developmentally normative changes in certain traits might masquerade as psychopathy in youth, and that this would lead to substantial instability of these traits from youth to adulthood. If this were the case, we would see large, age-related fluctuations in stability and predictive utility during adolescence. These kinds of dramatic fluctuations are not observed in the existing studies.

The moderate to high rank-order stability typically found during youth, and from youth to adulthood, clearly speaks in favor of some predictive utility of the youth psychopathy construct. However, the individual-level stability studies on both normal personality and psychopathic traits imply that one needs to be careful at the individual level (e.g., in clinical practice); that is, in any given individual case, it is difficult to know, based on the knowledge we have today from research, how high the risk is that a particular youth will continue to exhibit many psychopathic traits in adulthood.

Research focused on explaining why these traits are stable in some youth but not others should perhaps be of higher priority in future research than studies exclusively investigating stability. Future studies should move beyond a mere description of stability and change, and attempt to explain the *causes* of stability and change. At least a handful of studies have initiated this line of research. At least two twin studies have looked at the relative importance of genetic and environmental influences behind stability of psychopathic traits. Blonigen and colleagues (2006), using the two factors of the PPI (Lilienfeld & Andrews, 1996) as the measure of psychopathic traits, showed that 25% of the variation in the FD factor and 23% of the variation in the IA factor at 24 years are explained by genetic effects at 17 years, thus indicating a substantial genetic contribution to stability in these two factors. The second twin study by Forsman and colleagues (2008) examined the importance of genetic and environmental influence for the stability of psychopathy (a higher-order latent psychopathy construct consisting of the three dimensions of the YPI [Andershed et al., 2002]) between midadolescence and early adulthood, and showed that genetic factors contributed substantially (almost entirely, in fact) to the stability of psychopathy, whereas environmental factors were of very little importance. Both of these twin studies indicate that some kinds of genetically built-in individual differences (e.g., neuropsychological or cognitive deficits, or temperamental difficulties) are quite important in explaining why psychopathic traits are stable over time. The identification and understanding of these genetically built factors or processes that explain why psychopathy is stable over time constitute an important area of future research. In fact, already there are several studies that focus on identifying specific factors related to stability (e.g., Frick et al., 2003; Lynam, Loeber, & Stouthamer-Loeber, 2008; Muñoz et al., 2008; Pardini & Loeber, 2008).

At least as important, or perhaps even more important, is to understand why psychopathy and psychopathic traits are not stable, that is, to understand change, and to identify and understand protective factors (Salekin & Lochman, 2008). In fact, one of the primary reasons for extending the concept of psychopathy to youth is to see whether a developmental period exists when these traits may be less stable and more responsive to treatment (Salekin, Chapter 14, this volume). If these periods and protective factors can be identified and understood, we will have crucial knowledge about when and what to target in prevention and treatment. Protective factors are important if they counteract psychopathic traits per se, or see to that psychopathic traits do not lead to or coexist with delinquency. This line of research has just begun, but important clues are appearing. Thus far, social competence in the child (Barry et al., 2008) and positive peers (Muñoz et al., 2008) are promising candidates that may well be important protective features to counteract psychopathic development or steer the young person with these traits away from delinquency. There is also evidence that CU traits can change during adolescence under certain circumstances. Whereas children exposed to lower levels of physical punishment have shown decreases in CU traits over time, those exposed to higher levels of child-reported parental warmth and involvement have been associated with decreases in both CU traits and antisocial behavior during adolescence. Also, in this study, lower levels of anxiety were uniquely related to increased CU traits for youth who described their primary caregiver as exhibiting low involvement and warmth (Pardini et al., 2007). Thus, how parents react and behave toward children seems to be of importance in the development of CU traits in children (Farrington, Ullrich, & Salekin, Chapter 9, this volume). There are now also indications that parent-training intervention can have positive effects on empathy and feelings of guilt, and decrease CU traits in children (Hawes & Dadds, 2007).

More research focused on individuals rather than variables is needed within this field because it is much more informative for clinical practice. An increase in individual-oriented methodology (e.g., Biesanz, West, & Kwok, 2003; Graziano, 2003; see also Bergman, Andershed, & Andershed, 2009) is thus needed. The focus should be on understanding the underlying causes of stable versus unstable paths of psychopathic personality development over time. The goal should be knowledge that informs practice about specific targets for prevention and treatment in youngsters, so that full-blown psychopathy in adulthood can be avoided in as many cases as possible.

In conclusion, psychopathic traits are quite stable over time in some, perhaps in most, people but not in others. This seems to be the case for both males and females, although most research has focused on males to date. Future research needs to continue the work of understanding why these traits are stable in some people, and why they change in others.

Acknowledgment

The author was supported by funds from the Swedish Research Council during the preparation of this chapter.

References

American Psychiatric Association. (2000). *Diagnostic and statistical manual of mental disorders* (4th ed., text rev.). Washington, DC: Author.

Andershed, H., & Andershed, A.-K. (2008). The implications of heterogeneity among individuals with antisocial behavior. In D. Canter & R. Zukauskiene (Eds.), *Psychology, crime, and law: New horizons—international perspectives* (pp. 103–118). Aldershot, UK: Ashgate.

Andershed, H., Kerr, M., Stattin, H., & Levander, S. (2002). Psychopathic traits in non-referred youths: Initial test of a new assessment tool. In E. Blaauw & L. Sheridan (Eds.), *Psychopaths: Current international perspectives* (pp. 131–158). Hague, The Netherlands: Elsevier.

Asendorpf, J. B., & van Aken, M. A. G. (1991). Correlates of the temporal consistency of personality patterns in childhood. *Journal of Personality, 59,* 689–703.

Barry, T. D., Barry, C. T., Deming, A. M., & Lochman, J. E. (2008). Stability of psychopathic characteristics in childhood: The influence of social relationships. *Criminal Justice and Behavior, 35,* 244–262.

Bergman, L., Andershed, H., & Andershed, A.-K. (2009). Types and continua in developmental psychopathology: Problem behaviors in school and their relationship to later antisocial behavior. *Development and Psychopathology, 21,* 975–992.

Biesanz, J. C., West, S. G., & Kwok, O.-M. (2003). Personality over time: Methodological approaches to the study of short-term and long-term development and change. *Journal of Personality, 71,* 905–942.

Block, J. (1971). *Lives through time.* Berkeley, CA: Bancroft Books.

Blonigen, D. M., Hicks, B. M., Krueger, R. F., Patrick, C. J., & Iacono, W. G. (2006). Continuity and change in psychopathic traits as measured via normal-range personality: A longitudinal-biometric study. *Journal of Abnormal Psychology, 115,* 85–95.

Cooke, D. J., Kosson, D. S., & Michie, C. (2001). Psychopathy and ethnicity: Structural, item and test generalizability of the Psychopathy Checklist—Revised

(PCL-R) in Caucasian and African-American participants. *Psychological Assessment, 13*, 531–542.

Cooke, D. J., & Michie, C. (2001). Refining the construct of psychopathy: Towards a hierarchical model. *Psychological Assessment, 13*, 171–188.

Dadds, M. R., Fraser, J., Frost, A., & Hawes, D. J. (2005). Disentangling the underlying dimensions of psychopathy and conduct problems in childhood: A community study. *Journal of Consulting and Clinical Psychology, 73*, 400–410.

Durbin, C. E., & Klein, D. N. (2006). Ten-year stability of personality disorders among outpatients with mood disorders. *Journal of Abnormal Psychology, 115*, 75–84.

Edens, J. F., Marcus, D. K., Lilienfeld, S. O., & Poythress, N. G. (2006). Psychopathic, not psychopath: Taxometric evidence for the dimensional structure of psychopathy. *Journal of Abnormal Psychology, 115*, 131–144.

Edens, J. F., Skeem, J. L., Cruise, K. R., & Cauffman, E. (2001). Assessment of "juvenile psychopathy" and its association with violence: A critical review. *Behavioral Sciences and the Law, 19*, 53–80.

Forsman, M., Lichtenstein, P., Andershed, H., & Larsson, H. (2008). Genetic effects explain the stability of psychopathic personality from mid- to late adolescence. *Journal of Abnormal Psychology, 117*, 606–617.

Forth, A. E., & Book, A. S. (2007). Psychopathy in youth: A valid construct. In H. Hervé & J. C. Yuille (Eds.), *The psychopath: Theory, research, and practice* (pp. 369–387). Mahwah, NJ: Erlbaum.

Fraley, R. C., & Roberts, B. W. (2005). Patterns of continuity: A dynamic model for conceptualizing the stability of individual differences in psychological constructs across the life course. *Psychological Review, 112*, 60–74.

Frick, P. J., & Hare, R. D. (2001). *Antisocial Process Screening Device.* Toronto: Multi-Health Systems.

Frick, P. J., Kimonis, E. R., Dandreaux, D. M., & Farrell, J. M. (2003). The 4-year stability of psychopathic traits in non-referred youth. *Behavioral Sciences and the Law, 21*, 713–736.

Graziano, W. G. (2003). Personality development: An introduction toward process approaches to long-term stability and change in persons. *Journal of Personality, 71*, 893–904.

Hare, R. D. (1991). *The Hare Psychopathy Checklist—Revised.* Toronto: Multi-Health Systems.

Hare, R. D. (2003). *The Hare Psychopathy Checklist—Revised* (2nd ed.). Toronto: Multi-Health Systems, Inc.

Hart, S. D., Cox, D., & Hare, R. D. (1995). Manual for the Psychopathy Checklist: Screening Version (PCL:SV). Toronto: Multi-Health Systems.

Hawes, D. J., & Dadds, M. R. (2007). Stability and malleability of callous–unemotional traits during treatment for childhood conduct problems. *Journal of Clinical Child and Adolescent Psychology, 36*, 347–355.

Lenzenweger, M., Johnson, M., & Willett, J. (2004). Individual growth curve analysis illuminates stability and change in personality disorder features. *Archives of General Psychiatry, 61*, 1015–1024.

Lewis, M. (1999). On the development of personality. In L. A. Pervin & O. P. John

(Eds.), *Handbook of personality: Theory and research* (pp. 327–346). New York: Guilford Press.

Lilienfeld, S. O., & Andrews, B. P. (1996). Development and preliminary validation of a measure of psychopathic personality traits in noncriminal populations. *Journal of Personality Assessment, 66,* 488–524.

Loeber, R., Farrington, D. P., Stouthamer-Loeber, M., & Van Kammen,W. B. (1998). *Antisocial behavior and mental health problems: Explanatory factors in childhood and adolescence.* Mahwah, NJ: Erlbaum.

Loney, B. R., Taylor, J., Butler, M. A., & Iacono, W. G. (2007). Adolescent psychopathy features: 6–year temporal stability and the prediction of externalizing symptoms during the transition to adulthood. *Aggressive Behavior, 33,* 242–252.

Lynam, D. R. (1997). Pursuing the psychopath: Capturing the fledgling psychopath in a nomological net. *Journal of Abnormal Psychology, 106,* 425–438.

Lynam, D. R., Caspi, A., Moffitt, T. E., Loeber, R., & Stouthamer-Loeber, M. (2007). Longitudinal evidence that psychopathy scores in early adolescence predict adult psychopathy. *Journal of Abnormal Psychology, 116,* 155–165.

Lynam, D. R., & Derefinko, K. (2006). Psychopathy and personality. In C. J. Patrick (Ed.), *Handbook of psychopathy* (pp. 133–155). New York: Guilford Press.

Lynam, D. R., & Gudonis, L. (2005). The development of psychopathy. *Annual Review of Clinical Psychology, 1,* 381–407.

Lynam, D. R., Loeber, R., & Stouthamer-Loeber, R. (2008). The stability of psychopathy from adolescence into adulthood: The search for moderators. *Criminal Justice and Behavior, 35,* 228–243.

Lynam, D. R., & Widiger, T. A. (2007). Using a general model of personality to identify the basic elements of psychopathy. *Journal of Personality Disorders, 21,* 160–178.

McCrae, R. R., Costa, P. T., Jr., Ostendorf, F., Angleitner, A, Hrebícková, M., Avia, M. D., et al. (2000). Nature over nurture: Temperament, personality, and life span development. *Journal of Personality and Social Psychology, 78,* 173–186.

Millon, T., Meagher, S. E., & Grossman, S. D. (2001). Theoretical perspectives. In W. J. Livesley (Ed.), *Handbook of personality disorders: Theory, research, and treatment* (pp. 39–59). New York: Guilford Press.

Muñoz, L. C., & Frick, P. J. (2007). The reliability, stability, and predictive utility of the self-report version of the Antisocial Process Screening Device. *Scandinavian Journal of Psychology, 48*, 299–312.

Muñoz, L. C., Kerr, M., & Bésic, N. (2008). A matter of perspective: The peer relationships of youths with psychopathic personality traits. *Criminal Justice and Behavior, 35*, 212–227.

Murrie, D. C., Marcus, D. K., Douglas, K. S., Lee, Z., Salekin, R. T., & Vincent, G. M. (2007). Youth with psychopathy features are not a discrete class: A taxometric analysis. *Journal of Child Psychology and Psychiatry, 48,* 714–723.

Obradović, J., Pardini, D., Long, J. D., & Loeber, R. (2007). Measuring interpersonal callousness in boys from childhood to adolescence: An examination of longitudinal invariance and temporal stability. *Journal of Clinical Child and Adolescent Psychology, 36,* 276–292.

Ozer, D. J. (1993). The Q-sort method and the study of personality development. In D. C. Funder, R. D. Parke, C. Tomlinson-Keasey, & K. Widaman (Eds.), *Studying lives through time: Personality and development* (pp. 147–168). Washington, DC: American Psychological Association.

Ozer, D. J., & Gjerde, P. F. (1989). Patterns of personality consistency and change from childhood through adolescence. *Journal of Personality, 57,* 483–507.

Pardini, D., Obradović, J., & Loeber, R. (2006). Interpersonal callousness, hyperactivity/impulsivity, inattention, and conduct problems as precursors to delinquency persistence in boys: A comparison of three grade-based cohorts. *Journal of Clinical Child and Adolescent Psychology, 35,* 46–59.

Pardini, D. A., Lochman, J. E., & Powell, N. (2007). The development of callous–unemotional traits and antisocial behavior in children: Are there shared or unique predictors? *Journal of Clinical Child and Adolescent Psychology, 36,* 319–333.

Pardini, D. A., & Loeber, R. (2008). Interpersonal and affective features of psychopathy in children and adolescents: Advancing the developmental perspective, *Journal of Clinical Child and Adolescent Psychology, 36,* 269–275.

Roberts, B. W., Caspi, A., & Moffitt, T. (2001). The kids are alright: Growth and stability in personality development from adolescence to adulthood. *Journal of Personality and Social Psychology, 81,* 670–683.

Roberts, B. W., & DelVecchio, W. F. (2000). The rank-order consistency of personality traits from childhood to old age: A quantitative review of longitudinal studies. *Psychological Bulletin, 126,* 3–25.

Roberts, B. W., Walton, K. E., & Viechtbauer, W. (2006). Patterns of mean-level change in personality traits across the life course: A meta-analysis of longitudinal studies. *Psychological Bulletin, 132,* 1–25.

Robins, R. W., Fraley, C, Roberts, B. W., & Trzesniewski, K. (2001). A longitudinal study of personality change in young adulthood. *Journal of Personality, 69,* 617–640.

Rutherford, M., Cacciola, J. S., Alterman, A. I., McKay, J. R., & Cook, T. G. (1999). The 2-year test–retest reliability of the Psychopathy Checklist—Revised in methadone patients. *Assessment, 6,* 285–291.

Salekin, R. T. (2006). Psychopathy in children and adolescents: Key issues in conceptualization and assessment. In C. J. Patrick (Ed.), *Handbook of psychopathy* (pp. 389–414). New York: Guilford Press.

Salekin, R. T., Leistico, A. R., Trobst, K. K., Schrum, C. L., & Lochman, J. E. (2005). Adolescent psychopathy and personality theory—the interpersonal circumplex: Expanding evidence of a nomological net. *Journal of Abnormal Psychology, 33,* 445–460.

Salekin, R. T., & Lochman, J. E. (2008). Child and adolescent psychopathy: The search for protective factors. *Criminal Justice and Behavior, 35,* 159–172.

Salekin, R. T., Rosenbaum, J., & Lee, Z. (2008). Child and adolescent psychopathy: Stability and change. *Psychiatry, Psychology, and Law, 15*, 224–236.

Seagrave, D., & Grisso, T. (2002). Adolescent development and the measurement of juvenile psychopathy. *Law and Human Behavior, 26*, 219–240.

Skeem, J. L., & Cauffman, E. (2003). Views of the downward extension: Comparing the youth version of the Psychopathy Checklist with the Youth Psychopathic Traits Inventory. *Behavioral Sciences and the Law, 21*, 737–770.

Walters, G. D., Duncan, S. A., & Mitchell-Perez, K. (2007). The latent structure of psychopathy: A taxometric investigation of the Psychopathy Checklist—Revised in a heterogeneous sample of male prison inmates. *Assessment, 14*, 270–278.

11

Psychopathic Traits in Children and Adolescents

The Relationship with Antisocial Behaviors and Aggression

ADELLE E. FORTH
ANGELA S. BOOK

Until about a decade ago, relatively little attention was focused on the possibility of psychopathic traits in children or youth. Other than Hervey Cleckley's rich clinical descriptions of the emergence of psychopathic features during childhood and adolescence in his book *The Mask of Sanity* (1941), and pioneering research by Robins (1966), who followed up a sample of children classified as sociopathic to adulthood to determine the developmental precursors of this disorder, research on childhood psychopathic traits has been limited. Recently, however, a growing number of studies have encompassed a wide range of research with children and youth to understand the etiology and developmental factors underlying psychopathy. In this chapter, we review the literature on psychopathic traits in children, and then the literature on adolescents. Specifically, we (1) examine how psychopathic traits relate to conduct problems and antisocial behavior; (2) explore the link between motives for aggression and psychopathic traits; and (3) compare the predictive utility of psychopathy measures for future conduct problems, institutional maladjustment, and general and violent recidivism. Although much of the research on the relationship between psychopathy and correlates of antisocial behaviors and recidivism mirrors the literature on adult psychopaths, some important differences exist. We provide suggestions for future research that may elucidate the association between psychopathic traits and aggression, and the applied significance of this link.

Psychopathic Traits in Children

Research on psychopathic traits in children has focused on describing a subgroup of children with conduct disorder who have especially severe behavioral problems (Frick & Hare, 2001). The reasons for studying these traits in children are numerous. Identifying children with these traits allows for the possibility of prevention, clinical interventions, and effective risk management (Johnstone & Cooke, 2004; Salekin, Chapter 14, this volume). However, for this to be possible, a reliable and valid measure of psychopathic traits in children must exist (Farrington, 2005). Johnstone and Cooke (2004) suggest that we are only in the beginning stages of creating such a measure. One issue in establishing the validity of a measure of psychopathic traits in children is whether the instrument correlates with external criteria in the same manner as adult psychopathy measures do, such as the Psychopathy Checklist—Revised (PCL-R; Hare, 1991/2003). For example, much like their adult counterparts, children and youth with psychopathic traits show little remorse for the negative consequences of their behavior on others (Frick & Morris, 2004; Salekin, 2006), show impaired moral reasoning and empathetic concern (Blair, 1999; Fisher & Blair, 1998; Pardini, Lochman, & Frick, 2003), are more likely to be aggressive, and especially, are more likely to use proactive aggression (Flight & Forth, 2007; Frick, Cornell, Barry, Bodin, & Dane, 2003). Given that psychopathy in adults is highly predictive of aggression, crime, and antisocial behavior, it would not be unreasonable to expect that psychopathic traits in childhood would be similarly related to these outcomes.

Research in this area has focused on two measures of psychopathic traits in children: (1) the Antisocial Process Screening Device (APSD; Frick & Hare, 2001), and (2) the Childhood Psychopathy Scale (CPS; Lynam, 1997). Both measures have separate forms for self-report, parent, and teacher ratings. Our purpose in this section is to describe these scales and assess their validity, especially in relation to aggression and conduct problems in childhood.

The APSD

The APSD is the most widely used scale of psychopathic traits in children (Johnstone & Cooke, 2004). Originally known as the Psychopathy Screening Device (PSD; Frick, O'Brien, Wootton, & McBurnett, 1994), it was modeled after the PCL-R (Hare, 1991/2003). As with its adult counterpart, the APSD consists of 20 items rated on a 3-point scale (0: *Not at all true*, 1: *Sometimes true*, 2: *Definitely true*), that measures the degree to which each item is applicable to the child. This scoring system results in a score ranging from 0 to 40, with higher scores indicating more psychopathic traits. Typically, this instrument has been utilized for children between the ages of 6 and 13, although a self-report version has been employed with some adolescent samples.

Early factor analyses indicated that the APSD is made up of two factors: (1) impulsivity–conduct problems (I/CP) and (2) callous–unemotional (CU) traits (Frick et al., 1994). Children who score high on I/CP are described as impulsive, as having poor impulse control, and as more likely to be involved in delinquent behavior. High CU scores are more indicative of superficial charm and a lack of social emotions (e.g., guilt and empathy). The two-factor solution demonstrates divergent validity, in that the two factors correlate with different variables. For example, CU is positively correlated with sensation seeking, while I/CP correlates more with conduct problems. As well, the two-factor solution is relatively parallel to the interpersonal/affective and social deviance components found in adult populations (Hare, 1991/2003). More recently, Frick, Bodin, and Barry (2000) settled on a three-factor solution: (1) narcissism, (2) impulsivity, and (3) CU traits. Even this change in factor structure is consistent with research on adults, in that three- and four-factor solutions have been found to be viable possibilities (see Hare, 1991/2003, for a review).

The internal consistency of the APSD is well established, with values ranging from .85 to .93 for the total score. Alpha coefficients for the subscales are also adequate, ranging from .64 to .89. The values are highest for teacher ratings and lowest for parent ratings (Frick & Hare, 2001). The APSD also demonstrates good interrater reliability, in that parent and teacher ratings were similar (r [797] = .428, $p < .01$; Frick & Hare, 2001).

As mentioned earlier, for the purposes of demonstrating construct validity, the APSD should be correlated with aggression, with general conduct problems, as well as with the risk for future conduct problems. Such relationships would add credence to measuring psychopathic traits in children.

Aggression

Several studies have examined the link between aggression and psychopathic traits in children. For example, Frick and colleagues (1994) investigated the relationship between the PSD and aggression (as measured by the Child Behavior Checklist [CBCL]; Achenbach, 1991). They found that the I/CP factor was strongly correlated with parent reports of aggression whereas the CU factor was moderately correlated with aggression. Clearly, both subscales of the PSD are able to predict aggression, and this relationship is especially strong for I/CP. This finding is not surprising, given the impulsivity and poor behavioral controls in children scoring high on I/CP (Frick et al., 1994).

In a similar study, Christian, Frick, Hill, Tyler, and Frazer (1997) looked at 120 children (also ages 6–13) referred to outpatient services at a university. Children were categorized into four groups based on their scores on I/CP and CU traits: (1) a clinic control cluster (low scores on both), (2) a CU cluster (high scores on CU traits only), (3) an impulsive conduct cluster (high scores on I/CP only), and (4) a psychopathic conduct cluster (high scores on both). Children in the last two groups scored higher on the Aggression scale of the CBCL (Achenbach, 1991). These results mirror those of the Frick and colleagues (1994) study, in that groups with high I/CP scores were rated as more aggressive.

While it is clear from these studies that children with psychopathic traits tend to be more aggressive, specific types of aggression were not investigated in these studies. Research on aggression has distinguished two primary types: reactive (hostile or affective) and proactive (instrumental or predatory) aggression (Kingsbury, Lambert, & Hendrickse, 1997; Meloy, 2006). *Reactive aggression* is defined as being impulsive, unplanned and driven by heightened emotional arousal, and occurring as a reaction to some perceived imminent provocation. *Proactive aggression* is planned, calculated behavior that is goal directed and characterized by an absence of emotion. Several researchers have incorporated this conceptualization in their examination of the relationship between psychopathic traits and aggression.

In one such study, Frick and colleagues (2003) recruited 98 children from the community (mean age = 12.43). Participants were measured on CU traits and conduct problems, and followed up after 1 year. Children with a combination of CU traits and conduct problems reported more delinquency and showed higher aggression, specifically, proactive aggression, as measured by the Aggressive Behavior Rating Scale (ABRS; Brown, Atkins, Osborne, & Milnamow, 1996).

Kimonis, Frick, Fazekas, and Loney (2006) also investigated the relationship between aggression and psychopathic traits. In their sample of 50 nonreferred boys and girls, the total APSD score was significantly related to proactive, reactive, and total aggression in both boys and girls (as measured by the ABRS; Brown et al., 1996), consistent with the findings of the previous study.

While most research in this area has focused on 6- to 13-year-olds, one study has examined these relationships in a preschool sample. Kimonis, Frick, Boris, and colleagues (2006) evaluated 49 children from Head

Start programs, and found that CU traits significantly predicted proactive aggression and overall aggression, but *not* reactive aggression on the ABRS (Brown et al., 1996). These results correspond to findings in adults that psychopathic offenders are more likely to use instrumental aggression than reactive aggression (e.g., Cornell et al., 1996; Williamson, Hare, & Wong, 1987).

While aggression can be separated into proactive versus reactive aggression, another typology distinguishes between "overt" and "relational" aggression. *Overt aggression* involves physical and/or verbal aggression, while *relational aggression* involves behaviors such as exclusion and spreading rumors (Coie & Dodge, 1998). Marsee, Silverthorn, and Frick (2005) looked at self- and teacher- ratings on the APSD in relation to overt and relational aggression in a sample of 200 children (grades 5–9). They found that psychopathic traits (self- and teacher-reported) were positively correlated with both types of aggression, and this pattern of results was found in both boys and girls, although the relationship between relational aggression and psychopathic traits (teacher ratings) was stronger for the sample of girls. Interestingly, the subscales (narcissism, impulsivity, and CU) were equally predictive.

One study has examined the relationship between psychopathic traits and a very specific type of aggression: cruelty to animals. Dadds, Whiting, and Hawes (2006) found evidence for the relationship between CU traits and animal cruelty in a community sample of 131 children. In contrast to what was predicted by the authors, family conflict was not related to cruelty to animals. For boys, CU traits and externalizing behaviors were related to child but not parental reports of animal cruelty. For girls, CU traits were associated with both child and parent reports of cruelty. Additional research is needed to determine if animal cruelty is an early manifestation of more generalized problems with empathy.

From the studies described here, it is clear that children with psychopathic traits are more likely to be aggressive. More specifically, they tend to use proactive (or instrumental) aggression. The following section examines whether this is true of conduct problems more generally.

Conduct Problems

Several studies have examined the link between psychopathic traits and conduct problems. In one such study, Frick and colleagues (2003) recruited 98 children from the community (mean age = 12.43). Children were measured on CU traits and conduct problems, and were followed up after 1 year. Children with a combination of CU traits and conduct problems reported significantly more delinquency. Similarly, Marsee and colleagues (2005) found that teacher ratings on the APSD were positively correlated with self-report ratings of delinquency.

Frick and colleagues (1994) examined whether the PSD was correlated with various measures of conduct problems in a sample of 95 clinic-referred children (ages 6–13). Children were assessed in terms of the DSM-III-R criteria for oppositional defiant disorder (ODD) and conduct disorder (CD). Parents also were asked to complete the CBCL (Achenbach, 1991). Frick and colleagues found that the I/CP factor was strongly related to CD symptoms and delinquency, while the CU factor showed moderate relationships with the same variables (*r* values between .30 and .45). Clearly, the results of this study suggest that both factors are related to conduct problems in children, and that the relationship is stronger in the case of I/CP. This finding is not surprising given the impulsivity and poor behavioral controls in children scoring high on I/CP.

Similarly, Christian and colleagues (1997) found that children who scored high on I/CP were significantly more likely to have been diagnosed with either CD or ODD. They also scored higher on the delinquency scale of the CBCL (Achenbach, 1991). In addition to diagnosis and ratings on the CBCL, Christian and colleagues examined behavioral evidence of conduct problems. First, number of lifetime school suspensions was predicted by psychopathic traits. In this study, the children were placed into one of four groups based on their scores on I/CP and CU traits: (1) a clinic control cluster (low scores on both), (2) a CU cluster (high scores on CU traits only), (3) an impulsive conduct cluster (high scores on I/CP only), and (4) a psychopathic conduct cluster (high scores on both). Children in the last three clusters (i.e., those who had relatively high scores on one or both of the subscales) had significantly more suspensions than the control group. Those individuals in the psychopathic cluster (high on CU and I/CP) also had more suspensions than those in the CU cluster. Finally, children in the psychopathic cluster had significantly more police contacts than children belonging to any of the other clusters. These results suggest that psychopathic traits (especially the I/CP factor) predict conduct problems in children.

Frick and colleagues (2000) also investigated the link between psychopathic traits and conduct problems, specifically, ODD, CD, and attention-deficit/hyperactivity disorder (ADHD), in two samples of children: (1) a nonreferred community sample (N = 1,136), and (2) a clinic sample (N = 160). Children were assessed for symptoms of these disorders and rated on the APSD (parent and teacher ratings). Narcissism and impulsivity were strongly correlated with symptoms of all of the disorders, even when researchers controlled for the other subscales. However, the relationships between CU and symptoms of ODD, CD, and ADHD were weak after researchers controlled for narcissism and impulsivity.

Most research on the validity of the APSD with children has focused on general conduct problems. However, Dadds and Fraser (2006) investigated fire setting and fire interest as dependent variables. Their sample consisted of 1,359 children (ages 4–9), recruited from elementary schools. Dadds and Fraser combined the Strengths and Difficulties Questionnaire (SDQ; Goodman, 1997) with the APSD, and the resulting instrument comprised five scales: (1) antisocial, (2) CU traits, (3) anxiety, (4) hyperactivity, and (5) peer problems (see Dadds, Fraser, Frost, & Hawes, 2005, for a description of scale construction). They found that the antisocial factor predicted fire setting in both boys and girls, while CU traits did not.

Risk for Future Conduct Problems

The studies cited in the previous section show a clear link between psychopathic traits and conduct problems, regardless of the measure used. Another important criterion is *risk* for antisocial behavior in the future. Three studies have specifically examined this issue.

Frick and Dantagnan (2005) measured conduct problems and psychopathic traits at four yearly intervals in 79 children from a communitywide screening for conduct problems. Using stability of antisocial behavior and CU traits, children were placed into one of five groups: (1) the control group (no conduct problems, low CU); (2) children with stable conduct problems but low on CU traits (CP stable); (3) children with unstable conduct problems and low CU traits (CP nonstable); (4) children with stable conduct problems and high CU traits (CU-CP stable); and (5) children with unstable conduct problems who were high on CU traits (CU-CP nonstable). Conduct problems at Time 1 and Time 4 were significantly higher for those in the CU-CP stable group, and next highest in the CP stable group. This study also provides important information regarding prediction of persistence of conduct problems. Children who persisted and did not show evidence of CU traits were more impulsive, had a lower socioeconomic status, and were marginally more likely to come from families evidencing dysfunctional parenting. On the other hand, children with CU traits who persisted in their antisocial behavior experienced more life stressors and showed *less* association with a deviant peer group. These findings suggest that children with persistent conduct problems are not a homogeneous group and strengthen the argument for using measures of psychopathic traits to locate a group of children characterized by predatory and severe antisocial behavior.

In another study, Enebrink, Långström, and Gumpert (2006) examined the link between psychopathic traits in children and short-term and long-term risk for antisocial behavior. Seventy-three boys who had been referred to psychiatric clinics were rated on the APSD and the Early Assessment Risk List for Boys (EARL-20B; Augimeri, Koegl, Webster, & Leverne, 2001), a measure of risk for antisocial behavior. Participants were followed up over 30 months. I/CP showed medium to large correlations with the total risk for antisocial behavior, short-term risk for antisocial behavior, and long-term risk for antisocial behavior (measured on the EARL-20B). These results are consistent with research on adult samples showing that scores on the PCL-R (Hare, 1991/2003) are highly correlated with risk for general, violent, and sexual recidivism (described in Quinsey, Harris, Rice, & Cormier, 2006).

Dadds and colleagues (2005) also looked at the ability of the APSD to predict future conduct problems, but combined the APSD with the SDQ (Goodman, 1997) using factor analysis. The participants were 1,359 children, ages 4–9, tested two separate times, 12 months apart. The analysis resulted in five scales: (1) antisocial, (2) CU traits, (3) anxiety, (4) hyperactivity, and (5) peer problems. CU traits predicted antisocial behavior 12 months later, even after researchers controlled for antisocial behavior at the time of initial assessment.

To sum up, the APSD is predictive of future conduct problems and antisociality, as evidenced by these studies. That this mirrors findings with adolescent samples (see section on adolescents) and adults (Quinsey et al., 2006) speaks to the validity of the APSD as a measure of psychopathic traits in children.

Summary

The APSD demonstrates concurrent and predictive validity for antisocial behavior. The validity of the APSD is further emphasized by the fact that studies varied in age of participants, design, and in choice of dependent variable. APSD studies have included participants from a variety of age groups, ranging from preschool (e.g., Kimonis, Frick, Boris, et al., 2006) to 13 years of age (e.g., Frick et al., 2003). These studies have included both longitudinal (e.g., Frick & Dantagnan, 2005) and nonlongitudinal (e.g., Kimonis, Frick, Fazekas, et al., 2006) designs. Finally, studies varied in their choice of dependent variable. Some researchers have examined general antisociality (conduct problems; e.g., Frick & Dantagnan, 2005), whereas others investigated more specific behaviors, such as proactive aggression (e.g., Kimonis, Frick, Boris, et al., 2006), fire setting (Dadds & Fraser, 2006) and animal cruelty (Dadds et al., 2006). Given the clear and consistent relationship between psychopathic traits and antisocial characteristics despite the heterogeneity of methodology, the APSD appears to have good construct validity in children.

The APSD has also demonstrated a parallel with adult psychopathy. The factor structure and relationships with key personality and behavioral variables are similar to those observed with measures of adult psychopathy (Kotler & McMahon, 2005). The APSD is also practical: It is short in length and easy to administer, making it a very useful tool for research and screening purposes.

The CPS

The CPS, developed by Lynam (1997), was based on the PCL-R, and consists of items from the CBCL (Achenbach, 1991) and the California Child Q-Set (CQS; Block & Block, 1980). Like the APSD, items on the CPS are scored on a 3-point scale. The CPS has two factors, but because they are highly correlated (r = .95), only the total score is utilized. Not surprisingly, the CPS does have relatively high internal consistency (Falkenbach, Poythress, & Heide, 2003), although parent reports are more internally consistent than self-reports.

Only three studies have examined the validity of the CPS. In a sample of 430 boys, ages 12–13, Lynam (1997) found that the CPS was positively correlated with a serious and stable offending pattern, impulsivity, and externalizing disorders, such as aggression and delinquency, as measured on the Youth Self-Report (YSR; Achenbach, 1991) and the Teacher's Report Form (TRF; Achenbach & Edelbrock, 1986), even after controlling for other possible predictors of delinquency.

In a second study, Lynam (1998) placed 508 boys from the Pittsburgh Youth Study (average age, 10 years) into one of four groups depending on self-, mother, and teacher ratings of symptoms for various behavior disorders. The four groups were (1) conduct problems and hyperactivity, impulsivity, attention problems (HIA-CP), (2) CP only, (3) HIA only, and (4) none (no evidence of either CP or HIA). Boys in the HIA-CP group scored significantly higher on the CPS, were more antisocial, more diverse in their delinquency, and more disinhibited than boys in the other groups.

Finally, Pardini, Obradović, and Loeber (2006) used parts of the CPS in combination with items from the CBCL (Achenbach, 1991) and the TRF (Achenbach & Edelbrock, 1986) to create a scale of Interpersonal Callousness (IC). Five of the eight items measuring IC were selected from the CPS, and the other three items were chosen from the other two measures because they appeared to be similar to items in other measures of callousness. This process resulted in an IC scale. They also created scales of conduct problems (CP), hyperactivity/impulsivity (HI), and inattention (IN) using the CBCL and TRF. Three cohorts from the Pittsburgh Youth Study were followed for 3 years: first grade (N = 849), fourth grade (N = 868), and seventh grade (N = 856). CP predicted delinquency persistence in the youngest sample. Both CP and IN were correlated with delinquency persistence in the middle sample. Interestingly, IC was the only predictor of persistence in the oldest sample. Based on these findings, CP is the best predictor in younger children, with IC becoming more important in adolescence.

Like the APSD, the CPS predicts conduct problems and delinquency. As well, it is related to the risk for future antisocial behavior. However, the limited number of studies examining the CPS may constrain its generalizability. Nonetheless, there is considerable empirical research being conducted with the newer, 55-item version of the CPS.

Psychopathic Traits in Adolescents

This section focuses on studies that have examined the association between psychopathy measures and indices of antisocial behavior and violence in adolescents. It is not possible to review every study on psychopathic traits and violence and crime in the space available, so our goal is to provide an overview of the key findings, with suggestions for future research.

Measures of Psychopathic Traits in Youth

Measurement of psychopathic traits in youth have used two methodologies: expert rater and self-report. Using the Psychopathy Checklist: Youth Version (PCL:YV; Forth, Kosson, & Hare, 2003), an expert rater uses a combination of a structured interview and file information to assess for psychopathic traits. Expert raters can provide highly reliable measures of psychopathy, but they impose two kinds of constraints: Experts should be trained in the use of the instrument, and assessments with such procedures tend to be time consuming. These constraints have led to the development of self-report measures of psychopathic traits. Concerns about the use of self-report measures of psychopathy focus on the potential for response distortion, lack of comprehensive content validity, and level of insight (see Edens, Hart, Johnson, Johnson, & Olver, 2000, for more general concerns about use of self-reports in forensic evaluations). Despite these concerns, a number of adolescent psychopathy measures have been developed, including the self-report version of the APSD (Frick & Hare, 2001), the Youth Psychopathic Traits Inventory (YPI; Andershed, Kerr, Stattin, & Levander, 2002), the modified CPS (mCPS; see Spain, Douglas, Poythress, & Epstein, 2004, for a description), the Millon Adolescent Clinical Inventory's (MACI; Millon, 1993) Psychopathy Content Scale (PCS; Murrie & Cornell, 2002), the Psychopathy–16 (P-16) Scale (Salekin, Ziegler, Larrea, Anthony, & Bennett, 2003), and the Survey of Attitudes and Life Experiences (SALE; Rogers, Vitacco, Cruise, Sewell, & Neumann, 2002). Because there is a limited amount of research on the association of the SALE with antisocial and violent behaviors, this measure will not be reviewed. A brief description of measures of psychopathic traits in youth is provided below.

The PCL:YV

The PCL:YV (Forth et al., 2003) consists of 20 items for the assessment of psychopathic traits in adolescents. It was adapted from the Hare Psychopathy Checklist—Revised (PCL-R; Hare, 1991/2003). The PCL:YV uses an expert rater format to rate items on a 3-point scale, using information from interview and collateral information. Factor analyses of the PCL:YV have revealed support for both the three- and four-factor models (Forth et al., 2003; Jones, Cauffman, Miller, & Mulvey, 2006; Neumann, Kosson, Forth, & Hare, 2006; Salekin, Brannen, Zalot, Leistico, & Neumann, 2006). The three factors common to the two models are an interpersonal factor, an affective factor, and a behavioral factor. The fourth factor is an antisocial behavior factor. Interrater reliability of PCL:YV scores is acceptable, with intraclass correlation coefficients typically around .85 for total scores and a range from .70 to .90 for factor scores (Andershed, Hodgins, & Tengström, 2007; Vitacco, Neumann, Caldwell, Leistico, & Van Rybroek, 2006). Adequate internal consistencies of around .85 are usually obtained (range .73–.92) for total scores. However, the alphas for the factor scores are more variable, ranging from .22 to .86 (Andershed et al., 2007; Flight & Forth, 2007; Skeem & Cauffman, 2003; Vitacco et al., 2006).

The APSD

An experimental self-report version of the APSD (Frick & Hare, 2001) was first described by Caputo, Frick, and Brodsky (1999). The content of the 20 items parallel the APSD scale, with the wording altered for first-person responses. Items are scored on a 3-point scale. Recent factor analyses of self-report APSD scores have found support for a three-factor structure (Vitacco, Rogers, & Neumann, 2003). These three factors are labeled narcissism (NAR), callous–unemotional (CU), and impulsivity (IMP). Measures of internal consistency using the self-report version of the APSD (Falkenbach et al., 2003; Muñoz & Frick, 2007; Murrie, Cornell, Kaplan, McConville, & Levy-Elkon, 2004; Spain et al., 2004) have been adequate for the total score (values ranging from .71 to .82) but lower for the factor scores (range = .36–.72).

The YPI

The YPI (Andershed, Kerr, et al., 2002) is a 50-item self-report measure designed to assess psychopathic traits in community adolescents. The

YPI consists of 10 scales, with five items per scale. Items are rated on a 4-point scale. Confirmatory factor analyses of the YPI scales revealed a three-factor structure: (1) a grandiose/manipulative factor, (2) a callous–unemotional factor, and (3) an impulsive/irresponsible factor (Andershed, Kerr, et al., 2002; Larsson et al., 2006). Alpha coefficients for the YPI total range from .87 to .92 (Andershed, Kerr, et al., 2002; Andershed et al., 2007; Skeem & Cauffman, 2003), and factor scores range from .66 to .93 (Andershed, Kerr, et al., 2002; Andershed et al., 2007; Skeem & Cauffman, 2003).

The PCS from the MACI

The PCS (Murrie & Cornell, 2000) consists of 20 items from the MACI (Millon, 1993). Items are scored as true or false. Coefficient alpha was .87 in the Murrie and Cornell (2000) study and .86 in the Murrie and colleagues (2004) study. The P-16 scale consists of 16 items and has a coefficient alpha of .86. The validity for the two measures appears to be comparable, although their conceptualizations differ somewhat.

The CPS

The CPS (Lynam, 1997) consists of 41 items that are rated by the youth's parents. A self-report, 55-item version used in a study by Spain and colleagues (2004) was called the modified CPS (mCPS). There have been no studies examining the factor structure of the mCPS. The alpha coefficient for the mCPS total score was .87 (Spain et al., 2004).

The relationship between different measures of psychopathic traits has not been extensively investigated. Murrie and Cornell (2002) compared self-report APSD scores and MACI PCS scores to PCL:YV scores. The PCL:YV correlated moderately with the MACI PCS (r = .49) and the self-report APSD score (r = .40). Dolan and Rennie (2006) reported the PCL:YV and YPI were correlated at .29. A slightly smaller correlation (r = .24) was obtained by Skeem and Cauffman (2003) between these two measures. Stronger correlations were reported by Andershed and colleagues (2007) in a community sample of male and female adolescents, with PCL:YV total and YPI scores being moderately correlated (male adolescents: r = .47; female adolescents: r = .48).

In contrast to the weak to moderate correlations between the PCL:YV and self-report measures in offender samples, self-report psychopathy measures are more strongly associated with each other. This stronger association is not surprising, since they share method variance. Murrie and

Cornell (2002) reported that the self-report APSD and the MACI PCS was correlated ($r = .54$). Poythress, Dembo, Wareham, and Greenbaum (2006) reported that the APSD and the YPI strongly correlated with each other ($r = .79$).

Because a substantial amount of research has used the PCL:YV as the psychopathy measure, studies are first reviewed using this measure. Any available studies using self-report measures are then summarized.

Association with Criminal Conduct and Aggression

A large body of research indicates that psychopathy is strongly associated with criminal behavior and aggression in adults. Several mechanisms have been suggested to explain this association (Hart, 1998). Psychopaths possess negative and procriminal attitudes that support their use of violence to meet their needs. In addition, they have few inhibitions against committing violence. For example, they lack empathy for others, do not feel significant remorse concerning their actions, and experience little anxiety. Finally, they are attracted to high-risk situations and people, which in combination with their heightened impulsivity, increases their likelihood of violence.

In youth, psychopathic traits are associated with earlier onset of criminal activity, frequency, and versatility of crime, including violent offenses. Several studies with adolescent males have found support for this link between psychopathy and violent and criminal offenses. The PCL:YV has several items (e.g., 18, 19, and 20) that include a specific reference to criminal behavior, which is used to code these items. Inclusion of these item may inflate the correlation between PCL:YV and any measure of criminal history. In order to reduce this potential impact, most researchers examine the associations after removing the items that make explicit reference to criminal behavior.

Findings for age of onset of criminal conduct and its association with PCL:YV scores have been mixed. For example, Vincent, Vitacco, Grisso, and Corrado (2003) reported that male young offenders scoring high on the PCL:YV received their first convictions at significantly younger ages than those scoring lower. Brandt, Kennedy, Patrick, and Curtin (1997) using modified PCL-R scores reported a significant correlation with age of first arrest. Furthermore, Salekin and colleagues (2006) found a negative relationship between age of onset of antisocial behavior and PCL:YV scores, although the relationship was not statistically significant. However, Kosson and colleagues (2002) did not find a significant correlation with age at first trouble with the law and PCL:YV scores.

Adolescents with psychopathic traits tend to engage in more frequent offences and are more versatile in their offending. Campbell, Porter, and Santor (2004) found that PCL:YV scores were positively related with self-reported delinquency, aggressive behavior, and versatility of criminal history, although not related to official records for nonviolent and violent convictions. In a study of male adolescent probationers, Kosson, Cyterski, Stuerwald, Neumann, and Walker-Matthews (2002) found the PCL:YV scores correlated .27, .35, and .42 with previous violent, nonviolent, and total charges. As well, Murrie and colleagues (2004) found that the PCL:YV correlated both with adjudicated violent offense (r_{pb} = .24) and with unadjudicated violent offense (r_{pb} = .30). Finally, Vincent and colleagues (2003) reported that youth scoring higher on psychopathy have significantly more nonviolent and violent convictions than youth scoring lower on the PCL:YV.

Salekin (2008) recently evaluated the PCL:YV and examined its (and several other psychopathy scales) potential for incremental validity in light of 14 variables with theoretical and empirical links to antisocial conduct. The PCL:YV and a modified version of the Self-Report Psychopathy Scale (SRP-II-Mod; Benning, Patrick, Salekin, & Leistico, 2005) showed significant incremental power after these variables were considered. The Antisocial scale from the Personality Assessment Inventory (PAI-ANT; Morey, 1991) was also a predictor of general offending and accounted for 6% of the total variance.

With respect to self-report psychopathy scales, Skeem and Cauffman (2003) coded the institutional files of 160 male adolescent offenders for age of first contact with the police, and type and number of prior offenses. The YPI was not related to age at first contact (r = .11), number of offenses (r = –.09), or number of person-related offenses (r = .12). In contrast to Skeem and Cauffman's findings, other researchers have reported an association between self-report psychopathy scales and criminal conduct. For example, Poythress and colleagues (2006) examined the association between indices of criminal conduct and the YPI, and self-report APSD in a sample of 165 male and female youth in a juvenile diversion program. A self-report delinquency scale assessed whether the youth had committed 23 different delinquent behaviors in the past year and the age of onset of these behaviors. Both the YPI and the APSD were moderately correlated with indices of past-year offending (log transformed total number of past-year self-reported delinquent behaviors; both scales correlated at .44). The earliest age of onset for any delinquent behavior was correlated (–.29 for the APSD and –.28 for the YPI total scores). In addition, Murrie and colleagues (2004) reported that APSD (r_{pb} = .22) and MACI PCS (r_{pb} = .18) scores were associated with whether the youth had been adjudicated for a violent offense.

The association between self-report APSD scores and antisocial behaviors was investigated in a community sample of 91 young adolescents (Muñoz & Frick, 2007). Parental and youth self-report APSD scores, self-reported delinquency, parent-rated conduct problems, and occurrence of police contacts were studied annually across 3 years. Within each of these time periods, self-report APSD was related to self-reported delinquency (r's = .58, .42, and .38) and police contacts (r_{pb}'s = .25, .34, and .29). Parental APSD was related to parent-reported conduct problems (r's = .25, .34, and .55) but not to the occurrence of police contacts (r_{pb}'s = .11, .08, and .16). With respect to predictive validity, self-report APSD scores at Time 1 predicted self-reported delinquency and violence at Time 3 (r's = .50 and .43), and parent-reported conduct problems and aggression (r's = .62 and .47).

To summarize, research indicates a relation between PCL:YV scores and criminal conduct, although the magnitude of the association varies across the different measures of criminal conduct. In addition, more recent work using self-report measures of psychopathic traits indicates that these measures are related to delinquency in youth.

Psychopathic Traits and Motives for Violence

Consistent with findings reported for children (discussed earlier) and adults (Cornell et al., 1996; Porter & Woodworth, 2007; Williamson et al., 1987; Woodworth & Porter, 2002), research suggests that psychopathic traits are related to instrumental aggression in adolescents.

To date three studies (Flight & Forth, 2007; Murrie et al., 2004; Vitacco et al., 2006) have examined the nature of aggression and psychopathic traits in adolescent samples using a classification system for aggression developed by Cornell and colleagues (1996). This coding system assesses the aggressive act based on six dimensions: (1) planning, (2) goal directedness, (3) provocation, (4) anger, (5) victim injury, and (6) victim relationship. In a sample of 113 incarcerated youth, Murrie and colleagues (2004) reported a moderate correlation between PCL:YV scores and instrumental motives for prior violence (r = .36) and victim injury (r = .30).

Flight and Forth (2007) assessed a sample of 51 male adolescent offenders and found that PCL:YV total scores were related both to instrumental violence (r_{pb} = .59) and to reactive violence (r_{pb} = .55) but negatively to a self-report measure of empathy (r = –.55). To examine the relative contributions of empathy and psychopathic traits in predicting instrumental violence, logistic regressions were conducted. When psychopathic traits were entered first in the regression, empathy accounted for no additional variance in predicting instrumental violence. However, when empathy was entered first, psychopathic traits did account for significantly more variance.

Vitacco and colleagues (2006) examined the factor structure of a five-item measure of instrumental aggression, and the link between instrumental aggression and psychopathic traits in a sample of 122 incarcerated male adolescents. Based on confirmatory factor analysis, the three items most strongly related to instrumental aggression were goal directed, unprovoked by victim, and limited relationship with the victim. Instrumental aggression was related positively to the interpersonal factor (r = .20) but negatively to the antisocial factor (r = –.24), and not significantly related to the affective or lifestyle factor. Based on structural equation modeling, the association between PCL:YV three- and four-factor models and instrumental aggression, the pattern of findings differed. The four-factor model resulted in an excellent fit, accounting for 20% of the variance, with the interpersonal factor related positively and the antisocial factor related negatively to instrumental violence. The three-factor model resulted in a good fit, accounting for 8% of the variance, and only the lifestyle factor was related to instrumental violence. The differential pattern of results that occurred, whether the antisocial factor was included or not, points to the need for other researchers to analyze their data in a similar fashion.

Only recently have researchers begun to explore the association between psychopathic traits and victim injury. Vitacco, Caldwell, Van Rybroek, and Gabel (2007) examined which variables were most strongly related to level of victim injury in a sample of incarcerated violent youth. Using regression analyses, the following variables accounted for 17% of the variance associated with victim injury: PCL:YV affective factor, PCL:YV lifestyle factor, age of onset, and criminal versatility.

Researchers have begun to investigate the relationship between self-reported psychopathic traits and instrumental violence in youth. For instance, Loper, Hoffschmidt, and Ash (2001) found that adolescent offenders who committed instrumentally motivated violence scored higher on the MACI PCS. Likewise, using the APSD (Frick & Hare, 2001) to measure psychopathic traits, Kruh, Frick, and Clements (2005) reported that young adults who committed unprovoked aggression exhibited more psychopathic traits compared to those who committed aggression in response to provocation. In contrast, Murrie and colleagues (2004) found that neither the self-report nor staff ratings of the APSD or the MACI PCS was significantly related to instrumental violence or victim injury.

It is clear that because youth with psychopathic traits commit violence for multiple reasons, intervention strategies must also be multifaceted to target psychopathic youth's engagement in both reactive and goal-directed violence.

Sexual Aggression and Psychopathic Traits

Among adult sexual offenders the dichotomy between those who victimize children and those who victimize adults has generated research that assesses differences in the prevalence of psychopathy. In general, offenders who commit sexual homicides are the most psychopathic, followed by *mixed sexual offenders* (those who sexually assault both children and adults), followed by rapists, with the lowest psychopathy scores found among child molesters (Brown & Forth, 1997; Firestone, Bradford, Greenberg, Larose, & Curry, 1998; Porter et al., 2000; Quinsey, Rice, & Harris, 1995). Adolescent sexual offenders are also a diverse group that victimizes both children and adults or same-age peers. Recently, Parks and Bard (2006) investigated the differences in psychopathic traits and recidivism among three groups of 156 male adolescent offenders: offenders who victimized children, offenders who victimized peers and adults, and a mixed type. Consistent with the adult literature, the mixed group was more psychopathic than the other two groups.

Only one study has used a self-report psychopathy measure with juvenile sexual offenders. Caputo and colleagues (1999) used the self-report APSD, and found that juvenile sexual offenders had more CU traits than nonsexual violent offenders and nonviolent offenders.

Psychopathic Traits and Institutional Adjustment

How well do youth with psychopathic traits adapt to an institutional environment? Do youth with higher psychopathic scores engage in more disruptive behaviors during institutionalization? In an early study, Forth, Hart, and Hare (1990) reported a strong association between institutional charges for misconduct and modified PCL-R scores ($r = .46$).

To date, the most comprehensive meta-analysis to study the association between Hare Psychopathy Checklist scores, institutional misconduct, and recidivism was by Leistico, Salekin, DeCoster, and Rogers (2008). This meta-analysis included 12,186 adults and 2,553 adolescents in the samples. Not surprisingly, psychopathic traits were positively related to institutional misconduct. The authors did not present effect sizes across adolescent and adult samples, since age was not a significant moderator for PCL total, Factor 1 (F1), or Factor 2 (F2) scores for predicting institutional misconduct or recidivism. This, of course, means that psychopathy was predictive, regardless of age, providing more evidence for the validity of measuring psychopathy in adolescents.

Recently, Edens, Campbell, and Weir (2007) conducted a meta-analysis of 13 adolescent studies measuring the association between psychopathy (PCL:YV or modified PCL-R scores) and the total number of incidents, a

TABLE 11.1. Weighted Mean Effect Sizes for Hare PCL Scales and Institutional Misconduct in Youth and Adults from Three Meta-Analyses

	Guy et al. (2005)—adults		Edens & Campbell (2007)—youth		Leistico et al. (2008) —adults and youth	
	k (*N*)	r_w	*k* (*N*)	r_w	*k* (*N*)	*d*
Total/any						
PCL Total score	38 (5,381)	.29	15 (1,310)	.24	45 (6,137)	0.53
PCL Factor 1 score	25 (3,219)	.21	—(1,002)	.21	30 (3,898)	0.41
PCL Factor 2 score	25 (3,219)	.27	—(1,002)	.28	29 (3,848)	0.51
Aggression						
PCL Total score	31 (4,483)	.23	14 (1,188)	.25		
PCL Factor 1 score	22 (2,786)	.15	—(880)	.22		
PCL Factor 2 score	22 (2,786)	.20	—(880)	.34		
Physical violence						
PCL Total score	22 (3,502)	.17	10 (1,001)	.28		
PCL Factor 1 score	16 (2,129)	.14	—(775)	.24		
PCL Factor 2 score	16 (2,129)	.15	—(775)	.37		

Note. k, number of studies.

combined verbal and physical aggression category, and for physical aggression only. Table 11.1 presents the results from the Edens and colleagues and Leistico and colleagues studies and, for comparison purposes, a meta-analysis performed on 38 adult samples using the PCL-R or PCL:SV (Guy, Edens, Anthony, & Douglas, 2005).

The weighted mean effect sizes for the relation between PCL:YV and the total number of incidents and number of aggressive incidents were similar to the effect sizes for adult samples using the PCL-R or PCL:SV. A weighted mean effect size of 0.28 demonstrates a significant association between PCL:YV and institutional physical violence, and is much stronger than that reported by Guy and colleagues (2005) with adult samples (0.17). In adults, association between psychopathy and institutional misconduct was strongest for total number of incidents and weakest for physical violence, whereas for adolescents, the opposite pattern was obtained. It appears that youth with psychopathic traits are more likely to engage in overt aggression than their adult counterparts. Consistent with adults, it was shown that F2 consistently had greater predictive value than F1 across each of the three categories of institutional incidents.

Various studies have examined the factors underlying the PCL:YV in adolescent samples (Jones et al., 2006; Neumann et al., 2006; Salekin et al., 2006). These studies do not find support for the two-factor model but instead for the three- and four-factor models. In these more recent models, F1 is divided into an interpersonal factor (new F1) and an affective factor (new F2). F3 (behavior) is composed of behavioral traits, and F4 (antisocial) consists of early-onset externalizing problems, anger control, and delinquency. Research on the predictive value of each of these four factors is limited. A recent study by Dolan and Rennie (2006) compared the predictive validity of the PCL:YV and YPI in a sample of 115 institutionalized male CD adolescents. All disciplinary infractions were coded during a 12-month follow-up period. PCL:YV total, F1 (interpersonal) and F4 (antisocial) were all significantly correlated with any infractions (.33, .36, and .25, respectively) and physical assault (.25, .26, and .20, respectively). Das, de Ruiter, Lodewijks, and Doreleijers (2007) examined the association between the Dutch version of the PCL:YV and institutional disruptive behaviors in two samples of male adolescents provided with treatment. The behavioral and antisocial factors were more strongly related to institutional misconduct (including any physical violence and rule violations) than to interpersonal or affective factors.

Few studies have examined the association between self-report measures of psychopathic traits and institutional maladjustment. Spain and colleagues (2004) were the first to compare two self-report measures of psychopathy (APSD and mCPS) and the PCL:YV, and their relationship to institutional disciplinary infractions. In a sample of 85 male adjudicated adolescents, self-reports were more strongly related to any infractions (APSD: $r = .38$; mCPS: $r = .43$) as than the PCL:YV ($r = .27$). The same pattern of correlations was found with physical violence incidents, with the APSD ($r = .35$) and mCPS ($r = .35$) exhibiting stronger relationships than the PCL:YV ($r = .27$). Dolan and Rennie (2006) reported that there were no significant correlations between YPI total or subscales and institutional infractions.

In summary, studies examining the association between institutional infractions and psychopathic traits in youth have yielded findings that parallel those reported in adults. However, there are too few studies to make firm conclusions about the differential associations with the different psychopathy factors and institutional infractions.

Psychopathic Traits and Recidivism

Are psychopathic traits predictive of reoffending? One of the more common forensic clinical uses of the PCL-R with adults has been for risk assessment. Archer, Buffington-Vollum, Stredny, and Handel (2006) surveyed 152 forensic psychologists about test usage in forensic evaluations. The most frequently used test for risk assessment was the PCL-R or the PCL:SV. Although it was not designed as a risk assessment measure, several studies have measured the predictive utility of the PCL:YV for general and violent reoffending, including several narrative reviews (Edens, Skeem, Cruise, & Cauffman, 2001; Forth & Book, 2006; Forth & Mailloux, 2000; Vitacco & Vincent, 2006) and three meta-analyses (Edens et al., 2007; Leistico et al., 2008; Schwalbe, 2007). As compared to narrative reviews, which have been criticized for lacking methodological and statistical rigor and being susceptible to bias (Lipsey & Wilson, 2001), applying meta-analytic methods can help to address these concerns. Meta-analytical approaches allow the use of statistical means to compare and aggregate studies, and can control for moderator variables that may help to explain the variability among effect sizes.

In a meta-analysis of 21 studies using either the PCL:YV or modified PCL-R as the measure of psychopathic traits, Edens and colleagues (2007) reported effect sizes of 0.26, 0.23, and 0.07, respectively, for general, violent, and sexual recidivism (when one outlier study was removed for each general and violent recidivism, the effect sizes were 0.24 and 0.25, respectively). As can be seen in Table 11.2, these effect sizes are similar to meta-analytic studies with primarily adult samples using the Hare Psychopathy Checklists. The results of Edens and colleagues suggest that the relationship between psychopathic traits and both general and violent recidivism in adolescent offenders is statistically significant and in the "medium" effect range, as defined by Cohen (1988). This also holds true for the large-scale meta-analysis by Leistico and colleagues (2008). Although these results suggest optimism, there was moderate- to high-level heterogeneity among the recidivism effect sizes. To determine what might account for the variation in effect sizes in the Edens and colleagues meta-analysis, they conducted several moderator analyses, including methodological rigor, publication status, nationality, ethnicity, and gender. There were no statistically significant gender effects across these moderators for general recidivism. However, in female samples, when one outlier study was removed, the effect size dropped from 0.24 to 0.13. For violent recidivism, the moderator analysis for gender was significant and approached significance for ethnicity. With respect to female samples, the effect size based on five studies and 288 cases was 0.10, indicating a small effect for predicting violent recidivism. Edens and colleagues concluded that "at present, it would be difficult to defend ethically the use of the PCL:YV with female adolescents for risk assessment purposes" (p. 68). Several other authors have also raised concerns about the use of the PCL:YV with female adolescents for risk decision making (see Odgers, Reppucci, & Moretti, 2005; Vincent, 2006).

Noteworthy in Edens and colleagues (2007) was the finding that in those studies with a greater proportion of nonwhite adolescents, the relationship between total PCL:YV total scores and violent recidivism was

TABLE 11.2. Weighted Mean Effect Sizes for Hare PCL Scales and Recidivism in Youth and Adults from Six Meta-Analyses

	Salekin et al. (1996)—adults		Hemphill et al. (1998)—adults		Gendreau et al. (2002)—primarily adults		Walters (2003a, 2003b)—primarily adults		Edens et al. (2007)—youth		Leistico et al. (2008)—adults and youth	
	k (*N*)	*d*	*k* (*N*)	r_w	*k* (*N*)	r_w	*k* (*N*)	r_w	*k* (*N*)	r_w	*k* (*N*)	*d*
General recidivism												
PCL Total score	10	0.55	7 (1,275)	.25	30 (4,365)	.23	33 (4,870)	.26	20 (2,787)	.24	62 (11,140)	0.50
PCL Factor 1 score			5 (1,072)	.13	14	.10	26 (4,360)	.15	15 (2,157)	.18	29 (5,439)	0.37
PCL Factor 2 score			5 (1,072)	.31	14	.24	26 (4,360)	.32	15 (2,157)	.29	29 (5,439)	0.64
Violent recidivism												
PCL Total score	13	0.79	6 (1,374)	.21	26 (4,823)	.21	—	—	14 (2,067)	.25	68 (12,359)	0.47
PCL Factor 1 score			3 (370)	.13	13	.13	27 (6,356)	.18	12 (1,776)	.19	39 (6,437)	0.40
PCL Factor 2 score			3 (370)	.18	13	.19	27 (6,356)	.26	12 (1,776)	.26	38 (6,387)	0.57
Sexual recidivism												
PCL Total score	3	0.61	1 (178)	.23	—	—	—	—	4 (654)	.07	—	—
PCL Factor 1 score			—	—	—	—	5 (726)	.05	3 (437)	.03	—	—
PCL Factor 2 score			—	—	—	—	5 (726)	.08	3 (437)	.08	—	—

Note. Salekin et al. (1996)—effect sizes reported as Cohen *d*s. Gendreau et al. (2002)—six studies done with youth ($N = 789$). Walters (2003a)—four studies done with youth ($N = 476$). Walters (2003b)—four studies done with youth ($N = 554$). *k*, number of studies.

weaker. Leistico and colleagues (2008) also found that effect sizes for PCL total and F2 scores were larger for studies with more white participants.

As can be seen in Table 11.2, in youth, the behavioral and antisocial features (labeled Factor 2) of psychopathy were more strongly predictive of general and violent recidivism than were the interpersonal and affective features (labeled Factor 1). The differential predictive utility of the four factors of psychopathy has only rarely been studied. Parks and Bard (2006) investigated the differential predictive validity of the PCL:YV factor scores in a sample of juvenile sexual offenders. Both the interpersonal and antisocial factors of the PCL:YV were predictive of sexual recidivism, and the behavioral and antisocial factors were significant predictors of nonsexual recidivism.

Adolescence is a period of increased involvement in antisocial activities. However, the majority of youth do not continue their antisocial activities into adulthood. Two published studies have examined the long-term predictive ability of the PCL:YV. Using file-only coding of the PCL:YV, Gretton, Hare, and Catchpole (2004) followed up a sample of 157 adolescent offenders for 10 years, into early adulthood. The majority of youth (79%) were white, and as adolescents all had been referred for mental health assessment. Youth with high PCL:YV scores were more likely to commit violent offenses than were those with low scores, but they did not commit more general or sexual offenses. A high PCL:YV score was significantly associated with violent recidivism.

More recently, Edens and Cahill (2007) examined the long-term predictive utility of the PCL:YV in a sample of 75 male adolescent offenders for 10 years. PCL:YV total and factor scores did not predict general or violent recidivism during the follow-up period. The youth in the Gretton and colleagues (2004) and the Edens and Cahill (2007) studies differed in a number of ways. Gretton and colleagues studied Canadian youth, who were primarily white and had been referred for mental health assessments, and whose base-rate of violent reoffending was relatively high (68%). Youth in the Edens and Cahill study were Americans, primarily members of ethnic minorities (43% African American, 30% Hispanic), and had relatively high rates of gang affiliation (43% were current or former gang members), and a lower base rate of violent recidivism (32%).

Only with future research in different countries, using diverse ethnic samples of youth, will the long-term predictive utility of the PCL:YV be established. To date, no research has examined the long-term predictive ability of self-report measures of psychopathic traits.

Research on the association between psychopathic traits and future recidivism in females is equivocal. Leistico and colleagues (2008) reported that samples with a greater proportion of females (including adults and adolescents) had PCL Total and F1 scores that were more strongly related to negative outcomes (institutional misconduct and recidivism). However, Edens and colleagues (2007) reported that PCL:YV scores were not related to violent recidivism in adolescent females. It is not clear what accounts for the PCL:YV's lack of predictive validity for violent recidivism with female adolescents. Although many of the risk and protective factors have been identified in male adolescents, "the utility of those risk factors for female populations deserves further empirical inquiry" (Graves, 2007, p. 138). Males and females develop differently, both emotionally and physically, and are exposed to different socialization practices. Thus, it is not surprising that there are differences in the types of aggression exhibited by male and female adolescents. For example, adolescent females engage more in relational forms of aggression, while adolescent males engage more in overt aggression. Are females who display more overt aggression more psychopathic than those who engage in relational aggression? Additional research using measures others than official recidivism may help to elucidate the association between psychopathic traits and functions of aggression.

Does the PCL:YV Provide Incremental Validity in Prediction of Violence or Recidivism?

Can the PCL:YV predict institutional violence or reoffending over and above other predictors? Several studies have examined this by assessing the predictive ability of PCL:YV after controlling for other diagnoses (e.g., CD), other risk assessment instruments, or known risk predictors (e.g., past history of violence).

For example, in a series of regression analyses, Murrie and colleagues (2004) examined whether or not the adjusted PCL:YV total score (with three items relating to antisocial behavior removed) could improve the prediction of institutional violence when either previous violence variables or self-report psychopathic measures were entered first. In both regressions, the adjusted PCL:YV scores resulted in statistically significant improvement.

As well, in a 10-year follow-up study, Gretton and colleagues (2004) reported that PCL:YV scores predicted risk for violent reoffense, even after controlling for CD symptoms, but PCL:YV scores were not predictive of nonviolent or sexual recidivism.

Also recall that Salekin (2008), in a prospective study, found that psychopathy is predictive of recidivism from midadolescence to adulthood even when accounting for 14 variables that are typically linked with offending. In addition, this relation appeared to hold across measures.

Additional research is needed on the interaction between psychopathic traits and other risk factors. For example, Gretton, McBride, Hare, O'Shaughnessy, and Kumka (2001) examined the recidivism rates for four groups of juvenile sexual offenders based on a median split on the PCL:YV and evidence of deviant sexual arousal. The group with high PCL:YV scores and evidence for deviant sexual arousal was most likely to reoffend generally and violently, although not sexually.

Comparison with Other Risk Assessment Measures

Numerous instruments have been developed to assess risk for recidivism in adolescents. Schwalbe (2007) coded 28 studies that used a prospective design to test the predictive validity of juvenile risk assessment instruments. The area under the curve (*AUC*) was used as the index of predictive validity. Although 28 different risk assessment instruments were used in the studies, only four instruments had multiple effect sizes (used in two or more studies). The most widely studied measure was the Youth Level of Service Inventory/Case Management Inventory, used in 11 studies (AUC_w = .641). This was followed by the PCL:YV (AUC_w = .695) and the North Carolina Assessment of Risk (AUC_w = .603), each of which was used in three studies. Finally, the Orange County Risk Assessment was employed in two studies (AUC_w = .585). Schwalbe concluded that "the study supports the use of risk assessment as a decision-aid in jurisdictions that base placement decisions on assessment of risk for recidivism" (p. 460). Other measures are also emerging, such as the Risk–Sophistication–Treatment Inventory (RST-I; Salekin, 2004) and the Structured Assessment of Violence Risk in Youth (SAVRY; Borum, Bartel, & Forth, 2003). However, Schwalbe also notes that most of the risk assessment instruments have not been validated in multiple samples; thus, practitioners should be cautious when selecting and interpreting the findings they obtain from risk assessments. Table 11.3 summarizes the correlations across different risk measures within institutional violence and violent recidivism for adolescents and adults.

Future Directions and Summary

Research clearly demonstrates that psychopathic traits in children predict later antisocial behavior and aggression. Nevertheless, several aspects of this relationship require clarification. First, although the presence of psychopathic characteristics is associated with later violence and aggression, not all children go on to demonstrate violent or aggressive behavior. Future work must investigate what factors enable the transformation of psychopathic characteristics into violent or aggressive behavior in some children but not in others. The focus of most researchers is on identifying risk factors for crime and violence, but the flip side is to identify factors related to desistance (see Salekin, Lee, Schrum-Dillard, & Kubak, in press; Salekin &

TABLE 11.3. Weighted Mean Effect Size Comparisons of Psychopathy and Risk Measures for the Prediction of Institutional Violence and Violent Recidivism

	Institutional violence			Violent recidivism		
	Study	*k* (*N*)	r_w	Study	*k* (*N*)	r_w
PCL/PCL-R	Campbell et al. (2009)	5 (626)	.15	Campbell et al. (2009)	24 (4,757)	.24
PCL:SV	Campbell et al. (2009)	7 (504)	.25	—	—	—
PCL/PCL-R/ PCL:SV	Guy et al. (2005)	31 (4,483)	.23	—	—	—
LSI/LSI-R	Campbell et al. (2009)	6 (650)	.24	Campbell et al. (2009)	19 (4,361)	.25
HCR-20	Campbell et al. (2009)	11 (758)	.31	Campbell et al. (2009)	11 (1,395)	.25
VRAG	Campbell et al. (2009)	2 (222)	.17	Campbell et al. (2009)	14 (2,082)	.27
PCL:YV	Edens & Campbell (2007)	14 (1,188)	.25	Edens et al. (2007)	4 (727)	.24
YLS/CMI	—	—		Edens et al. (2007)	4 (727)	.21

Note. HCR-20, Historical/Clinical/Risk Management 20-item scale; LSI, Level of Service Inventory; LSI-R, Level of Service Inventory—Revised; VRAG, Violence Risk Appraisal Guide; YLS/CMI, Youth Level of Service/Case Management Inventory; *k*, number of studies.

Lochman, 2008). Thus, future research should identify factors that might buffer against the propensity for youth with many psychopathic traits to reoffend. If we knew more about the protective factors, we would be in a better position to create strategies to enhance the development of these factors. To do this would require longitudinal studies that follow young children into adulthood.

Second, assessments of psychopathy appear to identify a group of high-risk adolescents. However, it is essential that research continue to investigate the association between psychopathic traits and antisocial conduct in youth in different ethnic minorities and in female adolescents. Without increased knowledge of the function that psychopathic traits play in the onset and maintenance of crime and violence in minority youth and females, successful treatment planning will be difficult.

Third, the majority of predictive validity research has been retrospective in design. Additional prospective studies that measure both psychopathic traits and criminal behavior over longer periods of time are needed. Also, although psychopathic traits are predictive of future criminal behavior, many important domains have yet to be studied, such as school, work, family, and relationships. Are psychopathic traits in youth also related to these other areas of functioning?

Although psychopathic traits in children and adolescents are related to future antisocial and criminal conduct, this does not mean we should "weed out, or indefinitely lock up" (Seagrave & Grisso, 2002, p. 230) youth with many psychopathic traits. It is clear that without effective intervention, many youth with psychopathic traits will likely graduate to more serious criminal behaviors. Although there is little available research on the impact of treatment interventions for psychopathic youth, from a developmental perspective, they are likely to be more malleable, and thus more likely than adults to respond to intervention efforts (e.g., Caldwell, Skeem, Salekin, & Van Rybroeck, 2006). Our challenge is not to give up but to try our utmost to do everything we can to encourage their successful integration into society.

References

Achenbach, T. M. (1991). *The Child Behavior Checklist—1991*. Burlington: University of Vermont.

Achenbach, T. M., & Edelbrock, C. S. (1986). *Manual for the Teacher's Report Form and teacher version of the Child Behavior Profile*. Burlington: University of Vermont.

Andershed, H., Gustafson, S. B., Kerr, M., & Stattin, H. (2002). The usefulness of self-reported psychopathy-like traits in the study of antisocial behaviour among non-referred adolescents. *European Journal of Personality, 16*, 383–402.

Andershed, H., Hodgins, S., & Tengström, A. (2007). Convergent validity of the Youth Psychopathy Inventory (YPI): Association with the Psychopathy Checklist: Youth Version (PCL:YV). *Assessment, 14*, 144–154.

Andershed, H., Kerr, M., Stattin, H., & Levander, S. (2002). Psychopathic traits in non-referred youths: A new assessment tool. In E. Blaauw & L. Sheridan (Eds.), *Psychopaths: Current international perspectives* (pp. 131–158). Hague, The Netherlands: Elsevier.

Archer, R. P., Buffington-Vollum, J. K., Stredny, R. V., & Handel, R. W. (2006). A survey of psychological test use patterns among forensic psychologists. *Journal of Personality Assessment, 87*, 84–94.

Augimeri, L. K., Koegl, C. J., Webster, C. D., & Leverne, K. S. (2001). *Early Assessment Risk List for Boys: EARL-20B, Version 2*. Toronto: Earlscourt Child and Family Centre.

Benning, S., Patrick, C. J., Salekin, R. T. & Leistico, A. R. (2005). Convergent and discriminant validity of psychopathy factors assessed via self-report: A comparison of three instruments. *Assessment, 12*, 270–289.

Blair, R. J. R. (1999). Responsiveness to distress cues in the child with psychopathic tendencies. *Personality and Individual Differences, 27*, 135–145.

Block, J. H., & Block, J. (1980). *The California Child Q Set*. Palo Alto, CA: Consulting Psychologists.

Borum, R., Bartel, P., & Forth, A. (2003). *Manual for the Structured Assessment for Violence Risk in Youth (SAVRY): Version 1.1*. Tampa: Louis de la Parte Florida Mental Health Institute, University of South Florida.

Brandt, J. R., Kennedy, W. A., Patrick, C. J., & Curtin, J. J. (1997). Assessment of psychopathy in a population of incarcerated adolescent offenders. *Psychological Assessment, 9*, 429–435.

Brown, K., Atkins, M., Osborne, M., & Milnamow, M. (1996). A revised teacher rating scale for reactive and proactive aggression. *Journal of Abnormal Child Psychology, 24*, 473–480.

Brown, S. L., & Forth, A. E. (1997). Psychopathy and sexual assault: Static risk factors, emotional precursors, and rapist subtypes. *Journal of Consulting and Clinical Psychology, 65*, 848–857.

Caldwell, M., Skeem, J. L., Salekin, R. T., & Van Rybroeck, G. (2006). Treatment response of adolescent offenders with psychopathy features: A two-year follow-up. *Criminal Justice and Behavior, 33*, 571–596.

Campbell, M. A., French, S., & Gendreau, P. (2009). The prediction of violence in adult offenders: A meta-analytic comparison of instruments and methods of assessment. *Criminal Justice and Behavior, 36*, 567–590.

Campbell, M. A., Porter, S., & Santor, D. (2004). Psychopathic traits in adolescent offenders: An evaluation of criminal history, clinical, and psychosocial correlates. *Behavioral Sciences and the Law, 22*, 23–47.

Caputo, A. A., Frick, P. J., & Brodsky, S. L. (1999). Family violence and juvenile sex offending: Potential mediating roles of psychopathic traits and negative attitudes toward women. *Criminal Justice and Behavior, 26*, 338–356.

Christian, R. E., Frick, P. J., Hill, N. L., Tyler, L., & Frazer, D. R. (1997). Psychopathy and conduct problems in children: II. Implications for subtyping children with conduct problems. *Journal of the American Academy of Child and Adolescent Psychiatry, 36*, 233–241.

Cleckley, H. (1941). *The mask of sanity: An attempt to clarify some issues about the so called psychopathic personality*. St. Louis, MO: Mosby.

Cohen, J. (1988). *Statistical power analysis for the behavioral sciences* (2nd ed.). Hillsdale, NJ: Erlbaum.

Coie, J., & Dodge, K. (1998). Aggression and antisocial behavior. In W. Damon & N. Eisenberg (Eds.), *Handbook of child psychology: Social, emotional, and personality development* (pp. 779–862). Toronto: Wiley.

Cornell, D., Warren, J., Hawk, G., Stafford, E., Oram, G., & Pine, D. (1996). Psychopathy in instrumental and reactive violent offenders. *Journal of Consulting and Clinical Psychology, 64*, 783–790.

Dadds, M. R., & Fraser, J. (2006). Fire interest, fire setting and psychopathology in Australian children: A normative study. *Royal Australian and New Zealand College of Psychiatrists, 40*, 581–586.

Dadds, M. R., Fraser, J., Frost, A., & Hawes, D. J. (2005). Disentangling the underlying dimensions of psychopathy and conduct problems in childhood: A community study. *Journal of Consulting and Clinical Psychology, 73*, 400–410.

Dadds, M. R., Whiting, C., & Hawes, D. J. (2006). Associations among cruelty to animals, family conflict, and psychopathic traits in childhood. *Journal of Interpersonal Violence, 21*, 411–429.

Das, J., de Ruiter, C., Lodewijks, H., & Doreleijers, T. (2007). Predictive validity of the Dutch PCL:YV for institutional disruptive behavior: Findings from two samples of male adolescents in a juvenile justice treatment institution. *Behavioral Sciences and the Law, 25*, 739–755.

Dolan, M.C., & Rennie, C. E. (2006). Reliability and validity of the Psychopathy Checklist: Youth Version in a UK sample of conduct disordered boys. *Personality and Individual Differences, 40*, 65–75.

Edens, J. F., & Cahill, M. A. (2007). Psychopathy in adolescence and criminal recidivism in young adulthood: Longitudinal results from a multi-ethnic sample of youthful offenders. *Assessment, 14*, 57–64.

Edens, J. F., Campbell, J. S., & Weir, J. M. (2007). Youth psychopathy and criminal recidivism: A meta-analysis of the Psychopathy Checklist measures. *Law and Human Behavior, 31*, 53–75.

Edens, J. F., Hart, S. D., Johnson, D. W., Johnson, J. K., & Olver, M. E. (2000). Use of the Personality Assessment Inventory to assess psychopathy in offender populations. *Psychological Assessment, 12*, 132–139.

Edens, J. F., Skeem, J. L., Cruise, K. R., & Cauffman, E. (2001). Assessment of "juvenile psychopathy" and its association with violence: A critical review [Special issue]. *Behavioral Sciences and the Law, 19*, 53–80.

Enebrink, P., Långström, N., & Gumpert, C. H. (2006). Predicting aggressive and disruptive behavior in referred 6– to 12-year-old boys. *Assessment, 13*, 356–367.

Falkenbach, D. M., Poythress, N. G., & Heide, K. M. (2003). Psychopathic features in a juvenile diverse population: Reliability and validity of two self-report measures. *Behavioral Sciences and the Law, 21*, 787–805.

Farrington, D. (2005). The importance of child and adolescent psychopathy. *Journal of Abnormal Child Psychology, 33*, 489–497.

Firestone, P., Bradford, J., Greenberg, D., Larose, M., & Curry, S. (1998). Homicidal and nonhomicidal child molesters: Psychological, phallometric, and criminal features. *Sexual Abuse: Journal of Research and Treatment, 10*, 305–323.

Fisher, L., & Blair, R. J. R. (1998). Cognitive impairment and its relationship to psychopathic tendencies in children with emotional and behavioral difficulties. *Journal of Abnormal Child Psychology, 26*, 511–519.

Flight, J. I., & Forth, A. E. (2007). Instrumentally violent youths: The roles of psychopathic traits, empathy, and attachment. *Criminal Justice and Behavior, 34*, 739–751.

Forth, A. E., & Book, A. S. (2006). Psychopathy in youth: A valid construct? In H. Hervé & J. Yuille (Eds.), *The psychopath: Theory, research, and practice* (pp. 369–388). Mahwah, NJ: Erlbaum.

Forth, A. E., Hart, S. D., & Hare, R. D. (1990). Assessment of psychopathy in male young offenders. *Psychological Assessment, 2*, 342–344.

Forth, A. E., Kosson, D. S., & Hare, R. D. (2003). *The Psychopathy Checklist: Youth Version*. Toronto: Multi-Health Systems.

Forth, A. E., & Mailloux, D. L. (2000). Psychopathy in youth: What do we know?

In C. B. Gacono (Ed.), *The clinical and forensic assessment of psychopathy: A practitioner's guide* (pp. 25–54). Mahwah, NJ: Erlbaum.

Frick, P. J., Bodin, S. D., & Barry, C. T. (2000). Psychopathic traits and conduct problems in community and clinic referred samples of children: Further development of the Psychopathy Screening Device. *Psychological Assessment, 12*, 382–393.

Frick, P. J., Cornell, A. H., Barry, C. T., Bodin, S. D., & Dane, H. E. (2003). Callous–unemotional traits and conduct problems in the prediction of conduct problem severity, aggression, and self-report delinquency. *Journal of Abnormal Child Psychology, 31*, 457–470.

Frick, P. J., & Dantagnan, A. L. (2005). Predicting the stability of conduct problems in children with and without callous–unemotional traits. *Journal of Child and Family Studies, 14*, 469–485.

Frick, P. J., & Hare, R. D. (2001). *The Antisocial Process Screening Device*. Toronto: Multi-Health Systems.

Frick, P. J., & Morris, A. (2004). Temperament and developmental pathways to conduct problems. *Journal of Clinical and Adolescent Psychology, 33*, 54–68.

Frick, P. J., O'Brien, B. S., Wootton, J. M., & McBurnett, K. (1994). Psychopathy and conduct problems in children. *Journal of Abnormal Psychology, 103*, 700–707.

Gendreau, P., Goggin, C., & Smith, P. (2002). Is the PCL-R really the "unparalleled" measure of offender risk?: A lesson in knowledge cumulation. *Criminal Justice and Behavior, 29*, 397–426.

Goodman, R. (1997). The Strengths and Difficulties Questionnaire: A research note. *Journal of Child Psychology and Psychiatry, 38*, 581–586.

Graves, K. (2007). Not always sugar and spice: Expanding theoretical and functional explanations for why females aggress. *Aggression and Violent Behavior, 12*, 131–140.

Gretton, H. M., Hare, R. D., & Catchpole, R. E. H. (2004). Psychopathy and offending from adolescence to adulthood: A 10-year follow-up. *Journal of Consulting and Clinical Psychology, 72*, 636–645.

Gretton, H. M., McBride, M., Hare, R. D., O'Shaughnessy, R., & Kumka, G. (2001). Psychopathy and recidivism in adolescent sex offenders. *Criminal Justice and Behavior, 28*, 427–449.

Guy, L. S., Edens, J. F., Anthony, C., & Douglas, K. S. (2005). Does psychopathy predict institutional misconduct among adults?: A meta-analytic investigation. *Journal of Consulting and Clinical Psychology, 73*, 1056–1064.

Hare, R. D. (1991). *The Hare Psychopathy Checklist—Revised*. Toronto: Multi-Health Systems.

Hart, S. D. (1998). The role of psychopathy in assessing risk for violence: Conceptual and methodological issues. *Legal and Criminological Psychology, 3*, 121–137.

Hemphill, J. F., Hare, R. D., & Wong, S. (1998). Psychopathy and recidivism: A review. *Legal and Criminological Psychology, 3*, 141–172.

Johnstone, L., & Cooke, D. (2004). Psychopathic-like traits in childhood: Conceptual and measurement concerns. *Behavioral Sciences and the Law, 22,* 103–125.

Jones, S., Cauffman, E., Miller, J. D., & Mulvey, E. (2006). Investigating different factor structures of the Psychopathy Checklist: Youth Version: Confirmatory factor analytic findings. *Psychological Assessment, 18,* 33–48.

Kimonis, E. R., Frick, P. J., Boris, N. W., Smyke, A. T., Cornell, A. H., Farrell, J. M., et al. (2006). Callous–unemotional features, behavioral inhibition, and parenting: Independent predictors of aggression in a high-risk preschool sample. *Journal of Child and Family Studies, 15,* 745–756.

Kimonis, E. R., Frick, P. J., Fazekas, H., & Loney, B. R. (2006). Psychopathy, aggression and the processing of emotional stimuli in non-referred girls and boys. *Behavioral Sciences and the Law, 24,* 21–37.

Kingsbury, S. J., Lambert, M. T., & Hendrickse, W. (1997). A two-factor model of aggression. *Psychiatry, 60,* 225–232.

Kosson, D. S., Cyterski, T. D., Steurwald, B. L., Neumann, C. S., & Walker-Matthews, S. (2002). The reliability and validity of the Psychopathy Checklist: Youth Version in nonincarcerated males. *Psychological Assessment, 14,* 97–109.

Kotler, J. S., & McMahon, R. J. (2005). Child psychopathy: Theories, measurement, and relations with the development and persistence of conduct problems. *Clinical Child and Family Psychology Review, 8,* 291–325.

Kruh, I, P., Frick, P. J., & Clements, C. B. (2005). Historical and personality correlates to the violence of juveniles tried as adults. *Criminal Justice and Behavior, 32,* 69–96.

Larsson, H., Andershed, H., & Lichtenstein, P. (2006). A genetic factor explains most of the variation in psychopathic personality. *Journal of Abnormal Psychology, 115,* 230–231.

Leistico, A. R., Salekin, R. T., DeCoster, J., & Rogers, R. (2008). A large-scale meta-analysis relating the Hare measures of psychopathy to antisocial conduct. *Law and Human Behavior, 32,* 28–45.

Lipsey, M., & Wilson, D. (2001). *Practical meta-analysis* (Applied Social Research Methods Series, No. 49). Thousand Oaks, CA: Sage.

Loper, A. B., Hoffschmidt, S. J., & Ash, E. (2001). Personality features and characteristics of violent events committed by juvenile offenders. *Behavioral Sciences and the Law, 19,* 81–96.

Lynam, D. R. (1997). Pursuing the psychopath: Capturing the fledgling psychopath in a nomological net. *Journal of Abnormal Psychology, 106,* 425–438.

Lynam, D. R. (1998). Early identification of the fledgling psychopath: Locating the psychopathic child in the current nomenclature. *Journal of Abnormal Psychology, 107,* 566–575.

Meloy, J. R. (2006). Empirical basis and forensic application of affective and predatory violence. *Australian and New Zealand Journal of Psychiatry, 40,* 539–547.

Marsee, M. A., Silverthorn, P., & Frick, P. J. (2005). The association of psychopathic traits with aggression and delinquency in non-referred boys and girls. *Behavioral Sciences and the Law, 23,* 803–817.

Millon, T. (1993). *Millon Adolescent Clinical Inventory manual.* Minneapolis, MN: National Computer Systems.

Morey, L. C. (1991). *Personality Assessment Inventory professional manual.* Odessa, FL: Psychological Assessment Resources.

Muñoz, L. C., & Frick, P. J. (2007). The reliability, stability, and predictive utility of the self-report version of the Antisocial Process Screening Device. *Scandinavian Journal of Psychology, 48,* 299–312.

Murrie, D. C., & Cornell, D. G. (2000). The Millon Adolescent Clinical Inventory and psychopathy. *Journal of Personality Assessment, 75,* 110–125.

Murrie, D. C., & Cornell, D. G. (2002). Psychopathy screening of incarcerated juveniles: A comparison of measures. *Psychological Assessment, 14,* 390–396.

Murrie, D. C., Cornell, D. G., Kaplan, S., McConville, D., & Levy-Elkon, A. (2004). Psychopathy scores and violence among juvenile offenders: A multi-measure study. *Behavioral Sciences and the Law, 22,* 49–67.

Neumann, C. S., Kosson, D. S., Forth, A. E., & Hare, R. D. (2006). Factor structure of the Hare Psychopathy Checklist: Youth Version (PCL:YV) in incarcerated adolescents. *Psychological Assessment, 18,* 142–154.

Odgers, C. L., Reppucci, N., & Moretti, M. M. (2005). Nipping psychopathy in the bud: An examination of the convergent, predictive, and theoretical utility of the PCL:YV among adolescent girls. *Behavioral Science and the Law, 23,* 743–763.

Pardini, D., Lochman, A., & Frick, P. J. (2003). Callous/unemotional traits and social-cognitive processes in adjudicated youths. *Journal of the American Academy of Child and Adolescent Psychiatry, 42,* 364–371.

Pardini, D., Obradović, J., & Loeber, R. (2006). Interpersonal callousness, hyperactivity/impulsivity, inattention, and conduct problems as precursors to delinquency persistence in boys: A comparison of three grade-based cohorts. *Journal of Clinical Child and Adolescent Psychology, 35,* 46–59.

Parks, G. A., & Bard, D. E. (2006). Risk factors for adolescent sex offender recidivism: Evaluation of predictive factors and comparison of three groups based upon victim type. *Sex Abuse, 18,* 319–342.

Porter, S., Fairweather, D., Drugge, J., Hervé, H., Birt, A., & Boer, D. P. (2000). Profiles of psychopathy in incarcerated sexual offenders. *Criminal Justice and Behavior, 27,* 216–233.

Porter, S., & Woodworth, M. (2007). "I'm sorry I did it ... but he started it": A comparison of official and self-reported homicide descriptions of psychopaths and non-psychopaths. *Law and Human Behavior, 31,* 91–107.

Poythress, N. G., Dembo, R., Wareham, J., & Greenbaum, P. E. (2006). Construct validity of the Youth Psychopathic Traits Inventory and the Antisocial Process Screening Device (APSD) with justice-involved adolescents. *Criminal Justice and Behavior, 33,* 26–55.

Quinsey, V. L., Harris, G. T., Rice, M. E., & Cormier, C. A. (2006). *Violent offenders: Appraising and managing risk.* Washington, DC: American Psychological Association.

Quinsey, V. L., Rice, M. E., & Harris, G. T. (1995). Actuarial prediction of sexual recidivism. *Journal of Interpersonal Violence, 10,* 85–105.

Robins, L. N. (1966). *Deviant children grown up: A sociological and psychiatric study of sociopathic personality.* Baltimore: Williams & Wilkins.

Rogers, R., Vitacco, M., Cruise, K., Sewell, K., & Neumann, C. (2002). Screening for adolescent psychopathy among at-risk youth: Initial validation of the Survey of Attitudes and Life Experiences. *Assessment, 9,* 343–350.

Salekin, R. T. (2004). *Risk–Sophistication–Treatment Inventory: Professional manual.* Lutz, FL: Psychological Assessment Resources.

Salekin, R. T. (2008). Psychopathy and recidivism from mid-adolescence to young adulthood: Cumulating legal problems and limiting life opportunities. *Journal of Abnormal Psychology, 117,* 386–395.

Salekin, R. T., Brannen, D. N., Zalot, A. A., Leistico, A. M., & Neumann, C. S. (2006). Factor structure of psychopathy in youth: Testing the applicability of the new four-factor model. *Criminal Justice and Behavior, 33,* 135–157.

Salekin, R. T., Lee, Z., Schrum-Dillard, C. L., & Kubak, F. A. (in press). Child psychopathy and protective factors: IQ and motivation to change. *Psychology, Public Policy, and Law.*

Salekin, R. T., & Lochman, J. E. (2008). Child and adolescent psychopathy: The search for protective factors. *Criminal Justice and Behavior, 35,* 159–172.

Salekin, R. T., Ziegler, T. A., Larrea, M. A., Anthony, V. L., & Bennett, A. (2003) Predicting dangerousness with two Millon Adolescent Clinical Inventory Psychopathy scales: The importance of egocentric and callous traits. *Journal of Personality Assessment, 80,* 154–163.

Schwalbe, C. S. (2007). Risk assessment for juvenile justice: A meta-analysis. *Law and Human Behavior, 31,* 449–462.

Seagrave, D., & Grisso, T. (2002). Adolescent development and the measurement of juvenile psychopathy. *Law and Human Behavior, 26,* 219–239.

Skeem, J. L., & Cauffman, E. (2003). Views of the downward extension: Comparing the Youth Version of the Psychopathy Checklist with the Youth Psychopathic Traits Inventory. *Behavioral Sciences and the Law, 21,* 737–770.

Spain, S. E., Douglas, K. S., Poythress, N. G., & Epstein, M. (2004). The relationship between psychopathic features, violence, and treatment outcome: The comparison of three youth measures of psychopathic features. *Behavioral Sciences and the Law, 22,* 85–102.

Vincent, G. M. (2006). Psychopathy and violence risk assessment in youth [Special issue]. *Child Psychiatric Clinics of North America, 15*(2), 407–428.

Vincent, G. M., Vitacco, M. J., Grisso, T., & Corrado, R.R. (2003). Subtypes of adolescent offenders: Affective traits and antisocial behavior patterns. *Behavioral Sciences and the Law, 21,* 695–712.

Vitacco, M. J., Caldwell, M. J., Van Rybroek, G. J., & Gabel, J. (2007). Psychopathy and behavioral correlates of victim injury in serious juvenile offenders. *Aggressive Behavior, 33,* 537–544.

Vitacco, M. J., Neumann, C. S., Caldwell, M. F., Leistico, A. M., Van Rybroek, G. J. (2006). Testing factor models of the Psychopathy Checklist: Youth Version and their association with instrumental aggression. *Journal of Personality Assessment, 87,* 74–83.

Vitacco, M. J., Rogers, R., & Neumann, C. S. (2003). The Antisocial Process Screening Device: An examination of its construct and criterion-related validity. *Assessment, 10,* 143–150.

Vitacco, M. J., & Vincent, G. M. (2006). Understanding the downward extension of psychopathy to youth: Implications for risk assessment and juvenile justice. *International Journal of Forensic Mental Health, 5,* 29–38.

Walters, G. D. (2003a). Predicting criminal justice outcomes with the Psychopathy Checklist and Lifestyle Criminality Screening Form: A meta-analytic comparison. *Behavioral Sciences and the Law, 21,* 89–102.

Walters, G. D. (2003b). Predicting institutional adjustment and recidivism with the Psychopathy Checklist factor scores: A meta-analysis. *Law and Human Behavior, 27,* 541–558.

Williamson, S., Hare, R. D., & Wong, S. (1987). Violence: Criminal psychopaths and their victims. *Canadian Journal of Behavioral Science, 19,* 454–462.

Woodworth, M., & Porter, S. (2002). In cold blood: Characteristics of criminal homicides as a function of psychopathy. *Journal of Abnormal Psychology, 111,* 436–445.

12

Relationships of Child and Adolescent Psychopathy to Other Forms of Psychopathology

KATHRIN SEVECKE
DAVID S. KOSSON

Several studies have examined relationships between psychopathic traits and symptoms of other psychiatric disorders. However, there have been few comprehensive reviews of this issue. Therefore, in this chapter, we review theoretical relationships between the syndrome of psychopathic traits in youth and other disorders of childhood and adolescence. Because several different measures of psychopathic traits have been employed, we review evidence obtained with several distinct measures. The Psychopathy Checklist: Youth Version (PCL:YV), like the Psychopathy Checklist—Revised (PCL-R), is an expert rater measure of psychopathic traits in adolescents. Expert rater measures require substantial training time because they depend on a trained rater integrating information across multiple contexts and sources of information. The PCL:YV also requires substantial time and effort to administer and score because PCL:YV ratings are completed following a semistructured interview, as well as collateral information. However, research has documented that the PCL:YV provides reliable and valid measures of psychopathic traits that correlate with criminal activity, interpersonal behavior, and laboratory anomalies in ways similar to PCL-R scores (Forth, Kosson, & Hare, 2003). As discussed in other chapters in this book (see Patrick, Chapter 2; Salekin, Chapter 14), evidence suggests that the same dimensions underlie PCL:YV scores in male adolescents and PCL-R scores in adults; in particular, there is evidence that the pattern of intercorrelations between item scores can be explained by arrogant, deceptive interpersonal behavior (*interpersonal dimension*); callousness, remorselessness, and lack of empathy (*affective dimension*); an impulsive, irresponsible lifestyle (*lifestyle dimension*); and early, versatile, and persistent antisocial behavior (*antisocial dimension*).[1] Frick and colleagues developed the Antisocial Process Screening Device (APSD; Frick & Hare, 2001) to identify markers of psychopathic traits (e.g., callous and unemotional traits) in childhood (Frick, 1998; Frick, Cornell, Barry, Bodin, & Dane, 2003). Similarly, the Childhood Psychopathy Scale (CPS; Lynam, 1998) was designed to extend assessment of psychopathy to children. The APSD and CPS permit ratings of psychopathic traits by parents and teachers who are familiar with children's behavior over time. The APSD has three dimensions: the callous–unemotional (CU) dimension, the narcissism dimension, and the impulsivity dimension (Frick, Bodin, & Barry, 2000). Both the APSD and CPS demonstrate similar patterns of correlations with antisocial behavior, physiological anomalies, and laboratory deficits similar to those seen with the PCL-R in adults (see Kotler and McMahon, Chapter 4, this volume; see also Frick et al., 2003; Loney, Frick, Clements, Ellis, & Kerlin, 2003). Instruments also exist for assessing self-reported psychopathic traits in adolescents (e.g., Youth Psychopathic Traits Inventory [YPI]; Andershed, Gustafson, Kerr, & Stattin, 2002). A self-report version of the APSD has also yielded preliminary evidence of validity (Muñoz & Frick, 2007). The findings from the adult and adolescence psychopathy literatures find resonance in research on children with psychopathic traits.

Implications and Pitfalls of Comorbidity in Psychopathology

The associations of psychopathic features with other forms of psychopathology are of interest for several reasons. First, to the extent that correlations between psychopathic features and symptoms of other disorders are high, they raise the possibility that syndromes may reflect common or overlapping etiological factors; that is, patterns of comorbidity may provide guidance to understanding the pathophysiology underlying psychopathy. In addition, given suggestions that individuals with psychopathic features represent a heterogeneous group comprising several distinct, albeit related, syndromes, distinct patterns of comorbidity within samples of individuals with psychopathic features may aid in the identification of subtypes of psychopathy.

Alternatively, other disorders may produce symptoms that resemble psychopathic features. For example, bipolar disorder is associated with impulsivity and poor judgment. Individuals with psychoactive substance dependence often exhibit irresponsibility and a lack of commitment to schoolwork, jobs, and friends and family. In short, individuals with other disorders may appear to be characterized by psychopathic features that actually reflect another psychiatric syndrome. Consequently, presence of a concurrent psychiatric disorder increases the difficulty of diagnosis. It is important in assessing psychopathic features to distinguish features of psychopathy from features of other mental illnesses. However, it must also be recognized that psychopathology is not always discrete: A given anomaly or symptom may reflect the common influence of two or more different disorders.

A related issue is that, beyond any contributions to symptoms that may appear to represent psychopathic features (as noted earlier), other psychiatric syndromes may influence the expression of psychopathic features in ways that make it easier or more difficult to assess psychopathy. For example, although it is commonly believed that depressive disorders are negatively correlated with psychopathy in adulthood, as we discuss below, there is actually very little evidence for such negative relationships among youth. To the extent that a youth exhibits both depressive and psychopathic features, it is likely that the affective disorder will blunt approach behaviors and, therefore, reduce the likelihood of disinhibited behavior in social interactions; similarly, to the extent that affective disorder reduces bragging, it may be more difficult to identify grandiosity, even if underlying grandiosity remains a serious problem. Despite their importance, these issues have received little systematic attention to date, and they await future research efforts.

One way to disentangle the influence of different syndromes is to examine their appearance and impact over time. When features of psychopathy appear only after the onset of another form of psychopathology, it is more likely that the initial syndrome has influenced the appearance of these psychopathic features. Longitudinal methods are essential for clarifying the onset and developmental trajectories associated with different forms of psychopathology. Unfortunately, there have been few prospective studies of psychopathic features in youth, and these represent a critical need in the field. Similarly, such studies could be used to track the developmental trajectory of psychopathic features and compare it to the trajectory for other disorders. Frick and colleagues (2003) reported that CU features initially assessed by parent ratings when boys were in third through seventh grade exhibited very high stability over the following 4-year period. Moreover, they reported that degree of childhood conduct problems is one of the best predictors of stability in psychopathic traits (see also Pardini, Lochman, & Powell, 2007). However, no prior studies have reported on the independence versus relatedness of developmental trajectories for a syndrome associated with psychopathic traits versus other disorders over time.

Because most studies address only concurrent comorbidity, our review emphasizes what we have learned from such studies. Nevertheless, in examining comorbidity cross-sectionally, it is important to bear in mind that we cannot discern which of two or more disorders developed first, and it remains possible that both disorders reflect the same pathophysiology, or that a disease process associated with one of the disorders ultimately contributes to the development of the other disorder. As we mention again at the end of this chapter, we recommend that researchers conducting such studies examine the age of onset of each symptom.

One additional limitation on the work to be reviewed here must be underscored. Most studies of psychopathic features in youth have recruited clinical and court-involved or incarcerated samples. Although such samples have the advantage that they contain a higher proportion of youth with psychopathic features, they are susceptible to a form of bias commonly called Berkson's bias, or treatment-seeking bias, which refers to the finding that comorbidity is generally higher in clinical samples and in samples selected on the basis of maladaptive functioning (e.g., criminal activity). In brief, each sort of problem or illness that characterizes an individual can impair his or her functioning, and not all individuals with such problems exhibit such severe maladaptation that they seek treatment (or are hospitalized or arrested). The more problems that someone exhibits, the greater the likelihood that he or she will ultimately seek treatment or end up in a clinical sample. Consequently, studies of clinical and treatment samples (e.g., probationers, inpatients) are likely to obtain inflated estimates of comorbidity rates. For this reason, community and nonselected samples are especially valuable because they are not subject to this bias. However, we should also state that it is possible that incarcerated and more severe samples may also truly exhibit significant co-occurring psychopathology. Thus, these samples will also be important in future research.

In the sections that follow, we first review studies addressing relationships between the psychopathy syndrome and other externalizing disorders. Subsequent sections consider relationships between psychopathy and internalizing disorders, and personality pathology; we close with an examination of links between psychopathy and traumatization.

Externalizing Disorders

Several recent studies have documented that early behavior problems commonly precede the development of severe antisocial behavior. Externalizing behavior problems occur with elevated prevalence in not only those youth who grow up to exhibit adult criminality and substance abuse (Rasmussen, Storsaeter, & Levander, 1999; Roesler et al., 2004) but also in children who are later diagnosed with antisocial personality disorder (APD) and psychopathy (Vitelli, 1998).

In a community-based sample of adjudicated youth, Schmidt, McKinnon, Chattha, and Brownlee (2006) found that PCL:YV scores also demonstrated concurrent validity with externalizing behavior problems. Of all the disorders in the externalizing spectrum, psychopathy is the syndrome associated with the most severe negative outcomes, including violence, recidivism, and apparent refractoriness to treatment efforts. In this context, the prominence of disruptive behavior disorders in the childhoods of individuals who later display psychopathy has led to the suggestion that the same biological and environmental factors that lead to attention-deficit/hyperactivity disorder (ADHD) and conduct disorder (CD) may also represent contributing factors to or causes of psychopathy.

Conduct Disorder

CD is commonly diagnosed in youth, particularly in males. Recently, several researchers have argued that the early appearance of CD is a particularly serious indicator of the likelihood of participation in criminal activities throughout the lifespan. The prevalence of CD in the general population ranges from 1.8 to 16.0% in boys and from 0.8 to 9.2% in girls (Loeber, Green, Lahey, Frick, & McBurnett, 2000). In comparison, investigators report a substantially elevated CD prevalence of 31 to 100% in delinquent adolescents (Ollendick, Seligman, & Butcher, 1999; Ruchkin, Koposov, Vermeiren, & Schwab-Stone, 2003; Timmons-Mitchell et al., 1997, Vermeiren, 2003).

Several review articles note a retrospective link between adult psychopathy and childhood conduct problems, such as early onset of antisociality, frequent and versatile offending, stable and impulsive violence, and impulsivity (e.g., Lynam, 1996). However, these associations are derived primarily from follow-back studies, not from prospective longitudinal studies. Studies with youth samples also suggest links between psychopathic traits and childhood disruptive behavior disorders. For example, prior North American studies with the PCL:YV have shown that incarcerated adolescent males with high PCL:YV scores display an elevated prevalence of a variety of externalizing behaviors, including more aggressiveness (Gretton, McBride, Lewis, O'Shaughnessy, & Hare, 1994), more CD symptoms, and greater alcohol and substance abuse compared to low-scoring adolescent males (Forth & Burke, 1998).

Enebrink, Andershed, and Longstöm (2005) investigated whether high levels of CU traits would differentiate clinic-referred boys with conduct problems from those low on such traits. In a sample of Swedish boys with CD, ages 6–13, boys with many CU traits had more pervasive, varied, and aggressive disruptive behavioral problems than boys low on these traits. Moreover, higher levels of CD problems in boys with CU traits were not explained by the confounding presence of ADHD symptoms. Dadds, Fraser, Frost, and Hawes (2005), examining CU traits in young boys (mean age, 6.29 years) assigned to a 10-week parent-training intervention, reported that CU traits were associated with greater CD problems at pretreatment and uniquely predicted posttreatment CD problem severity.

There has been much less research exploring links between oppositional defiant disorder (ODD) and psychopathic features. However, given the very strong links between CD and ODD, such links may be expected. Salekin, Neumann, Leistico, DiCicco, and Duros (2004) reported moderate correlations between PCL:YV scores and number of ODD symptoms and high correlations (*r*'s ≥ .50) between scores on self-report measures of PCL:YV and ODD symptoms. Similar high correlations have been reported for the correlation between ODD symptoms and APSD ratings based on a composite of parent and teacher ratings (*r* = .67; Frick et al., 2000). Burns (2000) suggested that these very high correlations reflect item overlap between APSD items and DSM-IV diagnostic criteria. Christian, Frick, Hill, Tyler, and Frazer (1997) found that among children with conduct problems, those with CU traits had more ODD and CD symptoms than those without CU traits. In fact, some researchers have argued that ODD simply reflects a temperamental dimension that promotes participation in antisocial activities as part of a general lack of agreeableness: irritability, antagonism, stubbornness, and lack of cooperation (Lahey, Waldman, & McBurnett, 1999). From this perspective, ODD is the negative pole of the major personality dimension of agreeableness, which appears to be largely heritable (Dick, Viken, Kaprio, Pulkkinen, & Rose, 2005), and may represent a distal cause of psychopathic features.

Attention-Deficit/Hyperactivity Disorder

ADHD represents one of the most frequently observed disorders in child and adolescent psychiatry, with prevalence rates ranging from 3 to 9% in the normal population (Spencer, Biederman, Wilens, & Faraone, 2002). Follow-up studies involving children with ADHD suggest that 10–60% of the cases persist into adult life as an incomplete or full syndrome (Manuzza, Klein, Bessler, Malloy, & LaPadula, 1993; Spencer et al., 2002; Wender, Wolf, & Wasserstein, 2001). Prevalence rates of ADHD are also elevated in antisocial adolescent samples. Vermeiren (2003) reported that 4% of detained adolescents, 14–19% of adjudicated adolescents, and 20–72% of incarcerated adolescents met diagnostic criteria for ADHD. Similarly, whereas the overall prevalence of ADHD in adults is estimated at 2–5% (Barkley & Murphy, 1998), Roesler and colleagues (2004) found a prevalence of 45%

in the histories of young adult prison inmates. Moreover, ADHD is associated with executive dysfunction and socioemotional difficulties that may contribute to poor adult outcomes.

Furthermore, although ADHD shares a genetic diathesis with other conditions in the externalizing spectrum (e.g., CD), there is also evidence for a unique genetic contribution to ADHD. Several researchers have suggested that the link between disruptive behavior and adult psychopathy may be especially strong for youth with both ADHD or impulsivity and CD (Lynam, 1996). Compared to children with pure ADHD, pure CD, and controls, a subgroup with comorbid ADHD and CD (ADHD-CD) displays early-onset, frequent, severe, cross-situational, and versatile forms of externalizing behavior, ranging from aggression to stealing to substance use (Piatigorsky & Hinshaw, 2004). Children with ADHD-CD also show response patterns on physiological measures that suggest less reactive autonomic systems, more rapid habituation to orienting and to aversive startling stimuli (Herpertz et al., 2001), and deficits in executive functioning that resemble the neurocognitive and psychophysiological functioning seen in adult psychopathy (Lynam, 1998).

Similarly, Barry and colleagues (2000) showed that in a clinic-referred sample of children ages 6–13, those with symptoms of ADHD in combination with severe conduct problems were most likely to also show features associated with psychopathy. These children showed high rates of CU traits, a preference for thrill- and adventure-seeking activities (i.e., fearlessness), and were more likely to show a reward-dominant response style. Frick and colleagues (2000) also examined associations between the APSD scales and ADHD in community and clinic samples. In the community sample, all three dimensions (CU, narcissism, and impulsivity) and the total score were moderately to strongly correlated with impulsive/hyperactive and inattentive/disorganized symptoms. In the clinic sample, a similar pattern was found: Correlations between APSD scales and ADHD symptoms ranged from $r = .27$ (CU) to $r = .57$ (impulsivity).

Colledge and Blair (2001) conducted the first study to examine shared and unique relationships between ADHD symptoms and psychopathic traits in boys (age range, 9–16 years) assessed with the APSD (Teacher version). They noted that there were significant correlations between ADHD ratings and both CU and impulsivity/conduct problems scores. However, partial correlations between ADHD and CU ratings were no longer significant after they controlled for impulsivity/conduct problems, whereas correlations between ADHD ratings and impulsivity scores remained significant after they controlled for CU traits. Consequently, these results are consistent with the proposal by Lilienfeld and Waldman (1990) that most of the relationship between ADHD and psychopathy is likely mediated by CD.

Lynam (1996, 1998) has argued that the joint presence of ADHD and CD confers specific vulnerability to psychopathy. His perspective, here referred to as the *comorbid subtype hypothesis*, predicts greater prevalence of psychopathy among those characterized by ADHD-CD during childhood or adolescence. The studies reviewed above appear consistent with the suggestion that youth with ADHD and conduct problems are at heightened risk for psychopathy. However, these studies did not distinguish between the possibility that ADHD and CD interact to increase the likelihood of psychopathic traits, and the alternative possibility that each has main effects that increase the likelihood of psychopathic traits. One study of adults appears to point to the interaction predicted by Lynam. Johansson, Kerr, and Andershed (2005) compared psychopathic and nonpsychopathic violent male offenders (mean age, 30 years) on retrospective reports of CD problems and ADHD symptoms as youth. Their results showed that adult criminals diagnosed as psychopaths were highly likely to have had histories of both problems in combination (four times more likely than chance) but were not more likely than nonpsychopaths to have had CD or ADHD alone.

However, not all studies have reported findings consistent with this hypothesis. Abramowitz, Kosson, and Seidenberg (2004) reported that, in a sample of adult males, relationships between retrospective reports of childhood ADHD and CD symptoms and adult PCL-R ratings were consistent with main effects for both ADHD and CD but not with interactions between ADHD and CD. In addition, most (but not all) of the variance between ADHD and adult psychopathy was shared with CD; that is, consistent with Colledge and Blair (2001) and Lilienfeld and Waldman (1990), most of the relationship between ADHD and psychopathy appeared to be mediated by CD. Nevertheless, there was a small independent contribution of ADHD to elevated PCL-R scores. The other major finding of this study was that both CD and ADHD symptoms were primarily related to PCL-R Factor 2 scores. These disruptive behavior disorder symptoms were only slightly related to scores on Factor 1, the core interpersonal and affective symptoms of psychopathy. This finding suggests that it is probably necessary to move beyond the externalizing disorders to understand fully the mechanisms that contribute to the development of psychopathy.

Because it is possible that the relationships between externalizing disorders and psychopathic features may be different in youth than in adults, Sevecke, Kosson, and Krischer (2009) reexamined these issues in samples of male and female adolescents. Their findings were generally quite similar to those reported by Abramowitz and colleagues (2004). First, among both males and females, psychopathic traits correlated with symptoms of both ADHD and CD. Second, relationships between ADHD and psychopathy were largely mediated by CD symptoms for total scores and for all of the dimensions of psychopathy. Third, the mediation was not complete for the affective and lifestyle dimensions (for girls) or the antisocial dimension (boys and girls). Thus, results are somewhat consistent with the independent prediction position for the girls because both ADHD and CD contributed uniquely to predicting girls' scores on most dimensions of psychopathy. Fourth, Sevecke, Kosson, and Krischer also found that the combined presence of ADHD and CD symptoms interacted to reduce the likelihood of elevations on psychopathy (and on the antisocial dimension of psychopathy) but only in girls. In other words, there was evidence for ADHD × CD interactions with respect to PCL:YV total scores and scores on the antisocial dimension of psychopathy; however, the direction of these interactions was opposite to that predicted by the comorbid subtype hypothesis. Finally, although few studies have addressed the similarity of relationships between psychopathic traits and externalizing disorders in boys versus girls, this study reported that relationships between CD and psychopathy could be confirmed for both genders.

One additional recent study merits brief mention. Hipwell, Pardini, Loeber, Sembower, and Stouthamer-Loeber (2007), using a large community-based sample of young girls, recently reported that after they controlled for demographic variables, hyperactivity/impulsivity was positively associated with conduct problems and with CU traits, but it was not uniquely associated with CU traits after they controlled for co-occurring conduct problems. They also examined the CU × conduct problems interaction and found no evidence for such an interaction in their sample.

In summary, three of four recent studies addressing the comorbid subtype hypothesis failed to identify evidence for the sort of interaction predicted by Lynam. Nevertheless, because only two youth studies to date have examined the interaction hypothesis, it remains important to examine this possibility in other youth samples and in samples in other cultures.

Substance Abuse and Dependence Disorders

Substance abuse and dependence are related to psychopathy in men (Hare, 1991; Hare, Clark, Grann, & Thornton, 2000; Hart & Hare, 1989; Stalenheim & von Knorring, 1996), and several studies have replicated relationships between psychopathy and substance abuse in male adolescents (e.g., Mailloux, Forth, & Kroner 1997). Roussy and Toupin (2000) reported that violent incarcerated male offenders scoring high on the PCL:YV (30 or greater) were more likely to be diagnosed with alcohol or drug abuse (56%) than offenders scoring low on the PCL:YV (20 or lower; 21%). Multiple substance abusers in a sample of adolescent male inpatients had significantly higher psychopathy scores than did alcohol abusers (Harvey, Stokes, Lord, & Pogge, 1996). In a sample of 80 female offenders, PCL:YV scores correlated weakly with a diagnosis of alcohol dependence (r = .22) and did not correlate significantly with diagnoses of drug dependence (Bauer, Whitman, & Kosson, 2008). PCL:YV scores were also unrelated to various indices of drug abuse in one study of adolescent males (O'Neill, Lidz, & Heilbrun, 2003).

Genetic and Environmental Mechanisms Related to Externalizing Pathology

In light of recent evidence that common genetic factors contribute to variance in alcohol and substance abuse/dependence, APD, and CD (Kendler, Prescott, Myers, & Neale, 2003), along with the high heritabilities for externalizing pathology (Dick et al., 2005), and recent reports for genetic contributions to variance in psychopathic traits as assessed by either self-report measures or teacher ratings (Blonigen, Hicks, Krueger, Patrick, & Iacono, 2005; Viding, Blair, Moffitt, & Plomin, 2005), the relationships between psychopathic features and symptoms of various externalizing disorders argue that the same genetic factors that contribute to externalizing disorders probably also contribute to the development of psychopathic features. A number of twin studies have examined the importance of genetic, shared environmental and nonshared environmental factors for psychopathic traits and for antisocial behavior. These studies overall suggest that psychopathic personality traits are highly heritable, and that shared environmental factors are relatively unimportant (see Viding & Larrson, Chapter 5, this volume).

Internalizing Disorders

There is a well-documented positive correlation between anxiety and antisocial behavior in children (Zoccolillo, Pickles, Quinton, & Rutter, 1992), adolescents, and adults (Robins, 1991). The rates of anxiety disorders in children with CD range from 22 to 33% in community samples and from 60 to 75% in clinic-referred or institutionalized samples (see Zoccolillo et al., 1992, for reviews). Similarly, APD correlates positively with trait anxiety scores and with anxiety disorder diagnoses (Lilienfeld, 1994).

However, in contrast to externalizing disorders, internalizing disorders are often assumed to vary inversely with psychopathic traits. Dating back to Cleckley's (1941/1976) clinical description of the adult psychopath, "the absence of 'nervousness' or psychoneurotic manifestations" has often been considered a core characteristic of the psychopathic individual. Nevertheless, theoretical perspectives provide two very different explanations for the expected negative correlation between anxiety and psychopathy. In Cleckley's account, the absence of anxiety has usually been interpreted as one aspect of a general absence of emotional experience. However, other authors have argued that fearlessness or the absence of behavioral inhibition and anxiety is a central disposition underlying psychopathy (Cloninger, 1987; Fowles, 1980; Lykken, 1995), a perspective often referred to as the *low-fear hypothesis*.

Other researchers have approached the issue by positing two distinct kinds of psychopathic individuals. Adult psychopathic individuals characterized by low anxiety have been labeled *primary psychopaths* (Blackburn, 1998; Karpman, 1948), whereas youth with psychopathic traits and low anxiety have been referred to as *undersocialized delinquents* (e.g., Quay, Routh, & Shapiro, 1987). In contrast, whereas adult psychopathic individuals with high levels of anxiety have been labeled *secondary psychopaths* (e.g., Blackburn, 1998), highly antisocial children and adolescents with high anxiety have been referred to as *neurotic delinquents* (Quay et al., 1987). In fact, recent cluster analyses of adults have reported that measures of anxiety contribute to differentiation between groups of so-called primary psychopaths and secondary psychopaths (Hicks, Markon, Patrick, Krueger, & Newman, 2004; Lee, Salekin, & Iselin, 2010; Skeem et al., 2004; Swogger & Kosson, 2007; Vassileva, Kosson, Abramowitz & Conrod, 2005). Similarly, Newman and his colleagues have often argued that psychopathic individuals characterized by a lack of anxiety or negative affectivity exhibit cognitive deficits and other anomalies that psychopathic individuals with these traits do not (e.g., Newman, MacCoon, Vaughn, & Sadeh, 2005; Newman, Schmitt, & Voss, 1997). However, the results with children and adolescents are not always as clear-cut (see Kubak & Salekin, 2009; Lee et al., 2010).

Anxiety and Affective Disorders

In spite of substantial interest in the importance of anxiety in the assessment of psychopathy, few studies have examined the relationship between anxiety disorders and psychopathic traits, and even fewer have addressed this issue in youth and child samples. One prior adult study suggested negative correlations between psychopathy and diagnoses of internalizing disorders (Stalenheim & von Knorring, 1996). Similarly, in a Swiss sample of male inmates ages 17–27 years, the prevalences of affective disorder and posttraumatic stress disorder (PTSD) were significantly higher among inmates with fewer psychopathic traits than among inmates with more psychopathic traits (Moeller & Hell, 2003).

In contrast, among a sample of male juvenile offenders, Epstein, Douglas, Poythress, Spain, and Falkenbach (2002) and Jack (2000) found that PCL:YV total scores were unrelated to mood disorder diagnoses and ratings. Similarly, Bauer and colleagues (2008) found that PCL:YV scores were unrelated to diagnoses of major depression and dysthymia among female adolescent offenders. Enebrink and colleagues (2005) reported that boys with CU traits were more often diagnosed with dysthymia than were boys low on CU traits. Hipwell and colleagues (2007) also reported a positive correlation between CU traits and parent and teacher ratings of depressed mood, after controlling for variance in demographic variables. Moreover, the partial correlation between CU and depressed mood remained significant even after researchers controlled for conduct problems. Hipwell and colleagues also reported a positive correlation between CU ratings and parent–teacher ratings of negative emotionality; however, this correlation was no longer significant after they controlled for conduct problems.

Frick, O'Brien, Wootton, and McBurnett (1994) and Hipwell and colleagues (2007) also reported inverse relationships between CU scores and some, but not other, measures of anxiety. For example, Frick and colleagues examined parent and teacher ratings of anxiety and anxiety/depression, and found that although both correlations with CU ratings were negative, the correlation was significant only for teacher-reported anxiety, not for parent-rated anxiety/depression. Hipwell and colleagues reported negative partial correlations between CU traits and parent–teacher ratings of generalized anxiety symptoms but no correlations with ratings of panic and social phobia symptoms. However, it is noteworthy that the correlation with generalized anxiety symptoms was negative only after researchers controlled for conduct problems, indicating a suppressor effect. Lynam, Hoyle, and Newman (2006) have argued for caution in interpreting partial correlations that appear discrepant from zero-order correlations.

Negative Affectivity

A greater number of studies have examined correlations between measures of psychopathic traits and self-report measures of negative affectivity. These studies also suggest the possibility of important differences between the correlates of psychopathic features in youth versus adults. Adult studies generally report no relationships between psychopathy and scores on self-report measures of anxiety or negative affectivity (Hare, 2003; Schmitt & Newman, 1999), although a small number of studies have identified positive correlations between PCL-R scores and scores on some measures of negative affectivity (Hale, Goldstein, Abramowitz, Calamari, & Kosson, 2004) or symptoms of PTSD (Sullivan & Patrick, 2005).

In contrast, studies of these relationships in adolescents have yielded quite discrepant results. Some studies of adolescents have reported negative relationships between psychopathic traits and internalizing psychopathology. For example, Murrie and Cornell (2000) found that adolescent male inpatients with high scores on the PCL:YV scored significantly lower on an anxiety scale than did those with low PCL:YV scores. Similarly, Dolan and Rennie (2007) reported that PCL:YV scores correlated negatively with fearfulness scores in a sample of incarcerated adolescent males.

Consistent with adult findings, several studies have reported no relationships between psychopathic traits and self-report measures of negative affectivity or internalizing psychopathology (e.g., Frick et al., 1994). In a sample of male juvenile offenders, O'Neill and colleagues (2003) reported that PCL:YV scores were unrelated to scores on self-report measures of depression and anxiety. Similarly, Day (1996), using the Mood and Feeling Questionnaire (Angold et al., 1987) to assess depressive symptoms in a sample of children at high-risk for juvenile delinquency, reported that depression was not associated with ratings on either the CU or the impulsivity/conduct problems scales of the APSD. Valentine (2001) also reported no significant relationships between Psychopathy Screening Device scores and self-reported depression in a mixed sample of male and female adolescents with CD, and Campbell, Porter, and Santor (2004) reported no correlation between PCL:YV scores and scores on the internalizing subscales of the Youth Self-Report. Last, Brandt, Kennedy, Patrick, and Curtin (1997) also reported no significant relationships between a modified version of the adult PCL-R and measures of anxiety and internalizing psychopathology in male adolescents. However, it is noteworthy that all the nonsignificant correlations were positive.

Still other studies have reported significant positive associations between psychopathic traits and self-reports of negative affectivity, although findings are not entirely consistent across studies. Positive correlations between PCL:YV scores and self-reports of negative affectivity have been found in samples of adolescent males on probation (Kosson, Cyterski, Steuerwald, Neumann, & Walker-Matthews, 2002) and samples of incarcerated female adolescents (Bauer et al., 2008). Schmidt and colleagues (2006) also reported significant positive correlations between PCL:YV scores and both parental ratings and self-reports of internalizing pathology. However, in that study, both kinds of positive correlations were observed only in males.

Other studies have reported positive correlations with internalizing problems for some but not other measures of psychopathic traits. For example, Salekin, Neumann, and colleagues (2004) found no relationships between PCL:YV scores and self-reported depression or internalizing problem scale scores, but they reported positive relationships between scores on the self-report APSD and symptoms of internalizing disorders. Moreover, the nonsignificant correlations for the PCL:YV were also positive and, in some cases, relatively similar to those for the APSD. Similarly, whereas Salekin, Leistico, Trobst, Schrum, and Lochman (2005) reported no correlations between PCL:YV scores and measures of anxiety, they noted significant positive correlations between scores on two self-report measures of psychopathic traits and self-report measures of anxiety. Kosson and colleagues (2007) reported significant positive correlations between PCL:YV scores and scores on the Children's Depression Inventory, but the positive correlation between PCL:YV and Taylor Manifest Anxiety Scale scores fell short of statistical significance.

Finally, we note that although few studies have addressed which dimensions of psychopathic traits are associated with internalizing pathology, Kosson and colleagues (2007) noted that in a mixed-sex sample of detained adolescents (83% male), self-reported depression scores were significantly correlated with scores on the Interpersonal dimension but were not significantly correlated with scores on the other dimensions of psychopathy. In contrast, Bauer and colleagues (2008) reported that correlations with self-reported depression and negative affectivity were significant only for Lifestyle dimension scores.

In summary, relationships between psychopathic traits and internalizing disorders (diagnoses, symptoms, and traits) in youth are much less consistent than relationships between psychopathic traits and externalizing disorders. In addition, despite this variability, current evidence suggests that, among youth, relationships between internalizing disorders and psychopathic traits are often quite different than those reported in adult samples. Instead of negative correlations with diagnoses and symptoms of depressive and anxiety disorders, several studies report zero correlations. Instead of zero correlations with general measures of negative trait affectivity, several studies report small to moderate positive correlations. On the basis of such findings in one study, Kosson and colleagues (2002) hypothesized that youth with psychopathic traits may differ in important ways from adults with such traits. Whereas adult psychopaths are characterized by a "mask of sanity," a relatively normal-seeming facade that conceals underlying emotional deficits (Cleckley, 1941/1976), adolescents with psychopathic features might not yet have developed such a "mask"; consequently, they may be more troubled by negative affect and more amenable to therapeutic intervention (see Salekin, Chapter 14, this volume). However, the inconsistency in findings for different samples and different measures of psychopathic traits and internalizing problems represents an important obstacle to drawing firm conclusions. Not only is additional research needed, but research using multiple measures of each of these constructs is also critical. Only such studies can establish the extent to which the inconsistencies noted here reflect differences among measures versus heterogeneity among youth with psychopathic traits. Recently, Kubak and Salekin's (2009) examination of psychopathy (multimeasurement) and its relation to anxiety and offending through meditational models may provide some new insights.

Self-Directed Aggression

The specific relationship between suicidal behavior and adult psychopathy has been examined in several studies (see Douglas, Herbozo, Poythress, Belfrage, & Edens, 2006, for a review). Whereas Cleckley (1941/1976) argued that suicidal behavior in psychopathic individuals is generally manipulative, studies of psychopathic inmates have sometimes found positive correlations between psychopathy and suicide attempts. Danish male prisoners with high PCL-R scores had more often made previous suicidal attempts than those with low PCL-R scores (Andersen, Sestoft, Lillebæk, Mortensen, & Kramp, 1999). Among American adult male prisoners, suicide attempts and history were positively associated with Antisocial Lifestyle scores but were independent of Interpersonal–Affective scores (Verona, Patrick, & Joiner, 2001). Verona, Hicks, and Patrick (2005) replicated these results partially among adult female prisoners: Suicide attempts were associated positively with antisocial lifestyle scores but negatively with interpersonal–affective scores. Finally, Stafford and Cornell (2003) reported a small positive correlation between PCL-R total scores and staff ratings of self-directed aggression in 72 male and female inpatients; data were not analyzed separately for males and females. Douglas and colleagues (2006) concluded that the small positive association between suicidality and the antisocial lifestyle component of psychopathy is robust but that, in general, there is no relationship between scores on the interpersonal–affective component and suicidality.

To our knowledge, only two studies have directly examined self-directed aggression and psychopathic traits in adolescents. Sevecke, Pukrop, and Krischer (2009) reported that high scores on the PCL:YV were associated with suicidal behavior in incarcerated female adolescents but not in incarcerated male adolescents. In addition, among females, correlations with Affective, Lifestyle, and Antisocial dimension scores were all significant. Chabrol and Saint-Martin (2009), using the YPI, evaluated the contribution of psychopathic traits to the prediction of suicidal ideation among community male and female adolescents. They found that scores on the affective component of the YPI uniquely correlated with suicidal ideation. Therefore, they suggested that, in adolescents, psychopathic traits are not always a protective factor against suicidality. This finding is consistent with evidence reviewed earlier, suggesting that relations between psychopathic features and internalizing pathology appear different in adolescents than in adults. However, because they did not report separate analyses for male and female adolescents, it is not clear whether this finding characterized the males or females examined separately. Douglas and colleagues (2006) also included two adolescent male samples in their review. In both samples, analyses yielded positive correlations between psychopathic traits and suicidality for most measures of psychopathic traits and, in both cases, positive correlations appeared to be specific to antisocial lifestyle features. Although the small number of studies prohibits definitive conclusions, current evidence suggests that relationships between psychopathic traits and suicidality seen in adults are replicated in two of three samples of male adolescents. Findings in one sample of females suggest more positive correlations between affective components and suicidality in adolescents than in adults. Clearly, additional research examining male and female adolescent samples is needed.

Personality Disorders

Personality pathology has been shown to be relevant to understanding offending. Epidemiological studies have established that personality pathology is highly prevalent (40% to 60%) in adult criminal populations in Western societies (Casey, 2000; Hiscoke, Langstrom, Ottosson, & Grann, 2003; Windle & Windle, 1995). Moreover, in adult samples, psychopathy scores have correlated positively with personality pathology. For example, among adult male offenders, Hart and Hare (1989) reported significant correlations between psychopathy scores and diagnoses of APD and histrionic personality disorder (HPD). However, they also noted that PCL-R scores correlated with prototypicality ratings for APD, HPD, and narcissistic personality disorder (NPD). Among adult male violent offenders, Huchzermeier and colleagues (2007) found significant relationships between APD and borderline personality disorder (BPD) diagnoses, and scores on the antisocial lifestyle dimension of psychopathy; they also reported a significant positive correlation between NPD diagnoses and affective–interpersonal scores. Similarly, Soderstrom, Nilsson, Sjodin, Carlstedt, and Forsman (2005) showed that, among male offenders, PCL-R total scores, as well as Affective factor and Lifestyle factor scores, were significantly correlated with Cluster B personality disorder diagnoses. Weizmann-Henelius, Viemerö, and Eronena (2004) reported similar relationships in adult women for psychopathy total scores and for factor scores using the two-factor model, and also reported relationships between psychopathy and schizotypal personality disorder.

Investigators testing the validity and stability of personality pathology in adolescents have argued that in youth 14 years of age and older, personality disorders can be reliably and validly assessed (Bernstein, Cohen, & Velez, 1993; Grilo, Becker, Edell, & McGlashan, 2001; Kasen, Cohen, Skodol, Johnson, & Brook, 1999; Levy et al., 1999; Westen, Shedler, Durrett, Glass, & Martens, 2003). Although it has been argued that the stability of personality disorders increases from adolescence to adulthood (Roberts & DelVecchio, 2000) and is lower than previously assumed (Zanarini, Frankenburg, Hennen, Bradford Reich, & Silk, 2005), several longitudinal studies suggest that the stability of maladaptive personality traits relative to age peers may be roughly equivalent to that found in adulthood (Cohen, Crawford, Johnson, & Kasen, 2005; Johnson, Cohen, & Kasen, 2000; Zanarini et al., 2005).

Few studies have examined associations between psychopathic traits and personality pathology in youth samples. However, several authors have reported links between personality disorders and violence (Myers, Burket, & Harris, 1995). For example, Johnson, Cohen, Smailes, and colleagues (2000) reported associations between both Cluster A and Cluster B personality disorder symptoms and violence in a sample of community youth. However, there are also some specific findings relevant to psychopathy. In a sample of 30 adolescent psychiatric inpatients, those who met DSM-III-R criteria for NPD possessed significantly more psychopathic traits than those who did not meet diagnostic criteria (Myers et al., 1995). In addition, patients who met criteria for avoidant or self-defeating personality disorder had lower psychopathy scores than did youth who did not meet diagnostic criteria, and there was no difference in psychopathy scores between those who met versus did not meet criteria for BPD. In addition, Lynam and colleagues have demonstrated that CU traits in youth are negatively related to scores on the agreeableness and conscientiousness factors of the Big Five model of personality (Miller & Lynam, 2001; Miller, Lynam, Widiger, & Leukefeld, 2001).

On the basis of the existing results, however, one cannot decide whether personality traits or personality pathology play(s) a causal role in the pathway to psychopathic traits, or whether psychopathy and personality pathology are the outcome of some other, common process, such as parental neglect, social context or genetic predisposition. It is clear that in psychopathic adults, negative emotionality is primarily related to the lifestyle and antisocial dimensions of psychopathy. One recent study indicated that fearlessness and lack of inhibition at age 3 predict higher psychopathy scores in adulthood (Glenn, Raine, Venables, & Mednick, 2007). Nevertheless, it is premature to state whether temperamental factors and personality traits are related to all dimensions of psychopathy in youth, and it remains possible that observed correlations reflect the influence of other factors not examined.

Psychopathy and Traumatization

To date, few studies have addressed relationships between early traumatic experiences and the syndrome of psychopathy. However, in addition to adverse family conditions (Marmorstein & Iacono, 2005), early traumatization is commonly regarded as a causal or mediating risk factor for aggressive and violent behavior (Jaffee, Caspi, Moffitt, & Taylor, 2004; Loeber & Stouthamer-Loeber, 1998; Pollock, 1999). In addition, researchers have argued that early traumatization has a negative influence on development of the ability to regulate anger and affect (Erwin, Newman, McMackin, Morrissey, & Kaloupek, 2000; Novaco & Chemtob, 1998). Effective emotion and anger regulation contributes to reduced aggressiveness, whereas impaired regulation leads to heightened aggression.

Several studies have now linked child maltreatment with adult psychopathy (Marshall & Cooke, 1999). For example, Lang, Klinteberg, and Alm (2002) studied the implications of childhood neglect and/or abuse for adults' scores on the PCL-R (Hare, 2003) and violent offending. They found that those with more victimization had higher psychopathy scores than those with less severe victimization histories. Similarly, Bernstein, Stein, and Handelsman (1998) reported that in a substance-abusing sample, physical abuse and physical neglect, measured with the Childhood Trauma Questionnaire (CTQ), were related to a subcluster of "psychopathic" personality disorders consisting of childhood and adult sadistic and antisocial personality traits. In a Swiss sample of younger male offenders (ages 17–27), PCL-R total scores were correlated with the number of prior threatening events experienced (Moeller & Hell, 2003). Verona and colleagues (2005) reported that, among female offenders, both experiences of physical and sexual abuse correlated with PCL-R total scores and with scores on the affective–interpersonal and antisocial lifestyle dimensions of psychopathy. However, after controlling for the Factor 2 scores, the unique relationships between maltreatment and Factor 1 scores were no longer significant, suggesting that shared variance between the factors and variance specific to Factor 2 accounted for the significant zero-order correlations.

Campbell and colleagues (2004) evaluated the clinical, psychosocial and criminal correlates of psychopathic traits in a sample of 226 male and female incarcerated adolescent offenders. Although higher PCL:YV scores were associated with histories of physical abuse, the only specific psychosocial factor to predict PCL:YV scores was a history of nonparental living arrangements (e.g., foster care). Forth and colleagues (2003) summarize findings from several unpublished doctoral dissertations documenting an association between childhood victimization and PCL:YV scores in adolescents (McBride, 1998; O'Neill, 2001).

As for gender differences, a variety of studies have reported a heightened prevalence of traumatization in female delinquent juveniles compared to males (Abram et al., 2004; Cauffman, Feldman, Waterman, & Steiner, 1998; Dixon, Howie, & Starling, 2004). Only recently has the psychopathy construct been explicitly applied to women and adolescent girls (Salekin, Rogers, & Sewell, 1997; Vitale & Newman, 2001). Recently, Krischer and Sevecke (2008) examined relationships between psychopathic traits and histories of abuse in male and female adolescent delinquents. The analyses revealed an association between early physical and emotional traumatic experiences and psychopathy in detained boys. In girls, however, other family-related variables, such as nonparental living arrangements, seemed to be more highly associated with the psychopathy syndrome than traumatization. To our knowledge, the only study focusing on the relationship among violence, traumatization and psychopathy in delinquent girls was by Odgers, Reppucci, and Moretti (2005), who found a strong association between trauma and aggression, and between psychopathy and aggression, but they showed that the relation between psychopathic traits and violence was fully mediated by the relationship between psychopathic traits and victimization. Odgers and coworkers argued that the psychopathy syndrome in girls is not yet well understood, and their findings raise important questions about the complex relationship among trauma, psychopathy, and aggression.

Conclusion

Although research on the comorbidity between psychopathic traits and other forms of psychopathology is still in its infancy, available data appear to permit a few tentative conclusions. First, the heterogeneity among youth exhibiting psychopathic features is an important outcome of this literature review. Although it remains possible that the inconsistent findings across studies simply reflect the use of different instruments, different samples, and/or different procedures, it appears more likely that at least some of this heterogeneity reflects the need for improved assessment of youth with psychopathic traits. Because authors of other chapters in this volume have addressed the measurement of psychopathic traits in detail, we avoid speculating about the directions that improved assessment of these traits should take (see Kotler & McMahon, Chapter 4). Nevertheless, our review underscores the dramatic need for studies that include multiple measures of psychopathic traits and of external constructs. In addition, we recognize the likelihood of subtypes of youth that differ in psychopathic traits. Although it is beyond the scope of this review, evidence for subtypes of adults with psychopathic traits has now been reported in studies using a variety of different measures and different clustering methods (e.g., Hicks et al., 2004; Skeem et al., 2004; Swogger & Kosson, 2007). It seems likely that these subtypes originate in childhood or adolescence (Lee et al., 2010).

Second, associations between psychopathic traits and externalizing pathology are as strong in youth as in adults. Current findings suggest that the association with CD is stronger than that with ADHD. In addition, much of the relation between ADHD and psychopathic traits appears to be mediated by CD, and most of the shared variance between ADHD, CD, and psychopathy reflects the antisocial and lifestyle features of the psychopathy syndrome, not the core interpersonal and affective features. Although some studies cast doubt on the utility of the comorbid subtype hypothesis, the strong likelihood of heterogeneity among adolescents with psychopathic features encourages caution before we dismiss a hypothesis that may yet be corroborated in some samples.

Third, although our review revealed striking variance in the magnitude and direction of the relations between psychopathic traits and anxiety, and depression symptomatology, the evidence for positive relationships between psychopathic traits and internalizing psychopathology in a substantial number of the studies we reviewed, and across a variety of investigators and laboratories, argues persuasively that internalizing psychopathology may well represent an important area of discontinuity between the nomological networks associated with psychopathy in youth versus adulthood. It is important to note that the discrepant findings cannot be attributed simply to rater biases or self-presentation biases. Disparate findings have been reported in studies employing ratings by trained diagnosticians, parent and teacher ratings, and self-reports; in short, conflicting results have been obtained with all the assessment approaches employed. Additional research is needed to explore the developmental trajectories associated with psychopathic features in youth. One especially intriguing possibility is that features of depression or negative affectivity may moderate developmental outcomes for adolescents with psychopathic traits.

Fourth, personality pathology and child maltreatment represent important new domains for examining relationships between psychopathic features and other forms of psychopathology. In these domains the scarcity of findings provides the chief reason for caution. However, the provocative finding of Verona and colleagues (2005) that child maltreatment may partly reflect shared variance between the interpersonal–affective and antisocial lifestyle components of psychopathy points to the importance of additional research examining this possibility in youth.

Finally, we note that many important questions about relationships between psychopathic traits and other disorders cannot yet be answered. With respect to the mechanisms underlying comorbidity, behavior genetic studies suggest the possibility that there are specific genetic contributions to the development of CU traits. However, the extent to which these genetic influences overlap with other externalizing, internalizing, and personality disorders has received alarmingly little attention. More follow-up studies are also important to examine the influence of different parenting and socialization factors related to child and parent psychopathology, child management practices, and other environmental influences that may contribute to the development of a stable maladaptive psychopathic pathway. Although many early influential factors have been identified that predict antisocial behavior in adolescence, we still do not know enough about different patterns of pathways into adulthood to customize intervention strategies according to comorbid diagnoses and psychosocial risk factors. Furthermore, consistent with recommendations of Viding (2004) and Larsson and colleagues (2007), we wish to highlight the importance of studies that permit assessment of gene × environment correlations and interactions in the area of psychopathic traits. Therefore, additional research is needed that attempts to examine familial, social, and biological dimensions, with the aim of developing new integrative theories of the etiology of antisocial disorders.

In addition, several of the conceptual issues raised at the beginning of this chapter continue to suggest the need for additional research. Prior studies have not addressed the extent to which presence of a concurrent psychiatric disorder increases the difficulty of assessing psychopathic features. Such research may require the availability of multiple criteria for psychopathy. In addition, studies that examine the age of onset and course of different symptoms and syndromes over time are invaluable for disentangling the influences of different syndromes over time. Such information may ultimately warrant application in the assessment process. However, basic descriptive and longitudinal work is necessary before the pragmatic and theoretical implications of co-occurring forms of psychopathology can be disambiguated. The extent to which correlations between psychopathic features and symptoms of other disorders are very high raises the possibility that these syndromes reflect common or overlapping etiological factors. To avoid Berkson's, or treatment-seeking, bias it is also imperative that studies with clinical samples be counterbalanced by community studies. Some of the recent studies of psychopathic features in youth have begun to address this issue. To the extent that findings generalize across community and clinical samples, they provide confidence in the stability of relationships.

Finally, our review highlights our lack of knowledge about sex differences in the expression of psychopathic features and in patterns of comorbidity. Among girls, little is known about the shared and unique associations that CU behaviors and conduct problems have with aspects of emotional and behavioral dysregulation, and with parenting practices. However, current findings suggest that relationships between psychopathic traits and both externalizing (ADHD) and internalizing (self-directed aggression) problems may be different in girls than in boys. Further research examining sex differences in internalizing and personality disorders over time will help to address whether these sex differences contribute to differences in the construct validity of psychopathic traits among adolescents.

Note

1. As discussed elsewhere, the centrality of the antisocial dimension to the psychopathy construct has been the subject of some controversy, with some authors arguing that antisocial behavior is a consequence of the development of a psychopathy syndrome (e.g., Cooke, 1998), and others arguing that early and unusual antisocial behavior is one early marker of the phenotype that ultimately develops the full constellation of psychopathic traits.

References

Abram, K. M., Teplin, L. A., Charles, D. R., Longworth, S. L., McClelland, G. M., & Dulcan, M. K. (2004). Posttraumatic stress disorder and trauma in youth in juvenile detention. *Archives of General Psychiatry, 61*, 403–410.

Abramowitz, C. S., Kosson, D. S., & Seidenberg, M. (2004). The relationship between childhood attention deficit hyperactivity disorder, conduct problems and adult psychopathy. *Personality and Individual Differences, 36*, 1031–1037.

Andersen, H. S., Sestoft, D., Lillebæk, T., Mortensen, E. L., & Kramp, P. (1999). Psychopathy and psychopathological profiles in prisoners on remand. Acta *Psychiatrica Scandinavica, 99*, 33–39.

Andershed, H., Gustafson, S. B., Kerr, M., & Stattin, H. (2002). Understanding the abnormal by studying the normal. *Acta Psychiatrica Scandinavica Supplementum, 412*, 75–80.

Angold, A., Weissman, M. M., John, K., Merikangas, K. R., Prusoff, B. A., Wickramaratne, P., et al. (1987). Parent and child reports of depressive symptoms in children at low and high risk of depression. *Journal of Child Psychology and Psychiatry and Allied Disciplines, 28*, 901–915.

Barkley, R. A., & Murphy, K. R. (1998). *Attention-deficit/hyperactivity disorder: A clinical workbook.* New York: Guilford Press.

Barry, C. T., Frick, P. J., DeShazo, T. M., McCoy, M. G., Ellis, M., & Loney, B. R. (2000). The importance of callous–unemotional traits for extending the concept of psychopathy to children. *Journal of Abnormal Psychology, 109*, 335–340.

Bauer, D., Whitman, L. A., & Kosson, D. S. (2008). *Reliability and construct validity of the Psychopathy Checklist: Youth Version in incarcerated adolescent girls.* Manuscript in preparation.

Bernstein, D. P., Cohen, P., & Velez, C. N. (1993). Prevalence and stability of DSM-III-R personality disorders in a community-based survey of adolescents. *American Journal of Psychiatry, 150*, 1237–1243.

Bernstein, D. P., Stein, J. A., & Handelsman, L. (1998). Predicting personality pathology among adult patients with substance use disorders: Effects of childhood maltreatment. *Addictive Behaviors, 23*(6), 855–868.

Blackburn, R. (1998). Psychopathy and personality disorder: Implications of interpersonal theory. In D. J. Cooke, A. E. Forth, & R. D. Hare (Eds.), *Psychopathy: Theory, research and implications for society* (pp. 269–301). Dordrecht, The Netherlands: Kluwer Academic.

Blonigen, D. M., Hicks, B. M., Krueger, R. F., Patrick, C. J., & Iacono, W. G. (2005). Psychopathic personality traits: Heritability and genetic overlap with internalizing and externalizing psychopathology. *Psychological Medicine, 35*, 637–648.

Brandt, J. R., Kennedy, W. A., Patrick, C. J., & Curtin, J. J. (1997). Assessment of psychopathy in a population of incarcerated adolescent offenders. *Psychological Assessment, 9*, 429–435.

Burns, G. L. (2000). Problem of item overlap between the Psychopathy Screening Device and attention deficit hyperactivity disorder, oppositional defiant disorder, and conduct disorder rating scales. *Psychological Assessment, 12*, 447–450.

Campbell, M. A., Porter, S., & Santor, D. (2004). Psychopathic traits in adolescent offenders: An evaluation of criminal history, clinical, and psychosocial correlates. *Behavioral Sciences and the Law, 22*, 23–47.

Casey, P. (2000). The epidemiology of personality disorders. In P. Tyrer (Ed.), *Personality disorders: Diagnosis, management and course* (pp. 71–79). London: Arnold.

Cauffman, E., Feldman, S. S., Waterman, J., & Steiner, H. (1998). Posttraumatic stress disorder among female juvenile offenders. *Journal of the American Academy of Child and Adolescent Psychiatry, 37*(11), 1209–1216.

Chabrol, H., & Saint-Martin, C. (2009). Psychopathic traits and suicidal ideation in high school students. *Archives of Suicide Research, 13*(1), 64–73.

Christian, R. E., Frick, P. J., Hill, N. L., Tyler, L., & Frazer, D. R. (1997). Psychopathy and conduct problems in children: II. Implications for subtyping children with conduct problems. *Journal of the American Academy of Child and Adolescent Psychiatry, 36*, 233–241.

Cleckley, H. (1976). *The mask of sanity* (5th ed.). St Louis, MO: Mosby. (Original work published 1941)

Cloninger, C. R. (1987). A systematic method for clinical description and classification of personality variants: A proposal. *Archives of General Psychiatry, 44*, 573–588.

Cohen, P., Crawford, T. N., Johnson, J. G., & Kasen, S. (2005). The children in the Community Study of Developmental Course of Personality Disorder. *Journal of Personality Disorders, 19*, 131–140.

Colledge, E., & Blair, R. J. R. (2004). The relationship in children between the inattention and impulsivity component of attention deficit and hyperactivity disorder and psychopathic tendencies. *Personality and Individual Differences, 30*, 1175–1187.

Cooke, D. J. (1998). Psychopathy across cultures. In D. J. Cooke, A. E. Forth, & R. D. Hare (Eds.), *Psychopathy: Theory, research, and implications for society* (pp. 13–45). Dordrecht, The Netherlands: Kluwer.

Day, D. M. (1996). *A small validation study of the Psychopathy Screening Device (PSD) with children at risk for juvenile delinquency*. Toronto: Earlscourt Child Family Center.

Dick, D. M., Viken, R. J., Kaprio, J., Pulkkinen, L., & Rose, R. J. (2005). Understanding the covariation among childhood externalizing symptoms: Genetic and environmental influences on conduct disorder, attention deficit hyperactivity disorder, and oppositional defiant disorder symptoms. *Journal of Abnormal Child Psychology, 33,* 219–229.

Dixon, A., Howie, P., & Starling, J. (2004). Psychopathology in female juvenile offenders. *Journal of Child Psychology and Psychiatry, 45*(6), 1150–1158.

Dolan, M. C., & Rennie, C. E. (2007). Is juvenile psychopathy associated with low anxiety and fear in conduct disordered male offenders? *Journal of Anxiety Disorders, 21*(8), 1028–1038.

Douglas, K. S., Herbozo, S., Poythress, N. G., Belfrage, H., & Edens, J. F. (2006). Psychopathy and suicide: A multisample investigation. *Psychological Services, 3*, 97–116.

Enebrink, P., Andershed, H., & Langström, N. (2005). Callous–unemotional traits are associated with clinical severity in referred boys with conduct problems. *Nordic Journal of Psychiatry, 59*(6), 431–440.

Epstein, M. K., Douglas, K. S., Poythress, N. G., Spain, S. E., & Falkenbach, D. M. (2002). *A discriminant study of juvenile psychopathy and mental disorder*. Presented at the annual meeting for the American Psychology–Law Society, Austin, TX.

Erwin, B. A., Newman, E., McMackin, R., Morrissey, C., & Kaloupek, D. G. (2000). PTSD, malevolent environment, and criminality among criminally involved male adolescents. *Criminal Justice and Behavior, 27*, 196–215.

Forth, A. E., & Burke, H. C. (1998). Psychopathy in adolescence: Assessment, violence and developmental precursors. In D. J. Cooke, A. E. Forth, & R. D. Hare (Eds.), *Psychopathy: Theory, research and implications for society* (pp. 205–229). Boston: Kluwer Academic.

Forth, A. E,, Kosson, D., & Hare, R. (2003). *The Hare Psychopathy Checklist: Youth Version*. Toronto: Multi-Health Systems.

Fowles, D. C. (1980). The three arousal model: Implications of Gray's two-factor learning theory for heart rate, electrodermal activity, and psychopathy. *Psychophysiology, 17*(2), 87–104.

Frick, P. J. (1998). *Conduct disorders and severe antisocial behavior*. New York: Plenum Press.

Frick, P. J., Bodin, S. D., & Barry, C. T. (2000). Psychopathic traits and conduct problems in community and clinic-referred samples of children: Further development of the psychopathy screening device. *Psychological Assessment, 12*(4), 382–393.

Frick, P. J., Cornell, A. H., Barry, C. T., Bodin, S. D., & Dane, H. E. (2003). Callous–unemotional traits and conduct problems in the prediction of conduct problem severity, aggression, and self-report of delinquency. *Journal of Abnormal Child Psychology, 31,* 457–470.

Frick, P. J., & Hare, R. (2001). *The Antisocial Process Screening Device (ASPD)*. Toronto: Multi-Health Systems.

Frick, P. J., O'Brien, B. S., Wootton, J. M., McBurnett, K. (1994). Psychopathy and conduct problems in children. *Journal of Abnormal Psychology, 103*, 700–707.

Glenn, A. L., Raine, A., Venables, P. H., & Mednick, S. A. (2007). Early temperamental and psychophysiological precursors of adult psychopathic personality. *Journal of Abnormal Psychology, 116*, 508–518.

Gretton, H. M., McBride, M., Lewis, K., O'Shaughnessy, R., & Hare, R. D. (1994). Predicting patterns of criminal activity in adolescent sexual psychopaths. *Canadian Psychology, 35*, 50.

Grilo, C. M., Becker, D. F., Edell, W. S., & McGlashan, T. H. (2001). Stability and change of DSM-III-R personality disorder dimensions in adolescents followed up 2 years after psychiatric hospitalization. *Comprehensive Psychiatry, 42*, 364–368.

Hale, L. R., Goldstein, D. S., Abramowitz, C. S., Calamari, J. E., & Kosson, D. S. (2004). Psychopathy is related to negative affectivity but not to anxiety sensitivity. *Behavioural Research and Therapy, 42*, 679–710.

Hare, R. D. (2003). *The Hare Psychopathy Checklist—Revised (PCL-R)*. Toronto: Multi-Health Systems.

Hare, R. D., Clark, D., Grann, M., & Thornton, D. (2000). Psychopathy and the predictive validity of the PCL-R: An international perspective. *Behavioral Science and the Law, 18*, 623–645.

Hart, S. D., & Hare, R. D. (1989). Discriminant validity of the Psychopathy Checklist in a forensic psychiatric population. *Psychological Assessment: A Journal of Consulting and Clinical Psychology, 1*, 211–218.

Harvey, P. D., Stokes, J. L., Lord, J., & Pogge, D. L. (1996). Neurocognitive and personality assessment of adolescent substance abusers: A multidimensional approach. *Assessment, 3*, 241–253.

Herpertz, S. C., Wenning, B., Mueller, B., Qunaibi, M., Sass, H., & Herpertz-Dahlmann, B. (2001). Psychophysiological responses in ADHD boys with and without conduct disorder: Implications for adult antisocial behaviour. *Journal of the American Academy of Child Adolescent Psychiatry, 40*, 1222–1230.

Hicks, B. M., Markon, K. E., Patrick, C. J., Krueger, R. F., & Newman, J. P. (2004). Identifying psychopathy subtypes on the basis of personality structure. *Psychological Assessment, 16*, 276–288.

Hipwell, A. E., Pardini, D. A., Loeber, R., Sembower, M. K., & Stouthamer-Loeber, M. (2007). Callous–unemotional behaviors in young girls: Shared and unique effects relative to conduct problems. *Journal of Clinical Child and Adolescent Psychology, 36*, 293–304.

Hiscoke, U. L., Langstrom, N., Ottosson, H., & Grann, M. (2003). Self-reported personality traits and disorders (DSM-IV) and risk of criminal recidivism: A prospective study. *Journal of Personality Disorders, 17*, 293–305.

Huchzermeier. C., Geiger, F., Bruss, E., Godt, N., Köhler, D., Hinrichs, G., et al. (2007). The relationship between DSM-IV Cluster B personality disorders and psychopathy according to Hare's criteria: Clarification and resolution of previous contradictions. *Behavioral Sciences and the Law, 25*, 901–911.

Jack, L. A. (2000). *Psychopathy, risk/need factors, and psychiatric symptoms in high-risk youth: Relationships between variables and their link to recidivism.* Unpublished doctoral dissertation, Simon Fraser University, Burnaby, BC, Canada.

Jaffee, S. R., Caspi, A., Moffitt, T. E., & Taylor, A. (2004). Physical maltreatment victim to antisocial child: Evidence of an environmentally mediated process. *Journal of Abnormal Psychology, 113*(1), 44–55.

Johansson, P., Kerr, M., & Andershed, H. (2005). Linking adult psychopathy with childhood hyperactivity–impulsivity–attention problems and conduct problems through retrospective self-reports. *Journal of Personality Disorders, 19,* 94–101.

Johnson, J. G., Cohen, P., Kasen, S., Skodol, A. E., Hamagami, F., & Brook, J. S. (2000). Age-related change in personality disorder trait levels between early adolescence and adulthood: A community-based longitudinal investigation. *Acta Psychiatrica Scandinavica, 102,* 265–275.

Johnson, J. G., Cohen, P., Smailes, E., Kasen, S., Oldham, J. M., Skodol, A. E., et al. (2000). Adolescent personality disorders associated with violence and criminal behavior during adolescence and early adulthood. *American Journal of Psychiatry, 157,* 1406–1412.

Karpman, B. (1948). On the need for separating psychopathy into two distinct clinical types: Symptomatic and idiopathic. *Journal of Criminology and Psychopathology, 3,* 112–137.

Kasen, S., Cohen, P., Skodol, A. E., Johnson, J. G., & Brook, J. S. (1999). Influence of child and adolescent psychiatric disorders on young adult personality disorder. *American Journal of Psychiatry, 156,* 1529–1535.

Kendler, K. S., Prescott, C. A., Myers, J., & Neale, M. C. (2003). The structure of genetic and environmental risk factors for common psychiatric and substance use disorders in men and women. *Archives of General Psychiatry, 60,* 929–937.

Kosson, D. S., Allen, L., McBride, C. K., Walsh, Z., Tercek, R., & Greco, J. (2007, April). *Preliminary evidence for negative affectivity and maladaptive emotion regulation strategies in youth with psychopathic traits.* Presented at the 2nd annual meeting of the Society for the Scientific Study of Psychopathy, St. Pete Beach, FL.

Kosson, D. S., Cyterski, T. D., Steuerwald, B. L., Neumann, C., & Walker-Matthews, S. (2002). The reliability and validity of the Psychopathy Checklist: Youth Version in nonincarcerated adolescent males. *Psychological Assessment, 14,* 97–109.

Krischer, M., & Sevecke, K. (2008). The influence of early traumatization on psychopathy dimensions in female and male juvenile offenders. *International Journal of Law and Psychiatry, 31*(3), 253–262.

Kubak, F. A., & Salekin, R. T. (2009). Psychopathy and anxiety in children and adolescents: New insights and hints of a developmental trend. *Journal of Psychopathology and Behavioral Assessment, 31*(4), 271–284.

Lahey, B. B., Waldman, I. D., & McBurnett, K. (1999). Annotation: The development of antisocial behavior: An integrative causal model. *Journal of Child Psychology and Psychiatry, 40,* 669–682.

Lang, S., Klinteberg, B., & Alm, P. O. (2002). Adult psychopathy and violent behavior in males with early neglect and abuse. *Acta Psychiatrica Scandinavica, 412,* 93–100.

Larsson H., Tuvblad, C., Rijsdik, V. F., Andershed, H., Grann, M., & Lichtenstein, P. (2007). A common genetic factor explains the association between psychopathic personality and antisocial behavior. *Psychological Medicine, 37,* 1–12.

Lee, Z., Salekin, R. T., & Iselin, A. M. (2010). Psychopathic traits in youth: Is there evidence for primary and secondary subtypes? *Journal of Abnormal Child Psychology, 38*, 381–393.

Levy, K. N., Becker, D. F., Grilo, C. M., Mattanah, J. J. F., Garnet, K. E., Quinlan, D. M., et al. (1999). Concurrent and predictive validity of the personality disorder diagnosis in adolescent inpatients. *American Journal of Psychiatry, 156*, 1522–1528.

Lilienfeld, S. O. (1994). Conceptual problems in the assessment of psychopathy. *Clinical Psychology Review, 14*, 17–38.

Lilienfeld, S. O., & Waldman, I. D. (1990). The relationship between childhood attention-deficit hyperactivity disorder and adult antisocial behavior reexamined: The problem of heterogeneity. *Clinical Psychology Review, 10*, 699–725.

Loeber, R., Green, S. M., Lahey, B. B., Frick, P. J., & McBurnett, K. (2000). Findings on disruptive behaviour disorders from the first decade of the Developmental Trends Study. *Clinical Child and Family Psychology Review, 3*(1), 37–60.

Loeber, R., & Stouthamer-Loeber, M. (1998). Development of juvenile aggression and violence. Some common misconceptions and controversies. *American Psychologist, 53*(2), 242–259.

Loney, B. R., Frick, P. J., Clements, C. B., Ellis, M. L., & Kerlin, K. (2003). Callous–unemotional traits, impulsivity, and emotional processing in adolescents with antisocial behavior problems. *Journal of Clinical Child and Adolescent Psychology, 32*, 66–80.

Lykken, D. T. (1995). *The antisocial personalities*. Hillsdale, NJ: Erlbaum.

Lynam, D. R. (1996). The early identification of chronic offenders: Who is the fledgling psychopath? *Psychological Bulletin, 120*, 209–234.

Lynam, D. R. (1998). Early identification of the fledging psychopath: Locating the psychopathic child in the current nomenclature. *Journal of Abnormal Psychology, 107*, 566–575.

Lynam, D. R., Hoyle, R. H., & Newman, J. P. (2006). The perils of partialling: Cautionary tales from aggression and psychopathy. *Assessment, 13*, 328–341.

Mailloux, D. L., Forth, A. E., & Kroner, D. G. (1997). Psychopathy and substance use in adolescent male offenders. *Psychological Reports, 81*(2), 529–530.

Mannuzza, S., Klein, R. G., Bessler, A., Malloy, P., & LaPadula, M. (1993). Adult outcome of hyperactive boys: educational achievement, occupational rank and psychiatric status. *Archives of General Psychiatry, 50*, 565–576.

Marmorstein, N. R., & Iacono, W. G. (2005). Longitudinal follow-up of adolescents with late-onset antisocial behavior: A pathological yet overlooked group. *Journal of the American Academy of Child and Adolescent Psychiatry, 44*(12), 1284–1291.

Marshall, L. A., & Cooke, D. J. (1999). The childhood experiences of psychopaths: A retrospective study of familial and societal factors. *Journal of Personality Disorders, 13*(3), 211–225.

McBride, M. (1998). *Individual and familial risk factors for adolescent psychopathy.* Unpublished doctoral dissertation, University of British Columbia.

Miller, J. D., & Lynam, D. R. (2001). Structural models of personality and their relations to antisocial behavior: A meta-analytic review. *Criminality, 39*, 765–797.

Miller, J. D., Lynam, D. R., Widiger, T. A., & Leukefeld, C. (2001). Personality disorders as extreme variants of common personality dimensions: Can the five-factor model adequately represent psychopathy? *Journal of Personality, 69*, 253–276.

Moeller, A. A., & Hell, D. (2003). Affective disorder and "psychopathy" in a sample of younger male delinquents. *Acta Psychiatrica Scandinavica, 107*(3), 203–207.

Muñoz, L. C., & Frick, P. J. (2007). The reliability, stability, and predictive utility of the self-report version of the Antisocial Process Screening Device. *Scandinavian Journal of Psychology, 48*(4), 299–312.

Murrie, D. C., & Cornell, D. G. (2000). Psychopathy screening of incarcerated juveniles: A comparison of measures. *Psychological Assessment, 14*, 390–396.

Myers, W. C., Burket, R. C., & Harris, H. E. (1995). Adolescent psychopathy in relation to delinquent behaviors, conduct disorder, and personality disorders. *Journal of Forensic Sciences, 40*, 435–439.

Newman, J. P., MacCoon, D. G., Vaughn, L. J., & Sadeh, N. (2005). Validating a distinction between primary and secondary psychopathy with measures of Gray's BIS and BAS constructs. *Journal of Abnormal Psychology, 114*(2), 319–323.

Newman, J. P., Schmitt, W. A., & Voss, W. D. (1997). The impact of motivationally neutral cues on psychopathic individuals: Assessing the generality of the response modulation hypothesis. *Journal of Abnormal Psychology, 106*(4), 563–575.

Novaco, R. W., & Chemtob, C. M. (1998). Anger and trauma: Conceptualization, assessment, and treatment. In V. M. Follette, J. I. Ruzek, & F. R. Abueg (Eds.), *Cognitive-behavioral therapies for trauma* (pp. 162–190). New York: Guilford Press.

Odgers, C. L., Reppucci, N. D., & Moretti, M. M. (2005). Nipping psychopathy in the bud: An examination of the convergent, predictive, and theoretical utility of the PCL-YV among adolescent girls. *Behavioral Sciences and the Law, 23*, 1–21.

Ollendick, T. H., Seligman, L. D., & Butcher, A. T. (1999). Does anxiety mitigate the behavioral expression of severe conduct disorder in delinquent youths? *Journal of Anxiety Disorders, 13*(6), 565–574.

O'Neill, M. L. (2001). *Adolescents with psychopathic characteristics in a substance abusing cohort: Predictors, correlates, and treatment process and outcome.* Unpublished doctoral dissertation, MCP Hahnemann University, Philadelphia.

O'Neill, M. L., Lidz, V., & Heilbrun, K. (2003). Predictors and correlates of psychopathic characteristics in substance abusing adolescents. *International Journal of Forensic and Mental Health, 2*, 35–46.

Pardini, D. A., Lochman, J. E., & Powell, N. (2007). The development of callous–unemotional traits and antisocial behavior in children: Are there shared and/or unique predictors? *Journal of Clinical Child and Adolescent Psychology, 36*(3), 319–333.

Piatigorsky, A., & Hinshaw, S. P. (2004). Psychopathic traits in boys with and without attention-deficit/hyperactivity disorder: Concurrent and longitudinal correlates. *Journal of Abnormal Child Psychology*, *32*, 535–550.

Pollock, P. H. (1999). When the killer suffers. Post-traumatic stress reactions following homicide. *Legal and Criminological Psychology*, *4*, 185–202.

Quay, H. C., Routh, D. K., & Shapiro, S. K. (1987). Psychopathology of childhood: From description to validation. *Annual Review of Psychology*, *38*, 491–532.

Rasmussen, K., Storsaeter, O., & Levander, S. (1999). Personality disorders, psychopathy, and crime in a Norwegian prison population. *International Journal of Law and Psychiatry*, *22*, 91–97.

Roberts, B. W., & DelVecchio, W. F. (2000). The rank-order consistency of personality traits from childhood to old age: A quantitative review of longitudinal studies. *Psychological Bulletin*, *126*, 3–25.

Robins, L. N. (1991). Conduct disorder. *Journal of Child Psychology and Psychiatry*, *32*, 193–212.

Roesler, M., Retz, W., Retz-Junginger, P., Hengesch, G., Schneider, M., Supprian, T., et al. (2004). Prevalence of attention-deficit/hyperactivity disorder (ADHD) and comorbid disorders in young male prison inmates. *European Archives of Psychiatry and Clinical Neuroscience*, *254*, 365–371.

Roussy, S., & Toupin, J. (2000). Behavioral inhibition deficits in juvenile psychopaths. *Aggressive Behavior*, *26*, 413–424.

Ruchkin, V., Koposov, R., Vermeiren, R., & Schwab-Stone, M. (2003). Psychopathology and age at onset of conduct problems in juvenile delinquents. *Journal of Clinical Psychiatry*, *64*, 913–920.

Salekin, R. T., Neumann, C. S., Leistico, A. M., DiCicco, T. M., & Duros, R. L. (2004). Psychopathy and comorbidity in a young offender sample: Taking a closer look at psychopathy's potential importance over disruptive behavior disorders. *Journal of Abnormal Psychology*, *3*, 416–427.

Salekin, R. T., Neumann, C. S., Leistico, A. M., & Zalot, A. A. (2004). Psychopathy in youth and intelligence: An investigation of Cleckley's hypothesis. *Journal of Clinical Child and Adolescent Psychology*, *33*, 731–742.

Salekin, R. T., Rogers, R., & Sewell, K. W. (1997). Construct validity of psychopathy in a female offender sample: A multitrait–multimethod evaluation. *Journal of Abnormal Psychology*, *106*, 576–585.

Schmidt, F., McKinnon, L., Chattha, H. K., & Brownlee, K. (2006). Concurrent and predictive validity of the psychopathy checklist: Youth version across gender and ethnicity. *Psychological Assessment*, *18*(4), 393–401.

Schmitt, W. A., & Newman, J. P. (1999). Are all psychopathic individuals low-anxious? *Journal of Abnormal Psychology*, *108*(2), 353–358.

Sevecke, K., Kosson, D. S., & Krischer, M. (2009). The relationship between attention deficit hyperactivity disorder, conduct disorder and psychopathy in adolescent male and female detainees. *Journal of Behavioral Science and the Law*, *27*(4), 577–598.

Sevecke, K., Krischer, M., & Lehmkuhl, G. (2009). Relations between psychopathology and psychopathy dimensions: Findings from an adolescent female and male offender sample. *European Journal of Child and Adolescent Psychiatry, 18*, 85–95.

Sevecke, K., Pukrop, R., Kosson, D. S., & Krischer, M. (2009). Factor structure of the Hare Psychopathy Checklist: Youth Version in female and male detainees and community adolescents. *Psychological Assessment, 21*(1), 45–56.

Skeem, J. L., Mulvey, E. P., Appelbaum, P., Banks, S., Grisso, T., Silver, E., et al. (2004). Identifying subtypes of civil psychiatric patients at high risk for violence. *Criminal Justice and Behavior, 31*, 392–437.

Soderstrom, H., Nilsson, T., Sjodin, A. K., Carlstedt, A., & Forsman, A. (2005). The childhood-onset neuropsychiatric background to adulthood psychopathic traits and personality disorders. *Comprehensive Psychiatry, 46*, 111–116.

Spencer, T. J., Biederman, J., Wilens, T. E., & Faraone, S. V. (2002). Overview and neurobiology of attention-deficit/hyperactivity disorder. *Journal of Clinical Psychiatry, 63*(12), 3–9.

Stafford, E., & Cornell, D. G. (2003). Psychopathy scores predict adolescent inpatient aggression. *Assessment, 10*(1), 102–112.

Stalenheim, E. G., & von Knorring, L. (1996). Psychopathy and Axis I and Axis II psychiatric disorders in a forensic psychiatric population in Sweden. *Acta Psychiatrica Scandinavica, 94*, 217–223.

Sullivan, E. A., & Patrick, C. J. (2005, July). *Psychopathy, PTSD and personality.* Paper presented at the first annual meeting of the Society for the Scientific Study of Psychopathy, Vancouver, BC, Canada.

Swogger, M. T., & Kosson, D. S. (2007). Identifying subtypes of criminal psychopaths: A replication and extension. *Criminal Justice and Behavior, 34*, 953–970.

Timmons-Mitchell, J., Brown, C., Schulz, S. C., Webster, S. E., Underwood, L. A., & Semple, W. E. (1997). Comparing the mental health needs of female and male incarcerated juvenile delinquents. *Behavioral Sciences and the Law, 15*, 195–202.

Valentine, I. S. (2001). The relationship between depression, self-esteem, trauma, and psychopathy in understanding conduct disordered adolescents. *Dissertation Abstracts International B: Sciences and Engineering, 61*(10-B), 5585.

Vassileva, J., Kosson, D. S., Abramowitz, C., & Conrod, P. (2005). Psychopathy versus psychopathies in classifying criminal offenders. *Legal and Criminological Psychology, 10*, 27–43.

Vermeiren, R. (2003). Psychopathology and delinquency in adolescents: A descriptive and developmental perspective. *Clinical Psychological Review, 23*, 277–318.

Verona, E., Hicks, B. M., & Patrick, C. J. (2005). Psychopathy and suicidality in female offenders: Mediating influences of personality and abuse. *Journal of Consulting and Clinical Psychology, 73*, 1065–1073.

Verona, E., Patrick, C. J., & Joiner, T. E. (2001). Psychopathy, antisocial personality, and suicide risk. *Journal of Abnormal Psychology, 110*, 462–470.

Viding, E. (2004). Annotation: Understanding the development of psychopathy. *Journal of Child Psychology and Psychiatry, 45*(8), 1329–1337.

Viding, E., Blair, R. J., Moffitt, T. E., & Plomin, R. (2005). Evidence for substantial genetic risk for psychopathy in 7-year-olds. *Journal of Child Psychology and Psychiatry, 46*(6), 592–597.

Vitale, J. E., & Newman, J. P. (2001). Using the Psychopathy Checklist—Revised with female samples: Reliability, validity, and implications for clinical utility. *Journal of Clinical Psychology: Science and Practice, 7,* 117–132.

Vitelli, R. (1998). Childhood disruptive behavior disorders and adult psychopathy. *American Journal of Forensic Psychology, 16,* 29–37.

Weizmann-Henelius, G., Viemerö, V., & Eronen, M. (2004). Psychopathy in violent female offenders in Finland. *Psychopathology, 37,* 213–221.

Wender, P. H., Wolf, L. E., & Wasserstein, J. (2001). Adults with ADHD: An overview. *Annals of the New York Academy of Sciences, 931,* 1–16.

Westen, D., Shedler, J., Durrett, C., Glass, S., & Martens, A. (2003). Personality diagnoses in adolescence: DSM-IV Axis II diagnoses and an empirically derived alternative. *American Journal of Psychiatry, 160,* 952–966.

Windle, R. C., & Windle, M. (1995). Longitudinal patterns of physical aggression: Associations with adult social, psychiatric and personality functioning and testosterone levels. *Developmental Psychopathology, 7,* 563–585.

Zanarini, M. C., Frankenburg, F. R., Hennen, J., Bradford Reich, D., & Silk, K. D. (2005). The McLean Study of Adult Development (MSAD): Overview and implications of the first six years of prospective follow-up. *Journal of Personality Disorders, 19,* 505–523.

Zoccolillo, M., Pickles, A., Quinton, D., & Rutter, M. (1992). The outcome of childhood conduct disorder: Implications for defining adult personality disorder and conduct disorder. *Psychological Medicine, 22,* 971–1086.

Part IV

Special Populations, Treatment, and Forensic Applications

13

The Influences of Gender and Culture on Child and Adolescent Psychopathy

EDELYN VERONA
NAOMI SADEH
SHABNAM JAVDANI

Although there has been increasing interest in understanding developmental trajectories and childhood precursors of psychopathy, the study of the syndrome and its manifestations in female or nonwhite youth has lagged behind this broader surge. Given the already controversial nature of downward translations of psychopathy to children and adolescents (Falkenbach, Poythress, & Heide, 2003), it is not surprising that the main priority in the literature thus far has been to establish the validity of existing conceptualizations of youth psychopathy rather than to extend the construct fully to incorporate gender and culture. Nonetheless, several pioneering researchers have studied the relevance and validity of psychopathic traits in female and ethnic/minority youth.

This chapter reviews the admittedly sparse literature that examines gender and cultural moderators in the study of youth psychopathy. We review and evaluate the growing literature on the psychometric properties and functioning of instruments used to measure the psychopathy construct, and the correlates of these psychopathy assessments and their predictive utility. In the process of reviewing this literature, we (1) attend to the degree to which these studies have addressed key distinctions relevant to issues of gender and sex, ethnicity, culture, and class that are typically ignored in the mainstream psychopathy literature, and (2) highlight similarities between the youth psychopathy literature focused on gender and culture and the mainstream literature that has focused on white males.

Clarification and Distinctions in Terms of Gender and Culture

To understand the potential array of influences that gender and culture might have on the etiology, manifestation, and outcomes associated with youth psychopathy and antisocial behavior more broadly, it is necessary to clarify the meaning of gender and culture.

Gender and Sex

Gender refers to characteristics that are socially acquired and speaks to acquisition of particular roles and behaviors that occur throughout development (Krieger, 2001). The influence of gender in youth psychopathy may be particularly relevant with respect to gender norms and gender socialization. For instance, it is less socially acceptable for girls to display aggression, and there is evidence to suggest that parental socialization of girls may work to increase the likelihood of the development of internalizing rather than externalizing behaviors (Keenan & Shaw, 1997). The social construct of gender is related to, but also distinct from, the construct of *sex*, which refers to the biological and reproductive characteristics of individuals. For example, biological influences on male aggression have been evidenced with respect to high levels of sex-linked hormones such as testosterone (Olweus, Mattson, Schalling, & Low, 1988); likewise, there is evidence that prenatal exposure to high levels of androgens results in increased rough-and-tumble play during childhood in girls (Benton, 1992). Though these distinctions are important, it is often impossible to clearly differentiate their causal roles because socialization and biology are generally mutually reinforcing and mutually influence the environment. This is indeed the current state of the literature on youth psychopathy. Thus, throughout our review, we use the term *gender* primarily for the sake of efficiency, and because the literature reviewed often does not distinguish between gender- and sex-related influences.

Culture, Ethnicity, Race, and Social Class

Culture refers to the set of socially constructed and learned norms, values, beliefs, and behaviors shared by a group of individuals. *Culture* is a broad and potentially limitless term that is not necessarily defined by shared geography or history (e.g., an Internet culture). Nevertheless, much of the limited research to date on cultural factors related to youth psychopathy has focused on ethnicity and race. *Ethnicity* has been defined as a common group identity based on nationality, language, and other cultural factors (Betancourt & Lopez, 1993), and includes individuals' subjective sense of identity with a particular group and/or sense of being marginalized from the dominant culture (Phinney, 1996). *Race* is often defined by the shared biological and physical characteristics (e.g., skin tone, facial features) of groups (Betancourt & Lopez, 1993), though it is argued that race is also a social construct determined historically. We avoid use of the term *race* in this review given the difficulties in distinguishing biological influences per se.

It is important to note that the terms *culture*, *ethnicity*, and *race* are often confounded with, or used as proxies for, *social class* (Phinney, 1996). For instance, the effects associated with low socioeconomic status can be mistakenly attributed to characteristics of a particular race or ethnicity. In addition, an overreliance on studying incarcerated populations runs the risk of limiting the scope of our knowledge to individuals who come from both low socioeconomic status and are ethnic minorities (given disproportionate minority confinement). We note this important confound because of the implications it can have for understanding antisocial behavior and take caution to avoid such misinterpretations in the review of the literature that follows.

Many of the studies we review compare groups that share Western cultural heritage. As such, we take caution to specify the ethnic identity of the groups to which we refer (e.g., Canadian), and avoid using all-encompassing terms (e.g., Caucasian). We use the term *ethnic minority* to refer to African American, African decent, Hispanic/Latin(a), Asian American, Native American, and Aboriginal (or Native Canadian) individuals. In addition, the term *non–North American* is sometimes used to distinguish European from North American individuals.

Validity and Measurement of Youth Psychopathy across Gender and Ethnicity

Researchers have borrowed from the more established nomological network of psychopathy in male offenders to modify adult psychopathy assessment instruments to make them developmentally appropriate for use with youth. Although empirical evidence provides some support for adopting a downward-translation approach to measuring psychopathic tendencies in youth, the use of a construct developed for, and tested on, an adult population for conceptualizing psychopathic traits in children and adolescents remains controversial. For example, research suggests that symptoms of the disorder may be expressed differently, more difficult to assess, and less stable in childhood and adolescence than in adulthood (Salekin, Rosenbaum, & Lee, 2009; Edens, Skeem, Cruise, & Cauffman, 2001).

Although there is evidence for the generalizability of psychopathy assessment instruments to adult females, research suggests that psychopathy instruments that have been well-validated with male offenders (i.e., the Psychopathy Checklist—Revised [PCL-R]) may not fully capture the psychopathic syndrome as well in females (Bolt, Hare, Vitale, & Newman, 2004; Salekin, Rogers, & Sewell, 1997; Verona & Vitale, 2006). Research on the cross-cultural functioning of psychopathy measures in adults has revealed similar findings, though only a handful of studies exist across cultures (e.g., North American vs. European samples; Cooke, Michie, Hart, & Clark, 2005) and ethnic groups (for a review, see Sullivan & Kosson, 2006). Some cross-cultural comparisons on the prevalence rates of psychopathic traits have revealed that African American males receive slightly elevated scores on the PCL-R relative to European Americans (Cooke et al., 2005), although this difference may be negligible (Skeem, Edens, Camp, & Colwell, 2004). Thus, adult psychopathy measures appear to function comparably across cultures. To extend this work to children and adolescents, we next review data pertaining to the prevalence of psychopathic tendencies in boys and girls, ethnic minorities, and non–North American cultures. Subsequently, we examine the differential functioning of youth psychopathy instruments across gender and culture.

Prevalence of Prototypical Psychopathic Traits across Gender and Ethnicity

Gender Differences

In contrast to the adult literature, research on the relative prevalence rates of psychopathic traits in boys and girls is mixed, with some researchers noting overall higher psychopathic tendencies among boys than among girls, and others finding no gender differences. Comparisons of parent or teacher rating scales of psychopathy, such as Lynam's (1997) Child Psychopathy Scale (CPS; Baker, Jacobson, Raine, Lozano, & Bezdjian, 2007) and Frick and Hare's (2001) Antisocial Process Screening Device (APSD; Dadds, Fraser, Frost, & Hawes, 2005; Frick, Bodin, & Barry, 2000; Marsee, Silverthorn, & Frick, 2005) in schoolchildren indicate that boys are on average rated higher than girls on psychopathic traits. Consistent with this finding, a survey of child clinical psychologists demonstrated lower ratings for girls than boys on criteria compiled from multiple widely used youth psychopathy measures, including the APSD, CPS and Psychopathy Checklist: Youth Version (PCL:YV; Salekin, Rogers, & Machin, 2001). Similarly, Schrum and Salekin (2006) reported that only 8.8% of delinquent girls scored in the psychopathic cutoff range (i.e., a score of 30 or above) on the PCL:YV, which is lower than the 12–15% prevalence rate for delinquent boys observed in other studies (Murrie & Cornell, 2002; Vincent, Vitacco, Grisso, & Corrado, 2003).

However, other investigations of prevalence rates in youth only report gender differences on certain facets of psychopathy, or fail to observe any significant gender differences at all. For instance, Frick, O'Brien, Wootton, and McBurnett (1994) found that girls scored lower than boys on the impulsivity/conduct problems (I/CP) subscale of the APSD but not on the callous–unemotional (CU) subscale in both clinical and community samples. In contrast, analysis of the APSD with adjudicated delinquents has resulted in *higher* scores for girls than for boys on the I/CP subscale but not the CU subscale (Pardini, Lochman, & Frick, 2003). Using the PCL:YV, Penney and Moretti (2007) reported that girls scored lower than boys on the Interpersonal and Affective traits ("arrogant and deceitful interpersonal style" and "deficient affective experience," using Cooke & Michie's [2001] three-factor model), but similarly to boys on the Impulsivity facet. Other studies with adjudicated youth have not observed gender differences in psychopathic tendencies as indexed by total scores on the APSD, CPS, or PCL:YV (Salekin, Leistico, Trobst, Schrum, & Lochman, 2005) or on Factor 1 and Factor 2 scores on the PCL:YV (Campbell, Porter, & Santor, 2004).

Inconsistent findings in terms of gender differences in prevalence rates may be dependent upon the developmental period in which psychopathic traits are assessed (i.e., childhood vs. adolescence), sample selection (i.e., community vs. forensic), or the particular facets of psychopathy being assessed (i.e., CU traits vs. I/CP traits). Table 13.1 summarizes the results of existing studies examining prevalence rates of psychopathic traits in youth of different genders and ethnicities. As shown in Table 13.1, the pattern of findings across studies indicates that higher psychopathy scores for boys than for girls tend to emerge in samples recruited from clinical and community settings, which mostly involve preadolescent children. In contrast, the studies that examined psychopathic tendencies in adjudicated adolescents recruited from detention centers reported fewer differences in psychopathic scores across the genders, suggesting that both the sample and developmental period in which gender differences are assessed are important and may partially account for the equivocal findings in the literature. Additionally, studies with preadolescent children typically utilize the APSD, whereas most of the studies of adjudicated youth utilize the PCL:YV (see Table 13.1).

TABLE 13.1. Summary of Research Studies Reporting Gender and Ethnicity Differences in the Prevalence of Psychopathic Tendencies in Youth

Study authors	Measure	Age group	Sample	Gender/ethnic differences
		Studies comparing genders		
Dadds et al. (2005)	APSD Total	Children (ages 4–9)	Australia community	Boys > girls
Marsee et al. (2005)	APSD Total	Adolescents (ages 10–17)	Community	Boys > girls
Frick et al. (2000)	APSD CU and Narcissism	Children and early teens (third to seventh graders)	Clinical and community	Boys > girls
Frick et al. (1994)	APSD I/CP	Children and early teens (ages 6–13)	Clinical and community	Boys > girls
Frick et al. (1994)	APSD CU	Children and early teens (ages 6–13)	Clinical and community	Boys = girls
Baker et al. (2007)	CPS factors	Children (ages 9–10)	Community	Boys > girls
Salekin et al. (2001)	Salekin Survey of Prototypicality	Children and adolescents (ages 6–18)	Child clinical psychologists	Boys > girls
Schrum & Salekin (2006)	PCL:YV	Adolescents (ages 11–18)	Detention center	Boys > girls
Penney & Moretti (2007)	PCL:YV Factors 1 and 2	Adolescents (ages 12–18)	Community and forensic centers	Boys > girls
Pardini et al. (2003)	APSD I/CP	Adolescents (mean age = 15.8)	Detention center	Boys < girls
Pardini et al. (2003)	APSD CU	Adolescents (mean age = 15.8)	Detention center	Boys = girls
Cruise et al. (2003)	Salekin Survey of Prototypicality	Children and adolescents (ages 8–21)	Juvenile justice personnel	Boys = girls
Salekin et al. (2005)	APSD, CPS, and PCL:YV Total	Adolescents (ages 11–18)	Detention center	Boys = girls

TABLE 13.1. *(continued)*

Campbell et al. (2004)	PCL:YV Factors 1 and 2	Adolescents (ages 12–19)	Detention center in Novia Scotia	Boys = girls
Penney & Moretti (2007)	PCL:YV Factor 3	Adolescents (ages 12–18)	Forensic centers	Boys = girls
		Studies comparing ethnic groups[a]		
Frick et al. (1999)	APSD CU and I/CP	Children and early teens (ages 6–13)	Clinical	Ethnic minority > European American
Frick et al. (2000)	APSD CU and NAR	Children and early teens (third to seventh graders)	Clinical and community	Ethnic minority > European American
Frick et al. (2003)	APSD CU	Children and early teens (third to seventh graders)	Community	Ethnic minority > European American
Christian et al. (1997)	APSD CU and I/CP	Children and early teens (ages 6–13)	Clinical	Ethnic minority = European American

Note. APSD, Antisocial Process Screening Device (Frick & Hare, 2001); CU, callous–unemotional; I/CP, impulsivity/conduct problems; NAR, narcissism; CPS, Childhood Psychopathy Scale (Lynam, 1997); PCL:YV, Psychopathy Checklist: Youth Version (Forth, Kosson, & Hare, 2003).

[a]The ethnic/minority groups in these studies mostly comprised African American youth, although a small number of unspecified non–African American ethnic/minority youth were also included.

Indices of prevalence rates may also be affected by how well a particular psychopathy assessment instrument captures the construct of psychopathy across groups. Salekin, Rogers, and Machin (2001) asked child clinical psychologists to rate the most prototypical case of youth psychopathy they had encountered on 61 traits compiled from widely utilized youth psychopathy assessments. Results indicated that 23 prototypical items were identified for males but only 14 for females. Moreover, only two items emerged as specific to psychopathy in girls: "stays out at night without parental permission" and "sexual promiscuity," which suggests that psychopathic traits are either less prevalent in girls or the items used to index the traits in youth did not adequately capture psychopathic tendencies in girls. On the other hand, these results could be accounted for by the raters' gender biases or beliefs about the types of behaviors girls engage in when they misbehave. Salekin and colleagues also observed gender differences in the factor structures extracted from the assessment items, with child psychologists rating prototypical psychopathy as more strongly associated with the antisocial deviance features of psychopathy (aggressive criminal behavior) in boys, and with the affective–interpersonal features (superficial charm, conning, lying, shallow affect, and a lack of empathy) in girls.

Expanding on these findings, Cruise, Colwell, Lyons, and Baker (2003) surveyed juvenile detention workers and probation officers about the prototypical manifestation of psychopathy in girls and boys using the measure developed by Salekin and colleagues (2001). Consistent with the latter's findings, status offenses (i.e., "runs away from home overnight," "truant from school") and interpersonal items (i.e., "sexual promiscuity," "charming in insincere ways") were considered highly prototypical for girls but not for boys. Furthermore, juvenile justice personnel viewed prototypical psychopathic girls as more likely to engage in self-harm and exhibit comorbid psychopathology than prototypical psychopathic boys. The factor structures extracted by Cruise and colleagues were similar for boys and girls, except that, like the child clinical psychologists surveyed by Salekin and colleagues, juvenile justice personnel perceived prototypical psychopathy as a manifestation of criminally diverse behaviors in boys and nonviolent status offenses in girls.

Cultural and Ethnic Differences

Only a few studies have examined differences in prevalence rates for psychopathic tendencies in ethnic/minority groups and non–North American samples (see Table 13.1 for a summary). However, preliminary evidence suggests that, like ethnically diverse adult males, ethnic/minority youth receive slightly elevated ratings on measures of psychopathic tendencies. For instance, analysis of the APSD by Frick and colleagues (2000; Frick, Lilienfeld, Ellis, Loney, & Silverthorn, 1999) produced higher ratings for ethnic/minority youth, predominately African Americans, on the CU, narcissism (NAR), and I/CP subscales relative to non–ethnic/minority youth in clinic-referred and community samples. Replication of these findings were only observed for the CU subscale in a follow-up investigation by Frick and colleagues (2003) using a community sample. Not all empirical evidence, however, supports the presence of differential rates of psychopathic tendencies among ethnic groups (e.g., Christian, Frick, Hill, Tyler, & Frazer, 1997). Given the limited data on this topic and mixed findings, it is unclear whether the elevated scores observed in ethnic/minority groups are meaningful for understanding psychopathic tendencies in youth or are an artifact of other forces (i.e., socioeconomic status). To date, no studies in our literature review have examined cross-cultural differences in prevalence rates of psychopathic tendencies in youth. Thus, more research is needed to determine whether research in North American samples can be generalized to other cultures.

Psychopathy Factor Structure across Gender, Ethnicity, and Culture

Before using an assessment instrument with a population for which it was not developed, it is necessary for researchers to evaluate the validity of an instrument with a new population by examining its factor structure in relation to the structural model derived from the original population. According to Sue (1999), the more an instrument functions differently across groups, the more difficult it is to draw conclusions regarding the consistency and validity of the construct purportedly being assessed.

Gender Differences

In a sample of girls who identified predominately as African American (62%), Schrum and Salekin (2006) examined the applicability of the two-factor (Hare, 1991; Harpur, Hare, & Hakstian, 1989), three-factor (Cooke & Michie, 2001), and four-factor (Hare, 2003) models derived from the PCL-R with adult offenders to the PCL:YV with delinquent youth. According to the authors, both the three- and four-factor models fit the data adequately, although facets one (i.e., arrogant and deceitful interpersonal style) and two (i.e., deficient affective experience) demonstrated more structural stability (i.e., higher Cronbach's coefficient alphas) than facets three (i.e., impulsive and irresponsible behavioral style) and four (i.e., antisocial behavior). Similarly, items that indexed traits traditionally encompassed in Factor 1 of the PCL-R (e.g., "callous/lack of empathy," "conning/manipulative," "grandiose sense of self-worth") were most discriminating of the underlying psychopathy construct, which is consistent with research on adult males (Hare, 2003). Conversely, "poor anger control," "shallow affect," and "serious violation of conditional release" were the least discriminating in this sample of African American girls. In a sample of adjudicated youth, Jones, Cauffman, Miller and Mulvey (2006) observed measurement invariance across the genders for the three-factor model, suggesting that this factor structure is appropriate for use with both boys and girls.

The factor structure of the APSD, however, may not be as stable as the PCL:YV across genders. Indeed, research indicates that the NAR and IMP subscales—in the APSD three-factor model—show less differentiation in girls than boys (i.e., the items from each scale cross-load; Frick et al.,

2000), signifying that the two-factor solution (i.e., CU, NAR/IMP) may be more justifiable for girls than boys. Thus, although the factor structures of widely utilized psychopathy assessments instruments appear to capture the construct of psychopathy adequately for both boys and girls, more work is needed to determine whether the underlying trait structure varies across the genders.

Ethnic and Cultural Differences

Little research exists on the functioning of youth psychopathy instruments in ethnic/minority groups, making it impossible to draw conclusions regarding the generalizability of these assessments to nonwhite youth. Investigations on the topic are beginning to emerge, though, with a recent study by Jones and colleagues (2006) indicating that the three- and four-factor models of the PCL:YV fit the data moderately well for African American adolescents adjudicated for serious crimes. Both factor structures resulted in a poor fit, however, for the Latino boys recruited from the same adjudicated sample, indicating that these factor structures may need to be modified before they are used with this underrepresented population.

Cross-cultural research on the structural variance of youth psychopathy measures is also beginning to emerge in non–North American countries. For example, Dadds and colleagues (2005) examined the factor structure of the APSD in Australia and found that the three-factor solution (i.e., CU, NAR, IMP) exhibited adequate fit to the data. Conversely, confirmatory factor analysis of the APSD by Enebrink, Andershed, and Langstrom (2005) revealed a better fit for the two-factor solution (i.e., CU, NAR/IMP) than the three-factor solution in a sample of Swedish boys with emotional and behavioral problems.

Summary

Few studies have investigated how youth psychopathy measures function across gender, ethnicity, and culture. Across the genders, preliminary evidence indicates that PCL:YV and APSD function similarly in both boys and girls, although the factor structure may vary somewhat more in the latter than the former measure. Similarly, research with African American and Australian youth suggests that comparable factor structures emerge for the PCL:YV and APSD in these groups. However, in the only available study, the factor structures for Latino youth demonstrated poor fit. Although promising, additional studies are needed to confirm that the factor structures adopted from research on North American white boys demonstrate enough stability to justify the use of youth psychopathy measures with Latino and other ethnic/minority populations.

Correlates of Child/Adolescent Psychopathic Traits across Gender and Ethnicity

Although several studies have investigated differences in prevalence rates and the factor structure of psychopathic traits in girls and boys (and much less across cultures), fewer studies have examined the construct validity of the psychopathy instruments across genders and ethnic groups. Exceptions to this are studies investigating the utility of psychopathy instruments in predicting criminal recidivism and violence in adjudicated youth. Indeed, the increasing popularity of the PCL-based assessments in the forensic community and wide use in correctional institutions is mostly due to demonstrated utility in predicting long-term criminality and violence (Gretton, Hare, & Catchpole, 2004; Salekin, 2008). Does this utility among youth differ in terms of gender and ethnicity? The following sections review research on the differential relationships between youth psychopathy and criminal recidivism or aggression across groups. We also review a growing body of literature on gender and ethnic differences in youth psychopathy associations with laboratory and psychophysiological indices of affective and behavioral abnormalities (e.g., emotional processing, response modulation, selective attention).

Criminal Recidivism and Aggression

Gender

Analyses of the PCL-R in women have revealed limited evidence for the predictive validity of the instrument in terms of violence and criminal recidivism (Salekin et al., 1997; see Verona & Vitale, 2006). A similar trend has been found in the youth literature. Although PCL-based measures of youth psychopathy (mostly the PCL:YV) seem reliably to predict general and violent recidivism (but negligibly to predict sexual recidivism) in adjudicated boys, the effects for girls are smaller and often not significant across studies conducted in the United States, Canada, and Scotland (Marshall, Egan, English, & Jones, 2006; Schmidt, MacKinnon, Chattha, & Brownlee, 2006). Admittedly, this conclusion is based on the few studies that included adolescent girls (Edens, Campbell, & Weir, 2006). Nonetheless, existing risk assessment instruments, including the PCL:YV, may not tap into features (e.g., relational aggression) that make antisocial girls more likely to commit future violence.

In fact, in a study examining the relative contributions of the PCL:YV and history of victimization (maternal abuse, exposure to domestic violence) on aggression and criminal recidivism in female juvenile offenders (half of whom identified as African American), Odgers, Reppucci, and Moretti

(2005) found that the PCL:YV was not predictive of future offending, as determined by official records, but victimization significantly increased the odds of criminal reoffending in these girls. These data suggest that psychopathy traits, as currently assessed, may not be key predictors of female criminal behavior compared to family history variables, especially victimization and early adversity, which have been shown in several studies to be more strongly associated with aggression in female than in male participants (Mulder, Wells, Joyce, & Bushnell, 1994; Verona & Vitale, 2006). This does not necessarily mean that psychopathy is not a valid construct among female youth, but it does limit its potential utility in understanding the persistence of criminal behavior in girls.

Unlike the evidence for recidivism, reviewed earlier, higher PCL-R scores have been reliably associated with higher levels of prior violent and nonviolent criminal behavior, with greater numbers of prior convictions for violent and nonviolent offenses (Vitale, Smith, Brinkley, & Newman, 2002), and with self-reported violence (Weiler & Widom, 1996) in adult females. A similar trend emerges in the youth psychopathy literature. Marsee and colleagues (2005) measured psychopathic traits using the teacher-reported APSD in public school fifth to ninth graders. APSD total scores predicted aggression and delinquency equally for girls and boys; however, the APSD Narcissism subscale was more strongly associated with relational aggression in girls than in boys. Overt aggression (hitting, fighting) was equally associated with teacher-reported APSD scores in girls and boys, though self-reported APSD total scores were more strongly associated with overt aggression for boys than for girls. Odgers and colleagues (2005) found that among female juvenile offenders, the deficient affective experience facet of the PCL:YV was the only psychopathy facet associated with physical and relational aggression, and this facet was similarly related to both types of aggression in these adjudicated girls. Penney and Moretti (2007) also examined relationships between the facets of the PCL:YV and different forms of aggression (overt, relational, peer-directed) in 12- to 18-year-old adolescents held in Canadian forensic facilities (22% of whom were Native or "Aboriginal"). Girls and boys had comparable mean scores on overt aggression; however, girls had higher mean levels of aggression directed toward their mothers and romantic partners, whereas the boys showed higher levels of peer-directed aggression. PCL:YV total scores were associated with overt, relational, and peer-directed aggression, as well as violent and nonviolent offenses similarly in girls and boys. Thus, these studies do not find gender differences in the relation between different dimensions of psychopathy and relevant aggression outcomes among high-risk youth, despite the fact that girls may be more likely to be violent against intimates and people they know. These findings concur to some degree with a large-scale meta-analysis of studies on general and violent offending (Leistico, Salekin, DeCoster, & Rogers, 2008).

In both adults and youth, psychopathy traits are associated with higher rates of proactive (or instrumental) aggression (Woodworth & Porter, 2002). In contrast, reactive (or hostile) aggression is more generally demonstrated by youth with conduct problems. Unfortunately, no research study has examined these distinctions among psychopathic youth of different genders and ethnicities. Frick and colleagues (2003) reported that third- to seventh-grade children who scored high on CU traits of the APSD were *less* likely to react with hostile attributions to provocation (less reactive), whereas those who scored high on conduct problems (oppositional and antisocial behaviors) were generally more likely to attribute hostile intent to others following provocation (more reactive). Interestingly, this was the case only for boys, and not girls scoring high on conduct problems. Girls showed little variation in mean levels of hostile attribution across groups scoring low and high on CU or conduct problems. Thus, this study showed that (1) CU traits in girls and boys were similarly associated with less reactive hostility, and (2) compared to boys, girls who exhibit conduct problems did not show high levels of reactive aggressive thoughts.

Ethnicity and Culture

Most of the studies on youth psychopathy have included a substantial proportion of minority youth, especially those identifying as African American. However, only a handful of studies have attempted to examine the differential predictive role of psychopathy traits across ethnic or cultural groups. A meta-analysis by Edens and colleagues (2006) found that PCL-based instruments in youth were weak predictors of violent recidivism in more ethnically heterogeneous samples (more nonwhites in the sample). However, the PCL was equally and reliably predictive of recidivism across American, Canadian, and European youth samples, suggesting that the instrument had similar utility with white youth from different nationalities.

Edens and Cahill (2007) conducted a 10-year follow-up study of 67 male juvenile offenders (43% African American, 30% Hispanic, and 25% European American). Surprisingly, the PCL:YV did not predict violent or nonviolent recidivism across the 10-year follow-up period (*r*'s = –.01 to –.07). This finding contradicts previous research by Gretton and colleagues (2004), who found a correlation of .32 between the PCL:YV and violent recidivism across a 10-year follow-up period in a sample of Canadian youth, even after covarying conduct disorder and prior criminal history. However, this latter sample comprised 79% white and 19% Native (or

"Aboriginal") Canadians and was not ethnically heterogeneous. Together, these studies are consistent with the meta-analysis by Edens and colleagues (2006), in that the PCL:YV shows limited predictive validity among more ethnically diverse samples. On the other hand, Edens and Cahill found no evidence that ethnicity predicted rates of recidivism or that it moderated the relationship between psychopathy and any form of recidivism (violent or nonviolent) in their study. Also, at least one other study has reported adequate predictive validity for the PCL:YV among ethnic/minority groups in Canada. Schmidt and colleagues (2006) reported that the PCL:YV was more predictive of recidivism in Native Canadian youth compared to Canadian youth of European descent.

Thus, it seems that the ethnic composition of the sample plays a role in the potential utility of PCL-based instruments in predicting dangerousness and recidivism. In U.S. studies, the PCL:YV may be less effective in predicting recidivism among ethnic minorities, particularly African American youth, although in samples that have included Native Canadians, predictive validity is similar to that for Canadian samples of European descent. None of these studies, however, has taken into account the role of social class or socioeconomic status (SES) in moderating or mediating the effects of ethnicity on youth psychopathy in relation to recidivism. In the adult literature, Walsh and Kosson (2007) reported that SES interacted with both PCL-R scores and ethnicity in predicting violent reoffending; that is, psychopathy was a predictor of reoffending only at lower SES levels for European Americans; whereas psychopathy was predictive of violent reoffending at all levels of SES among African Americans. It is possible that a broader range of SES among European Americans relative to African Americans accounted for the prophylactic effect of SES for one group and not the other. However, it is also possible that African Americans may generally be more likely to be apprehended and convicted of future crimes, regardless of financial resources (Walsh & Kosson, 2007) or psychopathic traits (Edens et al., 2006). If accurate, this conclusion suggests the importance of systemic forces (e.g., race bias) shaping the relationship between youth psychopathy and recidivism across ethnic groups.

Unfortunately, no studies thus far have examined ethnic or cultural moderators of links between psychopathy traits and different forms (relational, physical) or functions (proactive vs. reactive) of aggression in youth.

Behavioral and Psychophysiological Correlates

Relatively few studies have examined youth psychopathy correlates in the laboratory. Thus, we do not include separate subsections for studies of gender and cultural differences.

Affective Processing Deficits

In view of Cleckley's (1976) observation that psychopaths lack the normal range and depth of emotion, numerous studies in the adult literature have confirmed deficits in affective responding among psychopathic compared with nonpsychopathic individuals (Hare, 1978). In general, these results have generalized to psychopathic women (Verona & Vitale, 2006). Only a subset of studies has investigated affective processes in youth with psychopathic traits, and most have not examined differences between genders or ethnic groups. In one exception, Loney, Butler, Lima, Counts, and Eckel (2006) found blunted cortisol reactions to stress among 12- to 18-year-old boys (62% white) who scored high on the CU subscale of the APSD. However, this effect was not found among the girls in this sample. Limitations of this study include not controlling for girls' menstrual cycles when examining cortisol responses and uneven distribution of ethnic groups across youth scoring high and low on CU or conduct problems. Thus, it is possible that the differential ethnic composition of the subgroups may have contributed to the gender differences in this study. Recently, O'Leary, Loney, and Eckel (2007) replicated these findings in college students: Psychopathic traits measured via a self-report psychopathy measure were associated with blunted cortisol responses to stress in young men but not in young women. Although O'Leary and colleagues controlled for women's menstrual cycles, the ethnic composition of the different psychopathic groups was still uneven across men and women, confounding the effects of gender and ethnicity on the findings.

Kimonis, Frick, Fazekas, and Loney (2006) examined gender and ethnic differences in response facilitation to emotional pictures in 6- to 13-year-old children (70% white). They found a significant interaction between psychopathy and aggressive traits in predicting facilitation to distressing pictures, in that the negative correlation between psychopathy and facilitation was significant at high but not low levels of aggressive traits. However, consistent with the adult literature (Sutton, Vitale, & Newman, 2002; Verona & Vitale, 2006), boys and girls high on these traits showed similar deficits in emotional facilitation. Thus, although gender differences in psychopathic affective deficits emerged in studies of cortisol response, this was not the case when behavioral responses to emotional pictures were measured.

Kimonis and colleagues (2006) also observed that the interaction between ethnicity and psychopathy in facilitation to distressing pictures was relatively substantial in size (6% of the variance), indicating that the negative correlation between psychopathy and response facilitation to distress was present for white but not ethnic/minority children (22% African American, 4% Hispanic). This latter result stands in contrast to Loney, Frick, Clementes, Ellis, and Kerlin (2003), who found robust effects of psychopathy (specifically, high CU traits on the APSD) on response facilitation to emotional words among mostly African American youth, replicating in a youth sample the findings from a study using predominantly white adult males. Of note, Loney and colleagues studied adolescents in a police juvenile diversion program, and Kimonis and colleagues studied preadolescent children of high-achieving adults, which may account for the differences in the results regarding ethnicity.

In summary, deficits in emotional facilitation to distressing pictures are observed similarly in psychopathic boys and girls. However, this is not the case for blunted cortisol responses to stress among girls scoring high on CU traits. Not enough studies have been conducted to make firm conclusions about ethnic differences in associations between psychopathic traits and affective processing. It is important to note that all studies reviewed in this section were conducted by Frick or his current/former colleagues.

Attentional and Behavioral Abnormalities

Psychopathic adults also show attentional abnormalities, including enhanced selective attention and reduced reactivity to irrelevant peripheral cues (e.g., Hiatt, Schmitt, & Newman, 2004), that have been linked to well-replicated behavioral deficits involving passive avoidance or response perseveration (e.g., Newman & Kosson, 1986). There have been some recent attempts to replicate these results in females and ethnic/minority groups; however, only one of these studies has been conducted with youth.

Vitale, Newman, Bates, and colleagues (2005) examined both selective attention and behavioral inhibition (or passive avoidance deficits) in a community sample of adolescents assessed for psychopathic traits using the APSD. Girls, as well as boys, with psychopathic traits showed attentional abnormalities (lack of interference from irrelevant peripheral cues) in a picture–word Stroop task. On the other hand, only psychopathic boys showed behavioral disinhibition (increased passive avoidance errors) on a go/no-go task. Thus, although female psychopathy is also associated with attentional deficits, there is less evidence for response perseveration or behavioral disinhibition in psychopathic females, as reported in one study with youth. Work by Newman and colleagues (Lorenz & Newman, 2002) has indicated that response modulation deficits are typically found in European American but not African American psychopathic inmates, though this ethnic difference has not always been reported by other research groups (Epstein, Poythress, & Brandon, 2006). To date, no study with youth has confirmed whether ethnicity influences attentional and/or behavioral abnormalities among youth with psychopathic traits. Further studies with youth, as well as those using newer technologies, are needed to resolve differential findings in response modulation and impulsivity in male and female youth.

CU Traits as a Developmental Pathway to Psychopathy

Frick and colleagues (1999, 2003) have proposed a developmental trajectory to psychopathy, especially among youth with early-onset conduct problems (see Moffitt, 1993; Moffitt & Caspi, 2001). Frick suggested that the antisocial behavior of youth scoring high on CU traits is qualitatively different from that of children or adolescents who exhibit conduct problems but not CU traits. In a series of studies, he has demonstrated that antisocial and aggressive behaviors of children who score high on CU traits are less strongly related to adversity factors, such as bad parenting or low intelligence, and more strongly related to thrill and adventure seeking (Frick et al., 2003), a reward-dominant response style, and deficits in processing negative emotional stimuli (Kimonis et al., 2006; Loney et al., 2003). As we reported earlier, several studies have attempted to analyze the extent to which CU traits have adequate construct validity in girls and in youth of different ethnicities, although findings across studies have been inconsistent (Frick et al., 2003; Loney et al., 2006). In the only systematic study to examine gender differences in the correlates of CU traits, Frick and colleagues (2003) found that third- to seventh-grade boys and girls (77% European Americans) scoring high on CU traits generally showed the same pattern of responses, including higher thrill seeking and reward dominance, and deficient response facilitation to negative emotional words, relative to control children or children scoring high only on conduct problems. On the other hand, boys who scored high on conduct problems showed higher levels of hostile attributions in response to provocation, but this was not the case for girls. This study suggests that although the affective deficits associated with psychopathy may lead to a similar trajectory in girls and boys, behavioral or impulsive features associated with conduct disorder may more generally be associated with differential outcomes (less aggression or hostility) in girls than in boys. No studies have examined these different trajectories in ethnic/minority youth.

Conclusions and Future Directions

Conclusions from Existing Literature

Research on the relative prevalence rates of psychopathic tendencies in boys versus girls is mixed. However, differences in sampling procedures and developmental period may help to account for some of the inconsistent findings. In particular, our review of the literature suggests that higher scores on youth psychopathy for boys than for girls tend to arise in studies that measure these traits in children and young adolescents (13 or younger) recruited from clinic-referred or community samples. Conversely, gender differences in the prevalence of psychopathic tendencies seem to diminish in studies of adjudicated adolescents, implicating potentially more severe manifestations of psychopathic traits among females than males placed in detention centers. This finding is interesting given research that indicates adult females exhibit fewer psychopathic traits than adult males, even among incarcerated offenders. Many of the studies also indicate that CU or interpersonal–affective traits are similarly represented across the genders, and gender differences are most robust on the behavioral or delinquent traits (males > females). Available research suggests that psychopathy scores are slightly higher in ethnic/minority youth in North America, particularly in African Americans. Due to a scarcity of research, it is unclear whether the elevated scores are meaningful for understanding psychopathic tendencies in youth or are an artifact of other forces (i.e., SES).

Research on the correlates of psychopathic traits in children and youth of different genders and cultures provides ideas about how to strengthen existing measures. Psychopathy assessments, particularly the PCL:YV, do not predict criminal recidivism as well in female or nonwhite youth. Also, girls with psychopathic traits show the typical affective (emotional facilitation; Kimonis et al., 2006) and attentional (lack of distractor interference; Vitale et al., 2005) abnormalities often observed in male psychopaths, but they may not show expected deficits in behavioral responding (passive avoidance errors; Vitale et al., 2005) and exhibit more relational than overt aggression (Marsee et al., 2005). This research on the correlates of psychopathic traits across groups may indicate differential manifestations of psychopathy depending on gender and culture. For example, professionals who work closely with antisocial youth (juvenile justice staff, child psychologists) perceive prototypical psychopathy as a manifestation of criminally diverse behaviors in boys (e.g., fighting, stealing) and nonviolent status offenses in girls. These differences in the types of antisocial behavior for which psychopathic boys and girls are apprehended may differentiate their psychopathic profiles; thus, it is essential that youth psychopathy measures include a diverse array of antisociality items that capture behavioral symptoms of psychopathy across the genders. The observed gender differences in studies of recidivism or passive avoidance errors among incarcerated female youth suggest that the assessment strategies and experimental tasks commonly used to measure behavioral disinhibition and reoffending in psychopaths may not adequately tap into the underlying mechanisms associated with real-life psychopathic behaviors in females.

In fact, reports of divergent behavioral manifestations of psychopathic tendencies in boys and girls are not surprising given research showing that girls are more likely to engage in covert forms of aggression, such as relational aggression (see Crick & Grotpeter, 1995), that involve the manipulation of their social network to inflict harm (e.g., spreading rumors, refusing friendship). Boys, on the other hand, more often employ overt forms of aggression (e.g., kicking, hitting) to cause harm (Björkqvist, Lagerspetz, & Kaukiainen, 1992). Additionally, the interpersonal context may be a stronger correlate of delinquent outcomes for girls than for boys given evidence that victimization history is an especially strong predictor of criminality in girls (Odgers et al., 2005). One hypothetical trajectory specific to girls might indicate that they commit (and recommit) status offenses in response to victimization, which begin with running away from a violent home (Chesney-Lind & Shelden, 2004). Since psychopathy measures often do not include relational aggression items, and researchers typically do not examine female-specific risk factors such as victimization, existing work may be missing aspects of antisociality in girls that are important to understanding psychopathy and criminal reoffending. Studies of psychopathic tendencies in youth should incorporate evolving indices of female-specific manifestations of antisocial behavior and environmental correlates of these behaviors rather than relying on existing methods predominantly developed for and tested on male offenders.

Limitations and Elaborations for Future Research

As with all areas, future studies are needed. Major limitations of the existing literature include (1) limited recruitment of ethnically diverse samples, as well as little explication of culture- or gender-based differences in existing samples; (2) incomplete elaboration of the processes by which cultural and gender-based differences may operate; (3) limited attention to the influences of social context or SES on the development and manifestations of youth psychopathy; and (4) lack of comparability across studies due to the use of different youth psychopathy assessment instruments and overreliance on forensic samples. Below, we elaborate on ways future research may address these overlapping limitations.

1. An obvious but important starting point is to increase recruitment and sample sizes across diverse cultural groups, and to report more fully on cultural characteristics of research samples. The majority of studies we reviewed have examined psychopathy and antisocial behavior in European American and North American youth. Broadening this approach to include youth from different, non-Western cultures, representing different languages, historical backgrounds, and exposure to different norms (e.g., around gen-

der socialization), would help us understand culture-specific manifestations of psychopathic traits in youth and validate cross-cultural aspects of the syndrome. Similarly, researchers can attend more closely to potentially meaningful interactions between the demographics of interviewers/researchers and participants. This information was not provided in most of the studies we reviewed, but such interactions may affect researchers' interpretations of gender or ethnic differences, as well as participants' responses to interview/research questions. Future research may work to vary systematically the match between researchers and participants on indicators such as gender and ethnic identity.

2. To explicate better the meaning of culture or gender-based differences, researchers may consider using an *emic* approach to understanding psychopathic traits in different groups of youth (e.g., Phinney, 1996). In such an approach, the group under study is investigated in detail and "from within," and conclusions drawn are not based on between-group comparisons. As such, "gender" or "culture" would be held constant (Phinney, 1996) and potentially problematic comparisons to one group that provides an arbitrary standard (i.e., white males) might be avoided. For example, our review demonstrates mixed findings on prevalence of psychopathic traits in boys versus girls. However, the construct of psychopathy has yet to be fully validated in girls. An emic approach could centralize the examination of "what psychopathy looks like" in girls rather than focus on relative comparisons (e.g., compare scores on existing psychopathy measures between boys and girls).

3. Researchers should attend to the influence of social context. Gender and culture can influence antisocial behavior by operating through larger social systems (e.g., courts). It is important to recognize that institutionalized forms of oppression, such as disproportionate minority confinement, can, and do, influence individual behavior (Prilleltensky & Gonick, 1996), and the influence of oppression is especially important for ethnic/minority and female youth (e.g., ethnic/minority youth may experience institutionalized racism, and female youth may be perceived as particularly deviant given the violation of gender norms). On the other hand, it is problematic to explain away youth behavior by attributing it to broad and encompassing variables (e.g., "context"). Instead, we advocate for the delineation of *particular* contextual variables likely to influence psychopathy in female and ethnic/minority youth that can be incorporated into a theory-driven nomological net.

4. Importantly, we recommend that more studies investigate non-incarcerated youth, using multiple measures of psychopathy (APSD, PCL:YV). Though it is often useful to study forensic samples due to the relatively low base rates of youth psychopathy in the general population,

an overreliance on forensic samples can be problematic because youth from forensic samples are more likely to have low SES *and* be ethnic minorities. This form of sampling would increase the likelihood that SES and ethnicity are conflated and capture a restricted range of a particular ethnic group and class. Moreover, the choice of assessment instrument is often confounded with the age group studied and the recruitment method used. For example, most research that has used the APSD has studied school-age children (under 13 years old) referred from mental health centers or recruited from the community or public schools. On the other hand, studies utilizing the PCL:YV involved adolescent samples, particularly adjudicated and detained youth. Thus, it is impossible to know whether disparate findings across studies are due to age, recruitment method, or psychopathy instrument.

In summary, future studies should avoid obvious confounds that influence interpretations of group differences. In keeping with the preceding recommendations, we strongly advocate for deliberate efforts to avoid problematic confounds, including the conflation of (1) culture and socioeconomic class, (2) social context versus individual-level factors (e.g., temperament), and (3) gender and sex. We recognize that these variables are often intricately related and mutually influential, but their relation does not mean that a more nuanced understanding of their unique contributions cannot be reached. One important means of avoiding such confounds is to operationalize and measure them directly in order to understand better the effects of each—especially since many studies include youth of different ethnicities, but few investigate results in light of ethnicity. In this way, we hope to avoid misunderstandings of the nature and extent of influence accorded by gender and culture on youth psychopathy.

References

Baker, L. A., Jacobson, K. C., Raine, A., Lozano, D. I., & Bezdijan, S. (2007). Genetic and environmental bases of childhood antisocial behavior: A multi-informant twin study. *Journal of Abnormal Psychology, 116,* 219–235.

Benton, D. (1992). Hormones and human aggression. In K. Björkqvist & P. Niemela (Eds.), *Of mice and women: Aspects of female aggression* (pp. 37–46). San Diego, CA: Academic Press.

Betancourt, H., & Lopez, S. R. (1993). The study of culture, ethnicity, and race in American psychology. *American Psychologist, 48,* 629–637.

Björkqvist, K., Lagerspetz, K., & Kaukiainen, A. (1992). Do girls manipulate and boys fight?: Developmental trends in regard to direct and indirect aggression. *Aggressive Behavior, 18,* 117–127.

Bolt, D. M., Hare, R. D., Vitale, J. E., & Newman, J. P. (2004). A multigroup item response theory analysis of the Psychopathy Checklist—Revised. *Psychological Assessment, 16*(2), 155–168.

Campbell, M. A., Porter, S., & Santor, D. (2004). Psychopathic traits in adolescent offenders: An evaluation of criminal history, clinical and psychosocial correlates. *Behavioral Sciences and the Law, 22,* 23–47.

Chesney-Lind, M., & Shelden, R. G. (2004). *Girls, delinquency, and juvenile justice.* Belmont, CA: Wadsworth/Thomson Learning.

Christian, R. E., Frick, P. J., Hill, N. L., Tyler, L., & Frazer, D. R. (1997). Psychopathy and conduct problems in children: Implications for subtyping children with conduct problems. *Journal of American Academy of Child and Adolescent Psychiatry, 36*, 233–241.

Cleckley, H. (1976). *The mask of sanity* (5th ed.). St. Louis, MO: Mosby.

Cooke, D. J., & Michie, C. (2001). Refining the construct of psychopathy: Towards a hierarchical model. *Psychological Assessment, 13*, 171–188.

Cooke, D. J., Michie, C., Hart, S. D., & Clark, D. (2005). Assessing psychopathy in the UK: Concerns about cross-culturally generalizability. *British Journal of Psychiatry, 186*, 335–341.

Crick, N. R., & Grotpeter, J. K. (1995). Relational aggression, gender, and social-psychological adjustment. *Child Development, 66*, 710–722.

Cruise, K., Colwell, L., Lyons, P., & Baker, M. (2003). Prototypical analysis of adolescent psychopathy: Investigating the juvenile justice perspective. *Behavioral Sciences and the Law,* 21, 829–846.

Dadds, M. R., Fraser, J., Frost, A., & Hawes, D. J. (2005). Disentangling the underlying dimensions of psychopathy and conduct problems in childhood: A community study. *Journal of Consulting and Clinical Psychology, 73*, 400–410.

Edens, J., Skeem, J., Cruise, K., & Cauffman, E. (2001). Assessment of "juvenile psychopathy" and it's association with violence: a critical review. *Behavioral Sciences and the Law, 19*, 53–80.

Edens, J. F., & Cahill, M. A. (2007). Psychopathy in adolescence and criminal recidivism in young adulthood: Longitudinal results from a multiethnic sample of youthful offenders. *Assessment, 14*, 57–64.

Edens, J. F., Campbell, J. S., & Weir, J. M. (2006). Youth psychopathy and criminal recidivism: A meta-analysis of the psychopathy checklist measures. *Law and Human Behavior, 31*, 53–75.

Enebrink, P., Andershed, H., & Langstrom, N. (2005). Callous–unemotional traits are associated with clinical severity in referred boys with conduct problems. *Nordic Journal of Psychiatry, 59,* 431–440.

Epstein, M. K., Poythress, N. G., & Brandon, K. O. (2006). The Self-Report Psychopathy Scale and passive avoidance learning: A validation study of race and gender effects. *Assessment, 13,* 197–207.

Falkenbach, D. M., Poythress, N. G., & Heide, K. M. (2003). Psychopathic features in a juvenile diversion population: Reliability and predictive validity of two self-report measures. *Behavioral Sciences and the Law, 21,* 787–805.

Forth, A. E., Kosson, D. S., & Hare, R. D. (2003). *The Psychopathy Checklist: Youth Version*. Toronto: Multi-Health Systems. (Original work published 1996)

Frick, P. J., Bodin, S. D., & Barry, C. T. (2000). Psychopathic traits and conduct problems in community and clinic-referred samples of children: Further development of the Psychopathy Screening Device. *Psychological Assessment, 12*(4), 382–393.

Frick, P. J., Cornell, A. H., Bodin, S. D., Dane, H. E., Barry, C. T., & Loney, B. R. (2003). Callous–unemotional traits and developmental pathways to severe conduct problems. *Developmental Psychology, 39*, 246–260.

Frick, P. J., & Hare, R. D. (2001). *The Antisocial Process Screening Device.* Toronto: Multi-Health Systems.

Frick, P. J., Lilienfeld, S. O., Ellis, M., Loney, B., & Silverthorn, P. (1999). The association between anxiety and psychopathy dimensions in children. *Journal of Abnormal Child Psychology, 27*, 383–392.

Frick, P. J., O'Brien, B. S., Wootton, J. M., & McBurnett, K. (1994). Psychopathy and conduct problems in children. *Journal of Abnormal Psychology, 103*, 700–707.

Gretton, H. M., Hare, R. D., & Catchpole, R. E. H. (2004). Psychopathy and offending from adolescence to adulthood: A 10-year follow-up. *Journal of Consulting and Clinical Psychology, 72*, 636–645.

Hare, R. D. (1978). Electrodermal and cardiovascular correlates of psychopathy. In R. D. Hare & D. Schalling (Eds.), *Psychopathic behavior: Approaches to research* (pp. 107–143). Chichester, UK: Wiley.

Hare, R. D. (1991). *Manual for the Revised Psychopathy Checklist.* Toronto: Multi-Health Systems.

Hare, R. D. (2003). *The Psychopathy Checklist—Revised* (2nd ed.). Toronto: Multi-Health Systems.

Harpur, T., Hare, R. D., & Hakstian, A. (1989). Two-factor conceptualization of psychopathy: Construct validity and assessment implications. *Psychological Assessment, 1*, 6–17.

Hiatt, K. D., Schmitt, W. A., & Newman, J. P. (2004). Stroop tasks reveal abnormal selective attention among psychopathic offenders. *Neuropsychology, 18*, 50–59.

Jones, S., Cauffman, E., Miller, J. D., & Mulvey, E. (2006). Investigating different factor structures of the Psychopathy Checklist: Youth Version—confirmatory factor-analytic findings. *Psychological Assessment, 18*, 33–48.

Keenan, K., & Shaw, D. (1997). Developmental and social influences on young girls' early problem behavior. *Psychological Bulletin, 121*, 95–113.

Kimonis, E. R., Frick, P. J., Fazekas, H., & Loney, B. R. (2006). Psychopathy, aggression, and the processing of emotional stimuli in non-referred girls and boys. *Behavioral Sciences and the Law, 24*, 21–37.

Krieger, N. (2001). A glossary for social epidemiology. *Journal of Epidemiological Community Health, 55*, 693–700.

Leistico, A. R., Salekin, R. T., DeCoster, J., & Rogers, R. (2008). A large-scale meta-analysis relating the Hare measures of psychopathy to antisocial conduct. *Law and Human Behavior, 32*, 28–45.

Loney, B. R., Butler, M. A., Lima, E. N., Counts, C. A., & Eckel, L. A. (2006). The relation between salivary cortisol, callous–unemotional traits, and conduct problems in an adolescent non-referred sample. *Journal of Child Psychology and Psychiatry, 47*, 30–36.

Loney, B. R., Frick, P. J., Clementes, C. B., Ellis, M. L., & Kerlin, K. (2003). Callous–unemotional traits, impulsivity, and emotional processing in adolescents with antisocial behavior problems. *Journal of Clinical Child and Adolescent Psychology, 32*, 66–80.

Lorenz, A. R., & Newman, J. P. (2002). Utilization of emotion cues in male and female offenders with antisocial personality disorder: Results from a lexical decision task. *Journal of Abnormal Psychology, 111*, 513–516.

Lynam, D. R. (1997). Pursuing the psychopathy: Capturing the psychopathy in a nomological net. *Journal of Abnormal Psychology, 106*, 425–438.

Marsee, M. A., Silverthorn, P., & Frick, P. J. (2005). The association of psychopathic traits with aggression and delinquency in non-referred boys and girls. *Behavioral Sciences and the Law, 23*, 803–817.

Marshall, J., Egan, V., English, M., & Jones, R. M. (2006). The relative validity of psychopathy versus risk/needs-based assessments in the prediction of adolescent offending behavior. *Legal and Criminological Psychology, 11*, 197–210.

Moffitt, T. E. (1993). Adolescence-limited and life-course-persistent antisocial behavior: A developmental taxonomy. *Psychological Review, 100*, 674–701.

Moffitt, T. E., & Caspi, A. (2001). Childhood predictors differentiate life-course persistent and adolescent-limited antisocial pathways among males and females. *Development and Psychopathology, 13*, 355–375.

Mulder, R. T., Wells, J. E., Joyce, P. R., & Bushnell, J. A. (1994). Antisocial women. *Journal of Personality Disorders, 8*, 279–287.

Murrie, D. C., & Cornell, D. G. (2002). Psychopathy screening of incarcerated individuals: A comparison of measures. *Psychological Assessment, 14*, 390–396.

Newman, J. P., & Kosson, D. S. (1986). Passive avoidance learning in psychopathic and non-psychopathic offenders. *Journal of Abnormal Psychology, 95*, 252–256.

Odgers, C. L., Reppucci, N. D., Moretti, M. M. (2005). Nipping psychopathy in the bud: An examination of the convergent, predictive, and theoretical utility of the PCL-YV among adolescent girls. *Behavioral Sciences and the Law, 23*, 743–763.

O'Leary, M. M., Loney, B. R., & Eckel, L. A. (2007). Gender differences in the association between psychopathic personality traits and cortisol response to reduced stress. *Psychoneuroendocrinology, 32*, 183–191.

Olweus, D., Mattsson, A., Schalling, D., & Low, H. (1988). Circulating testosterone levels and aggression in adolescent males. *Psychosomatic Medicine, 50*, 261–272.

Pardini, D. A., Lochman, J. E., & Frick, P. J. (2003). Callous/unemotional traits and social-cognitive processes in adjudicated youths. *Journal of the American Academy of Child and Adolescent Psychiatry, 42*, 364–371.

Penney, S. R., & Moretti, M. M. (2007). The relation of psychopathy to concurrent aggression and antisocial behavior in high-risk adolescent girls and boys. *Behavioral Sciences and the Law, 25*, 21–41.

Phinney, J. S. (1996). When we talk about American ethnic groups, what do we mean? *American Psychologist, 51*, 918–927.

Prilleltensky, I., & Gonick, L. (1996). Politics change, oppression remains: On the psychology and politics of oppression. *Political Psychology, 17*, 127–148.

Salekin, R. T. (2008). Psychopathy and recidivism from mid-adolescence to young adulthood: Cumulating legal problems and limiting life opportunities. *Journal of Abnormal Psychology, 117,* 386–395.

Salekin, R. T., Leistico, A. R., Trobst, K. K., Schrum, C. L., & Lochman, J. E. (2005). Adolescent psychopathy and personality theory—the interpersonal circumplex: Expanding evidence of a nomological net. *Journal of Abnormal Child Psychology, 33,* 445–460.

Salekin, R. T., Rogers, R., & Machin, D. (2001). Psychopathy in youth: Pursuing diagnostic clarity. *Journal of Youth and Adolescence, 30,* 173–195.

Salekin, R. T., Rogers, R., & Sewell, K. W. (1997). Construct validity of psychopathy in a female offender sample: A multitrait–multimethod evaluation. *Journal of Abnormal Psychology, 106,* 576–585.

Salekin, R. T., Rosenbaum, J., & Lee, Z. (2009). Child and adolescent psychopathy: Stability and change. *Psychiatry, Psychology and Law, 15,* 224–236.

Schmidt, F., McKinnon, L., Chattha, H. K., & Brownlee, K. (2006). Concurrent and predictive validity of the PCL:YV across gender and ethnicity. *Psychological Assessment, 18,* 393–401.

Schrum, C. L., & Salekin, R. T. (2006). Psychopathy in adolescent female offenders: An item response theory analysis of the Psychopathy Checklist: Youth Version. *Behavioral Sciences and the Law, 24,* 39–63.

Skeem, J. L., Edens, J. F., Camp, J., & Colwell, L. H. (2004). Are there ethnic differences in levels of psychopathy?: A meta-analysis *Law and Human Behavior, 28,* 505–527.

Sue, S. (1999). Science, ethnicity, and bias: Where have we gone wrong? *American Psychologist, 54,* 1070–1077.

Sullivan, E. A., & Kosson, D. S. (2006). Ethnic and cultural variations in psychopathy. In C. J. Patrick (Ed.), *Handbook of psychopathy* (pp. 437–458). New York: Guilford Press.

Sutton, S. K., Vitale, J. E., & Newman, J. P. (2002). Emotion among females with psychopathy during picture presentation. *Journal of Abnormal Psychology, 111,* 610–619.

Verona, E., & Vitale, J. (2006). Psychopathy in women: Assessment, manifestations, and etiology. In C. J. Patrick (Ed.), *Handbook of psychopathy* (pp. 415–436). New York: Guilford Press.

Vincent, G. M., Vitacco, M. J., Grisso, T., & Corrado, R. R. (2003). Subtypes of adolescent offenders: Affective traits and antisocial behavior patterns. *Behavioral Sciences and the Law, 21,* 695–712.

Vitale, J. E., Newman, J. P., Bates, J. E., Goodnight, J., Dodge, K. A., & Pettit, G. S. (2005). Deficient behavioral inhibition and anomalous selective attention in a community sample of adolescents with psychopathic traits and low-anxiety traits. *Journal of Abnormal Child Psychology, 33,* 461–470.

Vitale, J. E., Smith, S. E., Brinkley, C. A., & Newman, J. P. (2002). The reliability and validity of the Psychopathy Checklist—Revised in a sample of female offending. *Criminal Justice and Behavior, 29,* 202–231.

Walsh, Z., & Kosson, D. S. (2007). Psychopathy and violent crime: A prospective study of the influence of socioeconomic status and ethnicity. *Law and Human Behavior, 31*, 209–229.

Weiler, B. L., & Widom, C. S. (1996). Psychopathy and violent behavior in abused and neglected young adults. *Criminal Behavior and Mental Health, 6*, 253–271.

Woodworth, M., & Porter, S. (2002). In cold blood: Characteristics of criminal homicides as a function of psychopathy. *Journal of Abnormal Psychology, 111*, 436–445.

14

Treatment of Child and Adolescent Psychopathy

Focusing on Change

RANDALL T. SALEKIN

Psychopathy: Differing Conceptions

Cleckley (1941) offered what some consider a clear and well-accepted description of psychopathy. Specifically, he outlined 16 symptoms that captured interpersonal, affective, and behavioral aspects of the disorder. These symptoms included superficial charm and good intelligence, absence of nervousness, lack of empathy, and lack of remorse, as well as failure to follow a specific life plan. Via descriptive case examples, Cleckley articulated how psychopathic individuals engage in legal and moral transgressions, while maintaining a "mask of sanity." Robins (1966) and Cloninger (1978) suggested that psychopathy might best be measured by examining behavior rather than personality. This model moved the field away from personality features and focused on characteristics such as those that make up antisocial personality disorder delineated in DSM-IV (American Psychiatric Association, 2000). It was believed that behavioral characteristics indirectly tapped the personality features of the disorder. Symptoms included characteristics such as irresponsible and reckless behavior that violated the rights of others. Hare (1991/2003) offered a two-factor model for psychopathy that incorporated both Cleckley's model for psychopathy and antisocial behavior as delineated by Robins and her colleagues. Some researchers have argued that the two-factor model for psychopathy captures both Cleckley's (1941) and Robins's (1966) notions of psychopathy in a single, two-factor framework. Hare's model serves as one example of the multidimensionality of psychopathy and has most recently been divided into four facets that maintain the two broad traditional factors but parses them into smaller facets (see Figure 14.1).

For intervention science, varying conceptualizations (and factor structures) may have relevance to treatment responsiveness. Take, for one key example, the difference between Hare's (1991/2003) model, which is based on offenders, and compare it to Cleckley's (1941) model, which discussed many successful individuals in the business and medical fields. The two models may reflect various psychopathic subtypes, such as successful versus nonsuccessful, emotionally stable versus unstable, and primary versus secondary psychopathic individuals. Thus, definitional issues as well as the setting to which they are being applied, may have different real-world meaning, including potential differences in amenability to treatment.

High achievers in Cleckley's model may be viewed as less in need of treatment for severe antisocial behavior per se than those who engage in serious and varied criminality in Hare's model. Even, within a single model, there can be disagreements, as has been seen with the lively controversy regarding what underpins the Psychopathy Checklist model (see Hare, 1991/2003; Salekin, Brannen, Zalot, Leistico, & Neumann, 2006; Skeem & Cooke, 2009), with some researchers believing that antisocial behavior is a necessary component of the disorder, and others believing that it is not essential to psychopathy, but rather a potential behavioral consequence. Key descriptive items may also be omitted in some models, such as "absence of nervousness," which could play a chief role in treatment amenability.

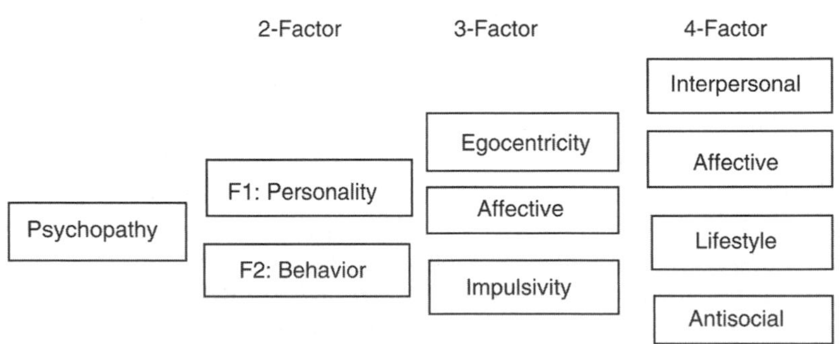

FIGURE 14.1. Components of psychopathy.

Two other issues are important to consider in examining treatment of psychopathy. Related to factor-analytic work, examining specific aspects of psychopathy (e.g., affective deficits) alone may be helpful for understanding the treatment of that particular component of the syndrome, but it may not equate to treating psychopathy as a whole. While dismantling of psychopathy may be important to understand treatment better, it is also important to investigate treatment of psychopathy as a broader construct. Comparing treatments that focus on component parts versus combined types, much like the work on attention-deficit/hyperactivity disorder (ADHD; i.e., inattentive, hyperactive, and combined types), will help researchers sort through issues regarding which aspects of psychopathy are in need of treatment and amenable to treatment.

Although beyond the scope of this chapter, another key and related issue is how psychopathy is measured (see Kotler & McMahon, Chapter 4, this volume; Lynam, 1997); because this is an important issue for treatment studies, I briefly discuss measurement issues. Specifically, there exist considerable heterogeneity and differences in research findings across assessment tools. Part of the heterogeneity and disparate research findings may be due not only to differing conceptualizations of the disorder but also to disparities in the methods in which psychopathy is measured. For example, self-report measures of psychopathy may not result in the same findings as clinician interview methods. Also, self-report screens may not result in the same findings as longer, more in-depth self-report measures. Moreover, newer self-report measures, such as the Child Psychopathy Scale (CPS; Lynam, 1997) and Youth Psychopathy Inventory (YPI; Andershed et al., 2002) at the child level, or the Multidimensional Personality Questionnaire (MPQ), Psychopathic Personality Inventory (PPI; Lilienfeld & Andrews, 1996), and Self-Report Psychopathy Scale–II (SRP-II; Hare, 1991/2003) and SRP-III (Williams, Paulhaus, & Hare, 2007) at the adult level, may differ from PCL models with respect to conceptualization, further complicating this issue. Nonetheless, such models, if further researched, could provide more detail about what is, and what is not, treatable with respect to psychopathic personality. To the extent that there are method effects, research needs to continue to determine whether self-, parent, clinical interview, or some combination (multimeasurement) of assessment is best. So long as researchers document which conceptualization–subtype–measure they are utilizing, such an approach to investigating the treatment outcome of psychopathy in youth may be justifiable, viable, and most comprehensive.

Hare's Model as a Starting Point

Because Hare's work, initiated in the 1970s (Hare, 1970), generated considerable theoretical and empirical study on the topic of psychopathy, it seems like a natural starting point. A good portion of this research focused on the structure of psychopathy, its external correlates, and more recent investigations have begun to examine psychopathy from new research perspectives. These perspectives include cognitive neuroscience to determine the particular structures and neurochemical functioning that may be implicated in the development and maintenance of psychopathy (Intrator et al., 1997; Kheil, Hare, Liddle, & McDonald, 1999; Newman, Curtin, Bertsch, & Baskin-Sommers, in press) and behavioral genetic research (Waldman & Rhee, 2006). Research on adults has shown that psychopathy has coherence (homogeneity of symptoms), a relatively stable factor structure, a genetic component, and meaningful external correlates (Salekin, Rogers, & Sewell, 1996).

The migration of the concept to children has shown many similar findings, with raters evidencing independent agreement, measures demonstrating structural stability and concurrent and predictive meaning (see Salekin, 2006), as well as a genetic basis (Larsson, Andershed, & Lichtenstein, 2006; Viding & Larsson, Chapter 5, this volume). Several research findings have shown, however, that there may be some developmental differences in the concept of psychopathy in childhood, in that studies tend to indicate only modest levels of stability, greater levels of comorbidity (Kubak & Salekin, 2009; Salekin, Leistico, Trobst, Schrum, & Lochman, 2005; Salekin, Neumann, Leistico, DiCiccio, & Duros, 2004; Salekin, Rosenbaum, & Lee, 2009; Salekin, Rosenbaum, Lee, & Lester, 2009), and dissimilar correlates with internalizing symptoms and some performance tasks (see Forth, Kosson, & Hare, 2003; Lee, Salekin, & Iselin, in press; Salekin, 2006; Salekin & Frick, 2005; Salekin, Rosenbaum, Lee, & Lester, 2009). While it remains unclear to what extent research findings will continue to elucidate similarities and differences with respect to the concept of child psychopathy, scientific findings are thus far encouraging for the treatment of psychopathy in children and adolescents; that is, research results, such as the overlap with internalizing disorders and potentially less stability may be indicative of better amenability (Kubak & Salekin, 2009; Lee, Salekin, & Iselin, 2010; Murrie et al., 2007; Salekin & Lochman, 2008; Salekin, Rosenbaum, Lee, & Lester, 2009). This is because such differences (concern about predicament) may provide important leads that may help to unravel the potential causal mechanisms linked to the development of psychopathy (Rutter, Tizard, & Whitmore, 1987). However, these are, admittedly, mostly suppositions at this point—which leads to the question: What do we really know about the treatment of psychopathy, on a general level, and what do we know about the treatment of child psychopathy?

Reviews and Past Perspectives: No Shortage of Opinion

A perusal of the literature on child psychopathy shows that there is little in the way of research on the topic of treatment, especially in comparison to the number of descriptive, structural, and etiological studies at the level of both adults and children. What is clear, however, is that there exist strong opinions and potentially ingrained beliefs regarding the potential impact treatment might have on psychopathy. In the absence of abundant and strong research on the topic, it is difficult to ascertain which beliefs may be correct. Nonetheless, some history on the psychopathy–treatment relation can be helpful in determining where we currently stand on this topic, and where we need to go with respect to research development in the field of child and adolescent psychopathy.

In one of the first chapters on psychopathy and treatment, Suedfeld and Landon (1978) commented that a "review of the literature suggests that a chapter on effective treatment should be the shortest in any book concerned with psychopathy. In fact, it has been suggested that one sentence would suffice: No demonstrably effective treatment has been found" (p. 347). Blackburn (1993) later arrived at two primary conclusions regarding the treatability of psychopathy: "First, while classical psychopaths have been shown to respond poorly to some traditional therapeutic interventions, it has yet to be established that 'nothing works' with this group [and] second, some offenders with personality disorders do appear to change with psychological treatment" (p. 202). Lösel (1998) noted there are "more question marks" than answers regarding the treatment of psychopathy (p. 303). Other reviewers of the literature have continued to delineate similar conclusions regarding the lack of sufficient data in this area (e.g., D'Silva, Duggan, & McCarthy, 2004; Kristiansson, 1995; Tennent, Tennent, Prins, & Bedford, 1993).[1]

Salekin (2002), utilizing a data-driven review, generated more optimistic conclusions. Following a review of 42 studies, Salekin found that, on average, 62% of patients benefited from psychotherapy; removing cases studies, 60% of patients benefited from therapy. Psychotherapy appeared to be effective for major classes of therapy (psychoanalytic, cognitive behavioral,[2] and eclectic) and a variety of outcomes (improving interpersonal relationships, increasing the capacity for feeling remorse and empathy, reducing the amount of lying, being released from probation, and maintaining a job). In addition, effective treatments were found to be intensive, including an average of four sessions of individual psychotherapy per week, for at least 1 year. Individual psychotherapy, when augmented with group psychotherapy, appeared to be beneficial. In addition, treatment programs that incorporated family members appeared to produce better effects. Salekin concluded the results indicated that for complex problems such as psychopathy, more elaborate and intensive intervention programs involving individual psychotherapy, treatment of family members, and input from groups may be needed. Thus, scope, intensity, and duration of treatment for psychopathy were important in the overall adjustment of psychopathic individuals.

The Salekin review and meta-analysis had strengths and limitations. With respect to strengths, the study examined a host of treatment modalities and a variety of life outcomes. The review included the time-honored methodology of case studies, quasi-experimental designs, and, to a lesser extent, control studies. The literature search drew widely from psychopathy treatment research, including studies such as Albert Ellis's (1961) case study, and Ingram, Gerard, Quay, and Levison's (1970) controlled intervention study. The review was broad but also limited in terms of the number of randomized treatment control studies. This aforementioned limitation, and other limitations, were clearly articulated in the discussion section of the review, and the author suggested that a second generation of research was needed.

Harris and Rice (2006) critiqued the Salekin (2002) meta-analysis and, in response, conducted their own review of the psychopathy treatment literature. Harris and Rice acknowledged the existence of studies showing positive results for the treatment of psychopathy, but noted that many of the studies demonstrating positive effects were case studies. They criticized the use of therapist opinion regarding client change and measures other than the PCL, and believed treatment studies that did not include recidivism as an outcome were unacceptable, and deemphasized their importance. Finally, Harris and Rice believed that the heterogeneity in outcome variables was problematic. Instead, these authors focused on several treatment studies that met with their specific considerations for appropriateness.

With the aforementioned inclusion–exclusion criteria, Harris and Rice (2006) adopted a blend of two conclusions: "No clinical intervention will ever be helpful" and "no effective interventions yet exist for psychopaths" (p. 563). Moreover, they maintained their original conclusion that treatment, as it currently exists, could "make psychopathic individuals worse" (p. 563). Because Harris and Rice viewed most of the treatment outcome studies in the Salekin (2002) meta-analysis as inadequate, and the Skeem, Monahan, and Mulvey (2002) study as flawed, their affirmatively stated conclusions regarding the treatability of psychopathy were based on the few studies they viewed as adequate (possibly a scant two studies). One study on which they based their conclusions was their own, which utilized a retrospective design and has been criticized extensively in the literature (see Caldwell, Skeem, Salekin, & Van Rybroek, 2006; Skeem et al., 2002).

One primary criticism is the retrospective design, and another is having an "intervention" that many researchers viewed as nontherapeutic. In addition, the authors supported their conclusion regarding the treatability of psychopathy with a very broad etiological theory (i.e., evolutionary strategy) advanced in their chapter, which has not been adequately validated and does not necessarily lead to conclusions that psychopathy is untreatable (Vaillant, 1975).

Moving to other reviews, Wong and Hare (2005) briefly reviewed a portion of the research on psychopathy and treatment. Their view regarding the treatment of psychopathy is slightly more positive than that of Harris and Rice (2006), as evidenced by their initiation and development of a treatment program. However, Wong and Hare (2005) are cautious regarding how much progress can be made with institutional offenders. In addition, they, too, believe that only PCL studies should be considered in outcome research, and that management might be the most optimal consideration for offenders. There appeared to be limited theory guiding their treatment program beyond the preexistent general correctional psychology programs for general offenders. Wong and Hare, like other reviewers of the psychopathy–treatment research, did not comment on the potential treatability of child and adolescent psychopathy in their program manual.

Summarizing and Integrating Past Reviews

The previously mentioned reviews collectively inform us that regardless of how limited the data might be, strong opinions about the treatability of psychopathy remain. Opinions range from the notion that the treatment of psychopathy (1) will have no effect on the condition (inert) (Harris & Rice, 2006), (2) will worsen the condition (iatrogenic; Harris & Rice, 2006), or (3) will potentially improve the condition (Salekin, 2002; Skeem et al., 2002). Several studies have now shown some evidence of positive outcomes for psychopathic youth following intervention (Caldwell et al., 2006; Hawes & Dadds, 2005; Salekin, 2002; Skeem et al., 2002), but, clearly, much more work is needed in this area.

In addition, the previously mentioned reviews differ in what, they suggest, may be viewed as "in bounds" with regard to psychopathy classifications and life outcomes. Some reviews viewed heterogeneity in classification of psychopathy as a positive aspect of intervention science (e.g., Salekin, 2002). Others believed that PCL tests should be the only indices used for inclusion criteria. With respect to outcome variables, some suggested that the only outcome that matters is recidivism (Harris & Rice, 2006; Wong & Hare, 2005). Others saw a host of outcome as important.

In this chapter, Psychopathy Checklist: Youth Version (PCL:YV) and PCL-based models are used to examine psychopathy treatment management and outcome studies. In some ways, these studies could be referred to as second-generation research, in that they use structured assessments of psychopathy with PCL versions (Salekin, 2002). However, I later present evidence to argue that some diversity in psychopathy measurement (Benning, Patrick, Salekin, & Leistico, 2005; Cleckley, 1941; Lilienfeld & Andrews, 1996; Salekin, 2008) and examination of outcome variables may be helpful in the future as research starts to expand on the psychopathy–treatment relation.

Review of Child and Adolescent Treatment Studies

Previous work on the treatment of psychopathy can be separated into roughly two categories. The first category is studies that consider compliance issues for psychopathic individuals in treatment settings. The second category represents studies that focus on treatment outcome for psychopathy. As mentioned, I present studies that focus on the PCL and its derivatives (Antisocial Process Screening Device [APSD]), but I later contrast this approach to findings from the Salekin (2002) meta-analysis, which is broader in its recruitment of research studies on psychopathy.

Treatment Compliance with Adolescents

In one of the first examinations of the issue, Forth, Hart, and Hare (1990) found that scores on a modified version of the Psychopathy Checklist—Revised (PCL-R; Hare, 1991/2003) were significantly correlated with the number of institutional charges for violent behavior in a group of 75 male offenders (mean age = 16.3; *SD* = 1.1; 77.3% white and 22.7% Native American). This study suggested that there may be treatment compliance issues with those youth scoring high on a psychopathy scale in typical juvenile justice settings. Brandt, Kennedy, Patrick, and Curtin (1997) used a modified version of the PCL-R in a sample of 130 adolescent offenders (mean age = 16.1; *SD* = 1.0; 70% African American, 28% white, and 2% Hispanic) and found that psychopathy scores were significantly correlated with verbal and physical rule violations, with intensive supervision placements for more serious misconduct.

In a prospective investigation of 72 adolescent psychiatric patients (mean age = 14.1; *SD* = 1.50; 37 males and 35 females; 83% white and 17% denoted as minorities), Stafford and Cornell (2003) found that scores on the PCL-R predicted staff ratings of overall institutional aggression, verbal and covert aggression, and aggression directed toward peers. In a series of studies, Rogers and his colleagues (Murdock-Hicks, Rogers, & Cashel, 2000; Rogers, Jackson, Sewell, & Johansen, 2004; Rogers, Johansen, Chang, & Salekin, 1997) examined the relation between psychopathy (PCL-R) and several treatment-related variables at a state hospital. Rogers and colleagues (1997) tested 81 adolescents (mean age = 15.62 years; *SD* = 1.03; 17.3% African Americans, 33.3% Hispanic Americans, 46.9% Anglo Americans, and 2.4% referred to as other) in a residential program in which treatment typically spanned 6 months. Psychopathy was modestly associated with treatment noncompliance ($r = .25$) and physical aggression ($r = .28$).

Similarly, Murdock-Hicks and colleagues (2000) examined 82 adolescent inpatients (mean age = 15.78; *SD* = 1.02; 58 African Americans, 31 Anglo Americans, 29 Hispanic Americans, and 2 other) from a state hospital mandated for treatment of substance abuse with comorbid disruptive behavior disorders. These authors used the Psychopathy Checklist: Screening Version (PCL:SV) and the Minnesota Multiphasic Personality Inventory for Adolescents (MMPI-A) to predict total, violent, and nonviolent infractions in this treatment-oriented facility for delinquent youth. Murdock-Hicks and colleagues found that psychopathic youth manifested a significantly higher rate of violent infractions than nonpsychopathic individuals. They also found that ethnic differences in PCL:SV scores raised concerns about the generalizability of the measure in this study because differences found in the relationship between psychopathy and infractions were based on ethnicity. The results from this study showed that psychopathy contributed very little to the prediction of total infractions. Specifically, in a multiple regression, Factor 2 (F2) added some to the prediction of infractions ($R^2 = .07$), while Factor 1 (F1) was nonsignificant ($R^2 = .01$).

Treatment Outcome (and Compliance) with Adolescent Offenders

Gretton, McBride, Hare, O'Shaughnessy, and Kumka (2001) retrospectively examined 220 adolescent males (mean age = 14.7; *SD* = 1.5) in an outpatient sex offender program. Files, including treatment notes, were used to rate the PCL:YV, code criminal history, and record demographic data for each participant. During the 10-year follow-up, adolescents with high PCL:YV scores committed significantly more violent offenses in the community and were relatively more likely to attempt to escape from custody. The effects were reported to be attributable to premature dropout or termination for adolescents with high PCL:YV scores. Only 64% of those with high PCL:YV scores completed treatment, compared to 79–80% of those with low-to-medium scores (Gretton, McBride, Hare, & O'Shaughnessy, 2000). Of those with high PCL:YV scores, only 30% who completed the treatment program were violent recidivists, compared to 80% who did not complete the program (Gretton et al., 2000). Thus, psychopathic-like youth who received sufficient doses of treatment appeared to benefit from it; that

TABLE 14.1. Child and Adolescent Treatment Outcome and Compliance Studies

Researchers	No./sample	Treatment type	Treatment compliance/treatment outcome	Compliance outcome	Treatment outcome
Forth, Hart, & Hare (1990)	75 male adolescent offenders	Maximum security detention center; treatment type not specified	Number of institutional charges for violent and aggressive behavior was higher in those scoring high on the PCL-R (r = .46).	X	—
Brandt, Kennedy, Patrick, & Curtin (1997)	130 male adolescent offenders	Treatment-intensive supervision placements for more serious misconduct	Psychopathy scores were significantly correlated with verbal (r = .31) and physical (r = .28) rule violations.	X	—
Rogers, Johansen, Chang, & Salekin (1997)	81 male adolescent offenders	Residential treatment facility for DBDs and substance abuse problems; treatment typically spanned 6 months	Psychopathy was associated with noncompliance (r = .25) and physical aggression (r = .28).	X	—
Murdock-Hicks, Rogers, & Cashel (2000)	82 male adolescent offenders	State hospital where mandated treatment for substance abuse and DBDs	Psychopathic individuals exhibited a higher rate of violent infractions than nonpsychopathic individuals (African American: r = .57; Anglo American: r = –.06). Nonviolent infractions had similar r's (African American: r = .51; Anglo American: r = .20) This was predicted by ethnicity in this study.	X	—
Stafford & Cornell (2003)	72 male and female adolescent psychiatric patients	Inpatient treatment for adolescents	PCL-R predicted institutional aggression (r = .49), verbal (r = .48) and covert aggression (r = .60), and aggression directed toward peers (r = .33).	X	—

Gretton, McBride, et al. (2001)	220 adolescent male sex offenders	Outpatient sex offender program for adolescents	Psychopathy-like youth who received sufficient doses of treatment appeared to benefit from it; that is, offenders with a high PCL:YV score who had remained in treatment reoffended at a rate that was not significantly different from that of offenders with a low PCL:YV score. It is possible that treatment had a beneficial effect in the psychopathic offenders, but it is also possible that those who remained in treatment were more motivated to change than were those who dropped out of treatment.	—	√
Catchpole (2003)	119 violent male adolescent offenders	Residential treatment for young offenders in Canadian facility	Treatment was associated with a similar reduction of general and violent recidivism across the range of psychopathy scores. The Catchpole (2003) study provided evidence for the treatment amenability of adolescents scoring high on the PCL:YV with two primary outcome variables.	—	√
O'Neill, Lidz, & Heilbrun (2003)	64 male adolescent offenders with substance abuse problems	Partial hospital program for substance-abusing adolescents	PCL:YV scores correlated negatively with days in the program ($r = -.42$) quality of participation ($r = -.55$), and researchers' ratings (from discharge summaries) of clinical improvement ($r = -.58$). Offenders were followed up for 1 year after release from the treatment facility. PCL:YV scores were significantly correlated with the number of times they were arrested ($r = .33$). Limited consideration for the treatment of psychopathy.	X	X
Falkenbach, Poythress, & Heide (2003)	69 male and female adolescent offenders	Court diversion treatment program	Psychopathy was correlated with program noncompliance ($r = .22$–$.36$) and rearrest ($r = .33$–$.56$) during a 1-year follow-up.	X	X

TABLE 14.1. *(continued)*

Researchers	No./sample	Treatment type	Treatment compliance/treatment outcome	Compliance outcome	Treatment outcome
Rogers, Jackson, Sewell, & Johansen (2004)	82 male adolescent offenders	State hospital that treated DBDs and substance abuse	Psychopathic traits did predict course of treatment and level of improvement, but the primary predictor for all outcome variables was breadth of substance abuse. Approximately 26% of the sample showed a significant decrease in psychopathic traits, with only 3.7% showing an exacerbation of symptoms. Management problems during the hospital course and the eventual outcome of treatment were improved even for those scoring high on a psychopathy measure.	X	X
Spain, Douglas, Poythress, & Epstein (2004)	85 adjudicated delinquent male adolescents remanded for rehabilitation services	Psychiatric dual-diagnosis services that spanned 9–12 months; treatment included medical and behavioral components (rational-emotive behavior therapy); the program was a multistep program based on point earned (lost) that could result in advancement or demotion in the program.	Psychopathy measures (PCL:YV, CPS, and APSD) were generally related to physical and verbal aggression and administration infraction, but results were highly variable in terms of treatment progress. Specifically, psychopathy did not appear to be predictive of number of days to promotion (PCL:YV was not predictive and only the behavioral components of the CPS and APSD were predictive of outcome). Psychopathy also did not predict whether individuals would have a treatment level dropped.	X	√

Hawes & Dadds (2005)	53 boys	Children being treated for ODD/CD with a program for DBDs. Treatment consisted of a manualized parent training intervention delivered by a clinical psychologist across 9 weeks (1 hour sessions).	Boys with callous–unemotional (CU) traits were reported to be less responsive to discipline with time out than boys without CU. CU traits did evidence a drop from Time 1 to Time 2 and at a 6-month follow-up ($d = .5$).	X	√
Caldwell, Skeem, Salekin, & Van Rybroek (2006)	85 adolescent males, treatment 79 adolescent males, treatment as usual	Mendota treatment center for young offenders	Treatment was associated with relatively slower and lower rates of serious recidivism, even after controlling for the effects of nonrandom assignment to treatment groups and release status.	—	√

Note. √, positive effect from therapy, X, no or negative effect from therapy; —, not measured. This table is not meant to be an extensive list of treatment studies but rather the treatment studies available through psychology search engines and published in scientific journals. This group of studies does not include dissertations, which may provide even further information on this topic once they pass through the peer-review process. DBDs, disruptive behavior disorders; CD, conduct disorder; ODD, oppositional defiant disorder; PCL-R, Psychopathy Checklist—Revised; PCL:YV, Psychopathy Checklist: Youth Version; CPS, Child Psychopathy Scale; APSD, Antisocial Process Screening Device.

is, offenders with high PCL:YV scores who remained in treatment reoffended at a rate that was not significantly different from that of offenders with low PCL:YV scores. It is possible that treatment had a beneficial effect in the psychopathic offenders, but it is also possible that those who remained in treatment were more motivated to change than were those who dropped out of treatment in this study. Either way, results from one of the first investigations on the topic likely argue for the importance of keeping psychopathic adolescent offenders in treatment.

Catchpole (2003) examined 119 violent adolescent offenders (mean age of the treatment group = 17. 6; *SD* = 1.3; 58.9% white, 25% First Nations, 5.4% Asian, and 10.7% other; mean age of the control group = 17.2; *SD* = 1.2; ethnicity: 59.3% white, 35.2% First Nations, 3.7% Asian, and 1.9% other) at three different treatment facilities in Canada. Treatment programs were primarily cognitive-behavioral in nature and lasted 6–8 months. Findings from this study showed that treatment groups had lower rates of violent and nonviolent reoffending than controls, and PCL:YV scores predicted latency to the first reoffense. Psychopathy was not found to moderate treatment response. Treatment was associated with a similar reduction of general and violent recidivism across the range of psychopathy scores. The Catchpole study provided evidence for the treatment amenability of adolescents scoring high on the PCL:YV, with two primary outcome variables. One potential problem was that this investigation was a retrospective–prospective design. The risk here is that treatment notes can affect psychopathy ratings, and there is the possibility for treatment contamination when one chart and two issues (assessment of psychopathy and treatment outcome) are being assessed, and sources of information might be difficult to separate completely.

O'Neill, Lidz, and Heilbrun (2003) examined 64 male adolescents (mean age = 16.0; *SD* = 1.0; approximately 52% African American, 28% Hispanic, and 20% white) in an intensive outpatient treatment program for substance abuse. The program was the Youth Opportunities Program in Philadelphia, Pennsylvania, a pretrial, partial hospital program for substance-abusing disruptive youth with behavior problems. The program involved 7 hours of scheduled programming per day, 5 days a week. The programming followed a comprehensive treatment model that included a number of structured intervention modalities addressing a broad range of problems and needs, in addition to treatment for the use of illicit substances. The major treatment modalities included a daily community meeting, 1-hour individual therapy sessions twice weekly (based on a cognitive-behavioral framework), 1-hour sessions of group therapy twice daily, 3 hours of classroom education per day, and daily recreational activities. The authors noted that youth showed some benefit from the program, but that psychopathy scores predicted worse attendance, lower quality of participation, fewer clean drug tests, lower clinical improvement ratings, and higher recidivism. Several problems with this study should be noted, however, in that it was a treatment program primarily for substance-abusing, adjudicated youth, and it was not designed for psychopathic youth. Perhaps even more concerning is that it would be difficult to rate the PCL:YV with file information that contained many of the outcome variables without having these variables influence psychopathy ratings, thereby conflating the two.

Rogers, Jackson, Sewell, and Johansen (2004) examined 82 male and female adolescents (mean age = 15.37; *SD* = 0.91; 12.2% African American, 26.8% Hispanic American, 41.5 European American, and 19.5% other/missing) undergoing treatment at a state hospital. Treatment consisted of psychoeducation and therapeutic groups, and provided youth with increased privileges based on program performance. The primary finding from this study was that while psychopathic traits did predict course of treatment and level of improvement, the primary predictor for all outcome variables was breadth of substance abuse. Importantly, in this study, approximately 26% of the sample showed a significant decrease in scores on a measure of psychopathic traits, with only 3.7% showing an exacerbation of symptoms. Rogers and colleagues concluded that breadth of polysubstance abuse appeared to be the best predictor of both management problems during the hospital course and the eventual outcome of treatment. Nonetheless, this study did show that conduct disorder (CD) with aggressive symptoms were predictive of hospital course, and psychopathic traits were predictive of the level of improvement.

Falkenbach, Poythress, and Heide (2003) examined the relation between psychopathic features and treatment program compliance, and outcomes in a sample of 69 adolescents in a court diversion program (mean age = 14.4; *SD* = 1.9; mixed gender: 60% boys, 40% girls; 55.1% white, 30.4% African American, 7.2% biracial, 1.4% Asian American, and 1.4% Native American). Psychopathic traits were assessed with the APSD and a modified version of the CPS. Falkenbach and colleagues found significant correlations with psychopathy and program noncompliance, and rearrest during a 1-year follow-up for both measures and across raters (parent and self-report).

In a similar study, Spain, Douglas, Poythress, and Epstein (2004) examined 85 adjudicated delinquents (mean age = 15.77; *SD* = 1.35; 79% white, 16% African American, and 4.9% Hispanic) in west central Florida, who were remanded for rehabilitation services. Length of stay for youth was approximately 9–12 months. Psychiatric dual-diagnotic services included day treatment, family therapy, onsite academics, and career counseling. The program included medical and behavioral components, with the behavioral component based on a rational-emotive behavioral treatment philosophy.

The program also utilized a multistep system based on points earned (or lost) that could result in advancement or demotion in program levels. Three psychopathy scales (PCL:YV, APSD, and CPS) were utilized to test the effects of treatment on psychopathy. Spain et al. found that psychopathy measures were generally positively linked to physical, verbal, and administrative infractions, but results were highly variable across psychopathy scales for two treatment outcome variables. Specifically, psychopathy did not appear to be predictive number of days to promotion (PCL:YV was not predictive, and only the behavioral components of the self-reports were predictive), and psychopathy scales did not predict whether a participant would have a treatment-level drop (only the *modified* CPS [mCPS] Affective scale predicted this outcome). Potential limitations of this study include its cross-sectional nature and whether self-report measures indicate state rather than trait effects within correctional settings.

To avoid this potential pitfall of retrospective designs, Caldwell and his colleagues (2006) used prospective designs and did not examine psychopathy as a moderator of treatment, but rather examined high psychopathy scorers in treatment settings. Specifically, they examined the treatment response of 141 juvenile offenders with high scores on the PCL:YV (*M* total > 27). Two groups of potentially psychopathic offenders were compared: one that participated in the Mendota Juvenile Treatment Center (MJTC), an intensive treatment program (*n* = 56), and another that received "treatment as usual" in a conventional juvenile correctional institution (JCI) setting (*N* = 85). Offenders in the JCI group (mean age at release = 17.2; *SD* = 1.0; 71.8% African American) were more than twice as likely to engage in violent recidivism in the community during a 2-year follow-up as those who participated in MJTC treatment (mean age at release = 17.0; *SD* = 0.87; 41.1% African American). Treatment was associated with relatively slower and lower rates of serious recidivism, even after researchers controlled for the effects of nonrandom assignment to treatment groups and release status. Other work by Caldwell and his colleagues has shown similar results (see Caldwell, McCormick, Umstead, & Van Rybroek, 2007; Caldwell & Van Rybroeck, 2001). The next step for this treatment is to see whether it can be transported to other programs, and to other clinicians and researchers.

Treatment of Psychopathy in Children

Although the studies reviewed here are adolescent focused and primarily use the PCL:YV, one study has used the APSD with children who have disruptive behavior disorder (DBD). It examined the effects of a standard DBD treatment on callousness, as indexed by the APSD and the Strengths and Weaknesses Questionnaire (Goodman, 1997), in children. Hawes and Dadds (2005) tested the impact of callous–unemotional (CU) characteristics on treatment outcomes and processes in a 10-week behavioral parent-training intervention with young boys referred for conduct problems and oppositional defiant disorder. This sample was relatively small and young ($N = 53$; mean age = 6.29). The authors found that CU characteristics[3] were associated with greater conduct problems at pretreatment. CU was also associated with poor outcomes at 6-month follow-up. CU characteristics uniquely predicted clinical outcomes when analyzed in relation to conduct problem severity, other predictors of antisocial behavior, and parents' implementation of treatment. Boys with high scores on CU traits were also reported to be less responsive to discipline with time-out than boys without CU characteristics. Interestingly, despite these difficulties, CU scores dropped from pretreatment to posttreatment ($d = 0.5$) for these children, and this drop was significant and maintained at a 6-month follow-up assessment.

What Do These "Second-Generation" Studies Tell Us?

Overall, the findings from the studies reviewed here do not make a strong case for the notion that psychopathy is untreatable in children and adolescents. They do speak to some of the problems encountered when dealing with psychopathic youth. Specifically, five of the five reviewed studies found that psychopathy scores were correlated with institutional misconduct in treatment settings. However, with respect to progress in psychotherapy, six out of eight studies showed that psychopathic youth benefited from treatment or did no worse than nonpsychopathic youth. These results suggest that psychopathic youth may pose more problems in treatment settings, but, on a note of encouragement, they may also make progress in treatment settings. These findings may do little to alleviate the concerns of those who suggest that psychopathic individuals have so many inherent personality and interpersonal difficulties that they lack the capacity to undergo real change. I review some of these characteristics below and delineate their association with negative treatment outcomes.

Integration to This Point in the Chapter

The preceding set of treatment articles provides a good example of what can be gleaned from PCL-focused studies, and examines institutional infractions and recidivism alone as outcome variables. To be sure, as a first step, these are important and necessary studies. However, they do not supply a great deal of information regarding different conceptualizations of psychopathy (successful vs. nonsuccessful, forensic vs. nonforensic) and what other factors may or may not be experiencing change. Thus, the potential mediators of change are essentially uninvestigated in such research. Much more could be gleaned from a richer intervention science on psychopathy. With broader conceptualizations of psychopathy and, importantly, a broad outlook on design and outcomes, we stand a better chance to learn more about how the disorder might operate in treatment (Salekin, 2002).

In light of the dearth of research on this topic of treatment outcome, critics may view any positive outcomes as unlikely to stand the test of time. Critics will point to psychopathy characteristics themselves as a reason that treatment will not work. Specifically, there are suppositions that certain characteristics of psychopathic individuals naturally make them less than ideal candidates for psychotherapy. These important points should not be ignored. And they will likely require attention in the development of appropriate interventions. However, such characteristics are not necessarily reasons for conclusions about inertness or iatrogenic effects of therapy.

Practical Problem Areas When Working with Psychopathic Youth

Psychopathy traits are potentially problematic in treatment settings. Researchers and clinicians should not be naive about this. However, whether they make treatment impossible is less clear. A number of potential problems have been outlined about the treatability of the psychopathic personality in previous reviews. These factors likely also apply to youth, although there may be developmental differences. Common therapist areas of concern include motivation to change, manipulation and deceit (being fooled), lack of real emotion in psychopathic youth, and the risk associated with therapy with psychopathic individuals. Numerous reviews (e.g., Lösel, 1998; Skeem, Polashek, & Manchak, 2009; Thornton & Blud, 2007; Wong & Burt, 2007) have addressed these topics, citing psychopathy items that align with each of the problem areas (e.g., manipulation, shallow affect), so I cover these issues briefly here, with the intent of finding potential inroads.

Motivation to Change

It has been frequently noted that psychopathic individuals are unlikely to perform well in psychotherapy because they are not particularly motivated to change. While this may be true to some extent, it does not necessarily mean that interventions would not be effective with children and adolescents. Also, if level of motivation to change were used as a reason for not proceeding with psychotherapy, mental health professionals would eliminate a good portion of psychotherapy cases, even though we now know such disorders (e.g., depression) may benefit from treatment in mental health clinics.

Fortunately, a wave of research has designed treatment to help motivate unmotivated clients, and it is possible that such treatments would also work for psychopathic youth. That being said, there could very well be something about psychopathic individuals' particular lack of motivation that is problematic for treatment. Until further evidence indicates that this particular lack of motivation is any worse than that in other disorders (including other DBDs, substance abuse disorders, etc.) there is no reason not to embark on, or offer, treatment. Instead, motivation needs to be tested, and innovative treatment studies should be designed to enhance motivation.

Deception and Manipulation

There is also concern that psychopathic individuals will deceive others, and that they are not likely to benefit from therapy because they just play along with the interventionist. It is possible that this will occur. But this likely occurs with other disorders, too, when patients feign improvement to impress therapists or family members, or to gain early release for restricted settings (e.g., inpatient units), or for a host of other reasons. The question is not whether this will occur with psychopathic youth, but rather how it might be treated. Better decision making is needed in high-risk situations when releasing patients, especially those who previously experienced symptoms, but if clinicians can learn to distinguish candid and honest reporting of symptoms from manipulation, they will be in a better position to treat and to make disposition recommendations for psychopathic youth. Note that there has also been speculation that treatment may teach psychopathic individuals the social and emotional skills that increase their likelihood of committing "successful" crime. This speculation is largely based on theory (Gough, 1971) and perhaps on the one study by Rice, Harris, and Cormier (1992). Whether social and emotional abilities actually increase or decrease with treatment is still unknown. More research is needed on this topic and a better understanding of psychopathy and deception in general in child populations is also needed (Salekin, Kubak, & Lee, 2008; Skeem et al., 2009).

Lack of Deep or Lasting Emotion

Another concern about the treatment of psychopathic individuals is that because they cannot form strong attachments to others, they are not able to do well in psychotherapy. Although some of the hallmark symptoms of psychopathy are lack of remorse and lack of empathy, there is not great deal of evidence about the stability of these characteristics at the individual and trait levels. In addition, there is little evidence that alterations in affective reactions cannot be made by individuals with psychopathic characteristics. However, research on emotion in psychopathic individuals requires much more attention to determine whether such youth completely lack emotion, or whether they are likely to have pockets of short-lived versus long-lived emotions, some other emotional capability, and so forth. Treatment might also help us to further understand the emotional functioning of the youth with psychopathic characteristics, by showing which areas can be built upon and which seem less likely to improve.

New Directions for the Science of Treatment of Psychopathy

The natural conclusion from this review is that we should be doing more to understand and potentially intervene with psychopathy, especially as it occurs in youth. Many researchers (e.g., Harris & Rice, 2006; Lösel, 1998; Salekin, 2002) have pointed out that the study designs need to be improved. Since these concerns have been outlined elsewhere, I do not cover them in great detail here. Rather, I suggest other areas that could be improved upon, which are more conceptual in nature. I provide some thoughts regarding new directions for research in this important area. I emphasize even more the need for theory and how successful programs will likely need to weave theory into program development if they are to advance research in this area.

Examining the previous reviews on the topic of psychopathy and treatment provides important information regarding future directions. There appear to be common themes in what previous researchers view as problematic in psychopathy treatment studies. First, there is the concern about how to define psychopathy. This problem has been noted by numerous scholars in the past (Blackburn, 1998a; Harris & Rice, 2006; Lösel, 1998; Salekin, 2002; Thorton & Blud, 2007). There has also been concern about what the appropriate outcome variables might be. Specifically, how do we know that a psychopathic individual got better? And, relatedly, there are concerns about the lack of treatment protocols specifically designed for psychopathy. Finally, there has been much concern about the methodological rigor of psychopathy treatment designs. Excluding the need for more rigorous research designs, perhaps most divergent views on these other issues are those of Salekin (2002) and Harris and Rice (2006).

Harris and Rice (2006) suggest that the PCL should be the only model used to assess psychopathy, and that the outcome to examine is recidivism. With respect to theory, they are less optimistic regarding treatment because of its evolutionary style. However, I would hope that future research be broader in scope, including an unrestrained mix of psychopathy definitions (e.g., Lynams's CPS; Patrick's triarchic model; Lilienfeld's eight-factor model) and many outcome variables. I use the next section to outline how this could be important for building theory in this area and, ultimately, for improving our understanding of the psychopathy–treatment relation.

Defining Psychopathy in the Upcoming Years

Previous research (Harris & Rice, 2006; Skeem et al., 2002) has criticized studies and reviews for using differing conceptualizations of psychopathy. At the same time, researchers have also contended that the PCL-R should not be the only measure used to examine psychopathy research questions (Harris & Rice, 2006; Skeem & Cooke, 2009). The best way to advance science in this area is to generate studies that assess the differing conceptions of psychopathy, and to examine how psychopathic youth might benefit from treatment. As mentioned earlier in this chapter, Cleckley's (1941) model of psychopathy was developed in the community, and Hare's (1991/2003) was developed in forensic populations. It will be important to examine the respective models' responsiveness to treatment. Moreover, recent models of psychopathy that branch out even further from more traditional models of psychopathy may require study to determine whether they are invariant with respect to intervention efforts. Heterogeneity regarding the concept of psychopathy can be helpful in examining what works (or does not work) with what type of psychopathic individual.

Evaluating Outcome in the Upcoming Years: Benefits from Using a Wider Net

In examining whether psychopathic individuals improve in therapy, it would be beneficial to look at a variety of outcomes. Mixing outcome variables has been viewed both positively and negatively in review papers and commentaries on the psychopathy treatment literature (Harris & Rice, 2006; Salekin, 2002). According to some, there is only one variable that matters in psychopathy treatment outcome studies—whether or not psychopathic individuals' experience recidivism (Harris & Rice, 2006; Wong & Hare, 2005). However, it could be argued that studying various outcome variables in youth could be important in furthering our understanding of the psychopathic personality and advancing treatment. There are numerous examples in the field in which using one outcome may be counterindicated. For instance, research on expressed emotion for patients with schizophrenia would not have resulted in interventions for patients if a return of psychotic symptoms were a marker for failure in a treatment program. Similarly, Marlatt (1987) would likely not have pursued relapse prevention research and treatment for substance abusers if he had held any subsequent substance use as a criterion for program failure. Beck (see Clark & Beck, 1990) would not have pursued the cognitive-behavioral theory of changing cognitions for depressed patients if recurrent depressed mood and suicidal ideation were markers of treatment failure. Few treatment programs would ever have advanced if recurrence of a problem were used as a marker for failure. Thus, a broad set of treatment outcome variables can be informative and advance intervention science.

To elaborate on this point, rearrest or recidivism, or even institutional infractions, are coarse indicators of improvement. Thus, a youth who begins to make friends at school, improve his or her grades, and have better relations with family members could be deemed a failure in therapy if he or she had one incident that brought him or her into contact with the law. Although recidivism is, without a doubt, a key outcome variable, other variables, such as job performance, interpersonal relationships, productive use of sports and hobbies, success in early romance, and other social factors, are also important. Moreover, they are likely to have a synergistic effect on each other, building competence in youth. At this point in research on child psychopathy, the question should be: What effect does psychotherapy have on any aspect of the condition? If other progress, beyond a reduction in contact with the law, is not noticed and built upon, then little in the way of protective factors will be discovered, few skills will be developed, and few life successes attained.

Finding Out What Works

A valid concern of past research in this area (a concern of the Salekin [2002] meta-analysis) is that meta-analytic researchers include studies of researchers who evaluate the therapy they like best, who pick clients, circumstances, and outcome measures that show therapy in the best light. Nonetheless, major differences among therapies can appear through this procedure, providing information about which methods may work better than others. For instance, as noted earlier, Salekin (2002) showed that therapeutic communities appear to be much less effective than dynamic and cognitive-behavioral paradigms with psychopathic individuals. Also, some basic classes of therapy seem to effectively reduce some aspects of psychopathy. So, why is this the case? The reason may be that at least some of the needed ingredients for change exist within the approaches previously used to treat psychopathic individuals.

Evidence for this might be reflected in more contemporary research. For instance, recent research that has focused on the promotion of conscience development (e.g., Kochanska, 1993) is salient. Kochanska (1995) has examined the importance of relationships between parents and youth in the development of conscience. Her term *reciprocal cooperation* and instruction of children about right and wrong may parallel what psychoanalytic therapists view as conscience development in working with parents and family members.

The other major class of therapy to have an effect was cognitive-behavioral therapy. Cognitive control could very well be key in containing and reducing antisocial behavior. Other important aspects of treatment gleaned from past studies include the importance of family members in the treatment process. Again, we know from past research that these factors do seem to increase the chances of improving client well-being.

It is likely that many current treatments for DBDs could also have some effect on psychopathic individuals. Well-known programs, including McMahon and Forehand's (2003) and Kazdin's (2009) suggestions for helping the noncompliant child, functional family therapy (Alexander & Parsons, 1973; Sexton & Alexander, 2003), the Incredible Years series (Webster-Stratton, 2001), and multisystemic therapy (Henggeler & Borduin, 1990; Henggeler, Schoenwald, Borduin, Rowland, & Cunningham, 1998), may have beneficial effects on psychopathic symptoms. Some of the ingredients in these programs, which have commonalities, may effect change in oppositionally defiant, conduct disordered, and perhaps even psychopathic youth. Although each therapy might be investigated to determine its relative effect on psychopathy, it will be ultimately informative to know which ingredients in common across programs are able to effect change in psychopathic youth. Smith and Glass (1977) referred to the use of *superclasses*—grouping therapies by their common ingredients—to determine impact on client well-being. By using a superclass approach, much more could be learned about how to treat psychopathy in youth (see also Weisz, Donenberg, Han, & Weiss, 1995; Weisz, Jensen-Doss, & Hawley, 2006; Weisz, Weiss, Han, Granger, & Morton, 1995).

In the event that therapies designed for specific DBDs (e.g., oppositional defiant disorder) do not work well for child psychopathy cases, more specific treatment programs will be needed to protect psychopathic individuals from themselves (academic failure, trouble with the law, substance abuse) and the community (aggression, offending). I now discuss how this could be done.

Specific Treatment Programs for Psychopathy: Providing Optimal Interventions

If treatments designed for disruptive youth are not optimal for psychopathic youth, then it will be important to tailor treatments specifically to this group. Intervention research specific to child psychopathy might draw on theory, including the conceptualization of how psychopathy starts out, how it is maintained, and how it ends or reappears for youth. Two foci of theory are particularly pertinent to the treatment question. First, researchers need to map out adequately the *theory of dysfunction,* which refers to the conceptual underpinnings and hypotheses about the likely factors leading to psychopathy in youth (brain anomalies, attachment difficulties, etc.) (Bowlby, 1969), the process involved, and how these processes emerge or operate. Although much work has been conducted in this area, researchers are still a long way from understanding the development of psychopathy in children and adolescents. Nonetheless, the focus is likely to be on various risk and protective factors, paths and trajectories, and how early development results in subsequent dysfunction (Kazdin, 1999, 2009; Salekin & Lochman, 2008). Models of development will likely be complex (Salekin, 2006); posing a single influence (i.e., construct) or mediator that leads to a single outcome is unlikely consistently to be the answer to how psychopathy develops.

Second, *theories of therapeutic change* for psychopathy in youth are needed, and these refer to the conceptual underpinnings of the process of change during treatment. The focus is on what therapy is designed to accomplish and through what means and processes.

Integration and Concluding Comments

The studies presented in this chapter are informative and offer a first step in showing that something works with psychopathic youth. However, the studies are also flawed in numerous ways. Past studies that used case study formats or quasi-experimental designs offer some important information regarding directions, and past research on treatment also may be interpreted as suggesting that change is possible. However, tightening up research methodology for a second generation of research in this area could be beneficial.

The field is likely in a much better position to design such studies on the treatment of psychopathy, and major classes of therapy could in fact be tested in controlled studies. Studies might focus on the current treatment programs to determine whether they can alleviate the symptoms of psychopathy in children and adolescents. These broad classes, as mentioned earlier, likely have had some success, although it is difficult to know what the therapists were doing, specifically, in each of the sessions to bring about change. Also, as mentioned, there are many different outcomes, and although this is a plus in research studies, the unilateral reduction of psychopathy symptoms ought to be the goal.

Notions of what progress is, exactly, in therapy need further consideration. Much like the lines that represent company earnings, there is not a steep and straight line indicating an increase or decrease in earnings but rather gradual rigid lines that represent a climb or reduction in earnings. So, too, is the process of growth or decline in human functioning that occurs in psychotherapy or when treatment is not undertaken by a given individual. Thus, a realistic goal for treating youth with psychopathic characteristics would not be to eradicate all symptoms at once, but rather to make gradual progress over the course of therapy, acknowledging that there will also be some bumps along the road.

Our research group has started to study the treatment of psychopathy in children and adolescents, and results thus far are promising. We hope other researchers might also be open to investigating psychopathy in generic conduct programs and other interventions that might help to reduce the problem behavior of psychopathic children and adolescents. We believe that some change is possible with this group, and that the focus, for now, should be on change. Key developmental differences may make children more available to treatment options (Rutter, 1989; Rutter et al., 1970), and such efforts to develop and advance treatment technology in this area should be pursued.

Notes

1. D'Silva and colleagues (2004) offered a rating system for the quality of the studies used in their meta-analyses. They noted why they rated each study as high or low in quality. The Rice and colleagues (1992) study was rated as highest in quality and carried some weight in their review. However, it should be noted that this study was a retrospective investigation involving a treatment that was not likely to have a positive intervening effect.
2. Harris and Rice (2006) questioned categorizing treatments as *cognitive-behavioral* because the term had not yet been invented. Our use of the term refers not to when it was invented but rather to what the treatment mostly characterized. Psychologists and psychiatrists used cognitive frameworks for many years prior to the formalization of the term. In fact, Alfred Adler is often credited with the founding of cognitive psychology.
3. CU for their study was tapping primarily affective traits.

References

Alexander, J. F., & Parsons, B. V. (1973). Short-term behavioral intervention with delinquent families: Impact on family process and recidivism. *Journal of Abnormal Psychology, 81*, 219–225.

American Psychiatric Association. (2000). *Diagnostic and statistical manual of mental disorders* (4th ed., text rev.). Washington, DC: Author.

Andershed, H., Kerr, M., Stattin, H., & Levander, S. (2002). Psychopathic traits in non-referred youths: A new assessment tool. In E. Blauuw & L. Sheridan (Eds.), *Psychopaths: Current international perspectives* (pp. 131–158). The Hague: Elsevier.

Benning, S. D., Patrick, C. J., Salekin, R. T., & Leistico, A. R. (2005). Convergent and discriminant validity of psychopathy factors assessed via self-report: A comparison of three instruments. *Assessment, 12*, 270–289.

Blackburn, R. (1993). *The psychology of criminal conduct*. Chichester, UK: Wiley.

Blackburn, R. (1998a). Psychopathy and the contribution of personality to violence. In T. Millon, E. Simonsen, M. Birket-Smith, & R. D. Davis (Eds.), *Psychopathy: Antisocial, criminal, and violent behavior* (pp. 50–68). New York: Guilford Press.

Blackburn, R. (1998b). Psychopathy and personality disorder: Implications of interpersonal theory. In D. J. Cooke, A. E. Forth, & R. D. Hare (Eds.), *Psychopathy: Theory, research, and implications for society* (pp. 269–302). Dordrecht: Kluwer.

Bowlby, J. (1969). *Attachment and loss: Vol. 1. Attachment* (2nd ed.). New York: Basic Books.

Brandt, J. R., Kennedy, W. A., Patrick, C. J., & Curtin, J. (1997). Assessment of psychopathy in a population of incarcerated adolescent offenders. *Psychological Assessment, 9*, 429–435.

Caldwell, M. F., McCormick, D. J., Umstead, D., & Van Rybroek, G. J. (2007). Evidence of treatment progress and therapeutic outcomes among adolescents with psychopathic features. *Criminal Justice and Behavior, 34*, 573–587.

Caldwell, M., Skeem, J. L., Salekin, R. T., & Van Rybroek, G. (2006). Treatment response of adolescent offenders with psychopathy features: A 2-year follow-up. *Criminal Justice and Behavior, 33*, 571–596.

Caldwell, M. F., & Van Rybroek, G. J. (2001). Efficacy of a decompression treatment model in the clinical management of violent juvenile offenders. *International Journal of Offender Therapy and Comparative Criminology, 45*, 469–477.

Catchpole, R. E. H. (2003). *Psychopathy and recidivism following treatment among previously violent youth*. Unpublished thesis, Simon Fraser University, Burnaby, BC.

Clark, D. A., & Beck, A. T. (1990). Cognitive therapy of anxiety and depression. In R. E. Ingram (Ed.), *Contemporary psychological approaches to depression: Theory, research, and treatment* (pp. 155–167). New York: Plenum Press.

Cleckley, H. (1941). *The mask of sanity*. St Louis, MO: Mosby.

Cloninger, C. R. (1978). The antisocial personality. *Hospital Practice, 13*, 97–106.

D'Silva, K., Duggan, C., & McCarthy, L. (2004). Does treatment really make psychopaths worse?: A review of the evidence. *Journal of Personality Disorders, 18*, 163–177.

Ellis, A. (1961). The treatment of a psychopath with rational psychotherapy. *Journal of Psychology, 51*, 141–150.

Falkenbach, D., Poythress, N., & Heide, K. (2003). Psychopathic features in a juvenile diversion population: Reliability and predictive validity of two self-report measures. *Behavioral Sciences and the Law, 21,* 787–805.

Forth, A. E., Hart, S. D., & Hare, R. D. (1990). Assessment of psychopathy in male young offenders. *Psychological Assessment, 2,* 342–344.

Forth, A. E., Kosson, D., & Hare, R. D. (2003). *Psychopathy Checklist: Youth Version.* Toronto: Multi-Health Systems.

Goodman, R. (1997). The Strengths and Difficulties Questionnaire: A research note. *Journal of Child Psychology and Psychiatry, 38,* 581–586.

Gough, H. G. (1971). Scoring high on an index of social maturity. *Journal of Abnormal Psychology, 77,* 236–241.

Gretton, H., McBride, M., Hare, R. D., & O'Shaughnessy, R. (2000, November). *The developmental course of offending in adolescent sex offenders: A ten-year follow-up study.* Paper presented at the Association for the Treatment of Sexual Abusers, San Diego, CA.

Gretton, H. M., McBride, M., Hare, R. D., O'Shaughnessy, R., & Kumka, G. (2001). Psychopathy and recidivism in adolescent sex offenders. *Criminal Justice and Behavior, 28,* 427–449.

Hare, R. D. (1970). *Psychopathy: Theory and research.* New York: Wiley.

Hare, R. D. (2003). *Manual for the revised Psychopathy Checklist.* Toronto: Multi-Health Systems. (Original work published 1991)

Harris, G. T., & Rice, M. E. (2006). Treatment of psychopathy: A review of empirical findings. In C. J. Patrick (Eds.), *Handbook of psychopathy* (pp. 555–572). New York: Guilford Press.

Hawes, D. J., & Dadds, M. R. (2005). The treatment of conduct problems in children with callous–unemotional traits. *Journal of Consulting and Clinical Psychology, 73,* 737–741.

Hawes, D. J., & Dadds, M. R. (2007). Stability and malleability of callous–unemotional traits during treatment for childhood conduct problems. *Journal of Clinical Child and Adolescent Psychology, 36,* 347–355.

Henggeler, S. W., & Borduin, C. M. (1990). *Family therapy and beyond: A multisystemic approach to treating the behavior problems of children and adolescents.* Pacific Grove, CA: Brooks/Cole.

Ingram, G. L., Gerard, R. E., Quay, H. C., & Levison, R. B. (1970). An experimental program for the psychopathic delinquent: Looking in the "correctional wastebasket." *Journal of Research in Crime and Delinquency, 7,* 24–30.

Intrator, J., Hare, R. D., Stritzke, P., Brichstwein, K., Dorfman, D., Harpur, T., et al. (1997). A brain imaging (SPECT) study of semantic and affective processing in psychopaths. *Biological Psychiatry, 42,* 96–103.

Kazdin, A. E. (1999). Current (lack of) status of theory in child and adolescent psychotherapy research. *Journal of Clinical Child Psychology, 28,* 533–543

Kazdin, A. E. (2009). *The Kasdin method for parenting the defiant child.* New York: Houghton Mifflin.

Kiehl, K. A., Hare, R. D., Liddle, P. F., & McDonald, J. J. (1999). Reduced P300 responses in criminal psychopaths during a visual oddball task. *Biological Psychiatry, 45,* 1498–1507.

Kochanska, G. (1993). Toward a synthesis of parental socialization and child temperament in early development of conscience. *Child Development, 64,* 325–347.

Kochanska, G. (1995). Children's temperament, mothers' discipline, and security of attachment: Multiple pathways to emerging internalization. *Child Development, 66,* 597–615.

Kristiansson, M. (1995). Incurable psychopaths? *Bulletin of the American Academy of Psychiatry and the Law, 23,* 555–562.

Kubak, F. A., & Salekin, R. T. (2009). Psychopathy and anxiety in children and adolescents: New insights and developmental pathways to offending. *Journal of Psychopathology and Behavioral Assessment, 31,* 271–284.

Larsson, H., Andershed, H., & Lichtenstein, P. (2006). A genetic factor explains most of the variation in the psychopathic personality. *Journal of Abnormal Psychology, 115,* 221–230.

Lee, Z., Salekin, R. T., & Iselin, A. R. (2010). Psychopathic traits in youth: Is there evidence for primary and secondary subtypes? *Journal of Abnormal Child Psychology, 38,* 381–393.

Lilienfeld, S. O., & Andrews, B. P. (1996). Development and preliminary validation of a self-report measure of psychopathic personality traits in noncriminal population. *Journal of Personality Assessment, 66,* 488–524.

Lösel, F. (1998). Treatment and management of psychopaths. In D. J. Cooke, A. E. Forth, & R. D. Hare (Eds.), *Psychopathy: Theory, research, and implications for society* (pp. 303–354). Dordrecht: Kluwer.

Lykken, D. T. (1995). *The antisocial personalities.* Hillsdale, NJ: Erlbaum.

Lynam, D. R. (1997). Pursuing the psychopath: Capturing the fledgling psychopath in a nomological net. *Journal of Abnormal Psychology, 106,* 425–438.

Marlatt, G. A. (1987). Alcohol, the magic elixir: Stress, expectancy, and the transformation of emotional states. In E. Gottheil, K. A. Druly, S. Pashko, & S. P. Weinstein (Eds.), *Stress and addiction* (pp. 302–322). New York: Brunner/Mazel.

McMahon, R. J., & Forehand, R. L. (2003). *Helping the noncompliant child: Family-based treatment for oppositional behavior* (2nd ed.). New York: Guilford Press.

Murdock-Hicks, M., Rogers, R., & Cashel, M. L. (2000). Predictions of violent and total infractions among institutionalized male juvenile offenders. *Journal of the American Academy of Psychiatry and Law, 28,* 183–190.

Murrie, D. C., Marcus, D. K., Douglas, K. S., Salekin, R. T., Lee, Z., & Vincent, G. (2007). Youth with psychopathy features are not a discrete class: A taxometric analysis. *Journal of Child Psychology and Psychiatry, 48,* 714–723.

Newman, J. P., Curtin, J. J., Bertsch, J. D., & Baskin-Sommers, A. R. (in press). Attention moderates the fearlessness of psychopathic offenders. *Biological Psychiatry.*

O'Neill, M. L., Lidz, V., & Heilbrun, K. (2003). Adolescents with psychopathic characteristics in a substance abusing cohort: Treatment process and outcomes. *Law and Human Behavior, 27,* 299–313.

Patrick, C. J., Curtin, J., & Tellegen, A. (2002). Development and validation of a brief form of the Multidimensional Personality Questionnaire. *Psychological Assessment, 14*, 150–163.

Rice, M. E., Harris, G. T., & Cormier, C. (1992). Evaluation of a maximum security therapeutic community for psychopaths and other mentally disordered offenders. *Law and Human Behavior, 16*, 399–412.

Robins, L. N. (1966). *Deviant children grown up: A sociological and psychiatric study of sociopathic personality.* Baltimore: Williams & Wilkins.

Rogers, R., Jackson, R. L., Sewell, K. W., & Johansen, J. (2004). Predictors of treatment outcome in dually diagnosed antisocial youth: An initial study of forensic inpatients. *Behavioral Sciences and the Law, 22*, 215–222.

Rogers, R., Johansen, J., Chang, J. J., & Salekin, R. T. (1997). Predictors of adolescent psychopathy: Oppositional and conduct-disordered symptoms. *Journal of the American Academy of Psychiatry and the Law, 25*, 261–271.

Rutter, M. (1989). Pathways from childhood to adult life. *Journal of Child Psychology and Psychiatry, 30*, 23–51.

Rutter, M., Tizard, J., & Whitmore, K. (Eds.). (1987). *Education, health, and behavior: Psychological and medical study of childhood development.* New York: Wiley.

Salekin, R. T. (2002). Psychopathy and therapeutic pessimism: Clinical lore or clinical reality? *Clinical Psychology Review, 22*, 79–112.

Salekin, R. T. (2006). Psychopathy in children and adolescents: Key issues in conceptualization and assessment. In C. J. Patrick (Ed.), *Handbook of psychopathy* (pp. 389–414). New York: Guilford Press.

Salekin, R. T. (2008). Psychopathy and recidivism from mid-adolescence to young adulthood: Cumulating legal problems and limiting life opportunities. *Journal of Abnormal Psychology, 117*, 386–395.

Salekin, R. T., Brannen, D., Zalot, A., Leistico, A. R., & Neumann, C. S. (2006). Factor structure of psychopathy in youth: Testing the applicability of the new four-factor model. *Criminal Justice and Behavior, 33*, 135–157.

Salekin, R. T., & Frick, P. J. (2005). Child and adolescent psychopathy: The need for a developmental perspective. *Journal of Abnormal Child Psychology, 33*, 403–409.

Salekin, R. T., Kubak, F. A., & Lee, Z. (2008). Deception in children and adolescents. In R. Rogers (Ed.), *Clinical assessment of malingering and deception* (3rd ed., pp. 343–364). New York: Guilford Press.

Salekin, R. T., & Leistico, A. R., Tobst, K. K., Schrum, C. L., & Lochman, J. E. (2005). Adolescent psychopathy and personality—the interpersonal circumplex: Expanding evidence of a nomological net. *Journal of Abnormal Child Psychology, 33*, 445–460.

Salekin, R. T., & Lochman, J. E. (2008). Child and adolescent psychopathy: The search for protective factors. *Criminal Justice and Behavior, 35*, 159–172.

Salekin, R. T., Neumann, C. S., Leistico, A. M., DiCicco, T. M., & Duros, R. L. (2004). Psychopathy and comorbidity in a young offender sample: Taking a closer look at psychopathy's potential importance over disruptive behavior disorders. *Journal of Abnormal Psychology, 113*, 416–427.

Salekin, R. T., Neumann, C. S., Leistico, A. R., & Zalot, A. A. (2004). Psychopathy in youth and intelligence: An investigation of Cleckley's hypothesis. *Journal of Clinical Child and Adolescent Psychology, 33,* 731–742.

Salekin, R. T., Rogers, R., & Sewell, K. W. (1996). A review and meta-analysis of the Psychopathy Checklist and Psychopathy Checklist—Revised. *Clinical Psychology: Science and Practice, 3,* 203–215.

Salekin, R. T., Rosenbaum, J., & Lee, Z. (2009). Psychopathy in children and adolescents: Stability and change. *Psychology, Psychiatry and Law, 15,* 224–236.

Salekin, R. T., Rosenbaum, J., Lee, Z., & Lester, W. S. (2009). Child and adolescent psychopathy: Like a painting by Monet. *Youth Violence and Juvenile Justice, 7,* 239–255.

Sexton, T. L., & Alexander, J. F. (2003). Functional family therapy: A mature model for working with at-risk adolescents and their families. In T. L. Sexton, G. R. Weeks, & M. S. Robbins (Eds.), *Handbook of family therapy: The science and practice of working with families and couples* (pp. 323–350). New York: Brunner/Routledge.

Skeem, J. L., Monahan, J., & Mulvey, E. P. (2002). Psychopathy, treatment involvement, and subsequent violence among civil psychiatric patients. *Law and Human Behavior, 26,* 577–603.

Skeem, J. L., Polaschek, D. L. L., & Manchak, S. (2009). Appropriate treatment works, but how?: Rehabilitating general, psychopathic, and high-risk offenders. In J. L. Skeem, K. S. Douglas, & S. O. Lilienfeld (Eds.), *Psychological science in the courtroom: Consensus and controversy* (pp. 358–384). New York: Guilford Press.

Smith, M. L., & Glass, G. V. (1979). Meta-analysis of psychotherapy outcome studies. *American Psychologist, 32,* 752–760.

Spain, S. E., Douglas, K. S., Poythress, N. G., & Epstein, M. K. (2004). The relationship between psychopathy, violence, and treatment outcome: A comparison of three youth psychopathy measures. *Behavioral Sciences and the Law, 22,* 85–102.

Stafford, E., & Cornell, D. G. (2003). Psychopathy scores predict adolescent inpatient aggression. *Assessment, 10,* 102–112.

Suedfeld, P., & Landon, P. B. (1978). Approaches to treatment. In R. D. Hare & D. Schalling (Eds.), *Psychopathic behavior: Approaches to research* (pp. 347–378). New York: Wiley.

Tennent, G., Tennent, D., Prins, H., & Bedford, A. (1993). Is psychopathic disorder a treatable condition? *Medicine, Science and the Law, 33,* 63–66.

Thornton, D., & Blud, L. (2007). The influence of psychopathic traits on response to treatment. In H. Herve & J. C. Yuille (Eds.), *The psychopath: Theory, research, and practice* (pp. 505–539). Mahwah, NJ: Erlbaum.

Vaillant, G. E. (1975). Sociopathy as a human process: A viewpoint. *Archives of General Psychiatry, 32,* 178–183.

Waldman, I. D., & Rhee, S. H. (2006). Genetic and environmental influences on psychopathy and antisocial behavior. In C. J. Patrick (Ed.), *Handbook of psychopathy* (pp. 205–228). New York: Guilford Press.

Webster-Stratton, C. (2001). The Incredible Years: Parents, teachers, and children training series. *Residential Treatment for Children and Youth, 18,* 31–45.

Weisz, J. R., Donenberg, G. R., Han, S. S., & Weiss, B. (1995). Bridging the gap between lab and clinic in child and adolescent psychotherapy. *Journal of Consulting and Clinical Psychology, 63*, 688–701.

Weisz, J. R., Jensen-Doss, A., & Hawley, K. M. (2006). Evidence-based youth psychotherapies versus usual clinical care: A meta-analysis of direct comparisons. *American Psychologist, 61*, 671–689.

Weisz, J. R., Weiss, B., Han, S. S., Granger, D. A., & Morton, T. (1995). Effects of psychotherapy with children and adolescents revisited: A meta-analysis of treatment outcome studies. *Psychological Bulletin, 117*, 450–468.

Williams, K. M., Paulhus, D. L., & Hare, R. D. (2007). Capturing the four-factor structure of psychopathy in college students via self-report. *Journal of Personality Assessment, 88*, 205–219.

Wong, S., & Hare, R. D. (2005). *Guidelines for a psychopathy treatment program.* Toronto: Multi-Health Systems.

Wong, S. C. P., & Burt, G. (2007). The heterogeneity of incarcerated psychopaths: Differences in risk, need, recidivism, and management approaches. In H. Hervé & J. C. Yuille (Eds.), *Psychopath: Theory, research, and practice* (pp. 461–484). Mahwah, NJ: Erlbaum.

15

Forensic Issues for Child and Adolescent Psychopathy

MICHAEL J. VITACCO
RANDALL T. SALEKIN
RICHARD ROGERS

Programmatic research with adults has established psychopathy as a critical construct in areas of violence prediction, and risk assessment and management (Vitacco & Neumann, 2008). Psychopathy's application to issues involving child and adolescent forensic psychology is significantly less well established. Many salient questions as to how best to utilize this construct in forensic applications with youth remain unanswered. Of course, some scholars have suggested that the construct should never be applied to youth. However, it has become apparent that the downward extension of psychopathy to adolescents has generated significant research on which forensic clinicians can draw in their forensic practices.

Psychopathy's relevance to forensic assessment lies in its usefulness for the prediction of violent and other negative outcomes, and its possible incremental validity over traditional DSM diagnoses in predicting antisocial behavior and violence in adolescents (Salekin, Leistico, Neumann, DiCicco, & Duros, 2004). This starting point provides the foundation for this chapter on forensic issues related to adolescent psychopathy.

This chapter does not advocate for the broad-based application of psychopathy assessment for the majority of child or adolescent forensic evaluations (*Miranda* rights, competency to stand trial, or an insanity defense) (Grisso, 1998). Instead, our goal is to provide a review of theoretical issues and empirical studies that can inform the clinician conducting forensic evaluations in which risk is a concern with children and adolescents. We posit that the evaluation of psychopathy in youth may be able to provide salient information in circumscribed situations (Forth & Book, Chapter 11, this volume). Forensic evaluators can use the knowledge gained from psychopathy assessments to impart specialized knowledge concerning risk and treatment needs that can be used to assist in the decision-making process. With this framework, the aims of this chapter are relatively straightforward:

- Review issues in developmental psychopathology that should influence the manner in which psychopathic traits are assessed in youth.
- Explain psychopathy assessment concerning issues related to risk assessment, treatment planning, and their potential impact on informing juvenile justice decisions.
- Review modalities to assess adolescent psychopathy and their potential utility in forensic assessment.
- Discuss issues related to report writing and diagnostic labeling associated with youth psychopathy.
- Provide a set of recommendations after each section that forensic evaluators can integrate into their clinical practices.

Developmental Issues and Psychopathy: Implications for Forensic Assessment

In assessing psychopathic traits in adolescents, forensic clinicians must be cognizant of developmental issues that influence the expression of psychopathy in youth. These developmental issues are relevant to understanding most childhood disorders, yet they are of particular importance in assessing psychopathy. Seagrave and Grisso (2002) cogently observed the importance of developmental issues in the initiation and continued expression of psychopathic traits. Primarily, we deem it to be of the utmost importance that forensic evaluators recognize the potential for change in psychopathy and antisocial behavior in even the most seemingly intractable antisocial adolescent (Moffitt, 1993; Salekin & Lochman, 2008). Failure to consider developmental issues when assessing psychopathy leads to a greater likelihood of committing serious and substantial errors. Our concern is that clinicians will place too much importance on a single psychopathy "score" at one point in time. Recognizing the malleability of psychopathy scores in youth (Andershed, Chapter 10, this volume) will place the forensic clinician in a better position to conduct appropriate and ethical assessments, and make appropriate treatment recommendations. A review of the concepts of discontinuity and heterotypic continuity can assist the forensic clinician in developing a more complete understanding of psychopathy and tempering expectations of what psychopathic traits can offer in evaluating youth (Forth & Book, Chapter 11, this volume; Vincent & Grisso, 2005; Vitacco & Vincent, 2006).

Discontinuity allows for the possibility that once a disorder is expressed in childhood or adolescence, it is subject to a great deal of change, including complete remission. Discontinuity is perhaps especially likely in early expressions of psychopathology. As noted by Vitacco and Vincent (2006), discontinuity manifests itself in two specific ways. *Equifinality* refers to the fact that several pathways that can lead to the expression of the disorder. One need only consider research demonstrating developmental links between psychopathic traits and genetics (Larsson, Andershed, & Lichtenstein, 2006; Viding & Larrson, Chapter 5, this volume), abuse (Poythress, Skeem, & Lilienfeld, 2006), disturbances in parenting (Fite, Greening, & Stoppelbein, 2008), and stress and sex hormones (Ellis, 1991; Cima, Smeets, & Jelicic, 2008) to realize the many developmental factors that might influence the etiology and expression of psychopathy. *Multifinality* refers to the notion that the same pathways or experiences can lead to dramatically different expressions or behavior. A prime example is the case of resilience. For instance, some individuals who have experienced stressful and catastrophic situations come away relatively unscathed. The National Survey of Child and Adolescent Well-Being (NSCAW), a large-scale study on multiple facets of behavior, has found that many children and adolescents with significant abuse histories do not engage in antisocial behaviors. However, we know from other research that abuse is associated with the expression of psychopathic behaviors in youth.

The *heterotypic continuity* concept is consistent with the idea that the expression of any childhood disorder, including psychopathic traits, can change midstream. One must consider that the early expression of psychopathy may be associated with other pathology at a later time (Sevecke & Kosson, Chapter 12, this volume; Salekin et al., 2004). In contrast, *homotypic continuity* refers to a correlation between a disorder at a specific time and the expression of the same traits or symptoms at a later point. Both of these factors warrant consideration when evaluating psychopathic traits in youth. On the one hand, it has been speculated that many children will appear less psychopathic through the process of development (Seagrave & Grisso, 2002); however, there is also some stability to psychopathy (Andershed, Chapter 10, this volume), and a portion of youth may continue to show dysfunction into adulthood and engage in antisocial conduct (Forth & Book, Chapter 11, this volume; Loney, Taylor, Butler, & Iacono, 2007; Rutter & Sroufe, 2000; Salekin, 2008). What is apparent is that the stability of psychopathy is generally consistent with other personality constructs measured in childhood and followed longitudinally (Shiner, 2000). Likewise, in a review of studies focusing on antisocial girls, Pajer (1998) noted that heterotypic and homotypic continuities are factors warranting consideration when developing an understanding of female antisociality. We posit that these factors are relevant to understanding the development of psychopathy in both males and females.

The assessment of psychopathic traits in youth is complicated by developmental issues. Forensic evaluators must be guided by the fact that the children or adolescents in front of them may appear different in a few short years. As such, clinicians should refrain from basing long-term predictions of violence risk on any single psychopathy score. How do we define *long term*? Although forensic evaluators are likely to differ on this key terminology, one option would be to define *short term* as less than 6 months and *long term* as exceeding 12 months.

Forensic evaluators should be guided by developmental considerations in their assessment that include the following:

1. A careful review of potential etiological factors.
2. Detailed documentation regarding the expression of the psychopathic traits from their onset to the current time.
3. A systematic review of potential protective factors that may serve to decrease the expressions of psychopathy over time.

Measurement Issues

Several years ago, an article or book section on adolescent psychopathy and measurement issues would either have been incredibly short or potentially unnecessary. However, that is no longer the case because even a cursory review of the literature reveals that forensic evaluators have several available measures that purport to capture the construct of youth psychopathy (see Kotler & McMahon, Chapter 4, this volume). Highlighting the example of this recent increase can be seen in Vaughn and Howard (2005), who have reviewed self-report measures used to assess psychopathic traits in adolescence. Their review yielded 30 articles focusing on nine separate measures. In the last 3 years, the large number of published research studies would have substantially increased that initial number. Theoretically, measurement of adolescent psychopathy plays a major role in defining the field and setting directions for future research (Farrington, 2005; Johnstone & Cooke, 2004; Salekin & Lynam, Chapter 1, this volume). For the forensic clinician, the reliability and validity of a measure ensures that it is appropriate for use and presentation to the court. Within the space confines of a single book chapter, we cannot discuss all measures in circulation. However, we wish to point out that four measures, one structured interview and three self-reports, have generated substantial research: Psychopathy Checklist: Youth Version (PCL:YV; Forth, Kosson, & Hare, 2003) Antisocial Process Screening Device (APSD; Frick & Hare, 2001), modified Childhood Psychopathy Scale (mCPS; Lynam, 1997), and the Youth Psychopathic Trait Inventory (YPI; Andershed, Kerr, Stattin, & Levander, 2002).

Prior to using any measure in clinical practice, forensic evaluators must review and consider the psychometric properties and ensure that the measure is relevant to the nature and purpose of the evaluation. Clinicians who decide to assess for psychopathy in forensic settings must be aware of the measure's literature base, as well as its strengths and limitations. Moreover, a clinician must be prepared to discuss the limitations of the assessment, both in the report and during direct and cross examination. We strongly recommend that clinicians readily acknowledge both the controversy of the psychopathy construct applied to youth and its inherent limitations.

Forensic Assessment

As we have previously stated, psychopathy will not necessarily assist the trier of fact in many forensic issues involving children and adolescents. However, psychopathy may have a circumscribed role in select forensic cases where risk or deception/manipulation is a concern. In this section, we consider whether psychopathy may add needed information to forensic evaluations. Specifically, we discuss psychopathy's role in the following issues involving adolescents: (1) risk assessments in which the aim is to predict negative outcomes, such as recidivism and violence; (2) transfer decisions in which an adolescent is under consideration for transfer to adult court; and (3) provision of information concerning treatment goals to administrators and therapists in the juvenile justice system. This information can assist in balancing issues such as protecting society and deciding on appropriate treatment and treatment settings for youth, as well as allocating limited resources. We present data suggesting that treatment provides an opportunity for long-term change, and psychopathy assessments may be useful in identifying at-risk adolescents most in need of intensive mental health treatment.

Psychopathy and Risk for Violence Assessment

A key aspect of many forensic practitioners' practices is the prediction of antisocial behavior and violence. Increasingly, forensic evaluators are being called upon to predict whether an adolescent is likely to engage in antisocial behavior or violence (Borum & Verhaagen, 2006; Conroy & Murrie, 2007) and what, if any, interventions would likely reduce that risk. The use of psychopathy to inform such decisions relative to risk is not without controversy. Some scholars have advocated for the abolition of psychopathy and its application to youth. In fact, an entire chapter would be needed to elucidate this argument and its counterargument. However, psychopathy has emerged as a relatively good predictor of antisocial outcomes and violence in youth (Forth & Book, Chapter 11, this volume; Leistico, Salekin, DeCoster, & Rogers, 2008; Vincent, 2006). This section of the chapter focuses on four issues germane to the forensic evaluator's use of psychopathy in evaluation of risk for antisocial behavior or violence assessment. First, we review the evidence that youth psychopathy is a moderate predictor of general and violent recidivism in youth. Second, we review the relationship between psychopathy and inpatient violence, which is a critical concern for clinicians working within the confines of juvenile correctional facilities or secure hospitals. Third, we discuss research linking psychopathy to instrumental aggression (Fontaine, 2007). Finally, we discuss research on the application of psychopathy to adolescent females, specifically noting how available research limits the generalizability of psychopathy to this understudied group.

In conducting risk assessments with youth, a key question centers on the incremental validity of adding a measure of psychopathy. This question is especially salient due to recent advances in the field of violence risk assessment, which has included the development of a number of specialized instruments to assess youth violence (see Borum & Verhaagen, 2006). As such, the assessment of psychopathy should be considered part of a risk evaluation that can inform the clinician about certain personality and behavioral characteristics of the adolescent. However, psychopathy should never be used in isolation or in lieu of comprehensive assessment of risk. To that end, several available measures that assess both dynamic and static risk factors in youth can be used in combination with psychopathy.

Another consideration is that the relationship between youth psychopathy and subsequent aggression is not as robust as once thought. As noted by Edens, Skeem, Cruise, and Cauffman (2001) there are "moderate associations" (p. 53) between measures of youth psychopathy and violence. Given this finding, it is salient that forensic evaluators do not inflate the meaning of a psychopathy score. We review findings relevant to psychopathy and risk assessment, and conclude the section with several recommendations for the appropriate use of psychopathy measurement in the assessment and prediction of youth violence.

Psychopathic Traits and Violence

A review of extant research clearly shows a relationship between PCL:YV/modified PCL scores and youth antisocial behavior and violence (see Leistico et al., 2008). In an early study, Forth, Hart, and Hare (1990) employed a modified, 18-item Psychopathy Checklist—Revised (PCL-R) in a sample of young male offenders (mean age = 16.3) placed in a maximum security facility. Although this study predated the creation of the PCL:YV, the authors were encouraged by the psychometric properties of the PCL-R in this sample of youthful offenders and its significant correlation ($r = .26$) with subsequent charges and convictions for violence.[1] Likewise, Brandt, Kennedy, Patrick, and Curtin (1997) used a modified PCL-R with 130 male delinquents, ranging in age from 14 to 18. Higher scores on the PCL-R were associated with quicker arrest for violent offenses. Both personality and behavior factors demonstrated incremental validity in the prediction of violence.

The development and introduction of the PCL:YV has moved the field away from modified versions of the adult instrument to a measure designed specifically for youth. Murrie, Cornell, Kaplan, McConville, and Levy-Elkon (2004) looked at the PCL:YV, along with other measures of adolescent psychopathy, in demonstrating that the PCL:YV (minus three items measuring antisocial behavior) was positively associated with history of violence and institutional aggression. Notably, the PCL:YV was more associated with violent behavior than either the APSD or a scale of the Millon Adolescent Clinical Inventory (Millon, 1993).

Beyond cross-sectional comparisons, several studies have recently begun evaluating the longitudinal power of the PCL:YV to predict violence and other antisocial behavior. Corrado, Vincent, Hart, and Cohen (2004) followed 182 male adolescent offenders for an average of 14.5 months postrelease. The PCL:YV was a significant predictor of both overall and violent recidivism. Items measuring behavioral dysfunction accounted for a greater amount of the variance associated with recidivism predictions. Another key finding was that adolescents with higher PCL:YV scores demonstrated a tendency to commit offenses quicker after release. Penney and Moretti (2007) found that PCL:YV scores predicted aggression in high-risk boys and girls. The research indicated that both affective and behavioral features of psychopathy were related to predictions of aggressive behavior. In a study of 157 boys, Gretton, Hare, and Catchpole (2004) scored PCL:YVs with a file review and evaluated criminal behavior over a 10-year period. Results indicated that total PCL:YV scores were associated with violent recidivism and provided incremental validity over age of onset of criminal behavior, diagnosis of conduct disorder, and history of violent and nonviolent offending.

Edens and Cahill (2007) assessed 75 males with the PCL:YV. Their results indicated that neither total nor factor scores of the PCL:YV were related to general or violent recidivism. Edens and Cahill attributed the nonsignificant findings partially to the diverse ethnicity of the sample. A potential problem with this study was the very small sample, and youth were not assessed for rearrest across an important time span (from adolescent to adulthood). In contrast, a meta-analysis that included 21 nonoverlapping studies found psychopathy to significantly predict general and violent recidivism (Edens, Campbell, & Weir, 2007; see also Leistico et al., 2008).

Salekin (2008) conducted a sophisticated study of adolescent psychopathy and its potential for incremental validity in light of 14 variables with theoretical and empirical links to antisocial behavior. The PCL:YV and a modified version of the Self-Report Psychopathy Scale–II (SRP-II-Mod) showed a small (3% of the variance) but significant incremental increase after these variables were considered. The Antisocial scale from the Personality Assessment Inventory (PAI-ANT; Morey, 1991) was the strongest predictor of general offending, accounting for 6% of the total variance. However, this study showed that psychopathy, as a concept, whether indexed by self-report or clinician interview, appeared to have predictive merit.

Another possibility that warrants consideration is the usefulness of self-report instruments for assessing the potential for violence in young offenders. Self-report instruments are gaining some support in the field of psychopathy (Lilienfeld & Fowler, 2006). In predicting violence in youth, self-report measures have shown some utility. Spain, Douglas, Poythress, and Epstein (2004) found both the APSD and mCPS to be more predictive of institutional aggression and treatment progress than the PCL:YV. However, in a study of justice system–involved youth, Boccaccini and colleagues (2007) found mixed results for the APSD and mCPS in 477 individuals from multiple settings. These authors were not convinced that self-report assessment of psychopathy provided the most predictive validity (see also Murrie et al., 2004). More recently, Douglas, Epstein, and Poythress (2008) found that the CPS and APSD were predictive of recidivism in a sample of 83 adolescent offenders followed over an average of 874 days, whereas the PCL was not. However, the significance of the psychopathy measures disappeared when other variables (e.g., substance abuse, conduct disorder) were employed as covariates.

A factor in the use of self-report instruments in the measurement of psychopathy is their transparency. Rogers and colleagues (2002) found that adolescents were able to alter their psychopathy scores significantly based on their desired outcome. Understanding the strengths and limitations of self-report tests is essential. For the clinician, one possibility is to assess psychopathy through various modalities (e.g., structured interview and self-report) in an attempt to obtain the most complete and accurate information.

A final concern relates to cutoff scores and psychopathy. As noted in the opening paragraphs of this chapter, psychopathy is often considered to have incremental power over antisocial personality disorder in the prediction of antisocial and violent behavior. Rogers, an author of this chapter and psychopathy researcher, recently questioned whether this long-held belief was proven. Rogers, Jordan, and Harrison (2007) questioned whether psychopathy actually has incremental power, or is it simply a matter of cutoff scores? Consider for the moment the disparity in cutoff scores: PCL-based measures, including the PCL:YV, impose a stringent 75% criterion (i.e., ≥ 30 of 40 points) for a cutoff score, whereas DSM-IV adult symptoms offer a comparatively lax 43% criterion (i.e., ≥ 3 of 7 symptoms). Even more dramatic are comparisons of PCL-based measures with their 75% criterion to the very lax 20% criterion (i.e., ≥ 3 of 15 symptoms) for conduct disorder (CD). The crucial and unaddressed issue is whether psychopathy has any incremental power when considered on a level playing field (e.g., 75% for PCL:YV vs. 75% for CD). Again, researchers should consider these issues in their work, and evaluators must be mindful of this in clinical practice. Specifically, this might mean that psychopathy is comparable in predicting antisocial outcomes, but perhaps not better at this task.

Institutional Violence

The issue of institutional violence is especially relevant to clinicians who work with incarcerated or hospitalized antisocial adolescents on a regular basis and may be personally subjected to their violence. Whether psychopathy is an effective predictor of institutional violence remains an open question. Hicks, Rogers, and Cashel (2000) used the Psychopathy Checklist: Screening Version (PCL:SV; Hart, Cox, & Hare, 1996) to evaluate 120 juvenile male offenders in a maximum-security institution. After a 6-month follow-up, it was determined that the PCL:SV accounted for a small and nonsignificant amount of the overall variance associated with institutional infractions. Notably, select scales from the Minnesota Multiphasic Personality Inventory for Adolescents (see Butcher & Williams, 2000) were better predictors of institutional infractions. Stafford and Cornell (2003), using a modified PCL-R, found that psychopathy was a significant predictor of violence in 72 adolescents placed in a mental health hospital. Psychopathy provided incremental validity over clinical diagnoses and scores from other self-report inventories.

Since the early research, a great deal more has been accomplished in regard to the relationship between psychopathic traits and inpatient violence. A meta-analysis by Edens and Campbell (2007) evaluated the relationship between psychopathy and institutional aggression. Using 15 nonoverlapping studies, with a total of 1,310 participants, Edens and Campbell found moderate relationships between psychopathy assessment and aggression and physical violence (r_w = .25 and .28, respectively). Not surprisingly, the authors found larger effect sizes for published studies compared to unpublished ones. They stated, "Considerable heterogeneity also was noted for the effect sizes for the aggression category, and this degree of variability could not be attributed to any individual study" (p. 23). The authors echoed the concern of many others and recommended caution in predicting inpatient violence on the basis of psychopathy assessments. Despite their call for caution, the overall evidence at this point indicates that psychopathic traits may have predictive value in inpatient violence in adolescents, but the relation is modest to moderate and, as such, this area is especially ripe for further research. Because of its moderate relationship, many other factors may play a major role in inpatient violence.

Instrumental Aggression

Recent research has explored the relationship between psychopathic traits and their relationships to two subtypes of violence, reactive and instrumental. *Reactive violence* is more common, is committed in response to provocation, and tends to be impulsive in nature. In contrast, *instrumental violence* is planned and proactive (see Fontaine, 2007). The value of measuring characteristics associated with instrumental aggression matters because adolescents engaging in instrumental aggression tend to have longer-term dysfunction and engage in more antisocial behavior (see Vitaro, Gendreau, Tremblay, & Oligny, 1998).

In adults, high scores on the affective and interpersonal facets of psychopathy have been linked to higher levels of instrumental aggression in adult forensic patients (Cornell et al., 1996). Notably, similar results have been demonstrated in hospitalized and incarcerated adolescents. In an early study using the PCL-R, Stafford and Cornell (2003) studied 72 adolescents in an inpatient facility and found total PCL-R score was related (r = .47) to instrumental aggression among adolescent inpatients. Other studies (Flight & Forth, 2007; Vitacco, Neumann, Caldwell, Leistico, & Van Rybroek, 2006) have also supported the relationship between facets of psychopathy and instrumental aggression in adolescent offenders.

While the relationship of psychopathy to instrumental aggression has considerable theoretical interest, its practical value remains to be seen. Instrumental violence is easy to categorize based on the characteristics of the offenses, simply by examining the level of planning, lack of reactivity, and criminal intent. Psychopathy studies predicting instrumental violence may be unnecessary or add little value. No researchers have begun to ask the more challenging question: Among offenders with histories of instrumental violence, do specific measures of psychopathy have incremental power over

CD symptoms and other relevant variables mentioned earlier in predicting future instrumental violence? If research continues to back the findings mentioned earlier, then forensic clinicians should be aware of the relationship between psychopathy and instrumental aggression. Furthering the relationship between psychopathy and instrumental violence requires additional validation, prospective research designs, and the use of larger samples to gain a better understanding of this relationship. Forensic clinicians should be alert to the potential impact of interpersonal and affective (i.e., personality) traits of psychopathy on understanding aggression and predicting future dysfunction.

Females and Psychopathy

The last issue we discuss in this section is the relevance of the psychopathy construct to adolescent females. This idea is not new. Salekin, Rogers, and Sewell (1997) pointed out over 10 years ago that psychopathy is manifested differently in female adults (see Verona & Vitale, 2006). The question as it applies to adolescent females has recently garnered attention with similar findings. Marsee, Silverthorn, and Frick (2005) found that a high score on the APSD was related to aggression in school-age males and females; however, its scores were related primarily to relational aggression in the adolescent females. Odgers, Reppucci, and Moretti (2005), in a sample of 125 females, and found that the PCL:YV was of limited use in predicting future offending and aggression. A finding that warrants attention is that the affective component of the PCL:YV was predictive of recidivism; however, that effect was eliminated once victimization was added to the equation. Penney and Moretti (2007) determined that the PCL:YV was predictive of negative outcomes, including violence, in female adolescents. In contrast, Schmidt, McKinnon, Chattha, and Brownlee (2007) established that the ability of the PCL:YV to predict violence in females was much weaker.

Schrum and Salekin (2006) conducted an item response theory analysis on the PCL:YV with 123 female adolescents. The results are very informative in that (1) personality factors and items provided more information than behavioral factors and items, (2) a lower prevalence was found for females than what was typically found in male samples, and (3) greater structural stability was found for the personality factors. The authors concluded that "the findings of the current study indicate that it is possible that psychopathy may be a viable construct in adolescent females for several reasons" (p. 59). Primarily, the authors were encouraged by the structural properties of the items in this completely female sample, but they did not evaluate the predictive power of the PCL:YV, which appears to be more limited in females. In the Leistico and colleagues (2008) meta-analysis, the relationship between Factor 1 (F1) traits and violence was stronger in females than in males. Specifically, they found "our finding that effect sizes were stronger for samples with larger numbers of females specifically contradicts Edens et al.'s (2007) observation that psychopathy was more predictive for males" (p. 39). The study of females and psychopathy is a growing area of research.

Recommendations

Clinically, a summary of this research is needed by forensic clinicians who examine psychopathy in the assessment of risk in adolescents. Several aspects warrant consideration when making predictions of risk. Forensic clinicians must be aware that although research shows a relationship among psychopathic traits and violence and recidivism in adolescent males, they need to learn significantly more to understand how psychopathy should be used in juvenile forensic evaluations. We offer forensic evaluators some basic recommendations for using psychopathy as part of a comprehensive risk assessment of antisocial behavior and violence.

1. Predictions of future antisocial behavior and violence based on psychopathy scores must be tentative and short-term. Vincent (2006) noted that a high psychopathy score may compel a conclusion of high-risk over the short term; however, even with significant research focusing on long-term outcomes, the field of adolescent psychopathy is not sufficiently advanced to speculate regarding the likelihood of future risk on the basis of a psychopathy score. Also, and critically, it is important to note that the magnitude of the correlations in these studies suggest that even though high scorers on a psychopathy scale may be more likely to reoffend, the vast majority of high scorers do not reoffend. This means that even if psychopathy is one of our better predictors of antisocial outcomes, such evaluations should include such a cautionary statement.

2. Forensic evaluators using the PCL:YV have the comfort of some evidence demonstrating the predictive power of the PCL:YV for violence and recidivism, and that it may provide incremental validity over traditional DSM externalizing diagnoses (see Salekin et al., 2004). However, there is not a great deal of prospective research on the incremental validity of psychopathy over the disruptive behavior disorders (DBDs), and many more validation studies are needed on this topic. Forensic psychologists would benefit from being very cautious about not overstating that psychopathy is more predictive of violence and recidivism than the DBDs.

3. Using multiple measures includes structured interviews, as well as both self-report and informant rating scales. Multimethod coverage ensures that various aspects of psychopathy are measured.

4. For short-term predictions of future antisociality and violence, forensic evaluators should consider using low scores as predictors of positive outcomes.

5. Evidence on the applicability of psychopathy to adolescent females is extremely mixed (see Verona, Sadeh, & Javdani, Chapter 13, this volume). As such, additional cautions are warranted when conducting risk assessments with this understudied population, until further research is available.

6. Clinicians involved in forensic risk assessment with adolescents must have a comprehensive knowledge of the literature and recent research findings, which are in a constant state of flux. In addition, we urge clinicians to undergo specialized training regarding child and adolescent development and risk assessment.

Psychopathy and Juvenile Transfer to Adult Court

Statutory changes in the juvenile justice system have created an environment in which adolescents are routinely transferred to adult court. Salekin and Grimes (2008) noted that three standards are used to guide transfer decisions: (1) risk for dangerousness, (2) sophistication–maturity, and (3) amenability to treatment (see also Salekin, Rogers, & Ustad, 2001). With dangerousness as one of the waiver criteria, evidence of psychopathy is sometimes used to support the transfer of a juvenile to adult court (see Seagrave & Grisso, 2002; Vitacco & Vincent, 2006). On this point, Steinberg (2002) provided an especially salient critique of problems that occur when applying the psychopathy construct to adolescents undergoing waiver evaluations. He noted that serious questions remained unanswered that potentially undermine psychopathy's applicability to adolescents.

This section on juvenile transfers is especially important because psychopathy is often misused in these evaluations (see Salekin & Debus, 2008). In a test of the influence of psychopathy in transfer decisions, Marczyk, Heilbrun, Lander, and DeMatteo (2005), in an archival study with 95 adolescents, found that total score on the PCL:YV, as well as other measures of risk and mental health, were retrospectively related to transfer status. The authors concluded, "generally, this study provided some empirical support for the use of these instruments in the juvenile justice system by demonstrating that these instruments have some utility in predicting certification status" (p. 296). Given the archival, retrospective nature of this study and relatively small sample size, these results need further validation and may be overstated given the limitations of the study. Instead, it might be more accurate to indicate that there were post hoc differences on the PCL:YV[3] between adolescents transferred to adult court and those remaining in juvenile court.

We have several concerns with using psychopathy as a measure to justify transfer decisions. Specifically, psychopathy has only marginal relevance to two of the three transfer criteria: sophistication–maturity and treatment amenability. Instead, forensic evaluators who conduct transfer evaluations could be assisted by instruments that systematically assess a broader set of psychological constructs (maturity, risk, amenability) that would help the courts address their criteria for transfer. For instance, the Risk–Sophistication–Treatment Inventory (RST-I; Salekin, 2004) provides a comprehensive assessment of factors related to transfer and has been empirically validated for assisting in juvenile disposition decision making (Salekin, Salekin, Clements, & Leistico, 2005). Importantly, the RST-I considers psychopathic features; however, the scale is only one of three that figure into dangerousness ratings and does not load onto the other factors related to transfer.

Given the complicated nature of transfer evaluations, forensic evaluators must be aware of the following. First, psychopathy can be used as one component in the assessment of dangerousness; however, as we discussed in the risk assessment section, comprehensive assessment requires the utilization of additional measures. Second, the presence of psychopathic traits does not address the treatment amenability or sophistication criteria. As such, forensic evaluators must realize that psychopathic traits only address one of the transfer criteria. Moreover, assessment should not be considered static; even psychopathy's applicability to future dangerousness is not static. Thus, measurement across multiple time points to assess constructs such as risk, sophistication, and amenability to treatment could benefit forensic clinicians and the courts.

In addition, psychologists should also be aware that even though they may be considering a broader array of factors, judges may not incorporate all this information in their decision making. In a study by Brannen and colleagues (2006), judges stated that they viewed amenability to treatment and maturity as the most important variables to consider in transfer decisions. However, when asked whether they would transfer youth in which dangerousness, maturity, and amenability were varied, an opinion of dangerousness that contained psychopathy characteristics carried much more weight in their decisions to waive youth. This may mean psychologists would need to be aware of this potential problem, raise this concern in reports, and highlight aspects of maturity and amenability in both their reports and testimony.

Psychopathy and Treatment

The treatment of youth with psychopathic traits has traditionally been viewed as a formidable challenge. A fundamental part of the problem is that clinicians have widely recognized that the presence of psychopathy often complicates standard treatments, but they have never designed treatments to address psychopathy per se (Rogers & Shuman, 2005). As an analogy, lung cancer likely complicates the treatment of heart disease. Can you imagine a cardiologist ignoring this comorbidity and just providing standard interventions for heart disease?

In past decades, the prevailing attitude that individuals with psychopathy were untreatable became a self-fulfilling prophecy (see Salekin, Chapter 14, this volume). In this section, several aspects of treatment relevant to the forensic clinician include (1) recent studies that focus on treating adolescents with psychopathic traits, (2) knowledge of treatment studies that informs clinical recommendations, and (3) considerations about at-risk adolescents that consider economic, social, and political viewpoints.

We need to acknowledge that treating adolescents with high levels of psychopathic traits is challenging. O'Neill, Lidz, and Heilbrun (2003) studied 64 adolescents placed in a partial hospitalization program for adjudicated adolescents with comorbid substance abuse problems. High PCL:YV scores were linked to higher attrition from treatment, less participation in treatment, and higher levels of recidivism once discharged from the program. Such factors highlight special issues surrounding adolescents with psychopathic traits.

A meta-analysis by Salekin (2002) on treatment and antisocial behavior in children and adolescents provided some reason for optimism. Salekin found that a variety of treatments were effective at treating antisocial behavior, including psychopathy, in youth. Although Salekin's meta-analysis was criticized for his inclusion of certain studies and their definition of treatment success (Harris & Rice, 2006, p. 561), the review challenged long-standing assumptions, associated with psychopathy and adolescents, and there may be valid reasons to consider a broader definition of psychopathy and outcome variables, one of the criticisms of the study (see Salekin, Chapter 14, this volume).

Work by Caldwell and colleagues (Caldwell, McCormick, Umstead, & Van Rybroek, 2007; Caldwell, McCormick, Vitacco, Van Rybroek, & Wolff, 2010; Caldwell, Skeem, Salekin, & Van Rybroek, 2006; Caldwell, Vitacco, & Van Rybroek, 2006) has demonstrated treatment success for males with high levels of psychopathic traits. Combining the traditional security of a juvenile correctional facility with treatment resources, they achieved treatment success with adolescents with average PCL:YV scores in the psychopathic range ($M = 31.80$). Not surprisingly, these adolescents also had significant histories of antisocial behavior, with the typical adolescent in these studies having committed multiple violent crimes (Vitacco, Caldwell, Van Rybroek, & Gabel, 2007). Of major significance, this research demonstrated substantial improvements in behavior and decreases in psychopathic traits in what were previously thought to be intractable adolescent offenders with little hope for the future.

Caldwell, Skeem, and colleagues (2006) compared specialized and standard treatment of comparable offender groups at a secure detention facility. Those receiving specialized treatment had significantly fewer violent acts after release and had relatively slower recidivism. In a related study, Caldwell and colleagues (2007) found that modified PCL:YV scores did not predict treatment success or recidivism. Instead, recidivism was predicted by final behavioral rating scores at the time of discharge from the institution. Moreover, even adolescents with extremely high PCL:YV scores improved with treatment, and a high percentage of them did not experience recidivism for several years after release.

Adolescents with high levels of psychopathic traits may be amenable to treatment if placed in a specialized treatment program designed to minimize or prevent the further development of psychopathy and antisocial behavior. Preliminary evidence suggests that one of the cores of psychopathy, callous traits, may actually decrease over the course of long-term treatment, which may form the basis for the improved behavior (Caldwell et al., 2007). Although it requires replication, this finding is especially salient to high-risk offenders. Significantly decreasing these traits may be critical to long-term success.

A related issue warranting our attention is that treatment is actually cost-effective when compared with the long-term effects of continued violence and incarceration (Caldwell, Vitacco, et al., 2006). Although it requires more funds initially, treatment provides more opportunity for change than the traditional route of incarceration at a juvenile correctional facility. Moreover, this comparison does not take into account the economic impact of additional victimizations resulting from high recidivism rates.

Forensic evaluators and clinicians must be cognizant of current research on treatment successes for youth with psychopathic traits (see Salekin, Chapter 14, this volume). Their efforts are needed to combat therapeutic pessimism and judicial cynicism with respect to adolescents with high levels of psychopathic traits. We present four recommendations for utilizing this research when making treatment recommendations within forensic practice:

1. Even the most serious adolescent offender should not be considered a "throw away." Intensive treatment may provide the best opportunity to eliminate future antisocial behavior and violence. Forensic evaluators may be in a unique position to highlight the potential for success and provide treatment recommendations.

2. Treatment research using a developmental perspective of psychopathy indicates that many high-risk adolescents will desist offending. Moreover, specialized treatment may further diminish the risk of recidivism.

3. Although treatment for high-risk psychopathic youth is initially expensive, the overall treatment is cost-effective. This is especially true if it minimizes subsequent incarceration or violent behavior. Juvenile authorities and policymakers need to be educated about long-term cost savings in designing specialized programs.

4. Forensic evaluators must consider the potential advantages of therapeutic programs over traditional placements in juvenile settings when evaluating individuals.

Psychopathy, Diagnostic Labeling, and Report Writing

One of the most significant controversies regarding adolescent psychopathy concerns labeling youth as psychopathic. The forensic evaluator must be concerned about the potential pejorative influence of a label. For example, the label "psychopath" may prevent adolescents from receiving needed mental health services or may, by itself, justify longer sentences. For example, Edens, Guy, and Fernandez (2003) found that individuals reviewing case material that labeled a juvenile as a psychopath were more likely to recommend the death penalty in a mock case[4] (see also Edens, Petrila, & Buffington-Vollum, 2002). However, other labels can also be damaging. In a study of 260 juvenile probation officers, Murrie, Cornell, and McCoy (2005) found that a diagnosis of antisocial personality disorder had a far greater impact than psychopathy on recommendations.[5]

Such labels also influence judges and clinicians who serve the family court. Murrie, Boccaccini, McCoy, and Cornell (2007) found that judges were more influenced by descriptions of antisocial behavior than by psychopathy diagnosis in rendering their decision on a hypothetical case. Rockett, Murrie, and Boccaccini (2007) used vignettes with 109 clinicians with juvenile justice experience. As expected, clinicians rated adolescents with histories of antisocial behavior and a diagnosis of psychopathy as having greater risk for violence. However, in the absence of antisocial behavior, the presence of psychopathy still influenced ratings of future risk. As reported by Jones and Cauffman (2008), psychopathy independently predicted less treatment amenability, higher perceptions of dangerousness, and recommendations for restrictive placement in a survey of 100 judges in the southeastern United States. When dangerousness ratings were added, the effect of psychopathy on more restrictive placement was no longer significant.

Forensic clinicians should consider avoiding in their reports and testimony, terms whose emotional impact may unduly influence triers of fact and other decision makers. To that end, we offer the following recommendations for report writing and diagnostic labels:

1. Forensic evaluators may best refrain from referring to or classifying youth as "psychopathic." If used, evaluators should provide explicit cautions that this term cannot be equated with dangerousness or poor treatment outcomes.

2. In addition, any categorization of psychopathy or related constructs must take into account the standard error of measurement (SEM). Using the PCL-YV, SEMs range from 1.89 to 2.91 depending on the sample. As such, although a score of 30 is typically used as a cutoff score for psychopathy, when considering the SEM, it may be more appropriate to use a score of 33 to minimize false positives further.

3. Forensic evaluators who assess adolescent psychopathy should discuss the limitations of the construct when applied to youth. These limitations include lack of information about long-term stability of the disorder (although this research base is growing; see Andershed, Chapter 10, this volume) and the positive influence that treatment may have on minimizing future dangerousness.

4. To the extent possible, forensic evaluators must be prepared to educate the trier of fact and other decision makers about the nature of psychopathy in youth. To that end, forensic evaluators must keep in mind documented treatment successes and developmental limitations to provide a full and accurate picture of the adolescent and risk factors.

Summary

This chapter has documented both the promising and not-so-promising aspects of applying the construct of psychopathy to adolescents. Steeped in controversy, the evidence for adolescent psychopathy as a predictor of recidivism and violence has been growing and demonstrates moderate relations with antisocial behavior (Forth & Book, Chapter 11, this volume, Leistico et al., 2008; Vincent, 2006). One thing is certain: Forensic evaluators must be cautious in the tone of their findings, being careful to not overstate the robustness of the relationship between psychopathy and violent and general recidivism. We hope we alerted the reader to the overall tone of the chapter, which is one of caution. Given the ramifications associated with psychopathy and the potential for harm that can occur when an adolescent is assessed as having high psychopathic traits, forensic clinicians must be especially careful not to misuse the construct of psychopathy and to identify limitations appropriately when it is used. To that end, we believe the recommendations we have provided allow for a balance between taking appropriate precautions and using psychopathy in forensic contexts. It is our hope that with further research on this topic, information about how child and adolescent psychopathy may assist in forensic evaluations will be further elucidated.

Notes

1. Other correlations for overall recidivism (r = .14) and charges and convictions for nonviolent offenses (r = .00) were not significant.
2. The authors also classified offenders by the frequency of instrumental aggression (i.e., never, once or twice, or frequently). Consistent with the initial analysis, adolescents who committed more instrumental aggression had higher scores on the PCL:YV than adolescents with few or no acts of instrumental aggression.
3. Other instruments in the study included the Youth Level of Service Case Management Inventory, the Massachusetts Youth Screening Instrument, and a host of criminological and demographic information.
4. This research was conducted prior to the U.S. Supreme Court decision outlawing capital punishment in juvenile offenders. Nonetheless, this study demonstrated how psychopathy can have a life-altering influence.
5. This result is difficult to interpret because antisocial personality disorder is usually inapplicable to juveniles.

References

Andershed, M., Kerr, H., Stattin, H., & Levander, S. (2002). Psychopathic traits in non-referred youths: A new assessment tool. In E. Blaauw & L. Sheridan (Eds.), *Psychopaths—Current international perspectives* (pp. 131–158). Hague, The Netherlands: Elsevier.

Boccaccini, M., Epstein, M., Poythress, N., Douglas, K., Campbell, J., Gardner, G., et al. (2007). Self-report measures of child and adolescent psychopathy as predictors of offending in four samples of justice-involved youth. *Assessment, 14*(4), 361–374.

Borum, R., & Verhaagen, D. (2006). *Assessing and managing violence risk in juveniles*. New York: Guilford Press.

Brandt, J., Kennedy, W., Patrick, C., & Curtin, J. (1997). Assessment of psychopathy in a population of incarcerated adolescent offenders. *Psychological Assessment, 9*(4), 429–435.

Butcher, J. N., & Williams, C. L. (2000). *Essentials of MMPI-2 and MMPI-A interpretation* (2nd ed.). Minneapolis: University of Minnesota Press.

Caldwell, M., McCormick, D., Umstead, D., & Van Rybroek, G. (2007). Evidence of treatment progress and therapeutic outcomes among adolescents with psychopathic features. *Criminal Justice and Behavior, 34*(5), 573–587.

Caldwell, M., McCormick, D., Vitacco, M. J., Van Rybroek, G., & Wolff, J. (2010). *The change of callous traits in juvenile offenders with intensive treatment.* Manuscript under review.

Caldwell, M., Skeem, J., Salekin, R., & Van Rybroek, G. (2006). Treatment response of adolescent offenders with psychopathy features: A 2-year follow-up. *Criminal Justice and Behavior*, *33*(5), 571–596.

Caldwell, M., Vitacco, M., & Van Rybroek, G. (2006). Are violent delinquents worth treating?: A cost–benefit analysis. *Journal of Research in Crime and Delinquency*, *43*(2), 148–168.

Cima, M., Smeets, T., & Jelicic, M. (2008). Self-reported trauma, cortisol levels, and aggression in psychopathic and non-psychopathic prison inmates. *Biological Psychology*, *78*(1), 75–86.

Conroy, M., & Murrie, D. (2007). *Forensic assessment of violence risk: A guide for risk assessment and risk management*. Hoboken, NJ: Wiley.

Cornell, D., Warren, J., Hawk, G., Stafford, E., Oram, G., & Pine, D. (1996). Psychopathy in instrumental and reactive violent offenders. *Journal of Consulting and Clinical Psychology*, *64*(4), 783–790.

Corrado, R., Vincent, G., Hart, S., & Cohen, I. (2004). Predictive validity of the Psychopathy Checklist: Youth Version for general and violent recidivism. *Behavioral Sciences and the Law*, *22*(1), 5–22.

Douglas, K., Epstein, M., & Poythress, N. (2008). Criminal recidivism among juvenile offenders: Testing the incremental and predictive validity of three measures of psychopathic features. *Law and Human Behavior*, *32*(5), 423–438.

Edens, J., & Cahill, M. (2007). Psychopathy in adolescence and criminal recidivism in young adulthood: Longitudinal results from a multiethnic sample of youthful offenders. *Assessment*, *14*(1), 57–64.

Edens, J., & Campbell, J. (2007). Identifying youths at risk for institutional misconduct: A meta-analytic investigation of the Psychopathy Checklist measures. *Psychological Services*, *4*(1), 13–27.

Edens, J., Campbell, J., & Weir, J. (2007). Youth psychopathy and criminal recidivism: A meta-analysis of the Psychopathy Checklist measures. *Law and Human Behavior*, *31*(1), 53–75.

Edens, J., Guy, L., & Fernandez, K. (2003). Psychopathic traits predict attitudes toward a juvenile capital murderer. *Behavioral Sciences and the Law*, *21*(6), 807–828.

Edens, J., Petrila, J., & Buffington-Vollum, J. (2001). Psychopathy and the death penalty: Can the Psychopathy Checklist—Revised identify offenders who represent "a continuing threat to society"? *Journal of Psychiatry and Law*, *29*(4), 433–481.

Edens, J., Skeem, J., Cruise, K., & Cauffman, E. (2001). Assessment of "juvenile psychopathy" and its association with violence: A critical review. *Behavioral Sciences and the Law*, *19*(1), 53–80.

Ellis, L. (1991). Monoamine oxidase and criminality: Identifying an apparent biological marker for antisocial behavior. *Journal of Research in Crime and Delinquency*, *28*(2), 227–251.

Farrington, D. (2005). The importance of child and adolescent psychopathy. *Journal of Abnormal Child Psychology*, *33*(4), 489–497.

Fite, P., Greening, L., & Stoppelbein, L. (2008). Relation between parenting stress and psychopathic traits among children. *Behavioral Sciences and the Law*, *26*(2), 239–248.

Flight, J., & Forth, A. (2007). Instrumentally violent youths: The roles of psychopathic traits, empathy, and attachment. *Criminal Justice and Behavior*, *34*(6), 739–751.

Fontaine, R. (2007). Disentangling the psychology and law of instrumental and reactive subtypes of aggression. *Psychology, Public Policy, and Law*, *13*(2), 143–165.

Forth, A., Hart, S., & Hare, R. (1990). Assessment of psychopathy in male young offenders. *Psychological Assessment: A Journal of Consulting and Clinical Psychology*, *2*(3), 342–344.

Forth, A. E., Kosson, D. S., & Hare, R. D. (2003). *Hare Psychopathy Checklist: Youth Version technical manual*. Toronto: Multi-Health Systems.

Frick, P. J., & Hare, R. D. (2001). *Manual for the Antisocial Process Screening Device*. Toronto: Multi-Health Systems.

Gretton, H., Hare, R., & Catchpole, R. (2004). Psychopathy and offending from adolescence to adulthood: A 10-year follow-up. *Journal of Consulting and Clinical Psychology*, *72*(4), 636–645.

Grisso, T. (1998). *Forensic evaluation of juveniles*. Sarasota, FL: Professional Resource Press/Professional Resource Exchange.

Harris, G. T., & Rice, M. (2006). Treatment of psychopathy: A review of empirical findings. In C. J. Patrick (Ed.), *Handbook of psychopathy* (pp. 555–572). New York: Guilford Press.

Hart, S., Cox, D., & Hare, R. D. (1995). *Manual for the Psychopathy Checklist: Screening Version (PCL:SV)*. Toronto: Multi-Health Systems.

Hicks, M., Rogers, R., & Cashel, M. (2000). Predictions of violent and total infractions among institutionalized male juvenile offenders. *Journal of the American Academy of Psychiatry and the Law*, *28*(2), 183–190.

Johnstone, L., & Cooke, D. (2004). Psychopathic-like traits in childhood: Conceptual and measurement concerns. *Behavioral Sciences and the Law*, *22*(1), 103–125.

Jones, S., & Cauffman, E. (2008). Juvenile psychopathy and judicial decision making: An empirical analysis of an ethical dilemma. *Behavioral Sciences and the Law*, *26*(2), 151–165.

Larsson, H., Andershed, H., & Lichtenstein, P. (2006). A genetic factor explains most of the variation in the psychopathic personality. *Journal of Abnormal Psychology*, *115*(2), 221–230.

Leistico, A., Salekin, R., DeCoster, J., & Rogers, R. (2008). A large-scale meta-analysis relating the Hare measures of psychopathy to antisocial conduct. *Law and Human Behavior*, *32*(1), 28–45.

Lilienfeld, S. O., & Fowler, K. A. (2006). The Self-Report Assessment of Psychopathy: Problems, pitfalls, and promises. In C. J. Patrick (Ed.), *Handbook of the psychopathy* (pp. 107–132). New York: Guilford Press.

Loney, B., Taylor, J., Butler, M., & Iacono, W. (2007). Adolescent psychopathy features: 6-year temporal stability and the prediction of externalizing symptoms during the transition to adulthood. *Aggressive Behavior*, *33*(3), 242–252.

Lynam, D. R. (1997). Pursuing the psychopath: Capturing the fledgling psychopath in a nomological net. *Journal of Abnormal Psychology, 106*, 425–438.

Marczyk, G., Heilbrun, K., Lander, T., & DeMatteo, D. (2005). Juvenile decertification: Developing a model for classification and prediction. *Criminal Justice and Behavior*, *32*(3), 278–301.

Marsee, M., Silverthorn, P., & Frick, P. (2005). The association of psychopathic traits with aggression and delinquency in non-referred boys and girls. *Behavioral Sciences and the Law*, *23*(6), 803-817.

Millon, T. (1993). *The Millon Adolescent Clinical Inventory manual*. Minneapolis, MN: National Computer Systems.

Moffitt, T. (1993). Adolescence-limited and life-course-persistent antisocial behavior: A developmental taxonomy. *Psychological Review*, *100*(4), 674–701.

Morey, L. C. (1991). *The Personality Assessment Inventory professional manual*. Odessa, FL: Psychological Assessment Resources.

Murrie, D., Boccaccini, M., McCoy, W., & Cornell, D. (2007). Diagnostic labeling in juvenile court: How do descriptions of psychopathy and conduct disorder influence judges? *Journal of Clinical Child and Adolescent Psychology*, *36*(2), 228–241.

Murrie, D., Cornell, D., Kaplan, S., McConville, D., & Levy-Elkon, A. (2004). Psychopathy scores and violence among juvenile offenders: A multi-measure study. *Behavioral Sciences and the Law*, *22*(1), 49–67.

Murrie, D., Cornell, D., & McCoy, W. (2005). Psychopathy, conduct disorder, and stigma: Does diagnostic labeling influence juvenile probation officer recommendations? *Law and Human Behavior*, *29*(3), 323–342.

Odgers, C., Moretti, M., & Reppucci, N. (2005, February). Examining the science and practice of violence risk assessment with female adolescents. *Law and Human Behavior*, *29*(1), 7–27.

O'Neill, M., Lidz, V., & Heilbrun, K. (2003). Adolescents with psychopathic characteristics in a substance abusing cohort: Treatment process and outcomes. *Law and Human Behavior*, *27*(3), 299–313.

Pajer, K. (1998). What happens to "bad" girls?: A review of the adult outcomes of antisocial adolescent girls. *American Journal of Psychiatry*, *155*(7), 862–870.

Penney, S., & Moretti, M. (2007). The relation of psychopathy to concurrent aggression and antisocial behavior in high-risk adolescent girls and boys. *Behavioral Sciences and the Law*, *25*(1), 21–41.

Rockett, J., Murrie, D., & Boccaccini, M. (2007). Diagnostic labeling in juvenile justice settings: Do psychopathy and conduct disorder findings influence clinicians? *Psychological Services*, *4*(2), 107–122.

Rogers, R., Jordan, M., & Harrison, K. (2007). Facets of psychopathy, Axis II traits, and behavioral dysregulation among jail detainees. *Behavioral Sciences and the Law*, *25*(4), 471–483.

Rogers, R., & Shuman, D. W. (2005). *Fundamentals of forensic practice: Mental health and criminal law*. New York: Springer.

Rogers, R., Vitacco, M., Jackson, R., Martin, M., Collins, M., & Sewell, K. (2002). Faking psychopathy?: An examination of response styles with antisocial youth. *Journal of Personality Assessment*, *78*(1), 31–46.

Rutter, M., & Sroufe, L. (2000). Developmental psychopathology: Concepts and challenges. *Development and Psychopathology*, *12*(3), 265–296.

Salekin, R. T. (2002). Psychopathy and therapeutic pessimism: Clinical lore or clinical reality? *Clinical Psychology Review*, *22*(1), 79–112.

Salekin, R. T. (2008). Psychopathy and recidivism from mid-adolescence to young adulthood: Cumulating legal problems and limiting life opportunities. *Journal of Abnormal Psychology*, *117*(2), 386–395.

Salekin, R. T., & Debus, S. (2008). Assessing child and adolescent psychopathy. In R. Jackson (Ed.), *Learning forensic assessment* (pp. 347–383). New York: Routledge.

Salekin, R. T., & Grimes, R. (2008). Clinical forensic evaluations for juvenile transfer to adult criminal court. In R. Jackson (Ed.), *Learning forensic assessment* (pp. 313–346). New York: Routledge/Taylor & Francis Group.

Salekin, R. T., & Lochman, J. (2008). Child and adolescent psychopathy: The search for protective factors. *Criminal Justice and Behavior, 35*(2), 159–172.

Salekin, R. T., Neumann, C., Leistico, A., DiCicco, T., & Duros, R. (2004). Psychopathy and comorbidity in a young offender sample: Taking a closer look at psychopathy's potential importance over disruptive behavior disorders. *Journal of Abnormal Psychology*, *113*(3), 416–427.

Salekin, R. T., Rogers, R., & Sewell, K. (1997). Construct validity of psychopathy in a female offender sample: A multitrait–multimethod evaluation. *Journal of Abnormal Psychology, 106*(4), 576–585.

Salekin, R. T., Rogers, R., & Ustad, K. (2001). Juvenile waiver to adult criminal courts: Prototypes for dangerousness, sophistication-maturity, and amenability to treatment. *Psychology, Public Policy, and Law*, *7*(2), 381–408.

Salekin, R. T., Salekin, K. L., Clements, C. B., & Leistico, A.-M. R. (2005). The Risk–Sophistication–Treatment Inventory. In T. Grisso, G. Vincent, & D. Seagrave (Eds.), *Mental health screening and assessment in juvenile justice* (pp. 341–356). New York: Guilford Press.

Schmidt, F., McKinnon, L., Chattha, H., & Brownlee, K. (2006). Concurrent and predictive validity of the Psychopathy Checklist: Youth Version across gender and ethnicity. *Psychological Assessment*, *18*(4), 393–401.

Schrum, C., & Salekin, R. T. (2006). Psychopathy in adolescent female offenders: An item response theory analysis of the Psychopathy Checklist: Youth Version. *Behavioral Sciences and the Law*, *24*(1), 39–63.

Seagrave, D., & Grisso, T. (2002). Adolescent development and the measurement of juvenile psychopathy. *Law and Human Behavior*, *26*(2), 219–239.

Shiner, R. (2000). Linking childhood personality with adaptation: Evidence for continuity and change across time into late adolescence. *Journal of Personality and Social Psychology*, *78*(2), 310–325.

Steinberg, L. (2002). *Juvenile psychopath: Fads, fact, and fictions*. Rockville, MD: National Institute of Justice.

Spain, S., Douglas, K., Poythress, N., & Epstein, M. (2004). The relationship between psychopathic features, violence and treatment outcome: The comparison of three youth measures of psychopathic features. *Behavioral Sciences and the Law*, *22*(1), 85–102.

Stafford, E., & Cornell, D. (2003). Psychopathy scores predict adolescent inpatient aggression. *Assessment*, *10*(1), 102–112.

Task Force on Community Preventive Services. (2007). Recommendation against policies facilitating the transfer of juveniles from juvenile to adult justice systems for the purpose of reducing violence. *American Journal of Preventive Medicine, 32*, S7–S28.

Vaughn, M., & Howard, M. (2005). Self-report measures of juvenile psychopathic personality traits: A comparative review. *Journal of Emotional and Behavioral Disorders, 13*(3), 152–162.

Verona, E., & Vitale, J. (2006). Psychopathy in women: Assessment, manifestations, and etiology. In C. J. Patrick (Ed.), *Handbook of psychopathy* (pp. 415–436). New York: Guilford Press.

Vincent, G. (2006). Psychopathy and violence risk assessment in youth. *Child and Adolescent Psychiatric Clinics of North America, 15*(2), 407–428.

Vincent, G., & Grisso, T. (2005). A developmental perspective on adolescent personality, psychopathology, and delinquency. In T. Grisso, G. Vincent, & D. Seagrave (Eds.), *Mental health screening and assessment in juvenile justice* (pp. 22–43). New York: Guilford Press.

Vitacco, M. J., & Neumann, C. S. (2008). The clinical assessment of psychopathy. In R. Jackson (Ed.), *Learning forensic assessment* (pp. 129–152). New York: Routledge/Taylor & Francis.

Vitacco, M. J., Neumann, C. S., Caldwell, M., Leistico, A., & Van Rybroek, G. (2006). Testing factor models of the Psychopathy Checklist: Youth Version and their association with instrumental aggression. *Journal of Personality Assessment, 87*(1), 74–83.

Vitacco, M. J., & Vincent, G. M. (2006). Applying adult concepts to youthful offenders: Psychopathy and its implications for risk assessment and juvenile justice. *International Journal of Forensic Mental Health Services, 5*, 29–38.

Vitaro, F., Gendreau, P., Tremblay, R., & Oligny, P. (1998). Reactive and proactive aggression differentially predict later conduct problems. *Journal of Child Psychology and Psychiatry, 39*(3), 377–385.

Part V

Conclusions and Future Directions

16

Child and Adolescent Psychopathy

The Road Ahead

RANDALL T. SALEKIN
DONALD R. LYNAM

Child psychopathy, without a doubt, has emerged as an important clinical construct. This has been evidenced by the burst of research on the topic, as well as information gleaned from this research. The excitement that surrounds the topic of child psychopathy stems from the possibility that it may hold the key to a better understanding of youth with chronic and severe disruptive behavior disorder (see Leistico, Salekin, DeCoster, & Rogers, 2008). Chapters in this book contain major work on how to define and measure psychopathy (Kotler & McMahon, Chapter 4; Lochman, Powell, Boxmeyer, Young, & Baden, Chapter 3; Patrick, Chapter 2); knowledge gained on the etiology of psychopathy, including information on genetics, brain anomalies, links to general models of personality and environmental influence (e.g., Blair, Chapter 7; Farrington, Ullrich, & Salekin, Chapter 9; Lynam, Chapter 8; Viding & Larsson, Chapter 5; see also DeBrito et al., 2009) and knowledge about comorbidity (Sevecke & Kosson, Chapter 12) and the stability of psychopathy from childhood to young adulthood (e.g., Andershed, Chapter 10; White & Frick, Chapter 6; see also Lynam, Caspi, Moffitt, Loeber, & Stouthamer-Loeber, 2007). The current volume on child psychopathy also contains chapters that show the work initiated on the applicability of psychopathy across ethnic and other minority groups (Verona, Sadeh, & Javdani, Chapter 13) and how predictive psychopathy is of negative outcomes, such as recidivism (Forth & Book, Chapter 11; see also Leistico et al., 2008). This Handbook also provides an update on intervention for child and adolescent psychopathy (Salekin, Chapter 14). Finally, this book provides information on how psychopathy might be used in clinical and forensic settings (Vitacco, Salekin, & Rogers, Chapter 15; see also Salekin & Debus, 2008). In a nutshell, the chapters in this Handbook show the considerable progress that has been made toward understanding child and adolescent psychopathy.

While scientific progress has been tremendous, we use this closing chapter to address the questions raised in the introductory chapter (Salekin & Lynam, Chapter 1) and previous debates on child and adolescent psychopathy (e.g., Frick, 2002; Hart, Watt, & Vincent, 2002; Lynam, 2002; Salekin, Rosenbaum, Lee, & Lester, 2009; Seagrave & Grisso, 2002; Skeem & Petrila, 2004) because these questions provide a good framework for determining how much progress has been made in the field of child and adolescent psychopathy. In addition, these questions provide a useful framework to chart the research course left ahead. Recall that the questions stemming from early debates on psychopathy and other, more recent papers on the topic (Farrington, 2005; Rutter, 2005; Salekin, 2006; Salekin, Rosenbaum, & Lee, 2009) have centered on four main issues. First, can psychopathy be reliably assessed in youth? Second, what does the psychopathy construct mean for children and adolescents (i.e., construct validity)? Third, does child psychopathy carry through to adulthood (i.e., stability)? And, fourth, is the concept predictive of anything important? As can be seen in the previous pages of this handbook, many significant advances have been made in this regard.

A Look at Child and Adolescent Psychopathy through a Developmental Psychopathology Lens

When interpreting the research findings in this handbook, much depends on the theoretical context from which one operates in determining the extent to which progress has been made. Put another way, the degree to which the construct has been shown to be "valid" or "invalid" depends somewhat on the lens one is looking through. We suggest that the construct be embedded within the principles of a developmental psychopathology. Developmental psychopathology, a macroparadigm, is useful because it allows for the incorporation and integration of multiple single paradigms (biological, cognitive, personality, and interpersonal theory). The developmental psychopathology framework also allows us to understand development across the lifespan. Thus, while individual frameworks have, to some extent, different origins (e.g., personality theory, temperament theory, biology), they may be complementary and allow for consideration of a much wider research base to integrate into the developmental psychopathology macropardigm, which will be primary in helping us better understand psychopathy in the future. We briefly delineate some of the major progress with respect to research on child and adolescent psychopathy, interjecting the developmental psychopathology framework to help determine the degree of progress that the field has made before discussing the research agenda that lies ahead of us.

Research Findings

The Structure of Child Psychopathy

Research within this book and elsewhere has frequently tested the structure and reliability of psychopathy instruments, allowing us to examine more closely questions regarding the overrepresentation of symptoms, as well as the general reliability of the concept. This research has demonstrated that the indices of child psychopathy have structural homogeneity, interrater reliability, and a factor structure similar to that of adult psychopathy (Andershed, Kerr, Stattin, & Levander, 2002; Forth, Hare, & Hart, 1990; Frick, Bodin, & Barry, 2000; Salekin, Brannen, Zalot, Leistico, & Neumann, 2006; Vincent & Hart, 2002). This research has been a necessary and important first step in extending the adult construct downward into childhood and adolescence. Other questions, such as the prevalence of psychopathy, have been examined to address the concern that all adolescents are by the very nature "egocentric" or "impulsive." To date, research has not borne this relationship out, and the prevalence rate for youth psychopathy is no higher than it is for adult psychopathy. There is evidence that the prevalence rate tends to be lower, approximately 7–15% (e.g., Cruise, 2000; Salekin, Leistico, Neumann, DiCiccio, & Duros, 2004), although in some samples, the rate is similar to that of adults, at around 20% (see Forth, Kosson, & Hare, 2003).

These previously mentioned research findings would suggest that psychopathy symptoms are not normative or mimicked by the developmental stage of adolescence.[1] In addition to these data, item response theory has contributed to our understanding of the psychopathy concept in both boys and girls (Schrum & Salekin, 2006; Vincent, 2002). This research has shown that the items indexing psychopathy, as defined by the Psychopathy Checklist: Youth Version (PCL:YV; Forth et al., 2003), function similarly to those of adult psychopathy: At high levels of the construct, most youth receive a top score (2); at low levels of the construct, youth receive a low score (0); and, at medium levels of the concept, youth receive a midlevel score (1) on the measure. Together, these findings suggest that child and adolescent psychopathy has similar prevalence rates and structural properties to those of adult psychopathy findings (supported by the research reviewed in this book by Kotler and McMahon, Chapter 4). While this research serves to address part of the youth psychopathy query (i.e., Is it overrepresented? Can it be reliably assessed?), it does not address two important points raised by researchers in the recent past (Farrington, 2005; Hart et al., 2002; Rutter, 2005; Seagrave & Grisso, 2002; Skeem & Petrila, 2004): What is it, exactly, that we are measuring? And, if it is psychopathy, do child and adolescent psychopaths grow up to be adult psychopaths? These questions can be partially addressed with construct validity and the temporal stability research presented in this handbook.

Child and Adolescent Psychopathy: What Is Its Meaning?

Lynam (1997) cogently referred to the construct validity work with children as capturing fledgling psychopathy in a nomological net. Along with his early study attempting to look at correlates linked to those scoring high on child indices of psychopathy, other research has been designed to test whether psychopathy has a nomological net similar to that of adult psychopathy. The bulk of research detailed in this handbook and elsewhere has shown that child and adolescent psychopathy is similar in appearance to adult psychopathy (e.g., Blair, Chapter 7; Lynam, Chapter 8; White & Frick, Chapter 6; Viding & Larsson, Chapter 5; see also Viding, Blair, Moffitt, & Plomin, 2005). Research has shown that psychopathy in youth appears to be linked to aberrant cognitive and affective processes (Blair, Chapter 7; see also Blair & Coles, 2000; Blair, Peschardt, Budhuani, Mitchell, & Pine, 2006), shares common traits from models of general personality (Lynam, Chapter 8; see also Lynam et al., 2005; Salekin, Leistico, Trobst, Schrum, & Lochman, 2005), and is linked to inhibition (Lynam et al., 2005; Salekin, Leistico, et al., 2004; Vitale et al., 2005). This research has shown that the nomological net surrounding child psychopathy appears similar to that of adult psychopathy.

However, there are dissimilarities, and while it is interesting looking for similarities to adult psychopathy, we suggest that there should also be some searching for differences rather than sweeping discrepant findings under the carpet. One important difference appears to be greater levels of comorbidity in children. Moreover, this comorbidity appears to span both externalizing and internalizing disorders. Although overlap with externalizing disorders might be expected, overlap with internalizing disorders is less coherent with adult theories of psychopathy. The higher than expected scores with anxiety occur across a variety of studies (e.g., Kosson, Cyterski, Steverwald, Neumann, & Walker-Matthews, 2002; Kubak & Salekin, 2009; Lee, Salekin, & Iselin, 2010; Lynam et al., 2007; Salekin, Neumann, et al., 2004; Vitale et al., 2005) and suggest the need for further investigation. In addition, psychopathy and negative affect in general appears to be higher than expected in youth (see Kosson et al., 2002; Salekin, Neumann, et al., 2004; Salekin et al., 2005). Another area in which dissimilarities have been noted between adult and child psychopathy is performance tasks (see Forth et al., 2003; Muñoz, Kerr, & Besic, 2008; Salekin & Debus, 2008). Specifically, some studies have shown that, unlike adults, psychopathic youth may not show all the same deficits in executive, dorsolateral frontal, or orbitofrontal functioning as do their adult counterparts (e.g., Forth et al., 2003). In summary, although child and adolescent psychopathy has general construct validity, some aspects to the construct require further research and inquiry.

Psychopathy and Stability Studies

Robins (1966) investigated the temporal stability of sociopathy based on child guidance cases and interviews with those same individuals over 20 years after their initial assessment. She found that over half the individuals diagnosed with conduct problems in childhood continued to evidence problems in adulthood. This early study, and others, were used to identify criteria for antisocial personality disorder, outlined in the *Diagnostic and Statistical Manual of Mental Disorders*. Despite its importance, this study was not designed to detect the etiological underpinnings of psychopathy and thus sheds little light on the development and maintenance of psychopathy. Nonetheless, it did show moderate continuity in antisocial behavior across a significant period of time.

More recently, emergent studies have attempted to investigate the stability of psychopathy from contemporary viewpoints. Frick, Kimonis, Dandreaux, and Farrell (2003) examined the stability of psychopathy in 100 nonreferred community children over a 4-year period. They found high parent (.80) and cross-informant (average of .53) stability. Some work from this study has been used to address parenting practices with respect to the maintenance of the disorder and thus provides some initial information on parenting practices and the etiology and/or maintenance of psychopathy. Lynam and colleagues (2007) examined the connection between childhood psychopathy at age 13 (assessed by the Childhood Psychopathy Scale) and adult psychopathy at age 24 (assessed by the Psychopathy Checklist: Screening Version) with over 200 participants. Modest stability ($r = .31$) was noted, and stability across the four-facet model showed slightly stronger correlations for traditional Factor 2 items: the correlations were .17 (Interpersonal), .15 (Affective), .30 (Lifestyle), and .33 (Antisocial). This study offered a significant advance in temporal stability data because it addressed the question of stability into young adulthood.

Glenn, Raine, Venables, and Mednick (2007) examined whether temperament and psychophysiology served as early indicators for psychopathic personality in adulthood. Three hundred thirty-five 3-year-olds were indexed on temperament and electrodermal activity in response to both orienting and aversive tones. In adulthood (age 28), the Hare Self-Report Psychopathy Scale–II (SRP-II; Hare, 1991) was administered. The authors discovered that individuals scoring high on the SRP-II had been significantly less fearful and inhibited at age 3, were more sociable, and displayed longer skin conductance to aversive stimuli when compared with controls. An unexpected finding was noted: Participants showed increased autonomic arousal and skin conductance orienting. This study offers some information on the physiological mechanisms of psychopathy.

These studies, also presented in greater detail in this volume by Andershed (Chapter 10), advanced our knowledge about the stability of psychopathy. The results indicate a modest link between child and adult psychopathy (Lynam et al., 2007) and a weak-to-moderate prospective link between childhood temperament and psychophysiology, and psychopathic personality in adulthood (Glenn et al., 2007).[2] Other studies have also emerged to show similar stability estimates (e.g., Barry, Barry, Deming, & Lochman, 2008; Burke, Loeber, & Lahey, 2007; Loney, Taylor, Butler, & Iacono, 2007; Pardini & Loeber, 2008). In general, although the findings in this book (Andershed, Chapter 10) partially support the notion that a portion of child psychopaths, as currently indexed, "grow up" to be adult psychopaths, according to stability research, a significant portion do not. This is, however, a complex research question that is not easily answered simply by administering psychopathy instruments at two points in time. We go into greater depth on the stability of psychopathy question in the latter part of this chapter to determine what can be done in the future to address these important questions. We now turn to antisocial outcomes before addressing why some youth may (or may not) follow a life course from child psychopathy to adult psychopathy.

Psychopathy and Antisocial Outcomes

Psychopathy is viewed as an important concept, in part because it can help to forecast behavior, which can then serve to protect society from certain personality types that are apt to break the law and be violent. It can also protect youth from cumulating negative outcomes. The expectation that these forecasts accurately predict character and behavior as late as adulthood may be too unrealistic for any psychological construct, and particularly for specific negative outcomes such as violence (see Monahan & Steadman, 1996, 2001). But, as indicated in this volume, psychopathy in child and adolescent samples may perform relatively well at more immediate forecasts of behavior (Forth & Book, Chapter 11). Specifically, we know that within the adult literature, psychopathy has been associated with negative outcomes such as violent and nonviolent offending (see Hemphill & Hare, 2004; Hemphill, Hare, & Wong 1998; Salekin, Rogers, & Sewell, 1996). Forth and Book's Chapter 11 in this handbook indicated a similar relation in adolescents (see also Edens, Campbell, & Weir, 2007; Leistico et al., 2008). Specifically, Forth and Book show that adolescent psychopathy evidences a similar magnitude of association to that of adult studies.

In the Leistico and colleagues (2008) meta-analysis, age did not moderate the effect between psychopathy and offending. In addition, prospective studies controlling for other potential factors that might account for recidivism have shown that psychopathy is associated with general and violent recidivism from adolescence to young adulthood (see Salekin, 2008). These findings, along with other concurrent construct validity findings, lend support to the construct of psychopathy in youth. Nonetheless, it is also important to note that there is considerable heterogeneity in the effect sizes reported in meta-analytic studies, and much more research is needed to determine what accounts for this heterogeneity (Vitacco, Salekin, & Rogers, Chapter 15). In addition, the predictive accuracy of other negative outcomes (beyond reoffense rates) has not been examined as thoroughly. Alcohol and drug use, unsafe sexual practices, sport injuries, work accidents, academic shortfalls, and other health risk concerns need much more research attention. We now return to the factors that might account for change in psychopathy scores and negative outcomes such as antisocial behavior.

Continuity and Discontinuity

Although evidence indicates modest stability (i.e., some continuity in the child psychopathy construct) and utility with respect to antisocial behavior, it may also be reasonable to assume there should be alterations in behavior and even aspects of one's personality. Research by Caspi and Shiner (2006) emphasizes the importance of acknowledging growth (including change) in personality development across time. This developmental psychopathology perspective is important in terms of better understanding and validating the psychopathy concept, and mapping out what might be expected for the nomological net across the life course (Farrington, 2005; Johnstone & Cooke, 2005; Rutter, 2005; Salekin, 2006; Salekin & Frick, 2005). Instability is also important to acknowledge because it tells us there are different trajectories for youth, with key life factors taking them off a rather destructive personality course (Lynam; 2002; Salekin & Frick, 2005).

The next important question for researchers to determine is the factors that account for change (both increases and decreases in psychopathy symptoms), as well as factors that allow for the maintenance of a disorder. In a recent special journal issue on child psychopathy in *Criminal Justice and Behavior* (Salekin & Lochman, 2008; see also Lynam, Loeber, & Stouthamer-Loeber, 2008; Pardini & Loeber, 2008), the focus was on trying to identify psychopathy trajectories (e.g., high to low psychopathy) and factors that influence change. Findings indicated that parenting (early on) is important and that friendships, social competence, and living in affluent neighborhoods may play a protective role against the development of psychopathy. These findings are consistent with the developmental psychopathology framework and the work on personality development by Caspi and Shiner (2006), acknowledging both stability and growth (change). Continued research on stability and change in children and adolescent psychopathic traits will provide important insights into the different trajectories of psychopathic personality and areas to target in interventions.

Treatment Research

Treatment research has often been utilized to some extent to build the case further for the nomological net surrounding psychopathy. Because bits of theory and research suggest that psychopathy may be an intractable disorder, studies showing negative treatment results are thought to support the notion that the disorder is chronic, and why little change ought to be expected. In addition, a number of researchers feel that if change does occur, it is because the psychopath has duped the clinician or the researcher. We do not know, however, whether this supposition is true about the treatment of child and adolescent psychopathy. What we do know is that several studies have shown that youth with psychopathic traits can be difficult in treatment settings (Salekin, Chapter 14). In other words, they are more likely to be disruptive and noncompliant with treatment than nonpsychopathic youth. However, previous treatment studies have utilized samples of convenience (e.g., O'Neill, Lidz, & Heilbrun, 2003; Rogers, Johansen, Chang, & Salekin, 1997; Spain, Douglas, Poythress, & Epstein, 2004) that have resulted in examination of generic treatment programs as applied to psychopathic youth, who might need more specialized interventions. Although these studies show, at least tentatively, that psychopathic youth make some progress in treatment programs, they do not address the key question of whether broader and more in-depth changes might occur in specialized programs that optimize treatment gains.

Thus far, the limited research examining the treatment of child and adolescent psychopathic traits is not strong enough in either direction to determine with certainty whether psychopathy is a treatable condition (Salekin, Chapter 14). However, some preliminary research indicating a dose–response effect (e.g., Caldwell, Skeem, Salekin, & Van Rybroek, 2006; Salekin, 2002) suggests that some aspects of psychopathy are treatable and, we would argue, that clinicians/researchers are not necessarily being duped with respect to their intervention work. Furthermore, observable behavioral indicators (i.e., recidivism) suggest that the change is real. Although we recognize that it is still possible for psychopathic youth to feign improvement or to skirt the law, it seems that these research questions require much more scientific inquiry. Evidence that psychopathy at this developmental stage is difficult to treat or causes unease should be utilized beyond construct validity to assist in developing appropriate interventions to manage children and adolescents with the condition. In addition, more stringent tests of this hypothesis require treatment programs that directly target psychopathic traits. Until a larger body of research emerges, a lack of therapeutic optimism does little to advance the field and is detrimental to the continued healthy development of youth.

An Integration of the Research Findings

Although there has been considerable debate about the appropriateness (e.g., overrepresentation of symptoms) of the concept of psychopathy in children and adolescents, the research in this handbook suggests that the syndrome appears to be a reliable one as currently indexed. In addition, the structure of psychopathy in children looks similar to that of adults. Moreover, there are some remarkable similarities in the nomological net that surrounds child and adolescent psychopathy (Blair, Chapter 7; Forth & Book, Chapter 11; Lynam, Chapter 8; see also DeBrito et al., 2009; Edens et al., 2007; Leistico et al., 2008; Lynam et al., 2005; Salekin et al., 2005; Vitale et al., 2005). There are also some dissimilarities, such as higher rates of co-occurring trait anxiety, negative affect, and performance task results, that do not necessarily parallel results found with adults (Forth et al., 2003; Kubak & Salekin, 2009; Lee et al., 2010).

As mentioned in the opening pages of this chapter, a developmental psychopathology framework can help us understand both similar and dissimilar results. Specifically, embedding child psychopathy within a developmental psychopathology model helps us understand the potential differences in the nomological net across different developmental periods. Numerous researchers have argued that with application of the developmental principle of heterotypic continuity, this is exactly what we would expect—the same underlying construct expressed differently across developmental stages. Considering this developmental principle and the extent to which construct validity has been established, it could be argued that the concept may be quite useful in explaining a subtype of youth (i.e., the theoretical net associated with the condition) and concomitant negative behaviors (e.g., antisocial conduct).

As for the question—Do all child psychopaths become adult psychopaths?—current data as reviewed by Andershed (Chapter 10) in this handbook suggest an answer: A few likely do, but a good portion do not, or at least they do not in the ways we expect.[3] Many of the longitudinal studies show that a significant portion of youth's psychopathic characteristics deescalate over time. And, if one examines negative outcome data, such as recidivism, research findings suggest that while youth scoring high on psychopathy scales are at risk for increased offending, a good portion of youth scoring high on psychopathy scales do not reoffend. This, again, may stress not only the importance of heterotypic continuity but also multifinality and equifinality, developmental principles that suggest youth can start out at a similar point but end up on quite different life paths, or, alternatively, can start on different paths but find themselves at the same end point (adult psychopathy). However, we must couch these statements regarding the extent to which child psychopaths become adult psychopaths in a great deal of caution. This caution is necessary because the research question is complex. Research and theory need to continue to map out what psychopathy looks like across development. For instance, one possibility is that many youth continue to have psychopathic personalities but vary greatly in the roles they take within society, including, as Cleckley put it, medical, political, and business roles, to mention a few. At present, we simply lack the sophistication to tap the psychopathic personality, and all its potential developmental manifestations across the life course (heterotypic continuity).

The debate on child psychopathy has served to stimulate research in this area, resulting in a large number of studies on child psychopathy to fill many of the needed research gaps, and our understanding of the child psychopathy construct has, without a doubt, greatly improved. However, we are still fairly unclear about the concept in terms of long-term outcomes. Data, thus far, represent rough estimates of the construct, with limited outcome data giving us the sense that we have very little in the way of clear, end-to-end follow-up of youth who might be psychopathic. As such, much more research is needed if we are to provide greater clarity regarding some of the important queries about child and adolescent psychopathy.

The Journey Ahead

Although considerable progress has been made toward better understanding of the child psychopathy construct, much more work is needed on measurement, temporal stability, and life outcomes for psychopathic youth. We suggest, as did Farrington (2005), that these questions will require "big science" to further the field of knowledge on this topic. There are several steps that we researchers can take to improve our understanding of the syndrome.

First, our measurement of psychopathy continues to be imprecise, and a number of researchers have now raised questions about this issue, as well as suggested better ways to rate the trait (Farrington, 2005; Johnstone & Cooke, 2004; Rutter, 2005). Very low correlations among psychopathy scales within single studies often highlight this important point (see Murrie & Cornell, 2003; Salekin, Neumann, Leistico, & Zalot, 2004). Rutter (2005) also raised the question of whether self-report measures alone may adequately tap the psychopathy construct. It may be that a return to multimethod assessment approaches with large samples, selecting only those scoring high on two or three elements, may provide greater clarity on the child psychopathy concept.

Second, conceptualization of psychopathy remains an issue. Whether it be Cleckley's classic model for psychopathy; Hare's two-factor framework; Lilienfeld's eight-factor model; Patrick's model of boldness, meanness, and impulsivity; or some other newer theory, each model is likely to have different correlates. This does not necessarily mean that one model is better than the next; it simply means that they are different (perhaps different variants of a broader psychopathy family of disorders). Several years ago, we described the Hare model as having conceptual drift (Rogers, 1995; Salekin, 2002), and Patrick (2006) echoed these key differences between Cleckley (1941) and Hare (2003). Although this can be detected from examining the items themselves, it need not necessarily continue to be a point of debate regarding the most accurate model. Reserving judgment as to what is the best model may be the one important way to proceed with future research on child and adolescent psychopathy and gain information on multiple psychopathy models. However, it is important to note that one's starting point with respect to psychopathy results in very different nomological nets, including differences such as brain abnormalities for some definitions and no (or subtle) brain anomalies for others, substance abuse correlates for some models and no substance abuse problems for others, and so forth. Future research should continue to examine the various models of psychopathy in different research settings.

Third, as Rutter (2005) notes, there may be a need to integrate biology better into the study of child and adolescent psychopathy. Much more research is needed on this topic, including functional magnetic resonance imaging, electroencephalography, galvanic skin conductance, and other biological measurements. However, we suggest that biological studies such as neuroimaging will likely only take us part way to better understanding the child psychopathy concept. For instance, neuroimaging studies are not likely to address deeper issues, such as the different envelopes of responses that different individuals may draw upon when specific parts of their brains are activated. Task development and the inferences drawn from tasks to real-life situations will also require greater scrutiny and much more attention in future child psychopathy work.

Fourth, behavior genetics and the activation and deactivation of genes in particular environmental conditions will require much more scrutiny and further sophisticated study. For example, as this research moves forward, much more care in indexing *behaviors* in genetic studies will be needed to determine what is genetically linked, or what components of psychopathy evidence a biological liability, and the extent to which the environment continues to play a role across development. Other important questions include the following: Are callousness characteristics alone truly representative of psychopathy? Or can some other heritable trait/characteristic result in psychopathy, as well as other conditions that differ from psychopathy (e.g., a hardy but moral personality)? Also, are all components of psychopathy necessary for the concept to be referred to as psychopathy? That is, are interpersonal characteristics necessary (the mask; superficial charm and good intelligence) to define psychopathy or does a deficit in affect alone suffice?

Fifth, determining how psychopathy fits with the current nomological system requires more research effort. Although we started this handbook with a discussion of the disruptive behavior disorders, determining how psychopathy may be formally codified in DSM-V and future DSM versions could be worth consideration if it ultimately helps us distinguish a certain type of youth with conduct problems. Although there is a great deal of interesting research into each of these issues, very little of it has been aimed directly toward answering questions that help to determine specific distinctions between oppositional defiant disorder (ODD) and conduct disorder (CD). More research is needed on the extent to which psychopathy offers additional information beyond CD. In terms of predictive validity, more detailed information is needed about how modifications to current criteria may aid in determining children's long-term prognosis and response to available treatments.

Sixth, protective factor research will need more attention in the future. As research moves forward, it will also be important to bear in mind the significant complexity in identifying factors that account for stability, inclines and declines in psychopathic traits, and positive and negative outcomes over time. Research that centers on examining inclines, maintenance, and declines may be key to intervention research. If we are to make new discoveries in the child psychopathy field, research needs to extend beyond single time point studies, to more extensive longitudinal investigations. One aim of such research would be to chart "deficits" as they begin to emerge across development (cognitive deficits that could be brought on by substance use; affective deficits that could be the result of environmental impacts, etc.) rather than assume that they all exist from birth and, thus, at each developmental stage of the disorder. Another important aim would be to examine aspects of the construct that are dissimilar in youth to see how these differences drop off or are maintained in subsets of youth over time (see Kubak & Salekin, 2009; Lee et al., 2010).

To give several examples, much more work is also needed on how psychopathic youth select their peers (whether some are delinquent) and whether they are influenced by their peers' delinquency (and vice versa). In addition, research is needed on factors that account for youth having nondelinquent peers. Previous research has shown that the peers of youth who score high on psychopathic traits tend to be neighborhood peers. This indicates that the rewards may be greater and the consequences less severe for youth to engage in delinquency in unstructured environments outside of school grounds (Muñoz et al., 2008). Protective factors may point to some of the key factors that researchers should consider when designing scientific investigations. Where possible, longitudinal designs, with the inclusion of multiple protective indices, could improve opportunities for uncovering protective mechanisms. In addition, and relatedly, how we think about the treatability of the condition will impact how we conduct research in this area, with greater optimism potentially producing more intervention innovations (Salekin, Chapter 14). Thus, although some researchers have been concerned about studying psychopathy in youth because of its potential harming effects, research has shown that claims about the disorder (e.g., poor treatment prognosis) have not been fully grounded in science (see Salekin, Chapter 14; see also Salekin, 2002; Salekin, Rogers, & Machin, 2001; Skeem, Monahan, & Mulvey, 2002).

Examining positive outcomes for psychopathy traits could also prove fruitful; that is, whether some psychopathy traits might also be linked to positive outcomes in youth is not known exactly. Specifically, superficial charm, intelligence, manipulation, and so forth, all could potentially have some positive aspects to them. We illustrate some possibilities in Table 16.1 that researchers should also potentially consider in their research programs.

While we do not intend to minimize all significant negative outcomes that can result from the personality style of psychopathy; we nonetheless feel that it is important to sketch out some of the positive outcomes that could result from this personality style. This might also help us account for the *multifinality developmental principle* of many youth starting out on a psychopathy trajectory, but only some being detected at a later point with measures of psychopathy designed primarily to detect a criminal lifestyle. This may also help us locate individuals who have made a positive adjustment in society. A recent study from our lab suggests that motivation may be one key factor (see Salekin, Lee, Schrum-Dillard, & Kubak, in press).

Finally, this concluding chapter underscores the point that, from a developmental psychopathology perspective, a chief reason for studying

TABLE 16.1. Potential Positive Outcomes Linked to Psychopathy Traits

Psychopathy trait	Potentially positive outcomes
Superficial charm	Good conversation skills; lighthearted in social settings; fun and entertaining to be around; good at interacting with others; improved romantic opportunities; power to please or delight others; attractiveness.
Intelligence	Can solve problems with greater ease; is open to novel experiences; has intelligent conversations.
Manipulation	Able to change environment to obtain resources; can lead, convincing others of the importance of an idea; can retract out of bad situations; a means of gaining control or social influence over others; win others over; persuade.
Absence of nervousness	Able to perform tasks without high levels of anxiety that detract from performance; able to engage in social settings without fear; has healthier presentation; easier on autonomic nervous system and better for healthy development (mental and physical).
Sensation seeking	May enjoy sports, such as skiing, football, skydiving, kayaking, rock climbing, hang gliding, scuba diving, and skate boarding, that are somewhat demanding but also provide good athletic conditioning; may also do well in careers that involve some risk, such as police officer, firefighter, and so forth, large circle of friends.

Note. This is not an exhaustive list, but it represents a few examples of potentially positive, related characteristic and outcomes.

psychopathic features earlier in development is to understand better the potential change that can occur in these features over time.

As research continues to unearth the developmental processes that can lead to the characteristics of psychopathy in youth and to discover the sources of both stability and change in these features over time, these findings will have important theoretical and practical implications, such as improving the well-being of youth with psychopathy.

Notes

1. This statement regarding prevalence is based on Psychopathy Checklist: Youth Version studies, and more research is needed to determine whether self-report measures might result in higher rates or higher scores on psychopathy scales than what is typically found with adult indices.
2. We use the term *moderate* here based on Hemphill's (2003) research on interpreting the magnitude of correlation coefficients. We also recognize that in terms of clinical assessments these estimates might be considered low.

3. This statement is based on current stability estimates and the manner in which psychopathy is indexed. We recognize that there are limitations to the way we currently measure psychopathy, and that the disorder can manifest in ways that are not detected by current assessment technology and/or current scientific techniques.

References

Andershed, H., Kerr, M., Stattin, H., & Levander, S. (2002). Psychopathic traits in non-referred youths: A new assessment tool. In E. Blauuw & L. Sheridan (Eds.), *Psychopaths: Current international perspectives* (pp. 131–158). The Hague: Elsevier.

Barry, T. D., Barry, C. T., Deming, A. M., & Lochman, J. E. (2008). Stability of psychopathic characteristics in childhood: The influence of social relationships. *Criminal Justice and Behavior, 35,* 244–262.

Blair, R. J. R., & Coles, M. (2000). Expression recognition and behavioural problems in early adolescence. *Cognitive Development, 15,* 421–434.

Blair, R. J. R., Peschardt, K. S., Budhani, S., Mitchell, D. G. V., & Pine, D. S. (2006). The development of psychopathy. *Journal of Child Psychology and Psychiatry, 47,* 262–275.

Burke, J. D., Loeber, R., & Lahey, B. B. (2007). Adolescent conduct disorder and interpersonal callousness as predictors of psychopathy in young adults. *Journal of Clinical Child and Adolescent Psychology, 36,* 334–346.

Caldwell, M., Skeem, J. L., Salekin, R. T., & Van Rybroek, G. (2006). Treatment response of adolescent offenders with psychopathy features: A 2–year follow-up. *Criminal Justice and Behavior, 33,* 571–596.

Capsi, A., & Shiner, R. L. (2006). Personality development. In N. Eisenberg, W. Damon, & R. M. Lerner (Eds.), *Handbook of child psychology: Vol. 3, Social, emotional, and personality development* (6th ed., pp. 300–365). Hoboken, NJ: Wiley.

Cleckley, H. (1941). *The mask of sanity.* St. Louis, MO: Mosby.

Cruise, K. R. (2000). *Measurement of adolescent psychopathy: Construct and predictive validity in two samples of juvenile offenders.* Unpublished doctoral dissertation, University of North Texas, Denton.

De Brito, S. A., Mechelli, A., Wilke, M., Jones, A. P., Hodgins, S., Viding, E., et al. (2009). Size matters: Increased grey matter in boys with conduct problems and callous–unemotional traits. *Brain: A Journal of Neurology, 132,* 843–852.

Edens, J. F., Campbell, J. S., & Weir, J. M. (2007). Youth psychopathy and criminal recidivism: A meta-analysis of the Psychopathy Checklist measures. *Law and Human Behavior, 13,* 53–75.

Farrington, D. P. (2005). The importance of child and adolescent psychopathy. *Journal of Abnormal Child Psychology, 33,* 489–497.

Forth, A. E., Hare, R. D., & Hart, S. D. (1990). Assessment of psychopathy in male young offenders. *Psychological Assessment, 2,* 342–344.

Forth, A. E., Kosson, D. S., & Hare, R. D. (2003). *The Psychopathy Checklist: Youth Version.* Toronto: Multi-Health Systems.

Frick, P. J. (2002). Juvenile psychopathy from a developmental perspective: Implications for construct development and use in forensic assessments. *Law and Human Behavior, 26*, 247–253.

Frick, P. J., Bodin, S. D., & Barry, C. T. (2000). Psychopathic traits and conduct problems in a community sample of clinic referred sample of children: Further development of the Psychopathy Screening Device. *Psychological Assessment, 12*, 382–393.

Frick, P. J., Kimonis, E. R., Dandreaux, D. M., & Farrell, J. M. (2003). The 4-year stability of psychopathic traits in non-referred youth. *Behavioral Sciences and the Law, 21*, 713–736.

Glenn, A. L., Raine, A., Venables, P. H., & Mednick, S. A. (2007). Early temperament and psychophysiological precursors of adult psychopathic personality. *Journal of Abnormal Psychology, 116*, 508–518.

Hare, R. D. (1991). *The Self-Report Psychopathy Scale–II*. Unpublished test, University of British Columbia, Vancouver.

Hare, R. D. (2003). *The Hare Psychopathy Checklist—Revised* (2nd ed.). Toronto: Multi-Health Systems.

Hart, S. D., Watt, K. A., & Vincent, G. M. (2002). Commentary on Seagrave and Grisso: Impressions of the state of the art. *Law and Human Behavior, 26*, 241–245.

Hemphill, J. F. (2003). Interpreting the magnitude of correlation coefficients. *American Psychologist, 58*, 78–79.

Hemphill, J. F., & Hare, R. D. (2004). Some misconceptions about the Hare PCL-R and risk assessment: A reply to Gendreau, Goggin, and Smith. *Criminal Justice and Behavior, 31*, 203–243.

Hemphill, J. F., Hare, R. D., & Wong, S. (1998). Psychopathy and recidivism: A review. *Legal and Criminological Psychology, 3*, 141–172.

Johnson, L., & Cooke, D. J. (2004). Psychopathic-like traits in childhood: Conceptual and measurement concerns. *Behavioral Sciences and the Law, 22*, 103–125.

Kosson, D. S., Cyterski, T. D., Steuerwald, B. L., Neumann, C. S., & Walker-Matthews, S. (2002). The reliability and validity of the Psychopathy Checklist: Youth Version (PCL:YV) in nonincarcerated adolescent males. *Psychological Assessment, 14*, 97–109.

Kubak, F. A., & Salekin, R. T. (2009). Psychopathy and anxiety in children and adolescents: New insights and hints of a developmental trend. *Journal of Psychopathology and Behavioral Assessment, 31*, 271–284.

Lee, Z., Salekin, R. T., & Iselin, A. R. (2010). Psychopathic traits in youth: Is there evidence for primary and secondary subtypes? *Journal of Abnormal Child Psychology, 38*, 381–393.

Leistico, A. R., Salekin, R. T., DeCoster, J., & Rogers, R. (2008). A large-scale meta-analysis relating the Hare measures of psychopathy to antisocial conduct. *Law and Human Behavior, 32*, 28–45.

Loeber, R., Burke, J. D., & Lahey, B. B. (2002). What are the antecedants to antisocial personality disorder? *Criminal Behavior and Mental Health, 12*, 24–36.

Loney, B. R., Taylor, J., Butler, M. A., & Iacono, W. G. (2007). Adolescent psychopathy features: 6–year temporal stability and the prediction of externalizing symptoms during the transition to adulthood. *Aggressive Behavior, 33*, 242–252.

Lynam, D. R. (1997). Pursuing the psychopath: Capturing the psychopath in a nomological net. *Journal of Abnormal Psychology, 106*, 425–438.

Lynam, D. R. (2002). Fledgling psychopathy: A view from personality theory. *Law and Human Behavior, 26*, 255–259.

Lynam, D. R., Caspi, A., Moffitt, T. E., Loeber, R., & Stouthamer-Loeber, M. (2007). Longitudinal evidence that psychopathy scores in early adolescence predict adult psychopathy. *Journal of Abnormal Psychology, 116*, 155–165.

Lynam, D. R., Caspi, A., Moffitt, T. E., Raine, A., Loeber, R., & Stouthamer-Loeber, M. (2005). Adolescent psychopathy and the Big Five: Results from two samples. *Journal of Abnormal Child Psychology, 33*, 431–443.

Lynam, D. R., Loeber, R., & Stouthamer-Loeber, M. (2008). The stability of psychopathy from adolescence into adulthood: The search for moderators. *Criminal Justice and Behavior, 35*, 228–243.

Monahan, J., & Steadman, H. J. (1996). Violent storms and violent people: How can meteorology inform risk communication in mental health law. *American Psychologist, 51*, 931–938.

Monahan, J., & Steadman, H. J. (2001). Violence risk assessment: A quarter century of research. In L. E. Frost & R. J. Bonnie (Eds.), *The evolution of mental health law* (pp. 195–211). Washington, DC: American Psychological Association.

Muñoz, L. C., Kerr, M., & Besic, N. (2008). The peer relationships of youths with psychopathic personality traits: A matter of perspective. *Criminal Justice and Behavior, 35*, 212–227.

Murrie, D. C., & Cornell, D. G. (2003). Psychopathy screening of incarcerated juveniles: A comparison of measures. *Psychological Assessment, 14*, 390–396.

O'Neill, M. L., Lidz, V., & Heilbrun, K. (2003). Adolescents with psychopathic characteristics in a substance abusing cohort: Treatment process and outcomes. *Law and Human Behavior, 27*, 299–313.

Pardini, D. A., & Loeber, R. (2008). Interpersonal callousness trajectories across adolescence: Early social influences and adult outcomes. *Criminal Justice and Behavior, 35*, 173–196.

Patrick, C. J. (2006). Back to the future: Cleckley as a guide to the next generation of psychopathy research. In C. J. Patrick (Ed.), *Handbook of psychopathy* (pp. 605–617). New York: Guilford Press.

Robins, L. N. (1966). *Deviant children grown up: A sociological and psychiatric study of sociopathic personality*. Baltimore, MD: Williams & Wilkins.

Rogers, R. (1995). *Diagnostic and structured interviewing: A handbook for psychologists*. Odessa, FL: Psychological Assessment Resources.

Rogers, R., Johansen, J., Chang, J. J., & Salekin, R. T. (1997). Predictors of adolescent psychopathy: Oppositional and conduct-disordered symptoms. *Journal of the American Academy of Psychiatry and the Law, 25*, 261–271.

Rutter, M. (2005). What is the meaning and utility of the psychopathy concept? *Journal of Abnormal Child Psychology, 33*, 499–503.

Salekin, R. T. (2002). Psychopathy and therapeutic pessimism: Clinical lore or clinical reality? *Clinical Psychology Review, 22*, 79–112.

Salekin, R. T. (2006). Psychopathy in children and adolescents: Key issues in conceptualization and assessment. In C. J. Patrick (Ed.), *Handbook of psychopathy* (pp. 389–414). New York: Guilford Press.

Salekin, R. T. (2008). Psychopathy and recidivism from mid-adolescence to young adulthood: Cumulating legal problems and limiting life opportunities. *Journal of Abnormal Psychology, 117,* 386–395.

Salekin, R. T. (2009). Psychopathology and assessment: Contributing knowledge to science and practice. *Journal of Psychopathology and Behavioral Assessment, 31,* 1–6.

Salekin, R. T., Brannen, D. A., Zalot, Z. A., Leistico, A. R., & Neumann, C. S. (2006). Factor structure of psychopathy in youth: Testing the new four factor model. *Criminal Justice and Behavior, 33,* 135–157.

Salekin, R. T., & Debus, S. A. (2008). Assessing child and adolescent psychopathy. In R. Jackson (Ed.), *Learning forensic assessment* (pp. 347–383). New York: Routledge/Taylor & Francis.

Salekin, R. T., & Frick, P. J. (2005). Psychopathy in children and adolescence: The need for a developmental perspective. *Journal of Abnormal Child Psychology, 33,* 403–409.

Salekin, R. T., Lee, Z., Schrum-Dillard, C. L., & Kubak, F. A. (in press). Child psychopathy and protective factors: IQ and motivation to change. *Psychology, Public Policy, and Law.*

Salekin, R. T., Neumann, C. S., Leistico, A. R., DiCicco, T. M., & Duros, R. L. (2004). Psychopathy and comorbidity in a young offender sample: Taking a closer look at psychopathy's potential importance over disruptive behavior disorders. *Journal of Abnormal Psychology, 113,* 416–427.

Salekin, R. T., Leistico, A. M., Trobst, K. K., Schrum, C., & Lochman, J. E. (2005). Adolescent psychopathy and personality theory—the interpersonal circumplex: Expanding evidence of a nomological net. *Journal of Abnormal Child Psychology, 33,* 445–460.

Salekin, R. T., & Lochman, J. E. (2008). Child and adolescent psychopathy: The search for protective factors. *Criminal Justice and Behavior, 35,* 159–172.

Salekin, R. T., Neumann, C. S., Leistico, A. R., & Zalot, A. A. (2004). Psychopathy in youth and intelligence: An investigation of Cleckley's hypothesis. *Journal of Clinical Child and Adolescent Psychology, 33,* 731–742.

Salekin, R. T., Rogers, R., & Machin, D. (2001). Psychopathy in youth: Pursuing diagnostic accuracy. *Journal of Youth and Adolescence, 30,* 173–195.

Salekin, R. T., Rogers, R., & Sewell, K. W. (1996). A review and meta-analysis of the Psychopathy Checklist and Psychopathy Checklist—Revised: Predictive validity of dangerousness. *Clinical Psychology: Science and Practice, 3,* 203–215.

Salekin, R. T., Rosenbaum, J., & Lee, Z. (2009). Psychopathy in children and adolescents: Stability and change. *Psychology, Psychiatry, and Law, 15,* 224–236.

Salekin, R. T., Rosenbaum, J., Lee, Z., & Lester, W. S. (2009). Child and adolescent psychopathy: Like a painting by Monet. *Youth Violence and Juvenile Justice, 7,* 239–255.

Schrum, C. L., & Salekin, R. T. (2006). Psychopathy in adolescent female offenders: An item response theory analysis of the Psychopathy Checklist: Youth Version. *Behavioral Sciences and the Law, 24,* 39–63.

Seagrave, D., & Grisso, T. (2002). Adolescent development and the measurement of juvenile psychopathy. *Law and Human Behavior, 26,* 219–239.

Skeem, J. L., Monahan, J., & Mulvey, E. P. (2002). Psychopathy, treatment involvement, and subsequent violence among civil psychiatric patients. *Law and Human Behavior, 26,* 577–603.

Skeem, J. L., & Petrila, J. (2004). Introduction to the special issue on juvenile psychopathy: Vol 2. Juvenile psychopathy: Informing the debate. *Behavioral Sciences and the Law, 22,* 1–4.

Spain, S. E., Douglas, K. S., Poythress, N. G., & Epstein, M. (2004). The relationship between psychopathic features, violence, and treatment outcome: The comparison of three youth measures of psychopathic features. *Behavioral Sciences and the Law, 22,* 85–102.

Viding, E., Blair, R. J. R., Moffitt, T. E., & Plomin, R. (2005). Evidence for substantial genetic risk for psychopathy in 7-year olds. *Journal of Child Psychology and Psychiatry, 46,* 592–597.

Vincent, G. M. (2002). *Investigating the legitimacy of adolescent psychopathy assessments: Contributions of item response theory.* Unpublished doctoral dissertation, Simon Fraser University, Burnaby, BC.

Vincent, G. M., & Hart, S. D. (2002). Psychopathy in childhood and adolescence: Implications for the assessment and management of multi-problem youths. In R. R. Corrado, R. Roesch, S. D., Hart, & J. K. Gierowski (Eds.), *Multi-problem youth: A foundation for comparative research on needs, interventions, and outcomes* (pp. 150–163). Amsterdam: IOS Press.

Vitale, J. E., Newman, J. P., Bates, J. E., Goodnight, J., Dodge, K. A., & Pettit, G. S. (2005). Deficient behavioral inhibition and anomalous selective attention in a community sample of adolescents with psychopathic traits and low-anxiety traits. *Journal of Abnormal Child Psychology, 33,* 461–470.

Author Index

Subject Index

Page numbers followed by *f* indicate figure, *t* indicate table.